W9-AQK-926

NOTES

ON THE

OLD TESTAMENT

EXPLANATORY AND PRACTICAL

BY

ALBERT BARNES

ENLARGED TYPE EDITION

EDITED BY

ROBERT FREW, D.D.

JOB

VOL. II

BAKER BOOK HOUSE
GRAND RAPIDS, MICHIGAN

Library of Congress Catalog Card Number: 55-11630

ISBN: 0-8010-0580-9

First Printing, January 1950
Second Printing, February 1956
Third Printing, March 1959
Fourth Printing, June 1961
Fifth Printing, May 1966
Sixth Printing, May 1968
Seventh Printing, April 1970
Eighth Printing, June 1971
Ninth Printing, September 1971
Tenth Printing, August 1972

PRINTED IN THE UNITED STATES OF AMERICA

THE BOOK OF JOB

CHAPTER XXII.

ANALYSIS OF THE CHAPTER.

THIS chapter commences the third series in the controversy. As before, Eliphaz begins the argument, and replies to Job. He maintains his former sentiments, and does it with great energy, and is evidently roused by the argument of Job. Job had attacked their main position in the previous chapter, and it became necessary now to fortify it if possible. There is, also, much severity in this discourse, and far more than usual that is personal. Job is openly charged with aggravated guilt, which. before, had been rather *implied* than *said*. But here is no concealment; and, perhaps, this is an instance, such as often occurs, where, when a man has the worst of the argument, he resorts to a personal attack on him who has confuted him. The argument of Eliphaz comprises the following points:—(1.) That it could not be any advantage to God that a man was righteous, and that he set up a claim to perfection. God had nothing to *lose* in treating men as they deserve, and could not be deterred by fear from dealing with them according to their real character, ver. 1—4. By these remarks, he seems to be replying to Job, as if it must be true, that if God did *not* deal with them according to their real character in this life, as Job had maintained, it must be either because he *feared* the wicked man, or because there was some *advantage* which he expected to derive from the fact that he lived. Instead of meeting the *facts*, to which Job had appealed, he goes into an abstract argument, of a very sophistical character, to show that it *could not* be so—a very common mode with controversialists. (2.) Eliphaz then openly attacks Job; appeals to him as an instance of the truth of his position; says that it was an indisputable fact, that he was a great sinner, that his iniquities were infinite, and that, therefore, he had been overwhelmed with these calamities, ver. 5—11. He argues from it, as a point which could not be called in question, that Job's calamities had come upon him in consequence of a guilty life; and that whatever he might say about the *theory* of the divine government, his own case was one which would confute it all. Job was himself, he maintains, a full demonstration that God would punish the wicked in this life. In these unkind remarks, the course of the argument is somewhat changed. Before this, the friends of Job had maintained the abstract position, that the wicked would be dealt with in this life according to their deserts, and had given a great variety of illustrations of this. But it had been left to be *inferred* that Job had this character BECAUSE these calamities had come upon him. But, *now*, the argument is changed. It is maintained, as an indisputable point, that he is an eminently wicked man, and that these calamities have come upon him in consequence of his crimes; and that, therefore, *his own case* showed that God would punish the wicked in this life. (3.) In ver. 12—14, Eliphaz says, that it was implied in the argument of Job that God *could* not distinguish between the actions of men, and the reasons why he did not treat them as they deserved must be, that thick clouds interposed between them and God, so that he could not see their conduct, or that the distance between God and man was so great that he was not able to mark what man was doing. Job had, in fact, maintained no such position; but Eliphaz *inferred* that this must be his meaning, or that his sentiments must lead to this. (4.) Eliphaz then (ver. 15—20) refers Job to the case of those who perished in the flood, and speaks as if Job had adopted their sentiments. They lived in prosperity. They said to God, Depart from us. Their houses were filled with good things. Yet, he says they were suddenly destroyed, and that at so signal a judgment the righteous rejoiced—implying that it was not improper to be gratified when so heavy calamities had come upon one who had shown himself as wicked as Job was now proved to be. (5.) In the conclusion, Eliphaz urges Job to become truly acquainted with God, assuring him that he would then be at peace, and then gives a glowing description of the prosperity to which he might look, as a reward, ver. 21—30. He would be rich; the Almighty would be his defence; he would find happiness in God; his prayer would be heard; light would shine upon his ways; and when others were humbled, he would be exalted.

THEN Eliphaz the Temanite answered and said,

2 Can a man be profitable [a] unto God, as [1] he that is wise may be profitable unto himself?

a Ps.16.2. 1 or, *if he may be profitable, doth his good success depend thereon.*

CHAPTER XXII.

2. *Can a man be profitable unto God?* Can a man confer any favour on God, so as to lay him under obligation? Eliphaz supposes that Job sets up a *claim* to the favour of God, because he was of service to him, or because God had something to fear if he was cut off. He maintains, therefore, that a man can confer no favour on God, so as to lay him under obligation. God is independent and supreme. He has nothing to gain if man is righteous—he has nothing to apprehend if he is punished. He is not dependent at all on man. ¶ *As he*

3 *Is it* any pleasure to the Almighty that thou art righteous? or *is it* gain *to him* that thou makest thy ways perfect?

---

that is wise. Marg. or, *if he may be profitable, doth his goodness* depend *thereon.* The meaning of the passage is, a wise man may promote his own advantage, but he cannot be of advantage to God. All the result of his wisdom must terminate on himself, and not on God; comp. Ps. xvi. 2. Of the correctness of this sentiment there can be no doubt. It accords with reason, and with all that is said in the Scriptures. God is too great to be benefited by man. He is infinite in all his perfections; he is the original fountain of blessedness; he is supremely wise; he has all resources in himself, and he cannot be dependent on his creatures. He cannot, therefore, be deterred from punishing them by any dread which he has of losing their favour—he cannot be induced to bless them because they have laid him under obligation. Eliphaz meant this as a reply to what Job had said. He had maintained, that God did *not* treat men according to their character in this life, but that, in fact, the wicked were often prospered, and suffered to live long. Eliphaz at once *infers*, that if this were so, it must be because they could render themselves *serviceable* to God, or because he must have something to dread by punishing them. In the general sentiment, he was right; in the *inference* he was wrong—since Job had not affirmed that they are spared from any such cause, and since many *other* reasons may be assigned.

3. Is it *any pleasure to the Almighty that thou art righteous?* This is the same sentiment which was advanced in the previous verse. The meaning is, that it can be no advantage to God that a man is righteous. He is not dependent on man for happiness, and cannot be deterred from dealing justly with him because he is in danger of losing any thing. In this sense, it is true. God *has* pleasure in holiness wherever it is, and is pleased when men are righteous; but it is not true that he is dependent on the character of his creatures for his own happiness, or that men can lay him under obligation by their own righteousness. Eliphaz applies this general truth to Job, probably, because he understood him as complaining of the dealings of God with him, *as if* he had laid God under obligation by his upright life. He supposes that it was implied in the remarks of Job, that he had been so upright, and had been of so much consequence, that God *ought* to have continued him in a state of prosperity. This supposition, if Job ever had it, Eliphaz correctly meets, and shows him that he was not so profitable to God that he could not do without him. Yet, do men not often feel thus? Do ministers of the gospel not sometimes feel thus? Do we not sometimes feel thus in relation to some man eminent for piety, wisdom, or learning? Do we not feel as if God could not do without him, and that there was a sort of necessity that he should keep him alive? Yet, how often are such men cut down, in the very midst of their usefulness, to show (1) that God is not dependent on them; and (2) to keep them from pride, as if they were necessary to the execution of the divine plans; and (3) to teach his people their dependence on *Him,* and not on frail, erring mortals. When the church places its reliance on a human arm, God very often suddenly knocks the prop away.

4. *Will he reprove thee for fear of thee?* Or, rather, will he come into trial, and argue his cause before a tribunal, because he is afraid that his character will suffer, or because he feels himself bound to appear, and answer to the charges which may be brought? The language is all taken from courts of justice, and the object is, to reprove Job as if he felt that it was necessary that God should appear and answer to what he alleged against him. ¶ *Will he enter with thee into judgment?* Will he condescend to enter on a trial with one like thee?

4 Will he reprove thee for fear of thee? will he enter with thee into judgment?

5 *Is* not thy wickedness great? and thine iniquities infinite?

6 For thou hast taken a pledge

Will he submit his cause to a trial with man, as if he were an equal, or as if man had any right to such an investigation? It is to be remembered, that Job had repeatedly expressed a desire to carry his cause before God, and that God would meet him as an equal, and not take advantage of his majesty and power to overwhelm him; see Notes on chap. xiii. 3, 20, 21. Eliphaz here asks, whether God could be expected to meet *a man*, one of his own creatures, in this manner, and to go into a trial of the cause. He says that God was supreme; that no one could bring him into court; and that he could not be restrained from doing his pleasure by any dread of man. These sentiments are all noble and correct, and worthy of a sage. Soon, however, he changes the style, and utters the language of severe reproach, because Job had presumed to make such a suggestion. Perhaps, also, in this verse, a special emphasis should be placed on "*thee*." "Will God enter into trial with *thee* — a man whose wickedness is so great, and whose sin is infinite?" ver. 4, 5.

5. Is *not thy wickedness great?* That is, "Is it not utter presumption and folly for a man, whose wickedness is undoubtedly so great, to presume to enter into a litigation with God?" Eliphaz here *assumes* it as an undeniable proposition, that Job was a great sinner. This charge had not been directly made before. He and his friends had argued evidently on that supposition, and had maintained that one who was a great sinner would be punished in this life for it, and they had left it to be implied, in no doubtful manner, that they so regarded Job. But the charge had not been before so openly made. Here Eliphaz argues as if that were a point that could not be disputed. The only *proof* that he had, so far as appears, was, that Job had been afflicted as they maintained great sinners *would be*, and they, therefore, concluded that he must be such. No facts are referred to, except that he was a great sufferer, and yet, on the ground of this, he proceeds to take for granted that he *must have been* a man who had taken a pledge for no cause; had refused to give water to the thirsty; had been an oppressor, &c. ¶ *And thine iniquities infinite?* Heb. "And there is no end to thine iniquities,"—that is, they are without number. This does not mean that sin is *an infinite evil*, or that his sins were infinite in degree; but that if one should attempt to reckon up the number of his transgressions, there would be no end to them. This, I believe, is the only place in the Bible where sin is spoken of, in any respect, as "*infinite;*" and this cannot be used as a proof text, to show that sin is an infinite evil, for (1) that is not the meaning of the passage even with respect to Job; (2) it makes no affirmation respecting sin in general; and (3) it was untrue, even in regard to Job, and in the sense in which Zophar meant to use the phrase. There is no intelligible sense in which it can be said that sin is *an infinite evil;* and no argument should be based on such a declaration, to prove that sin demanded an infinite atonement, or that it deserves eternal sufferings. Those doctrines can be defended on solid grounds — they should not be made to rest on a false assumption, or on a false interpretation of the Scriptures.

6. *For thou hast taken a pledge from thy brother for nought.* The only evidence which Eliphaz seems to have had of this was, that this was a heinous sin, and that as Job seemed to be severely punished, it was to be *inferred* that he must have committed some such sin as this. No way of treating an unfortunate and a suffering man could be more unkind. A *pledge* is that which is given by a debtor to a creditor, for security for the payment of a debt, and would be, of course, that which was regarded

from thy brother for nought, and stripped the naked [1] of their clothing.

7 Thou hast not given water to the weary to drink, and thou hast withholden bread from the hungry.

8 But *as for* [2] the mighty man, he had the earth; and the [3] honourable man dwelt in it.

9 Thou hast sent widows away empty, and the arms of the fatherless have been broken.

1 *clothes of the naked.* 2 *man of arm.* 3 *eminent,* or, *accepted for countenance.*

as of value. Garments, which constituted a considerable part of the wealth of the Orientals, would usually be the pledge which would be given. With us, in such cases, watches, jewelry, notes, mortgages, are given as collateral security, or as pledges. The law of Moses required, that when a man took the garment of his neighbour for a pledge, it should be restored by the time the sun went down, Ex. xxii. 26, 27. The crime here charged on Job was, that he had exacted a pledge from another where there was no just claim to it; that is, where no debt had been contracted, where a debt had been paid, or where the security was far beyond the value of the debt. The injustice of such a course would be obvious. It would deprive the man of the use of the property which was pledged, and it gave him to whom it was pledged an opportunity of doing wrong, as he might retain it, or dispose of it, and the real owner see it no more. ¶ *And stripped the naked of their clothing.* Marg. *clothes of the naked.* That is, of those who were poorly clad, or who were nearly destitute of clothes. The word *naked* is often used in this sense in the Scriptures; see Notes, John xxi. 7. The meaning here is, that Job had taken away by oppression even the garments of the poor in order to enrich himself.

7. *Thou hast not given water to the weary.* That is, thou hast withheld the rites of hospitality—one of the most grievous offences which could be charged on an Arabian; comp. Notes on Isa. xxi. 14. In all the Oriental world, hospitality was regarded, and is still, as a duty of the highest obligation.

8. *But* as for *the mighty man;* Heb. as in the margin, *man of arm.* The *arm,* in the Scriptures, is the symbol of power; Ps. x. 15, "Break thou the arm of the wicked;" Ezek. xxx. 21, "I have broken the arm of Pharaoh;" Ps. lxxxix. 13, "Thou hast a mighty arm;" Ps. xcvii. 1, "His holy arm hath gotten him the victory." The reason of this is, that the sword and spear were principally used in war, and success depended on the force with which they were wielded by the arm. There can be no doubt that this is intended to be applied to Job and that the meaning is, that he had driven the poor from their possessions, and he had taken forcible occupancy of what belonged to them. The idea is, that he had done this by *power,* not by *right.* ¶ *Had the earth.* Took possession of the land, and drove off from it those to whom it belonged, or who had an equal right to it with him. ¶ *And the honorable man.* Marg. *eminent,* or *accepted of countenance.* Heb. "Lifted up of countenance;" that is, the man whose countenance was elevated either by honour or pride. It may be used to describe either; but, perhaps, there is more force in the former, in saying that it was the great man, the man of rank and office, who had got possession. There is, thus, some sarcasm in the severe charge: "*The* great man — *the* man of rank, and wealth, and office, has got possession, while the humble and poor are banished." Job had had great possessions; but this charge as to the manner in which he had acquired them seems to be wholly gratuitous. Eliphaz takes it for granted, since he was so severely punished, that it *must have been* in some such way.

9. *Thou hast sent widows away empty.* That is, without regarding their wants, and without doing any thing to mitigate their sorrows. The

10 Therefore snares [a] *are* round about thee, and sudden fear troubleth thee ;

11 Or darkness, *that* thou canst not see ; and abundance of waters cover thee.

12 *Is* not God in the height of

a chap.18.8—10; Ps. 11. 6.

oppression of the widow and the fatherless is, in the Scriptures, every where regarded as a crime of peculiar magnitude ; see Notes on Isa. i. 17. ¶ *The arms of the fatherless have been broken.* Thou hast taken away all that they relied on. Thou hast oppressed them and taken advantage of their weak and defenceless condition to enrich yourself. This charge was evidently gratuitous and unjust. It was the result of an *inference* from the fact that he was thus afflicted, and about as just as inferences, in such cases, usually are. To all this, Job replies in beautiful language in chap. xxix. 11—16, when describing his former condition, and in justice to him, we may allow him to speak *here*, and to show what was, in fact, the course of his life.

When the ear heard me, then it blessed me ;
And when the eye saw me, it gave witness to me :
Because I delivered the poor that cried,
And the fatherless, and him that had none to help him.
The blessing of him that was ready to perish came upon me:
And I caused the widow's heart to leap for joy.
I put on righteousness, and it clothed me ;
My judgment was as a robe and a diadem.
I was eyes to the blind,
And feet was I to the lame ;
I was a father to the poor,
And the cause which I knew not, I searched out.

10. *Therefore snares* are *round about thee. Snares* were used for catching wild animals and birds, and the word then came to denote any sudden calamity; see chap. xviii. 8—10. Eliphaz here says, that it *must be* that these calamities came upon Job in consequence of such sins as he had specified. About that he took it for granted there could be no dispute. ¶ *And sudden fear.* The calamities of Job came upon him suddenly, chap. i. It was to this, doubtless, that Eliphaz alluded.

11. *Or darkness.* Darkness and night in the Scriptures are emblems of calamity. ¶ That *thou canst not see.* Deep and fearful darkness ; total night, so that nothing is visible. That is, the heaviest calamities had overwhelmed him. ¶ *And abundance of waters.* An emblem, also, of calamities; chap. xxvii. 20; Ps. lxix. 1, 2; lxxiii. 10.

12. Is *not God in the height of heaven ?* In the highest heaven. That is, Is not God exalted over all worlds? This seems to be intended to refer to the sentiments of Job, as if he had maintained that God was so exalted that he could not notice what was occurring on earth. It should, therefore, be read in connection with the following verse : " God is so exalted, that thou sayest, How can he know ? Can he look down through the thick clouds which intervene between him and man ?" Job had maintained no such opinion, but the process of thought in the mind of Eliphaz seems to have been this. Job had maintained that God did *not* punish the wicked in this life as they deserved, but that they lived and prospered. Eliphaz *inferred* that he could hold that opinion only because he supposed that God was so exalted that he could not attend to worldly affairs. He knew no other way in which the opinion could be held, and he proceeds to argue *as if* it were so. Job had in the previous chapter appealed to plain *facts*, and had rested his whole argument on them. Eliphaz, instead of meeting the *facts* in the case, or showing that they did not exist as Job said they did, considered his discourse as a denial of Divine Providence, and as representing God to be so far above the earth that he could not notice what was occurring here. How common is this in theological controversy ! One man, in defending his opinions, or in searching for the truth, appeals to *facts*, and endeavours to ascertain their nature and bearing. His adversary, instead of meeting them, or showing that they are not so, at once appeals to some admitted doctrine, to some established article of a creed, or to

heaven? and behold the [1] height of
the stars, how high they are!
13 And thou sayest, [2] How [a] doth
God know? can he judge through
the dark cloud?
14 Thick clouds *are* a covering to him, that he seeth not;

1 *head.* 2 or, *what.* a Ps.10.11; 73.11.

some tradition of the fathers, and says that the appeal to fact is but a denial of an important doctrine of revelation. It is easier to charge a man with denying the doctrine of Providence, or to call him by a harsh name, than it is to meet an argument drawn from fact and from the plain meaning of the Bible. ¶ *And behold the height of the stars.* Marg. as in Heb. *head*—ראש. God is more exalted than the highest of the stars. The stars are the highest objects in view, and the sense, therefore, is, that God is infinitely exalted.

13. *And thou sayest, How doth God know?* That is, it *follows* from what you have said; or the opinion which you have advanced is *the same* as if you had affirmed this. How common it is to charge a man with holding what we *infer*, from something which he has advanced, he must hold, and then to proceed to argue *as if* he actually held that. The philosophy of this is plain. He advances a certain opinion. *We* infer at once that he can hold that only on certain grounds, or that if he holds that he must hold something else also. We can see that if *we* held that opinion, we should also, for the sake of consistency, be compelled to hold something which seems to follow from it, and we cannot see how this can be avoided, and we at once charge him with holding it. But the truth may be, that *he* has not seen that such consequences follow, or that he has some other way of accounting for the fact than we have; or that he may hold to the fact and yet deny wholly the consequences which legitimately follow from it. Now we have a right to show him *by argument* that his opinions, if he would follow them out, would lead to dangerous consequences, but we have a right to charge him with holding only what he *professes* to hold. He is not answerable for our inferences; and we have no right to charge them on him as being his real opinions. Every man has a right to avow what he actually believes, and to be regarded as holding that, and that only. ¶ *How doth God know?* That is, How can one so exalted see what is done on the distant earth, and reward and punish men according to their deserts? This opinion was actually held by many of the ancients. It was supposed that the supreme God did not condescend to attend to the affairs of mortals, but had committed the government of the earth to inferior beings. This was the foundation of the Gnostic philosophy, which prevailed so much in the East in the early ages of the Christian church. Milton puts a similar sentiment into the mouth of Eve in her reflections after she had eaten the forbidden fruit:

And I, perhaps, am secret: heaven is high,
High and remote from thence to see distinct
Each thing on earth; and other care perhaps
May have diverted from continual watch
Our great Forbidder, safe with all his spies
about him. Par. Lost, B. ix.

¶ *Can he judge through the dark cloud?* Can he look down through the clouds which interpose between man and him? Eliphaz could not see how Job could maintain his opinions without holding that this was impossible for God. He could see no other reason why God did not punish the wicked than because *he did not see them,* and he, therefore, charges this opinion on Job.

14. *Thick clouds* are *a covering to him.* This is to be understood as expressing what Eliphaz regarded as the sentiment of Job—that so thick clouds intervened between him and man that he could not take cognizance of what was going forward on earth. ¶ *And he walketh in the circuit of heaven.* Upon the arch of heaven, as it seems to be bent over our heads. He walks above that cerulean, so high, that he cannot see what occurs on earth, and to punish mortals. This was not an uncommon sentiment among the ancients,

and he walketh in the circuit of
heaven.
15 Hast thou marked the old way
which wicked men have trodden?
16 Which were cut down out of
time, whose [1] foundation was overflown with a flood;
17 Which [a] said unto God, Depart from us: and what can the
Almighty do [2] for them?

1 or, *a flood was poured upon their foundation*, Ge.7.10, &c.; 2Pe.2.5.

a ch.21.14. 2 or, *to*.

though it is here, with the greatest injustice, attributed to Job. A similar sentiment is expressed by Lucretius, as quoted by Rosenmüller and Noyes:

Omnis enim per se Divum natura necesse est
Immortali ævo summa cum pace fruatur,
Semota a nostris rebus, sejunctaque longe.
Nam privata dolore omni, privata periclis,
Ipsa suis pollens opibus, nihil indiga nostri,
Nec bene promeritus capitur, nec tangitur ira.

comp. Isa. xxix. 15.

15. *Hast thou marked the old way which wicked men have trodden?* Hast thou seen what has happened in former times to wicked men? Job had maintained that God did not deal with men in this world according to their character. To meet this, Eliphaz now appeals to ancient facts, and especially refers to the deluge, when the wicked were cut off by a flood for their sins. Schultens, Dr. Good, Noyes, and Reiske, however, suppose that the word here rendered "mark," means to *pursue*, or *imitate*, and that the sense is, "Are you willing to adopt the principles of those wicked men who lived in the time of the deluge?" But the sense is not materially affected. The general design is to refer Job to the case of the impious generation that was swept off by a flood. The judgments of God on them were a full refutation, in his view, of the sentiments of Job.

16. *Which were cut down.* Who were suddenly destroyed by a flood. On the word here used (קמט) see Notes on chap. xvi. 8. It occurs only in that place and this. Its primary notion is that of drawing together or contracting—as the feet of a lamb or calf are drawn together and tied preparatory to being killed; and the meaning here is, probably, "who were *huddled together* by the waters," or who were driven in heaps by the deluge, so rapidly and suddenly did it come upon them. ¶ *Out of time.* Heb. "And there was no time;" that is, it was done in a moment, or suddenly. No time was given them; no delay was granted. The floods rushed over them, and nothing could stay them. ¶ *Whose foundation was overflown.* Marg. or, *a flood was poured upon their foundation.* That is, all on which they relied was swept away. The word *foundation* refers to that on which their happiness and security rested, as a house rests on its foundation, and when that is swept away the house falls. ¶ *With a flood.* Heb. (נהר) *river*. The word is commonly applied to a river; and in the Scriptures, by way of eminence, to the Euphrates; see Notes on Isa. vii. 20; viii. 7. It may be used, however, to denote a river which is swollen, and then a flood—and it is several times rendered *flood* in the Scriptures; Job xiv. 11; Jonah ii. 3 (where it means the sea); Josh. xxiv. 2, 3, 14, 15; Ps. lxvi. 6; Job xxviii. 11; Ps. xxiv. 2; xciii. 3; Cant. viii. 7. Prof. Lee supposes that the allusion here is to some overflowing of the Euphrates, but the reference seems to be decidedly to the deluge in the time of Noah. The *language* is such as would be used in referring to that, and the *fact* is just such an one as would be pertinent to the argument of Eliphaz. The fact was undoubtedly well known to all, so that a bare allusion to it would be enough.

17. *Which said unto God, Depart from us;* Notes, chap. xxi. 14. A very correct description of the old world. They had no wish to retain God in their knowledge. Probably Eliphaz here refers to what Job had said, chap. xxi. 14, 15. He had remarked, in describing the wicked, that they said unto God, "Depart from us," and yet they lived prosperously. "But see," says Eliphaz, "*a case* where they did this. It was done by the

18 Yet [a] he filled their houses with good *things;* but the counsel of the wicked is far from me.

a Ac.14.16,17.

19 The righteous see *it,* and are glad: and the innocent laugh them to scorn.

inhabitants of the world before the deluge, and their houses were filled, as you say the houses of the wicked are, with good things, but God swept them all suddenly away." ¶ *And what can the Almighty do for them?* Marg. or, *to.* That is, they demanded what the Almighty could do for them. They did not feel their dependence on him; they did not admit that they needed his aid; they cast off all reliance on him. This whole passage is a most sarcastic retort on what Job had said in chap. xxi. 14, 15. He had affirmed that though wicked men used this language, yet that they prospered. Eliphaz takes the same language and applies it to the sinners before the deluge, and says that they expressed themselves just in this manner. The language which Job puts into the mouths of the wicked, had indeed, says Eliphaz, been used. But by whom? By those who lived in security and prosperity. "By the men before the deluge," says he, "the race that was so wicked that it was necessary to cut them off by the flood. These are the men to whose sentiments Job appeals; these the men with whom he has sympathy!"

18. *Yet he filled their houses with good things.* This is undoubtedly a biting sarcasm. Job had maintained that such men were prosperous. "Yes," says Eliphaz, "their houses *were* well filled! They were *signally* blessed and prospered!" ¶ *But the counsel of the wicked is far from me.* This is the very language of Job, chap. xxi. 16. It is here used sarcastically. "Far from ME," you say, "be the counsel of the wicked. Thus you defend them, and attempt to show that they are the favourites of heaven! You attempt to prove that God must and will bless them! Far from ME, say *I*, be the counsel of the wicked! With them *I* have no part, no lot. I will not defend them—I will not be their advocate!" The object is, to show that, notwithstanding all that Job had said, he was secretly the advocate of the wicked, and stood up as their friend.

19. *The righteous see* it, *and are glad;* see the destruction of the wicked; comp. Rev. xv. 3; xvi. 7; xix. 1, 2. This is designed by Eliphaz, probably, not only to state a fact about the righteous of other times who saw the wicked punished, but, also, to vindicate his own conduct and that of his two friends in regard to Job. If the righteous of other times had rejoiced when the wicked were punished, they inferred that it was not improper for them to manifest similar rejoicings when God had overtaken one who was so signally depraved as they supposed Job to be. Their want of sympathy for him, therefore, they would defend by a reference to the conduct of the men of other times. There *is* a sense in which good men rejoice when the wicked are detected and punished. It is not (1) that they rejoice that the sin was committed; nor (2) that they rejoice in misery; nor (3) that they would not rejoice more if the wicked had been righteous, and had escaped suffering altogether. But it is the kind of joy which we have when a murderer, a robber, or a pirate is seized—when a counterfeiter is detected—when a man who prowls around the dwelling at night to murder its inmates is brought to punishment. It is joy, not that the sin was committed, but that the laws are executed; and who should not rejoice in that? We have joy in the character of an upright judge when he impartially and faithfully administers the laws; and why should we not rejoice in God when he does the same? We rejoice in the manifestation of truth and justice among men—why should we not in the exhibition of the same things in God? We rejoice in a police that can ferret out every form of iniquity, and bring offenders to justice; and why should we not

20 Whereas [1] our substance is not cut down, but [2] the remnant of them the fire consumeth.

1 or, *estate*. 2 or, *their excellency*.

21 Acquaint now thyself with [3] him, and be at peace:[a] thereby good shall come unto thee.

3 i.e. *God*. a Is.27.5; Phi.4.7.

rejoice in that government which is infinitely more perfect than any police ever was among men? ¶ *And the innocent laugh them to scorn.* This is another way of saying that they exult or rejoice; comp. Prov. i. 26, 27. No consideration can justify men in deriding and mocking those who are subjected to punishment; and it is by no means certain that the speaker meant to refer to such derision.

20. *Whereas our substance is not cut down.* Marg. or, *estate.* Gesenius supposes that this means our adversary or enemy. The word here used (קִים) he regards as derived from קוּם—to rise, to rise up; and, hence, it may have the sense of rising up against, or an enemy. So Noyes understands it, and renders it,

"Truly, our adversary is destroyed;
And fire hath consumed his abundance."

Rosenmüller accords with this, and it seems to me to be the correct view. According to this, it is the language of the righteous (ver. 19) when exulting over the punishment of the wicked, saying, "Our foe is cut down." Jerome renders it, Nonne succisa est erectio eorum, &c. The LXX., "Has not their substance (ὑπόστασις) disappeared?" The sense is not materially different. If the word *substance*, or *property*, is to be retained, it should be read as a question, and regarded as the language of the righteous who exult. "Has not their substance been taken away, and has not the fire consumed their property?" Dr. Good strangely renders it, "For our tribe is not cut off." ¶ *But the remnant of them.* Marg. *their excellency.* Heb. יִתְרָם. Jerome, *reliquias eorum*—"*the remnants of them.*" Sept. κατάλειμμα—*the residue*, or *what is left.* The Hebrew word (יֶתֶר) means, *the remainder, the residue, the rest;* then, what is redundant, more than is needed, or that abounds; and then, *wealth*, the superabundant property which a man does not *need* for his own use or family. The word here probably means that which the rich sinner possessed. ¶ *The fire consumeth.* Or, hath consumed. It has been supposed by many that the allusion here is to the destruction of Sodom and Gomorrah, and it cannot be denied that such an allusion is possible. If it were *certain* that Job lived before that event, there could be little objection to such a supposition. The *only* objection would be, that a reference to such an event was not more prominent. It would be a case just in point in the argument of the three friends of Job, and one to which it might be supposed they would have appealed as decisive of the controversy. They lived in the vicinity. They could not have been strangers to so remarkable an occurrence, and it would have furnished just the argument which they wished, to prove that God punishes the wicked in this life. If they lived after that event, therefore, it is difficult to account for the fact, that they did not make a more distinct and prominent allusion to it in their argument. It is true, that the same remark may be made respecting the allusion to the flood, which was a case equally in point, and in reference to which the allusion, if it exist at all, is almost equally obscure. So far as the *language* here is concerned, the reference may be either to the destruction of Sodom, or to destruction by lightning, such as happened to the possessions of Job, chap. i. 16; and it is difficult, if not impossible, to determine which is correct. The *general* idea is, that the judgments of heaven, represented by fire, had fallen on the wicked, and that the righteous, therefore, had occasion to rejoice.

21. *Acquaint now thyself with him.* Marg. i. e. *with God.* Eliphaz takes it for granted now, that Job was a sinner wholly unreconciled to God, and unacquainted with him. This fact, he supposes, was the source of

all his calamities. As long as he remained thus unreconciled to God, he must be miserable. He proceeds, therefore, in a most beautiful manner, to exhort him to be at peace with God, and portrays the benefits which would result from such a reconciliation. There are few passages in the Bible of more exquisite beauty than this, and nothing could be sounder advice, on the supposition that Job was, as he supposed, a stranger to God. In this beautiful exhortation, he shows (1) what he means by becoming acquainted with God (ver. 21, 22, 23); and then (2) what would be the happy results of such reconciliation, ver. 24—30. The word rendered *acquaint thyself* (הסכן — from סכן) means, properly, *to dwell*, to be familiar with any one, to associate with one—from the idea of dwelling in the same tent or house; and in Hiphil, the form here used, to become familiar with any one, to be on terms of friendship. The meaning here is, "Secure the friendship of God. Become truly acquainted with him. Be reconciled to him. You are now estranged. You have no just views of him. You murmur and complain, and you are suffering under his displeasure as a sinner. But it is not too late to repent, and to return to him; and in so doing you will find peace." An acquaintance with God, in the sense of this passage, implies (1) a correct knowledge of his true character, and (2) reconciliation with him. There are two great difficulties among men in regard to God. The first is, that they have no just views of his real character. They think him harsh, stern, tyrannical. They regard his law as severe, and its penalty as unjust. They think his government to be arbitrary, and himself to be unworthy of confidence This erroneous view must be corrected before men can be reconciled to him—for how can they be brought to lay aside their opposition to him while they regard him as unjust and severe? Secondly, even when the character of God is explained, and his true character is set before men, they are opposed to it. They are opposed to him because he is so holy. Loving sin, they cannot love one who has no sin, and who frowns on evil; and this opposition to the *real* character of God must be removed before they can be reconciled to him. This requires a change of heart—a change from sin to holiness; and this is the work performed in regeneration. ¶ *And be at peace.* There can be no peace while you maintain a warfare with God. It is a war against your Maker, where he has control over your conscience, your intellect, your body, and all which can affect your welfare; and while this is maintained, there can be no peace. If the mind is reconciled to him, there will be peace. Peace of mind *always* follows reconciliation where there has been a variance, and nowhere is the peace so entire and full of joy as when man feels that he is reconciled to God. Eliphaz here has stated a doctrine which has been confirmed by all the subsequent revelations in the Bible, and by the experience of all those who have become reconciled to God; comp. Notes on Rom. v. i. It is peace, as opposed to the agitation and conflict of the mind before; peace resulting from acquiescence in the claims of God; peace in the belief that he is wholly right, and worthy of confidence; and peace in the assurances of his friendship and favour for ever. This doctrine, it seems, was thus understood in the early ages of the world, and, indeed, must have been known as early as religion existed after the fall. Man became alienated from God by the apostacy; peace was to be found again only by returning to God, and in reconciliation to him. ¶ *Thereby good shall come unto thee.* The benefits which he supposed would result from such reconciliation, he proceeds to state in the following verses. They relate chiefly to temporal prosperity, or to proofs of the divine favour in this life. This was in accordance with the views which then prevailed, and especially with their limited and obscure conceptions of the future state. They saw a part—*we* see more; and yet we by no means see all. The

22 Receive, I pray thee, the law from his mouth, and lay up [a] his words in thine heart.

23 If thou return [b] to the Almighty, thou shalt be built up, thou shalt put away [c] iniquity far from thy tabernacles.

24 Then shalt thou lay up gold [1] as dust, and the *gold* of Ophir as the stones of the brooks.

a Ps.119.11. b Ho.14.1,2. c 2Tim.2.19. 1 or, *on the dust.*

good which results from reconciliation with God consists in (1) pardon of sin; (2) peace of conscience; (3) the assurance that we shall have all that is needful in this life; (4) support in trial; (5) peace and triumph in death; (6) a part in the resurrection of the just; and (7) a crown incorruptible and undefiled in heaven. No man was ever *injured* by becoming reconciled to God; no one is reconciled to him who is not made a better and a happier man in this life, and who will not be crowned with immortal glory hereafter.

22. *Receive, I pray thee, the law from his mouth.* Listen to his commands, and obey his precepts. ¶ *And lay up his words in thine heart.* Embrace his truth, and do not forget it. Let it abide with you, and let it influence your secret feelings and the purposes of the soul.

23. *If thou return to the Almighty.* Assuming that he was an impenitent sinner, and wholly unreconciled to him. ¶ *Thou shalt be built up.* A figure taken from building up a house, in contradistinction from pulling one down, and denoting that he would be prospered and happy. ¶ *Thou shalt put away iniquity.* Rosenmüller, Good, Noyes, and Wemyss, suppose correctly, as it seems to me, that the word "if" is to be understood here to complete the sense—"*if* thou shalt put away iniquity." ¶ *From thy tabernacle.* From thy tent, or dwelling.

24. *Then shalt thou lay up gold as dust.* Marg. or, "*on the dust.*" Dr. Good renders this, "Thou shalt then count thy treasure as dust"—implying that he would have much of it. Noyes, "Cast to the dust thy gold"—implying that he would throw his gold away as of no account, and put his dependence on God alone. Kimchi, and, after him, Grotius, suppose that it means, "Thy gold thou shalt regard no more than dust, and gold of Ophir no more than the stones of the brook; God shall be to thee better than gold and silver." The editor of the Pictorial Bible supposes that there is here a distinct reference to the sources from which gold was formerly obtained, as being washed down among the stones of the brooks. The word rendered *gold* here (בֶּצֶר) is from בָּצַר — to *cut off,* Ps. lxxvi. 12, and was properly applied to the *ore* of precious metals in the rude state, as *cut* or *dug* out of mines. Hence, it properly refers to the metals in their crude state, and before they were subjected to the fire. Then it comes to mean precious metals, and is parallel with gold of Ophir in the other hemistich. The word occurs only in the following places; Job xxii. 24; xxxvi. 19, where it is rendered *gold,* and Job xxii. 25, where it is rendered *defence.* The literal translation here would be, "Cast to the dust the precious metals; on the stones of the brooks [the gold of] Ophir." The Vulgate renders it, "He shall give for earth flint, and for flint golden torrents." The LXX., "Thou shalt be placed on a mount in a rock, and as a rock of the torrent of Ophir." Chald. "And thou shalt place upon the dust thy strong tower (כרך תקיף), and as a rock of the torrents the gold of Ophir." The word here is probably synonymous with *precious treasure,* whether consisting in gold or silver; and the idea is, that he should cast to the dust all that treasure, or regard it as valueless; that he should cease to make it an object of solicitude to gain it, and *then* the Almighty would be to him a treasure of more value than gold According to this, the idea is, not that he would be recompensed with gold and silver as the consequence of returning to God, but that God would

25 Yea, the Almighty shall be thy [1] defence, and thou shalt have plenty [2] of silver.

26 For then shalt thou have thy delight in the Almighty, and shalt lift up thy face unto God.

1 or, *gold*.

2 *silver of strength.*

---

afford him more happiness than he had found in the wealth which he had sought, and on which Eliphaz supposed his heart had been set. He regarded Job as covetous of property, as mourning over that which he had lost, and he entreats him now to cease to grieve on account of that, and to come and put his trust in God. ¶ *And the* gold *of Ophir as the stones of the brooks.* Or, rather, "Cast the gold of Ophir to the stones of the valley, or let it remain in its native valley among the stones of the brook, as of no more value than they are." There is, probably, allusion here to the fact, that gold was then commonly found in such places, as it is often now. It was washed down by mountain torrents, and lodged among the stones of the valley, and was thence collected, and the sand being washed out, the gold remained. Ophir is uniformly mentioned in the Scriptures as a place abounding in gold, and as well known; see 1 Kings ix. 28; 2 Chron. viii. 18; ix. 10; 1 Kings x. 11; xxii. 48; 1 Chron. xxix. 4. Much perplexity has been felt in reference to its situation, and the difficulty has not been entirely removed. In regard to the opinions which have been held on the point, the reader may consult my Notes on Isa. xiii. 12, the Note in the Pictorial Bible on 2 Chron. xx. 36, and the Dissertation of Martin Lipenius *de Ophir*, in Ugolin's Thesaur. Sacr. Ant. Tom. vii. pp. 262—387; also, the Dissertation of J. C. Wichmanshausen, *de navigatione Ophiritica*, and Reland's Dissertation *de Ophir* in the same volume. From the mention of this place at a period so early as the time of Job, it is reasonable to suppose that it was not a very remote region, as there is no evidence that voyages were made then to distant countries, or that the knowledge of geography was very extensive. The *presumption* would be, that it was in the vicinity of Arabia.

25. *Yea, the Almighty shall be.* Or, rather, "then the Almighty shall be"—והיה. The meaning is, that if he would return to God, and cast off his anxiety for gold, *then* the Almighty would be his real treasure, and would impart to him solid happiness. ¶ *Thy defence.* Marg. *gold.* The margin is the more correct translation. The word is the same which occurs in the previous verse (בצר), and there rendered *gold.* The word *may* have the sense of *defence,* as the verb (בצר) is often used with such a reference; Num. xiii. 28; Deut. i. 28; iii. 5; ix. 1, *et al.* The meaning of such places, where the word is applied to walled towns or fortified places, is, that the enemy was, by means of walls, *cut off* from approach. Here, however, the idea of *gold* or *treasure* better suits the connection, and the meaning is, that *God* would be to him an invaluable *treasure* or source of happiness. ¶ *And thou shalt have plenty of silver.* Marg. *silver of strength.* The correct idea, however, is, "and the Almighty shall be treasures of silver unto thee;' that is, he shall be better to you than an abundance of the precious metals. The Hebrew is literally, "And silver of treasures unto thee."

26. *Shalt thou have thy delight in the Almighty.* Instead of complaining of him as you now do, you would then find calm enjoyment in contemplating his character and his moral government. This is a correct account of the effects of reconciliation. He who becomes truly "*acquainted*" with God has pleasure in his existence and attributes; in his law and administration. No longer disposed to complain, he confides in him when he is afflicted; flees to him when he is persecuted; seeks him in the day of prosperity; prefers him to all that this world can give, and finds his supremest joys in turning away from all created good to hold communion with the Uncreated One. ¶ *And shalt lift up thy face unto God.* An

27 Thou [a] shalt make thy prayer unto him, and he shall hear thee, and thou shalt pay thy vows.
28 Thou shalt also decree [b] a thing, and it shall be established unto thee: and the light shall shine upon thy ways.
29 When *men* are cast down, then thou shalt say, *There is* lifting up; and he shall save [1] the humble [c] person.

a Ps.66.17–20. b Mat.21.22.

1 *him that hath low eyes.* c 1Pe.5.5.

emblem of prosperity, happiness, and conscious innocence. We hang our face down when we are conscious of guilt; we bow the head in adversity. When conscious of uprightness; when blessed with prosperity, and when we have evidence that we are the children of God, we look up toward heaven. This was the natural condition of men—made to look upwards, while all other animals look grovelling on the earth. So Milton describes the creation of man:

There wanted yet the master-work, the end
Of all yet done; a creature, who, not prone
And brute as other creatures, but endued
With sanctity of reason, might erect
His stature, and upright with front serene
Govern the rest, self-knowing; and from thence
Magnanimous to correspond with heaven,
But grateful to acknowledge whence his good
Descends; thither with heart, and voice, and eyes,
Directed in devotion, to adore
And worship God supreme, who made him chief
Of all his works. Par. Lost, B. vii.

The classic reader will instantly recollect the description in Ovid:

Pronaque cum spectent animalia cætera terram;
Os homini sublime dedit; cœlumque tueri
Jussit, et erectos ad sidera tollere vultus.
Meta. i. 84.

27. *Thou shalt make thy prayer unto him.* God would then hear him, for he would be righteous. This was one of the blessings which would follow reconciliation. It is, in fact, one of the blessings of a return to God. He hears the cry of his people, and answers their supplications. To be permitted to go to God and to tell him all our wants, to plead for all we need and to implore blessings on our families and friends, is a privilege of far higher value than any thing which wealth can bestow; is worth more than all the honours of this world. ¶ *And thou shalt pay thy vows.* That is, thy vows shall be accepted; thou shalt obtain those blessings for which thou didst make thy vows.

28. *Thou shalt also decree a thing, and it shall be established unto thee.* Thou shalt form a purpose or plan, and it shall not be frustrated. It shall not be opposed by the events of divine Providence, but whatever you undertake shall prosper. ¶ *And the light shall shine upon thy ways.* Thou shalt be prospered in all things, instead of being overtaken with calamity.

29. *When* men *are cast down.* The meaning of this is, probably, when men are usually cast down, or in the times of trial and calamity, which prostrate others, you shall find support. You shall then be enabled to say, "there is lifting up, or there is support." Or, more probably still, it may mean, "in times when others are cast down and afflicted, thou shalt be able to raise them up, or to aid them. Thou shalt be able to go to them and say, 'Be of good cheer. Do not be cast down. There is consolation.' And thou shalt be able to procure important blessings for them by thy counsels and prayers;" see Notes on ver. 30. ¶ *And he shall save the humble person.* That is, either, "*Thou* shalt save the humble person," by a change from the second person to the third, which is not uncommon in Hebrew; or, "thou shalt be able from thine own experience to say, *He*, i. e. *God*, will save the humble person, or the one that is cast down." Marg. *him that hath low eyes*. The Hebrew is like the margin. In affliction the eyes are cast upon the ground; and so, also, a casting the eyes to the ground is indicative

30 He [1] shall deliver the island of the innocent: and it is delivered by the pureness of thine hands.

[1] or, *the innocent shall deliver the island*, Ge.18.26.

of dejection, of humility, or of modesty. It refers here to one who experiences trials; and Eliphaz says that Job would be able to save such an one; that is, to support him in his afflictions, and furnish the helps necessary to restore him again to comfort.

30. *He shall deliver the island of the innocent.* Marg. *the innocent shall deliver the island.* Never was there a more unhappy translation than this; and it is quite clear that our translators had no intelligible idea of the meaning of the passage. What can be meant by "saving the *island* of the innocent?" The word rendered *island* (אִי) commonly means, indeed, an island, or a maritime country; see Notes on Isa. xx. 6; xli. 1. It is, however, used as a *negative* in 1 Sam. iv. 21, in the name *I-chabod*—אִי־כָבוֹד. "And she named the child I-chabod (marg. i. e. *where* is *the glory?* or, there is *no glory*), saying, the glory is departed from Israel." This sense is frequent in the Rabbinic Hebrew, where it is used as connected with an adjective in a privative sense, like the English *un*. It is probably an abbreviated form of (אַיִן) *not, nothing;* and is used here as a *negative* to qualify the following word, "He shall deliver even him that is *not* innocent." So it is rendered by the Chaldee, by Le Clerc, Rosenmüller, Gesenius, Noyes, and others. The Vulgate and the Septuagint render it, "He shall deliver the innocent." The sense is, that the man who returns to God, and who is regarded by him as his friend, will be able to intercede for the guilty, and to save them from the punishment which they deserved. His prayers and intercessions will be heard in their behalf, and on his account favours will be shown to them, even when they did not personally deserve them. This sentiment accords with that expressed in Gen. xviii. 26, "If I find in Sodom fifty righteous within the city, then I will spare all the place for their sakes;" Ezek. xiv. 14, "Though these three men, Noah, Daniel, and Job were in it, they should deliver but their own souls;" comp. Ezek. xxii. 30; Jer. v. 1. The sentiment, also, had a beautiful illustration, though one which Eliphaz did not here think of, in his own case and that of his friends, where this very Job, to whom he was giving this counsel, was directed to intercede for them; chap. xlii. 7, 8. The sentiment, indeed, is found every where in the Scriptures, that the righteous are permitted to pray for others, and that they are thus the means of bringing down important blessings on them. In answer to those prayers, multitudes are saved from calamity here, and will be brought to eternal life hereafter. ¶ *And it is delivered by the pureness of thine hands.* Or, rather, he, *i. e.* the wicked, for whom you pray, will be delivered by the pureness of thine hands. That is, God will save him in answer to the prayers of a righteous man. Your upright and holy life; your pure hands stretched out in supplication, shall be the means of saving him. No one can tell how many blessings are conferred on wicked men *because* the righteous pray for them. No one can tell how many a wicked son is spared, and ultimately saved, in answer to the intercessions of a holy parent; nor can the wicked world yet know how much it owes its preservation, and the numberless blessings which it enjoys, to the intercessions of the saints. It is *one* of the innumerable blessings of being a child of God thus to be permitted to be the means of bringing down blessings on others, and saving sinners from ruin. All the friends of God may thus confer unspeakable benefits to others; and they who have "an interest at the throne of grace" should plead without ceasing for the salvation of guilty and dying men.

CHAPTER XXIII.

ANALYSIS OF CHAPTERS XXIII. AND XXIV.

These two chapters contain the answer of Job to the last speech of Eliphaz. The address is that of a mind agitated by deep and conflicting emotions. It consists in part in the expression of those emotions, and in part in an endeavour once more to convince his friends of the falsehood of their positions. The address comprises the following topics.

He expresses the depth of his sorrows, and says that his complaint is more bitter than he had yet expressed, chap. xxiii. 2. He then repeats his earnest desire to carry his cause before God, since he could obtain no justice from men, but he knows not where to find him. He is assured that if he could get his cause before him, justice would be done him, ver. 3—9. In this perplexity, however, he consoles himself with the reflection that though he had not the opportunity of pleading his cause as he wished before God, yet that he knew that he was sincere, and would yet appear for his vindication, and bring him forth as gold, ver. 10—12. Yet, he says, he is troubled at the dealings of God with him, notwithstanding his consciousness of integrity. He trembles at the contemplation of a Being who thus carries forward his eternal and unchangeable purpose; who has all power to execute his designs; and whose judgments are so fearful, ver. 13—17.

Having thus given vent to his feelings, he returns to the argument, chap. xxiv. He attempts by one more effort to convince his adversaries that it was not a *matter of fact* that God dealt with the wicked in this life as they deserved, and that *in fact* many of them lived in prosperity. He denies that judgments come universally upon wicked men, and maintains that they do not even frequently come; and he produces a catalogue of enormous crimes, and shows that they who committed them actually lived and were prospered. He specifies those who remove the landmarks; those who plunder flocks and herds; those who oppress the fatherless and the widow; those who are cruel; those who pluck the fatherless from the breast, and take a pledge of the poor; he mentions the murderer, the adulterer, the thief, and says that all these in fact live and flourish. Yet he maintains that, notwithstanding their present prosperity, they shall be brought down, and meet the rewards of their wickedness hereafter. As all this was indisputable, it ended the controversy Eliphaz and Zophar made no further reply, and Bildad only made (chap. xxv.) a feeble effort, without attempting to meet the facts, and uttered some vague generalities which showed that he in fact had no more to say.

THEN Job answered and said,
2 Even to-day *is* my complaint bitter: my [1] stroke is heavier than my groaning.
3 Oh [a] that I knew where I might find him! *that* I might come *even* to his seat!

1 *hand*. a Is.26.8; Je 14.8.

CHAPTER XXIII.

2. *Even to-day*. At the present time. I am not relieved. You afford me no consolation. All that you say only aggravates my woes. ¶ *My complaint;* see Notes on chap. xxi. 3. ¶ *Bitter*. Sad, melancholy, distressing. The meaning is, not that he made bitter complaints in the sense which those words would naturally convey, or that he meant to find fault with God, but that his case was a hard one. His friends furnished him no relief, and he had in vain endeavoured to bring his cause before God. This is now, as he proceeds to state, the principal cause of his difficulty. He knows not where to find God; he cannot get his cause before him. ¶ *My stroke*. Marg. as in Heb. *hand;* that is, the hand that is upon me, or the calamity that is inflicted upon me. The *hand* is represented as the instrument of inflicting punishment, or causing affliction; see Notes on chap. xix. 21. ¶ *Heavier than my groaning*. My sighs bear no proportion to my sufferings. They are no adequate expression of my woes. If you think I complain; if I am heard to groan, yet the sufferings which I endure are far beyond what these would seem to indicate. Sighs and groans are not improper. They are prompted by nature, and they furnish *some* relief to a sufferer. But they should not be (1.) with a spirit of murmuring or complaining; (2.) they should not be *beyond* what our sufferings demand, or the proper expression of our sufferings. They should not be such as to lead others to suppose we suffer more than we actually do. (3.) They should —when they are extorted from us by the severity of suffering—lead us to look to that world where no groan will ever be heard.

3. *Oh that I knew where I might find him!* Where I might find *God*. He had often expressed a wish to bring his cause directly before God, and to be permitted to plead his cause there; see Notes on chap. xiii. 3, 20, seq But this he had not yet been able to do. The argument had been with his three friends, and he saw that there was no use in attempting further to convince them. If he could get the cause before God, and be allowed to plead it there, he felt assured that justice would be done him. But he had not been able to do this. God

4 I would order *my* cause [a] before him, and fill my mouth with arguments.

5 I would know the words *which* he would answer me, and understand what he would say unto me.

6 Will [b] he plead against me with *his* great power? No; but he would put *strength* in me.

a Is 43.26. b Is 57.16.

had not come forth in any visible and public manner as he wished, so that the cause could be fairly tried before such a tribunal, and he was in darkness. The *language* here used will express the condition of a pious man in the times of spiritual darkness. He cannot find God. He has no near access as he once had to him. In such a state he anxiously seeks to find God, but he cannot. There is no light and no comfort to his soul. This language may further describe the state of one who is conscious of uprightness, and who is exposed to the suspicion or the unkind remarks of the world. His character is attacked; his motives are impugned; his designs are suspected, and no one is disposed to do him justice. In such a state, he feels that *God* alone will do him justice. *He* knows the sincerity of his heart, and he can safely commit his cause to him. It is always the privilege of the calumniated and the slandered to make an appeal to the divine tribunal, and to feel that whatever injustice our fellow-men may be disposed to do us, there is One who will never do a wrong. ¶ That *I might come* even *to his seat.* To his throne, or tribunal. Job wished to carry the cause directly before him. Probably he desired some manifestation of God—such as he was afterwards favoured with—when God would declare his judgment on the whole matter of the controversy.

4. *I would order* my *cause before* him; comp. Notes on Isa. xliii. 26. That is, I would arrange my arguments, or plead my cause, as one does in a court of justice. I would suggest the considerations which would show that I am not guilty in the sense charged by my friends, and that notwithstanding my calamities, I am the real friend of God. ¶ *And fill my mouth with arguments.* Probably he means that he would appeal to the evidence furnished by a life of benevolence and justice, that he was not a hypocrite or a man of distinguished wickedness, as his friends maintained.

5. *I would know the words* which *he would answer me.* That is, I wish to understand what would be *his* decision in the case—and what would be his judgment in regard to me. That was of infinitely more importance than any opinion which *man* could form, and Job was anxious to have the matter decided by a tribunal which could not err. Why should *we* not desire to know exactly what God thinks of us, and what estimate he has formed of our character? There is no information so valuable to us as that would be; for on *his* estimate hangs our eternal doom, and yet there is nothing which men more instinctively dread than to know what God thinks of their character. It would be well for each one to ask himself, *Why is it so?*

6. *Will he plead against me with* his *great power?* "Will he make use of his mere *power* to overwhelm me and confound me? Will he take advantage of omnipotence to triumph over me, instead of argument and justice? No: he will not do it. The discussion would be fair. He would hear what I have to say, and would decide according to truth. Though he is Almighty, yet he would not take advantage of that to prostrate and confound me." When Job (chap. xiii. 3) wished to carry the cause directly before God, he asked of Him two conditions only. One was, that he would take off his hand from him, or remove his afflictions for a time, that he might be able to manage his own cause; and the other was, that He would not take advantage of his power to overwhelm him in the debate, and prevent his making a fair statement of his case; see Notes on chap. xiii. 20, 21. He here expresses his firm conviction that his wish in

7 There the righteous might dispute with him; so shall I be delivered for ever from my judge.

8 Behold, I go forward, but he
is not *there;* and backward, but I
cannot perceive him;

---

this respect would be granted. He would listen, says he, to what I have to say in my defence as if I were an equal. ¶ *No; but he would put* strength *in me.* The word *strength* is not improperly supplied by our translators. It means that he would enable him to make a fair presentation of his cause. So far from taking advantage of his mere *power* to crush him, and thus obtain an ascendency in the argument, he would rather *strengthen* him, that he might be able to make his case as strong as possible. He would rather aid him, though presenting his own cause in the controversy, than seek to weaken his arguments, or so to awe him by his dread majesty as to prevent his making the case as strong as it might be. This indicates remarkable confidence in God.

7. *There the righteous might dispute with him.* One who is conscious of his integrity might carry his cause there, with the assurance that he would be heard, and that justice would be done him. There can be no doubt that Job here refers to himself, though he speaks in the third person, and advances this as a general proposition. ¶ *So shall I be delivered for ever from my judge.* From him who would judge or condemn me (מְשֹׁפְטִי). He does not here refer to *God,* as if he would be delivered from him, but to *any one* who would attempt to judge and condemn him, as his friends had done. The meaning is, that having, as he confidently expected he would, obtained the verdict of God in his favour, he would be ever after free from condemnation. The decision would be final. There was no higher tribunal, and no one would dare to condemn him afterwards. This shows his consciousness of integrity. It may be applied to ourselves—to all. If we can obtain, at the last day, when our cause shall be brought before God, the divine verdict in our favour, it will settle the matter for ever. No one, after that, will condemn us; never again shall our character or conduct be put on trial. The divine decision of that day will settle the question to all eternity. How momentous, then, is it that we should so live as to be acquitted in that day, and to have *an eternal sentence* IN OUR FAVOUR!

8. *Behold, I go forward.* The meaning of these verses is, I go in all directions, but I cannot find God. I am excluded from the trial which I seek, and I cannot bring my cause to his throne. Job expresses his earnest desire to see some visible manifestation of the Deity, and to be permitted to argue his cause in his presence. But he says he sought this in vain. He looked to all points of the compass where he might rationally expect to find God, but all in vain. The terms here used refer to the points of the compass, and should have been so rendered. The Oriental geographers considered themselves as facing the East, instead of the North, as we do. Of course, the West was behind them, the South on the right hand, and on the left the North. This was a more natural position than ours, as day begins in the East, and it is natural to turn the face in that direction. There is no reason why our maps should be made so as to require us to face the *North,* except that such is the custom. The Hebrew custom, in this respect, is found also in the notices of geography in other nations. The same thing prevails among the Hindoos. Among them, Para, or Purra, signifying "before," denotes the East; Apara and Paschima, meaning "behind," the West; Dacshina, or "the right hand," the South; and Bama, or "the left hand," the North; see Wilford's Inquiry respecting the Holy Isles in the West, Asiatic Researches, vol. viii. p. 275. The same thing occurred among the ancient Irish; see an Essay on the Antiquity of the Irish language, by an unknown author, Dublin, 1772; comp. on this subject, Rosenmüller's Alterthumskunde i. s.

9 On the left hand, where he doth work, but I cannot behold *him:* he hideth himself on the right hand, that I cannot see *him:*

136—144. The same custom prevailed among the Mongols. *Gesenius.* On the notices of the science of geography exhibited in the book of Job, comp. Intro. § viii. 2, 3. The phrase, therefore, "Behold, I go forward," means, "I go to the East. I look toward the rising of the sun. I see there the most wonderful of the works of the Creator in the glories of the sun, and I go towards it in hopes of finding there some manifestation of God. But I find him not, and, disappointed, I turn to other directions." Most of the ancient versions render this *the East.* Thus the Vulgate, *Si ad Orientem iero.* The Chaldee למדינחא, *to the sun-rising.* ¶ *But he is not* there. There is no manifestation of God, no coming forth to meet me, and to hear my cause. ¶ *And backward* (ואחור). To the West—for this was *behind* the individual when he stood looking to the East. Sometimes the West is denoted by this term *behind* (אחור), and sometimes by *the sea* (ים), because the Mediterranean was at the West of Palestine and Arabia; see Notes on Isa. ix. 12; comp. Ex. x 19; xxvii. 13; xxxviii. 12; Gen. xxviii. 14. ¶ *But I cannot perceive him.* The meaning is, "Disappointed in the East, the region of the rising sun, I turn with longing to the *West,* the region of his setting, and hope, as his last beams fade from the view, that I shall be permitted to behold some ray that shall reveal God to my soul. Before the night settles down upon the world, emblem of the darkness in my soul, I would look upon the last lingering ray, and hope that in that I may see God. In that vast region of the West, illuminated by the setting sun, I would hope somewhere to find him; but I am disappointed there. The sun withdraws his beams, and darkness steals on, and the world, like my soul, is enveloped in gloom. I can see no indications of the presence of God coming forth to give me an opportunity to argue my cause before him."

9. *On the left hand.* That is, in the North—at the left hand when the face was turned to the East. So the Chaldee, בציפונא—*on the North.* The other versions, the Vulgate, the Septuagint, the Syriac, Castellio, Luther, &c., render it *on the left hand.* The common term among the Hebrews for the *North* is צפון—*tzaphon* (from צפן—*to hide,* or *conceal*), meaning the hidden, concealed, or dark region, since the ancients regarded the North as the seat of gloom and darkness, (Hom. Od. ix. 25, seq.), while they supposed the South to be illuminated by the sun. *Gesenius.* Frequently, however, as here, the word "left," or "left hand," is used. The region of the North is intended. ¶ *Where he doth work.* Where there are such wonderful manifestations of his majesty and glory. May Job here not refer to the *Aurora Borealis,* the remarkable display of the power of God which is seen in those regions? May he not have felt that there was some special reason why he might hope to meet with God in that quarter, or to see him manifest himself amidst the brilliant lights that play along the sky, as if to precede or accompany him? And when he had looked to the splendour of the rising sun, and the glory of his setting, in vain, was it not natural to turn his eye to the *next* remarkable manifestation, as he supposed, of God, in the glories of the Northern lights, and to expect to find him there? There is reason to think that the ancient Chaldeans, and other heathens, regarded the regions of the North, illuminated with these celestial splendours, as the peculiar residence of the gods (see Notes on Isa. xiv. 13), and it seems probable that Job may have had allusion to some such prevailing opinion. ¶ *But I cannot behold* him. I can see the exhibition of remarkable splendour, but still *God* is unseen. He does not come amidst those glories to give me an opportunity to carry my cause before him. The meaning, then, of this is, "Disappointed in the East and the West, I turn to the North.

10 But he knoweth the way that [1] I take: *when* [a] he hath tried me I shall come forth as gold.

1 is *with me*. a 1 Pe.1.7.

There I have been accustomed to witness extraordinary manifestations of his magnificence and glory. There beautiful constellations circle the pole. There the Aurora plays, and seems to be the manifestation of the glory of God. Next to the glory of the rising and setting sun, I turn to those brilliant lights, to see if there I may not find my God, but in vain. Those lights are cold and chilly, and reveal no God to my soul. Disappointed, then I turn to the last point, the South, to see if I can find him there." ¶ *He hideth himself on the right hand.* On the South. The South was to the ancients an unknown region. The deserts of Arabia, indeed, stretched away in that region, and they were partially known, and they had some knowledge that the sea was beyond. But they regarded the regions farther to the South, if there was land there, as wholly impassable and uninhabitable on account of the heat. The knowledge of geography was slowly acquired, and, of course, it is impossible to tell what were the views which prevailed on the subject in the time of Job. That there was little accuracy of information about remote countries must be regarded as an indisputable fact; and, probably, they had little conception of distant parts of the earth, except that formed by conjecture. Interesting details of the views of the ancients, on this subject, may be found in the Encyclopedia of Geography, vol. i. pp. 10—68; compare particularly the Notes on chap. xxvi. 10. The earth was regarded as encompassed with waters, and the distant southern regions, on account of the impossibility of passing through the heat of the torrid zone, were supposed to be inaccessible. To those hidden and unknown realms, Job says he now turned, when he had in vain looked to each other quarter of the heavens, to see if he could find some manifestation of God. Yet he looked to that quarter equally in vain. God *hid* or *concealed* himself in those inaccessible regions, so that he could not approach him. The meaning is, "I am also disappointed here. He hides himself in that distant land. In the burning and impassable wastes which stretch themselves to an unknown extent there, I cannot find him. The feet of mortals cannot traverse those burning plains, and there I cannot approach him. To whatever point of the compass I turn, I am left in equal darkness." What a striking description is this of the darkness that sometimes comes over the Christian's soul, prompting to the language, "O that I knew where I *might* find him! That I *could* come to his throne!"

10. *But he knoweth the way that I take.* Marg. "is *with me*." That is, "I have the utmost confidence in him. Though I cannot see him, yet he sees me, and he knows my integrity; and whatever men may say, or however they may misunderstand my character, yet he is acquainted with me, and I have the fullest confidence that he will do me justice." ¶ When *he hath tried me.* When he has subjected me to all the tests of character which he shall choose to apply. ¶ *I shall come forth as gold.* As gold that is tried in the crucible, and that comes forth the more pure the intenser is the heat. The application of fire to it serves to separate every particle of impurity or alloy, and leaves only the pure metal. So it is with trials applied to the friend of God; and we may remark (1.) That all real piety will bear *any* test that may be applied to it, as gold will bear any degree of heat without being injured or destroyed. (2.) That the effect of all trials is to purify piety, and make it more bright and valuable, as is the effect of applying intense heat to gold. (3.) There is often much alloy in the piety of a Christian, as there is in gold, that needs to be removed by the fiery trial of affliction. Nothing else will remove it but trial, as nothing will be so effectual a purifier of gold as intense heat. (4.) A true Christian should not dread trial. It will not hurt him. He will be the

11 My foot hath held his steps,
his way have I kept, and not declined.
12 Neither have I gone back
from the commandment of his lips;
I [a] have [1] esteemed the words of
his mouth more than my [2] necessary *food*. [b]

a Ps. 19.9,10. 1 *hid*, or, *laid up*. 2 or, *appointed portion*. *b* Je. 15.16.

more valuable for his trials, as gold is for the application of heat. There is no danger of destroying true piety. It will live in the flames, and will survive the raging heat that shall yet consume the world.

11. *My foot hath held his steps.* Roberts, in his Oriental Illustrations, and the Editor of the Pictorial Bible, suppose that there is an allusion here to the active, grasping power which the Orientals have in their feet and toes. By constant usage they accustom themselves to make use of them in holding things in a manner which to us seems almost incredible, and they make the toes perform almost the work of fingers. We bind ours fast from early childhood in our close shoes, and they become useless except for the purpose of walking. But the Orientals use theirs differently. They seize upon an object with their toes, and hold it fast. If in walking along they see any thing on the ground which they desire to pick up, instead of stooping as we would, they seize it with their toes, and lift it up. Alypulle, a Kandian chief, was about to be beheaded. When he arrived at the place of execution, he looked round for some object on which to seize, and saw a small shrub, and seized it with his toes, and held it fast in order to be firm while the executioner did his office. *Roberts.* So an Arab in treading firmly, or in taking a determined stand, seems to lay hold of, to grasp the ground with his toes, giving a fixedness of position inconceivable to those whose feet are cramped by the use of tight shoes. This may be the meaning here, that Job had fixed himself firmly in the footsteps of God, and had adhered tenaciously to him; or, as it is rendered by Dr. Good, "In his steps will I *rivet* my feet." ¶ *And not declined.* Turned aside.

12. *Neither have I gone back.* I have not put away or rejected. ¶ *The commandment of his lips.* That which he has spoken, or which has proceeded out of his mouth. ¶ *I have esteemed.* Marg, *hid*, or, *laid up*. The Heb. is, "I have hid," as we hide or lay up that which is valuable. It is a word often applied to laying up treasures, or concealing them so that they would be safe. ¶ *More than my necessary* food. Marg, "or, *appointed portion*." Dr. Good renders it, "In my bosom have I laid up the words of his mouth." So Noyes, "The words of his mouth I have treasured up in my bosom." So Wemyss; and so it is rendered in the Vulgate, and by the LXX. The variety in the translation has arisen from the difference of reading in regard to the Hebrew word מחקי. Instead of this meaning "more than my portion" or "allowance, the Sept. and Vulgate appear to have read בחקי—*in my bosom.* But there is no authority for the change, and there seems to be no reason for it. The word חק, *hhoq*, means something decreed, designated, appointed; then an appointed portion, as of labour, Ex. v. 14; then of food—an allowance of food, Prov. xxx. 8; then a limit, bound, law, statute, &c. It seems to me that the word here means *purpose, intention, rule*, or *design*, and that the idea is. that he had regarded the commands of God more *than his own purposes.* He had been willing to sacrifice his own designs to the will of God, and had thus shown his preference for God and his law. This sense seems to be the most simple of any, and it is surprising that it has not occurred to any expositors. So the same word is used in ver. 14. If this be the meaning, it expresses a true sentiment of piety in all ages. He who is truly religious is willing to sacrifice and abandon his own plans at the command of God. Job says that he was conscious of having done this, and he thus had a firm conviction that he was a pious man.

13 But he *is* in one *mind*, and who can turn him? and *what* his soul desireth, even *that* he doeth.

14 For he performeth *the thing that is* appointed [a] for me: and many such *things are* with him.

a 1 Th.3.3.

13. *But he* is *in one* mind. He is unchangeable. He has formed his plans, and no one can divert him from them. Of the *truth* of this sentiment there can be no dispute. The only difficulty in the case is to see why Job adverted to it here, and how it bears on the train of thought which he was pursuing. The idea seems to be, that God was now accomplishing his eternal purposes in respect to him; that he had formed a plan far back in eternal ages, and that that plan must be executed; that he was a Sovereign, and that however mysterious his plans might be, it was vain to contend with them, and that man ought to submit to their execution with patience and resignation. Job expected yet that God would come forth and vindicate him; but at present all that he could do was to submit. He did not pretend to understand the reason of the divine dispensations; he felt that he had no power to resist God. The language here is that of a man who is perplexed in regard to the divine dealings, but who feels that they are all in accordance with the unchangeable purpose of God. ¶ *And* what *his soul desireth, even* that *he doeth.* He does what he pleases. None can resist or control him. It is vain, therefore, to contend against him. From this passage we see that the doctrine of divine sovereignty was understood at a very early age of the world, and entered undoubtedly into the religion of the patriarchs. It was then seen and felt that God was absolute; that he was not dependent on his creatures; that he acted according to a plan; that he was inflexible in regard to that plan, and that it was in vain to attempt to resist its execution It is, when properly understood, a matter of unspeakable consolation that God *has* a plan—for who could honour a God who had *no* plan, but who did everything by hap-hazard? It is matter of rejoicing that he has *one* great purpose which extends through all ages, and which embraces all things—for then every thing falls into its proper place, and has its appropriate bearing on other events. It is a matter of joy that God *does* execute all his purposes; for as they are all good and wise, it is *desirable* that they should be executed. It would be a calamity if a good plan were *not* executed. Why then should men murmur at the purposes or the decrees of God?

14. *For he performeth* the thing that is *appointed for me.* "I am now meeting only what has been determined by his eternal plan. I know not what is the *reason* why it was appointed; but I see that God had resolved to do it, and that it is vain to resist him." So when *we* suffer, we may say the same thing. It is not by chance or hap-hazard that we are afflicted; it is because *God* has "appointed" that it should be so. It is not by passion or caprice on his part; not by sudden anger or wrath; but it is because he had determined to do it as a part of his eternal plan. It is much, when we are afflicted, to be able to make this reflection. I had rather be afflicted, feeling that it is *the appointment of God*, than feeling that it is *by chance* or *hap-hazard.* I had rather think that it is a part of a plan calmly and deliberately formed by God, than that it is the result of some unexpected and uncontrollable cause. In the one case, I see that mind and thought and plan have been employed, and I infer that there is a *reason* for it, though I cannot see it; in the other, I can see no proof of reason or of wisdom, and my mind finds no rest. The doctrine of divine purposes or decrees, therefore, is eminently adapted to give consolation to a sufferer. I had infinitely rather be under the operation of a plan or decree where there *may* be a reason for all that is done, though I cannot see it, than to feel that I am subject to the tossings of blind chance, where there

15 Therefore am I troubled at his presence: when I consider, I am afraid [a] of him.
16 For God maketh my heart soft, and the Almighty troubleth me:
17 Because I was not cut off before the darkness, *neither* hath he covered the darkness from my face.

a Ps. 119.120.

can possibly be *no* reason. ¶ *And many such things are with him.* The purpose does not pertain to me alone. It is a part of a great plan which extends to others—to all things. He is executing his plans around me, and I should not complain that in the development of his vast purposes I am included, and that I suffer. The idea seems to be this, that Job found consolation in the belief that he was not alone in these circumstances; that he had not been marked out and selected as a special object of divine displeasure. Others had suffered in like manner. There were *many* cases just like his own, and why should he complain? If I felt that there was special displeasure against *me;* that no others were treated in the same way, it would make afflictions much more difficult to bear. But when I feel that there is an eternal plan which embraces all, and that I only come in for my share, in common with others, of the calamities which are judged necessary for the world, I can bear them with much more ease and patience.

15. *Therefore am I troubled at his presence.* The doctrine of divine purposes and decrees *is fitted to impress the mind with awe.* So vast are the plans of God; so uncertain to us is it what will be developed next; so impossible is it to resist God when he comes forth to execute his plans, that they fill the mind with reverence and fear. And this is one of the objects for which the doctrine is revealed. It is designed to rebuke the soul that is filled with flippancy and self-conceit; to impress the heart with adoring views of God, and to secure a proper reverence for his government. Not knowing what may be the next development of his plan, the mind should be in a state of holy fear—yet ready to submit and bow in whatever aspect his purposes may be made known. A Being, who has an eternal plan, and who is able to accomplish all that he purposes, and who makes known none of his dealings beforehand, should be an object of veneration and fear. It will not be the same *kind of dreadful fear* which we would have of one who had almighty power, but who had *no plan* of any kind, but profound veneration for one who is infinitely wise as well as almighty. The fear of an Almighty Being, who has an eternal plan, which we cannot doubt is wise, though it is inscrutable to us, is a fear mingled with confidence; it is awe leading to the profoundest veneration. His eternal counsels may take away *our* comforts, but they are right; his coming forth may fill us with awe, but we shall venerate and love him. ¶ *When I consider.* When I endeavour to understand his dealings; or when I think closely on them. ¶ *I am afraid of him.* This would be the effect on any mind. A man that will sit down alone and *think* of God, and on his vast plans, will see that there is abundant occasion to be in awe before him.

16. *For God maketh my heart soft.* That is, *faint.* He takes away my strength; comp. Notes on Isa. vii. 4. This effect was produced on Job by the contemplation of the eternal plan and the power of God.

17. *Because I was not cut off before the darkness.* Before these calamities came upon me. Because I was not taken away in the midst of prosperity, and while I was enjoying his smiles and the proofs of his love. His trouble is, that he was spared to pass through these trials, and to be treated as if he were one of the worst of men. This is what now perplexes him, and what he cannot understand. He does not know why God had reserved him to treat him as if he were the chief of sinners. ¶ Neither *hath he covered the darkness from my face.* The word

CHAPTER XXIV.

WHY, seeing times [a] are not hidden from the Almighty, do they that know him not see his days?

a Acts 1.7.

"neither" is supplied here by our translators, but not improperly. The difficulty with Job was, that God had not *hidden* this darkness and calamity so that he had not seen it. He could not understand why, since he was his friend, God had not taken him away, so that all should have seen, even in his death, that he was the friend of God. This feeling is not, perhaps, very uncommon among those who are called to pass through trials. They do not understand why they were *reserved* to these sufferings, and why God did not take them away before the billows of calamity rolled over them.

1. *Why, seeing times are not hidden from the Almighty.* Dr. Good renders this,

> "Wherefore are not doomdays kept by the Almighty,
> So that his offenders may eye his periods?"

Dr. Noyes,

> "Why are not times of punishment reserved by the Almighty,
> And why do not they, who regard him, see his judgments?"

Jerome, "Times are not hidden from the Almighty; but they who know him are ignorant of his days." The LXX., "But why have set times—ὧραι—escaped the notice—ἔλαθον—of the Almighty, and the wicked transgressed all bounds? The word עִתִּים, here translated *times*, is rendered by the Chaldee (עִדָּנַיָּא) *set times*, times appointed for an assembly or a trial, beforehand designated for any purpose. The Hebrew word properly means, set time, fit and proper times; and in the plural, as here used, means *seasons*, Est. i. 13; 1 Chron. xii. 32; and then vicissitudes of things, fortunes, destinies; Ps. xxxi. 16; 1 Chron. xxix. 30. Here it means, probably, the vicissitudes of things, or what actually occurs. All changes are known to God. He sees good and bad times; he sees the changes that take place among men. And since he sees all this, Job asks, with concern, Why is it that God does not come forth to deal with men according to their true character? That this was the fact, he proceeds to show farther in illustration of the position which he had maintained in chap. xxi. by specifying a number of additional cases where the wicked undeniably prospered. It was this which perplexed him so much, for he did not doubt that their conduct was clearly known to God. If their conduct had been unknown to God, it would not have been a matter of surprise that they should go unpunished. But since all their ways were clearly seen by him, it might well excite inquiry why they were permitted thus to prosper. *He* believed that they were reserved to a future day of wrath, chap. xxi. 30; chap. xxiv. 23, 24. They would be punished in due time, but it was not a fact as his friends alleged, that they were punished in this life according to their deeds. ¶ *Do they that know him?* His true friends; the pious. ¶ *Not see his days.* The days of his wrath, or the day when he punishes the wicked. Why are they not permitted to see him come forth to take vengeance on his foes? The phrase "*his* days" means the days when God would come forth to punish his enemies. They are called "*his* days," because at that time God would be the prominent object that would excite attention. They would be days when he would manifest himself in a manner so remarkable as to characterise the period. Thus the day of judgment is called the day "of the Son of Man," or "*his* day" (Luke xvii. 24), because at that time the Lord Jesus will be the prominent and glorious object that shall give character to the day. The *question* here seems to have been asked by Job mainly to call attention to *the fact* which he proceeds to illustrate. The fact was undeniable. Job did *not* maintain, as Eliphaz had charged on him (chap. xxii. 12—14), that the reason why God did not punish them was, that he could not

2 *Some* remove the land-marks ; they violently take away flocks, and feed [1] *thereof.*

3 They drive away the ass of the fatherless, they take [a] the widow's ox for a pledge.

4 They turn the needy out of the way ; the poor of the earth hide themselves together.

5 Behold, *as* wild asses in the desert, go they forth to their work, rising betimes for a prey ; the wilderness *yieldeth* food for them *and* for *their* children.

1 or, them.

a De.24.6,17.

see their deeds. He admitted most fully that God did see them, and understood all that they did. In this they were agreed. Since this was so, the question was why the wicked were spared, and lived in prosperity. The fact that it was so, Job affirms. The *reason* why it was so, was the subject of inquiry now. This was perplexing, and Job could solve it only by referring to what was to come hereafter.

2. Some *remove the land-marks.* Land-marks are pillars or stones set up to mark the boundaries of a farm. To remove them, by carrying them on to the land of another, was an act of dishonesty and robbery—since it was only by marks that the extent of a man's property could be known. Fences were uncommon ; the art of surveying was not well understood, and deeds describing land were probably unknown also, and their whole dependence, therefore, was on the stones that were erected to mark the boundaries of a lot or farm. As it was not difficult to remove them, it became a matter of special importance to guard against it, and to make it a crime of magnitude. Accordingly, it was forbidden in the strictest manner in the law of Moses. " Cursed be he that removeth his neighbour's land-mark ;" Deut. xxvii. 17 ; comp. Deut. xix. 14 ; Prov. xxii. 28 ; xxiii. 10. ¶ *And feed* thereof. Marg. " or, them." The margin is correct. The meaning is, that they drive off the flocks of others, and *pasture* them ; that is, they are at no pains to conceal what they do, but mingle them with their own herds, and feed them as if they were their own. If they drove them away to kill, and removed them wholly from view, it would be less shameful than to keep and claim them as their own, and to make the robbery so public.

3. *They drive away the ass of the fatherless.* Of the orphan, who cannot protect himself, and whose only property may consist in this useful animal. Injury done to an orphan is always regarded as a crime of peculiar magnitude, for they are unable to protect themselves ; see Notes, chap. xxii. 9. ¶ *They take the widow's ox for a pledge ;* see Notes, chap. xxii. 6. The widow was dependent on her ox to till the ground, and hence the crime of taking it away in pledge for the payment of a debt.

4. *They turn the needy out of the way.* They crowd the poor out of the path, and thus oppress and injure them. They do not allow them the advantages of the highway. ¶ *The poor of the earth hide themselves together.* For fear of the rich and mighty man. Driven from the society of the rich, without their patronage and friendship, they are obliged to associate together, and find in the wicked man neither protector nor friend. And yet the proud oppressor is not punished.

5. *Behold,* as *wild asses in the desert.* In regard to the wild ass, see Notes on chap. vi. 5. Schultens, Good, Noyes, and Wemyss, understand this, not as referring to the haughty tyrants themselves, but to the oppressed and needy wretches whom they had driven from society, and compelled to seek a precarious subsistence, like the wild ass, in the desert. They suppose that the meaning is, that these outcasts go to their daily toil seeking roots and vegetables in the desert for a subsistence, like wild animals. But it seems to me that the reference is rather to another class of wicked men : to the wandering tribes that

6 They reap *every one* his [1] corn
in the field, and [2] they gather the
vintage of the wicked.
7 They cause the naked to
lodge without clothing, that *they
have* no covering in the cold
8 They are wet with the showers of the mountains, and embrace [a] the rock for want of a shelter.

1 *mingled corn*, or *dredge*.
2 *the wicked gather the vintage*. a La.4.5.

live by plunder—who roam through the deserts, and live an unrestrained and a lawless life, like wild animals The wild ass is distinguished for its fleetness, and the comparison here turns principally on this fact. These marauders move rapidly from place to place, make their assault suddenly and unexpectedly, and, having plundered the traveller, or the caravan, as suddenly disappear. They have no home, cultivate no land, and keep no flocks. The only objection to this interpretation is, that the wild ass is not a beast of prey. But, in reply to this, it may be said, that the comparison does not depend on that, but on the fact that they resemble those animals in their lawless habits of life; see Notes on chap. xi. 12; xxxix. 5. ¶ *Go they forth to their work.* To their employment—to wit, plunder. ¶ *Rising betimes.* Rising early. It is a custom of the Orientals every where to rise by break of day. In journeys, they usually rise long before day, and travel much in the night, and during the heat of the day they rest. As caravans often travelled early, plunderers would rise early, also, to meet them. ¶ *For a prey.* For plunder—the business of their lives. ¶ *The wilderness.* The desert, for so the word wilderness is used in the Scriptures; see Notes on Isa. xxxv. 1; Matt iii. 1. ¶ Yieldeth *food.* To wit, by plunder. They obtain subsistence for themselves and their families by plundering the caravans of the desert. The idea of Job is, that they are seen by God, and yet that they are suffered to roam at large.

6. *They reap* every one *his corn.* Marg. *mingled corn*, or *dredge.* The word here used (בליל) denotes, properly, *meslin*, mixed provender, made up of various kinds of grain, as of barley, vetches, &c., prepared for cattle; see Notes on Isa. xxx. 24. ¶ *In the field.* They break in upon the fields of others, and rob them of their grain, instead of cultivating the earth themselves. So it is rendered by Jerome—Agrum non suum demerunt; et vineam ejus, quem vi oppresserint vindemiant. The LXX. render it, "A field, not their own, they reap down before the time—πρὸ ὥρας. ¶ *They gather the vintage of the wicked.* Marg. *the wicked gather the vintage.* Rather, they gather the vintage of the oppressor. It is not the vintage of honest industry; not a harvest which is the result of their own labour, but of plunder. They live by depredations on others. This is descriptive of those who support themselves by robbery.

7. *They cause the naked to lodge without clothing.* They strip others of their clothing, and leave them destitute. ¶ *That* they have *no covering in the cold.* All travellers tell us, that though the day is intensely hot in the deserts of Arabia, yet the nights are often intensely cold. Hence, the sufferings of those who are plundered, and who have nothing to defend themselves from the cold air of the night.

8. *They are wet with the showers of the mountains.* That is, the poor persons, or the travellers, whom they have robbed. Hills collect the clouds, and showers seem to pour down from the mountains. These showers often collect and pour down so suddenly that there is scarcely time to seek a shelter. ¶ *And embrace the rock for want of a shelter.* Take refuge beneath a projecting rock. The robbers drive them away from their homes, or plunder them of their tents, and leave them to find a shelter from the storm, or at night, beneath a rock. This agrees exactly with what Niebuhr says of the wandering Arabs near mount Sinai: "Those who cannot afford a tent, spread out a cloth

9 They pluck the fatherless from the breast, and take a pledge of the poor.
10 They cause *him* to go naked without clothing, and they take away the sheaf *from* the hungry;
11 *Which* made oil within their walls, *and* tread *their* wine-presses, and suffer thirst.

---

upon four or six stakes; and others spread their cloth near a tree, or endeavour to shelter themselves from the heat and the rain in the cavities of the rocks. Reisebeschreib. i. Th. s. 233.

9. *They pluck the fatherless from the breast.* That is, they steal away unprotected children, and sell them, or make slaves of them for their own use. If this is the correct interpretation, then there existed at that time, what has existed since, so much to the disgrace of mankind, the custom of kidnapping children, and bearing them away to be sold as slaves. Slavery existed in early ages; and it must have been in some such way that slaves were procured. The wonder of Job is, that such men were permitted to live—that God did not come forth and punish them. The *fact* still exists, and the ground of wonder is not diminished. Africa bleeds under wrongs of this kind; and the vengeance of heaven seems to sleep, though the child is torn away from its mother, and conveyed, amid many horrors, to a distant land, to wear out life in hopeless servitude. ¶ *And take a pledge of the poor.* Take that, therefore, which is necessary for the comfort of the poor, and retain it, so that they cannot enjoy its use; see Notes on chap. xxii. 6.

10. *And they take away the sheaf* from *the hungry.* The meaning of this is, that the hungry are compelled to bear the sheaf for the rich without being allowed to satisfy their hunger from it. Moses commanded that even the ox should not be muzzled that trod out the corn (Deut. xxv. 4); but here was more aggravated cruelty than that would be, in compelling men to bear the sheaf of the harvest without allowing them even to satisfy their hunger. This is an instance of the cruelty which Job says was actually practised on the earth, and yet God did not interpose to punish it.

11. Which *made oil within their walls.* Or rather, they compel them to express oil within their walls. The word יצהירו, rendered "made oil," is from צהר, to shine, to give light; and hence the derivatives of the word are used to denote light, and then oil, and thence the word comes to denote to press out oil for the purpose of light. Oil was obtained for this purpose from olives by pressing them, and the idea here is, that the poor were compelled to engage in this service for others without compensation. The expression "within their walls," means probably within the walls of the rich; that is, within the enclosures where such presses were erected. They were taken away from their homes; compelled to toil for others; and confined for this purpose within inclosures erected for the purpose of expressing oil. Some have proposed to read this passage, "Between their walls they make them toil at noonday;" as if it referred to the cruelty of causing them to labour in the sweltering heat of the sun. But the former interpretation is the most common, and best agrees with the usual meaning of the word, and with the connection. ¶ And *tread* their *wine-presses and suffer thirst.* They compel them to tread out their grapes without allowing them to slake their thirst from the wine. Such a treatment would, of course, be cruel oppression. A similar description is given by Addison in his letter from Italy:

Il povreo Abitante mira indarno
Il roseggiante Arancio e'l pingue grano,
Crescer dolente ei mira ed oli, e vini,
E de mirti odorar l' ombra si sdegna.
In mezzo alla Bonta della Natura
Maledetto languisce, e dentro a cariche
Di vino vigne muore per la sete.

"The poor inhabitant beholds in vain
The reddening orange and the swelling grain;
Joyless he sees the growing oils and wines,
And in the myrtle's fragrant shade repines;
Starves, in the midst of nature's bounty curst,
And in the loaden vineyard dies for thirst."

12 Men groan from out of the city, and the soul of the wounded crieth out: yet God layeth not folly *to them.*

13 They are of those that rebel against the light; they know not the ways thereof, nor abide in the paths thereof.

Addison's works, vol. i. pp. 51—53. Ed. Lond. 1721.

12. *Men groan from out of the city.* The evident meaning of this is, that the sorrows caused by oppression were not confined to the deserts and to solitary places; were not seen only where the wandering freebooter seized upon the traveller, or in the comparatively unfrequented places in the country where the poor were compelled to labour in the wine-presses and the olive presses of others, but that they extended to cities also. In what way this oppression in cities was practised, Job does not specify. It might be by the sudden descent upon an unsuspecting city, of hordes of freebooters, who robbed and murdered the inhabitants, and then fled, or it might be by internal oppression, as of the rich over the poor, or of masters over their slaves. The idea which Job seems to wish to convey is, that oppression abounded. The earth was full of violence. It was in every place, in the city and the country, and yet God did not in fact come forth to meet and punish the oppressor as he deserved. There would be instances of oppression and cruelty enough occurring in all cities to justify all that Job here says, especially in ancient times, when cities were under the control of tyrants. The word which is translated *men* here is מתים, which is not the usual term to denote men. This word is derived from מות, to *die;* and hence there may be here the notion of *mortals,* or of the *dying,* who utter these groans. ¶ *And the soul of the wounded crieth out.* This expression appears as if Job referred to some acts of violence done by robbers, and perhaps the whole description is intended to apply to the sufferings caused by the sudden descent of a band of marauders upon the unsuspecting and slumbering inhabitants of a city. ¶ *Yet God layeth not folly* to them. The word rendered *folly* (תִּפְלָה) means folly; and thence also wickedness. If this reading is to be retained, the passage means that God does not lay to heart, that is, does not regard their folly or wickedness. He suffers it to pass without punishing it; comp. Acts xvii. 30. But the same word, by a change of the points, (תְּפִלָּה), means *prayer;* and many have supposed that it means, that God does not regard the prayer or cry of those who are thus oppressed. This, in itself, would make good sense, but the former rendering agrees better with the connection. The object of Job is not to show that God does not regard the cry of the afflicted, but that he does not interpose to punish those who are tyrants and oppressors.

13. *They are of those that rebel against the light.* That is, they hate the light: comp. John iii. 20. It is unpleasant to them, and they perform their deeds in the night. Job here commences a reference to another class of wicked persons—those who perform their deeds in the darkness of the night; and he shows that the same thing is true of them as of those who commit crimes in open day, that God does not interpose directly to punish them. They are suffered to live in prosperity. This should be rendered, "Others hate the light;" or, "There are those also who are rebellious against the light." There is great force in the declaration, that those who perform deeds of wickedness in the night are *rebels* against the light of day. ¶ *They know not the ways thereof.* They do not see it. They work in the night. ¶ *Nor abide in the paths thereof.* In the paths that the light makes. They seek out paths on which the light does not shine.

14. *The murderer.* One of the instances, referred to in the previous verse, of those who perform their deeds in darkness. ¶ *Rising with the*

14 The [a] murderer rising with
the light killeth the poor and
needy, and in the night is as a
thief.

15 The eye also of the adulterer
waiteth for the twilight, [b] saying
no eye shall see me: and [1] disguiseth *his* face.

16 In the dark they dig through
houses, *which* they had marked for
themselves in the day-time: they
know [c] not the light.

a Ps.10.8–11. *b* Pr.7.8,9.

1 *setteth* his *face in secret* *c* John 8. 19.

light. Heb. לאור. Vulg. *Manè primo — in the earliest twilight.* The meaning is, that he does it very early; by daybreak. It is not in open day, but at the earliest dawn. ¶ *Killeth the poor and needy.* Those who are so poor and needy that they are obliged to rise early and go forth to their toil. There is a double aggravation—the crime of murder itself, and the fact that it is committed on those who are under a necessity of going forth at that early hour to their labour. ¶ *And in the night is as a thief.* The same man. Theft is usually committed under cover of the night. The idea of Job is, that though these crimes cannot escape the notice of God, yet that he does not interpose to punish those who committed them. A striking incidental illustration of the fact stated here, occurred in the journey of Messrs. Robinson and Smith, on their way from Akabah to Jerusalem. After retiring to rest one night, they were aroused by a sudden noise; and they apprehended an attack by robbers. "Our Arabs," says Dr. R, "were evidently alarmed. They said, if thieves, *they would steal upon us at midnight; if robbers they would come down upon us towards morning.*" Bibl. Research. i. 270. It would seem, therefore, that there was some settled time or order in which they are accustomed to commit their various depredations.

15. *The eye also of the adulterer waiteth for the twilight;* comp. the description in Prov. vii. 8, 9, "He went the way to her house; in the twilight, in the evening, in the black and dark night." ¶ *And disguiseth* his *face.* Marg. *setteth his face in secret.* The meaning is, that he put a mask on his face, lest he should be recognised. So Juvenal, Sat. viii. 144, as quoted by Noyes:

—— si nocturnus adulter
Tempora Santonico velas adoperta cucullo.

These deeds of wickedness were then performed in the night, as they are still; and yet, though the eye of God beheld them, he did not punish them. The meaning of Job is, that men were allowed to commit the blackest crimes, but that God did not come forth to cut them off.

16. *In the dark they dig through houses.* This refers, probably, to another class of wicked persons. The adulterer steals forth in the night, but it is not his way to "dig" into houses. But the persons here referred to are robbers, who conceal themselves by day, and who at night secretly enter houses for plunder. The phrase "dig through" probably has reference to the fact that houses were made of clay, or of bricks dried in the sun—a species of mud cottages, and whose walls, therefore, could be easily penetrated. In the East, nearly all the houses are made of unburnt brick, and there is little difficulty in making a hole in the wall large enough to admit the human body; comp. Ezek. xii. 7. In Bengal, says Mr. Ward, it is common for thieves to dig through the walls of houses made of mud, or under the house-floors, which are made merely of earth, and enter thus into the dwellings while the inmates are asleep. Rosenmüller's Alte u. neue Morgenland *in loc.* ¶ Which *they had marked for themselves in the day-time.* According to this translation the idea would be, that in the day-time they carefully observed houses, and saw where an entrance might be effected. But this interpretation seems contrary to the general sense of the passage. It is said that they avoid the light, and that the night is the time for accomplishing their purposes. Probably, therefore, the meaning of

17 For the morning *is* to them even as the shadow of death; if *one* know *them, they are in* the terrors of [a] the shadow of death.

a Ps.73 18,19.

18 He *is* swift as the waters; their portion is cursed in the earth: he beholdeth not the way of the vineyards.

this passage is, "in the day time they shut themselves up." So it is rendered by Gesenius, Rosenmüller, Noyes, and others. The word here used, and rendered "*marked*" (חָתַם), means *to seal, to seal up;* and hence the idea of shutting up, or making fast; see Notes on Job ix. 7; Isa. viii. 17. Hence it may mean to shut up *close* as if one was locked in; and the idea here is, that in the day-time they shut themselves up close in their places of concealment, and went forth to their depredations in the night. ¶ *They know not the light.* They do not see the light. They do all their work in the dark.

17. *For the morning* is *to them even as the shadow of death.* They dread the light as one does usually the deepest darkness. The morning or light would reveal their deeds of wickedness, and they therefore avoid it. ¶ *As the shadow of death.* As the deepest darkness; see Notes on chap. iii. 5. ¶ *If* one *know* them. If they are recognised. Or, more probably, this means "they," *i. e.* each one of them, "are familiar with the terrors of the shadow of death," or with the deepest darkness. By this rendering the common signification of the word (יַכִּיר) will be retained, and the translation will accord with the general sense of the passage. The meaning is, that they are familiar with the blackest night. They do not dread it. They dread only the light of day. To others the darkness is terrible; to them it is familiar. The word rendered "shadow of death" in the latter part of this verse, is the same as in the former. It may mean in both places the gloomy night that resembles the shadow of death. Such a night is "terrible" to most men, to them it is familiar, and they feel secure only when its deep shades are round about them.

18. *He* is *swift as the waters.* Noyes renders this, "They are as swift as the skiff upon the waters." Dr. Good, "Miserable is this man upon the waters." Wemyss, "Such should be as foam upon the waters." Le Clerc says that there is scarcely any passage of the Scriptures more obscure than this, and the variety of rendering adopted will show at once the perplexity of expositors. Rosenmüller supposes that the particle of comparison (כְּ) is to be understood, and that the meaning is, "he is *as* a light thing upon the waters;" and this probably expresses the true sense. It is a comparison of the thief with a light boat, or any other light thing that moves gently on the face of the water, and that glides along without noise. So gently and noiselessly does the thief glide along in the dark. He is rapid in his motion, but he is still. It is not uncommon to describe one who is about to commit crime in the night as moving noiselessly along, and as taking every precaution that the utmost silence should be preserved. So Macbeth, when about to commit murder, soliloquizes:

Now o'er the one half world
Nature seems dead ——
And withered murder,
Alarm'd by his sentinel, the wolf,
Who's howl'd his watch, thus with his stealthy pace,
With Tarquin's ravishing strides, towards his design
Moves like a ghost.
Thou sure and firm-set earth,
Hear not my steps, which way they walk, for fear
The very stones prate of my whereabout.

I do not know, however, that this comparison of a thief, with a light object on the waters, is to be found any where else, but it is one of great beauty. The word rendered "swift" (קַל) may denote either that which is *swift,* or that which is *light.* In Isa. xxx. 16, it is applied to a fleet horse. Here it may be rendered, "He is as a light thing upon the face of the waters." ¶ *Their portion is cursed in the earth.* That is, their manner

19 Drought and heat [1] consume the snow-waters; *so doth* the grave *those which* have sinned.

20 The womb shall forget him; the worm shall feed sweetly on him; he shall be no more [a] remembered; and wickedness shall be broken as a tree.

1 *violently take.*

a Pr.10.7; Is.26.14.

of life, their way of obtaining a livelihood, is deserving of execration. The result of humble toil and honest labour may be said to be blessed; but not the property which they acquire. Rosenmüller and Noyes, however, suppose that the word "portion" here refers to their habitation, and that the idea is, they have their dwelling in wild and uncultivated places; they live in places that are cursed by sterility and barrenness. The Hebrew will bear either construction. The word *lot,* as it is commonly understood by us, may perhaps embrace both ideas. "Theirs is a cursed *lot* on earth." ¶ *He beholdeth not the way of the vineyards.* That is, they do not spend their lives in cultivating them, nor do they derive a subsistence from them. They live by plunder, and their abodes are in wild retreats, far away from quiet and civilised society. The object seems to be to describe marauders, who make a sudden descent at night on the possessions of others, and who have their dwellings far away from fields that are covered with the fruits of cultivation.

19. *Drought and heat consume the snow-waters.* Marg. *violently take;* see Notes on chap. vi. 17. The word rendered "consume," and in the margin "violently take" (יִגְזְלוּ), means properly to strip off, as skin from the flesh; and then to pluck or tear away by force; to strip, to spoil, to rob. The meaning here is, that the heat seems to *seize* and carry away the snow waters—to bear them off, as a plunderer does spoil. There is much poetic beauty in this image. The "snow-waters" here mean the waters that are produced by the melting of the snow on the hills, and which swell the rivulets in the valleys below. Those waters, Job says, are borne along in rivulets over the burning sands, until the drought and heat absorb them all, and they vanish away; see the beautiful description of this which Job gives in chap. vi. 15—18. Those waters vanish away silently and gently. The stream becomes smaller and smaller as it winds along in the desert until it all disappears. So Job says it is with these wicked men whom he is describing. Instead of being violently cut off; instead of being hurried out of life by some sudden and dreadful judgment, as his friends maintained, they were suffered to linger on calmly and peaceably—as the stream glides on gently in the desert—until they quietly disappear by death—as the waters sink gently in the sands or evaporate in the air. The whole description is that of a peaceful death as contradistinguished from one of violence. ¶ So doth *the grave* those who *have sinned.* There is a wonderful terseness and energy in the original words here, which is very feebly expressed by our translation. The Hebrew is (שְׁאוֹל חָטָאוּ) "the grave, they have sinned." The sense is correctly expressed in the common version. The meaning is, that they who have sinned die in the same quiet and gentle manner with which waters vanish in the desert. By those who have sinned, Job means those to whom he had just referred—robbers, adulterers, murderers, &c., and the sense of the whole is, that they died a calm and peaceful death; see Notes on chap. xxi. 13, where he advances the same sentiment as here.

20. *The womb shall forget him.* His mother who bare him shall forget him. The idea here seems to be, that he shall fade out of the memory, just as other persons do. He shall not be overtaken with any disgraceful punishment, thus giving occasion to remember him by a death of ignominy. At first view it would seem to be a calamity to be soon forgotten by a mother; but if the above inter-

21 He evil-entreateth the barren *that* beareth not, and doeth not good to the widow.

22 He draweth also the mighty with his power: he riseth up, [1] and no *man* is sure of life.

1 or, *he trusteth not* his own *life*.

pretation be correct, then it means that the condition of his death would be such that there would be no occasion for a mother to remember him with sorrow and shame, as she would one who was ignominiously executed for his crimes. This interpretation was proposed by Mercer, and has been adopted by Rosenmüller, Noyes, and others. It accords with the general scope of the passage, and is probably correct. Various other interpretations, however, have been proposed, which may be seen in Good, and in the Critici Sacri. ¶ *The worm shall feed sweetly on him.* As on others. He shall die and be buried in the usual manner. He shall lie quietly in the grave, and there return to his native dust. He shall not be suspended on a gibbet, or torn and devoured by wild beasts; but his death and burial shall be peaceful and calm; see Notes on chap. xxi. 26; xix. 26. ¶ *He shall be no more remembered.* As having been a man of eminent guilt, or as ignominiously punished. The meaning is, that there is nothing marked and distinguishing in his death. There is no peculiar manifestation of the divine displeasure. There is some truth in this, that the wicked cease to be remembered. Men hasten to forget them; and having done no good that makes them the objects of grateful reminiscence, their memory fades away. This, so far from being a calamity and a curse, Job regards as a favour. It would be a calamity to be remembered as a bad man, and as having died an ignominious death. ¶ *And wickedness shall be broken as a tree. Evil* here or *wickedness* (עַוְלָה) means an evil or wicked man. The idea seems to be, that such a man would die as a tree that is stripped of its leaves and branches is broken down. He is not like a green tree that is violently torn up by the roots in a storm, or twisted off in a tempest, but like a dry tree that begins to decay, and that falls down gently by its own weight. It lives to be old, and then quietly sinks on the ground and dies. So Job says it is with the wicked. They are not swept away by the divine judgments, as the trees of the forest are torn up by the roots or twisted off by the tornado.

21. *He evil entreateth the barren.* The woman who has no children to comfort or support her. He increases her calamity by acts of cruelty and oppression. To be without children, as is well known, was regarded, in the patriarchal ages, as a great calamity. ¶ *And doeth not good to the widow;* see Notes on chap. xxiv. 3. Notwithstanding all this, he is permitted to live in prosperity, and to die without any visible tokens of the divine displeasure.

22. *He draweth also the mighty with his power.* The word here rendered *d aweth* (מָשַׁךְ), means *to draw;* and then, to lay hold of, to take, to take away, and, hence, to remove, to destroy; Ps. xxviii. 3; Ezek. xxii. 20. The idea here seems to be, that his acts of oppression and cruelty were not confined to the poor and the defenceless. Even the great and the mighty were also exposed, and he spared none. No one was safe, and no rights could be regarded as secure. The character here described is one that pertains to a tyrant, or a conqueror, and Job probably meant to describe some such mighty man, who was regardless alike of the rights of the high and the low. ¶ *He riseth up.* When he rises up; that is, when he enters on an enterprise, or goes forth to accomplish his wicked purposes. ¶ *And no* man *is sure of life.* From the dread of him even the great and mighty have no security. This language will well describe the character of an Oriental despot. Having absolute power, no man, not even the highest in rank, can feel that his life is safe if the monarch becomes in any way offended. Yet, Job says that

23 *Though* it be given him *to be*
in safety, whereon he resteth ; yet
his [a] eyes *are* upon their ways.
24 They are exalted for a little [b] while, but are [1] gone and
brought low ; they are taken
[2] out of the way as all *other*, and
cut off as the tops of the ears of
corn.
25 And if *it be* not *so* now, who
will make me a liar, and make my
speech nothing worth ?

a Ps. 11.4. *b* Ps.37.35,36. 1 *not.* 2 *closed up.*

even such a despot was permitted to live in prosperity, and to die without any remarkable proof of the divine displeasure.

23. Though *it be given him* to be *in safety*. That is, God gives him safety. The name *God* is often understood, or not expressed. The meaning is, that God gives this wicked man, or oppressor, safety. He is permitted to live a life of security and tranquillity. ¶ *Whereon he resteth.* Or, rather, "And he is sustained, or upheld"—(וישען). The meaning is, that he is sustained or upheld by God. ¶ *Yet his eyes* are *upon their ways.* "And the eyes of God are upon the ways of such men." That is, God guards and defends them. He seems to smile upon them, and to prosper all their enterprises.

24. *They are exalted for a little while.* This was the proposition which Job was maintaining. His friends affirmed that the wicked were punished for their sins in this life, and that great crimes would soon meet with great calamities. This Job denies, and says that *the fact* was, that they were "exalted." Yet he knew that it was to be but for a little time, and *he* believed that they would, at no distant period, receive the proper reward of their deeds. He maintains, however, that their death might be tranquil and easy, and that no extraordinary proof of the divine displeasure would be perceived in the manner of their departure. ¶ *But are gone and brought low.* Marg. *not.* Heb. ואיננו—"and are not;" comp. Gen. xlii. 13. "The youngest is this day with our father, and one is not;" Gen. xxxvii. 30. "The child is not, and I, whither shall I go?" That is, the child is dead ; comp. the expression *Troja fuit.* The meaning here is, that they soon disappear, or vanish. ¶ *They are taken out of the way as all* other. They die in the same manner as other men do, and without any extraordinary expressions of the divine displeasure in their death. This was directly contrary to what his friends had maintained. The Hebrew word here (קפץ) means, *to gather, to collect ;* and is often used in the sense of "gathering to one's fathers," to denote death. ¶ *And cut off as the tops of the ears of corn.* Of wheat, barley, or similar grain. *Corn,* in the sense in which the word is commonly used in this country, was not known in the time of Job. The allusion here is to the harvest. When the grain was ripe, it seems they were in the habit of cutting off the ears, and not of cutting it near the root, as we do. The body of the stalk was left, and, hence, there is so frequent allusion in the Scriptures to stubble that was burnt. So, in Egypt, the children of Israel were directed to obtain the stubble left in the fields, in making brick, instead of having straw furnished them. The meaning of Job here is, that they would not be taken away by a violent death, or before their time, but that they would be like grain standing in the field to the time of harvest, and then peacefully gathered ; comp. Ps. lxxiii. 4.

25. *And if* it be *not* so *now, who will make me a liar ?* A challenge to any one to prove the contrary to what he had said. Job had now attacked their main position, and had appealed to facts, in defence of what he held. He maintained that, as a matter of fact, the wicked were prospered, that they often lived to old age, and that they then died a peaceful death, without any direct demonstration of the divine displeasure. He boldly appeals, now, to any one

CHAPTER XXV.

ANALYSIS OF THE CHAPTER.

This short reply of Bildad closes what the three friends of Job had to say, for Zophar does not attempt to answer. Bildad does not attempt to meet the appeals which Job had made to facts, or reply to his arguments. He does not even reproach Job as he and his friends had done before, or even express his conviction that he was a wicked man. The speech is evidently that of one who felt that he must say *something*, but who did not know how to meet the course of argument which Job had pursued. He asserts, in a lofty strain, the majesty, dominion, and infinite perfection of the Deity, and then repeats the proposition, that in the sight of such a God the whole universe must be regarded as impure. It would seem to be implied that he supposed that Job's arguments went on the supposition that man was pure, and that all that was necessary to be said, was to re-affirm the impossibility that any should be holy in the sight of God. Many a man, when perplexed with some view of truth which wholly confounds all his reasoning and sets aside his maxims, but who lacks the ingenuousness to admit the force of the argument adduced, meets a case just as Bildad did. Unconvinced, he adheres to his own opinion; unable to meet the argument, he does not attempt to reply to it, yet feels that he must say *something* to show that he is not silenced. The feebleness of this reply, however only encourages Job to utter the triumphant sentiments expressed in the following chapters.

THEN answered Bildad the Shuhite and said,
2 Dominion [a] and fear *are* with
him; he maketh peace in his high
places.
3 Is there any number of his
armies? and upon whom [b] doth
not his light arise?

a Da.4.3,34; Jude 25. *b* Mat.5.45.

to deny this, or to prove the contrary. The appeal was decisive. The fact was undeniable, and the controversy was closed. Bildad (chap. xxv.) attempts a brief reply, but he does not touch the question about *the facts* to which Job had appealed, but utters a few vague and irrelevant proverbial maxims, about the greatness of God, and is silent. His proverbs appear to be exhausted, and the theory which he and his friends had so carefully built up, and in which they had been so confident, was now overthrown. Perhaps this was one design of the Holy Spirit, in recording the argument thus far conducted, to show that the theory of the divine administration, which had been built up with so much care, and which was sustained by so many proverbial maxims, was false. The overthrow of this theory was of sufficient importance to justify this protracted argument, for (1.) it was and is of the highest importance that correct views should prevail of the nature of the divine administration; and (2.) it is of especial importance in comforting the afflicted people of God. Job had experienced great aggravation, in his sufferings, from the position which his friends had maintained, and from the arguments which they had been able to adduce, to prove that his sufferings were proof that he was a hypocrite. But it is worth all which it has cost; all the experience of the afflicted friends of God, and all the pains taken to reveal it, to show that affliction is no certain proof of the divine displeasure, and that important ends may be accomplished by means of trial.

CHAPTER XXV.

2. *Dominion and fear* are *with him.* That is, God has a right to rule, and he ought to be regarded with reverence. The object of Bildad is to show that He is so great and glorious that it is impossible that man should be regarded as pure in his sight. He begins, therefore, by saying, that he is a Sovereign; that he is clothed with majesty, and that he is worthy of profound veneration. ¶ *He maketh peace in his high places.* "High places," here refer to the heavenly worlds. The idea is, that he preserves peace and concord among the hosts of heaven. Numerous and mighty as are the armies of the skies, yet he keeps them in order and in awe. The object is to present an image of the majesty and power of that Being who thus controls a vast number of minds. The phrase does not necessarily imply that there had been variance or strife, and that then God had made peace, but that he preserved or kept them in peace.

3. *Is there any number of his armies?* The armies of heaven; or the hosts of angelic beings, which are often represented as arranged or marshalled into armies; see Notes on Isa. i. 9. The word which is here used is not the common one which is rendered "hosts," (צבא), but is גדוד,

4 How then can man be justified [a] with God? or how can he
be clean [b] *that is* born of a woman?
5 Behold even to the moon, and
it shineth not; yea, the stars are
not pure in his sight;
6 How much less man, *that is* a
worm, and the son of man, *which*
is a worm?

a chap. 4 17,&c.; 9.2. &c.; Ps.143 2,&c.; Ro. 5.1,18.

b Zec.13.1; 1Co.6.11; 1John 1.9; Re.1.5.

which means properly a troop, band, or army. It may here mean either the constellations often represented as the army which God marshals and commands, or it may mean the angels. ¶ *And upon whom doth not his light arise?* This is designed evidently to show the majesty and glory of God. It refers probably to the light of the sun, as the light which he creates and commands. The idea is, that it pervades all things; that, as controlled by him, it penetrates all places, and flows over all worlds. The image is a striking and sublime one, and nothing is better fitted to show the majesty and glory of God.

4. *How then can man be justified with God?* see chap. iv. 17, 18; xv. 15, 16. Instead of meeting *the facts* to which Job had appealed, all that Bildad could now do was to *repeat* what had been said before. It shows that he felt himself unable to dispose of the argument, and yet that he was not willing to confess that he was vanquished. ¶ *Or how can he be clean?* This sentiment had been expressed by Job himself, chap. xiv. 4. Perhaps Bildad meant now to adopt it as undoubted truth, and to throw it back upon Job as worthy of his special attention. It has no bearing on the arguments which Job had advanced, and is utterly irrelevant except as Bildad supposed that the course of argument maintained by Job implied that he supposed himself to be pure.

5. *Behold even to the moon, and it shineth not.* Or, behold even the moon shineth not. That is, in comparison with God it is dark and obscure. The idea is, that the most beautiful and glorious objects become dim and fade away when compared with him. So Jerome renders it, *Ecce luna etiam non splendet.* The word here rendered *shineth* (יאהיל) frequently means to pitch or remove a tent, and is a form of the word אהל uniformly rendered *tent* or *tabernacle.* Some have supposed that the meaning here is, that even the moon and the stars of heaven—the bright canopy above—were not fit to furnish a *tent* or *dwelling* for God. But the parallelism seems to demand the usual interpretation, as meaning that the moon and stars faded away before God. The word אהל derives this meaning, according to Gesenius, from its relation to the word הלל, to be clear or brilliant, from the mutual relation of the verbs פא and עע. The Arabic has the same meaning. ¶ *Yea, the stars are not pure in his sight.* That is, they are not bright in comparison with him. The design is to show the glory of the Most High, and that nothing could be compared with him: see Notes, chap. iv. 18.

6. *How much less man;* see chap. iv. 19. Man is here mentioned as a worm; in chap. iv. 19 he is said to dwell in a house of clay and to be crushed before the moth. In both cases the design is to represent him as insignificant in comparison with God. ¶ *A worm,* רמה; see chap. vii. 5. The word is commonly applied to such worms as are bred in putridity, and hence the comparison is the more forcible. ¶ *And the son of man.* Another mode of speaking of man. Any one of the children of man is the same. No one of them can be compared with God; comp. Notes, Matt. i. 1. ¶ Which is *a worm.* תולעה; comp. Notes, Isa. i. 18. This word frequently denotes the worm from which the scarlet or crimson colour was obtained. It is, however, used to denote the worm that is bred on putrid substances, and is so used here; comp. Ex. xvi. 20; Isa. xiv. 11; lxvi. 24. It is also applied to a worm that destroys plants. Jonah iv. 7; Deut. xxviii. 39. Here it means, that man is poor, feeble,

CHAPTER XXVI.

ANALYSIS OF THE CHAPTER.

In this chapter Job commences a reply to all that had been said by his three friends, and concludes the controversy. At the close of this chapter, it would seem probable, that he paused for Zophar, whose turn came next to speak, but as he said nothing, he resumed his discourse, and continued it to the close of chap. xxxi.

This chapter consists of two parts. I. In the first part (ver. 1—4), Job begins the reply with sarcasms on his opponent as having offered nothing that in reality pertained to the dispute. He had made great pretensions, but he had not in any way met the difficulties of the case. He had not replied at all to his arguments, nor had he done any thing to relieve his mind in its embarrassments. II. In the second part (ver. 5—14) Job himself enters into a statement of the power and majesty of the Almighty. He shows that he could speak in as lofty a style of the greatness of God as his friends could. His object in this seems to be, not merely a trial of skill in the description which was given of God, but to show them that the views which *he* cherished were not produced by any low and grovelling conceptions of God. He had the most exalted ideas of him. He accorded with all that they said. He could even go beyond them in his descriptions of the divine majesty and glory. His views about his own character, therefore, were not inconsistent with the most exalted conceptions of the Deity, nor did he regard the most elevated views of God as any proof that he himself was eminently guilty or hypocritical, as they seemed to suppose. Having thus shown that his views of God were quite as exalted as those of his friends, in the next chapter he returns to his argument, and defends the positions which he had before advanced.

BUT Job answered and said,
2 How [a] hast thou helped *him that is* without power? *how* savest thou the arm *that hath* no strength?
3 How hast thou counselled

a Is.41. 6.

powerless. In comparison with God he is a crawling worm. All that is said in this chapter is true and beautiful, but it has nothing to do with the subject in debate. Job had appealed to the course of events in proof of the truth of his position. The true way to meet that was either to deny that the facts existed as he alleged, or to show that they did not prove what he had adduced them to establish. But Bildad did neither; nor did he ingenuously confess that the argument was against him and his friends. At this stage of the controversy, since they had nothing to reply to what Job had alleged, it would have been honourable in them to have acknowledged that they were in error, and to have yielded the palm of victory to him. But it requires extraordinary candour and humility to do that; and rather than do it, most men would prefer to say *something*—though it have nothing to do with the case in hand.

CHAPTER XXVI.

2. *How hast thou helped* him that is *without power?* It has been doubted whether this refers to Job himself, the two friends of Bildad, or to the Deity. *Rosenmüller*. The connection, however, seems to demand that it should be referred to Job himself. It is sarcastical. Bildad had come as a friend and comforter. He had, also, in common with Eliphaz and Zophar, taken upon himself the office of teacher and counsellor. He had regarded Job as manifesting great weakness in his views of God and of his government; as destitute of all strength to bear up aright under trials, and now all that he had done to aid one so weak was found in the impertinent and irrelevant generalities of his brief speech. Job is indignant that one with such pretensions should have said nothing more to the purpose. Herder, however, renders this as if it related wholly to God, and it cannot be denied that the Hebrew would bear this:

"Whom helpest thou? Him who hath no strength?
Whom dost thou vindicate? Him whose arm hath no power?
To whom give counsel? One without wisdom?
Truly much wisdom hast thou taught him."

¶ How *savest thou the arm* that hath *no strength?* That is, your remarks are not adapted to invigorate the feeble. He had come professedly to comfort and support his afflicted friend in his trials. Yet Job asks what there was in his observations that was fitted to produce this effect? Instead of declaiming on the majesty and greatness of God, he should have said something that was adapted to relieve an afflicted and a troubled soul.

3. *How hast thou counselled* him that hath *no wisdom?* As he had undertaken to give counsel to another, and to suggest views that might

him that hath no wisdom? and *how* hast thou plentifully declared the thing as it is?

4 To whom hast thou uttered words? and whose spirit [a] came from thee?

5 Dead *things* are formed from under the waters, [1] and the inhabitants thereof.

a Ec.12.7. 1 or, *with*.

be adapted to elevate his mind in his depression, and to console him in his sorrows, he had a right to expect more than he had found in his speech. ¶ *And* how *hast thou plentifully declared the thing as it is?* The word rendered "the thing as it is" (תּוּשִׁיָּה) denotes properly *a setting upright, uprightness*—from ישׁה; then help, deliverance, Job vi. 13; purpose, undertaking, enterprise, Job v. 12; then counsel, wisdom, understanding, Job xi. 6; xii. 16. Here it is synonymous with *reason, wisdom*, or *truth*. The word rendered "plentifully" (לָרֹב) means "for multitude," or abundantly, and the sense here is, that Bildad had made extraordinary pretensions to *wisdom*, and that this was the result. This short, irrelevant speech was all; a speech that communicated nothing new, and that met none of the real difficulties of the case.

4. *To whom hast thou uttered words?* Jerome renders this, *Quem docere voluisti?* "Whom do you wish to teach?" The sense is, "Do you attempt to teach me in such a manner, on such a subject? Do you take it that I am so ignorant of the perfections of God, that such remarks about him would convey any real instruction?" ¶ *And whose spirit came from thee?* That is, by whose spirit didst thou speak? What claims hast thou to inspiration, or to the uttering of sentiments beyond what man himself could originate? The meaning is, that there was nothing remarkable in what he had said that would show that he had been indebted for it either to God or to the wise and good on earth.

5. *Dead* things. Job here commences *his* description of God, to show that his views of his majesty and glory were in no way inferior to those which had been expressed by Bildad, and that what Bildad had said conveyed to him no real information. In this description he far surpasses Bildad in loftiness of conception, and sublimity of description. Indeed, it may be doubted whether for grandeur this passage is surpassed by any description of the majesty of God in the Bible. The passage here has given rise to much discussion, and to a great variety of opinion. Our common translation is most feeble, and by no means conveys its true force. The *object* of the whole passage is to assert the universal dominion of God. Bildad had said (chap. xxv.) that the dominion of God extended to the heavens, and to the armies of the skies; that God surpassed in majesty the splendour of the heavenly bodies; and that compared with him man was a worm. Job commences *his* description by saying that the dominion of God extended even to the nether world; and that such were his majesty and power that even the shades of the mighty dead trembled at his presence, and that hell was all naked before him. The word רְפָאִים—*Rephaim*—so feebly rendered "*dead things*," means *the shades of the dead; the departed spirits that dwell in Sheol;* see the word explained at length in the Notes on Isa. xiv. 9. They are those who have left this world and who have gone down to dwell in the world beneath—the great and mighty conquerors and kings; the illustrious dead of past times, who have left the world and are congregated in the land of Shades. Jerome renders it, *gigantes*, and the LXX., *γίγαντες*—*giants;* from a common belief that those shades were larger than life. Thus Lucretius says:

Quippe et enim jam tum divum mortalia secla
Egregias animo facies vigilante videbant;
Et magis in somnis, *mirando corporis auctu*.
Rer. Nat. ver. 1168.

The word *shades* here will express the sense, meaning the departed

6 Hell [a] *is* naked before him, and destruction hath no covering.

a Ps.139.8,11; Pr.15.11; He.4.13.

---

spirits that are assembled in Sheol. The Chaldee renders it, גבריא — mighty ones, or giants; the Syriac, in like manner, *giants.* ¶ *Are formed.* The Syriac renders this, *are killed.* Jerome, *gemunt*—groan; Sept., "Are giants born from beneath the water, and the neighbouring places?" What idea the authors of that version attached to the passage it is difficult to say. The Hebrew word here used (יחוללו, from חול), means to twist, to turn, to be in anguish - as in child-birth; and then it may mean to tremble, quake, be in terror; and the idea here seems to be, that the shades of the dead were in anguish, or trembled at the awful presence, and under the dominion of God. So Luther renders it—understanding it of giants—*Die Riesen ängsten sich unter den Wassern.* The sense would be well expressed, "The shades of the dead tremble, or are in anguish before him. They fear his power. They acknowledge his empire." ¶ *Under the waters.* The abode of departed spirits is always in this book placed beneath the ground. But why this abode is placed beneath *the waters,* is not apparent. It is usually under the ground, and the entrance to it is by the grave, or by some dark cavern; comp. Virgil's Æniad, Lib. vi. A different interpretation has been proposed of this verse, which seems better to suit the connection. It is to understand the phrase (מתחת) "*under*," as meaning simply *beneath*—"the shades beneath;" and to regard the word (מים) *waters* as connected with the following member:

"The shades beneath tremble;
The waters and the inhabitants thereof."

Thus explained, the passage means that the whole universe is under the control of God, and trembles before him. Sheol and its Shades; the oceans and their inhabitants stand in awe before him. ¶ *And the inhabitants thereof.* Of the waters — the oceans. The idea is, that the vast inhabitants of the deep all recognise the power of God and tremble before him. This description accords with that given by the ancient poets of the power and majesty of the gods, and is not less sublime than any given by them.

6. *Hell.* Heb. שאול, *Sheol;* Gr. ᾅδης, *Hades.* The reference is to the abode of departed spirits—the nether world where the dead were congregated; see Notes on chap. x. 21, 22. It does not mean here, as the word *hell* does with us, a place of punishment, but the place where all the dead were supposed to be gathered together. ¶ Is *naked before him.* That is, he looks directly upon that world. It is hidden from us, but not from him. He sees all its inhabitants, knows all their employments, and sways a sceptre over them all. ¶ *And destruction.* Heb. אבדון, *Abaddon;* comp. Rev. ix. 11, "And they had a king over them, which is the angel of the bottomless pit, whose name in the Hebrew is Abaddon, but in the Greek tongue hath his name Apollyon." The Hebrew word means *destruction,* and then *abyss,* or place of destruction, and is evidently given here to the place where departed spirits are supposed to reside. The word in this form occurs only here and in Prov. xv. 11; Ps. lxxxviii. 11; Job xxvi. 6, in all which places it is rendered *destruction.* The idea here is, not that this is a place where souls are *destroyed,* but that it is a place similar to destruction—as if all life, comfort, light, and joy, were extinguished. ¶ *Hath no covering.* There is nothing to conceal it from God. He looks down even on that dark nether world, and sees and knows all that is there. There is a passage somewhat similar to this in Homer, quoted by Longinus as one of unrivalled sublimity, but which by no means surpasses this. It occurs in the Iliad, xx. 61—66:

Ἔδδεισεν δ' ὑπένερθεν ἄναξ ἐνέρων Ἀιδωνεὺς, κ.τ.λ.

7 He stretcheth out [a] the north over the empty place, *and* hangeth the earth upon nothing.

a Ps.104.2.

Deep in the dismal regions of the dead,
Th' infernal monarch reared his horrid head,
Leaped from his throne, lest Neptune's arm should lay
His dark dominions open to the day,
And pour in light on Pluto's drear abodes,
Abhorred by men, and dreadful e'en to gods.
POPE.

7. *He stretcheth out the north.* This whole passage is particularly interesting as giving a view of the cosmology which prevailed in those early times. Indeed, as has been already remarked, this poem, apart from every other consideration, is of great value for disclosing to us the prevailing views on the subject of astronomy, geography, and many of the arts, at a much earlier period than we have an account of them elsewhere. The word *north* here denotes the heavens as they appear to revolve around the pole, and which seem to be stretched out as a curtain. The heavens are often represented as a veil, an expanse, a curtain, or a tent; see Notes on Isa. xxxiv. 4; xl. 22. ¶ *Over the empty place.* עַל-תֹּהוּ, *Upon emptiness, or nothing.* That is, without any thing to support it. The word here used (תֹּהוּ) is one of those employed Gen. i. 2, "And the earth was *without form* and void." But it seems here to mean emptiness, nothing. The north is stretched out and sustained by the mere power of God. ¶ And *hangeth the earth upon nothing.* It has nothing to support it. So Milton:

"And earth self-balanced from her centre hung."

There is no certain evidence here that Job was acquainted with the globular form of the earth, and with its diurnal and annual revolutions. But it is clear that he regarded it as not resting on any foundation or support; as lying on the vacant air, and kept there by the power of God. The Chaldee Paraphrast, in order to *explain* this, as that Paraphrase often does, adds the word *waters.* "He hangeth the earth עַלֵי מַיָא *upon the waters,* with no one to sustain it." The sentiment here expressed by Job was probably the common opinion of his time. It occurs also in Lucretius:

Terraque ut in media mundi regione quiescat
Evanescere paullatim, et decrescere, pondus
Convenit; atque aliam naturam subter habere,
Et ineunte aevo conjunctam atque uniter aptam
Partibus aeriis mundi, quibus insita vivit
Propterea, non est oneri, neque deprimit auras;
Ut sua quoique homini nullo sunt pondere membra,
Nec caput est oneri collo, nec denique totum
Corporus in pedibus pondus sentimus inesse.
v. 535.

In this passage the sense is, that the earth is self-sustained; that it is no burden, or that no one part is burdensome to another—as in man the limbs are not burdensome, the head is not heavy, nor the whole frame burdensome to the feet. So, again, Lucretius says, ii. 602:

Hanc, veteres Grajum docti cecinere poetæ,
Aeris in spatio magnam pendere—
Tellurem, neque posse in terra sistere terram.

——"in ether poised she hangs,
Unpropt by earth beneath."

So Ovid says:

Ponderibus librata suis.

Self-poised and self-balanced.

And again, Fastor, vi. 269:

Terra pilae similis, nullo fulcimine nixa,
Ære subjecto tam grave pendet onus.

From passages like this occurring occasionally in the classic writers, it is evident that the true figure of the earth had early engaged the attention of men, and that occasionally the truth on this subject was before their minds, though it was neither wrought into a system nor sustained then by sufficient evidence to make it an article of established belief. The description here given is appropriate now; and had Job understood all that is now known of astronomy, his language would have been appropriate to express just conceptions of the greatness and majesty of God. It *is* proof of amazing power and greatness that he has thus "hung" the earth, the planets, the vast sun himself, upon nothing, and that by his

8 He bindeth up [a] the waters in his thick clouds; and the cloud is not rent under them.

9 He holdeth back the face of his throne, *and* spreadeth his cloud [b] upon it.

a Ge.1.6,7; Pr.30.4.

b Ps.97.2.

---

own power he sustains and governs all.

8. *He bindeth up the waters in his thick clouds.* That is, he *seems* to do it, or to collect the waters in the clouds, as in bottles or vessels. The clouds appear to hold the waters, as if bound up, until he is pleased to send them drop by drop upon the earth ¶ *And the cloud is not rent under them.* The wonder which Job here expresses is, that so large a quantity of water as is poured down from the clouds, should be held suspended in the air without seeming to rend the cloud, and falling all at once. His image is that of a bottle, or vessel, filled with water, suspended in the air, and which is not rent. What were the views which he had of the *clouds,* of course it is impossible now to say. If he regarded them as they are, as vapours, or if he considered them to be a more solid substance, capable of holding water, there was equal ground for wonder. In the former case, his amazement would have arisen from the fact, that so light, fragile, and evanescent a substance as vapour should contain so large a quantity of water; in the latter case, his wonder would have been that such a substance should distil its contents drop by drop. There is equal reason for admiring the wisdom of God in the production of rain, now that the cause is understood. The clouds are collections of vapours. They contain moisture, or vapour, which ascends from the earth, and which is held in suspension when in small particles in the clouds; as, when a room is swept, the small particles of dust will be seen to float in the room. When these small particles are attracted, and form masses as large as *drops,* the air will no longer sustain them, and they fall to the earth. *Man* never could have devised a way for causing *rain;* and the mode in which it is provided that large quantities of water shall be borne from one place to another in the air, and made to fall when it is needed, by which the vapours that ascend from the ocean shall not be suffered to fall again into the ocean, but shall be carried on to the land, is adapted to excite our admiration of the wisdom of God now, no less than it was in the time of Job.

9. *He holdeth back the face of his throne.* That is, he does not exhibit it—he covers it with clouds. The idea seems to be, that God sometimes comes forth and manifests himself to mankind, but that he comes encompassed with clouds, so that his throne cannot be seen. So in Ps. xviii. 11, "He made darkness his secret place, his pavilion round about him were dark waters and thick clouds of the skies." God is often represented as encompassed with clouds, or as accompanied with tempests. ¶ And *spreadeth his cloud upon it.* That is, so that it cannot be seen. There is much poetic beauty in this image. It is, that the clouds are made to conceal the splendour of the throne of God from the sight of man, and that all their sublimity and grandeur, as they roll on one another, and all their beauty when painted with so many colours in the evening, are designed to hide that throne from mortal eyes. No one sees God; and though it is manifest that he is every where employed, and that he comes forth with amazing grandeur in the works of creation and providence, yet he is himself invisible.

10. *He hath compassed the waters with bounds.* The word rendered *compassed* (חג, or חוג), means to describe a circle—to mark out with a compass; and the reference is to the form of the horizon, which appears as a circle, and which seems to be marked out with a compass. A similar idea Milton has beautifully expressed in his account of the creation:

10 He hath compassed the waters
with bounds, [a] until the [1] day and
night come to an end.

a Pr.8.29. 1 end of light with darkness.

"Then staid the fervid wheels, and in his hand
He took the golden compasses, prepared
In God's eternal store, to circumscribe
This universe, and all created things:
One foot he centered, and the other turned
Round through the vast profundity obscure;
And said, 'Thus far extend thy bounds,
This be thy just circumference, O world!'"
Par. Lost, B. vii.

In the passage before us, we have a statement of the ancient views of geography, and of the outer limits of the world. The earth was regarded as a circular plane, surrounded by waters, and those waters encompassed with perpetual night. This region of night—this outer limit of the world, was regarded as at the outer verge of the celestial hemisphere, and on this the concave of heaven seemed to rest. See Virgil, Geor. i. 247.

Illic, ut perhibent, aut intempesta silet nox
Semper, et obtenta densantur, nocte tenebræ;
Aut redit a nobis Aurora, diemque reducit.

No *maps* are preserved constructed at so early an age as the time of Job; but maps have been constructed from the descriptions in Strabo, Herodotus, and others, which furnish illustrations of the prevailing views on the subject of geography in their times. The oldest geographical writer among the Romans is Mela, who lived in the reign of Claudius, and who died A. D. 54. In his work, *De Situ Orbis*, he gives a description of the world according to the prevailing views, and probably embodied the results of former investigations and discoveries. "We find him adopting, in its fullest extent, the belief of a circumambient ocean; and when he speaks of 'the high earth in this middle part of it, and describes the sea as going under and washing round it, we are led to believe, that he viewed the earth as a sort of cone, or as a high mountain raised by its elevation above the abyss of waters. Having made a vague division of the world into East, West, and North, he distributed it into five zones, two temperate, one torrid, and two frigid. Only the first two were habitable; and that on the South was inaccessible to man, on account of the torrid regions intervening. According to this system, however, there was on that side another earth, inhabited by people whom he calls *Antichthones*, from their opposite position with respect to that part which we inhabit. The form and boundaries of the known and habitable earth are thus delineated:— The Mediterranean, with its branches of the Straits, the Euxine, and the Palus Mœotis; its great tributaries, the Nile and the Tanais—these combine, in his conception, to form the grand line by which the universe is divided. The Mediterranean itself separates Europe from Africa; and these continents are bounded on the East, the former by the Tanais, the latter by the Nile; all beyond or to the East of these limits was Asia." The following cut is probably a correct representation of his system, and gives the view of the world which prevailed in his time.

The ancient Arabs supposed the earth to be encompassed with an ocean. This ocean was called the "sea of darkness;" and the Northern sea was regarded as particularly pitchy and gloomy, and was called "the sea of pitchy darkness." Edrisi, a distinguished Arabic geographer of the middle ages, supposed that the land floated on the sea, only a part of it appearing above the water, like an egg floating in the water. The following cut, taken from an Arabian manuscript, will furnish an interesting view of the prevailing conceptions of the figure of the world in his time:

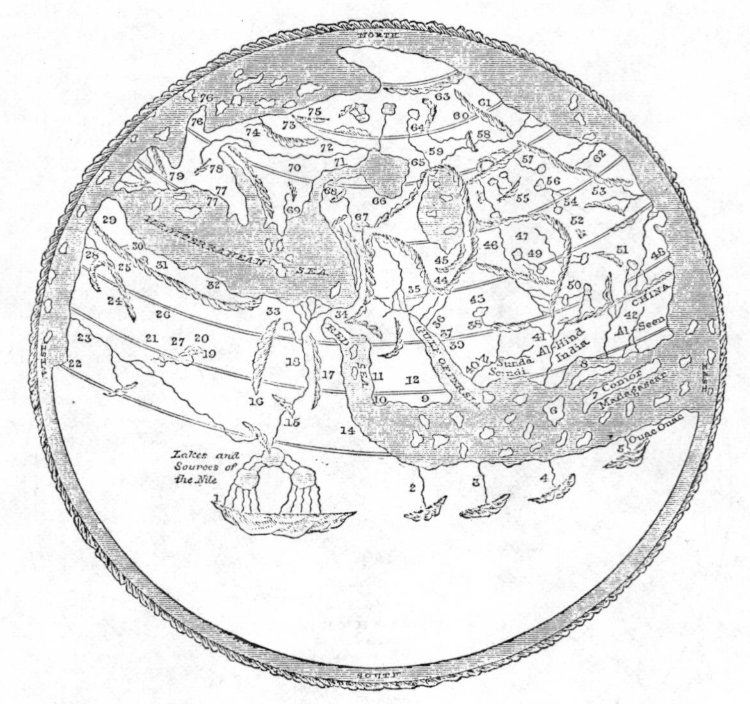

1 Mountains of the Moon and Sources of the Nile.
2 Berbara (kingdom of Adel).
3 Al-Zung (Zanguebar).
4 Sefala (Sofala).
5 Al-Wak Wak.
6 Serendeeb (Ceylon).
7 Al-Comor (Madagascar).
8 A-Dasi.
9 Al-Yeman (Arabia Felix).
10 Tehama.
11 Al-Hejaz (Arabia Deserta).
12 Al-Shujar (Seger).
13 Al-Imama (Yamama).
14 Al-Habesh(Ethiopia Abyssinia.)
15 Al-Nuba (Nubia).
16 Al-Tajdeen.
17 Al-Bejah.
18 Al-Saneed (Upper Egypt, Said).
19 Al-ouhat-what (Oasis).
20 Gowas.
21 Kanun.
22 Belad Al-lemlum.
23 Belad Mufrada.
24 Belad Nemaneh.
25 Al-Mulita u Sinhajeh.
26 Curan (Karooan, Kurene).
27 Negroland.
28 Al-Sous Nera.
29 Al-Mughrub Al Amkeen (Mogreb the West).
30 Afreekeea (Africa).
31 Belad El Gerid (Date Country).
32 Seharee, Bereneek (or Desert of Berenike).
33 Missur (Egypt).
34 Al-Sham (Syria).
35 Al-Irak (Persian empire).
36 Fars (Persia Proper).
37 Kirman(Carmania).
38 Alfazeh.
39 Mughan.
40 Al-Sunda (Scindi).
41 Al-Hind (India).
42 Al-Seen (China).
43 Khorasan.
44 Al-Beharus.
45 Azerbijan (Media).
46 Khuwarizm.
47 Al-Shash.
48 Khirkeez.
49 Al-Sefur.
50 Al-Tibut (Tibet).
51 Al-Nufuz Izz.
52 Kurjeea (Georgia).
53 Keymak.
54 Kulhœa.
55 Izzea.
56 Azkush.
57 Turkesh.
58 Iturab.
59 Bulghar (Bulgaria).
60 Al-Mutenah.
61 Yajooj (Gog).
62 Majooj (Magog.,
63 Asiatic (Russia).
64 Bejeerut.
65 Al-Alman.
66 Al-Khuzzus Khosrs (Caspian Sea).
67 Turkea (Turkey).
68 Albeian (Albania).
69 Makeduneeah (Macedonia).
70 Baltic Sea.
71 Jenubea (probably Sweden).
72 Germania (Germany).
73 Denmark.
74 Afranseeah(France).
75 Felowiah (Norway).
76 Burtea or Burtenea (Britain).
77 Corsica, Sardinia, &c.
78 Italy.
79 Ashkerineah (part of Spain, Q. Andalusia).

A map of the world, constructed during the Crusades, and embodying the views of the world prevailing then, exhibits the world, also, as surrounded by a dark ocean on every side—*mare tenebrosum*—and may be introduced as an illustration of this passage in Job. It is the map of Sanudo, annexed to Bongar's "Gesta Dei per Francos." In this map, Jerusalem, according to the prevailing views, "is placed in the centre of the world, as the point to which every other object is to be referred; the earth is made a circle, surrounded by the ocean, the shores of which are represented as every where nearly equidistant from that spiritual capital, the site of which is, indeed, remarkable for its relation to the three continents, Asia, Europe, and Africa. Persia stands in its proper place; but India, under the modifications of Greater and Lesser, is confusedly repeated at different points, while the river Indus is mentioned in the text as the Eastern boundary of Asia. To the North, the castle of Gog and Magog, an Arabian feature, crowns a vast range of mountains, within which, it is said, that the Tartars had been imprisoned by Alexander the Great. The Caspian appears, with the bordering countries of Georgia, Hyrcania, and Albania; but these features stand nearly at the Northern boundary of the habitable earth. Africa has a sea to the South, stated, however, to be inaccessible, on account of the intensity of the heat. The European countries stand in their due place, not even excepting Russia and Scandinavia, though some oversights are observable in the manner in which the two are connected together."

11 The pillars of heaven tremble, *a* and are astonished at his reproof.

a He.12.26

A similar view prevails among the modern Egyptians. "Of geography, the Egyptians, in general, and with very few exceptions, the best instructed among them, have scarcely any knowledge. Some few of the learned venture to assert that the earth is a globe, but they are opposed by a great majority of the 'Oolâma. The common opinion of all the Moos'lims is, that the earth is an almost plane expanse, surrounded by the ocean, which they say is encompassed by a chain of mountains called Cka'f." Lane's Modern Egyptians, vol. i. p. 281. A similar view of the world prevails, also, now among the Independent Nestorians, which may be regarded as the ancient prevailing opinion in Persia, handed down by tradition. "According to their views of geography," says Dr. Grant, "the earth is a vast plain, surrounded by the ocean, in which a *leviathan* plays around, to keep the water in motion, and prevent its becoming stagnant and putrid; and this leviathan is of such enormous length, that his head follows his tail in the circuit round the earth! That I had crossed the ocean, where I must have encountered the monster, was a thing almost incredible." The Nestorians, p. 100. In ancient times, it was regarded as impossible to penetrate far into the sea surrounding the earth, on account of the thick darkness, and it was believed that after sailing for any considerable distance on that sea, the light would wholly fail. In the ninth century, the Arabic historians tell us, that the brothers Almagrurim sailed from Lisbon due west, designing, if possible, to discover the countries beyond the "sea of darkness." For ten or eleven days, they steered westward; but, seeing a storm approaching, the light faint, and the sea tempestuous, they feared that they had come to the dark boundaries of the earth. They turned, therefore, south, sailed twelve days in that direction, and came to an island which they called Ganam, or the island of birds, but the flesh of these birds was too bitter to be eaten. They sailed on twelve days farther, and came to another island, the king of which assured them that their pursuit was vain; that his father had sent an expedition for the same purpose; but that, after a month's sail, the light had wholly failed, and they had been obliged to return. A great amount of interesting and valuable information, on the ancient views of the geography of the world, may be seen in the Encyclopedia of Geography, vol. i. pp. 9—68. It is not easy to ascertain what were the exact views in the time of Job, but it is quite probable, from the passage before us, that the earth was supposed to be surrounded by an ocean, and that the outer limits were encompassed with deep and impenetrable darkness ¶ *Until the day and night come to an end.* Marg. *end of light with darkness.* The true meaning is, to the confines of light and darkness. To the end, or extremity (תַּכְלִית—*perfection, completion*) of the light with the darkness; that is, where the light terminates in the darkness. *Where* that limit was, or *how* the sun was supposed to pass around it, or could pass over it, without illuminating it, it is now impossible to ascertain. The prevailing views on geography and astronomy must have been very obscure, and there must have been many things which they could not pretend to comprehend or explain.

11. *The pillars of heaven tremble.* That is, the mountains, which seem to bear up the heavens. So, among the ancients, Mount Atlas was represented as one of the pillars of heaven. Virgil speaks of "Atlas whose brawny back supports the skies." And Hesiod, ver. 785, advances the same notion:

> "Atlas, so hard necessity ordains,
> Great, the ponderous vault of stars sustains.
> Not far from the Hesperides he stands,
> Nor from the load retracts his head or hands."

The word "*reproof*" in this verse re-

12 He [a] divideth the sea with his power, and by his understanding he smiteth through [1] the proud. [b]

13 By his spirit he [c] hath garnished the heavens; his hand hath formed the crooked serpent.

a Ex.14.21; Is.51.15. 1 *pride.* *b* Da.4.37. *c* Ps.33.6 7.

fers to the language of God, as if spoken in anger to rebuke the mountains or the earth. Perhaps the reference is to thunder, to storms, and to winds, which seem to be the voice of God; comp. Ps. xxix. 3–8. Similar descriptions of the majesty and glory of God abound in the Scriptures, where he speaks to the earth, the mountains, the hills, and they tremble. Thus in Ps. civ. 32;

He looketh on the earth, and it trembleth;
He toucheth the hills, and they smoke.

So in Habak. iii. 10:

The mountains saw thee, and they trembled;
The overflowing of the water passed by;
The deep uttered his voice, and lift up his
hands on high.

So in Nahum i. 5, "The mountains quake at him, and the hills melt, and the earth is burnt at his presence."

12. *He divideth the sea with his power.* Herder renders this:

By his power he scourgeth the sea,
By his wisdom he bindeth its pride.

Jerome (Vulg.), "By his power the seas are suddenly congregated together." The LXX., "By his power—κατέπαυσε τὴν θάλασσαν—he makes the sea calm." Luther, Vor seiner Kraft wird das Meer plötzlich ungestüm—"By his power the sea becomes suddenly tempestuous." Noyes renders it, "By his power he stilleth the sea." This is undoubtedly the true meaning. There is no allusion here to the dividing of the sea when the Israelites left Egypt; but the idea is, that God has power to calm the tempest, and hush the waves into peace. The word here used (רָגַע) means, to make afraid, to terrify; especially, to restrain by threats; see Notes on Isa. li. 15; comp. Jer. xxxi. 35. The reference here is to the exertion of the power of God, by which he is able to calm the tumultuous ocean, and to restore it to repose after a storm—one of the most striking exhibitions of omnipotence that can be conceived of. ¶ *By his understanding.* By his wisdom. ¶ *He smiteth through.* He scourges, or strikes—as if to punish. ¶ *The proud.* The pride of the sea. The ocean is represented as enraged, and as lifted up with pride and rebellion. God scourges it, rebukes it, and makes it calm.

13. *By his spirit.* The word *spirit* here is either synonymous with *wisdom,*—referring to the wisdom by which God made the heavens; or with *breath*—meaning, that he did it by his own command. There is no evidence that Job refers to the Third Person of the Trinity—the Holy Spirit—as being specially engaged in the work of creation. The word *spirit* is often used to denote one's self; and the meaning here is, that *God* had done it. This was one of the exhibitions of his power and skill. ¶ *He hath garnished the heavens.* He has formed the stars which constitute so beautiful an ornament of the heavens. ¶ *His hand hath formed the crooked serpent.* Or, rather, the *fleeing serpent*—נָחָשׁ בָּרִחַ; see Notes on Isa. xxvii. 1. There can be no doubt that Job refers here to one of the constellations, which it seems was then known as the serpent or dragon. The practice of forming pictures of the heavens, with a somewhat fanciful resemblance to animals, was one of the most early devices of astronomy, and was evidently known in the time of Job; comp. Notes on chap. ix. 9. The object was, probably, to aid the memory; and though the arrangement is entirely arbitrary, and the resemblance wholly fanciful, yet it is still continued in the works of astronomy, as a convenient help to the memory, and as aiding in the description of the heavenly bodies. This is probably the same constellation which is described by Virgil, in language that strikingly resembles that here used by Job:

14 Lo, these *are* parts [a] of his ways; but how little a portion is heard of him? but the thunder of his power who can understand?

a 1Co.13.9,12.

Maximus hïc flexu sinuoso elabitur anguis
Circüm, perque duas in morem fluminis Arctos,
Arctos oceani metuentes æquore tingi.
Geor. i. 241.

Around our pole the spiry Dragon glides,
And, like a winding stream, the Bears divides;
The less and greater, who by Fate's decree
Abhor to die beneath the Southern sea.
DRYDEN.

The figure of the Serpent, or "the Dragon," is still one of the constellations of the heavens, and there can be little doubt that it is the same that is referred to in this ancient book. On the celestial globes it is drawn between the Ursa Major and Cepheus, and is made to embrace the pole of the ecliptic in its convolutions. The head of the monster is under the foot of Hercules; then there is a coil tending eastwardly about 17° north of Lyra; then he winds northwardly about 14° to the second coil, where he reaches almost to the girdle of Cepheus; then he loops down and makes a third coil somewhat in the shape of the letter U, about 15° below the first; and then he holds a westerly course for about 13°, and passes between the head of the Greater and the tail of the Lesser Bear. The constellation has eighty stars; including four of the second magnitude, seven of the third, and twelve of the fourth. The *origin* of the name given to this constellation, and the *reason* why it was given, are unknown. It has been supposed that the Dragon in his tortuous windings is symbolical of the oblique course of the stars, and particularly that it was designed to designate the motion of the pole of the equator around the pole of the ecliptic, produced by the precession of the equinoxes. It may be doubted, however, whether this is not a refinement; for the giving of a name for such a cause must have been based on knowledge much in advance of that which was possessed when this name was given. Mythologists say, that Draco was the watchful dragon which guarded the golden apples in the garden of the Hesperides, near Mount Atlas, in Africa, and which was slain by Hercules. Juno is said to have taken the Dragon up to heaven, and to have made a constellation of him, as a reward for his faithful services. The origin of the division of the stars into constellations is now unknown. It has been known from the earliest times, and is found in all nations; and it is remarkable that about the same mode of division is observed, and about the same names are given to the constellations. This would seem to indicate that they had a common origin; and probably that is to be found in Chaldea, Arabia, or Egypt. Sir Isaac Newton regards Egypt as the parental point; Sir William Jones, Chaldea; Mr. Montucla, Arabia. There is probably no book earlier than this of Job, and the mention here of the names of the constellations is probably the first on record. If so, then the first *intimation* that we have of them was from Arabia; but still it may have been that Job derived his views from Egypt or Chaldea. The *sense* in the passage before us is, that the greatness and glory of God are seen by forming the beautiful and the glorious constellations that adorn the sky.

14. *Lo, these* are *parts of his ways.* This is a small portion of his works. We see only the outlines, the surface of his mighty doings. This is still true. With all the advances which have been made in science, it is still true that we see but a small part of his works. What we are enabled to trace with all the aids of science, compared with what is unseen and unknown, may be like the analysis of a single drop of water compared with the ocean. ¶ *But how little a portion is heard of him?* Or, rather, "But what a faint whisper have we heard of him!" Literally, "What a whisper of a word,"—ומה־שמץ דבר. The word שמץ means a transient sound rapidly passing away; and then

CHAPTER XXVII.

ANALYSIS OF THE CHAPTER.

IT would seem to have been natural that Zophar should have replied here to what Job had said; and the commencement of this chapter appears to indicate that there had been a pause made here by Job, under an expectation that he would speak. It was now his turn, in the regular course of the controversy, but he was silent. Bildad had made a feeble reply (chap. xxv.), and Zophar did not attempt to say any thing, and the three friends return to the controversy no more. Seeing, therefore, that nothing was said in reply, Job resumes his remarks, and urges his sentiments at length. This reaches to the close of chap. xxxi.

Chaps. xxvii. and xxviii. have immediate reference to the controversy which had been maintained, and contain such suggestions as seem to have satisfied the friends of Job that he was right in his main positions, or at least such as to induce them to remain silent. The following points are introduced and discussed in this chapter.

He begins with a most solemn asseveration that he would speak only the truth, and would never be found the advocate for error. For the sincerity of this intention, he makes a direct appeal to the living God, ver. 2—4. He then as solemly re-asserts his own innocence, and says that he *could* not justify the sentiments which had been advanced, nor could he renounce his own consciousness of integrity, and concede, as his friends wished him to, that his sufferings were proof of extraordinary guilt, ver. 5, 6. He then proceeds to say, that he had no idea of justifying the wicked or the hypocrite. On account of the sentiments which he had advanced, his enemies had charged him with this; but he denies it now in the most solemn manner. He expresses his abhorrence of a wicked character; says that he believes their fate will be all that a man could wish his enemy to experience, and expresses a firm conviction that the hope of the hypocrite would fail. In this he accorded entirely with all that they had said, ver. 7—10. He then states that he himself held that the wicked would be punished, and proceeds to defend that position. This defence occupies the remainder of the chapter. He had maintained, in opposition to his friends, that it was not a regular and universal principle of the divine administration that men were dealt with in this world according to their character, and that *no certain* conclusion could be drawn respecting a man's character from the divine dealings with him in this world. In particular, he had shown, by an appeal *to facts*, that the wicked live and prosper; that they often reach a peaceful old age, and die surrounded by every circumstance of affluence and honour. The appeal to these facts, which his friends could not deny, had done much to settle the controversy. But now, having silenced them, he *admits* that this was not *an universal principle;* states that he does not mean to say that men are *never* dealt with according to their crimes, or to maintain that God has no moral government in this world. He goes on, therefore, to show (ver. 11—23) that it was a great principle of the divine administration that the wicked would be destroyed; that if they were prospered for a time, destruction would certainly come, and that they could not hope to escape with impunity. He does not deny *his* main position that the innocent suffer, and that the wicked are prospered, nor does he admit *their* main position, that great sufferings are necessarily proof of great guilt;—but he *does* concede that there was truth in the general principle that the wicked *would be punished.* This he was not disposed to deny; and having showed them before that their main positions were wrong, and their application of their position to him cruel and uncalled for, he now shows exactly where the truth is, and concedes that, however prosperous the wicked may be for a time, they will certainly be punished. In this way the controversy is brought to a close. He states, therefore, that though the children of a wicked man are multiplied, it will be for the sword . though he heap up silver, he shall not be permitted always to enjoy it; though he build his house, he shall soon lie down in the dust; though he be prospered, yet he shall be swept away as by a storm; and though men may honour him for a while, yet they shall hiss him finally out of the world. If there seems to be some inconsistency here with the views which he had before expressed, they are, nevertheless, not inconsistent with the general *principles* which he had maintained. It is only in some expressions which he may have formerly used in the heat of argument, and under the severity of suffering, that there seems to be any thing irreconcilable with what he here lays down. It was important that he should admit what he here states, lest it might be inferred that he denied altogether the government of God over the world. This is *one* mode of explaining a difficulty which has been felt in regard to the meaning of the latter part of this chapter, ver. 13—23; see, however, the Notes on ver. 13. Perhaps the solution there suggested will commend itself to many minds as being more probably correct.

---

a *whisper;* see Notes on chap. iv. 12. A "whisper of a word" means a word not fully and audibly spoken, but which is *whispered* into the ear; and the beautiful idea here is, that what we see of God, and what he makes known to us, compared with the full and glorious reality, bears about the same relation which the gentlest whisper does to words that are fully spoken. ¶ *The thunder of his power who can understand?* It is probable that there is here a comparison between the gentle "whisper" and the mighty "thunder;" and that the idea is, if, instead of speaking to us in gentle whispers, and giving to us in that way some faint indications of his nature, he were to speak out in thunder, who could understand him? If, when he speaks in such faint and gentle tones, we are so much impressed with a sense of his greatness and glory, who would not be overwhelmed if he were to speak out as in thunder? Thus explained, the expression does not refer to literal thunder, though there is much in the heavy peal to excite adoring views of God, and much that to Job must have been inexplicable. It may be asked, even now, who can understand all the philosophy of the thunder? But with much more impressiveness it may be asked, as Job probably meant to ask, who could understand

MOREOVER, Job [1] continued
his parable, and said,
2 *As* God liveth, *who* hath
taken away my judgment; and
the Almighty, *who* hath [2] vexed
my soul;

[1] *added to take up.*
[2] *made my soul bitter,* Ru.1.20.

3 All the while my breath *is* in
me, and the [3] spirit of God *is* in
my nostrils,
4 My lips shall not speak
wickedness, nor my tongue utter
deceit.

[3] i. e. *the breath which God gave him* Ge.2.7.

the great God, if he spoke out with the full voice of his thunder, instead of speaking in a gentle whisper?

1. *Job continued.* Marg. as in Heb. *added to take up.* Probably he had paused for Zophar to reply, but since he said nothing he now resumed his argument. ¶ *His parable.* A *parable* properly denotes a comparison of one thing with another, or a fable or allegorical representation from which moral instruction is derived. It was a favourite mode of conveying truth in the East, and indeed is found in all countries; see Notes on Matt. xiii. 3. It is evident, however, that Job did not deliver his sentiments in this manner; and the word rendered "*parable*" here (משׁל) means, as it often does, a sententious discourse or argument. The word is used in the Scriptures to denote *a parable,* properly so called; then a sententious saying; an apothegm; a proverb; or a poem or song; see Notes Isa. xiv. 4. It is rendered here by the Vulgate, parabolam; by the LXX., προοιμίῳ—"Job spake by preface;" Luther, *fuhr fort—Job continued;* Noyes, *discourse;* Good, *high argument.* The meaning is, that Job continued his *discourse;* but there is in the word a reference to the *kind* of discourse which he employed, as being sententious and apothegmatical.

2. As *God liveth.* A form of solemn adjuration, or an oath by the living God. "As certainly as God lives." It is the form by which God himself often swears; see Ezek. xiv. 16; xxxiii. 11, and is often employed by others; 1 Sam. xx. 3; xxv. 26. ¶ Who *hath taken away my judgment.* Who hath rejected my cause, or who has refused me justice; that is, who has treated me as though I was guilty, and withholds from me relief. The language is *forensic,* and the idea is, that he would make his solemn appeal to him, *even though* he had rejected his cause. Perhaps there is implied here more than the solemnity of an ordinary oath. A man might be supposed to be willing to make his appeal to one who had shown himself friendly or favourable to him, but he would manifest more reluctance to making his appeal in an important case to a judge who had decided against him, especially if that decision was regarded as severe, and if that judge had refused to hear what he had to say in self-defence. But Job here says, that such was his confidence in his own sincerity and truth, that he could make his appeal to God, *even though* he knew that he had hitherto gone against him, and treated him as if he were guilty. ¶ Who *hath vexed my soul.* Marg. as in Heb. *made my soul bitter.* That is, who has greatly afflicted me; comp. 2 Kings iv. 27, *Marg.,* and Ruth i. 20.

3. *And the spirit of God* is *in my nostrils.* As long as I live. The "spirit of God" here means the breath that God breathed into man when he created him, Gen. ii. 7. It would seem probable that there was an allusion to that fact by the language here, and that the knowledge of the way in which man was created was thus handed down by tradition.

4. *My lips shall not speak wickedness.* This solemn profession made on oath might have done something to allay the suspicions of his friends in regard to him, and to show that they had been mistaken in his character. It is a solemn assurance that he did not *mean* to vindicate the cause of wickedness, or to say one word in its favour; and that as long as he lived he would never be found

5 God forbid that I should justify you ; till I die I will not remove mine [a] integrity from me.
6 My righteousness I hold fast, and will not let it go ; my heart [b] shall not reproach *me* [1] so long as I live.
7 Let mine enemy be as the wicked, and he that riseth up against me as the unrighteous.

a chap.2.3,9.
b Ac.24.16 ; 1 John 3.19-21. 1 *from my days*.

advocating it. ¶ *Nor my tongue utter deceit.* I will never make any use of sophistry ; I will not attempt to make "the worse appear the better reason ;" I will not be the advocate of error. This had always been the aim of Job, and he now says that no circumstance should ever induce him to pursue a different course as long as he lived. Probably he means, also, as the following verse seems to imply, that no consideration should ever induce him to countenance error or to palliate wrong. He would not be deterred from expressing his sentiments by any dread of opposition, or even by any respect for his friends. No friendship which he might have for them would induce him to justify what he honestly regarded as error.

5. *God forbid.* חָלִילָה לִּי. "Far be it from me." Literally, "Profane be it to me ;" that is, I should regard it as unholy and profane ; I cannot do it. ¶ *That I should justify you.* That I should admit the correctness of your positions, and should concede that I am an hypocrite. He was conscious of integrity and sincerity, and nothing could induce him to abandon that conviction, or to admit the correctness of the reasoning which they had pursued in regard to him. Coverdale (A. D. 1535) has given this a correct translation, "God forbid that I should grant your cause to be right." ¶ *Till I die I will not remove mine integrity from me.* I will not admit that I am insincere and hypocritical. This is the language of a man who was conscious of integrity, and who would not be deprived of that consciousness by any plausible representations of his professed friends.

6. *My righteousness I hold fast.* I hold on to the consciousness of integrity and uprightness. I cannot, will not, part with that. Job had lost his property, his health, and his domestic comforts, but he had in all this one consolation—he felt that he was sincere. He had been subjected to calamity by God *as if* he were a wicked man, but still he was resolved to adhere to the consciousness of his uprightness. Property may leave a man ; friends may forsake him ; children may die ; disease may attack him ; slander may assail him ; and death may approach him ; but still he may have in his bosom *one* unfailing source of consolation ; he may have the consciousness that his aim has been right and pure. That nothing can shake ; of that, no storms or tempests, no malignant foe, no losses or disappointment, no ridicule or calumny, can deprive him. ¶ *My heart shall not reproach* me. That is, as being insincere, false, hollow. ¶ *So long as I live.* Marg. *from my days.* So the Hebrew—מִיָּמָי. Vulg. *in omni vita mea.* Sept., "I am not conscious to myself of having done any thing amiss"—ἄτοπα πράξας ; comp. Notes on 1 Cor. iv. 4. The idea is, that he had a consciousness of integrity, and that he meant to maintain it as long as he lived.

7. *Let mine enemy be as the wicked.* This is probably said that he might show that it was not his intention to justify the wicked, and that in all that he had said it was no part of his purpose to express approbation of their course. His friends had charged him with this ; but he now solemnly disclaims it, and says that he had no such design. To show how little he meant to justify the wicked, he says that the utmost that he could desire for an enemy would be, that he would be treated as he believed the wicked would be. A similar expression occurs in Dan. iv. 19, "My lord, the dream be to them that hate thee, and the interpretation thereof to thine enemies ;" that is, calamities are coming upon thee indicated by the dream,

8 For [a] what *is* the hope of the hypocrite, though he hath gained, when God taketh away his soul?

9 Will God hear [b] his cry when trouble cometh upon him?

a Matt.16.26. b Pr.1.28.

such as you would desire on your foes; so in Judges v. 31. After the mother of Sisera had anxiously looked for the return of her son from the battle, though he was then slain, the sacred writer adds, "So let all thine enemies perish, O Lord." Thus when a traitor is executed it is common for the executioner to hold up his head and say, "So let all the enemies of the king die." Job means to say that he had no sympathy with wicked men, and that he believed that they would be punished as certainly and as severely as one could desire his enemy to suffer. Schnurrer supposes that by the *enemy* here he refers to his friends with whom he had been disputing; but this is to give an unnecessarily harsh construction to the passage.

8. *For what* is *the hope of the hypocrite?* The same sentiment which Job here advances had before been expressed by Bildad; see it explained in the Notes on chap. viii. 13 seq. It had also been expressed in a similar manner by Zophar, Notes chap. xx. 5, and had been much insisted on in their arguments. Job now says that he fully accords with that belief. He was not disposed to defend hypocrisy; he had no sympathy for it. He knew, as they did, that all the joy of a hypocrite would be temporary, and that when death came it must vanish. He wishes that his remarks should not be construed so as to make him the advocate of hypocrisy or sin, and affirms that he relied on a more solid foundation of peace and joy than the hypocrite could possess. It was by explanations and admissions such as these that the controversy was gradually closed, and when they came fully to understand Job, they felt that they had nothing which they could reply to him. ¶ *Though he hath gained*—יִבְצָע. The Vulgate renders this, *si avarè rapiat*—"if he avariciously seizes upon." The LXX. ὅτι ἐπέχει—*that he persisteth.* Dr. Good, "That he should prosper;" and so Wemyss. The Hebrew word (בצע) means properly, to cut or dash in pieces; then to tear in pieces, or to plunder or spoil; then to cut off, to bring to an end, &c. It is applied to the action of a weaver, who, when his web is finished, cuts off the thrum that binds it to the beam. The web is then *finished;* it is all woven, and is then taken from the loom. Hence it is elegantly used to denote the close of life, when life is woven or finished—by the rapid passing of days like the weaver's shuttle (Job vii. 6), and when it is then, as it were, taken out of the loom; see this figure explained in the Notes on Isaiah xxxviii. 12. This is the idea here, that life would be cut off like the weaver's web, and that when that was done the hope of the hypocrite would be of no value. ¶ *When God taketh away his soul.* When he dies. There has been much perplexity felt in regard to the Hebrew word here rendered "taketh away"—יֵשֶׁל. A full explanation may be seen in Schultens and Rosenmüller. Some suppose it is the future from נשל for ישל—meaning *to draw out,* and that the idea is, that God *draws out* this life as a sword is drawn out of a sheath. Others, that it is from שָׁלָה—*to be secure,* or *tranquil,* or *at rest;* and that it refers to the time when God shall give *rest* in the grave, or that the meaning of the word שָׁלָה here is the same as שָׁלַל or נשל—to draw out; see Gesenius on the word שָׁלָה. Schnurrer conjectures that it is derived from שאל—*to ask, to demand,* and that the form here is contracted from the future ישאל. But the common supposition is, that it means to *draw out*—in allusion to drawing out a sword from a scabbard—thus drawing life or the soul from the body.

9. *Will God hear his cry when trouble cometh upon him?* Coverdale has rendered this (ver. 8, 9) so as to make excellent sense, though not strictly in accordance with the original. "What hope hath the hypocrite though he have great good, and though

10 Will he delight himself in the Almighty? will he always [a] call upon God?

[a] Matt. 13 21.

11 I will teach you [1] by the hand of God: *that* which *is* with the Almighty will I not conceal.

[1] or, *being in.*

God give him riches after his heart's desire? Doth God hear him the sooner, when he crieth unto him in his necessity?" The object of the verse is to show the miserable condition of a wicked man or a hypocrite. This is shown by the fact which Job asserts, that God will not hear his cry when he feels his need of aid, and when he is induced to call upon him. This is true only when his object in calling upon God is *merely* for help. If he has no relentings for his sin, and no real confidence in God; if he calls upon him in trouble, intending to return to his sins as soon as the trouble is over, or if such is the state of his mind that God sees that he *would* return to his sins as soon as his calamities cease, then he cannot be expected to hear him. But if he comes with a penitent heart, and with a sincere purpose to forsake his sins and to devote himself to God, there is no reason to doubt that he would hear him. The argument of Job is in the main sound. It is, that if a man wishes the favour of God, and the assurance that he will hear his prayer, he must lead a holy life. A hypocrite cannot expect his favour: comp. Notes on Isa. i. 15.

10. *Will he delight himself in the Almighty?* A truly pious man *will* delight himself in the Almighty. His supreme happiness will be found in God. He has pleasure in the contemplation of his existence, his perfections, his law, and his government. Coverdale renders this, "Hath he such pleasure and delight in the Almighty that he dare alway call upon God?" The idea of Job is that a hypocrite has not his delight in the Almighty; and, therefore, his condition is not such as *he* would defend or choose. Job had been charged with defending the character of the wicked and with maintaining that they were the objects of the divine favour. He now says that he maintained no such opinion. He was aware that the only real and solid happiness was to be found in God, and he knew that a hypocrite would not find delight there. This is true to the letter. A hypocrite has no real happiness in God. He sees nothing in the divine perfections to love; nothing in the divine plans that commands and secures his affections. The hypocrite, therefore, is a miserable man. He professes to love what he does not love; tries to find pleasure in what his heart hates; mingles with a people with whom he has no sympathy, and joins in services of prayer and praise which are disgusting and irksome to his soul. The pious man rejoices that there is just such a God as Jehovah is. He sees nothing in him which he desires to be changed, and he has supreme delight in the contemplation of his perfections. ¶ *Will he always call upon God?* That is, he will not always call upon God. This is literally true. The hypocrite prays (1,) when he makes a profession of religion; (2,) on some extraordinary occasion—as when a friend is sick, or when he feels that he himself is about to die, but he does not *always* maintain habits of prayer. He suffers his business to break in upon his times for prayer; neglects secret devotion on the slightest pretence, and soon abandons it altogether. One of the best tests of character is the feeling with which we pray, and the habit which we have of calling on God. The man who *loves* secret prayer has one of the most certain evidences that he is a pious man; comp. Notes chap. xx. 5.

11. *I will teach you by the hand of God.* Marg. "or, *being in.*" Coverdale, "In the name of God." So Tindal, Noyes, "Concerning the hand of God." Good, "Concerning the dealings of God." The Chaldee renders it בנבואת אלהא—"By the prophecy of God." Luther, "I will teach you by the hand of God." The idea evidently is, that Job would instruct them by what God *had done.* He would appeal to his works, and to

12 Behold, all ye yourselves have seen *it;* why then are ye thus altogether vain?

13 This is the portion of a wicked man with God, and the heritage of oppressors, *which* they shall receive of the Almighty.

the dispensations of his providence; and by the indications of wisdom and skill which were to be found there, he would derive important lessons for their instruction on the great principles of his administration. Accordingly, in the remainder of this chapter, he makes his appeal to what actually occurs in the dispensations of Providence, and in the next, he refers to various scientific subjects, evincing the wisdom which God had shown in the mineral kingdom. The *hand* is the instrument by which we accomplish any thing, and hence it is here used to denote *what God does.* ¶ That *which* is *with the Almighty will I not conceal.* That is, I will appeal to his works, and show what traces of wisdom there are in them.

12. *Behold, all ye yourselves have seen* it. You have had an opportunity of tracing the proofs of the wisdom of God in his works. ¶ *Why then are ye thus altogether vain.* Why is it that you maintain such opinions—that you evince no more knowledge of his government and plans—that you argue so inconclusively about him and his administration! Why, since you have had an opportunity of observing the course of events, do you maintain that suffering is necessarily a proof of guilt, and that God deals with all men, in this life, according to their character? A close observation of the course of events would have taught you otherwise. Job proceeds to state what he supposes to be the exact truth on the subject, and particularly aims, in the following chapter, to show that the ways of God are inscrutable, and that we cannot be expected to comprehend them, and are not competent to pronounce upon them.

13. *This is the portion of a wicked man with God.* There has been much diversity of view in regard to the remainder of this chapter. The difficulty is, that Job seems here to state the same things which had been maintained by his friends, and against which he had all along contended. This difficulty has been felt to be very great, and *is* very great. It cannot be denied, that there is a great resemblance between the sentiments here expressed and those which had been maintained by his friends, and that this speech, if offered by them, would have accorded entirely with their main position. Job *seems* to abandon all which he had defended, and to concede all which he had so warmly condemned. One mode of explaining the difficulty has been suggested in the "Analysis" of the chapter. It was proposed by Noyes, and is plausible, but, perhaps, will not be regarded as satisfactory to all. Dr. Kennicott supposes that the text is imperfect, and that these verses constituted the third speech of Zophar. His arguments for this opinion are, (1.) That Eliphaz and Bildad had each spoken three times, and that we are naturally led to expect a third speech from Zophar; but, according to the present arrangement, there is none. (2.) That the sentiments accord exactly with what Zophar might be expected to advance, and are exactly in his style; that they are expressed in "his fierce manner of accusation," and are "in the very place where Zophar's speech is naturally expected." But the objections to this view are insuperable. They are, (1.) The entire want of any authority in the manuscripts, or ancient versions, for such an arrangement or supposition. All the ancient versions and manuscripts make this a part of the speech of Job. (2.) If this had been a speech of Zophar, we should have expected a reply to it, or an allusion to it, in the speech of Job which follows. But no such reply or allusion occurs. (3.) If the form which is usual on the opening of a speech, "And Zophar answered and said," had ever existed here, it is incredible that it should have been removed.

14 If [a] his children be multiplied *it is* for the sword; and his offspring shall not be satisfied with bread.

15 Those that remain of him shall be buried in death; and his widows shall not weep.[b]

a De.28.41; 2 Ki.9.7,8; Hos.9.13. *b* Ps.78.64.

But it occurs in no manuscript or version; and it is not allowable to make such an alteration in the Scripture by conjecture. Wemyss, in his translation of Job, accords with the view of Kennicott, and makes these verses (13—23) to be the third speech of Zophar. For this, however, he alleges no *authority*, and no reasons except such as had been suggested by Kennicott. Coverdale, in his translation of the Bible (A. D. 1553), has inserted the word "saying" at the close of ver. 12, and regards what follows to the end of the chapter as an enumeration or recapitulation of the false sentiments which they had maintained, and which Job regards as the "vain" things (ver. 12) which they had maintained. In support of this view the following reasons may be alleged: (1.) It avoids all the difficulty of transposition, and the necessity of inserting an introduction, as we must do, if we suppose it to be a speech of Zophar. (2.) It avoids the difficulty of supposing that Job had here contradicted the sentiments which he had before advanced, or of conceding all that his friends had maintained. (3.) It is in accordance with the practice of the speakers in this book, and the usual practice of debaters, who enumerate at considerable length the sentiments which they regard as erroneous, and which they design to oppose. (4.) It is the most simple and natural supposition, and, therefore, most likely to be the true one. Still, it must be admitted, that the passage is attended with difficulty; but the above solution is, it seems to me, the most plausible. ¶ *This is the portion.* This is what he receives; to wit, what he states in the following verses, that his children would be cut off. ¶ *And the heritage of oppressors.* What tyrants and cruel men must expect to receive at the hand of God.

14. *If his children be multiplied,* it is *for the sword.* That is, they shall be slain in war. The first calamities which it is here said would come upon a man, relate to his family (ver. 14—18); the next are those that would come upon himself, ver. 19—23. All the sentiments here expressed are found in the various speeches of the friends of Job, and, according to the interpretation suggested above, this is designed to represent their sentiments. They maintained that if a wicked man was blessed with a numerous family, and seemed to be prosperous, it was only that the punishment might come the more heavily upon him, for that they certainly would be cut off; see chap. xviii. 19, 20; xx. 10. ¶ *And his offspring shall not be satisfied with bread.* This sentiment was advanced by Zophar, chap. xx. 10; see Notes on that verse.

15. *Those that remain of him.* Those that survive him. ¶ *Shall be buried in death.* Heb. "shall be buried *by* death" (במות), that is, "Death shall be the grave-digger"—or, they shall have no friends to bury them; they shall be unburied. The idea is highly poetical, and the expression is very tender. They would have no one to weep over them, and no one to prepare for them a grave; there would be no procession, no funeral dirge, no train of weeping attendants; even the members of their own family would not weep over them. To be unburied has always been regarded as a dishonour and calamity (comp. Notes on Isa. xiv. 19), and is often referred to as such in the Scriptures; see Jer. viii. 2; xiv. 16; xvi. 4, 6. The passage here has a striking resemblance to Jer. xxii. 18, 19:

"They shall not lament for him, saying,
Ah! my brother! or, Ah! sister!
They shall not lament for him, saying,
Ah! lord! or, Ah! his glory!
With the burial of an ass shall he be buried,
Drawn out and cast beyond the gates of Jerusalem."

¶ *And his widows shall not weep.* The *plural* here—"widows"—is a proof that polygamy was then practised. It

16 Though he heap up silver as
the dust, and prepare raiment as
the clay;
17 He may prepare *it*, but [a] the
just shall put *it* on, and the innocent shall divide the silver.
18 He buildeth his house as a
moth, and as a booth *that* the keeper maketh.

a Ec.2.26.

is probable that Job here alludes to the shrieks of domestic grief which in the East are heard in every part of the house among the females on the death of the master of the family, or to the train of women that usually followed the corpse to the grave. The standing of a man in society was indicated by the length of the train of mourners, and particularly by the number of wives and concubines that followed him as weepers. Job refers to this as the sentiment of his friends, that when a wicked man died, he would die with such evident marks of the divine displeasure, that even his own family would not mourn for him, or that they would be cut off before his death, and none would be left to grieve.

16. *Though he heap up silver as the dust.* That is, in great quantities—as plenty as dust; comp. 1 Kings x. 27, "And the king made silver to be in Jerusalem as stones." ¶ *And prepare raiment.* Oriental wealth consisted much in changes of raiment. Sir John Chardin says that in the East it is common to gather together immense quantities of furniture and clothes. According to D'Herbelot, Bokteri, an illustrious poet of Cufah in the ninth century, had so many presents made him in the course of his life, that when he died he was found possessed of an hundred complete suits of clothes, two hundred shirts, and five hundred turbans. comp. Ezra ii. 69, and Neh. vii. 70; see Bochart Hieroz. P. II. Lib. iv. c. xxv. p. 617. This species of treasure is mentioned by Virgil;

Dives equûm, dives pictaî vestis et auri.
Æn. ix. 26.

The *reason* why wealth consisted so much in changes of raiment, is to be found in the fondness for display in Oriental countries, and in the fact that as fashions never change there, such treasures are valuable until they are worn out. In the ever-varying fashions of the West such treasures are comparatively of much less value. ¶ *As the clay.* As the dust of the streets; or as abundant as mire.

17. *The just shall put* it *on.* The righteous shall wear it. It shall pass out of the hands of him who prepared it, into the hands of others. The meaning is, that the wicked, though they become rich, would not live to enjoy their ill-gotten gains. These two verses contain a beautiful illustration of what Dr. Jebb calls *the introverted parallelism*—where the fourth member answers to the first, and the third to the second:

Though he heap up silver as the dust,
  And prepare raiment as the clay,
  The just shall put it [raiment] on,
And the innocent shall divide the silver.

A similar instance occurs in Matth. vii. 6:

Give not that which is holy unto the dogs,
  Neither cast ye your pearls before swine,
  Lest they [the swine] trample them under their feet,
And [the dogs] turn again and rend you.

For a full illustration of the nature of Hebrew poetry, the reader may consult De Wette, Einleitung in die Psalmen, translated in the Biblical Repository, vol. iii. pp. 445, seqq. and Nordheimer's Hebrew Grammar, vol. ii. pp. 319, seqq; see also the Introduction to Job, § V. ¶ *The innocent shall divide the silver.* That is, the righteous shall come into possession of it, and divide it among themselves. The wicked who had gained it shall not be permitted to enjoy it.

18. *He buildeth his house as a moth.* The house which the moth builds is the slight fabric which it makes for its own dwelling in the garment which it consumes. On this verse comp. chap. viii. 14. The dwelling of the moth is composed of the materials of the garment on which it feeds, and there may be an allusion here not only to the fact that the house which

19 The rich [a] man shall lie down, but he shall not be gathered: he openeth his eyes, and he *is* not.

a Lu.16,22,23.

the wicked reared for themselves would be temporary, and that it would soon pass away like the dwelling of the moth, but that it was obtained—like the dwelling of the moth—at the expense of others. The idea of frailty, however, and of its being only a very temporary habitation, is probably the main thought in the passage. The allusion here is to the *moth-worm* as it proceeds from the egg, before it is changed into the chrysalis, aurelia, or nymph. "The young moth, upon leaving the egg which a papilio has lodged upon a piece of stuff, or a skin well dressed, and commodious for her purpose, immediately finds a habitation and food in the nap of the stuff, or hair of the skin. It gnaws and lives upon the nap, and likewise builds with it its apartment, accommodated both with a front door and a back one: the whole is well fastened to the ground of the stuff, with several cords and a little glue. The moth sometimes thrusts her head out of one opening, and sometimes out of the other, and perpetually demolishes all about her; and when she has cleared the place about her, she draws out all the stakes of the tent, after which she carries it to some little distance, and then fixes it with her slender cords in a new situation." *Burder.* It is to the insect in its larvæ or caterpillar state that Job refers here, and the slightness of the habitation will be easily understood by any one who has watched the operations of the silk worm, or of the moths that appear in this country. The idea is, that the habitation which the wicked constructed was temporary and frail, and would soon be left. The Chaldee and Syriac render this "the spider;" and so does Luther—*Spinne.* The slight gossamer dwelling of the spider would well correspond with the idea here expressed by Job. ¶ *And as a booth.* A tent, or cottage. ¶ That *the keeper maketh.* That one who watches vineyards or gardens makes as a temporary shelter from the storm or the cold at night. Such edifices were very frail in their structure, and were designed to be only temporary habitations; see the subject explained in Notes on Isa. i. 8. Niebuhr, in his description of Arabia, p. 158, says, "In the mountains of Yemen they have a sort of nest on the trees, where the Arabs sit to watch the fields after they have been planted. But in the Kehama, where they have but few trees, they build a light kind of scaffolding for this purpose." Mr. Southey opens the fifth part of his Curse of Kehama with a similar allusion:

"Evening comes on:—arising from the stream
Homeward the tall flamingo wings his flight;
And when he sails athwart the setting beam,
His scarlet plumage glows with deeper light.
The WATCHMAN, at the wish'd approach of night,
Gladly forsakes the field, where he all day,
To scare the winged plunderers from their prey,
With shout and sling, on yonder clay-built height,
Hath borne the sultry ray.

19. *The rich man.* That is, the rich man who is wicked. ¶ *Shall lie down.* Shall die—for so the connection demands. ¶ *But he shall not be gathered.* In an honourable burial. The slain in battle are gathered together for burial; but he shall be unburied. The expressions "to be gathered," "to be gathered to one's fathers," frequently occur in the Scriptures, and seem to be used to denote a peaceful and happy death and an honourable burial. There was the idea of a happy union with departed friends; of being honourably placed by their side in the grave, and admitted to companionship with them again in the unseen world; comp. Gen. xxv. 8; xxxv. 29; xlix. 29, 33; Num. xxvii. 13; Deut. xxxii. 50; Jud. ii. 10; 2 Kings xxii. 20. Among the ancients, the opinion prevailed that the souls of those who were not buried in the customary manner, were not permitted to enter Hades, or the abodes of the dead, but were doomed to wander for an hundred years upon the banks of the river Styx. Thus Homer (Iliad,

20 Terrors take hold on him as waters, a tempest stealeth him away in the night.

21 The east wind carrieth him away, and he departeth; and, as a [a] storm, hurleth him out of his place.

22 For *God* shall cast upon him, and not spare: [1] he would fain flee out of his hand.

23 *Men* shall clap their hands at him, and shall hiss him out of his place.

a Ps.58.9. 1 *in fleeing he would flee.*

xxiii. 71, seq.) represents the spirit of Patroclus as appearing to Achilles, and praying him that he would commit his body with proper honours to the earth. So Palinurus is represented by Virgil (Æneid, vi. 365) as saying, "Cast earth upon me, that I may have a calm repose in death." The Hindoos, says Dr. Ward, believe that the souls of those who are unburied wander about and find no rest. It is possible that such views may have prevailed in the time of Job. The sentiment here is, that such an honoured death would be denied the rich man of oppression and wickedness. ¶ *He openeth his eyes, and he* is *not.* That is, in the twinkling of an eye he is no more. From the midst of his affluence he is suddenly cut off, and hurried away in a moment.

20. *Terrors take hold on him as waters.* That is, as suddenly and violently as angry floods; comp. Notes on chap. xviii. 14. ¶ *A tempest stealeth him away.* He is suddenly cut off by the wrath of God. A tempest comes upon him as unexpectedly as a thief or robber comes at night. Death is often represented as coming upon man with the silence of a thief, or the sudden violence of a robber at midnight; see Note chap. xxi. 17; comp. Matt. xxiv. 42—44.

21. *The east wind carrieth him away.* He is swept off as by the violence of a tempest. Severe storms are represented in this book as coming from the East; comp. Notes on chap. xv. 2. The ancients believed that men might be carried away by a tempest or whirlwind; comp. Isa. xli. 16; see also Homer, Odys. xx. 63, seq.

"Snatch me, ye whirlwinds far from human race,
Tost through the void illimitable space;
Or if dismounted from the rapid cloud,
Me with his whelming wave let Ocean shroud!" Pope.

Comp. Notes on chap. xxx. 22. The parallelism here would seem to imply that the wind referred to was *violent*, but it is possible that the allusion may be to the burning winds of the desert, so well known in the East, and so frequently described by travellers. The Vulgate here renders the Hebrew word קָדִים, *ventus urens*, "burning wind;" the LXX. in like manner, καύσων; the Syriac simply *wind.* This east wind, or burning wind, is what the Arabians call *Samûm.* It is a hot wind which passes over the desert, and which was formerly supposed to be destructive of life. More recent travellers, however, tell us that it is not fatal to life, though exceedingly oppressive. ¶ *And as a storm*; see Ps. lviii. 9. ¶ *Hurleth him out of his place.* Takes him entirely away, or removes him from the earth.

22. *For* God *shall cast upon him.* That is, God shall bring calamities upon him, or cast his thunderbolts upon him, and shall not pity him. ¶ *He would fain flee.* He would gladly escape from the wrath of God, but he is unable to do it.

23. Men *shall clap their hands at him.* That is, they shall combine to drive him out of the world, and rejoice when he is gone. The same sentiment was also expressed by Bildad, chap. xviii. 18:

He shall be driven from light into darkness,
And chased out of the world.

There can be no doubt, I think, that Job alludes to that sentiment, and that his object in quoting it is to show its incorrectness. He does not indeed go into a formal reply to it in the following chapters, but he seems to consider that he had already replied to it by the statements which he had made, and which showed the incorrectness of the views which his

CHAPTER XXVIII.

ANALYSIS OF THE CHAPTER.

VARIOUS opinions have been entertained of the design of this chapter, and of the connection which it has with the preceding. A statement and examination of those opinions may be found in Schultens and Rosenmuller. The most probable opinion, as it seems to me, is, that the design is to show that we must acquiesce in the inscrutable dispensations of divine Providence, without being able fully to comprehend them. The ways of God are high and mysterious. Vast wisdom is shown in his works, and there is much which man cannot comprehend. All his works are such as to excite the admiration of man. There is great obscurity in his dealings, and every where God had shown that his plans are far above those of man. The friends of Job had pretended to understand the reason of the divine dispensations. They had maintained that when men suffered they clearly comprehended the cause, and that the reason was that God dealt with them strictly according to their character. This position Job had controverted. He had showed that it was not true in fact. The wicked, he said, often lived long, and died in peace. But still, he admitted, that there was much which he could not understand. He did not know why they were thus permitted to live, and he did not know why the righteous were subjected to trials so severe. All this, he now says, is to be resolved into the superior and infinite wisdom of God; and in that it becomes man to acquiesce, even though he cannot now explain it. In illustration of this, he labours to show that man had made surprising discoveries in the works of nature; that he had penetrated the bowels of the earth, and had overcome the greatest obstacle in the attainment of knowledge and in the investigation of science, but still all that he had done or could do did not disclose to him the plans of the divine administration, or the reason of the divine dealings, and therefore true wisdom was to be found in the fear of the Lord, and in profound veneration for the Almighty. In showing this, Job adverts to the following topics.

(1.) He refers to the skill which man had shown in operations of *mining*, and to the discoveries which he had made of the places of silver and gold; ver. 1, 2.

(2.) In these operations, man had penetrated to the greatest depths, so as to carry his discoveries far into the regions of night; ver. 3, 4.

(3.) He had wrought the earth, bringing food out of it; he had turned it up, and found out the places of precious stones; ver. 5, 6.

(4.) He had far surpassed the wisdom of the brute creation; he had gone where their sagacity could not lead them, and had penetrated into dark regions which the keen eye of the vulture had not seen, and where even the lion had not adventured; ver. 7, 8.

(5.) He had put forth extraordinary power. He had removed vast stones; had overturned mountains; had cut canals through mighty rocks, and had confined and bound the angry floods; ver. 9—11.

(6.) Yet still, Job says, none of these things revealed the secret plans of the divine administration. The wisdom which man sought was not to be found there. It was far above all the discoveries of science, and all the mere investigations of nature. It had not been found in the abyss or in the sea, it could not be bought with gold or silver, with the sapphire, with coral or pearls; rubies and the topaz could not purchase it. Even Destruction and Death said that they had only heard of it with their ears; ver. 12—22.

(7.) It was to be found, therefore, only *in God*. He only understood the way of true wisdom, and the reason of his own plans; and it became man to acquiesce in his inscrutable dealings. True wisdom was therefore to be found in the fear of the Lord, and in a profound veneration for the Almighty; ver. 23—28.

SURELY there is a [1] vein for the silver, and a place for gold *where* they fine *it*.

1 or, *mine*.

friends had taken. He had demonstrated in the previous chapters that their main position was incorrect, and he asks (in ver. 12 of this chapter), how it was possible that they could hold such sentiments as these, in the midst of all the *facts* which surrounded them? The whole current of events was against their opinion, and in the close of this chapter he enumerates the sentiments which they had advanced, which he regarded as so strange, and which he felt that he had now shown to be erroneous. Indeed, *they* seem to have regarded themselves as confuted, for they were silent. Job had attacked and overthrown their main position, that men were treated according to their character in this life, and that consequently extraordinary sufferings were proof of extraordinary guilt, and, that being overthrown, they had nothing more to say. Having silenced them, and shown the error of the opinions which he has here enumerated, he proceeds in the following chapters to state his own views on important topics connected with the providence of God, mainly designed to show that we are not to expect fully to comprehend the reason of his dispensations.

CHAPTER XXVIII.

1. *Surely there is a vein for silver.* Marg. *mine.* Coverdale renders this, "There are places where silver is molten." Prof. Lee renders it, "There is an outlet for the silver," and supposes it means the *coming out* or separation of the silver from the earthy particles by which it is surrounded in the ore, not the coming out from the mine. The word rendered *vein* (מוצא) means properly *a going forth,* as the rising of the sun, Ps. xix. 6; the promulgation of an edict, Dan. ix. 25; then a *place* of going forth—as a gate, door; Ezek. xlii. 11; xliii. 11, and thence a mine, a vein, or a place of the *going forth* of metals; that is, a place where they are procured. So the LXX. here, Ἔστι γὰρ ἀργυρίῳ τό

πος; ὅθεν γίνεται—"there is a place for silver whence it is obtained." The idea here is, that man had evinced his wisdom in finding out the mines of silver and working them. It was one of the instances of his skill that he had been able to penetrate into the earth, and bring out the ore of the precious metals, and convert it to valuable purposes. ¶ *And a place for gold.* A workshop, or laboratory, for working the precious metals. Job says, that even in *his* time such a laboratory was a proof of the wisdom of man. So now, one of the most striking proofs of skill is to be found in the places where the precious metals are purified, and wrought into the various forms in which they are adapted to ornament and use. ¶ Where *they fine* it—יָזֹקּוּ. The word here used (זָקַק) means properly to bind fast, to fetter; and then to *compress*, to *squeeze* through a strainer; and hence to strain, filter; and thence to purify—as wine that is thus filtered, or gold that is purified; Mal. iii. 3. It may refer here to any process of purifying or refining. It is commonly done by the application of heat. One of the instructive uses of the book of Job is the light which it throws incidentally on the state of the ancient arts and sciences, and the condition of society in reference to the comforts of life at the early period of the world when the author lived. In this passage it is clear (1) that the metals were then in general use, and (2.) that they were so wrought as to furnish, in the view of Job, a striking illustration of human wisdom and skill. Society was so far advanced as to make use not only of gold and silver, but also of copper and brass. The use of gold and silver commonly *precedes* the discovery of iron, and consequently the mention of *iron* in any ancient book indicates a considerably advanced state of society. It is of course, not known to what extent the art of working metals was carried in the time of Job, as all that would be indicated here would be that the method of obtaining the pure metal from the ore was understood. It may be interesting, however, to observe, that the art was early known to the Egyptians, and was carried by them to a considerable degree of perfection. Pharaoh arrayed Joseph in vestures of fine linen, and put a chain of gold about his neck; Gen. xli. 42, and great quantities of gold and silver ornaments were borrowed by the Israelites of the Egyptians, when they were about to go to the promised land. Gold and silver are mentioned as known in the earliest ages; comp. Gen. ii. 11, 12; xli. 42; Ex. xx. 23; Gen. xxiii. 15, 16. Iron is also mentioned as having been early known; Gen. iv. 22. Tubal Cain was instructor in iron and brass. Gold and silver mines were early wrought in Egypt, and if Moses was the compiler of the book of Job, it is possible that some of the descriptions here may have been derived from that country, and at all events the mode of working these precious metals was probably the same in Arabia and Egypt. From the mention of ear rings, bracelets, and jewels of silver and gold, in the days of Abraham, it is evident that the art of metallurgy was known at a very remote period. Workmen are noticed by Homer as excelling in the manufacture of arms, rich vases, and other objects inlaid or ornamented with vessels:

> Πηλείδης δ' αἶψ' ἄλλα τίθει ταχυτῆτος ἄεθλα,
> Ἀργύρεον κρατῆρα τετυγμένον.
>
> Il. xxiii. 741.

His account of the shield of Achilles (Il. xviii. 474) proves that the art of working in the precious metals was well known in his time; and the skill required to delineate the various objects which he describes was such as no ordinary artisan, even at this time, could be supposed to possess. In Egypt, ornaments of gold and silver, consisting of rings, bracelets, necklaces, and trinkets, have been found in considerable abundance of the times of Osirtasen I., and Thothmes III., the contemporaries of Joseph and of Moses. Diodorus (i. 49) mentions silver mines of Egypt which produced 3,200 myriads of minæ. The gold mines of Egypt remained long unknown, and their position has been as

2 Iron *is* taken out of the [1]earth, and brass *is* molten *out of* the stone.

1 or, *dust*.

certained only a few years since by M. Linant and M. Bonomi. They lie in the Bisháree desert, about seventeen days' journey to the South eastward from Derow. The matrix in which the gold in Egypt was found is quartz, and the excavations to procure the gold are exceedingly deep. The principal excavation is 180 feet deep. The quartz thus obtained was broken by the workmen into small fragments, of the size of a bean, and these were passed through hand mills made of granitic stone, and when reduced to powder the quartz was washed on inclined tables, and the gold was thus separated from the stone. Diodorus says, that the principal persons engaged in mining operations were captives, taken in war, and persons who were compelled to labour in the mines, for offences against the government. They were bound in fetters, and compelled to labour night and day. "No attention," he says, "is paid to these persons; they have not even a piece of rag to cover themselves; and so wretched is their condition, that every one who witnesses it, deplores the excessive misery which they endure. No rest, no intermission from toil, are given either to the sick or the maimed; neither the weakness of age, nor women's infirmities, are regarded; all are driven to the work with the lash, till, at last, overcome with the intolerable weight of their afflictions, they die in the midst of their toil." Diodorus adds, "Nature indeed, I think, teaches that as gold is obtained with immense labour, so it is kept with difficulty, creating great anxiety, and attended in its use both with pleasure and with grief." It was perhaps, in view of such laborious and difficult operations in obtaining the precious metals, and of the skill which man had evinced in extracting them from the earth, that Job alluded here to the process as a striking proof of human wisdom. On the early use of the metals among the ancient Egyptians, the reader may consult with advantage, Wilkinson's "Manners and Customs of the Ancient Egyptians," vol. iii. p. 215, seq.

2. *Iron.* As has been remarked above, iron was early known, yet probably its common use indicates a more advanced state of civilization than that of gold and silver. The Mexicans were ignorant of the use of iron, though ornaments of gold and silver elegantly wrought abounded among them. Iron is less easily discovered than copper, though more abundant, and is wrought with more difficulty. Among the ancient nations, copper was in general use long before iron; and arms, vases, statues, and implements of every kind were made of this metal alloyed and hardened with tin, before iron came into general use. Tubal Cain is indeed mentioned (Gen. iv. 22) as the "instructor of every artificer in brass and *iron*," but no direct mention is made of iron arms (Num xxxv. 16) or tools (Deut. xxvii. 5), until after the departure from Egypt. According to the Arundelian Marbles, iron was known one hundred and eig ty-eight years before the Trojan war, about 1370 years B. C.; but Hesiod, Plutarch, and others, limit its discovery to a much later period. Homer, however, distinctly mentions its use, Il. xxiii. 262:

Η δὲ γυναῖκας ἐϋζώνας, πολιόν τε σίδηρον.

That by the *sideros* of the poet is meant iron, is clear, from a simile which he uses in the Odyssey, derived from the quenching of iron in water, by which he illustrates the hissing produced in the eye of Polyphemus by piercing it with the burning stake:

> "And as when armourers temper in the ford
> The keen edged pole-axe or the shining sword,
> The red-hot metal hisses in the lake,
> Thus in the eye-ball hissed the plunging stake."
>
> Odyss. ix. 391. POPE.

Iron is mentioned in the time of Og king of Bashan, 1450 B.C. It was at first, however, regarded as of great value, and its use was very limited. It was presented in the temples of Greece as among the most valuable offerings,

3 He setteth an end to darkness, and searcheth out all perfection: the stones of darkness, and the shadow of death.

---

and rings of iron have been found in the tombs of Egypt that had been worn as ornaments, showing the value of the metal. One of the reasons why this metal comes so slowly into use, and why it was so rare in early times, was the difficulty of smelting the ore, and reducing it to a malleable state. "Its gross and stubborn ore," says Dr. Robertson (America, B. iv.), "must feel twice the force of fire, and go through two laborious processes, before it becomes fit for use." It was this fact which made it to Job such a proof of the wisdom of man that he had invented the process of making iron, or of separating it from the earthy portions in which it is found. ¶ *Is taken out of the earth.* Marg. *dust.* The form in which iron is found is too well known to need description. It is seldom, if ever, found in its purity, and the ore generally has so much the appearance of mere *earth*, that it requires some skill to distinguish them. ¶ *And brass.* נחושה. Brass is early and frequently mentioned in the Bible (Gen. iv. 22; Ex. xxv. 3; xxvi. 11, *et al.*), but there is little doubt that copper is meant in these places. Brass is a compound metal, made of copper and zinc—containing usually about one third of the weight in zinc—and it is hardly probable that the art of compounding this was early known; comp. Notes on chap. xx. 24. Dr. Good renders this, "And the rock poureth forth copper." Coverdale, "The stones resolved to metal." Noyes, "The stone is melted into copper." Prof. Lee, "Also the stone [is taken from the earth] from which one fuseth copper." The Hebrew is, literally, "And stone is poured out (יצוק) copper." The LXX. render it, "And brass is cut like stones;" that is, is cut from the quarry. The word *stone* here in the Hebrew (אבן) means, doubtless, *ore* in the form of stone; and the fact here mentioned, that such ore is fused into the נחושה, *nĕhhūshâ*, is clear proof that copper is intended. Brass is never found in ore, and is never compounded in the earth. A similar idea is found in Pliny, who probably uses the word *aes* to denote copper, as it is commonly employed in the ancient writings. Aes fit ex lapide aeroso, quem vocant Cadmiam; et igne lapides in aes solvantur. Nat. Hist. xxxiv. i. 22. On the general subject of ancient metallurgy, see Wilkinson's Manners and Customs of the Ancient Egyptians, vol. iii. chap. ix.

3. *He setteth an end to darkness.* That is, man does. The reference here is undoubtedly to the operations of mining, and the idea is, that man delves into the darkest regions; he goes even to the outer limits of darkness; he penetrates every where. Probably the allusion is derived from the custom of carrying torches into mines. ¶ *And searcheth out all perfection.* Makes a complete search; examines every thing; carries the matter to the utmost. The idea is not that he searches out all perfection—as our translation would seem to convey; but that he makes a complete and thorough search—and yet after all he does not come to the true and highest wisdom. ¶ *The stones of darkness.* The last stone, says Herder, in the mining investigations in the time of Job; the corner or boundary stone, as it were, of the kingdom of darkness and night. Prof. Lee supposes that there is allusion here to the fact that stones were used as *weights*, and that the idea is, that man had ascertained the *exact weight* of the gross darkness, that is, had taken an accurate admeasurement of it, or had wholly investigated it. But this solution seems far-fetched. Schultens supposes the centre of the earth to be denoted by this expression. But it seems to me that the words "stone" and "darkness" are to be separated, and that the one is not used to qualify the other. The sense is, that man searches out every thing; he perfectly and accurately penetrates every where, and examines all objects;—*the stone* (אבן), that is, the rocks, the mines; *the darkness* (אפל), that is, the darkness of the cavern,

4 The flood breaketh out from the inhabitant; *even the waters* forgotten of the foot: they are dried up, they are gone away from men.

---

the interior of the earth; *and the shadow of death* (צלמות), that is, the most dark and impenetrable regions of the earth. So it is rendered by Coverdale: "The stones, the dark, and the horrible shadow."

4. *The flood breaketh out from the inhabitant.* It would be difficult to tell what idea our translators affixed to this sentence, though it seems to be a literal version of the Hebrew. There has been a great variety of rendering given to the passage. Noyes translates it:

> "From the place where they dwell they open a shaft,
> Unsupported by the feet,
> They are suspended, they swing away from men."

Herder:

> "A flood goeth out from the realm of oblivion,
> They draw it up from the foot of the mountain,
> They remove it away from men."

According to this, the meaning, Herder says, would be, that "the dwelling of the forgotten would be the kingdom of the dead, and at greater depth than the deepest mines have reached. Streams break forth from the river of eternal oblivion beneath, and yet are overcome by the miners, pumped dry, and turned out of the way. "Yet I confess," says he, "the passage remains obscure to my mind." Coverdale renders it, "With the river of water parteth he asunder the strange people, that knoweth no good neighbourhood; such as are rude, unmannerly, and boisterous." The LXX. render it, "The channels of brooks are choked up with sand; when to such as know not the right way strength is unavailing, and they are removed from among men." The difficulty of interpreting the passage has been felt by every expositor to be great; and there are scarcely two expositions alike. There can be no doubt that Job refers to mining operations, and the whole passage should be explained with reference to such works. But the obscurity may possibly arise from the fact that mining operations were then conducted in a manner different from what they are now, and the allusion may be to some custom which was then well understood, but of which we now know nothing. A plausible interpretation, at least, has been furnished by Gesenius, and one which seems to me to be more satisfactory than any other. An explanation of the words in the passage will bring out this view. The word rendered "breaketh out" (פרץ) means to break, rend, tear through—and here refers to the act of breaking through the earth for the purpose of sinking a shaft or pit in a mine. The word rendered "flood" (נחל) means properly a stream or brook; then a valley in which a brook runs along; and here Gesenius supposes it means a shaft or pit of a mine. It may be called a נחל, *năhhăl*, or valley, from the resemblance to a *gully* which the water has washed away by a mountain-torrent. ¶ *From the inhabitant.* This conveys evidently no idea as it now stands. The Hebrew is מעם־גר. The word גור, from which גר is derived, means to sojourn for a time, to dwell, as a stranger or guest; and the phrase here means, "away from any dweller or inhabitant;" that is, from where men dwell, or from the surface of the ground as the abode of men; that is, under ground. Or the idea is, that it is done where no one could dwell. It could not be the abode of man. ¶ Even the waters *forgotten of the foot.* The words "even the waters" are supplied by the translators. The Hebrew is הנשכחים מני־רגל, and refers to being *unsupported* by the foot. They go into a place where the foot yields no support, and they are obliged to suspend themselves in order to be sustained. ¶ *They are dried up*—דלו. The word דלל, from which this is derived, means to hang down, to be pendulous, as boughs are on a tree, or as a bucket is in a well. According to this interpretation, the meaning is, that they *hang down* far from men in their mines, and swing to and fro like the branches of a tree in the wind. ¶ *They are gone away from men.* The

5 *As for* the earth, out of it cometh bread; and under it is turned up as it were fire.

6 The stones of it *are* the place of sapphires; and it hath [1] dust of gold.

1 or, *gold ore.*

---

word נָעוּ, from נוּעַ, means to move to and fro, to waver, to vacillate. Gr. and Latin *νεύω*, *nuo*, Germ. *nicken*, to nod backwards and forwards. The sense here is, that, far from the dwellings of men, they *wave to and fro* in their deep mines, suspended by cords. They descend by the aid of cords, and not by a firm foothold, until they penetrate the deep darkness of the earth. Other interpretations may be seen, however, defended at length in Schultens, and in Rosenmüller—who has adopted substantially that of Schultens—in Dr. Good, and in other commentaries. Few passages in the Bible are more obscure.

5. As for *the earth, out of it cometh bread.* That is, it produces food, or the materials for bread. The idea of Job seems to be, that it was proof of great wisdom and skill on the part of man that he had carried the arts of agriculture so far. The earth in producing grain, and the arts of husbandry, were illustrative of wisdom and skill, but they did not impart the wisdom about the government of God which was desired. That was reserved to be imparted more directly by God himself, ver. 23, seq. ¶ *And under it is turned up as it were fire.* That is, on being turned up it discloses precious stones that seem to glow like coals of fire. This is the obvious sense of this passage, though a different interpretation has been given by most expositors. Job is speaking of mining. He describes the search for gold, and silver, and precious stones. He says that one of the wonders of wisdom in the earth is, that it produces nutritious grain; another, that when the same earth is turned up it seems to rest on a bed of fire. The dark ground is made to glow by the quantity of jewels that are disclosed, and its deep recesses seem to be on fire. There is no reference here, therefore, as it seems to me, to any volcanic agency, or to any belief that the earth rests on a sea of fire. The idea has been expressed in Sergeant's "Mine:"

"Wheresoe'er our footsteps turn,
Rubies blush and diamonds burn."

Luther has given to the passage a different sense. Man bringet auch Feuer unten aus der Erde, da oben Speise auf wächst—"They bring fire from the earth beneath, where food grows up above." Coverdale, "He bringeth food out of the earth; that which is under he consumeth with fire." Herder, "And underneath it is changed as by fire." Dr. Good, "Below it [the earth] windeth a fiery region."

6. *The stones of it* are *the place.* Among the stones of the earth sapphires are found. "The situation of the sapphire is in alluvial soil, in the vicinity of rocks, belonging to the secondary floetz trap formation, and imbedded in gneiss." *Jameson.* "The sapphire occurs in considerable abundance in the granitic alluvion of Matura and Saffragam, in Ceylon." *Davy.* ¶ *Sapphires.* Comp. Note Isa. liv. 11. The sapphire is a precious stone, usually of a blue colour, though it is sometimes yellow, red, violet, green, or white. In hardness it is inferior to the diamond only:

"In unroll'd tufts, flowers purpled, blue and white,
Like sapphire, pearl, in rich embroidery."
SHAKSPEARE.

"He tinctures rubies with their rosy hue,
And on the sapphire spreads a heavenly blue."
BLACKMORE.

The mineral is, next to the diamond, the most valuable of the precious stones. The most highly prized varieties are the crimson and carmine red; these are the *Oriental ruby* of the traveller, and next to the diamond are the most valuable jewels hitherto discovered. The blue varieties—the sapphire of the jeweller—are next in value to the red. The yellow varieties—the *Oriental Topaz* of the jeweller—are of less value than the blue or true sapphire. *Edin. Ency.* Art.

7 *There* [a] *is* a path which no
fowl knoweth, and which the vulture's eye hath not seen:
8 The lion's whelps have not
trodden it, nor the fierce lion passed
by it.

a chap.11.6.

9 He putteth forth his hand upon
the rock; [1] he overturneth the
mountains by the roots.
10 He [b] cutteth out rivers among
the rocks; and his eye seeth every
precious thing.

1 or, *flint*. b Hab.3.9.

Mineralogy. ¶ *And it hath dust of gold.* Marg. or, *gold ore.* Literally, "The dusts of gold are in it." Gold is often found in the form of dust. It is obtained by washing it from the sand, and passing it over a fleece of wool, to which the gold adheres.

7. There is *a path which no fowl knoweth.* That is, a path in searching for gold and precious stones. The miner treads a way which is unseen by the bird of keenest vision. He penetrates into the deep darkness of the earth. The object of Job is to show the wisdom and the intrepidity of man in penetrating these dark regions in searching for sapphires and gold. The most far-sighted birds could not find their way to them. The most intrepid and fearless beasts of prey dared not adventure to those dangerous regions. The word rendered *fowl* (עיט) means either a ravenous beast, Jer. xii. 9, or more commonly a ravenous bird; see Notes on Isa. xlvi. 11. According to Bochart, Hieroz. P. II. L. II. c. viii. p. 195, the word here denotes a rapacious bird of any kind; a bird which has a keen vision. ¶ *Which the vulture's eye hath not seen.* The vulture is distinguished for the remarkable keenness of its vision. On the deserts of Arabia, it is said, when a camel dies, there is almost immediately discerned far in the distant sky, what seems at first to be a mere speck. As it draws nearer it is perceived to be a vulture that had marked the camel as he fell, and that comes to prey upon it. This bird is proverbial for the keenness of its sight.

8. *The lion's whelps.* The lion that ventures into the most dangerous places in pursuit of prey, has not dared to go where man has gone in pursuit of precious stones and gold. On the words here used to designate the lion, see Bochart Hieroz. P. I. Lib. iii. c. 1.

9. *He putteth forth his hand.* That is, the miner in securing the precious metals and gems. ¶ *Upon the rock.* Marg. *flint.* The word here used (חַלָּמִישׁ) occurs also in Ps. civ. 8. Deut. viii. 15; xxxii. 13. It means *flint, silex;* and the idea is, that the miner approaches the hardest substances. He penetrates even the flint in searching for precious stones. Dr. Good renders it, "Sparry ore." Michaelis renders the same word in Deut. vii. 15, porphyry, or red granite. The idea is that nothing, however difficult, not even cutting down the hardest rocks, deters the miner from pursuing his work. ¶ *He overturneth the mountains by the roots.* That is, he digs under them, and they fall. The *root* of a mountain means its base or foundation. The following passage from Pliny (Hist. Nat. xxxiii. c. iv. § 21) furnishes an admirable illustration of this passage: Tamen in silice facilior existimatur labor. Est namque terra ex quodam argillæ genere glaræ mixta, Candidam vocant, prope inexpugnabilis. Cuneis eam ferreis aggrediuntur, et iisdem malleis; nihilque durius putant, nisi quod inter omnia auri fama durissima est. Peracto opere cervices fornicum ab ultimo caedunt, dantque signum ruinæ, eamque solus intelligit in cacumine montis pervigil. Hic voce, ictuque, repente operarios revocari jubet, pariterque ipse devolat. Mons fractus cadit in sese longo fragore, qui concipi humana mente non possit, et flatu incredibili. Spectant victores ruinam naturæ.

10. *He cutteth out rivers among the rocks.* That is, in his operations of mining, he cuts channels for the water to flow off through the rocks. This was done, as it is now, for the purpose of drawing off the water that accumulates in mines. ¶ *His eye seeth every precious thing.* Every valuable mineral or precious stone that lies imbedded in the rocks. It is evident

11 He bindeth [a] the floods from [2] overflowing ; and *the thing that is* hid bringeth he forth to light.

a chap.26.8. 2 *weeping*.

from this, that mining operations were carried to a considerable extent in the time of Job. The art of thus penetrating the earth, and laying open its secret treasures, indicate an advanced stage of society—a stage much removed from barbarism.

11. *He bindeth the floods from overflowing.* Marg. *weeping.* The Hebrew also is "from weeping" מִבְּכִי; referring to the water which trickles down the shaft of the mine. The idea is, that even the large streams which break out in such mines, the fountains and springs which the miner encounters in his operations, he so effectually restrains that they do not even trickle down or *weep* on the sides of the shaft, but it is left perfectly dry. This is necessary in opening mines of coal or minerals, and in making tunnels or other excavations. Yet any one who has passed into a coal mine, through a tunnel, or into any one of the deep natural caves of the earth, will see how difficult it is to close all the places where water would trickle down. It is in fact seldom done ; and if done literally in the time of Job, it indicates a very advanced state of the art of mining. In sinking a shaft, it is often necessary to pass at different depths through strata of earth where the water oozes out in abundance, and where the operations would be necessarily suspended if it could not be stopped or drawn off. The machinery necessary for this constitutes a considerable part of the expense of mining operations. ¶ *And* the thing that is *hid he bringeth forth to light.* The concealed treasures ; the gold and gems that are buried deep in the earth. He brings them out of their darkness, and converts them to ornament and to use. This ends the description which Job gives of the operations of mining in his time. We may remark in regard to this description (1) that the illustration was admirably chosen. His object was to show that true wisdom was not to be found by human science, or by mere investigation. He selects a case, therefore, where man had shown the most skill and wisdom, and where he had penetrated farthest into darkness. He penetrated the earth ; drove his shaft through rocks ; closed up gushing fountains, and laid bare the treasures that had been buried for generations in the regions of night. Yet all this did not enable him fully to explain the operations of the divine government. (2.) The art of mining was carried to a considerable degree of perfection in the time of Job. This is shown by the fact that his description would apply very well to that art even as it is practised now. Substantially the same things were done then which are done now, though we cannot suppose with the same skill, or to the same extent, or with the same perfection of machinery. (3.) The time when Job lived was in a somewhat advanced period of society. The art of working metals to any considerable extent indicates such an advance. It is not found among barbarous tribes, and even where the art is to a considerable extent known, it is long before men learn to sink shafts in the earth, or to penetrate rocks, or to draw off water from mines. (4.) We see the wisdom and goodness which God has shown in regard to the things that are most useful to man. Those things which are *necessary* to his being, or which are very desirable for his comfort, are easily accessible ; those which are less necessary, or whose use is dangerous, are placed in deep, dark, and almost inaccessible places. The fruits of the earth are near to man ; water flows every where, and it is rare that he has to dig deep for it ; and when found by digging, it is a running fountain, not soon exhausted like a mine of gold ; and iron, also, the most valuable of the metals, is usually placed near the surface of the earth. But the pearl is at the bottom of the ocean ; diamonds and other precious stones are in remote regions or imbedded in rocks ; silver runs along in small veins, often in the fissures of rocks, and extending far into the bow-

12 But where [a] shall wisdom be
found? and where *is* the place of
understanding?
13 Man knoweth not the price
[b] thereof; neither is it found in the
land of the living.
14 The depth saith, It *is* not in
me: and the sea saith, *It is* not
with me.

a Ec.7.24. b Pr.3.13-15.

els of the earth. The *design* of placing the precious metals in these almost inaccessible fissures of the rocks, it is not difficult to understand. Had they been easily accessible, and limited in their quantity, they would long since have been exhausted—causing at one time a *glut* in the market, and at others absolute want. As they are now, they exercise the utmost ingenuity of man, first to *find* them, and then to *procure* them; they are distributed in small quantities, so that their value is always great; they furnish a convenient circulating medium in all countries; they afford all that is needful for ornament. (5) There is another proof of wisdom in regard to their arrangement in the earth, which was probably unknown in the time of Job. It is the fact that the most useful of the metals are found in immediate connection with the fuel required for their reduction, and the limestone which facilitates that reduction. This is now perfectly understood by mineralogists, and it is an instance of the goodness of God, and of the wisdom of his arrangements, which ought not to be disregarded or overlooked. They who wish to examine this subject more at length, may find some admirable views in Buckland's Geology and Mineralogy (Bridgewater Treatises), vol. i. pp. 392–415.

12. *But where shall wisdom be found?* That is, the full understanding of the plans of God—for this is the point of inquiry. The object of Job is to show that it is not to be found in the most profound science; by penetrating to the farthest extent of which man was capable in the earth, nor by any human investigations whatever. None of these things revealed the great plans of the Almighty in reference to his moral government, and particularly to the points which engrossed the attention of Job and his friends. Where true wisdom *is* to be found he proceeds to state in the subsequent verses.

13. *Man knoweth not the price thereof.* The word rendered *price* (ערך) means properly that which is set in a pile or row, or which is arranged in order. Here it means preparation, equipment—that is, any thing put in order, or ready, Judges xvii. 10. It is also used in the sense of estimation or valuation, Lev. v. 15, 18. The word *price* here, however, seems to form no proper answer to the question in the previous verse, as the question is, *where* wisdom is to be found, not what is its *value*. Many expositors have, therefore, introduced a different idea in their interpretation. Dr. Good renders it, "Man knoweth not its *source*." Prof. Lee, "Man knoweth not its *equal*." Herder, "Man knoweth not the *seat* thereof." Coverdale, "No man can tell how *worthy* a thing she is." The LXX. render it, "Man knoweth not—ὁδὸν αὐτῆς—her way." But the word here used is not employed to denote a *place* or *way*, and the true interpretation doubtless is, that Job does not confine himself to a strict answer of the question proposed in ver. 12, but goes on to say that man could not *buy* it; he could neither find it, nor had he the means of purchasing it with all the wealth of which he was the owner. ¶ *Neither is it found in the land of the living.* That is, it is not found among men. We must look to a higher source than man for true wisdom; comp. Isa. xxxviii. 11; liii. 8.

14. *The depth saith.* This is a beautiful personification. The object of this verse and the following is, to show that wisdom cannot be found in the deepest recesses to which man can penetrate, nor purchased by any thing which man possesses. It must come from God only. The word depth here (תהום) means properly a wave, billow, surge; then a mass of waters,

15 It [1] cannot be gotten for gold, [a] neither shall silver be weighed *for* the price thereof.

16 It cannot be valued with the gold of Ophir, with the precious onyx, or the sapphire.

17 The gold and the crystal cannot equal it; and the exchange of it *shall not be for* jewels [2] of fine gold.

1 *fine gold shall not be given for it.* a Pr.8. 10,19; 16.16. 2 or, *vessels.*

a flood, or the deep ocean, Deut. viii. 7; Gen. vii. 11; Ps. xxxvi. 6; and then a gulf, or abyss. It refers here to the sea, or ocean; and the idea is, that its vast depths might be sounded, and true wisdom would not be found there.

15. *It cannot be gotten for gold.* Marg. *fine gold shall not be given for it.* The word which is here rendered *gold*, and in the margin *fine gold* (סגור), is not the common word used to denote this metal. It is derived from סגר, to *shut*, to *close*, and means properly that which is *shut up* or *enclosed;* and hence Gesenius supposes it means pure gold, or the most precious gold, as that which is shut up or enclosed with care. Dr. Good renders it "solid gold," supposing it means that which is condensed, or beaten. The phrase occurs in nearly the same form (זהב סגור, "*gold shut up*," Marg.) in 1 Kings vi. 20, 21; vii. 49, 50; x. 21; 2 Chron. iv. 21, 22; ix. 20, and undoubtedly denotes there the most precious kind of gold. Its relation to the sense of the verb *to shut up* is not certain. Prof. Lee supposes that the idea is derived from the use of the word, and of similar words in Arabic, where the idea of heating, fusing, giving another colour, changing the shape, and thence of fixing, retaining, &c., is found; and that the idea here is that of fused or purified gold. Michaelis supposes that it refers to *native* gold that is pure and unadulterated, or the form of gold called *dendroides*, from its shooting out in the form of a tree—*baumartig gewachsenes Gold* (from the Arabic, *a tree*). It is not known, however, that the Hebrew word סגר was ever used to denote a tree. There can be no doubt that the word denotes *gold* of a pure kind, and it *may* have been given to it because gold of that kind was carefully *shut up* in places of safe keeping; but it would seem more probable to me that it was given to it for some reason now unknown. Of many of the names now given by us to objects which are significant, and which are easily understood by us, it would be impossible to trace the reason or propriety, after the lapse of four thousand years. ¶ *Neither shall silver be weighed.* That is, it would be impossible to weigh out so much silver as to equal its value. Before the art of coining was known, it was common to *weigh* the precious metals that were used as a medium of trade; comp. Gen. xxiii. 16.

16. *The gold of Ophir.* Uniformly spoken of as the most precious gold; see Notes on chap. xxii. 24. ¶ *With the precious onyx.* The onyx is a semi-pellucid gem, with variously coloured veins or zones. It is a variety of the chalcedony. The Arabic word denotes that which was of two colours, where the white predominated. The Greeks gave the name *onyx* (ὄνυξ) to the gem from its resemblance to the colour of the thumb-nail; see *Passow.* ¶ *Or the sapphire;* Notes on ver. 6.

17. *The gold and the crystal.* A crystal, in chemistry, is an inorganic body which, by the operation of affinity, has assumed the form of a regular solid, terminated by a number of plane and smooth surfaces. It is found in various forms and sizes, and is composed of a great variety of substances. The common *rock crystal* is a general name for all the transparent crystals of quartz, particularly of limpid or colourless quartz. *Webster.* The word here used (זכוכית) occurs nowhere else in the Bible. It is from זכך, to be clean, pure; and is given to the crystal on account of its transparency. In Arabic the word means either glass or crystal. Jerome translates it, *vitrum*—glass; the LXX. ὕαλος—crystal, or the *lapis crystallinus.* Hesychius says that the crystal

18 No mention shall be made of [1] coral, or of pearls; for the price of wisdom *is* above rubies.

1 or, *Ramoth.*

denotes λαμπρὸν κρύος—*clear ice* or, λίθον τίμιον—*a precious stone.* There is no reason to suppose that *glass* was known so early as this, and the probability is that the word here denotes something like the rock crystal, having a strong resemblance to the diamond, and perhaps then regarded as nearly of equal value. It cannot be supposed that the relative value of gems was then understood as it is now. ¶ *Jewels of fine gold.* Marg. *vessels.* The Hebrew word כְּלִי properly means vessels, or instruments. It may refer here, however, to ornaments for the person, as it was in that way chiefly that gold was employed.

18. *No mention shall be made of coral.* That is, as a price by which to purchase wisdom, or in comparison with wisdom. The margin here is, *Ramoth*—retaining the Hebrew word ראמות. Jerome renders it, *excelsa*—exalted or valuable things. So the LXX. Μετέωρα—exalted or sublime things; as if the word were from רום, to be exalted. According to the Rabbins, the word here means *red coral.* It occurs also in Ezek. xxvii. 16, where it is mentioned as a valuable commodity in merchandise in which Syria traded with Tyre, and occurs in connection with emeralds, purple, broidered work, fine linen, and agate. The coral is a well known marine substance, not valued now as if it were a precious stone, but probably in the time of Job regarded as of value sufficient to be reckoned with gems. It was not rare, though its uses were not known. As a beautiful object, it might at that time deserve to be mentioned in connection with pearls. It is now found in abundance in the Red Sea, and probably that which was known to Job was obtained there. Shaw says, "In rowing gently over it [the port *Tor*], while the surface of the sea was calm, such a diversity of *Madrepores Fucuses*, and other marine vegetables, presented themselves to the eye, that we could not forbear taking them, as Pliny [L. xiii. cap. 25] had done before us, for a forest under water. The branched Madrepores particularly contributed very much to authorize the comparison, for we passed over several that were eight or ten feet high, growing sometimes pyramidical, like the cypress, and at other times had their branches more open and diffused, like the oak; not to speak of others which, like the creeping plants, spread themselves over the bottom of the sea;" Travels, p. 384, Ed. Oxford, 1738. It should be added, however, that there is no absolute certainty that Job referred here to coral. The Hebrew word would suggest simply that which was *exalted in value,* or of great price; and it is not easy to determine to what particular substance Job meant to apply it. ¶ *Or of pearls.* גָּבִישׁ—*Gabish.* This word occurs nowhere else, though אֶלְגָּבִישׁ—*Elgabish,* is found in Ezek. xiii. 11, 13; xxxviii. 22, where it means hail-stones, or pieces of ice. Perhaps the word here means merely *crystal*—resembling ice. So Umbreit Gesenius, and others, understand it. Prof. Lee supposes that the word here used denotes that which is *aggregated* and then what is *massive,* or *vast*; see his Note on this place. Jerome renders it, *eminentia*—exalted, lofty things; the LXX. retain the word without attempting to translate it—γαβὶς—and the fact that they have not endeavoured to render it, is a strong circumstance to show that it is now hopeless to attempt to determine its meaning. ¶ *Above rubies.* The ruby is a precious stone of a carmine red colour, sometimes verging to violet. There are two kinds of rubies, the oriental or corundum, and the spinelle. The ruby is next in hardness to the diamond, and approaches it in value. The oriental ruby is the same as the sapphire. The ruby is found in the kingdom of Pegu, in the Mysore country, in Ceylon, and in some other places, and is usually imbedded in gneiss. It is by no means certain, however, that the word here used (פְּנִינִים) means rubies. Many of the Rabbins suppose that *pearls*

19 The topaz of Ethiopia shall
not equal it, neither shall it be
valued with pure gold.
20 Whence [a] then cometh wisdom? and where *is* the place of
understanding?
21 Seeing it is hid from the eyes
of all living, and kept close from
the fowls of the [1] air.

a ver.12.Ja.1.5,17. 1 or, *heaven*.

are meant by it; and so Bochart, Hieroz. ii. Lib. v. c. 6, 7, understands it. J. D. Michaelis understands it to mean *red corals,* and Gesenius concurs with this opinion. Umbreit renders it, *Perlen—pearls.* The word occurs in Prov. iii. 15; viii. 11; xx. 15; xxxi. 10; Lam. iv. 7. In the Proverbs, as here, it is used in comparison with *wisdom*, and undoubtedly denotes one of the precious gems.

19. *The topaz.* The topaz is a precious stone, whose colours are yellow, green, blue, and red. Its natural place is in various primitive rocks, such as the topaz-rock, gneiss, and clay-slate. It is found in the granite and gneiss districts of Mar and Cairngorm, in Cornwall, in Brazil, and in various other places. The most valuable stones of this kind now known are those which are found in Brazil. This gem is much prized by jewellers, and is considered as one of the more beautiful ornamental stones. The Hebrew word פִּטְדָה *pitdâ* occurs in Ex. xxviii. 17; xxxix. 10; Ezek. xxviii. 13. and in this place only. It is uniformly rendered *topaz*. It is not improbable that the English word *topaz*, and the Greek τοπάζιον, are derived from this, by a slight transposition of the letters—פטדה. The Vulgate and the LXX. render this *topaz*. ¶ *Of Ethiopia.* Heb. כוש—*Cush.* Coverdale here renders it, *India.* On the meaning of this word, and the region denoted by it, see Notes on Isa. xi. 11. It may mean either the part of Africa now known as Ethiopia, or Abyssinia and Nubia; the southern part of Arabia, or the Oriental Cush in the vicinity of the Tigris. It is better, since the word has such ambiguity, to retain the original, and to translate it *Cush.* For any thing that appears, this may have denoted, in the time of Job, the southern part of Arabia. It is known that the topaz was found there. Thus Pliny says, Lib. xxxvii. 32, Reperta est—in Arabiæ insula, quæ Citis vocatur; in qua Troglodytæ praedones, diutius fame—prossi cum herbas radicesque effoderant, eruerunt topazion.

20. *Whence then cometh wisdom?* This question is now repeated from ver. 12, in order to give it greater emphasis. It is designed to fix the attention on the inquiry as one which found no solution in the discoveries of science, and whose solution was hidden from the most penetrating human intellect.

21. *It is hid from the eyes of all living.* That is, of all men, and of all animals. Man has not found it by the most sagacious of all his discoveries, and the keenest vision of beasts and fowls has not traced it out. ¶ *And kept close.* Heb. *concealed.* ¶ *From the fowls of the air;* comp. Notes on ver. 7. Umbreit remarks, on this passage, that there is attributed to the fowls in Oriental countries a deep knowledge, and an extraordinary gift of divination, and that they appear as the interpreters and confidants of the gods. One cannot but reflect, says he, on the personification of the good spirit of Ormuzd through the fowls, according to the doctrine of the Persians (Comp. Creutzer's Symbolik Th. 1. s. 723); upon the ancient fowl-king (Vogelkönig) Simurg upon the mountain Kap, representing the highest wisdom of life; upon the discourses of the fowls of the great mystic poet of the Persians, Ferideddin Attar, &c. Among the ancient Greeks and Romans, also, a considerable part of their divinations consisted in observing the flight of birds, as if they were endowed with intelligence, and indicated coming events by the course which they took; comp. also, Eccles. x. 20, where wisdom or intelligence is ascribed to the birds of the air. "Curse not the king, no, not in thy thought; and curse not the rich in

22 Destruction and death say, We have heard the fame thereof with our ears.

23 God [a] understandeth the way thereof, and he knoweth the place thereof.

a Pr.2.6.

thy bed-chamber: for a bird of the air shall carry the voice, and that which hath wings shall tell the matter."

22. *Destruction.* This is a personification which is exceedingly sublime. Job had spoken of the wonderful discoveries made by science, but none of them had disclosed true wisdom. It had not been discovered in the shaft which the miner sank deep in the earth; in the hidden regions which he laid open to day, nor by the birds that saw to the farthest distance, or that were regarded as the interpreters of the will of the gods. It was natural to ask whether it might not have been discovered in the vast profound of the nether world—the regions of death and of night; and whether by making a bold appeal to the king that reigned there, a response might not be heard that would be more satisfactory. In ver. 14, the appeal had been made to the *sea*—with all its vast stores; here the appeal is to far deeper regions—to the nether world of darkness and of death. On the word used here (אבדון), *destruction,* see Notes on chap. xxvi. 6. It is employed here, as in that place, to denote the nether world—the abode of departed spirits—the world where those are who have been *destroyed* by death, and to which the destruction of the grave is the entrance. ¶ *And death.* Death is used here to denote *Sheol,* or the abode of the spirits of the dead. The sense is, that those deep and dark regions had simply heard the distant report of wisdom but they did not understand it, and that if one went down there it would not be fully revealed to him. Perhaps there is an allusion to the natural expectation that, if one could go down and converse with the *dead,* he could find out much more than can be known on earth. It was to be presumed that they would understand much more about the unseen and future world, and about the plans and government of God, than man can know here. It was on this belief, and on the hope that some league or alliance could be made with the dead, inducing them to communicate what they knew, that the science of necromancy was founded; see Notes on Isa. viii. 19. ¶ *We have heard the fame thereof.* We have heard the report of it, or a rumour of it. The meaning is, that they did not understand it fully, and that if man could penetrate to those dark regions, he could not get the information which he desired. Wisdom is still at such an immense distance that it is only a *report,* or rumour of it, which has reached us.

23. *God understandeth the way thereof.* These are doubtless the words of Job. The meaning is, that the reason of the divine dispensations could be known only to God himself. He had given no *clew* by which man could discover this. He might carry his investigations far into the regions of science; he could penetrate the earth, and look on the stars, but still all his investigations fell short of disclosing the reasons of the divine dispensations. The secret was lodged in his bosom, and he only could communicate it where and when he pleased. It may be added here, that this is as true now as it was in the time of Job. Man has carried the investigations of science almost infinitely farther than he had then, but still by the investigations of science he has by no means superseded the necessity of revelation, or shed light on the great questions that have, in all ages, so much perplexed the race. It is only by direct communication, by his word and by his Spirit, that man can be made to understand the reason of the divine doings, and nothing is better established by the course of events than the truth on which Job here so much insists, that *science* cannot answer the questions of so much interest to man about the divine government.

24 For he [a] looketh to the ends of the earth, *and* seeth under the whole heaven;

25 To make [b] the weight for the winds; and he weigheth the waters by measure.

26 When he made a decree for the rain, and a way for the lightning of the thunder;

27 Then did he see it, and [1] declare it; he prepared it, yea, and searched it out.

a Pr.15.3. *b* Ps.135.7.

1 or, *number*.

---

24. *For he looketh to the ends of the earth.* That is, God sees and knows every thing. He looks upon the whole universe. Man sees objects dimly; he sees but a few, and he little understands the bearing of one thing or another.

25. *To make the weight for the winds.* That is, to weigh the winds, and to measure the waters—things that it would seem most difficult to do. The idea here seems to be, that God had made all things by measure and by rule. Even the winds—so fleeting and imponderable—he had adjusted and balanced in the most exact manner, as if he had *weighed* them when he made them. The air has *weight*, but it is not probable that this fact was known in the time of Job, or that he adverted to it here. It is rather the idea suggested above, that the God who had formed every thing by exact rule, and who had power to govern the winds in the most exact manner, must be qualified to impart wisdom. ¶ *And he weigheth the waters;* comp. Notes on Isa. xl. 12, seq. The word rendered *weigheth* in this place (תכן) means either to *weigh*, or to *measure*, Isa. xl. 12. As the "measure" here is mentioned, it rather means probably to adjust, to apportion, than to weigh. The waters are dealt out by measure; the winds are weighed. The sense is, that though the waters of the ocean are so vast, yet God has adjusted them all with infinite skill, as if he had dealt them out by measure; and having done this, he is qualified to explain to man the reason of his doings.

26. *When he made a decree for the rain.* A statute or law (חק) by which the rain is regulated. It is not sent by chance or hap-hazard. It is under the operation of regular and settled laws. We cannot suppose that those laws were understood in the time of Job, but the *fact* might be understood that the rain *was* regulated by laws, and that fact would show that God was qualified to impart wisdom. His kingdom was a kingdom of settled law and not of chance or caprice, and if the *rain* was regulated by statute, it was fair to presume that he did not deal with his people by chance, and that afflictions were not sent without rule; comp. Notes on chap. v. 6. ¶ *And a way.* A path through which the rapid lightning should pass—referring, perhaps, to the apparent *opening* in the clouds in which the lightning seems to move along. ¶ *The lightning of the thunder.* The word lightning here (חזיז—hhâziz) properly means *an arrow*, from חזז, obsol., to pierce through, to transfix, to perforate; and hence the lightning—from the rapidity with which it passes—like an arrow. The word "thunder" (קֹלוֹת) means *voices*, and hence *thunder*, as being by way of eminence the voice of God; comp. Ps. xxix. 3—5. The whole expression here means "the thunder-flash." Coverdale renders this, "when he gave the mighty floods a law;" but it undoubtedly refers to the thunder-storm, and the idea is, that he who controls the rapid lightning, regulating its laws and directing its path through the heavens, is qualified to communicate truth to men, and can explain the great principles on which his government is administered.

27. *Then did he see it.* That is, then did he see wisdom. When in the work of creation he gave laws to the rain and the thunder storm; when he weighed out the winds and measured out the waters, *then* he saw and understood the principles of true wisdom. There is a remarkable similarity be-

28 And unto man he said, Behold, the fear [a] of the LORD that *is* wisdom; [b] and to depart from evil *is* understanding.

a De.4.6; Ps.111.10; Pr.1.7,9,10; Ec.12.13. *b* Ja.3.17.

tween the expression here and Prov. viii. 27—30, "When he prepared the heavens, I [wisdom] was there; when he set a compass upon the face of the depth; when he established the clouds above; when he strengthened the foundations of the deep; when he gave to the sea his decree, that the waters should not pass his commandment; when he appointed the foundations of the earth; then I was by him as one brought up with him; I was daily his delight, rejoicing always before him." ¶ *And declare it.* Marg. *number.* The word (ספר) means, however, rather to *declare*, or to *narrate;* and the idea is, that even then he made known to intelligent beings the true principles of wisdom, as consisting in the fear of the Lord, and in suitable veneration for the Most High. *In what way* this was made known, Job does not say; but there can be no doubt of the fact to which he adverts, that even in his time the great principles of all real wisdom were made known to created intelligences, as consisting in profound veneration of God, in a willingness to bow under his dispensations, and to confide in him. ¶ *He prepared it.* Made it a matter of *thought* and *inquiry* to find out what was real wisdom, and communicated it in a proper way to his creatures. The idea is, that it was not the result of chance, nor did it spring up of its own accord, but it was a matter of *intelligent investigation* on the part of God to know what constituted true wisdom. Probably, also, Job here means to refer to the attempts of *man* to investigate it, and to say that its value was enhanced from the fact that it had even required *the search of God* to find it out. Beautiful eulogiums of Wisdom may be seen in the Apocryphal book Ecclesiasticus, of which the following is a specimen:

Wisdom shall praise herself,
And shall glory in the midst of her people.
In the congregation of the Most High shall she open her mouth,
And triumph before his power.
I came out of the mouth of the Most High,
And covered the earth as a cloud.
I dwell in high places,
And my throne is in a cloudy pillar.
I alone compassed the circuit of heaven,
And walked in the bottom of the deep.
In the waves of the sea, and in all the earth,
And in every people and nation, I got a possession.
He created me from the beginning, before the world,
And I shall never fail. Chap. xxiv.

28. *And unto man he said.* At what time, or how, Job does not say. Prof. Lee supposes that this refers to the instruction which God gave in Paradise to our first parents; but it may rather be supposed to refer to the universal tenor of the divine communications to man, and to all that God had said about the way of true wisdom. The meaning is, that the substance of all that God had said to man was, that true wisdom was to be found in profound veneration of him. ¶ *The fear of the* LORD, *that is wisdom.* The word "Lord" here is improperly printed in small capitals, as if the word were יהוה—JEHOVAH. The original word is, however, אדני—*Adonai;* and the fact is worthy of notice, because one point of the argument respecting the date of the book turns on the question whether the word JEHOVAH occurs in it; see Notes on chap. xii. 9. The fear of the Lord is often represented as true wisdom; Prov. i. 7; xiv. 27; xv. 33; xix. 23; Ps. cxi. 10, *et al.* The meaning here is, that real wisdom is connected with a proper veneration for God, and with submission to him. We cannot understand his ways. Science cannot conduct us up to a full explanation of his government, nor can the most profound investigations disclose all that we would wish to know about God. In these circumstances, true wisdom is found in humble piety; in reverence for the name and perfections of God; in that veneration which leads us to adore him, and to believe that he is right, though clouds and darkness are round about him. To this conclusion Job, in all his perplexities, comes, and here his mind finds rest. ¶ *And*

CHAPTER XXIX.

ANALYSIS OF THE CHAPTER.

THIS chapter is closely connected with the two following, and they together constitute a continuous argument. Job returns to his own case, and probably designs to show that this is a striking illustration of the mysteriousness of the divine dealings to which he had adverted in the last chapter. His general aim is to vindicate his own integrity against the charges of his friends, and to show that all that he had said about the unprecedented nature of his afflictions was well founded. In chap. xxix. he beautifully descants on his former prosperity; in chap. xxx. he exhibits the striking contrast between that and his present condition; and in chap. xxxi. in answer to the accusations of his friends, he relates the principal transactions of his past life, asserts his integrity as displayed in the discharge of all the duties which he owed to God and man, and again appeals to the omniscience and justice of God in proof of his sincerity. *Lowth.*

This chapter is occupied with a description of his former prosperity. He refers particularly to the times when God smiled upon and blessed him; when he lifted the light of his countenance upon him, and his children were round about him, ver. 1—6; he speaks of the respect which was shown him when he went into the place of public concourse—when young men retired before him, when princes and nobles were silent in his presence, and when the ears and eyes of all blessed him for the good that he had done to the fatherless and to him that was ready to perish, ver. 7—13; he speaks of the time when he put on righteousness as a robe and a diadem, and when he was eyes to the blind and feet to the lame, ver. 14—17; and he refers to the fact that he then supposed that his prosperity would be permanent, and to the universal respect in which he was held by all classes of men, ver. 18—25. The whole picture in the chapter is one of uncommon beauty, and describes a state of the highest happiness and prosperity. It is the image of a venerable patriarch, a wise counsellor, a universal benefactor, a composer of difficulties, a man enjoying universal confidence and affection. It is an image of what was *aimed at* as constituting the highest state of earthly blessedness in the estimation of those who lived in patriarchal times, and is a beautiful portraiture of what would be regarded as the most honourable distinction in the hospitality and piety of the East. At the same time it is a beautiful description of piety and its effects every where; and of the respect shown to wisdom, virtue, and benevolence, in all ages.

MOREOVER, Job [1] continued his parable, and said,

2 O that I were as *in* months past, as *in* the days *when* God preserved me;

[1] added to take up.

---

to depart from evil is *understanding.* To forsake every evil way *must* be wise. In doing that, man knows that he cannot err. He walks safely who abandons sin, and in forsaking every evil way he knows that he cannot but be right. He may be in error when speculating about God, and the reasons of his government; he may be led astray when endeavouring to comprehend his dealings; but there can be no such perplexity in departing from evil. There he *knows* he is right. There his feet are on a rock. It is better to walk surely there than to involve ourselves in perplexity about profound and inscrutable operations of the divine character and government. It may be added here, also, that he who aims to lead a holy life, who has a virtuous heart, and who seeks to do always what is right, will have a clearer view of the government and truth of God, than the most profound intellect can obtain without a heart of piety; and that without that, all the investigations of the most splendid talents will be practically in vain.

CHAPTER XXIX.

1. *Moreover, Job continued his parable;* see Notes on chap. xxvii. 1. It is probable that Job had paused to see if any one would attempt a reply. As his friends were silent, he resumed his remarks and went into a more full statement of his sufferings. The fact that Job more than once paused in his addresses to give his friends an opportunity to speak, and that they were silent when they seemed called upon to vindicate their former sentiments, was what particularly roused the wrath of Elihu and induced him to answer; chap. xxxii. 2—5.

2. *Oh that I were.* Heb. "Who will give?" a common mode of expressing a wish; comp. chap. vi. 8; xi. 5; xiii. 5; xxiii. 3. ¶ *As in months past.* O that I could recall my former prosperity, and be as I was when I enjoyed the protection and favour of God. Probably one object of this wish was that his friends might see from what a state of honour and happiness he had been brought down. They complained of him as impatient. He may have designed to show them that his lamentations were not unreasonable, when it was borne in mind from what a state of prosperity he had been taken, and to what a condition of wo he had been brought. He, therefore, goes into this extended description of his former happiness, and dwells particularly upon the good which he was enabled then to do, and the respect which was shown him as

3 When [1] his candle shined
upon my head, *and when* by his
light I [a] walked *through* darkness;

1 or, *lamp*. a Ps.23 4.

4 As I was in the days of my
youth, when the secret [b] of God
was upon my tabernacle;

b Ps.25.14.

a public benefactor. A passage strikingly similar to this occurs in Virgil, Æn. viii. 560:

O mihi præteritos referat si Jupiter annos!
Qualis eram. cùm primam aciem Praeneste sub ipsâ
Stravi, scutorumque incendi victor acervos.

"O would kind heaven my strength and youth recall,
Such as I was beneath Praeneste's wall;
There where I made the foremost foes retire,
And set whole heaps of conquered shields on fire!"

3. *When his candle shined upon my head.* Marg. or, *lamp;* comp. Notes chap. xviii. 6. It was remarked in the Note on that place, that it was common to have lamps or lights always burning in a house or tent. When Job speaks of the lamps shining *on his head,* the allusion is probably to the custom of suspending a lamp from the ceiling—a custom which prevails among the wealthy Arabs. *Scott.* Virgil speaks of a similar thing in the palace of Dido:

——Dependent lychni laquearibus aureis
Incensi. Æn. i. 726.

"From gilded roofs depending lamps display
Nocturnal beams that imitate the day."
DRYDEN.

See, also Lucretius, ii. 24. Indeed the custom is common every where; and the image is a beautiful illustration of the divine favour—of light and happiness imparted by God, the great source of blessedness from above. The Hebrew word rendered "*shined*" (בְּהִלּוֹ) has been the occasion of some perplexity in regard to its form. According to Ewald, Heb. Gram. p. 471, and Gesenius, Lex, it is the Hiphil form of הלל—to shine, the He preformative being dropped. The sense is, "In his causing the light to shine." Others suppose that it is the infinitive of Kal, with a pleonastic suffix; meaning "when it shined;" *i. e.* the light. The sense is essentially the same; comp. Schultens and Rosenmüller *in loco.* ¶ And when *by his light.* Under his guidance and direction. ¶ *I walked* through *darkness.* "Here is reference probably to the fires or other lights which were carried before the caravans in their nightly travels through the deserts.' *Noyes.* The meaning is, that God afforded him protection, instruction, and guidance. In places, and on subjects that would have been otherwise dark, he counselled and led him. He enjoyed the manifestations of the divine favour; his understanding was enlightened, and he was enabled to comprehend subjects that would have been otherwise perplexing and difficult. He refers, probably, to the inquiries about the divine government and administration, and to the questions that came before him as a magistrate or an umpire—questions that he was enabled to determine with wisdom.

4. *As I was in the days of my youth.* The word here rendered *youth* (חֹרֶף), properly means *autumn—from* (חָרַף), to *pluck, pull,* as being the time when fruits are gathered. Then it means that which is mature; and the meaning here is probably *mature* or *manly*—"As I was in the days of my ripeness;' that is, of my vigour or strength. The whole passage shows that it does not mean *youth,* for he goes on to describe the honour and respect shown to him when in mature life. So the Septuagint—"Ὅτε ἤμην ἐπιβρίθων ὁδοὺς—"When I made heavy or laded my ways," an expression referring to autumn as being laden with fruit. So we speak of the spring, the autumn, and the winter of life, and by the autumn denote the maturity of vigour, experience, and wisdom. So the Greeks used the word ὀπώρα, Pindar, *Isthm.* 2, 7, 8; *Nem.* 5, 10, Æschyl. Suppl. 1005, 1022. So Ovid:

Excessit Autumnus posito fervore juventæ
Maturus, mitisque inter juvenemque senemque;
Temperie medius, sparsis per tempora canis.
Inde senilis hiems tremulo venit horrida passu.
Aut spoliata suos, aut, quos habet, alba capillos.
Metam. 15 200.

The wish of Job was, that he might be restored to the vigour of mature

5 When the Almighty *was* yet with me, *when* my children *were* about me;

6 When [a] I washed my steps with butter, and the rock poured [1] me out rivers of oil;

a De.33.24. 1 with me.

life, and to the influence and honours which he had then, or rather, perhaps, it was that they might have a view of what he was then, that they might see from what a height he had fallen, and what cause he had of complaint and grief. ¶ *When the secret of God* was *upon my tabernacle.* The meaning of this language is not clear, and considerable variety has obtained in the interpretation. The LXX. render it, "When God watched over—ἐπισκοπὴν ἐποιεῖτο—my house." Vulg., "When God was secretly in my tabernacle." Noyes, "When God was the friend of my tent." Coverdale renders the whole, "As I stood when I was wealthy and had enough; when God prospered my house." Umbreit, Als noch traulich Gott in meinem Zelte weilte—"When God remained cordially in my tent." Herder, "When God took counsel with me in my tent." The word rendered *secret* (סוֹד), means a *couch* or *cushion* on which one reclines, and then a divan, or circle of friends sitting together in consultation; see the word explained in the Notes on chap. xv. 8. The idea here probably is, that God came into his tent or dwelling as a friend, and that Job was, as it were, admitted to the secrecy of his friendship and to an acquaintance with his plans.

5. *When the Almighty* was *yet with me.* Job regarded God as withdrawn from him. He now looked back with deep interest to the time when he dwelt with him.

6. *When I washed my steps with butter.* On the word rendered *butter*, see Notes on Isa. vii. 15. It properly means *curdled milk.* Umbreit renders it, *Sahne; cream.* Noyes, *milk*, and so Wemyss. The LXX. "When my ways flowed with butter"—βουτύρῳ. So Coverdale, "When my ways ran over with butter." Herder, "And where I went a stream of milk flowed on." The sense may be, that cream or butter was so plenty that he was able to make use of it for the most common purposes—even for that of washing his feet. That butter was sometimes used for the purpose of anointing the feet—probably for comfort and health—as oil was for the head, is mentioned by Oriental travellers. Hassilquist (Travels in Palestine, p. 58), speaking of the ceremonies of the priests at Magnesia on Holy Thursday, says, "The priest washed and dried the feet, and afterward besmeared them with butter, which it was alleged was made from the first milk of a young cow." Bruce says that the king of Abyssinia daily anointed his head with butter. Burder in Rosenmüller's alte u. neue Morgenland, *in loc.* It is possible that this use of butter was as ancient as the time of Job, and that he here alludes to it, but it seems more probable that the image is designed to denote superfluity or abundance; and that where he trod, streams of milk or *cream* flowed—so abundant was it round him. The word rendered *steps* (הֲלִיכַי) does not properly denote *the feet* but *the tread, the going, the stepping.* This sense corresponds with that of the other member of the parallelism. ¶ *And the rock poured me out rivers of oil.* Marg. *with me.* The idea is, that the very rock near which he stood, seemed to pour forth oil. Instead of water gushing out, such seemed to be the abundance with which he was blessed, that the very rock poured out a running stream of oil. Oil was of great value among the Orientals. It was used as an article of food, for light, for anointing the body, and as a valuable medicine. To say, then, that one had abundance of oil, was the same as to say that he had ample means of comfort and of luxury. Perhaps by the word *rock* here, there is an allusion to the places where olives grew. It is said that those which produced the best oil grew upon rocky mountains. There may be, also, an allusion to this in

7 When I went out to the gate
through the city, *when* I prepared
my seat in the street!
8 The young men saw me, and
hid themselves; and the aged arose
and stood up.
9 The princes refrained talking,
and laid *their* hand on their mouth.
10 The [1] nobles held their peace,

[1] *The voice of the nobles was hid.*

Deut. xxxii. 13: "He made him to suck honey out of the rock, and oil out of the flinty rock." Prof. Lee, and some others, however, understand here by the *rock*, the press where oil was extracted from olives, and which it is supposed was sometimes made of stone.

7. *When I went out to the gate.* The *gate* of a city was a place of public concourse, and where courts were usually held. Job speaks here as a magistrate, and of the time when he went forth to sit as a judge, to try causes. ¶ When *I prepared my seat in the street.* That is, to sit as a judge. The seat or tribunal was placed in the street, in the open air, before the gate of the city, where great numbers might be convened, and hear and see justice done. The Arabs, to this day, hold their courts of justice in an open place, under the heavens, as in a field or a market-place. Norden's Travels in Egypt, ii. 140. There has been, however, great variety of opinion in regard to the meaning of this verse. Schultens enumerates no less than *ten* different interpretations of the passage. Herder translates it,

> "When from my house I went to the assembly,
> And spread my carpet in the place of meeting."

Prof. Lee translates it, "When I went forth from the gate to the pulpit, and prepared my seat in the broad place." He supposes that Job refers to occasions when he addressed the people, and to the respect which was shown him then. Dr. Good renders it, "As I went forth, the city rejoiced at me." It is probable, however, that our common version has given the true signification. The word rendered *city* (קרת), is a poetic form for (קריה) *city*, but does not frequently occur. It is found in Prov. viii. 3; ix. 3, 14; xi. 11. The phrase "*upon* the city"—Heb. עלי־קרת—or, "*over* the city," may refer to the fact that the gate was in an elevated place, or that it was the *chief* place, and, as it were, over or at the head of the city. The meaning is, that as he went out from his house toward the gate that was situated in the most important part of the city, all did him reverence.

8. *The young men saw me, and hid themselves.* That is, they retired as if awed at my presence. They gave place to me, or reverently withdrew as I passed along. ¶ *And the aged arose,* and *stood up.* They not merely rose, but they continued to stand still until I had passed by. "This is a most elegant description, and exhibits most correctly the great reverence and respect which was paid, even by the old and the decrepit, to the holy man, in passing along the streets, or when he sat in public. They not only rose, which in men so old was a great mark of distinction, but they stood; and they continued to do it, though the attempt was so difficult." *Lowth.* The whole image presents a beautiful illustration of Oriental manners, and of the respect paid to a man of known excellence of character and distinction.

9. *The princes refrained talking.* As a mark of respect, or in awe of his presence. ¶ *And laid* their *hand on their mouth.* To lay the finger or the hand on the mouth is every where an action expressive of silence or respect; Notes, chap. xxi. 5. "In one of the subterranean vaults of Egypt, where the mummies lie buried, they found in the coffin an embalmed body of a woman, before which was placed a figure of wood, representing a youth on his knees, laying a finger on his mouth, and holding in his other hand a sort of chafing dish, which was placed on his head, and in which, without doubt, had been some perfumes." *Maillet.*

10. *The nobles.* Marg., "*The voice of the nobles was hid.*" Literally, this may be rendered, "as to the voice the

and their tongue cleaved to the
roof of their mouth.
11 When the ear heard *me*, then
it blessed [a] me ; and when the eye
saw *me*, it gave witness to me :
12 Because I delivered [b] the poor
that cried, and the fatherless, and
him that had none to help him.
13 The blessing of him that was
ready to perish came upon me :
and I caused the widow's heart to
sing for joy.
14 I [c] put on righteousness, and
it clothed me ; my judgment *was*
as a robe and a diadem.

a Lu.4.22;11.27. *b* Ps.72.12 ; Pr.21.13;24.11,12. *c* Is.61.10 ; Ep.6.14.

---

nobles hid themselves ;" or the phrase here employed (נחבאו קול נגידים=) may be rendered, "the voice of the nobles was hid"—it being common in the Hebrew when two nouns come together, of different numbers and gender, for the verb to conform to the latter. *Rosenmüller*. The word "nobles" here is to be understood in the sense of *counsellors*, or men of rank. They would now be called *Emirs*, or *Sheïks*. ¶ *And their tongue cleaved to the roof of their mouth.* They were so awed by my presence that they could not speak.

11. *When the ear heard* me. A personification for "they who heard me speak, blessed me." That is, they commended or praised me. ¶ *And when the eye saw* me. All who saw me. ¶ *It gave witness to me.* That is, the fixed attention to what he said and the admiration which was shown by the eyes of the multitudes, were witnesses of the respect and honour in which he was held. Gray has a beautiful expression similar to this when he says,

"He reads his history in a nation's eyes."

12. *Because I delivered the poor that cried.* This is spoken of himself as a magistrate or judge—for the whole description relates to that. The meaning is, that when the poor man, who had no means of employing counsel, brought his cause before him, he heard him and delivered him from the grasp of the oppressor. He never made an appeal to him in vain ; comp. Prov. xxi. 13 ; xxiv. 11, 12. ¶ *And the fatherless.* The orphan who brought his cause before him. He became the patron and protector of those whose natural protectors—their parents—had been removed by death ; comp. Notes on Isa. i. 17. ¶ *And* him that had *none to help him.* The poor man who had no powerful patron. Job says that, as a magistrate, he particularly regarded the cause of such persons, and saw that justice was done them—a beautiful image of the administration of justice in patriarchal times. This is the sense in which our translators understood this. But the parallelism seems rather to require that this should be applied to the fatherless who had no one to aid him, and the Hebrew, by understanding the conjunctive ו as meaning *when*, will bear this construction. So it is understood by Rosenmüller, Umbreit, Herder, and Noyes.

13. *The blessing of him that was ready to perish*, &c. Of the man who was falsely accused, and who was in danger of being condemned, or of him who was exposed to death by poverty and want. ¶ *And I caused the widow's heart to sing for joy.* By becoming her patron and friend ; by vindicating her cause, and saving her from the oppressive exactions of others; comp. Isa. i. 17.

14. *I put on righteousness.* Or *justice*—as a magistrate, and in all his transactions with his fellow-men. It is common to compare moral conduct or traits of character with various articles of apparel ; comp. Notes on Isa. xi. 5 ; lxi. 10. ¶ *And it clothed me.* It was my covering ; I was adorned with it. So we speak of being "clothed with humility ;" and so, also, of the "garments of salvation." ¶ *My judgment.* Or rather justice—particularly as a magistrate. ¶ Was *as a robe.* The word *robe* (מעיל) denotes the *mantle* or outer garment that is worn by an Oriental. It constitutes the most elegant part of his dress ; Notes no Isa vi. 1. The idea is, that his strict justice was to

15 I was eyes [a] to the blind, and
feet *was* I to the lame.
16 I *was* a father to the poor;
and [b] the cause *which* I knew not
I searched out.
17 And I brake the [1] jaws of the
wicked, and [2] plucked the spoil out
of his teeth.
18 Then [c] I said, I shall die in

a Nu. 10.31. *b* Pr. 29.7. 1 *jaw-teeth, or, grinders.* 2 *cast.* *c* Ps. 30.7.

him what the full flowing robe was in apparel. It was that for which he was best known; that by which he was distinguished, as one would be by an elegant and costly robe. ¶ *And a diadem.* Or, turban. The word here used צניף—is from צנף, to roll, or wind around, and is applied to the turban, because it was thus wound around the head. It is applied to the mitre of the high-priest (Zech. iii. 5), and may also be to a diadem or crown. It more properly here, however, denotes the *turban,* which in the East is an essential part of dress. The idea is, that he was fully clad or adorned with justice.

15. *I was eyes to the blind.* An exceedingly beautiful expression, whose meaning is obvious. He became their counsellor and guide. ¶ *And feet* was *I to the lame.* I assisted them, and became their benefactor. I did for them, in providing a support, what they would have done for themselves if they had been in sound health.

16. *I* was *a father to the poor.* I took them under my protection, and treated them as if they were my own children. ¶ *And the cause* which *I knew not I searched out.* This is according to the interpretation of Jerome. But the more probable meaning is, "the cause of him who was unknown to me, that is, of the stranger, I searched out." So Rosenmüller, Herder, Umbreit, and Good. According to this, the sense is, that, as a magistrate, he gave particular attention to the cause of the stranger, and investigated it with care. It is possible that Job here designs specifically to reply to the charge brought against him by Eliphaz in chap. xxii. 6, seq. The duty of showing particular attention to the stranger is often inculcated in the Bible, and was regarded as essential to a character of uprightness and piety among the Orientals.

17. *And I brake the jaws of the wicked.* Marg. "*jaw-teeth,* or, *grinders.*" The Hebrew word מתלעות, the same, with the letters transposed, as מלתעות, is from לתע, to *bite*—and means *the biters,* the grinders, the teeth. It is not used to denote the jaw. The image here is taken from wild beasts, with whom Job compares the wicked, and says that he rescued the helpless from their grasp, as he would a lamb from a lion or wolf. ¶ *And plucked.* Marg. *cast.* The margin is a literal translation, but the idea is, that he violently seized the spoil or prey which the wicked had taken, and by force tore it from him.

18. *Then I said.* So prosperous was I, and so permanent seemed my sources of happiness. I saw no reason why all this should not continue, and why the same respect and honour should not attend me to the grave. ¶ *I shall die in my nest.* I shall remain where I am, and in my present comforts, while I live. I shall then die surrounded by my family and friends, and encompassed with honours. A *nest* is an image of quietness, harmlessness, and comfort. So Spenser speaks of a *nest:*

Fayre bosome! fraught with virtue's richest tresure,
The neast of love, the lodging of delight,
The bowre of bliss, the paradise of pleasure.
Sonnet LXXVI.

The image here expresses the firm hope of a long life, and of a peaceful and tranquil death. The LXX. render it, "My age shall grow old like the trunk of a palm tree"—στέλεχος φοίνικος—I shall live long; comp. Bochart, Hieroz. P. ii. Lib. vi. c. v. p. 820, for the reason of this translation. ¶ *And I shall multiply my days as the sand.* Herder renders this, "the Phœnix;" and observes that the Phœnix is obviously intended here, only through a double sense of the word, the figure of the bird is im-

my nest, and I shall multiply *my* days as the sand.
19 My root *was* [1] spread out by the waters, and the dew lay all night upon my branch.

[1] opened.

mediately changed for that of the palm-tree. The Rabbins generally understand by the word here rendered "sand" (חוֹל) the Phœnix—a fabulous bird, much celebrated in ancient times. Rabbi Osaiâ in the book *Bereshith Rabba*, or Commentary on Genesis, says of this bird, "that all animals obeyed the woman [in eating the forbidden fruit] except one bird only by the name of חול—*hhul*, concerning which it is said in Job, 'I will multiply my days as the *hhul*—כחול.'" Rabbi Jannai adds to this, that "this bird lives a thousand years, and in the end of the thousand years, a fire goes forth from its nest, and burns it up, but there remains, as it were, an egg, from which again the members grow, and it rises to life;" comp. Nonnus in Dionys. Lib. 40. Martial, Claudian, and others in Bochart, Hieroz. P. ii. Lib. vi. c. v. pp. 818—825. But the more correct rendering is, doubtless, the common one, and it is usual in the Scriptures to denote a great, indefinite number, by the sand; Gen. xxii. 17; Judges vii. 12; Habak. i. 9. A comparison similar to this occurs in Ovid, Metam. Lib. xiv. 136, seq.:

> ——Ego pulveris hausti
> Ostendens cumulum, quot haberet corpora pulvis,
> Tot mihi natales contingere vana rogavi.

The meaning is, that he supposed his days would be very numerous. Such were his expectations—expectations so soon to be disappointed. Such was his condition—a condition so soon to be reversed. The very circumstances in which he was placed were fitted to beget a too confident expectation that his prosperity would continue, and the subsequent dealings of God with him should lead all who are in similar circumstances, not to confide in the stability of their comforts, or to suppose that their prosperity will be uninterrupted. It is difficult, when encompassed with friends and honours, to realize that there ever will be reverses; it is difficult to keep the mind from confiding in them as if they *must* be permanent and secure.

19. *My root* was *spread out by the waters*. Marg. as the Hebrew, *opened*. The meaning is, that it was spread abroad or extended far, so that the moisture of the earth had free access to it; or it was like a tree planted near a stream, whose root ran down to the water. This is an image designed to denote great prosperity. In the East, such an image would be more striking than with us. Here green, large, and beautiful trees are so common as to excite little or no attention. In such a country as Arabia, however, where general desolation exists, such a tree would be a most beautiful object, and a most striking image of prosperity; comp. De Wette on Ps. i. 3. ¶ *And the dew lay all night upon my branch*. In the absence of rain—which seldom falls in deserts—the scanty vegetation is dependent on the dews that fall at night. Those dews are often very abundant. Volney (Travels i. 51) says, "We, who are inhabitants of humid regions, cannot well understand how a country can be productive without rain, but in Egypt, the dew which falls copiously in the night, supplies the place of rain." See, also, Shaw's Travels, p. 379. "To the same cause also [the violent heat of the day], succeeded afterwards by the coldness of the night, we may attribute the plentiful dews, and those thick, offensive mists, one or other of which we had every night too sensible a proof of. The dews, particularly, (as we had the heavens only for our covering), would frequently wet us to the skin." The sense here is, as a tree standing on the verge of a river, and watered each night by copious dews, appears beautiful and flourishing, so was my condition. The LXX. however, render this, "And the dew abode at night on my harvest"—*καὶ δρόσος αὐλισθήσεται ἐν τῷ θερισμῷ μου.* So the Chaldee—רבית בחצדי וטלא.

20 My glory *was* [1] fresh in me, and my [a] bow was [2] renewed in my hand.

21 Unto me *men* gave ear, and waited, and kept silence at my counsel.

22 After my words they spake not again; and my speech dropped upon them.

23 And they waited for me as for the rain; and they opened

1 *new*. *a* Ge. 49.24. 2 *changed*.

A thought, similar to the one in this passage, occurs in a Chinese Ode, translated by Sir William Jones, in his works, vol. ii. p. 351:

Vide illius aquæ rivum
Virides arundines jucundè luxuriant!
Sic est decorus virtutibus PRINCEPS NOSTER!

"Seest thou yon stream, around whose banks
The green reeds crowd in joyous ranks?
In nutrient virtue and in grace,
Such is the PRINCE that rules our race."
DR. GOOD.

20. *My glory* was *fresh in me*. Marg. *new*. "As we say, the man shall not *overlive* himself." *Umbreit*. The idea is, that he was not exhausted; he continued in vigour and strength. The image is probably taken from that suggested in the previous verse—from a tree, whose beauty and vigour were continued by the waters, and by the dew that lay on its branches. ¶ *And my bow*. An emblem of vigour and strength. The ancients fought with the bow, and hence a man who was able to keep his bow constantly drawn, was an image of undiminished and unwearied vigour; comp. Gen. xlix. 24: "But his bow abode in strength." ¶ *Was renewed in my hand*. Marg. as in Heb. *changed*. The meaning is, that it constantly renewed its strength. The idea is taken from a tree, which *changes* by renewing its leaves, beauty, and vigour; Isa. ix. 10; comp. Job xiv. 7. The sense is that his bow gathered strength in his hand. The figure is very common in Arabic poetry, many specimens of which may be seen in Schultens *in loco*.

21. *Unto me* men *gave ear*. Job here returns to the time when he sat in the assembly of counsellors, and to the respectful attention which was paid to all that he said. They listened when he spake; they waited for him to speak before they gave their opinion; and they were then silent. They neither interrupted him nor attempted a reply.

22. *After my words they spake not again*. The highest proof which could be given of deference. So full of respect were they that they did not dare to dispute him; so sagacious and wise was his counsel that they were satisfied with it, and did not presume to suggest any other. ¶ *And my speech dropped upon them*. That is, like the dew or the gentle rain. So in Deut. xxxii. 2:

My doctrine shall drop as the rain;
My speech shall distil as the dew,
As the small rain upon the tender herb,
And as the showers upon the grass.

So Homer speaks of the eloquence of Nestor,

Τοῦ καὶ ἀπὸ γλώσσης μέλιτος γλυκίων ῥέεν αὐδή.

"Words sweet as honey from his lips distill'd." POPE.

So Milton, speaking of the eloquence of Belial, says,

——— *Though his tongue*
Dropt manna, and could make the worse appear
The better reason, to perplex and dash
Maturest counsels. Par. Lost, B. ii.

The comparison in the Scriptures of words of wisdom or persuasion, is sometimes derived from honey, that drops or gently falls from the comb. Thus in Prov. v. 3:

For the lips of a strange woman drop as an honey-comb,
And her mouth is smoother than oil.

So in Cant. iv. 11:

Thy lips, O my spouse, drop as the honeycomb;
Honey and milk are under thy tongue.

23. *And they waited for me as for the rain*. That is, as the dry and thirsty earth waits for the rain. This is a continuation of the beautiful image commenced in the previous verse, and conveys the idea that his counsel was as necessary in the assemblies of men as the rain was to give growth to the seed, and beauty

their mouth wide *as* for the latter rain.

24 *If* I laughed on them, they believed *it* not; and the light of my countenance they cast not down.

---

to the landscape. ¶ *And they opened their mouth wide.* Expressive of earnest desire; comp. Ps. cxix. 131: "I opened my mouth and panted." ¶ As *for the latter rain.* The early and the latter rains are frequently spoken of in the Scriptures, and in Palestine and the adjacent regions are both necessary to the harvest. The early, or autumnal rains, commence in the latter half of October, or the beginning of November, not suddenly, but by degrees, so as to give the husbandman an opportunity to sow his wheat and barley. The rains come mostly from the west, or south-west, continuing for two or three days at a time, and falling especially during the nights. During the months of November and December, they continue to fall heavily; afterwards they return only at longer intervals, and are less heavy; but at no period during the winter do they entirely cease to occur. Rain continues to fall more or less during the month of March, but it is rare after that period. The latter rains denote those which fall in the month of March, and which are so necessary in order to bring forward the harvest, which ripens early in May or June. If those rains fail, the harvest materially suffers, and hence the expressions in the Scriptures, that "the husbandman waits for that rain;" comp. James v. 7; Prov. xvi. 15. The expression, "the early and the latter rain" seems, unless some material change has occurred in Palestine, not to imply that *no* rain fell in the interval, but that those rains were usually more copious, or were especially necessary, first for sowing, and then for bringing forward the harvest. In the interval between the "latter" and the "early" rains—between March and October—rain never falls, and the sky is usually serene; see Robinson's Bibl. Researches, vol. ii. pp. 96—100. The meaning here is, that they who were assembled in counsel, earnestly desired Job to speak, as the farmer desires the rain that will bring forward his crop.

24. If *I laughed on them, they believed* it *not.* There is considerable variety in the interpretation of this member of the verse. Dr. Good renders it, "I smiled upon them, and they were gay." Herder, If I laughed at them, they were not offended." Coverdale, "When I laughed, they knew well it was not earnest." Schultens, "I will laugh at them, they are not secure." But Rosenmüller, Jun. et Trem., Noyes and Umbreit, accord with the sense given in our common translation. The Hebrew literally is, "Should I laugh upon them, they did not confide;" and, according to Rosenmüller, the meaning is, "Such was the reverence for my gravity, that if at any time I relaxed in my severity of manner, they would scarcely believe it, nor did they omit any of their reverence towards me, as if familiarity with the great should produce contempt." Grotius explains it to mean, "Even my jests, they thought, contained something serious." The word here used, however (שׂחק), means not only to laugh or smile upon, but to laugh at, or deride; Ps. lii. 6: Job xxx. 1; comp. Job v. 22; xxxix 7; xxii. 19. It seems to me, that the sense is, that so great was his influence, that he was able to control them even with a smile, without saying a word; that if, when a measure was proposed in debate, he should even *smile*, though he said nothing, they would have no confidence in it, but would at once abandon it as unwise. No higher influence than this can be well conceived, and this exposition accords with the general course of remark, where Job traces along the various degrees of his influence till he comes to this, the highest of them all. ¶ *And the light of my countenance they cast not down.* His smile of favour on an undertaking, or his smile at the weakness or want of wisdom of any thing proposed, they could not resist. It

25 I chose out their way, and sat chief, and dwelt as a king in the army, as one *that* comforteth the mourners.

settled the matter. They had not power by their arguments or moral courage to resist him even if he did not say a word, or even to change the aspect of his countenance. A look, a token of approbation or disapprobation from him, was enough.

25. *I chose out their way.* That is, I became their guide and counsellor. Rosenmüller and Noyes explain this as meaning, "When I came among them;" that is, when I chose to go in their way, or in their midst. But the former interpretation better agrees with the Hebrew, and with the connection. Job is speaking of the honours shown to him, and one of the highest which he could receive was to be regarded as a leader, and to have such respect shown to his opinions that he was even allowed to select the way in which they should go; that is, that his counsel was implicitly followed. ¶ *And sat chief.* Heb. "Sat *head*." He was at the head of their assemblies. ¶ *And dwelt as a king in the army.* As a king, surrounded by a multitude of troops, all of whom were subservient to his will, and whom he could command at pleasure. It is not to be inferred from this, that Job was a king, or that he was at the head of a nation. The idea is, merely, that the same respect was shown to him which is to a monarch at the head of an army. ¶ *As one* that *comforteth the mourners.* In time of peace I was their counsellor, and in time of war they looked to me for direction, and in time of affliction they came to me for consolation. There were no classes which did not show me respect, and there were no honours which they were not ready to heap on me.

It may seem, perhaps, that in this chapter there is a degree of self-commendation and praise altogether inconsistent with that consciousness of deep unworthiness which a truly pious man should have. How, it may be asked, can this spirit be consistent with religion? Can a man who has any proper sense of the depravity of his heart, speak thus in commendation of his own righteousness, and recount with such apparent satisfaction his own good deeds? Would not true piety be more distrustful of self, and be less disposed to magnify its own doings? And is there not here a recalling to recollection of former honours, in a manner which shows that the heart was more attached to them than that of a man whose hope is in heaven should be? It may not be possible to vindicate Job in this respect altogether, nor is it necessary for us to attempt to prove that he was entirely perfect. We are to remember, also, the age in which he lived; we are not to measure what he said and did by the knowledge which we have, and the clearer light which shines upon us. We are to bear in recollection the circumstances in which he was placed, and perhaps we shall find in them a mitigation for what seems to us to exhibit such a spirit of self reliance, and which looks so much like the lingering love of the honours of this world. Particularly we may recall the following considerations:

(1.) He was vindicating himself from charges of enormous guilt and hypocrisy. To meet these charges, he runs over the leading events of his life, and shows what had been his general aim and purpose. He reminds them, also, of the respect and honour which had been shown him by those who best knew him—by the poor, the needy, the inhabitants of his own city, the people of his own tribe. To vindicate himself from the severe charges which had been alleged against him, it was not improper thus to advert to the general course of his life, and to refer to the respect in which he had been held. Who could know him better than his neighbours? Who could be better witnesses than the poor whom he had relieved; and the lame, the blind, the sorrowful, whom he had comforted? Who could better testify to his character than they who had followed his counsel in times of

CHAPTER XXX.

ANALYSIS OF THE CHAPTER.

The design of Job in this chapter is, to contrast his condition at the time when he spake it with his former happiness and prosperity. The afflictions which he describes are mainly those which result from the want of respect and honour which he had formerly enjoyed. He begins by saying (ver. 1—11) that the most vile and abject of society now treated him with disrespect and irreverence—the very outcasts and dregs of mankind now made him their song. He then goes on to say (ver. 12—14) that the youths, instead of showing him the respect and reverence which they had once done, now joined with others in adding to his calamities. He then (ver. 15—19) adverts to the depth of his bodily sufferings, and to the painful and loathsome nature of the disease which had come upon him. He says (ver. 20—24) that he cried in vain to God, and that he felt assured that he meant to bring him down to death. In the conclusion of the chapter (ver. 25—31) he says that notwithstanding he had shown compassion to the poor, and had as a consequence looked for some token of the divine favour and approbation, yet nothing but calamity came, and he was now plunged in the deepest distress; he was a brother to dragons, and a companion to owls.

BUT now *they that are* [1] younger than I have me in derision, whose fathers I would have disdained to have set with the dogs of my flock.

1 *of fewer days.*

perplexity and danger? Who would be more competent witnesses than the mourners whom he had comforted?

(2.) It was a main object with Job to show the greatness of his distress and misery, and for this purpose he went into an extended statement of his former happiness, and especially of the respect which had been shown him. This he contrasts beautifully with his present condition, and the colours of the picture are greatly heightened by the contrast. In forming our estimate of this chapter, we should take this object into the account, and should not charge him with a design to magnify his own righteousness, when his main purpose was only to exhibit the extent and depth of his present woes.

(3.) It is not improper for a man to speak of his former prosperity and happiness in the manner in which Job did. He does not speak of himself as having any merit, or as relying on this for salvation. He distinctly traces it all to God (ver. 2—5), and says that it was because *he* blessed him that he had enjoyed these comforts. It was not an improper acknowledgment of the mercies which he had received from his hand, and the remembrance was fitted to excite his gratitude. And although there may seem to us something like parade and ostentation in thus dwelling on former honours, and recounting what he had done in days that were past, yet we should remember how natural it was for him, in the circumstances of trial in which he then was, to revert to past scenes, and to recall the times of prosperity, and the days when he enjoyed the favour of God.

(4.) It may be added, that few men have ever lived to whom this description would be applicable. It must have required uncommon and very remarkable worth to have made it proper for him thus to speak, and to be able to say all this so as not to be exposed to contradiction. The description is one of great beauty, and presents a lovely picture of patriarchal piety, and of the respect which then was shown to eminent virtue and worth. It is an illustration of the respect that *will* be, and that *ought* to be, shown to one who is upright in his dealings with men, benevolent towards the poor and the helpless, and steady in his walk with God.

CHAPTER XXX.

1. *But now* they that are *younger than I.* Marg. *of fewer days.* It is not probable that Job here refers to his three friends. It is not possible to determine their age with accuracy, but in chap. xv. 10, they claim that there were with them old and very aged men, much older than the father of Job. Though that place may possibly refer not to themselves but to those who held the same opinions with them, yet none of those who engaged in the discussion, except Elihu (chap. xxxii. 6), are represented as young men. They were the contemporaries of Job; men who are ranked as his friends; and men who showed that they had had opportunities for long and careful observation. The reference here, therefore, is to the fact

2 Yea, whereto *might* the strength of their hands *profit* me, in whom old age was perished?

3 For want and famine *they were* [1] solitary; fleeing into the

1 or, *dark as the night.*

that while, in the days of his prosperity, even the aged and the honourable rose up to do him reverence, now he was the object of contempt even by the young and the worthless. The Orientals would feel this much. It was among the chief virtues with them to show respect to the aged, and their sensibilites were peculiarly keen in regard to any indignity shown to them by the young. ¶ *Whose fathers I would have disdained.* Who are the children of the lowest and most degraded of the community. How deep the calamity to be so fallen as to be the subject of derision by such men! ¶ *To have set with the dogs of my flock.* To have associated with my dogs in guarding my flock. That is, they were held in less esteem than his dogs. This was the lowest conceivable point of debasement. The Orientals had no language that would express greater contempt of any one than to call him a dog; comp. Deut. xxiii. 18; 1 Sam. xvii. 43; xxiv. 14; 2 Sam. iii. 8; ix. 8; xvi. 9; 2 Kings viii. 13; Note Isa. lxvi. 3.

2. *Yea, whereto* might *the strength of their hands* profit *me.* There has been much difference of opinion respecting the meaning of this passage. The general sense is clear. Job means to describe those who were reduced by poverty and want, and who were without respectability or home, and who had no power in any way to affect him. He states that they were *so* abject and worthless as not to be worth his attention; but even *this* fact is intended to show how low he was himself reduced, since even the most degraded ranks in life did not show any respect to one who had been honoured by princes. The Vulgate renders this, "The strength—*virtus*—of whose hands is to me as nothing, and they are regarded as unworthy of life." The LXX. "And the strength of their hands, what is it to me? Upon whom perfection—συντέλεια—has perished." Coverdale, "The power and strength of their hands might do me no good, and as for their age, it is spent and passed away without any profit." The literal translation is, "Even the strength of their hands, what is it to me?" The meaning is, that their power was not worth regarding. They were abject, feeble, and reduced by hunger—poor emaciated creatures, who could do him neither good nor evil. Yet this fact did not make him *feel* less the indignity of being treated by such vagrants with scorn. ¶ *In whom old age was perished.* Or, rather, in whom *vigour*, or the power of accomplishing any thing, has ceased. The word כלח—*kĕlăhh*, means *completion*, or the act or power of finishing or completing any thing. Then it denotes old age—age as *finished* or *completed;* Job v. 26. Here it means the maturity or vigour which would enable a man to complete or accomplish any thing, and the idea is, that in these persons this had utterly perished. Reduced by hunger and want, they had no power of effecting any thing, and were unworthy of regard. The word here used occurs only in this book in Hebrew (chap. v. 26; xxx. 2), but is common in Arabic; where it refers to the *wrinkles*, the *wanness*, and *the austere aspect* of the countenance, especially in age. See *Castell's Lex.*

3. *For want and famine.* By hunger and poverty their strength is wholly exhausted, and they are among the miserable outcasts of society. In order to show the depth to which he himself was sunk in public estimation, Job goes into a description of the state of these miserable wretches, and says that he was treated with contempt by the very scum of society, by those who were reduced to the most abject wretchedness, and who wandered in the deserts, subsisting on roots, without clothing, shelter, or home, and who were chased away by the respectable portion of the community as if they were thieves and robbers. The description is one of great power, and presents a sad picture of his own con-

wilderness [1] in former time desolate and waste ;

1 *yesternight.*

4 Who cut up mallows by the bushes and juniper-roots *for* their meat.

dition. ¶ They were *solitary.* Marg. or, *dark as the night.* Heb. גלמוד. This word properly means *hard,* and is applied to a dry, stony, barren soil. In Arabic it means a hard rock. *Umbreit.* In chap. iii. 7, it is applied to a night in which none are born. Here it seems to denote a countenance, dry, hard, emaciated with hunger. Jerome renders it, *steriles.* The LXX. ἄγονος—*sterile.* Prof. Lee, "Hardly beset." The meaning is, that they were greatly reduced—or *dried up*—by hunger and want. So Umbreit renders it, *gantz ausgedorrt—altogether dried up.* ¶ *Fleeing into the wilderness.* Into the desert or lonely wastes. That is, they *fled* there to obtain, on what the desert produced, a scanty subsistence. Such is the usual explanation of the word rendered *flee*—ערק. But the Vulgate, the Syriac, and the Arabic, render it *gnawing,* and this is followed by Umbreit, Noyes, Schultens, and Good. According to this the meaning is, that they were "gnawers of the desert;" that is, that they lived by gnawing the roots and shrubs which they found in the desert. This idea is much more expressive, and agrees with the connection. The word occurs in Hebrew only in this verse and in ver. 17, where it is rendered "My sinews," but which may more appropriately be rendered "My gnawing pains." In the Syriac and Arabic the word means to *gnaw,* or *corrode,* as the leading signification, and as the sense of the word cannot be determined by its usage in the Hebrew, it is better to depend on the ancient versions, and on its use in the cognate languages. According to this, the idea is, that they picked up a scanty subsistence as they could find it, by gnawing roots and shrubs in the deserts. ¶ *In the former time.* Marg. *yesternight.* The Hebrew word (אמש) means properly last night ; the latter part of the preceding day, and then it is used to denote night or darkness in general. Gesenius supposes that this refers to *the night of desolation,* the pathless desert being strikingly compared by the Orientals with darkness. According to this, the idea is not that they had gone but yesterday into the desert, but that they went into the shades and solitudes of the wilderness, far from the abodes of men. The sense then is, "They fled into the night of desolate wastes." ¶ *Desolate and waste.* In Hebrew the same word occurs in different forms, designed to give *emphasis,* and to describe the gloom and solitariness of the desert in the most impressive manner. We should express the same idea by saying that they hid themselves in the *shades* of the wilderness.

4. *Who cut up mallows.* For the purpose of eating. Mallows are common medicinal plants, famous for their emollient or softening properties, and the size and brilliancy of their flowers. It is not probable, however, that Job referred to what we commonly understand by the word mallows. It has been commonly supposed that he meant a species of plant, called by the Greeks Halimus, a saltish plant, or *salt wort,* growing commonly in the deserts and poor land, and eaten as a salad. The Vulgate renders it simply *herbas;* the LXX. ἄλιμα—*alima.* The Hebrew word, according to Umbreit, means a common salad of a saltish taste, whose young leaves being cooked, constituted food for the poorer classes. The Hebrew word מלוח—*măllūăhh* is from מלח—*mĕlăhh, salt,* and properly refers to a marine plant or vegetable. ¶ *By the bushes.* Or among the bushes ; that is, that which grew among the bushes of the desert. They wandered about in the desert that they might obtain this very humble fare. ¶ *And juniper-roots.* The word here rendered "juniper" (רתם—*rothem*), occurs only in this place, and in 1 Kings xix. 4, 5; Ps. cxx. 4. In each place it is rendered *juniper.* In 1 Kings it is mentioned as the tree under which Elijah sat down when he fled into the wilderness for his life ; In Ps cxx. 4, it is mentioned as a material for making *coals.* "Sharp

5 They were driven forth from among *men*, (they cried after them as *after* a thief.)

6 To dwell in the cliffs of the valleys, *in* caves [1] of the earth, and *in* the rocks.

[1] *holes.*

arrows of the mighty, with coals of juniper." It is rendered *juniper* by Jerome, and by the Rabbins. The verb (רתם) occurs in Micah i. 13, where it is rendered *bind*, and means to bind on, to make fast; and probably the plant here referred to received its name in some way from the notion of *binding*—perhaps because its long, flexible, and slender twigs were used for binding, or for *withes*. There is no evidence, however, that the *juniper* is in any case intended. It denotes a species of *broom*—*spartium junceum* of Linn., which grows abundantly in the deserts of Arabia. It is the *Genista rœtam* of Forskal. *Flora* Egypt. Arab. p. 214. It has small variegated blossoms, and grows in the water-courses of the Wadys. Dr. Robinson (Bibl. Researches, i. 299) says, "The *Retem* is the largest and most conspicuous shrub of these deserts, growing thickly in the water-courses and valleys. Our Arabs always selected the place of encampment (if possible) in a place where it grew, in order to be sheltered by it at night from the wind; and, during the day, when they often went on in advance of the camels, we found them not unfrequently sitting or sleeping under a bush of Retem, to protect them from the sun. It was in this very desert, a day's journey from Beersheba, that the prophet Elijah lay down and slept beneath the same shrub. The roots are very bitter, and are regarded by the Arabs as yielding the best charcoal. The Hebrew name רתם—*Rothem*, is the same as the present Arabic name." Burckhardt remarks, that he found several Bedawins in the Wady Genne collecting brushwood, which they burnt into charcoal for the Egyptian market, and adds that they preferred for this purpose the thick roots of the shrub Rethem, which grew there in abundance. Travels in Syria, p. 483. It could have been only those who were reduced to the utmost penury and want that could have made use of the roots of this shrub for food, and this is doubtless the idea which Job means to convey. It is said to have been occasionally used for food by the poor. See Gesenius, Lex.; Umbreit *in loc.*, and Schultens. A description of the condition of the poor, remarkably similar to this, occurs in Lucan, Lib. vii.;

——— Cernit miserabile vulgus
In pecudum cecidisse cibos, et carpere dumos
Et morsu spoliare nemus.

Biddulph (in the collection of Voyages from the Library of the Earl of Oxford, p. 807), says he had seen many poor people in Syria gather mallows and clover, and when he had asked them what they designed to do with it, they answered that it was for food. They cooked and ate them. Herodotus, viii. 115, says, that the army of Xerxes, after their defeat, when they had consumed all the corn of the inhabitants in Thessaly, "fed on the natural produce of the earth, stripping wild and cultivated trees alike of their bark and leaves, to such an extremity of famine were they come."

5. *They were driven forth from among* men. As vagabonds and outcasts. They were regarded as unfit to live among the civilized and the orderly, and were expelled as nuisances. ¶ (*They cried after them as* after *a thief.*) The inhabitants of the place where they lived drove them out with a loud outcry, as if they were thieves and robbers. A class of persons are here described who were mere vagrants and plunderers, and who were not allowed to dwell in civilized society, and it was one of the highest aggravations of the calamities of Job, that he was now treated with derision by such outcasts.

6. *To dwell in the cliffs of the valleys.* The word here rendered *cliffs* (ערוץ) denotes rather *horror*, or something *horrid*, and the sense here is, that they dwelt in *the horror of valleys;* that is, in horrid valleys.

7 Among the bushes they brayed; under the nettles they were
gathered together.

8 *They were* children of fools,
yea, children [a] of base [1] men; they
were viler than the earth.

a Ps.4·.10—13.

1 men of no name.

The idea is that of deep and frightful glens, where wild beasts ranged, far from the abodes of men, and surrounded by frightful wastes. The word rendered *valleys* (נחל) means properly a brook, stream, water-course—what is now called a *wady;* a place where the winter torrents run, but which is usually dry in summer; see Notes on chap. vi. 15. ¶ *In caves of the earth.* Marg. as in Heb. *holes.* Sept. "Whose houses are—τρῶγλαι πετρῶν—caverns of the rocks;" that is, who are *Troglodytes.* Caves furnished a natural dwelling for the poor and the outcast, and it is well known that it was not uncommon in Egypt, and in the deserts of Arabia, to occupy such caves as a habitation; see Diod. Sic. Lib. iii. xiv. and Strabo, Lib. xvi. ¶ *And in the rocks.* The caverns of the rocks. Dr. Richardson found a large number of such dwellings in the vicinity of Thebes, many of which were large and beautifully formed and sculptured with many curious devices. Mr. Rich, also, saw a large number of such caves not far from Mousal. Residence in Koordistan, vol. ii. p. 94.

7. *Among the bushes.* Coverdale, "Upon the dry heath went they about crying." The Hebrew word is the same which occurs in ver. 4, and means *bushes* in general. They were heard in the shrubbery that grew in the desert. ¶ *They brayed*—ינהקו. The Vulgate renders this, "They were concealed." The LXX. "Amidst sweet sounds they cry out." Noyes, "They utter their cries." The Hebrew word properly means to *bray.* It occurs only here and in chap. vi. 5, where it is applied to the *ass.* The sense here is, that the voices of this vagrant and wretched multitude was heard in the desert like the braying of asses. ¶ *Under the nettles.* Dr. Good, "Under the briers." Prof. Lee, "Beneath the broom-pea." Noyes, "Under the thorns." The Hebrew word חרול—*hhârûl,* occurs only here and in Zeph. ii. 9, and Prov. xxiv. 31, in each of which places it is rendered *nettles.* It is probably derived from חרל = חרר, to burn, to glow, and is given to nettles from the burning or prickling sensation which they produce. Either the word nettles, thistles, or thorns, would sufficiently answer to its derivation. It does not occur in the Arabic. *Castell.* Umbreit renders it, *unter Dornen—under thorns.* ¶ *They were gathered together.* Vulg., "They accounted it a delicacy to be in a thorn-hedge." The word here used (ספח) means *to add;* and then to be added or assembled together. The idea is, that they were huddled together quite promiscuously in the wild-growing bushes of the desert. They had no home; no separate habitation. This description is interesting, not only as denoting the depth to which Job had been reduced when he was the object of contempt by such vagrants, but as illustrative of a state of society existing then.

8. They were *children of fools.* The word rendered *fools* נבל—*Nâbâl,* means, (1) stupid, foolish; and (2) abandoned, impious; comp. 1 Sam. xxv. 3, 25. Here it means the worthless, the refuse of society, the abandoned. They had no respectable parentage. Umbreit, "A brood of infamy." Coverdale, "Children of fools and villains." ¶ *Children of base men.* Marg. as in Hebrew, *men of no name.* They were men of no reputation; whose ancestors had in no way been distinguished; possibly meaning, also, that they herded together as beasts without even a name. ¶ *They were viler than the earth.* Gesenius renders this, "They are frightened out of the land." The Hebrew word (כאה) means to chide, to upbraid, and then in Niph. to be chidden away, or driven off. The sense is, as an impious and low-born race they were driven out of the land.

9 And now am I [a] their song;
yea, I am their [b] by-word.
10 They abhor me, they flee far
from me, and [1] spare not to [c] spit
in my face.
11 Because he hath loosed my
cord, and afflicted me, they have
also let loose the bridle before me.
12 Upon *my* right *hand* rise the
youth; they push away my feet,
and they raise up against me the
ways of their destruction.

a Ps.69.12; La.3.14,63. b chap.17.6.

1 withho'd not spittle from.
c Is.50.6; Mat.26.67; 27.30.

9. *And now am I their song;* see chap. xvii. 6; comp. Ps. lxix. 12, "I was the song of the drunkards;" Lam. iii. 14, "I was a derision to all my people, and their song all the day." The sense is, that they made Job and his calamities the subject of low jesting, and treated him with contempt. His name and sufferings would be introduced into their scurrilous songs to give them pith and point, and to show how much they despised him now. ¶ *Yea, I am their by-word;* see Notes on chap. xvii. 6.

10. *They abhor me.* Heb. They regard me as abominable. ¶ *They flee far from me.* Even such an impious and low born race now will have nothing to do with me. They would consider it no honour to be associated with me, but keep as far from me as possible. ¶ *And spare not to spit in my face.* Marg. *withhold not spittle from.* Noyes renders this, "*Before* my face;" and so Luther, Wemyss, Umbreit, and Prof. Lee. The Hebrew may mean either to spit *in* the face, or to spit *in the presence* of any one. It is quite immaterial which interpretation is adopted, since in the view of Orientals the one was considered about the same as the other. In *their* notions of courtesy and urbanity, he commits an insult of the same kind who spits in the presence of another which he would if he spit on him. Are they not right? Should it not be so considered every where? Yet how different their views from the more refined notions of the civilized Occidentals! In America, more than in any other land, are offences of this kind frequent and gross. Of nothing do foreigners complain of us more, or with more justice; and much as we boast of our intelligence and refinement, we should gain much if in this respect we would sit down at the feet of a Bedawin Arab, and incorporate his views into our maxims of politeness.

11. *Because he hath loosed my cord.* According to this translation, the reference here is to God, and the sense is, that the reason why he was thus derided and contemned by such a worthless race was, that God had unloosened his cord. That is, God had rendered him incapable of vindicating himself, or of inflicting punishment. The figure, according to this interpretation, is taken from *a bow,* and Job means to say that his bow was relaxed, his vigour was gone, and they now felt that they might insult him with impunity. But instead of the usual reading in the Hebrew text יתרי — *Yithri — my nerve,* another reading יתרו — *Yithriv — his nerve,* is found in the keri or margin. This reading has been adopted in the text by Jahn, and is regarded as genuine by Rosenmüller, Umbreit, and Noyes. According to this, the meaning is, that the worthless rabble that now treated him with so much contempt, had relaxed all restraint, and they who had hitherto been under some *curb,* now rushed upon him in the most unbridled manner. They had cast off all restraint arising from respect to his rank, standing, moral worth, and the dread of his power, and now treated him with every kind of indignity. ¶ *And afflicted me.* By the disrespect and contempt which they have evinced. ¶ *They have also let loose the bridle before me.* That is, they have cast off all restraint—repeating the idea in the first member of the verse.

12. *Upon* my *right* hand *rise the youth.* The right hand is the place of honour, and therefore it was felt to

13 They mar my path, they set forward my calamity, they *have* no helper.

14 They came *upon me* as a wide breaking-in *of waters:* in the desolation they rolled themselves *upon me.*

---

be a greater insult that they should occupy even that place. The word rendered *youth* (פִּרְחַח) occurs nowhere else in the Hebrew Scriptures. It is probably from פָּרַח, to sprout, germinate, blossom; and hence would mean *a progeny,* and would be probably applied to beasts. It is rendered by Jerome, *calamities;* by the LXX. "Upon the right hand of the progeny, or brood (βλαστοῦ), they rise," where Schleusner conjectures that βλαστοὶ should be read, "On the right hand rise a brood or progeny." Umbreit renders it, *eine Brut – a brood.* So Rosenmüller, Noyes, and Schultens. The idea then is, that this rabble rose up, even on his right hand, as a brood of wild animals — a mere rabble that impeded his way. ¶ *They push away my feet.* Instead of giving place for me, they jostle and crowd me from my path. Once the aged and the honourable rose and stood in my presence, and the youth retired at my coming, but now this worthless rabble crowds along with me, jostles me in my goings, and shows me no manner of respect; comp. chap. xxix. 8. ¶ *And they raise up against me the ways of their destruction.* They raise up against me destructive ways, or ways that tend to destroy me. The figure is taken from an advancing army, that casts up ramparts and other means of attack designed for the destruction of a besieged city. They were, in like manner, constantly making advances against Job, and pressing on him in a manner that was designed to destroy him.

13. *They mar my path.* They break up all my plans. Perhaps here, also, the image is taken from war, and Job may represent himself as on a line of march, and he says that this rabble comes and breaks up his path altogether. They break down the bridges, and tear up the way, so that it is impossible to pass along. His plans of life were embarrassed by them, and they were to him a perpetual annoyance. ¶ *They set forward my calamity.* Luther renders this part of the verse, "It was so easy for them to injure me, that they needed no help." The literal translation of the Hebrew here would be, "they profit for my ruin;" that is, they bring as it were profit to my ruin; they help it on; they promote it. A similar expression occurs in Zech. i. 15, "I was but a little displeased, and they helped forward the affliction;" that is, they aided in urging it forward. The idea here is, that they hastened his fall. Instead of assisting him in any way, they contributed all they could to bring him down to the dust. ¶ *They* have *no helper.* Very various interpretations have been given of this phrase. It may mean, that they had done this alone, without the aid of others; or that they were persons who were held in abhorrence, and whom no one would assist; or that they were worthless and abandoned persons. Schultens has shown that the phrase, *one who has no helper,* is proverbial among the Arabs, and denotes a worthless person, or one of the lowest class. In proof of this, he quotes the Hamasa, which he thus translates, Videmus vos ignobiles, pauperes, quibus nullus ex reliquis hominibus adjutor. See, also, other similar expressions quoted by him from Arabic writings. The idea here then is, probably, that they were so worthless and abandoned that no one would help them — an expression denoting the utmost degradation.

14. *They came* upon me *as a wide breaking-in* of waters. The Hebrew here is simply, "Like a wide breach they came," and the reference may be, not to an inundation, as our translators supposed, but to an irruption made by a foe through a breach made in a wall. When such a wall fell, or when a breach was made in it, the besieging army would pour in in a tumultuous manner, and cut down all before them; comp. Isa. xxx. 13.

15 Terrors are turned upon me:
they pursue my [1] soul as the wind;
and my welfare passeth away as a
cloud.
16 And now my soul is poured
out upon [a] me: the days of affliction have taken hold upon me.
17 My bones are pierced in me
in the night-season; and my sinews
take no rest.

1 *principal one.*

a Ps.42.4.

This seems to be the idea here. The enemies of Job poured in upon him as if a breach was made in a wall. Formerly they were restrained by his rank and office, as a besieging army was by lofty walls; but now all these restraints were broken down, and they poured in upon him like a tumultuous army. ¶ *In the desolation they rolled themselves* upon me. Among the ruins they rolled tumultuous along; or they came pitching and tumbling in with the ruins of the wall. The image is taken from the act of sacking a city, where the besieging army, having made a breach in the wall, would seem to come tumbling into the heart of the city with the ruins of the wall. No time would be wasted, but they would follow suddenly and tumultuously upon the breach, and roll tumultuously along. The Chaldee renders this as if it referred to the rolling and tumultuous waves of the sea, and the Hebrew would admit of such a construction, but the above seems better to accord with the image which Job would be likely to use.

15. *Terrors are turned upon me.* As if they were all *turned* upon him, or made to converge towards him. Every thing fitted to produce terror seemed to have a direction given it *towards* him. Umbreit, and some others, however, suppose that God is here referred to, and that the meaning is, "God is turned against me; terrors drive as a storm against me." The Hebrew will bear either construction; but it is more emphatic and impressive to suppose it means that every thing adapted to produce terror seemed to be turned against him. ¶ *They pursue my soul as the wind.* Marg. *my principal one.* The word "they" here, refers to the *terrors.* In the original the word תרדף agrees with בלהות, *terrors* understood, for this word is often used as a collective noun, and with a singular verb, or it may agree with כל אחת—"each one of the terrors persecutes me." There is more difficulty about the word rendered *soul* in the text, and *principal one* in the margin—נדבתי. It properly means *willingness, voluntariness, spontaneity;* then a free-will offering, a voluntary sacrifice; then largeness, abundance. Rosenmuller renders it, "My vigour." Noyes, "My prosperity," and so Coverdale. Jerome, "My desire," and the LXX., "My hope passes away as the wind." Schultens translates it, "They persecute my generous spirit as the wind." It seems probable that the word refers to a generous, noble nature; to a large and liberal soul, evincing its magnanimity in acts of generosity and hospitality; and the idea seems to be, that his enemies rushed against that generous nature like a tempest. They wholly disregarded it, and a nature most generous and noble was exposed to the fury of the storm. ¶ *And my welfare.* Heb. my salvation; or my safety. ¶ *As a cloud.* As a cloud vanishes and wholly disappears.

16. *And now my soul is poured out upon me.* So in Ps. xlii. 4, "I pour out my soul in me." We say that one is *dissolved* in grief. The language is derived from the fact that the soul in grief seems to lose all firmness or consistence. The Arabs style a fearful person, *one who has a watery heart,* or *whose heart melts away like water. Noyes.*

17. *My bones are pierced in me.* The *bones* are often represented in the Scriptures as the seat of acute pain; Ps. vi. 2; xxii. 14; xxxi. 10; xxxviii. 3; xlii. 10; Prov. xiv. 30; comp. Job xx. 11. The meaning here is, that he had had shooting or piercing pains in the night, which disturbed and prevented his rest. It

18 By the great force *of my disease* is my garment changed: it bindeth me about as the collar of my coat.

19 He hath cast [a] me into the mire, and I am become like dust and ashes.

[a] chap. 9. 31.

is mentioned as a peculiar aggravation of his sufferings that they were *in the night*—a time when we expect repose. ¶ *And my sinews take no rest;* see the word here rendered *sinews* explained in the Note on ver. 3. The word literally means *gnawers,* and hence the teeth. The Vulgate renders it, *qui me comedunt, non dormiunt,* "they who devour me do not slumber." The LXX. νευρά μου—*my sinews,* or *arteries. Schleusner.* Luther, "They who gnaw me." Coverdale, *Sinews.* I see no reason to doubt that the *teeth* or the jaws are meant, and that Job refers to the violent pain in the tooth, among the acutest pains to which the body is subject. The idea is, that every part of the body was diseased and filled with pain.

18. *By the great force* of my disease. The words "of my disease" are not in the Hebrew. The usual interpretation of the passage is, that in consequence of the foul and offensive nature of his malady, his garment had become discoloured or defiled—changed from being white and clear to filthiness and offensiveness. Some have understood it as referring to the skin, and as denoting that it was so affected with the leprosy, that he could scarcely be recognised. Umbreit supposes it to mean, "Through the omnipotence of God has my white robe of honour been changed into a narrow garment of grief—*trauerkleid.* Dr. Good renders it, "From the abundance of the acrimony;" that is, of the fierce or acrimonious humour, "it is changed into a garment for me." Coverdale, "With all their power have they changed my garment, and girded me therewith, as it were with a coat." Prof. Lee, "With much violence doth my clothing bind me." According to Schultens, it means, "My affliction puts itself on in the form of my clothing;" and the whole passage, that without and within, from the head to the feet, he was entirely diseased. His affliction was his outer garment, and it was his inner garment—his mantle and his tunic. The Hebrew is difficult. The phrase rendered "by the great force," means, literally, "by the multitude of strength"—and may refer to the strength of disease, or to the strength of God, or to the force with which his garment girded him. The word rendered "is changed"—יתחפש, is from חפש, to seek, to search after, in Kal; in Hithpa. the form used here, to let one's self be sought; to hide one's self; to disguise one's self; 1 Kings xx. 38. According to this, it would mean that his garment was *disguised;* that is, its appearance was changed by the force of his disease. *Gesenius.* Jerome renders it, "In their multitude, my garment is consumed; the LXX., "With great force he took hold of my garment." Of these various interpretations, it is impossible to determine which is the correct one. The *prevailing* interpretation seems to be, that by the strength of his disease his garment was changed in its appearance, so as to become offensive, and yet this is a somewhat feeble sense to give to the passage. Perhaps the explanation of Schultens is the best, "By the greatness of power, pain or disease has become my garment; it girds me about like the mouth of my tunic." He has shown, by a great variety of instances, that it is common in Arabic poetry to compare pain, sickness, anxiety, &c., to clothing. ¶ *It bindeth me about as the collar of my coat.* The collar of my *tunic,* or under garment. This was made like a shirt, to be gathered around the neck, and the idea is, that his disease fitted close to him, and was gathered close around him.

19. *He hath cast me into the mire.* That is, God has done it. In this book the name of God is often understood where the speaker seems to avoid it, in order that it may not be

20 I cry unto thee, and thou
dost not hear me ; I stand up, and
thou regardest me *not*.
21 Thou art [1] become cruel to
me : with thy [2] strong hand thou
opposest thyself against me.
22 Thou liftest me up to the
wind ; thou causest me to ride *upon*
it, and dissolvest my [3] substance.

1 *turned to be.*
2 *the strength of thy hand.*
3 or, *wisdom.*

needlessly repeated. On the meaning of the expression here, see Notes on chap. ix. 31. ¶ *And I am become like dust and ashes.* Either in appearance, or I am regarded as being as worthless as the mire of the streets. Rosenmüller supposes it means, "I am more like a mass of inanimate matter than a living man."

20. *I cry unto thee, and thou dost not hear me.* This was a complaint which Job often made, that he could not get the ear of God ; that his prayer was not regarded, and that he could not get his cause before him ; comp. chap. xiii 3, 19, seq., and chap. xxvii. 9. ¶ *I stand up.* Standing was a common posture of prayer among the ancients ; see Heb. xi. 21 ; 1 Kings viii. 14, 55 ; Neh. ix. 2. The meaning is, that when Job stood up to pray, God did not regard his prayer.

21. *Thou art become cruel to me.* Marg. *turned to be.* This language, applied to God, seems to be harsh and irreverent, and it may well be inquired whether the word *cruel* does not express an idea which Job did not intend. The Hebrew word אכזר, is from an obsolete root כזר—not found in Hebrew. The Arabic root, nearly the same as this, means to break with violence ; to rout as an enemy ; then to be enraged. In the Syriac, the primary idea is, that of *a soldier*, and thence it may refer to such acts of violence as a soldier commonly commits. The word occurs in Hebrew in the following places, and is translated in the following manner. It is rendered *cruel* in Deut. xxxii. 33 ; Job xxx. 21 ; Prov. v. 9 ; xi. 17 ; xii. 10 ; xvii. 11 ; xxvii. 4 ; Isa. xiii. 9 ; Jer. vi. 23 ; l. 42; xxx. 14; and *fierce* in Job xli. 10. Jerome renders it, *mutatus mihi in crudelem*—"thou art changed so as to become cruel to me ;" the LXX. render it, ἀνελεημόνως — *unmerciful ;* Luther, Du bist mir verwandelt in einem Grausamen—"thou art changed to me into a cruel one ;" and so Umbreit, Noyes, and translators generally. Perhaps the word *fierce*, *severe* or *harsh*, would express the idea ; still it must be admitted that Job, in the severity of his sufferings, is often betrayed into language which cannot be a model for us, and which we cannot vindicate. ¶ *With thy strong hand.* Marg. *the strength.* So the Hebrew. The *hand* is the instrument by which we accomplish any thing ; and hence any thing which God does is traced to his *hand.* ¶ *Thou opposest thyself against me* — תשטמני. The word שטם — *Sâtam*, means to lie in wait for any one ; to lay snares ; to set a trap ; see chap. xvi. 9, where the same word occurs, and where it is rendered "who *hateth* me," but where it would be better rendered he *pursues*, or *persecutes* me. The meaning is, that God had become his adversary, or had set himself against him. There was a severity in his dealings with him *as if* he had become a foe.

22. *Thou liftest me up to the wind.* The sense here is, that he was lifted up as stubble is by a tempest, and driven mercilessly along. The figure of riding upon the wind or the whirlwind, is common in Oriental writers, and indeed elsewhere. So Milton says,

> "They ride the air in whirlwind."

So Addison, speaking of the angel that executes the commands of the Almighty, says,

> "Rides in the whirlwind, and directs the storm."

Coverdale renders this verse, "In times past thou didst set me up on high, as it were above the wind, but now hast thou given me a very sore fall." Rosenmüller thinks that the image here is not taken from straw or chaff that is driven by the wind, but that the meaning of Job is, that he is lifted up and borne aloft like a cloud. But the image of chaff or straw taken up by the whirlwind and driven about, seems best to accord with the scope of the passage. The idea is, that the tempest of calamity had swept every thing away, and had driven him about as a worthless object, until he was wasted away and ruined. It is possible that Job refers in this passage to the *sand-storm* which occurs sometimes in the deserts of Arabia. The following description of such a storm by Mr. Bruce (vol. iv. pp. 553, 554), will furnish an illustration of the force and sublimity of the passage. It is copied from Taylor's Fragments, in Calmet's Dictionary, vol. iii. 235: "On the fourteenth," says Bruce, "at seven in the morning, we left Assa Nagga, our course being due north. At one o'clock we alighted among some acacia trees at Waadi el Halboub, having gone twenty-one miles. We were here at once surprised and terrified by a sight, surely one of the most magnificent in the world. In that vast expanse of desert from west and to north-west of us, we saw a number of prodigious *pillars of sand* at different distances, at times *moving with great celerity,* at others stalking on with a majestic slowness; at intervals we thought they were coming in a very few minutes to overwhelm us, and small quantities of sand did actually more than once reach us. Again they would retreat so as to be almost out of sight—their tops *reaching to the very clouds.* There the tops often separated from the bodies; and these, once disjoined, *dispersed in the air,* and did not appear more. Sometimes they were broken near the middle, as if struck with a large cannon shot. About noon they began to advance with considerable swiftness upon us, the wind being very strong at north. Eleven of them ranged alongside of us about the distance of three miles. The greatest diameter of the largest appeared to me at that distance as if it would measure two feet. They retired from us with a wind at south-east, leaving an impression upon my mind to which I can give no name, though surely one ingredient in it was fear, with a considerable deal of wonder and astonishment. It was in vain to think of flying; the swiftest horse, or fastest sailing ship, could be of no use to carry us out of this danger, and the full persuasion of this riveted me as if to the spot where I stood, and let the camels gain on me so much in my state of lameness, that it was with some difficulty I could overtake them.

"The whole of our company were much disheartened, except Idris, and imagined that they were advancing into whirlwinds of moving sand, from which they should never be able to extricate themselves; but before four o'clock in the afternoon these phantoms of the plain had all of them fallen to the ground and disappeared. In the evening we came to Waadi Dimokea, where we passed the night, much disheartened, and our fear more increased, when we found, upon wakening in the morning, that one side was perfectly buried in the sand that the wind had blown above us in the night.

"The sun shining through the pillars, which were thicker, and contained more sand, apparently, than any of the preceding days, seemed to give those nearest us an appearance as if spotted with stars of gold. I do not think at any time they seemed to be nearer than two miles. The most remarkable circumstance was, that the sand seemed to keep in that vast circular space, surrounded by the Nile on our left, in going round by Chaigie toward Dougola, and seldom was observed much to the eastward of a meridian, passing along the Nile through the Magizan, before it takes that turn; whereas the simoom was always on the opposite side of our course, coming upon us from the south-east.

"The same appearance of moving pillars of sand presented themselves to us this day in form and disposition

23 For I know *that* thou wilt bring me *to* death, and *to* the house appointed [a] for all living.

[a] Ge.3.19.

like those we had seen at Waadi Halboub, only they seemed to be more in number, and less in size. They came several times in a direction close upon us, that is, I believe, within less than two miles. They began, immediately after sunrise, like a thick wood, and almost darkened the sun; his rays shining through them for near an hour, gave them an appearance of pillars of fire."

"If my conjecture," says Taylor, "be admissible, we now see a magnificence in this imagery, not apparent before: we see how Job's dignity might be exalted in the air; might rise to great grandeur, importance, and even terror, in the sight of beholders; might ride upon the wind, which bears it about, causing it to advance or to recede; and, after all, when the wind diminishes, might disperse, dissipate, melt this pillar of sand into the undistinguished level of the desert. This comparison seems to be precisely adapted to the mind of an Arab; who must have seen, or have been informed of, similar phenomena in the countries around him." ¶ *And dissolvest my substance.* Marg. or *wisdom.* The word rendered "*dissolvest,*" means to melt, to flow down, and then to cause to melt, to cause to pine away and perish; Isa. lxiv. 7. It is applied to a host or army that appears to melt away; 1 Sam. xiv. 16. It is also applied to one who seems to melt away with fear and terror; Ex. xv. 15; Josh. ii. 9, 24. Here the meaning probably is, that God caused Job to melt away, as it were, with terrors and alarms. He was like one caught up in a whirlwind, and driven along with the storm, and who, in such circumstances, would be dissolved with fear. The word rendered *substance* (תשיה) has been very variously interpreted. The word, as it is written in the text, means help, deliverance, purpose, enterprise, counsel, or understanding; see chap. v. 12; vi. 13; xi. 6. But by some, and among others. Gesenius, Umbreit, and Noyes, it is supposed that it should be read as a verb, תשוה from שוה—to fear. According to this, the meaning is, "thou terrifiest me." This agrees better with the connection; is more abrupt and emphatic, and is probably the true interpretation.

23. *For I know* that *thou wilt bring me* to *death.* This is the language of despair. Occasionally Job seems to have had an assurance that his calamities would pass by, and that God would show himself to be his friend on earth (comp. Notes on chap. xix. 25, seq.), and at other times he utters the language of despair. Such would be commonly the case with a good man afflicted as he was, and agitated with alternate hopes and fears. We are not to set these expressions down as contradictions. All that inspiration is responsible for, is the fair record of his feelings; and that he should have alternate hopes and fears is in entire accordance with what occurs when we are afflicted. Here the view of his sorrows appears to have been so overwhelming, that he says he *knew* they must terminate in death. The phrase "to death" means to the house of the dead, or to the place where the dead are. *Umbreit.* ¶ *And* to *the house appointed for all living.* The grave; comp. Heb. ix. 27. That house or home is "appointed" for all. It is not a matter of chance that we come there, but it is because the Great Arbiter of life has so ordained. What an affecting consideration it should be, that *such* a house is designated for all! A house so dark, so gloomy, so solitary, so repulsive! For all that sit on thrones; for all that move in the halls of music and pleasure; for all that roll along in splendid carriages; for all the beautiful, the gay, the vigorous, the manly; for all in the marts of business, in the low scenes of dissipation, and in the sanctuary of God; for every one who is young, and every one who is aged, this is the home! Here they come at last; and here they lie down in the narrow bed! God's hand will

24 Howbeit he will not stretch out *his* hand to the [1] grave, though they cry in his destruction.

[1] *heap.*

bring them all there; and there will they lie till his voice summons them to judgment!

24. *Howbeit he will not stretch out* his *hand to the grave.* Marg. *heap.* In our common version this verse conveys no very clear idea, and it is quite evident that our translators despaired of giving it a consistent sense, and attempted merely to translate it literally. The verse has been rendered by every expositor almost in his own way; and though almost no two of them agree, yet it is remarkable that the versions given are all beautiful, and furnish a sense that agrees well with the scope of the passage. The Vulgate renders it, "But not to their consumption wilt thou send forth their hand; and if they fall, thou wilt save them." The Sept., "For O that I could lay violent hands on myself, or beseech another, and he would do it for me." Luther renders it, "Yet he shall not stretch out the hand to the charnel-house, and they shall not cry before his destruction." Noyes:

> "When he stretcheth out his hand, prayer availeth nothing.
> When he bringeth destruction, vain is the cry for help."

Umbreit renders it:

> Nur mög' er nicht an den zerstörten Haufen Hand anlegen!
> Oder mussen jene selbst in ihrem Tode schreien?

> "Only if he would not lay his hand upon the heaps of the destroyed!
> Or must these also cry out in their death?"

According to this interpretation, Job speaks here in bitter irony. "I would gladly die," says he, "if God would only suffer me to be quiet when I am dead." He would be willing that the edifice of the body should be taken down, provided the ruins might rest in peace. Rosenmüller gives the same sense as that expressed by Noyes. Amidst this variety of interpretation, it is by no means easy to determine on the true meaning of the passage. The principal difficulty in the exposition lies in the word בעי, rendered in the text "in the grave," and in the margin "heap." If that word is compounded of the preposition ב and עי, it means literally, "in ruins, or in rubbish"—for so the word עי is used in Mic. i. 6; Jer. xxvi. 18; Mic. iii. 12; Ps. lxxix. 1; Nehem. iv. 2, 10. But Gesenius supposes it to be a single word, from the obsolete root בעה, Chaldee בעא, *to pray, to petition;* and according to this the meaning is, "Yea, prayer is nought when he stretches out his hand; and in his [God's] destruction, their cry availeth not." Prof. Lee understands the word (בעי) in the same sense, but gives a somewhat different meaning to the whole passage. According to him the meaning is, "Nevertheless, upon prayer thou wilt not lay thine hand; surely, when he destroyeth, in this alone there is safety." Schultens accords very nearly in the sentiment expressed by Umbreit, and renders it, "Yet not even in the tomb would he relax his hand, if in its destruction an alleviation were there." This sentiment is very strong, and borders on impiety, and should not be adopted if it is possible to avoid it. It looks as if Job felt that God was disposed to pursue his animosity even into the regions of the dead, and that he would have pleasure in carrying on the work of destruction and affliction in the ruins of the grave. After the most careful examination which I have been able to give of this difficult passage, it seems probable to me that the following is the correct sense. Job means to state a general and important principle—that there was *rest* in the grave. He said he knew that God would bring him down there, but that would be a state of repose. The hand of God producing pain, would not reach there, nor would the sorrows experienced in this world be felt there, provided there had been a praying life. Notwithstanding all his afflictions, therefore, and his certain conviction that he would die, he had unwavering confidence in God. Agreeably to

25 Did not I weep for him that
was [1] in trouble? was *not* my soul
grieved for the poor?
26 When [a] I looked for good,
then evil came *unto me;* and when
I waited for light, there came
darkness.
27 My bowels boiled, and rested
not; the days of affliction prevented
me.

1 *hard of day.* a Je.8.15.

this, the following paraphrase will convey the true sense. "I know that he will bring me to the grave. *Nevertheless* (אַךְ), *over the ruins* (בְעִי)—of my body, the ruins in the grave — *he will not stretch out his hand*—to afflict me there or to pursue those who lie there with calamity and judgment; *if in his destruction* (בְּפִידוֹ)—in the destruction or desolation which God brings upon men—*among them* (לָהֶן)—among those who are thus consigned to the ruins of the grave—*there is prayer* (שׁוּעַ); if there has been supplication offered to him, or a *cry* for mercy has gone up before him." This paraphrase embraces every word of the original; saves the necessity of attempting to change the text, as has been often done, and gives a meaning which accords with the scope of the passage, and with the uniform belief of Job, that God would ultimately vindicate him, and show that he himself was right in his government.

25. *Did not I weep,* &c. Job here appeals to his former life, and says that it had been a characteristic of his life to manifest compassion to the afflicted and the poor. His *object* in doing this is, evidently, to show how remarkable it was that he was so much afflicted. "Did I deserve," the sense is, "such a hard lot? Has it been brought on me by my own fault, or as a punishment for a life where no compassion was shown to others?" So far from it, he says, that his whole life had been distinguished for tender compassion for those in distress and want. ¶ *In trouble.* Marg. as in Hebrew, *hard of day.* So we say, "a man has a hard time of it," or has a hard lot.

26. *When I looked for good.* When I supposed that respect would be shown me; or when I looked forward to an honoured old age. I expected to be made happy and prosperous through life, as the result of my uprightness and benevolence; but, instead of that, calamity came and swept all my comforts away. He experienced the instability which most men are called to experience, and the divine dealings with him showed that no reliance could be placed on confident plans of happiness in this life.

27. *My bowels boiled.* Or rather, My bowels boil—for he refers to his present circumstances, and not to the past. It is clear that by this phrase he designs to describe deep affliction. The bowels, in the Scriptures, are represented as the seat of the affections. By this is meant the *upper* bowels, or the region of the heart and the lungs. The reason is, that deep emotions of the mind are *felt* there. The heart beats quick; or it is heavy and pained; or it seems to melt within us in the exercise of pity or compassion; comp. Notes on Isa. xvi. 11. The idea here is, that the seat of sorrow and of grief was affected by his calamities. Nor was the feeling slight. His emotions he compared with agitated, boiling water. It is possible that there is an allusion here to the inflammatory nature of his disease, producing internal heat and pain; but it is more probable that he refers to the mental anguish which he endured. ¶ *The days of affliction prevented me.* Literally, "have anticipated me"—for so the word *prevent* was formerly used, and so it is uniformly used in the Bible; Notes on Job iii. 12; comp. Ps. lix. 10; lxxix. 8; lxxxviii. 13; cxix. 148; 1 Thess. iv. 15. There is in the Hebrew word (קִדֵּם) the idea that days of anguish came in an unexpected manner, or that they anticipated the fulfilment of his plans. All his schemes and hopes of life had been *anticipated* by these overwhelming sorrows.

28 I went mourning without the sun: I stood up, *and* cried in the congregation

29 I am a brother to dragons, and a companion to [1] owls.

1 or, *ostriches*.

28. *I went mourning.* Or rather, "I go," in the present tense, for he is now referring to his present calamities, and not to what was past. The word rendered "*mourning*," however (קדר), means here rather to be dark, dingy, *tanned*. It literally means to be foul or turbid, like a torrent, Job vi. 16; then to go about in filthy garments, as they do who mourn, Job v. 11; Jer. xiv. 2; then to be dusky, or of a dark colour, or to become dark. Thus it is applied to the sun and moon becoming dark in an eclipse, or when covered with clouds, Jer. iv. 28; Joel ii. 10; iii. 15; Mic. iii. 6. Here it refers to the fact that, by the mere force of his disease, his skin had become dark and swarthy, though he had not been exposed to the burning rays of the sun. The wrath of God had *burned* upon him, and he had become black under it. Jerome, however, renders it *moerens*, mourning. The LXX., "I go groaning (στένων) without restraint, or limit"—ἄνευ φιμοῦ. The Chaldee translates it אוכם, *black*. ¶ *Without the sun.* Without being exposed to the sun; or without the agency of the sun. Though not exposed, he had become as dark as if he had been a day-labourer exposed to a burning sun. ¶ *I stood up.* Or, I stand up. ¶ And *cried in the congregation.* I utter my cries in the congregation, or when surrounded by the assembled people. Once I stood up to counsel them, and they hung upon my lips for advice; now I stand up only to weep over my accumulated calamities. This indicates the great change which had come upon him, and the depth of his sorrows. A man will weep readily in private; but he will be slow to do it, if he can avoid it, when surrounded by a multitude.

29. *I am a brother to dragons.* That is, my loud complaints and cries resemble the doleful screams of wild animals, or of the most frightful monsters. The word "brother" is often used in this sense, to denote *similarity* in any respect. The word *dragons* here (תנים, *tănnim*) denotes properly a sea-monster, a great fish, a crocodile; or the fancied animal with wings called a dragon; see Notes on Isa. xiii. 22. Gesenius, Umbreit, and Noyes, render this word here *jackals* — an animal between a dog and a fox, or a wolf and a fox; an animal that abounds in deserts and solitudes, and that makes a doleful cry in the night. So the Syriac renders it an animal resembling a dog; a wild dog. *Castell.* This idea agrees with the scope of the passage better than the common reference to a sea-monster or a crocodile. "The *Deeb*, or *Jackal*," says Shaw, "is of a darker colour than the fox, and about the same bigness. It yelps every night about the gardens and villages, feeding upon roots, fruit, and carrion." Travels, p. 247, Ed. Oxford, 1738. That some wild animal, distinguished for a mournful noise, or howl, is meant, is evident; and the passage better agrees with the description of a jackal than the hissing of a serpent or the noise of the crocodile. Bochart supposes that the allusion is to dragons, because they erect their heads, and their jaws are drawn open, and they *seem* to be complaining against God on account of their humble and miserable condition. Taylor (Concord.) supposes it means jackals or *thoes*, and refers to the following places where the word may be so used; Ps. xliv. 19; Isa. xiii. 22; xxxiv. 13; xxxv. 7; xliii. 20; Jer. ix. 11; x. 22; xlix. 33; li. 37; Lam. iv. 3; Mic. i. 8; Mal. i. 3. ¶ *And a companion to owls.* Marg. *ostriches.* The word *companion* here is used in a sense similar to *brother* in the other member of the parallelism, to denote resemblance. The Hebrew, here rendered *owls*, is, literally, *daughters of answering*, or *clamour*—בנות יענה. The name is given on account of the plaintive and mournful cry which is made. *Bochart.* Gesenius supposes, how-

30 My skin [a] is black upon me, and my bones are burnt with heat.
31 My harp also is *turned* to mourning, and my organ into the voice of them that weep.

CHAPTER XXXI.

ANALYSIS OF THE CHAPTER.

THIS chapter finishes the reply of Job, and closes the argument. Zophar should have answered in his turn, but he is silent, and the cause is then taken up by Elihu. The chapter is a beautiful vindication of the private life of Job. It is not to be regarded as uttered in the spirit of boasting or self-confidence, but as made necessary by the accusations of his friends. They had charged him with crimes of an aggravated character, and they regarded his sufferings as full proof that he was a wicked man In chap. xxix. he had spoken of his *public* life—his character as an Emir or magistrate, and of the honour that was shown him in that capacity; and in this chapter he goes into a detail of the principles on which his private conduct was regulated, and maintains his integrity in regard to his conduct there. While his main design was to meet the charges of his friends, it cannot be denied that there is an *implied* reflection on the dealings of God, as if they were severe and harsh; see ver. 35—37. But the picture which he has drawn of himself is exquisitely beautiful. Nothing can surpass it as a moral painting; and whatever may be thought of the propriety of his dwelling on the virtues of his own private life in the manner in which he here does, the description is a fine illustration of what was regarded in the patriarchal times as constituting true piety, and of the nature of true piety in all ages and lands.

The plan of the chapter is to specify certain of the leading virtues of piety, and to deny that he had been guilty of violating any of them, and to imprecate appropriate punishment on himself if he had been guilty. The following is a summary of the virtues specified.

(1.) *Chastity*, ver. 1—4. He says that he had so conscientiously adhered to that virtue, that he did not even allow himself to look on a maid, ver. 1. He knew that God would punish this sin, ver. 3; he knew that his eye saw all his ways, ver. 4.

(2.) *Seriousness and sincerity of life*, ver. 5, 6. He says that he had not walked in a vain and deceitful manner, ver. 5, and asks that he might on this subject be weighed in an even balance, ver. 6.

(3.) *Uprightness and purity of life*, ver. 7, 8. He says that his steps had not been turned out of the way, and that no stain cleaved to his hands, ver. 7; if there did,

[a] La.4.8; 5.10.

---

ever, that it is on account of its greediness and gluttony. The name "daughters of the ostrich" denotes properly the female ostrich. The phrase is, however, put for the ostrich of both sexes in many places; see Gesenius on the word יַעֲנָה; comp. Notes on Isa. xiii. 21. For a full examination of the meaning of the phrase, see Bochart, Hieroz. P. ii. L. 2. cap. xiv. pp. 218—231; see also chap. xxxix. 13—17. There can be little doubt that the ostrich is here intended, and Job means to say that his mourning resembled the doleful noise made by the ostrich in the lonely desert. Shaw, in his Travels, says that during the night "they [the ostriches] make very doleful and hideous noises; which would sometimes be like the roaring of a lion; at other times it would bear a nearer resemblance to the hoarser voice of other quadrupeds, particularly of the bull and the ox. I have often heard them groan as if they were in the greatest agonies."

30. *My skin is black upon me;* see ver. 28. It had become black by the force of the disease. ¶ *My bones are burnt with heat.* The bones, in the Scriptures, are often represented as the seat of pain. The disease of Job seems to have pervaded the whole body. If it was the elephantiasis (see Notes on chap. ii. 7, 8), these effects would be naturally produced.

31. *My harp also is* turned *to mourning.* What formerly gave cheerful sounds, now gives only notes of plaintiveness and lamentation. The harp was probably an instrument originally designed to give sounds of joy. For a description of it, see Notes on Isa. v. 12. ¶ *And my organ.* The *form* of what is here called the *organ*, is not certainly known. The word עֻגָב is doubtless from עָגַב, *to breathe, to blow;* and most probably the instrument here intended was the *pipe.* For a description of it, see Notes on Isa. v. 12. This instrument, also, was played, as would appear, on joyous occasions, but Job now says that it was turned to grief. All that had been joyous with him had fled. His honour was taken away; his friends were gone; they who had treated him with reverence now stood at a distance, or treated him with contempt; his health was departed, and his former appearance, indicating a station of affluence, was changed for the dark complexion produced by disease, and the instruments of joyousness now gave forth only notes of sorrow.

he asked that he might be compelled to sow while another reaped, and that his offspring might be rooted out, ver. 8.

(4.) *Fidelity to the marriage vow*, ver. 9—12. He affirms that his heart had not been allured by a woman, and that he had not attempted to destroy the peace of his neighbour by seducing his wife, ver. 9. If such a fault should be found against him, he consented that his own wife should be made to serve others in the most menial capacity, ver. 10. He adds, with peculiar emphasis, and in a manner that shows his sense of the magnitude of such an offence, that this was a crime which ought to be punished by the judges, and that it was a fire which consumed to destruction, ver. 11, 12.

(5.) *Fidelity to his servants*, ver. 13—15. He affirms that he had not been guilty of injustice or unkindness to either his man-servant or maid-servant, ver. 13. He says that he well knew that if he had been, he could not answer God when he should call him to judgment, ver. 14, for the same God had made him and them, ver. 15.

(6.) *Benevolence towards the poor, the widow, and the fatherless*, ver. 16—23. He says that if he had been guilty of neglecting them; if he had caused the widow to weep, or had eaten his morsel alone, or had refused to clothe the naked, or to vindicate the cause of the fatherless, he was willing that his arm should fall from his shoulder-blade.

(7.) *Freedom from idolatry*, ver. 24—23. He had not put his trust in gold, nor had he worshipped the sun or the moon, ver. 24—27. He says that *that* would have been an offence that should be punished by the judge, for he would have denied the God above, ver. 28.

(8.) *Kindness to his enemies*, ver. 29, 30. He had not rejoiced in their destruction, nor had he allowed his mouth to imprecate a curse on them.

(9.) *Hospitality*, ver. 31, 32. Even those that dwelt in his tent had been constrained to express their admiration at his hospitality, and he had not suffered the stranger to lodge in the street, nor refused to open his doors to the traveller.

(10.) *Freedom from secret sin*, ver. 33—37. He had not attempted to conceal his offences, nor to cloak them by hiding them in his bosom, ver. 33, 34. Here he could boldly make his appeal to God, and wished that the record were made, and that all his thoughts, motives, and plans were recorded. He says that it would be such a perfect vindication of his innocence, that he would take it triumphantly on his shoulder and bind it as a diadem on his head, ver. 35—37.

(11.) *Honesty towards others in the purchase and use of land*, ver. 38—40. He says that he had not seized upon the land of others by violence, or cultivated it without paying for its use, so that the land itself could not cry out against him, ver. 38, 39. If he had, he asked that on his own land thistles might spring up instead of wheat, and cockles instead of barley. Having thus asserted his integrity, he said that he was done. He regarded his character as vindicated, and he had no more to say.

I MADE a covenant with mine eyes; [a] why then should I think [b] upon a maid?

a Matt.5.28. b Pr.6.25.

CHAPTER XXXI.

1. *I made a covenant with mine eyes.* The first virtue of his private life to which Job refers is chastity. Such was his sense of the importance of this, and of the danger to which man was exposed, that he had solemnly resolved not to think upon a young female. The phrase here, "I made a covenant with mine eyes," is poetical, meaning that he *solemnly resolved*. A covenant is of a sacred and binding nature; and the strength of his resolution was as great as if he had made a solemn compact. A covenant or compact was usually made by slaying an animal in sacrifice, and the compact was ratified over the animal that was slain, by a kind of imprecation that if the compact was violated the same destruction might fall on the violators which fell on the head of the victim. This idea of *cutting up a victim* on occasion of making a covenant, is retained in most languages. So the Greek ὅρκια τέμνειν, τέμνειν σπονδάς, and the Latin *icere fœdus—to strike a league*, in allusion to the striking down, or slaying of an animal on the occasion. And so the Hebrew, as in the place before us, כרת ברית—*to cut a covenant*, from cutting down, or cutting in pieces the victim over which the covenant was made; see this explained at length in the Notes on Heb. ix. 16. By the language here, Job means that he had resolved, in the most solemn manner, that he would not allow his eyes or thoughts to endanger him by improperly contemplating a woman. ¶ *Why then should I think upon a maid?* Upon a virgin—על־בתולה; comp. Prov. vi. 25, "Lust not after her beauty in thine heart; neither let her take thee with her eyelids;" see, also, the fearful and solemn declaration of the Saviour in Matth. v. 28. There is much emphasis in the expression used here by Job. He does not merely say that he *had not* thought in that manner, but that the thing was morally impossible that he *should have done it*. Any charge of that kind, or any suspicion of it, he would repel with indignation. His purpose to lead a pure life, and to keep a pure heart, had been so settled, that it was *impossible* that he could have offended in that respect. His purpose, also, not to *think* on this subject, showed the extent of the restriction imposed on himself. It was not

2 For what portion of God *is*
there from above? and *what* inheritance of the Almighty from on
high?
3 *Is* not destruction to the wicked? and a strange *punishment* to
the workers of iniquity?
4 Doth [a] not he see my ways,
and count all my steps?

a John1.48; Je 32.19.

---

merely his intention to lead a chaste life, and to avoid open sin, but it was to maintain a pure heart, and not to suffer the mind to become corrupted by dwelling on impure images, or indulging in unholy desires. This strongly shows Job's piety and purity of heart, and is a beautiful illustration of patriarchal religion. We may remark here, that if a man wishes to maintain purity of life, he must make just such a covenant as this with himself—one so sacred, so solemn, so firm, that he will not suffer his mind *for a moment* to harbour an improper thought. "The very passage of an impure thought through the mind leaves pollution behind it;" and the outbreaking crimes of life are just the result of allowing the imagination to dwell on impure images. As the *eye* is the great source of danger (comp. Matth. v. 28; 2 Peter ii. 14), there should be a solemn purpose that *that* should be pure, and that any sacrifice should be made rather than allow indulgence to a wanton gaze: comp. Mark ix. 47. No man was ever too much guarded on this subject; no one ever yet made too solemn a covenant with his eyes, and with his whole soul to be chaste.

2. *For what portion of God* is there *from above?* Or, rather, "What portion should I then have from God who reigns above?" Job asks with emphasis, what portion or reward he should expect from God who reigns on high, if he had *not* made such a covenant with his eyes, and if he had given the reins to loose and wanton thoughts? This question he himself answers in the following verse, and says, that he could have expected only destruction from the Almighty.

3. Is *not destruction to the wicked?* That is, Job says that he was well aware that destruction would overtake the wicked, and that if he had given indulgence to impure desires he could have looked for nothing else. Well knowing this, he says, he had guarded himself in the most careful manner from sin, and had laboured with the greatest assiduity to keep his eyes and his heart pure. ¶ *And a strange* punishment—נֵכֶר. The word here used, means literally *strangeness*—a strange thing, something with which we were unacquainted. It is used here evidently in the sense of a strange or unusual punishment; something which does not occur in the ordinary course of events. The sense is, that for the sin here particularly referred to, God would interpose to inflict vengeance in a manner such as did not occur in the ordinary dealings of his providence. There would be some punishment adopted peculiarly to *this* sin, and which would mark it with his *especial* displeasure. Has it not been so in all ages? The Vulgate renders it, *alienatio*, and the LXX. in a similar manner—ἀπαλλοτρίωσις—and they seem to have understood it as followed by *entire alienation* from God; an idea which would be every where sustained by a reference to the history of the sin referred to by Job. There is no sin that so much poisons all the fountains of pure feeling in the soul, and none that will so certainly terminate in the entire wreck of character.

4. *Doth he not see my ways?* This either means that God was a witness of all that he did—his thoughts, words, and deeds, and would punish him if he had given indulgence to improper feelings and thoughts; or that since God saw all his thoughts, he could boldly appeal to him as a witness of his innocence in this matter, and in proof that his life and heart were pure. Rosenm ller adopts the latter interpretation; Herder seems to incline to the former. Umbreit renders it, "God himself must be a witness that I speak the truth." It is not

5 If [a] I have walked with vanity,
or if my foot hath hasted to deceit;
6 Let [1] me be weighed in an even
balance, that God may know mine
integrity.
7 If my step hath turned out of
the way, and mine heart [b] walked
after mine eyes, and if any blot
hath cleaved to mine hands;
8 *Then* let me sow, and let another eat; yea, let my offspring be
rooted out.

a Ps.44 20,21.
1 *him weigh me in balances of justice.*
b Eze.14 3,7.

easy to determine which is the true meaning. Either of them will accord well with the scope of the passage.

5. *If I have walked with vanity.* This is the second specification in regard to his private deportment. He says that his life had been sincere, upright, honest. The word *vanity* here is equivalent to *falsehood*, for so the parallelism demands, and so the word (שׁוא) is often used; Ps. xii. 3; xli. 7; Ex. xxiii. 1; Deut. v. 20; comp. Isa, i. 13. The meaning of Job here is, that he had been true and honest. In his dealings with others he had not defrauded them; he had not misrepresented things; he had spoken the exact truth, and had done that which was without deception or guile. ¶ *If my foot hath hasted to deceit.* That is, if I have gone to execute a purpose of deceit or fraud. He had never, on seeing an opportunity where others might be defrauded, *hastened* to embrace it. The LXX. render this verse, "If I have walked with scoffers—μετα γελοιαστῶν—and if my foot has hastened to deceit."

6. *Let me be weighed in an even balance.* Marg. *him weigh me in balances of justice.* That is, let him ascertain exactly my character, and treat me accordingly. If on trial it be found that I am guilty in this respect, I consent to be punished accordingly. Scales or balances are often used as emblematic of justice. Many suppose, however, that this verse is a parenthesis, and that the imprecation in verse 8, relates to verse 5, as well as to verse 7. But most probably the meaning is, that he consented to have his life tried in this respect in the most exact and rigid manner, and was willing to abide the result. A man may express such a consciousness of integrity in his dealings with others, without any improper self-reliance or boasting. It may be a simple fact of which he may be certain, that he has never meant to defraud any man.

7. *If my step hath turned out of the way.* The path in which I ought to walk—the path of virtue. ¶ *And mine heart walked after mine eyes.* That is, if I have coveted what my eyes have beheld; or if I have been determined by the *appearance* of things rather than by what is right, I consent to bear the appropriate punishment. ¶ *And if any blot hath cleaved to mine hands.* To have clean hands is emblematic of innocence; Job xvii. 9; Ps. xxiv. 4; comp. Matth. xxvii. 24. The word *blot* here means *stain, blemish;* Dan. i. 4. The idea is, that his hands were pure, and that he had not been guilty of any act of fraud or violence in depriving others of their property.

8. Then *let me sow, and let another eat.* This is the imprecation which he invokes, in case he had been guilty in this respect. He consented to sow his fields, and let others enjoy the harvest. The expression here used is common in the Scriptures to denote insecurity of property or calamity in general; see Lev. xxvi. 16: "And ye shall sow your seed in vain, for your enemies shall eat it;" comp. Deut. xxviii. 30; Amos ix. 13, 14. ¶ *Yea, let my offspring be rooted out.* Or, rather, "Let what I plant be rooted up." So Umbreit, Noyes, Schultens, Rosenmüller, Herder, and Lee understand it. There is no evidence that he here alludes to his children, for the connection does not demand it, nor does the word used here require such an interpretation. The word צאצאים—means properly *shoots;* that is, what springs out of any thing—as the earth, or a tree—from יצא—to go out, to go forth. It

9 If mine heart have been deceived
by a woman; or *if* I have laid
wait at my neighbour's door;
10 *Then* let my wife grind unto
another, and let others bow down
upon her.
11 For this is an heinous crime;
yea, it *is* [a] an iniquity *to be punished*
by the judges.

[a] Le.20.10.

is applied to the productions of the earth in Isa. xlii. 5; xxxiv. 1, and to children or posterity, in Isa. xxii. 24; lxi. 9; lxv. 23; Job v. 25; xxi. 8. Here it refers evidently to the productions of the earth; and the idea is, that if he had been guilty of dishonesty or fraud in his dealings, he wished that all that he had sowed should be rooted up.

9. *If mine heart have been deceived by a woman.* If I have been enticed by her beauty. The word rendered *deceived* (פתה) means *to open, to expand.* It is then applied to that which is open or ingenuous; to that which is unsuspicious—like a youth; and thence is used in the sense of being deceived, or enticed; Deut. xi. 16; Ex. xxii. 16; Prov. i. 10; xvi. 29. The word "woman" here probably means a married woman, and stands opposed to "virgin" in ver. 1. The crime which he here disclaims is adultery, and he says that his heart had never been allured from conjugal fidelity by the charms or the arts of a woman. ¶ *Or if I have laid wait at my neighbour's door.* That is, to watch when he would be absent from home. This was a common practice with those who were guilty of the crime referred to here; comp. Prov. vii. 8, 9.

10. Then *let my wife grind unto another.* Let her be subjected to the deepest humiliation and degradation. Probably Job could not have found language which would have more emphatically expressed his sense of the enormity of this crime, or his perfect consciousness of innocence. The *last* thing which a man would imprecate on himself, would be that which is specified in this verse. The word *grind* (טחן) means to crush, to beat small; then to grind, as in a hand-mill; Judges xvi. 21; Num. xi. 8. This was usually the work of females and slaves; see Notes on Isa. xlvii. 2. The meaning here is, "Let my wife be the mill-wench to another; be his abject slave, and be treated by him with the deepest indignity." This passage has been understood by many in a different sense, which the parallelism might seem to demand, but which is not necessarily the true interpretation. The sense referred to is this: Cogatur uxor mea ad patiendum alius concubitum, ut verbum molendi hoc loco eodem sensu sumatur, quo non raro a Latinis usurpatur ut in illo Horatii (Satyr. L. i. Ecl. ii. ver. 35), *alienas permolere uxores.* In this sense the Rabbinic writers understand Judges xvi. 21 and Lam. v. 13. So also the Chaldee renders the phrase before us (אתתי תשמש עם חורן) *coeat cum alio uxor mea;* and so the LXX. seem to have understood it—ἀρέσαι ἄρα καὶ ἡ γυνή μου ἑτέρῳ. But probably Job meant merely that his wife should be reduced to the condition of servitude, and be compelled to labour in the employ of another. We may find here an answer to the opinion of Prof. Lee (in his Notes on ver. 1), that the wife of Job was at this time dead, and that he was meditating the question about marrying again. May we not here also find an instance of the fidelity and forgiving spirit of Job towards a wife who is represented in the early part of this book as manifesting few qualities which could win the heart of an husband? There is no expression of impatience at her temper and her words on the part of Job, and he here speaks of it as the most serious of all calamities that could happen; the most painful of all punishments, that that same wife should be reduced to a condition of servitude and degradation.

11. *For this is an heinous crime.* This expresses Job's sense of the enormity of such an offence. He felt that there was no palliation for it; he would in no way, and on no pretence, attempt to vindicate it. ¶ *An iniquity* to be punished by *the judges.* A

12 For it *is* a fire *that* consumeth to destruction, [a] and would root out all mine increase.

a Mal.3.5; He.13.4.

13 If I did despise the cause of my man-servant, or of my maid-servant, when they contended with me;

crime for the judges to determine on and decide. The sins which Job had specified before this, were those of the *heart;* but here he refers to a crime against society—an offence which deserved the interposition of the magistrate. It may be observed here, that adultery has always been regarded as a sin "to be punished by the judges." In most countries it has been punished with death; see Notes on John viii. 5.

12. *For it* is *a fire* that *consumeth to destruction.* This may mean that such an offence would be a crime that would provoke God to send destruction, like a consuming fire upon the offender (*Rosenmüller* and *Noyes*), or more likely it is designed to be descriptive of the nature of the sin itself. According to this, the meaning is, that indulgence in this sin tends wholly to ruin and destroy a man. It is like a consuming fire, which sweeps away every thing before it. It is destructive to the body, the morals, the soul. Accordingly, it may be remarked that there is no one vice which pours such desolation through the soul as licentiousness. See Rush on the Diseases of the Mind. It corrupts and taints all the fountains of morals, and utterly annihilates all purity of the heart. An intelligent gentleman, and a careful observer of the state of things in society, once remarked to me, that on coming to the city of Philadelphia, it was his fortune to be in the same boarding-house with a number of young men, nearly all of whom were known to him to be of licentious habits. He has lived to watch their course of life; and he remarked, that there was not one of them who did not ultimately show that he was essentially corrupt and unprincipled in every department of morals. There is not any one propensity of man that spreads such a withering influence over the soul as this; and, however it may be accounted for, it is certain that indulgence in this vice is a certain evidence that the whole soul is corrupt, and that no reliance is to be placed on the man's virtue in any respect, or in reference to any relation of life. ¶ *And would root out all mine increase.* By its desolating effects on my heart and life. The meaning is, that it would utterly ruin him; comp. Luke xv. 13, 30. How many a wretched sensualist can bear testimony to the truth of this statement! How many a young man has been wholly ruined in reference to his worldly interests, as well as in reference to his soul, by this vice! comp. Prov. vii. No young man could do a better service to himself than to commit the whole of that chapter to memory, and so engrave it on his soul that it never COULD be forgotten.

13. *If I did despise the cause of my man-servant.* Job turns to another subject, on which he claimed that his life had been upright. It was in reference to the treatment of his servants. The meaning here is, "I never refused to do strict justice to my servants when they brought their cause before me, or when they complained that my dealings with them had been severe." ¶ *When they contended with me.* That is, when they brought their cause before me, and complained that I had not provided for them comfortably, or that their task had been too hard. If *in any respect* they supposed they had cause of complaint, I listened to them attentively, and endeavoured to do right. He did not take advantage of his *power* to oppress them, nor did he suppose that they had no rights of any kind. It is evident, from this, that Job had those who sustained to him the relation of *servants;* but whether they were *slaves,* or *hired servants,* is not known. The language here will agree with either supposition, though it cannot be doubted that slavery was known as early as the

14 What then shall I do when God riseth up? and, when he visiteth, what shall I answer him?

15 Did [a] not he that made me in the womb make him? and [1] did not one fashion us in the womb?

a Pr.22.2.

1 or, *did he not fashion us in one womb.*

time of Job. There is no certain evidence that he held any *slaves*, in the proper sense of the term, nor that he regarded slavery as right; comp. Notes on chap. i. 3. He here refers to the numerous persons that had been in his employ in the days of his prosperity, and says that he had never taken advantage of his power or rank to do them wrong.

14. *What then shall I do when God riseth up?* That is, when he rises up to pronounce sentence on men, or to execute impartial justice. Job admits that if he had done injustice to a servant, he would have reason to dread the divine indignation, and that he could have no excuse. "I tremble," said President Jefferson, speaking of slavery in the United States, "when I remember that God is just!" *Notes on Virginia.* ¶ *And when he visiteth.* When he comes to inspect human conduct. Umbreit renders it, "when he punishes." The word *visit* is often used in this sense in the Scriptures.

15. *Did not he that made me in the womb make him?* Had we not one and the same Creator, and have we not consequently the same nature? We may observe in regard to this sentiment, (1.) That it indicates a very advanced state of view in regard to man. The attempt has been always made by those who wish to tyrannize over others, or who aim to make slaves of others, to show that they are of a different race, and that in the design for which they were made, they are wholly inferior. Arguments have been derived from their complexion, from their supposed inferiority of intellect, and the deep degradation of their condition, often little above that of brutes, to prove that they were originally inferior to the rest of mankind. On this the plea has been often urged, and oftener *felt* than urged, that it is right to reduce them to slavery. Since this feeling so early existed, and since there is so much that may be plausibly said in defence of it, it shows that Job had derived his views from something more than the speculations of men, and the desire of power, when he says that he regarded all men as originally equal, and as having the same Creator. It is in fact a sentiment which men have been practically very reluctant to believe, and which works its way very slowly even yet on the earth; comp. Acts xvii. 26. (2.) This sentiment, if fairly embraced and carried out, would soon destroy slavery every where. If men *felt* that they were reducing to bondage those who were originally on a level with themselves—made by the same God, with the same faculties, and for the same end; if they felt that in their very origin, in their nature, there was that which could not be made mere *property*, it would soon abolish the whole system. It is kept up only where men endeavour to convince themselves that there is *some original inferiority* in the slave which makes it proper that he should be reduced to servitude and be held as property. But as soon as there can be diffused abroad the sentiment of Paul, that "God hath made of one blood all nations of men," (Acts xvii. 26), or the sentiment of the patriarch Job, that "the same God made us and them in the womb," that moment the shackles of the slave will fall, and he will be free. Hence it is apparent, how Christianity, that carries this lesson on its fore-front, is the grand remedy for the evils of slavery, and needs only to be universally diffused to bring the system to an end. ¶ *And did not one fashion us in the womb?* Marg. Or, *did he not fashion us in one womb?* The Hebrew will bear either construction, but the parallelism rather requires that given in the text, and most expositors agree in this interpretation. The sentiment is, whichever interpretation be adopted, that they had a common origin; that

16 If I have withheld the poor from *their* desire, or have caused the eyes of the widow to fail;
17 Or have eaten my morsel myself alone, and the fatherless hath not eaten thereof;
18 (For from my youth he was brought up with me, as *with* a

God would watch over them alike as his children; and that, therefore, they had equal rights.

16. *If I have withheld the poor from their desire.* Job now turns to another class of virtues, regarded also as of great importance in the patriarchal ages, kindness to the poor and the afflicted; to the fatherless and the widow. He appeals to his former life on this subject; affirms that he had a good conscience in the recollection of his dealings with them, and impliedly declares that it could not have been for any deficiency in the exercise of these virtues that his calamities had come upon him. The meaning here is, that he had not denied to the poor their wish. If they had come and desired bread of him, he had not withheld it; see chap. xxii. 7. ¶ *Or caused the eyes of the widow to fail.* That is, I have not frustrated her hopes, or disappointed her expectations, when she has looked intently upon me, and desired my aid. The "failing of the eyes" refers to *failing of the object of their expectation;* or the expression means that she had not looked to him in vain; see chap. xi. 20.

17. *Or have eaten my morsel myself alone.* If I have not imparted what I had, though ever so small, to others. This was in accordance with the Oriental laws of hospitality. It is regarded as a fixed law among the Arabians, that the guest shall always be helped first, and to that which is best; and no matter how needy the family may be, or how much distressed with hunger, the settled laws of hospitality demand that the stranger-guest shall have the first and best portion. Dr. Robinson, in his "Biblical Researches," gives an amusing instance of the extent to which this law is carried, and the sternness with which it is executed among the Arabs. In the journey from Suez to Mount Sinai, intending to furnish a supper for the Arabs in their employ, he and his fellow-travellers had bought a kid, and led it along to the place of their encampment. At night the kid was killed and roasted, and the Arabs were anticipating a savoury supper. But those of whom they had bought the kid, learned in some way that they were to encamp near, and naturally concluded that the kid was bought to be eaten, and followed them to the place of encampment, to the number of five or six persons. "Now the stern law of Arabian hospitality demands, that whenever a guest is present at a meal, whether there be much or little, the first and best portion must be laid before the stranger. In this instance the five or six guests attained their object, and had not only the selling of the kid, but also the eating of it, while our poor Arabs, whose mouths had long been watering with expectation, were forced to take up with the fragments." Vol. i. 118. There is often, indeed, much ostentation in the hospitality of the Orientals, but the law is stern and inflexible. "No sooner," says Shaw (Travels, vol. i. p. 20), "was our food prepared, than one of the Arabs, having placed himself on the highest spot of ground in the neighbourhood, called out thrice with a loud voice to all their brethren, *the sons of the faithful,* to come and partake of it; though none of them were in view, or perhaps within a hundred miles of them." The great law of hospitality Job says he had carefully observed, and had not withheld what he had from the poor and the fatherless.

18. *For from my youth he was brought up with me.* This verse is usually regarded as a parenthesis, though very various expositions have been given of it. Some have understood it as *denying* that he had in any way neglected the widow and the fatherless, and affirming that the orphan had always, even from his youth, found a father in him, and the widow a guide. Others, as our translators,

father, and I have guided [1] her from
my mother's womb;)
19 If I have seen any perish for
want of clothing, or any poor without covering;
20 If [a] his loins have not blessed
me, and *if* he were *not* warmed with
the fleece of my sheep;
21 If I have lifted up my hand
against the fatherless, when I saw
my help in the gate;
22 *Then* let mine arm fall from

1 i. e. *the widow.*

a De.24.13.

---

suppose that it is a parenthesis thrown in to indicate his general course of life, although the imprecation which he makes on himself, if he had neglected the widow and the orphan, is found in ver. 22. Luther reads the two previous verses as questions, and this as an answer to them, and so also do Rosenmüller and Noyes. Umbreit regards this verse as a parenthesis. This is probably to be considered as the correct interpretation, for this better agrees with the Hebrew than the other proposed. It *implies* a denial of having neglected the widow and the orphan, but the *full* expression of his abhorrence of a charge of having done so, is to be found in the strong language in ver. 22. The unusual Hebrew word גדלני stands probably for גדל עמי—"he was brought up with me." This form of the word does not elsewhere occur. ¶ *As with a father.* That is, he always found in me one who treated him as a father. The meaning is, that he had always had under his care those who were orphans; that from his very youth they had been accustomed to look up to him as a father; and that they had never been disappointed in him. It is the language of one who seems to have been born to rank, and who had the means of benefiting others, and who had done it all his life. This accords also with the Oriental notions of *kindness*—requiring that it should be shown especially to the widow and the fatherless. ¶ *I have guided her.* Marg. "*That is, the widow.*" The meaning is, that he had been her counsellor and friend. ¶ *From my mother's womb.* This cannot be *literally* true, but it means that he had done it from early life; or as we would say, he had *always* done it.

19. *If I have seen any perish,* &c. He turns to another virtue of the same general class—that of providing for the poor. The meaning is clear, that he had always assisted the poor and needy.

20. *If his loins have not blessed me.* This is a personification by which the part of the body that had been clothed by the benevolence of Job, is supposed to speak and render him thanks.

21. *If I have lifted up my hand against the fatherless.* That is, if I have taken advantage of my rank, influence, and power, to oppress and injure him. ¶ *When I saw my help in the gate.* The *gate* of a city was a place of concourse; a place where debates were held, and where justice was administered. Job speaks here of that part of his life when he was clothed with authority as a magistrate, or when he had power and influence as a public man. He says that he had never abused this power to oppress the fatherless. He had never taken advantage of his influence to injure them, because he saw he had a strong party under his control, or because he had power enough to carry his point, or because he had those under him who would sustain him in an oppressive measure. This is spoken with reference to the usually feeble and defenceless condition of the orphan, as one who is deprived of his natural protector and who is, therefore, liable to be wronged by those in power.

22. Then *let mine arm.* The strong language which Job uses here, shows his consciousness of innocence, and his detestation of the offences to which he here refers, ver. 16—22. The word rendered *arm* here (כָּתֵף) means properly the *shoulder.* Isa. xlvi. 7; xlix. 22; Num. vii. 9; comp. Notes on Isa. xi 14. There is no instance, it is believed, unless this is one, in which it means *arm,* and the meaning here is, that he wished, if he had been guilty, his shoulder might separate

my shoulder-blade, and mine arm
be broken from [1] the bone.
23 For [a] destruction *from* God
was a terror to me, and by reason
of his highness [b] I could not endure.

1 or, *the chanel-bone.* *a* Ps.119.120. *b* Ps 76. 7.

24 If [c] I have made gold my hope,
or have said to the fine gold, *Thou
art* my confidence;
25 If I rejoiced because my
wealth *was* great, and because mine
hand had [2] gotten much;

c 1 Ti.6.17. 2 *found.*

---

from the blade. So Herder, Rosenmüller, Umbreit, and Noyes render it; and so the Vulgate and the LXX. ¶ *From my shoulder-blade.* The scapula—the flat bone to which the upper arm is attached. The wish of Job is, that the shoulder might separate from that, and of course the arm would be useless. Such a strong imprecation implies a firm consciousness of innocence. ¶ *And mine arm.* The word *arm* here denotes the *forearm*—the arm from the elbow to the fingers. ¶ *From the bone.* Marg. "*the chanel bone.*" Literally, "from the reed"—מִקָּנָה. Umbreit renders it, *Schneller als ein Rohr—quicker than a reed.* The word קָנֶה—*kânâ*, means properly a *reed, cane, calamus* (Notes on Isa. xliii. 24), and is here applied to the upper arm, or arm above the elbow, from its resemblance to a reed or cane. It is applied, also, to the arm or branch of a chandelier, or candlestick, Ex. xxv. 31, and to the rod or beam of a balance, Isa. xlvi. 6. The meaning here is, that he wished that his arm should be broken at the elbow, or the forearm be separated from the upper arm, if he were guilty of the sins which he had specified. There is allusion, probably, and there is great force and propriety in the allusion, to what he had said in ver. 21: "If his arm had been lifted up against an orphan, he prayed that it might fall powerless."

23. *For destruction* from *God* was *a terror to me.* The destruction which God would bring upon one who was guilty of the crime here specified, awed and restrained me. He was deterred from this crime of oppressing the fatherless by the fear of God. He could have escaped the judgment of men. He had power and influence enough not to dread the penalty of human law. He could have done it in such a way as not to have been arraigned before any earthly tribunal, but he remembered that the eye of God was upon him, and that he was the avenger of the fatherless and the widow. ¶ *And by reason of his highness.* On account of his majesty, exaltation, glory. ¶ *I could not endure.* לֹא אוּכָל—*I could not;* that is, I could not *do it.* I was so much awed by his majesty; I had such a veneration for him, that I could not be guilty of such an offence.

24. *If I have made gold my hope.* That is, if I have put my trust in gold rather than in God; if I have fixed my affections with idolatrous attachment on riches rather than on my Maker. Job here introduces another class of sins, and says that his conscience did not charge him with guilt in respect to them. He had before spoken mainly of social duties, and of his manner of life towards the poor, the needy, the widow, and the orphan. He here turns to the duty which he owed to God, and says that his conscience did not charge him with *idolatry* in any form. He had indeed been rich, but he had not fixed his affections with idolatrous attachment on his wealth. ¶ *Or have said to fine gold.* The word here used (כֶּתֶם) is the same which is employed in chap. xxviii. 16, to denote the gold of Ophir. It is used to express that which was most pure—from the verb כָּתַם—*to hide, to hoard,* and then denoting that which was hidden, hoarded, *precious.* The meaning is, that he had not put his trust in that which was most sought after, and which was deemed of the highest value by men.

25. *If I have rejoiced because my wealth* was *great.* That is, if I have rejoiced *as if* I might now confide in it, or put my trust in it. He had not found his principal joy in his property, nor had he attempted to find in that the happiness which he ought to seek

26 If I beheld the [1] sun when it shined, or the moon walking [2] *in* brightness,

1 *light.* 2 *bright.*

---

in God. ¶ *And because mine hand had gotten much.* Marg. *found.* Prof. Lee translates this, "When as a mighty man my hand prevailed." But the usual interpretation is given in our translation, and this accords better with the connection. The word *found* better expresses the sense of the Hebrew than *gotten*, but the sense is not materially varied.

26. *If I beheld the sun when it shined.* Marg. *light.* The Hebrew word (אוֹר) properly means *light*, but that it here means the *sun* is manifest from the connection, since the *moon* occurs in the parallel member of the sentence. Why the word *light* is used here rather than *sun*, can be only a matter of conjecture. It may be because the worship to which Job refers was not primarily and originally that of the sun, the moon, or the stars, but of *light as such*, and that he mentions this as the essential feature of the idolatry which he had avoided. The worship of *light* in general soon became in fact the worship of the sun—as that is the principal source of light. There is no doubt that Job here refers to idolatrous worship, and the passage is particularly valuable, as it describes one of the forms of idolatry then existing, and refers to some of the customs then prevalent in such worship. The word *light* is used, also, to denote the sun in chap. xxxvii. 21; comp. Isa. xviii. 4; Habak. iii. 4. So, also, Homer speaks of the sun not only as λαμπρὸν φάος ἠελίοιο—*bright light of the sun*, but simply as φάος—*light*. Odyss. Γ. 335. The worship here referred to is that of the heavenly bodies, and it is known that this existed in the early periods of the world, and was probably one of the first forms of idolatry. It is expressly mentioned by Ezekiel as prevailing in his time, chap. viii. 16, "And they worshipped the sun towards the east." That it prevailed in the time of Moses, is evident from the caution which he gives in Deut. iv. 19; comp. 2 Kings xxiii. 5. It is well known, also, that the worship of the heavenly bodies was common in the East, and particularly in Chaldea—near to which Job is supposed to have lived, and it was a remarkable fact that one who was surrounded with idolaters of this description had been enabled always to keep himself pure. The principle on which this worship was founded was, probably, that of gratitude. Men adored the objects from which they derived important benefits, as well as deprecated the wrath of those which were supposed to exert a malignant influence. But among the objects from which men derived the greatest benefits were the sun and moon, and hence they were objects of worship. The stars, also, were supposed to exert important influences over men, and hence they also early became objects of adoration. An additional reason for the worship of the heavenly bodies may have been, that *light* was a natural and striking symbol of the divinity, and those shining bodies may have been at first honoured as representatives of the Deity. The worship of the heavenly bodies was called Sabaism, from the Hebrew word צבא *tzaba*—*host*, or *army*—as being the worship of the hosts of heaven. It is supposed to have had its origin in Persia, and to have spread thence to the West. That the moon was worshipped as a deity, is abundantly proved by the testimony of the ancient writers. Hottinger, Hist. Orient. Lib. i. c. 8, speaking of the worship of the Zabaists, adduces the testimony of Ali Said Vaheb, saying that the first day of the week was devoted to the sun; the second to the moon; the third to Mars, &c. Maimonides says that the Zabaists worshipped the moon, and that they also said that Adam led mankind to that species of worship. Mor. Nev. P. iii. Clemens Alexandr. says (in Protrept.) καὶ προσεκύνησαν ἥλιον ὡς ἰνδοὶ, καὶ σελήνην ὡς φρύγες. Curtius says of the people of Lybia (Liv. iv. in Melp.) θυοῦσι δὲ ἡλίῳ καὶ σελήνῃ μόυνοισι. Julius Cesar says of the Germans, that they worshipped the moon, Lib. vi. de B. G. p. 158. The Romans had a tem-

27 And my heart hath been secretly enticed, or [1] my mouth hath
kissed my hand;
28 This also [a] *were* an iniquity
to be punished by the judge: for I
should have denied the God *that is*
above.
29 If I rejoiced at the destruction

1 *my hand hath kissed my mouth.*

a De.17.2-7.

ple consecrated to the moon, Taci. Ann. Lib. xv. Livy, L. xl. See Geor. Frid. Meinhardi Diss. de Selenolatria, in Ugolin's Thesau. Sacr. Tom. xxiii. p. 831, seq. Indeed, we have a proof of the worship of the moon in our own language, in the name given to the second day of the week—*Monday, i. e. Moon-day,* implying that it was formerly regarded as devoted to the worship of the moon. The word "*beheld*" in the passage before us must be understood in an idolatrous sense. "If I have looked upon the sun as an object of worship." Schultens explains this passage as referring to splendid and exalted characters, who, on account of their brilliance and power, may be compared to the sun at noonday, and to the moon in its brightness. But the more obvious and common reference is to the sun and moon as objects of worship. ¶ *Or the moon walking* in *brightness.* Marg. *bright.* The word "walking," here applied to the moon, may refer either to its course through the heavens, or it may mean, as Dr. Good supposes, advancing to her full; "brightly, or splendidly progressive." The LXX. render the passage strangely enough. "Do we not see the shining sun eclipsed? and the moon changing? For it is not in them."

27. *And my heart hath been secretly enticed.* That is, away from God, or led into sin. ¶ *Or my mouth hath kissed my hand.* Marg. *my hand hath kissed my mouth.* The margin accords with the Hebrew. It was customary in ancient worship to kiss the idol that was worshipped; comp. 1 Kings xix. 18, "I have left me seven thousand in Israel—and every mouth which hath not kissed him." See, also, Hos. xiii. 2. The Mohammedans at the present day, in their worship at Mecca, kiss the black stone which is fastened in the corner of the Beat Allah, as often as they pass it, in going round the Caaba. If they cannot come near enough to kiss it, they touch it with the hand, and kiss that. An Oriental pays his respects to one of a superior station by kissing his hand and putting it to his forehead. *Paxton.* See the custom of kissing the hand of a Prince, as it exists in Arabia, described by Niebuhr, Reisebeschreib. 1, S. 414. The custom prevailed, also, among the Romans and Greeks. Thus Pliny (Hist. Nat. xxviii. 2) says, Inter adorandum dexteram ad osculum referimus, et totum corpus circumagimus. So Lucian in the book, περὶ ὀρχήσεως, says, "And the Indians, rising early, adore the sun—not as we, *kissing the hand*—τὴν χεῖρα κύσαντες—think that our vow is perfect." The foundation of the custom here alluded to, is the *respect* and *affection* which is shown for one by kissing; and as the heavenly bodies which were worshipped were so remote that the worshippers could not have access to them, they expressed their veneration by kissing the hand. Job means to say, that he had never performed an act of homage to the heavenly bodies.

28. *This also* were *an iniquity* to be punished by *the judge.* Note ver. 11. Among the Hebrews idolatry was an offence punishable by death by stoning; Deut. xvii. 2—7. It is possible, also, that this might have been elsewhere in the patriarchal times a crime punishable in this manner. At all events, Job regarded it as a heinous offence, and one of which the magistrate ought to take cognizance. ¶ *For I should have denied the God* that is *above.* The worship of the heavenly bodies would have been in fact the denial of the existence of any Superior Being. This, in fact, always occurs, for idolaters have no knowledge of the true God.

29. *If I rejoiced at the destruction of him that hated me.* Job here introduces another class of offences, of which he says he was innocent. The

of him that hated me, or lifted up
myself when evil found him ;
30 (Neither have I suffered my
[1] mouth to sin, [a] by wishing a curse
to his soul;)
31 If the men of my tabernacle

1 *palate.*

a Ec.5.6.

---

subject referred to is the proper treatment of those who injure us. In respect to this, he says that he was entirely conscious of freedom from exultation when calamity came upon a foe, and that he had never even wished him evil in his heart. The word "*destruction*" here, means calamity, disappointment, or affliction of any kind. It had never been pleasant to him to see one who hated him suffer. It is needless to remark how entirely this accords with the New Testament. And it is pleasant to find such a sentiment as this expressed in the early age of the world, and to see how the influence of true religion is at all times the same. The religion of Job led him to act out the beautiful sentiment afterwards embodied in the instructions of the Saviour, and made binding on all his followers; Matth. v. 44. True religion will lead a man to act out what is embodied in its precepts, whether they are expressed in formal language or not. ¶ *Or lifted up myself.* Been elated or rejoiced. ¶ *When evil found him.* When calamity overtook him.

30. *Neither have I suffered my mouth.* Marg. as in Hebrew, *palate.* The word is often used for the mouth in general, and especially as the organ of the voice—from the use and importance of the palate in speaking. Prov. viii. 7, "For my palate (חִכִּי) speaketh truth." It is used as the organ of taste, Job xii. 11; comp. vi. 30; Ps. cxix. 103. ¶ *By wishing a curse to his soul.* It must have been an extraordinary degree of piety which would permit a man to say this with truth, that he had never harboured *a wish* of injury to an enemy. Few are the men, probably, even now, who could say this, and who are enabled to keep their minds free from every wish that calamities and woes may overtake those who are seeking their hurt. Yet this is the nature of true religion. It controls the heart, represses the angry and revengeful feelings, and creates in the soul an earnest desire for the happiness even of those who injure us.

31. *If the men of my tabernacle.* The men of my tent; or those who dwell with me. The reference is doubtless to those who were in his employ, and who, being constantly with him, had an opportunity to observe his manner of life. On this verse there has been a great variety of exposition, and interpreters are by no means agreed as to its meaning. Herder connects it with the previous verse, and renders it,

> "No! my tongue uttered no evil word,
> Nor any imprecation against him,
> When the men of my tent said,
> 'O that we had his flesh, it would satisfy us.'"

That is, though he were the bitterest enemy of my house, and all were in open violence. Noyes translates it,

> "Have not the men of my tent exclaimed,
> 'Who is there that hath not been satisfied with his meat?'"

Umbreit supposes that it is designed to celebrate the benevolence of Job, and that the meaning is, that all his companions—the inmates of his house—could bear him witness that not one of the poor was allowed to depart without being satisfied with his hospitality. They were abundantly fed, and their wants supplied. The verse is undoubtedly to be regarded as connected, as Ikenius supposes, with the following, and is designed to illustrate the hospitality of Job. His object is to show that those who dwelt with him, and who had every opportunity of knowing all about him, could never say that the stranger was not hospitably entertained. The phrase, "if the men of my tabernacle said not," means, that *a case never occurred* in which they could not make use of the language which follows, they never could say that the stranger was not hospitably entertained. ¶ *Oh that we had.* The phrase מִי־יִתֵּן, commonly means, "O that"—as the *Latin Utinam*—implying a wish or said not, Oh that we had of his flesh! we cannot be satisfied.

32 (The stranger [a] did not lodge in the street; *but* I opened my doors to the traveller;) [1]

[a] Lev.19.34; He.13.2. [1] or, *way*.

desire. See chap. xix. 23; xxxi. 35. But here the phrase seems to be used in the sense of "Who will give, or who will show or furnish" (comp. chap. xiv. 4); and the sense is, "Who will refer to one instance in which the stranger has not been hospitably entertained?" ¶ *Of his flesh! we cannot be satisfied.* Or, rather, "Who will refer to an instance in which it can be said that we have not been satisfied from his flesh, *i. e.* from his table, or by his hospitality?" The word *flesh* here cannot mean, as our translation would seem to imply, the flesh of Job himself, as if it were to be torn and lacerated with a spirit of revenge, but that which his table furnished by a generous hospitality. The LXX. render this, "If my maid-servants have often said, O that we had some of his flesh to eat! while I was living luxuriously." For a great variety of opinions on the passage, see Schultens *in loc.* The above interpretation of Ikenius is the most simple, natural, and obvious of any which have been proposed, and is adopted by Schultens and Rosenmüller.

32. *The stranger did not lodge in the street.* This is designed to illustrate the sentiment in the previous verse, and to express his consciousness that he had showed the most generous hospitality. ¶ But *I opened my doors to the traveller.* Marg. or *way.* The word here used (ארח) means properly *way, path, road;* but it also denotes those who travel on such a way; see chap. vi. 19, "The troops of Tema looked," Heb. תמא ארחות—*the ways*, or *paths of Tema;* that is, those who travelled in those paths. Vulgate here, *viatori.* Sept. "To every one that came"—παντὶ ἐλθόντι. This was one of the methods of hospitality—the central and crowning virtue among the Arabs to this day, and among the Orientals in all ages. Among the boasts of hospitality, showing the place which this virtue had in their estimation, and the methods by which it was practised, we may refer to such expressions as the following:—"I occupy the public way with my tent;" that is, to every traveller without distinction, my tent is open and my table is spread. "He makes the public path the place for the cords of his tent;" that is, he fixed the pins and cords of his tent in the midst of the public highway, so that every traveller might enter. These examples are quoted by Schultens from the Hamasa. Another beautiful example may be taken from the same collection of Arabic poems. I give the Latin translation of Schultens:

> Quam sæpe latratum imitanti viatori, cui resonabat echo
> Suscitavi ignem, cujus lignum luculentum
> Properusque surrexi ad eum, ut prædæ mihi loco esset,
> Præ metu ne populus meus eum ante me occuparet.

That is, "How often to the traveller, imitating the bark of the dog, and the echo of whose voice was heard, have I kindled a fire, the shining wood of which I quick raised up to him, as one would hasten to the prey, in fear lest some one of my own people should anticipate me in the privileges and rites of hospitality." The allusion to the imitation of the barking of a dog here, refers to the custom of travellers at night, who make this noise when they need a place of rest. This sound is responded to by the dogs which watch around the tents of their masters, and the sound is the signal for a general rush to show hospitality to the stranger. Burckhardt, speaking of the inhabitants of the Houran—the country east of the Jordan, and south of Damascus, says, "A traveller may alight at any house he pleases; a mat will be immediately spread for him, coffee made, and a breakfast or dinner set before him. In entering a village it has often happened to me, that several persons presented themselves, each begging that I would lodge at his house. It is a point of honour with the host never to receive the smallest return from a guest. Besides the private habitations, which

33 If I covered my transgressions [1] as Adam, [a] by hiding mine
iniquity in my bosom;
34 (Did I fear a great multitude, [b] or did the contempt of
families terrify me, that I kept
silence, *and* went not out of the
door?

1 or, *after the manner of men.* a Ge.3.11,12.

b Ex.23.2.

offer to every traveller a secure night's shelter, there is in every village the Medhafe of the Sheikh, where all strangers of decent appearance are received and entertained. It is the duty of the Sheikh to maintain this Medhafe, which is like a tavern, with the difference that the host himself pays the bill. The Sheikh has a public allowance to defray these expenses, and hence a man of the Houran, intending to travel about for a fortnight never thinks of putting a single para in his pocket; he is sure of being every where well received, and of living better, perhaps, than at his own home." Travels in Syria, pp. 294, 295.

33. *If I covered my transgressions as Adam.* That is, if I have attempted to hide or conceal them; if, conscious of guilt, I have endeavoured to cloak my sins, and to appear righteous. There has been great variety of opinion about the meaning of this expression. The margin reads it, "After the manner of men." Luther, renders it, "Have I covered my wickedness as a man"—Habe ich meine Schalkheit wie ein Mensch gedecht. Coverdale, "Have I ever done any wicked deed where through I shamed myself before men." Herder, "Did I hide my faults like a mean man." Schultens, "If I have covered my sin as Adam." The Vulgate, *Quasi homo*—"as a man." The Sept., "If when I sinned unwillingly (ἀκουσίως—*inadvertently, undesignedly*) I concealed my sin." Noyes, "After the manner of men." Umbreit, *Nach Menschenart*—"After the manner of men." Rosenmüller, *As Adam.* The Chaldee, כאדם, meaning, as Rosenmüller remarks, as Adam; and the Syriac, *As men.* The meaning may either be, as men are accustomed to do when they commit a crime—referring to the common practice of the guilty to attempt to cloak their offences, or to the attempt of Adam to hide his sin from his Maker after the fall; Gen. iii. 7, 8. It is not possible to decide with certainty which is the correct interpretation, for either will accord with the Hebrew. But in favour of the supposition that it refers to the effort of Adam to conceal his sin, we may remark, (1.) That there can be little or no doubt that that transaction was known to Job by tradition. (2.) It furnished him a pertinent and striking illustration of the point before him. (3.) The illustration is, by supposing that it refers to him, much more striking than on the other supposition. It is true that men often attempt to conceal their guilt, and that it may be set down as a fact very general in its character; but still it is not *so* universal that there are no exceptions. But here was a specific and well-known case, and one which, as it was the first, so it was the most sad and melancholy instance that had ever occurred of an attempt to conceal guilt. It was not an attempt to hide it from *man*—for there was then no other man to witness it; but an attempt to hide it from *God.* From such an attempt Job says *he* was free. ¶ *By hiding mine iniquity in my bosom.* By attempting to conceal it so that others would not know it. Adam attempted to conceal his fault even from God; and it is common with men, when they have done wrong, to endeavour to hide it from others.

34. *Did I fear a great multitude.* Our translators have rendered this as if Job meant to say that he had not been deterred from doing what he supposed was right by the fear of others; as if he had been independent, and had done what he knew to be right, undeterred by the fear of popular fury, or the loss of the favour of the great. This version is adopted also by the Vulgate, by Herder, and substantially by Coverdale and Luther. Another interpretation has, however, been proposed, and is

35 Oh that one would hear me! behold [1] my desire *is, that* the Almighty would answer me, and *that* mine adversary had written a book;

1 or, *my sign* is that *the Almighty will answer me.*

adopted by Schultens, Noyes, Good, Umbreit, Dathe, and Scott, which is, that this is to be regarded as an *imprecation*, or that this is the punishment which he invoked and expected if he had been guilty of the crime which is specified in the previous verses. The meaning then would be "Then let me be confounded before the great multitude! Let the contempt of families cover me with shame! Let me keep silence, and let me never appear abroad!" The Hebrew will admit of either construction, and either of them will accord well with the connection. The *latter*, however, regarding it as an imprecation, seems to me to be preferable, for two reasons. (1.) It will accord more forcibly with what he had said in the previous verse. The sense then would be, as expressed by Patrick, "If I have studied to appear better than I am, and have not made a free confession, but, like our first parent, have concealed or excused my faults, and, out of self-love, have hidden mine iniquity, because I dread what the people will say of me, or am terrified by the contempt into which the knowledge of my guilt will bring me with the neighbouring families, then am I content my mouth should be stopped, and that I never stir out of my door any more." (2.) This interpretation seems to be required, in order to make a proper *close* of his remarks. The general course in this chapter has been to specify an offence, and then to utter an imprecation if he had been guilty of it. In the previous verses he had specified crimes of which he had declared himself innocent; but unless this verse be so regarded, there is no invocation of any corresponding punishment if he had been guilty. It seems probable, therefore, that this verse is so to be regarded. According to this, the phrase "Did I fear a great multitude" means, "Then let me be terrified by a multitude—by the opinions of the world, and let this be the punishment of my sin. Since by the fear of others I was led to hide my sin in my bosom, let it be my lot to lose all popular favour, and feel that I am the object of public scorn and contempt!" ¶ *Or did the contempt of families terrify me.* Let the contempt of families crush me; let me be despised and abhorred by them. If I was led to hide sins in my bosom because I feared them, then let me be doomed to the total loss of their favour, and become wholly the object of their scorn. ¶ *That I kept silence.* Or let me keep silence as a punishment. That is, let me not be admitted as a counsellor, or allowed to express my sentiments in the public assemblies. ¶ *And went not out at the door.* That is, "Let me not go out at the door. Let me be confined to my dwelling, and never be allowed to appear in public, to mingle in society, to take part in public affairs—*because* by the fear of the world I attempted to hide my faults in my bosom. Such a punishment would be appropriate to such an offence. The retribution would be no more than a suitable recompense for such an act of guilt—and I would not shrink from it."

35. *O that one would hear me!* This refers undoubtedly to God. It is, literally, "Who will give to me one hearing me;" and the wish is that which he has so often expressed, that he might get his cause fairly before God. He feels assured that there would be a favourable verdict, if there could be a fair judicial investigation; comp. Notes on chap. xiii. 3. ¶ *Behold, my desire* is. Marg. "Or, *my sign* is that *the Almighty will answer me*." The word rendered in the text *desire*, and in the margin *sign*, (תָּו, *Tāv*), means properly a mark, or sign, and is also the name of the last letter of the Hebrew alphabet. Then the word means, according to Gesenius (*Lex.*), a *mark*, or *cross*, as subscribed to a bill of complaint; hence the bill itself, or, as we should say, *the pleading*. According to this, Job means to say that he was ready for

36 Surely I would take it upon my shoulder, *and* bind it *as* a crown to me.

37 I would declare unto him the number of my steps; as a prince would I go near unto him.)

---

trial, and that there was his *bill of complaint*, or his *pleading*, or his *bill of defence*. So Herder renders it, "See my defence." Coverdale, "Lo, this is my cause." Miss Smith renders it, "Behold my gage!" Umbreit, *Meinel Kagschrift—My accusation*. There can be no doubt that it refers to the forms of a judicial investigation, and that the idea is, that Job was ready for the trial. "Here" says he, "is my defence, my argument, my pleading, my bill! I wait that my adversary should come to the trial." The *name* here used as given to the bill or pleading (תו, *Tāv*, *mark*, or *sign*), probably had its origin from the fact that some *mark* was affixed to it—of some such significance as a seal—by which it was certified to be the real bill of the party, and by which he acknowledged it as his own. This might have been done by signing his name, or by some conventional *mark* that was common in those times. ¶ *That the Almighty would answer me.* That is, answer me as on trial; that the cause might be fairly brought to an issue. This wish he had frequently expressed. ¶ *And that mine adversary.* God; regarded as the opposite party in the suit. ¶ *Had written a book.* Or, would write down his charge. The wish is, that what God had against him were in like manner entered in a bill, or pleading, that the charge might be fairly investigated. On the word *book*, comp. Notes, chap. xix. 23. It means here a pleading in court, a bill, or charge against any one. There is no irreverence in the language here. Job is anxious that his true character should be investigated, and that the great matter at issue should be determined; and he draws his language & illustrations from well-known practices in courts of law.

36. *Surely, I would take it upon my shoulder.* That is, the book or bill which the Almighty would write in the case. Job says that he has such confidence that what God would record in his case would be in his favour, such confidence that he had no charge of hypocrisy against him, and that he who knew him altogether would not bring such an accusation against him, that he would bear it off triumphantly on his shoulders. It would be all that he could desire. This does not refer to what a judge would decide if the cause were submitted to him, but to a case where an opponent or adversary in court should bring all that he could say against him. He says that he would bear even such a bill on his shoulders in triumph, and that it would be a full vindication of his innocence. It would afford him the best vindication of his character, and would be that which he had long desired. ¶ And *bind it* as *a crown to me.* I would regard it as an ornament—a diadem. I would bind it on my head as a crown is worn by princes, and would march forth exultingly with it. Instead of covering me with shame, it would be the source of rejoicing, and I would exhibit it every where in the most triumphant manner. It is impossible for any one to express a more entire consciousness of innocence from charges alleged against him than Job does by this language.

37. *I would declare unto him the number of my steps.* That is, I would disclose to him the whole course of my life. This is language also appropriate to a judicial trial, and the meaning is, that Job was so confident of his integrity that he would approach God and make his whole course of life known to him. ¶ *As a prince would I go near unto him.* With the firm and upright step with which a prince commonly walks. I would not go in a base, cringing manner, but in a manner that evinced a consciousness of integrity. I would not go bowed down under the consciousness of guilt, as a self-condemned malefactor, but with the firm and elastic foot-tread of one conscious of innocence. It must be remembered that all this is said with reference to the charges which had been brought against him by his friends,

38 If my land cry against me, or that the furrows likewise thereof [1] complain;

39 If I have eaten the [2] fruits thereof without money, or have caused [3] the owners thereof to lose their life; [a]

1 *weep.* 2 *strength.* 3 or, *the soul of the owners thereof to expire,* or, *breathe out.* a 1 Ki.21.19.

and not as claiming absolute perfection. He was accused of gross hypocrisy, and it was maintained that he was suffering the judicial infliction of Heaven on account of that. *So far as those charges were concerned,* he now says that he could go before God with the firm and elastic tread of a prince—with entire cheerfulness and boldness. We are not, however, to suppose that he did not regard himself as having the common infirmities and sinfulness of our fallen nature. The discussion does not turn at all on that point.

38. *If my land cry against me.* This is a new specification of an offence, and an imprecation of an appropriate punishment if he had been guilty of it. Many have supposed that these closing verses have been transferred from their appropriate place by an error of transcribers, and that they should have been inserted between ver. 23 and 24—or in some previous part of the chapter. It is certain that ver. 35—37 would make an appropriate and impressive close of the chapter, being a solemn appeal to God in reference to all the specifications, or to the general tenor of his life; but there is no authority from the MSS. to make any change in the present arrangement. All the ancient versions insert the verses in the place which they now occupy, and in this all versions agree, except, according to Kennicott, the Teutonic version, where they are inserted after ver. 25. All the MSS. also concur in the present arrangement. Schultens supposes that there is manifest pertinency and propriety in the present arrangement. The former specification, says he, related mainly to his *private* life, this to his more *public* conduct; and the design is to vindicate himself from the charge of injustice and crime in both respects, closing appropriately with the latter. Rosenmüller remarks that in a composition composed in an age and country so remote as this, we are not to look for or demand the observance of the same regularity which is required by the modern canons of criticism. At all events, there is no authority for changing the present arrangement of the text. The meaning of the phrase "if my land cry out against me" is, that in the cultivation of his land he had not been guilty of injustice. He had not employed those to till it who had been compelled to do it, nor had he imposed on them unreasonable burdens, nor had he defrauded them of their wages. The land had not had occasion to cry out against him to God, because fraud or injustice had been done to any in its cultivation; comp. Gen. iv. 10; Hab. ii. 11. ¶ *Or that the furrows likewise thereof complain.* Marg. *weep.* The Hebrew is, "If the furrows weep together," or "in like manner weep." This is a beautiful image. The very furrows in the field are personified as *weeping* on account of injustice which would be done them, and of the burdens which would be laid on them, if they were compelled to contribute to oppression and fraud.

39. *If I have eaten the fruits thereof.* Marg. *strength.* The *strength* of the earth is that which the earth produces or which is the result of its strength. We speak now of a "strong soil"—meaning that it is capable of *bearing* much. ¶ *Without money.* Heb. "without silver"—silver being the principal circulating medium in early times. The meaning here is, "without paying for it;" either without having paid for the land, or for the labour. ¶ *Or have caused the owners thereof.* Marg. *the soul of the owners thereof to expire,* or *breathe out.* The Hebrew is, "If I have caused the life of the owners [or lords] of it to breathe out." The meaning is, if I have appropriated to myself the land or labour of others without paying for it, so that their means of living are taken away.

40 Let thistles grow instead of wheat, and [1] cockle instead of barley. The words of Job are ended.

CHAPTER XXXII.

GENERAL ANALYSIS OF THE SPEECH OF ELIHU—CHAPS. XXXII—XXXVII.

This chapter commences the speech of Elihu, which is continued to the close of chap. xxxvii. He has not appeared before in the controversy, and his name is not mentioned as having been present, though it is evident, from the tenor of his own remarks, that he had heard what had been said. Nothing more is known of this new character than is here expressed. Whether he came with the others to condole with Job (chap. ii. 11, 12), or whether he was his personal friend, and had been with him through all his trials, or whether he was one who accidentally happened to be present at this discussion, is not intimated. The remarkable sufferings of a man who had been so prominent as Job, would undoubtedly excite considerable attention; and it is no unreasonable supposition that many persons may have been attracted by the controversy that was maintained between him and his friends. But nothing more is known of Elihu than is specified in this chapter. See Notes on ver 2. He is a young man, who had been restrained by modesty thus far from expressing his opinion, but who had listened attentively to all that had been said. An opportunity is now presented for his speaking when he could not be charged with impertinence, or with disrespect to his superiors in age, if he expressed his opinion. The three friends of Job had been completely silenced. The last speech of Bildad (chap. xxv.) had contained only a few very brief general reflections, which had nothing to do with the subject in dispute, and Zophar, whose turn would have been next, had not even attempted to reply. Eliphaz, of course—such were the notions of courtesy which prevailed in the East—would not presume to speak out of his regular turn. Job had waited for them to speak in their turn (chap. xxix. 1), and as they had not done it, he had gone on and made a full vindication of his life. He had no more which he wished to say, and so far as the original disputants were concerned, the controversy was ended.

At this stage of the argument, it was not improper for Elihu, though comparatively a youth, to speak. The reasons which he had for speaking, he himself states. They are, (1) Because Job had, as he supposed, justified himself rather than God, chap. xxxii. 2. He had indulged in severe reflections on the divine dealings; had dwelt improperly on his own integrity, and had been unwilling to confess that he was a sinner. Whatever *blame* there was, he apprehended Job was disposed to cast on his Maker; and Elihu interposes, therefore, to state *the truth* on the subject, and to vindicate the character of God. (2.) The three friends of Job had been equally to blame. They had in no measured terms condemned Job, and yet they had made no answer to what he had said, chap. xxxii. 3. They pertinaciously held to their opinion that he was an eminently wicked man; that all these judgments had come on him for his sins, and yet they had not specified his faults, nor had they replied to what he had said in self-defence. In such a state of things, this youthful bystander and observer of the controversy interposes. His mind was greatly excited. He could contain himself (ver. 19) no longer. Both parties he regarded as wrong; both as deserving rebuke; and both as ignorant of the truth in the case. He appears, therefore, not as the advocate of either, but professes to come in as a sort of arbiter, to take the place of God (chap. xxxiii. 6), and to state what was the truth. Yet he does not settle the whole controversy. So far as the book of Job may be regarded as a *poem*, the design of its composer appears to have been, to introduce Elihu partly to show the necessity of the divine interposition, and to prepare the way for the sublime introduction of God himself in the close of the book. It is God who ultimately determines the difficult controversy, and who appears to state the exact truth in the case. The introduction of Elihu contributes much to the beauty and variety of the poem, and at the same time it accords with the design of the author. The remarks of *Bouillier* on this point are worthy of attention. "The three men, driven on by a rash, and inconsiderate impulse, attacked the character of a most upright man, not only by cruel suspicions, but by skilful criminations, with little discrimination in regard to the truth. A fourth actor is introduced, superior in wis-

[1] or, *noisome weeds.*

He disclaims all injustice in the case. He had not deprived others of their land by violence or fraud, so that they had no means of subsistence.

40. *Let thistles grow;* Gen. iii. 18. Thistles are valueless; and Job is so confident of entire innocence in regard to this, that he says he would be willing, if he were guilty, to have his whole land overrun with noxious weeds. ¶ *And cockle.* Cockle is a well known herb that gets into wheat or other grain. It has a bluish flower, and small black seed, and is injurious because it tends to discolour the flour. It is not certain by any means, however, that this is intended here. The margin is, *noisome weeds.* The Hebrew word (באשה) is from באש, *Bâ'ash*, to *have a bad smell*, to *stink*, and was given to the weed here referred to on that account, comp. Isa. xxxiv. 3. The cockle however, has no unpleasant odour, and the word here probably means noxious weeds. So it is rendered by Herder and by Noyes. The Sept. has βάτος, *bramble;* the Vulg., *spina, thorn;* Prof. Lee, *prunus sylvestris*, "a bramble resembling the hawthorn;" Schultens, *labrusca, wild vine.* ¶ *The words of Job are ended.* That is, in the present speech or argument; his discussions with his friends are closed. He spoke afterwards, as recorded in the subsequent chapters, but not in controversy with them. He had vindicated his character, sustained his positions, and they had nothing to reply. The remainder of the book is occupied mainly with the speech of Elihu, and with the solemn and sublime address which God himself makes.

dom to the others, who, by a new and more cautious method, undertakes to unravel the difficulty in regard to Job. Those things were indubitable which he taught, that there was no one among men who was so perfect that he did not offend against the laws of God; that there was no one who, trusting to his own innocence, could affirm that he was not obnoxious to the divine displeasure, or that the calamities which he suffered were undeserved. Job would not have reason for complaining, if the exact truth in regard to him were known, and his affairs accurately weighed in a balance. Elihu, therefore, did not err in thus thinking, as he was not afterwards accused of fault. Yet in his own opinion or view he erred, for such was not the cause of the calamities of Job, as the beginning of his history shows. Elihu in fact did not err less than the others in his view, although he adduced a more probable conjecture, and sustained it by a true doctrine, that by this the great purpose of the author of this book might be accomplished, to wit, to show how little men can look into the secret reasons of divine Providence, in which they can with more safety acquiesce, than curiously to inquire into them." See Rosenmuller, Intro. to the chapter. Elihu professes entire impartiality. He speaks only because he feels constrained to do it, and because such sentiments have been advanced that he can no longer keep silence. He says that he will not be influenced by respect to any man's person; he will attempt to flatter no one; he will speak wholly in the fear of God. After the introduction in chap. xxxii., he reproves Job because he had claimed too much for himself, and had indulged in a spirit of complaining against God. He goes on to say, that it is not necessary for God to develop all his counsels and purposes to men; that he often speaks in visions of the night; and that the great purpose of his dealings is to take away pride from man, and to produce true humility. This he does also by the dispensations of his providence, and by the calamities with which he visits his people. Yet he says, if when man is afflicted he will be truly penitent, God will have mercy, and restore his flesh, so that it will be fresher than that of an infant. The true secret, therefore, of the divine dispensations, according to Elihu, the principle on which *he* explains all, is, that afflictions are DISCIPLINARY, or are designed to produce humility and penitence. They are not absolute proof of enormous wickedness and hypocrisy, as the friends of Job had maintained; nor could one in affliction lay claim to freedom from sin, or blame God, as he understood Job to have done, chap. xxxiii. He next reproves Job for evincing a proud spirit of scorning, and especially for having maintained that, according to the divine dealings with him, it would be no advantage to a man to be pious, and to delight himself in God. Such an opinion implied that God was severe and wrong in his dealings. To meet this, Elihu brings forward a variety of considerations to show the impropriety of remarks of this kind, and especially to prove that the Governor of the world can do nothing inconsistent with benevolence and justice. From these considerations he infers that the duty of one in the situation of Job was plain. It was, to admit the possibility that he had sinned, and to resolve that he would offend no more, chap. xxxiv. He then proceeds to consider the opinion of Job, that under the arrangements of divine Providence there could be no advantage in being righteous; that the good were subjected to so many calamities, that nothing was gained by all their efforts to be holy; and that there was no profit though a man were cleansed from sin, chap. xxxv. 3. To this Elihu replies, by showing that God is supreme; that the character of man cannot profit him; that he is governed by other considerations in his dealings than that man has a *claim* on him; and that there are great and important considerations which lead him to the course which he takes with men, and that to complain of these is proof of rebellion, chap. xxxv. Elihu then closes his address by stating (1,) the true principles of the divine administration, as he understood them, chap. xxxvi., and (2,) by saying that there is much in the divine government which is inscrutable, but that there are such evidences of greatness and wisdom in his government, there are so many things in the works of nature and in the course of events which we cannot understand, that we should submit to his superior wisdom, chap. xxxvii. See the Analyses to those chapters.

ANALYSIS OF CHAPTER XXXII.

THE chapter before us (xxxii.) is occupied mainly with a statement of the reasons which induced Elihu to speak at all. The first six verses are prose; the remainder, as well as the whole of the following chapters, consists of poetry. In ver. 1—6 an account is given of Elihu, and of his excited feelings when the three friends of Job ceased to answer him. In ver. 6 he himself speaks; he says that he was comparatively young, and that he knew that it was more appropriate that age should speak, ver 6, 7. Yet he says that he felt himself irresistibly urged to declare his views, ver. 8. Great as was the respect due to age and rank, yet even aged men were not always wise, and might err, and he was therefore emboldened to declare his sentiments, ver. 9, 10. He says that he had carefully attended to all that they had said, and that he had discovered that the three friends of Job had been perfectly silenced, ver. 11—13. It was incumbent on them, he says, to have replied to Job, rather than to have left the task to him, for the words of Job had not been directed against him, but them, ver. 14; but since they did not answer, he felt himself called upon to show his opinion, ver. 15—17. It would be a relief to him to be allowed to speak, for he was full of the subject—like fermenting wine in new bottles, ver. 18—20. He promises that his opinion shall be delivered with entire impartiality, and without respect to any man's person, and with no disposition to flatter, ver. 21, 22.

SO these three men ceased [1] to answer Job, because he *was* righteous in his own eyes.

[1] *from answering.*

CHAPTER XXXII.

1. *So these three men ceased to answer Job.* Each had had three opportunities of replying to him, though in the last series of the controversy Zophar had been silent. Now all were silent; and though they do not appear in the least to have been convinced, or to have changed their opinion, yet they found no arguments with which to sustain their views. It was this, among other things, which induced Elihu to take up the subject. ¶ *Because he was righteous in his own eyes.* Umbreit expresses the sense of this by adding, "and they could not convince him of his unrighteousness." It was not *merely* because he was righteous in his own estimation, that they ceased to answer him; it was because their arguments had no effect in convincing him, and they had nothing new to say. He seemed to be obstinately bent on maintaining his own good opinion of

2 Then was kindled the wrath of Elihu the son of Barachel the Buzite, of the kindred of Ram; against Job was his wrath kindled, because he [1] justified himself, rather than God.

[1] his soul.

himself in spite of all their reasoning, and they sat down in silence.

2. *Then was kindled the wrath.* Wrath or anger is commonly represented as kindled, or as burning. ¶ *Of Elihu.* The name *Elihu* (אליהוא) means, "God is he;" or, as the word He (הוא) is often used by way of eminence to denote the true God or JEHOVAH, the name is equivalent to saying, "God is my God," or "my God is JEHOVAH." On what account this name was given to him, is now unknown. The names which were anciently given, however, were commonly significant, and it was not unusual to incorporate the name of God in those given to men. See Notes, Isa. i. 1. This name was probably given as an expression of piety on the part of his parents. ¶ *The son of Barachel.* The name Barachel (ברכאל) means "God blesses," and was also probably given as expressive of the piety of his parents, and as furnishing in the name itself a valuable motto which the child would remember. Nothing more is known of him than the name; and the only propriety of remarking on the philology of the names arises from the fact that they seem to indicate the existence of piety, or of the knowledge of God, on the part of the ancestors of Elihu. ¶ *The Buzite.* Buz was the second son of Nahor, the brother of Abraham, Gen. xxii. 20, 21. A city of the name Buz is mentioned in Jer. xxv. 23, in connection with Dedan and Tema, cities of Arabia, and it is probable that Barachel, the father of Elihu, was of that city. If this name was given to the place after the son of Nahor, it will follow that Elihu, and consequently Job, must have lived after the time of Abraham. ¶ *Of the kindred of Ram.* Of Ram nothing is certainly known. The Chaldee renders this מן גניסת אברהם, *of the race of Abraham.* Some have supposed that the *Ram* here mentioned is the same as the ancestor of David mentioned in Ruth iv. 19, and in the genealogical table in Matt. i. 3, 4, under the name of *Aram.* Others suppose that he was of the family of Nahor, and that the name is the same as אֲרָם *Aram*, mentioned in Gen. xxii. 21. Thus, by aphæresis the Syrians are called רַמִּים, *Rammim*, (2 Chron. xxii. 6), instead of אֲרַמִּים, *Arammim*, as they are usually denominated; comp. 2 Kings viii. 29. But nothing certain is known of him who is here mentioned. It is worthy of observation that the author of the book of Job has given the genealogy of Elihu with much greater particularity than he has that of either Job or his three friends. Indeed, he has not attempted to trace their genealogy at all. Of Job he does not even mention the name of his father; of his three friends he mentions merely the place where they dwelt. Rosenmüller infers, from this circumstance, that Elihu is himself the author of the book, since, says he, it is the custom of the Turks and Persians, in their poems, to weave in, near the end of the poem, the name of the author in an artificial manner. The same view is taken by Lightfoot, *Chronica temporum et ord. Text. V. T.* A circumstance of this kind, however, is too slight an argument to determine the question of the authorship of the book. It may have been that Elihu was *less known* than either of the other speakers, and hence there was a propriety in mentioning more particularly his family. Indeed, this fact is morally certain, for he is not mentioned, as the others are, as the "friend" of Job. ¶ *Because he justified himself.* Marg. *his soul.* So the Hebrew; the word נֶפֶשׁ, *nĕphĕsh, soul*, being often used to denote one's self. ¶ *Rather than God.* Prof. Lee renders this, "justified himself with God;" and so also Umbreit, Good, and some others. And so the Vulgate renders it—*coram Deo.* The LXX. render it, ἐναντίον κυρίου—*against the Lord;* that is, rather than the Lord. The proper translation of

3 Also against his three friends
was his wrath kindled, because
they had found no answer, and *yet*
had condemned Job.
4 Now Elihu had [1] waited till
Job had spoken, because they *were*
elder [2] than he.
5 When Elihu saw that *there was*
no answer in the mouth of *these* three
men, then his wrath was kindled.
6 And Elihu the son of Barachel
the Buzite, answered and said, I
am [3] young, and ye *are* very old;
[a] wherefore I was afraid, and [4] durst
not show you mine opinion.
7 I said, Days should speak, and

1 *expected Job in words.* 2 *elder for days.* 3 *few of days.* *a* chap. 15.10. 4 *feared.*

the Hebrew (מאלהים) is undoubtedly *more than God:* and this was doubtless the idea which Elihu intended to convey. He *understood* Job as vindicating himself rather than God; as being more willing that aspersions should be cast on the character and government of God, than to confess his own sin.

3. *Because they had found no answer, and* yet *had condemned Job.* They held Job to be guilty, and yet they were unable to adduce the proof of it, and to reply to what he had said. They still maintained their *opinion,* though silenced in the *argument.* They were in that state of mind, not uncommon, in which they obstinately held on to an opinion which they could not vindicate, and believed another to be guilty, though they could not prove it.

4. *Now Elihu had waited.* Marg as in Heb., *expected Job in words.* The meaning is plain, that he had waited until all who were older than himself had spoken. ¶ *Because they* were *elder than he.* Marg. as in Heb., *elder for days.* It appears that they were *all* older than he was. We have no means of determining their respective ages, though it would seem probable that Eliphaz was the oldest of the three friends, as he uniformly spoke first.

6. *And Elihu—said, I* am *young.* Marg. *few of days.* The Hebrew is, "I am small (צעיר) of days;" that is, I am inexperienced. We have no means of ascertaining his exact age, though it is evident that there was a considerable disparity between them and him. ¶ *And ye* are *very old.* ישישים. The word used here is probably derived from the obsolete root שיש, *to be white, hoary;* and hence *to be hoary-headed,* or *aged;* comp. 2 Chron. xxxvi. 17. The whole of the discourses of the friends of Job seem to imply that they were aged men. They laid claim to great experience, and professed to have had opportunities of long observation, and it is probable that they were regarded as sages, who, by the long observation of events, had acquired the reputation of great wisdom. ¶ *Wherefore I was afraid.* He was timid, bashful, diffident. ¶ *And durst not show you mine opinion.* Marg. *feared.* He had that diffidence to which modesty prompts in the presence of the aged. He had formed his opinion as the argument proceeded, but he did not deem it proper that one so young should interfere, even when he thought he perceived that others were wrong.

7. *I said, Days should speak.* The aged ought to speak. They have had the advantage of long observation of the course of events; they are acquainted with the sentiments of past times; they may have had an opportunity of conversing with distinguished sages, and it is to them that we look up for counsel. This was eminently in accordance with the ancient Oriental views of what is right; and it is a sentiment which accords with what is obviously proper, however little it is regarded in modern times. It is one of the marks of urbanity and true politeness; of the prevalence of good breeding, morals, and piety, and of an advanced state of society, when respect is shown to the sentiments of the aged. They have had the opportunity of long observation. They have conversed much with men. They have seen the results of certain courses of conduct, and they have arrived at a period of life when they can look at the reality of things, and are uninflu-

multitude of years should teach
wisdom.
8 But *there is* a spirit [a] in man :
and the inspiration [b] of the Almighty giveth them understanding.
9 Great [c] men are not *always*
wise ; neither do the aged understand judgment.
10 Therefore I said, Hearken
to me ; I also will shew mine
opinion.
11 Behold, I waited for your
words ; I gave ear to your [1] rea-

a Pr.20.27. *b* Pr.2.6; Da.2.21. *c* Mat.11.25; 1Co.1.27. 1 *understandings.*

enced now by passion. Returning respect for the sentiments of the aged, attention to their counsels, veneration for their persons, and deference for them when they speak, would be an indication of advancement in society in modern times ; and there is scarcely any thing in which we have deteriorated from the simplicity of the early ages, or in which we fall behind the Oriental world, so much as in the want of this.

8. *But* there is *a spirit in man.* This evidently refers to a spirit imparted from above ; a spirit from the Almighty. The parallelism seems to require this, for it responds to the phrase "the inspiration of the Almighty" in the other hemistich. The Hebrew expression here also seems to require this interpretation. It is, רוח היא, *the Spirit itself ;* meaning the very Spirit that gives wisdom, or the Spirit of inspiration. He had said, in the previous verse, that it was reasonable to expect to find wisdom among the aged and the experienced. But in this he had been disappointed. He now finds that wisdom is not the attribute of rank or station, but that it is the gift of God, and therefore it may be found in a youth. All true wisdom, is the sentiment, is from above ; and where the inspiration of the Almighty is, no matter whether with the aged or the young, there is understanding. Elihu undoubtedly means to say, that though he was much younger than they were, and though, according to the common estimate in which the aged and the young were held, he might be supposed to have much less acquaintance with the subjects under consideration, yet, as all true wisdom came from above, he might be qualified to speak. The word "spirit" here, therefore, refers to the spirit which God gives ; and the passage is a proof that it was an early opinion that certain men were under the teachings of divine inspiration. The Chaldee renders it רוח נבואתא, *a spirit of prophecy.* ¶ *And the inspiration of the Almighty.* The "breathing" of the Almighty — נשמת שדי. The idea was, that God *breathed* this into man, and that this wisdom was the breath of God ; comp. Gen. ii. 7 ; John xx. 22. Sept., *πνοὴ, breath, breathing.*

9. *Great men are not* always *wise.* Though wisdom may in general be looked for in them, yet it is not universally true. Great men here denote those who are distinguished for rank, age, authority. ¶ *Neither do the aged understand judgment.* That is, they do not *always* understand it. The word *judgment* here means *right, truth.* They do not always understand what is the exact truth in regard to the divine administration. This is an apology for what he was about to say, and for the fact that one so young should speak. Of the *truth* of what he here said there could be no doubt, and hence there was a propriety that one who was young should also be allowed to express his opinion on important subjects.

11. *I gave ear to your reasons.* Marg. *understandings.* The meaning is, that he had given the most respectful attention to the views which they had expressed, implying that he had been all along present, and had listened to the debate. ¶ *Whilst ye searched out what to say.* Marg. as in Heb., *words.* It is implied here that they had bestowed much attention on what they had said. They had carefully sought out all the arguments at their command

sons, whilst ye searched out [1] what
to say.
12 Yea, I attended unto you;
and, behold, *there was* none of you
that convinced Job, *or* that answered his words:

13 Lest ye should say, [a] We
have found out wisdom; God
thrusteth him down, not man.
14 Now, he hath not [2] directed
his words against me; neither will
I answer him with your speeches.

1 *words.*

a Jer.9.23. 2 or, *ordered.*

to confute Job, and still had been unsuccessful.

12. There was *none of you that convinced Job.* There was no one to produce conviction on his mind, or rather, there was no one to *reprove him by answering him* — מוכיח עונה. They were completely silenced, and had nothing to reply to the arguments which he had advanced, and to his reflections on the divine government.

13. *Lest ye should say, We have found out wisdom.* That is, this has been permitted and ordered in such a manner that it might be manifest that the truths which are to convince him come from God and not from man. You were not permitted to refute or convince him, for if you had been you would have been lifted up with pride, and would have attributed to yourselves what belongs to God. This is in accordance with the entire drift of the book, which is to introduce the Almighty himself to settle the controversy when human wisdom failed. They could not arrogate to themselves the claim that they had found out wisdom. They had been completely silenced by Job; they had no power to drive him from his positions; they could not explain the divine dealings so as to settle the great inquiry in which they had been engaged. Elihu proposes to do it, and to do it in such a way as to show that it could be accomplished only by that wisdom which is from above. ¶ *God thrusteth him down, not man.* These are the words of Elihu. The meaning is, "God only can drive Job from his position, and show him the truth, and humble him. The wisdom of man fails. The aged, the experienced, and the wise have been unable to meet his arguments and bring him down from the positions which he has taken. That work can be done only by God himself, or by the wisdom which he only can give." Accordingly Elihu, who proposes to meet the arguments of Job, makes no appeal to experience or observation; he does not ground what he says on the maxims of sages or the results of reflection, but proposes to adduce the precepts of wisdom which God had imparted to him; chap. xxxiii. 4, 6. Other interpretations have, however, been given of this verse, but the above seems to me the most simple, and most in accordance with the scope of the passage.

14. *Now, he hath not directed* his *words against me.* Marg. *ordered.* The meaning of this expression is, "I can approach this subject in a wholly dispassionate and unprejudiced manner. I have had none of the provocations which you have felt; his harsh and severe remarks have not fallen on me as they have on you, and I can come to the subject with the utmost coolness." The object is to show that he was not irritated, and that he would be under no temptation to use words from the influence of passion or any other than those which conveyed the simple truth. He seems disposed to admit that Job had given some occasion for severe remarks, by the manner in which he had treated his friends. ¶ *Neither will I answer him with your speeches.* They also had been wrong. They had given way to passion, and had indulged in severity of language, rather than pursued a simple and calm course of argument. From all this, Elihu says he was free, and could approach the subject in the most calm and dispassionate manner. He had had no temptation to indulge in severity of language like theirs, and he would not do it.

15. *They were amazed.* These also

15 They were amazed; they answered no more; they [1] left off speaking.

16 When I had waited, (for they spake not, but stood still, *and* answered no more,)

1 *removed speeches from themselves.*

17 *I said,* I will answer also my part; I also will shew mine opinion.

18 For I am full of [2] matter; the spirit within [3] me constraineth me.

2 *words.* 3 *of my belly.*

are the words of Elihu, and are designed to express his astonishment that the three friends of Job did not answer him. He says that they were completely silenced, and he repeats this to call attention to the remarkable fact that men who began so confidently, and who still held on to their opinion, had not one word more to say. There is some reason to suppose, from the change of person here from the second to the third, that Elihu turned from them to those who were present, and called *their* attention to the fact that the friends of Job were completely silenced. This supposition, however, is not absolutely necessary, for it is not uncommon in Hebrew poetry to change from the second person to the third, especially where there is any censure or rebuke implied; comp. chap. xviii. 4. ¶ *They left off speaking.* Marg. *removed speeches from themselves.* The marginal reading accords with the Hebrew. The sense is the same as in the common version, though the Hebrew is more poetic. It is not merely that they ceased to speak, but that they put words *at a great distance* from them. They could say absolutely nothing. This fact, that they were wholly silent, furnished an ample apology for Elihu to take up the subject.

17. *I also will show mine opinion.* In this language, as in ver. 6, there is a delicate expression of modesty in the Hebrew which does not appear in our translation. It is אף־אני—*even I.* "Even one *so* young, and *so* humble as I, may be permitted to express my sentiments, when the aged and the great have nothing more to say. It will be no improper intrusion for even *me* to speak when no other one more aged and honourable desires to." In all this we may discern a degree of courtesy, and a delicate sense of propriety, which may be commended to the imitation of all, and especially to the young. In the manners of the pious men whose biography is recorded in the Bible, there is a degree of refinement, delicacy, and courtesy, in their treatment of others, such as will seldom be found even in the most elevated walks of life, and such as religion only can produce. The outward form may be obtained by the world; the living principle is found only in the heart which is imbued with love to God and man.

18. *For I am full of matter.* Marg. as in Heb. *words.* The three friends of Job had been silenced. They had not *one word* more to say. Elihu says that the reverse was true of him. He was full of *words,* and felt constrained to speak. It was not because he forced himself to do it, nor because he did it as a mere matter of duty, but he was so impressed with the subject that it would be a relief for him to give utterance to his views. ¶ *The spirit within me.* Referring, probably, to the conviction that it was the divine Spirit which urged him to speak; see Notes on ver. 8; comp. chap. xxxiii. 4. A similar constraint in regard to the necessity of speaking, when under the influence of the Holy Spirit, is expressed in Jer. xx. 9, "His word was in my heart as a burning fire shut up in my bones, and I was weary with forbearing, and I could not stay;" comp. Intro. to Isaiah § 7. (3.) The phrase "within me" is in the margin, as in Heb. *my belly*—where the belly is spoken of as the seat of the mind; see chap. xv. 2. We speak of the *head* as the seat of the intellect, and the *heart* as the seat of the affections. The Hebrews were much in the habit of representing the region of

19 Behold, my belly *is* as wine *which* hath [1] no vent; it is ready to burst like new bottles.

1 *is not opened.*

---

the heart as the seat of all mental operations.

19. *Behold, my belly* is *as wine* which *hath no vent.* Marg. as in Heb., *is not opened*—לא יפתח. The reference is to a bottle, in which there is no opening, or no vent for the fermenting wine to work itself off. It is usual to leave a small hole in barrels and casks when wine, cider, or beer is fermenting. This is necessary in order to prevent the cask from bursting. Elihu compares himself to a bottle in which new wine had been put, and where there was no vent for it, and when in consequence it was ready to burst. That *new wine* is here intended is apparent from the connection, and has been so understood by the ancient versions. So Jerome renders it, *Mustum, must,* or new wine. The LXX. ἀσκὸς γλεύκους ζέων δεδεμένος—"a bottle filled with sweet wine, fermenting, bound;" that is, which has no vent. ¶ *It is ready to burst like new bottles.* The LXX. render this, "As the rent (ἐῤῥηγώς) bellows of a smith." Why this version was adopted, it is not easy to say. The comparison would be pertinent, but the version could not be made from the present Hebrew text. It is possible that the copy of the Hebrew text which the Septuagint had may have read חרשים—*artificers,* instead of חדשים—*new,* and then the meaning would be, "as the bottles, or skins of artificers;" that is, as their bellows, which were doubtless at first merely the skins of animals. The reference of Elihu, however, is undoubtedly to skins that were used as bottles, and *new* skins are here mentioned as ready to burst, not because they were more likely to burst than old ones—for that was by no means the case—but because new and unfermented wine would naturally be placed in them, thus endangering them. Bottles in the east, it is well known, are usually made of the skins of goats; see Notes on Matth. ix. 17. The annexed cut represents the usual form of bottles in the East:

The process of manufacturing them at present is this: The skins of the goats are striped off whole except at the neck. The holes at the feet and tail are sewed up. They are first stuffed out full, and strained by driving in small billets and chips of oak wood; and then are filled with a strong infusion of oak bark for a certain time, until the hair becomes fixed, and the skin sufficiently tanned. They are sold at different prices, from fifteen up to fifty piastres. Robinson's Bibli. Research. ii. 440. Elihu, perhaps, could not have found a more striking illustration of his meaning. He could no longer restrain himself, and he gave utterance, therefore, to the views which he deemed so important. The word *belly* in this verse (בטן) is rendered by Umbreit and Noyes, *bosom.* It not improbably has this meaning and the reference is to the fact that in the East the words are uttered forth much more *ab imo pectore,* or are much more *guttural* than *with us.* The voice seems to come from the lower part of the throat, or from the bosom, in a manner which the people of Western nations find it difficult to imitate.

20 I will speak, that I may [1] be
refreshed: I will open my lips,
and answer.
21 Let me not, I pray you, accept any man's person; neither
let me give flattering titles unto
man.
22 For [a] I know not to give
flattering titles; *in so doing* my
Maker [b] would soon take me away.

1 *breathe.*

a Gal.1.10. *b* Ps.12 3,4

20. *I will speak, that I may be refreshed.* Marg. *breathe.* The meaning is, that he would then have room to breathe again; he would feel relieved.

21. *Let me not, I pray you.* This is not to be regarded as an address to them, or a prayer to God, but as an expression of his determination. It is similar to the phrase which we use when we say, "may I never do this;" implying the strongest possible purpose *not* to do it. Elihu means to say that on no account would he use partiality or flattery in what he said. ¶ *Accept any man's person.* Treat any with partiality. That is, "I will not be influenced by rank, age, wealth, or personal friendship, in what I say. I will state the truth impartially, and will deliver my sentiments with entire freedom;" see the phrase explained in the Notes on chap. xiii. 8. ¶ *Neither let me give flattering titles unto man.* The word here used (כנה—not used in Kal, but found only in Piel), means to address in a friendly and soothing manner; to speak kindly to any one, Isa. xliv. 5; xlv. 4; and then to flatter. That is, undoubtedly, its meaning here. Elihu says he did not know how to flatter any one. He meant to state the exact truth; to treat each one impartially; and not to be influenced by the rank or wealth of those whom he addressed. He meant to deal in plain and simple truth.

22. *For I know not to give flattering titles.* I do not know how to flatter. It is not in my character; it has not been my habit. ¶ In so doing. These words are not in the Hebrew, and they greatly mar the sense, and give a different idea from that which was intended by the speaker. ¶ *My Maker would soon take me away.* Or, rather, "My Maker will soon take me away." That is, "I know that I must soon be removed, and must stand before my Maker. I must give an account for all that I say. Knowing that I am to go to the realities of another state of being, I cannot flatter men. I must tell them the exact and simple truth." There could be no better preventive of flattery than this. The conviction that we are soon to appear before God, where all are on a level, and where every mask will be stripped off, and every thing appear as it is, would prevent us from ascribing to others qualities which we know they do not possess, and from giving them titles which will only exalt them in their own estimation, and hide the truth from their minds. Titles which properly belong to men, and which pertain to office, religion does not forbid us to confer—for the welfare of the community is promoted by a proper respect for the names and offices of those who rule. But no good end is answered in ascribing to men titles as *mere* matters of distinction, which serve to keep before them the idea of their own talents or importance; or which lead them to forget that they like others are soon to be "taken away," and called to give up their account in another world. The deep conviction that we are all soon to try the realities of a bed of death and of the grave, and that we are to go to a world where there is no delusion, and where the ascription of qualities to us here which do not belong to us will be of no avail, would prompt to a wish to state always the simple truth. Under that conviction, we should never so ascribe to another any quality of beauty, strength, or talent, any name or title, as to leave him for one moment under a deception about himself. If this rule were followed, what a change would it produce in the social, the political, the literary, and even the religious world!

CHAPTER XXXIII.

ANALYSIS OF THE CHAPTER.

THE discourse in this chapter is directed entirely to Job. In the following chapter Elihu addresses particularly the friends of Job. In this chapter, the main design is to convince Job that he had erred in the views which he had expressed of God, and to state the true design of affliction—which he supposes had not been understood either by him or his friends. The three friends of Job regarded it as a mere punishment—as always expressive of the divine displeasure. Job had resisted this opinion, but was not able to state *why* good men are afflicted. Sometimes he seemed to suppose that it must be resolved into mere sovereignty; sometimes he had indulged in language of severity in regard to God; and sometimes he held that God would yet come forth and vindicate the afflicted, and appear as the friend of his people. Elihu interposes and says that neither understood the true object of affliction. It was to accomplish what nothing else would do; to produce effects on the mind and life which could not be reached in any other way; and if the afflicted would turn from their sins, God would be still merciful to them. In stating these views, Elihu dwells on the following points:

I. He addresses himself to Job, and urges reasons why he should listen to what he had to say, ver. 1—7. He says that he would speak in uprightness and truth; that the Spirit of God had taught him, and that he was in God's stead; and that as Job had often wished that he might be permitted to bring his cause before God, he now had the opportunity, and in such a way that he would not be overawed by the divine majesty, as if he had visibly appeared. If he desired to vindicate himself, he had now the opportunity.

II. He refers, briefly, to the sentiments which Job had advanced, and particularly to his severe reflections on the divine dealings, as if God had been unjust and severe, ver. 8—11. Job, he says, had maintained his own perfect purity; he had denied that he deserved what had come upon him; he had charged God with "finding occasions" against him, and with having pleasure in bringing trials on him without any sufficient cause; and had said that God regarded him as an enemy, and narrowly watched all his paths.

III. Elihu proposes, therefore, to meet all this, and show Job that his opinion was unjust, and to state to him the real design of his affliction, to suggest some principle which would explain it all without these injurious reflections on the character of God. This occupies the remainder of the chapter, ver. 12—33 In doing this, he adverts to the following points:

(1.) He says that Job could not be vindicated in what he had said; that God was greater than man; and that even *if* man could not see the reason of his doings he ought to acquiesce in them, since God did not give account of any of his matters, ver. 12, 13.

(2.) He observes that God speaks in various ways to men; that he often addresses them by direct revelation in the visions of the night; and that his *object* is to benefit man—to withdraw him from an evil purpose, and to make him humble, ver. 14—17.

(3.) In the prosecution of the same object, and with a view to the same result, he often visits men with affliction. His object is to keep back man from the pit, and he therefore chastens him so that his life abhors bread, so that his flesh pines away, and so that he draws near to the grave, ver. 18—22.

(4.) If this is effectual—if man receives it in a proper manner, and is disposed to come back to God, he is willing to receive and forgive him. *Here is the real clew to the design of affliction.* It is to bring the offender to repentance, and to save his soul. If the afflicted man has some one to explain the design of trial, then God will be gracious; his flesh will be restored fresher than an infant's, and if he confesses his sin, God will be merciful to him, and save him, ver. 23—28. All these things, he says, are done by God to accomplish a single purpose—to bring back man from his wanderings, and to restore him to the favour of Heaven, ver. 29, 30.

(5.) In the conclusion of his address to Job, Elihu calls on him to reply to this, if he had any answer to make. He professes a desire to vindicate Job if he could, but says that if he had nothing to say in reply, he would teach him what true wisdom was, ver. 31—33.

WHEREFORE, Job, I pray thee, hear my speeches, and hearken to all my words.
2 Behold, now I have opened
my mouth, my tongue hath spoken
in my [1] mouth.
3 My words [a] *shall be of* the

1 *palate.* a Pr.8.6-9.

CHAPTER XXXIII.

1. *Wherefore, Job, I pray thee.* In the next chapter he addresses the three friends of Job. This is addressed particularly to him. ¶ *My speeches.* Heb. *my words*—מִלָּי. This is the usual word in the Aramæn languages to express a saying or discourse, though in Hebrew it is only a poetic form. The meaning is, not that he would address separate *speeches*, or distinct *discourses*, to Job, but that he called on him to attend to what he had to say.

2. *My tongue hath spoken in my mouth.* Marg. *palate.* The meaning is, that since he had ventured to speak, and had actually commenced, he would utter only that which was worthy to be heard. This is properly the commencement of his argument, for all that he had before said was merely an introduction. The word *palate*—"in my palate" (בְחִכִּי) is here used because of the importance of that organ in the act of speaking. Perhaps also, there may be reference to the fact that the Hebrews made much more use of the lower organs of enunciation—the palate, and the throat, than we do, and much less use of the teeth and lips. Hence their language was strongly guttural.

3. *My words* shall be of *the uprightness of my heart.* I will speak in sincerity. I will utter nothing that shall be hollow and hypocritical. What I speak shall be the real suggestion of my heart—what I feel and know to be true. Perhaps Elihu was the more

uprightness of my heart; and my lips shall utter knowledge [a] clearly.

4 The Spirit of God hath made me, and the breath of the Almighty hath given me life.

a Ti.2.7,8.

5 If thou canst answer me, set *thy words* in order before me; stand up;

6 Behold I *am* according to thy
1 wish in [b] God's stead; I also am
2 formed out of the clay.

1 *mouth.* *b* chap.31.35. 2 *cut.*

anxious to make this point entirely clear, because the three friends of Job might be supposed to have laid themselves open to the suspicion that they were influenced by passion or prejudice; that they had maintained their opinions from mere obstinacy and not from conviction; and that they had been sometimes disposed to cavil. Elihu claims that all that *he* was about to say would be entirely sincere. ¶ *Shall utter knowledge clearly.* Shall state things just as they are, and give the true solution of the difficulties which have been felt in regard to the divine dealings. His object is to guard himself wholly from the suspicion of partiality.

4. *The Spirit of God hath made me;* see Notes, chap. xxxii. 8. There is an evident allusion in this verse to the mode in which man was created, when God breathed into him the breath of life and he became a living being; Gen. ii. 7. But it is not quite clear why Elihu adverts here to the fact that God had made him, or what is the bearing of this fact on what he proposed to say. The most probable supposition is, that he means to state that he is, like Job, a man; that both were formed in the same way—from the same breathing of the Almighty, and from the same clay (ver. 6); and that although he had undertaken to speak to Job in God's stead (ver. 6), yet Job had no occasion to fear that he would be overawed and confounded by the Divine Majesty. He had dreaded that, if he should be permitted to bring his case before him (Notes, ver. 7), but Elihu says that now he would have no such thing to apprehend. Though it would be in fact the same thing as carrying the matter before God—since he came in his name, and meant to state the true principles of his government, yet Job would be also really conducting the cause *with a man* like himself, and might, unawed, enter with the utmost freedom into the statement of his views.

5. *If thou canst answer me.* The meaning of this verse is this: "The controversy between you and me, if you choose to reply, shall be conducted in the most equitable manner, and on the most equal terms. I will not attempt, as your three friends have done, to overwhelm you with reproaches; nor will I attempt to overawe you as God would do, so that you could not reply. I am a man like yourself, and desire that if any thing *can* be said against what I have to advance, it should be offered with the utmost fairness and freedom." ¶ *Stand up.* That is, "maintain your position, unless you are convinced by my arguments. I wish to carry nothing by mere authority or power."

6. *Behold, I am according to thy wish in God's stead.* Marg. as in Heb. *mouth.* The *mouth* is that by which we express our desires, and the word here is equivalent to *wish.* Some have, however, rendered this differently. Umbreit translates it, ich bin, wie du, von Gott—*I am, as thou art, from God.* So Noyes, "I, like thee, am a creature of God." Wemyss, "I am thine equal in the sight of God." Coverdale, "Behold, before God am I even as thou, for I am fashioned and made even of the same mould." The Vulgate renders it, "Behold God made me as he made thee; and of the same clay am I formed." So the LXX, "From clay am I formed as well as thou, and we are formed from the same." This interpretation seems to be demanded also by the parallelism, where he says that he was made of the same clay with Job; that is, that he was a man like him. Still, it seems to me, that the fair and obvious meaning of the Hebrew is that which is expressed in our common version. The Hebrew is, לאל הן־אני כפיך—"lo, I am, according to

7 Behold, my [a] terror shall not make thee afraid, neither shall my hand be heavy upon thee.

[a] chap. 9.34.

thy mouth [word, or wish] for God;" that is, I am in his place; I speak in his name; I am so commissioned by him that you may regard yourself as in fact speaking to him when you address his ambassador. This will also accord with what is said in ver. 7, and with what Job had so earnestly desired, that he might be allowed to bring his cause directly before God; see Notes, chap. xiii. 3. ¶ *I also am formed out of the clay.* Marg. *cut.* The figure is taken from the act of the potter, who *cuts off* a portion of clay which he moulds into a vessel, and there is manifest allusion here to the statement in Genesis, that God made man of the dust of the ground. The meaning in this connection is, "Though I am in the place of God, and speak in his name, yet I am also a man, made of the same frail material as yourself. In me, therefore, there is nothing to overawe or confound you as there would be if God spake himself."

7. *Behold my terror shall not make thee afraid.* Job had earnestly desired to carry his cause directly before God, but he had expressed the apprehension that he would overawe him by his majesty, so that he would not be able to manage his plea with the calmness and self-possession which were desirable. He had, therefore, expressed it as his earnest wish, that if he were so permitted, God would not take *advantage* of his majesty and power to confound him; see Notes chap. xiii. 21. Elihu now says, that the wish of Job in this could be amply gratified. Though he spake in the name of God, and it might be considered that the case was fairly carried before him, yet he was also *a man.* He was the fellow, the equal with Job. He was made of the same clay, and he could not overawe him as the Almighty himself might do. There would be, therefore, in his case all the advantage of carrying the cause directly up to God, and yet none of the disadvantage which Job apprehended, and which must ensue when a mere man undertook to manage his own cause with the Almighty. ¶ *Neither shall my hand be heavy upon thee.* Alluding, evidently, to what Job had said, chap. xiii. 21, that the hand of God was heavy upon him, so that he could not conduct his cause in such a manner as to do justice to himself. He had asked, therefore (see Notes on that place), as a special favour, if he was permitted to carry his cause before God, that his hand would be so far lightened that he could be able to state his arguments with the force which they required. Elihu says now that that wish could be gratified. Though he was in the place of God, yet he was a man, and his hand would not be upon him to crush him down so that he could not do justice to himself. The noun rendered *hand* (אֶכֶף) does not elsewhere occur. The verb אָכַף occurs once in Prov. xvi. 26, where it is rendered "*craveth*"—"He that laboureth, laboureth for himself; for his mouth *craveth* it of him"—where the margin is *boweth unto.* The word in Arabic means to load a beast of burden; to bend, to make to bow under a load; and then to impel, to urge on; and hence it means, "his mouth, *i. e. hunger,* impels, or urges him on to labour." In like manner the meaning of the word here (אכף) *may* be a load or burden, meaning "my load, i. e. my weight, dignity, authority, shall not be burdensome or oppressive to you." But the parallel place in chap. xiii. 21, is "hand," and that meaning seems to be required here. Kimchi supposes it is the same as כַּף—*hand,* and the LXX. have so rendered it, ἡ χείρ μου. In the view of the speech of Elihu thus far, we cannot but remark that there is much that is peculiar, and especially that he lays decided claim to inspiration. Though speaking for God, yet he was in human nature, and Job might speak to him as a friend, unawed and unterrified by any dread of overwhelming majesty and power. On what grounds

8 Surely thou hast spoken in
mine hearing, [1] and I have heard
the voice of *thy* words, *saying*,
9 I am clean[a] without transgression, I *am* innocent; neither *is*
there iniquity in me.
10 Behold, he findeth occasions
against me, he [b] counteth me for
his enemy;

1 *ears*. *a* chap.10.7;16.17;23.11,12;27 5,6;29.14. *b* chap.19.11.

Elihu based these high pretensions does not appear, and his claim to them is the more remarkable from his youth. It does not require the aid of a very lively imagination to fancy a resemblance between him and the Lord Jesus—the great mediator between God and man—and were that mode of interpretation which delights to find types and figures every where a mode that could be vindicated, there is no character in the Old Testament that would more obviously suggest that of the Redeemer than the character of Elihu. His comparative youth, his modesty, his humility, would suggest it. The fact that he comes in to utter his sentiments where age and wisdom had failed to suggest the truth, and when pretending sages were confounded and silenced, would suggest it. The fact that he claims to be in the place of God, and that a cause might be managed before him *as if* it were before God, and yet that he was a man like others, and that no advantage would be taken to overawe by mere majesty and power, are all circumstances that would constitute a strong and vivid resemblance. But I see no *evidence* that this was the design of the introduction of the character of Elihu, and interesting as the comparison might be, and desirable as it may seem that the book of Job should be found to contain some reference to the great work of mediation, yet the just and stern laws of interpretation exclude such a reference in the absence of proof, and do not allow us to luxuriate in the conceptions of fancy, however pious the reflections might be, or to search for typical characters where the Spirit of inspiration has not revealed them as such, however interesting or edifying might be the contemplation.

8. *Surely thou hast spoken in mine hearing*. Marg. as in Heb. *ears*. This shows that Elihu had been present during the debate, and had attentively listened to what had been said. He now takes up the main point on which he supposed that Job had erred—the attempt to justify himself. He professes to adduce the very words which he had used, and disclaims all design of judging from mere hearsay.

9. *I am clean*. I am pure and holy. ¶ *Without transgression*. Job had not used these very expressions, nor had he intended to maintain that he was absolutely free from sin; see chap. ix. 20. He had maintained that he was not chargeable with the transgressions of which his three friends maintained that he was guilty, and in doing that he had used strong language, and language which even *seemed* to imply that he was without transgression; see chap. ix. 30; x. 7; xiii. 23; xvi. 17. ¶ *I am innocent*. The word here used (חַף) is from the verb חָפַף—*to cover, to protect;* and also, as a secondary meaning, from the Arabic, to rub, to wipe off; to wash away; to lave. Hence it denotes that which is rubbed clean, washed, pure – and then innocent. The word occurs only in this place. It is not the exact language which Job had used, and there seems to be some injustice done him in saying that he had employed such language. Elihu means, doubtless, that he had used language which *implied* this, or which was equivalent to it.

10. *Behold, he findeth occasions against me*. That is, God. This is not exactly the language of Job, though much that he had said had seemed to imply this. The idea is, that God sought opportunity to oppose him; that he was desirous to find in him some ground or reason for punishing him; that he wished to be hostile to him, and was narrowly on the watch to find an opportunity which would justify his bringing calamity upon him. The word rendered *occasions*—תְּנוּאוֹת, is

11 He [a] putteth my feet in
the stocks, he marketh [b] all my
paths.
12 Behold, *in* this thou art not
just: I will answer thee, that God
is greater than man.
13 Why dost thou strive [c]
against him? for he [1] giveth not
account [d] of any of his matters.

a chap.13 27. *b* Ps. clxxxix.3. *c* Isa.45.9. 1 *answereth not.* *d* Da.4.35.

from נוא, in Hiphil הניא—to refuse, decline; to hinder, restrain, Num. xxx. 6, 9, 12; and hence the noun means, *a holding back, a withdrawal, an alienation;* and hence the idea is, that God *sought* to be *alienated* from Job. The Vulgate renders it, "He seeks *complaints* (*querales*) against me." The LXX. μέμψιν—accusation. Umbreit, *Feindshaft, enmity.* So Gesenius and Noyes. ¶ *He counteth me for his enemy.* This is language which Job had used; see chap. xix. 11.

11. *He putteth my feet in the stocks.* This also is language which Job had used; see chap. xiii. 27. ¶ *He marketh all my paths*; in chap. xiii. 27, "Thou lookest narrowly unto all my paths;" see Notes on that verse.

12. *Behold,* in *this thou art not just.* In this view of God, and in these reflections on his character and government. Such language in regard to the Deity cannot be vindicated; such views cannot be right. It cannot be that he wishes to be the foe of man; that he watches with a jealous eye every movement with a view to find something that will justify him in bringing heavy calamities upon his creatures, or that he sets himself as a spy upon the way in which man goes, in order to find out something that shall make it proper for him to treat him as an enemy. It cannot be denied that Job *had* indulged in language making substantially such representations of God, and that he had thus given occasion for the reproof of Elihu. It can as little be denied that such thoughts frequently pass through the minds of the afflicted, though they do not express them in words, nor is it less doubtful that they should be at once banished from the soul. *They cannot be true.* It CANNOT be that God thus regards and treats his creatures; that he *wishes* to find "occasion" in them to make it proper for him to bring calamity upon them, or that he desires to regard them as his foes. ¶ *I will answer thee.* That is, I will show that this view is unjust." This he does in the subsequent verses by stating what he supposes to be the real design of afflictions, and by showing that God in these trials had a good and benevolent object. ¶ *That*—כי. Rather, *because,* or *for.* The object is not to show *that* God was greater than man—for that could not be a matter of information, but to show that *because* he was far above man he had great and elevated objects in his dealings with him, and man should submit to him without a murmur. ¶ *God is greater than man.* The meaning of this is, that man should suppose that God has good reasons for all that he does, and that he might not be qualified to understand the reason of his doings. He should therefore acquiesce in his arrangements, and not call in question the equity of the divine dealings. In all our trials it is well to remember that *God is greater* than we are. He knows what is best; and though we may not be able to see the reason of his doings, yet it becomes us to acquiesce in his superior wisdom.

13. *Why dost thou strive against him?* By refusing to submit to him, and by calling in question his wisdom and goodness. ¶ *For he giveth not account of any of his matters.* Marg. as in Heb. *answereth not.* The idea is, that it is as useless as it is improper to contend with God. He does his own pleasure, and deals with man as he deems best and right. The reason of his doings he does not state, nor has man any power to extort from him a statement of the causes why he afflicts us. This is still true. The *reason* of his doings he does not often make known to the afflicted, and it is impossible to know *now* the causes why he has brought on us the calamity with which we are visited. The

14 For God speaketh once, yea, twice, *yet man* perceiveth it not.
15 In a dream, in a vision of the night, when deep sleep falleth upon men, in slumberings upon the bed,

general reasons why men are afflicted may be better known now than they were in the time of Elihu, for successive revelations have thrown much light on that subject. But when he comes and afflicts us as individuals; when he takes away a beloved child; when he cuts down the young, the vigorous, the useful, and the pious, it is often impossible to understand *why* he has done it. All that we can do then is to SUBMIT to his sovereign will, and to believe that though we cannot see the reasons why he has done it, yet that does not prove that there *are* no reasons, or that we may *never* be permitted to understand them. We are required to submit to *his will*, not *to our own reason;* to acquiesce because *he does it*, not because *we see it to be right.* If we always understood the reasons why he afflicts us, our resignation would be not *to the will of God*, but to our own knowledge of what is right; and God, therefore, often passes before us in clouds and thick darkness to see whether we have sufficient confidence in him to believe that he does right, even when we cannot see or understand the reason of his doings. So a child reposes the highest confidence in a parent, when he believes that the parent will do right, though he cannot understand why he does it, and the parent does not choose to let him know. May not a father see reasons for what he does which a child could not understand, or which it might be proper for him to withhold from him?

14. *For God speaketh once.* The object of what is here said is, to show the reason why God brings affliction upon men, or to explain the principles of his government which Elihu supposed had been sadly misunderstood by Job and his friends. The reason why he brings affliction, Elihu says, is because all other means of reclaiming and restraining men fail. He communicates his will to them; he speaks to them again and again in dreams and visions; he warns them of the error of their course (ver. 14—17), and when this is all ineffectual he brings upon them affliction. He lays them upon their bed where they must reflect, and where there is hope that they may be reclaimed and reformed, ver. 18—28. ¶ *Yea, twice.* He does not merely admonish him once. He repeats the admonition when man refuses to hear him the first time, and takes all the methods which he can by admonition and warning to withdraw him from his wicked purpose, and to keep him from ruin. ¶ Yet man *perceiveth it not.* Or, rather, "Although he does not perceive it or attend to it." Though the sinner is regardless of the admonition, yet still God repeats it, and endeavours to save him from the commission of the crimes which would lead him to ruin. This is designed to show the patience and forbearance of God, and how many means he takes to save the sinner from ruin. Of the *truth* of what Elihu here says, there can be no difference of opinion. It is one of the great principles of the divine administration that the sinner is often warned, though he heeds it not; and that God sends repeated admonitions even when men will not regard them, but are bent on their own ruin.

15. *In a dream.* This was one of the methods by which the will of God was made known in the early periods of the world; see Notes on chap. iv. 12—17. And for a fuller account of this method of communicating the divine will, see Introduction to Isaiah, § 7. (2.) ¶ *In a vision of the night*, Notes, chap. iv. 13; comp. Intro. to Isa. § 7. (4.) ¶ *When deep sleep falleth upon men.* This may be designed to intimate more distinctly that it was from God. It was not the effect of disturbed and broken rest; not such fancies as come into the mind between sleeping and waking, but the visitations of the divine Spirit in the profoundest repose of the night. The word rendered "deep sleep" (תרדמה) is one that

16 Then he [1] openeth the ears of men, and sealeth their instruction.

1 *revealeth*, or *uncovereth*.

17 That he may withdraw [a] man *from his* [2] purpose, and hide pride [b] from man.

a chap 17.11. 2 *work*. *b* Isa.23.9.

denotes the most profound repose. It is not merely sleep, but it is sleep of the soundest kind—that kind when we do not usually dream; see Notes on chap. iv. 13. The Chaldee has here rendered it correctly, עמיקתא שינתא—*sleep that is deep*. The LXX. render it, δεινὸς φόβος—*dread horror*. The Syriac renders this verse, "Not by the lips does he teach; by dreams and visions of the night," &c. ¶ *In slumberings upon the bed.* The word rendered *slumberings* (תנומות) means a light sleep, as contradistinguished from very profound repose. Our word *slumber* conveys the exact idea. The meaning of the whole is, that God speaks to men when their senses are locked in repose—alike in the profound sleep when they do not ordinarily dream, and in the gentle and light slumbers when the sleep is easily broken. In what way, however, they were to distinguish such communications from ordinary dreams, we have no information. It is scarcely necessary to remark that what is here and elsewhere said in the Scriptures about dreams, is no warrant for putting any confidence in them now as if they were revelations from heaven.

16. *Then he openeth the ears of men.* Marg. as in Heb. *revealeth*, or *uncovereth*. The idea is, that he then reveals to the ear of man important admonitions or counsels. He communicates valuable truth. We are not to understand this as saying that the sleeper actually *hears* God speak, but as the ear is the organ of hearing, it is employed here to denote that God then communicates his will to men. In what way he had access to the souls of men by dreams, it is impossible to explain. ¶ *And sealeth their instruction.* Literally, "In their admonition he seals;" or he affixes a seal. The idea is, that he makes the admonition or instruction as secure as if a seal were affixed to it. A *seal* ratified or confirmed a contract, a will, or a deed, and the sense here is, that the communications of God to the soul were as firm as if they had been ratified in like manner. Or possibly it may mean, that the warnings of God were communicated to the soul like a sealed letter or message unknown to any other; that is, were made privately to the individual himself in the slumbers of the night. Others have understood the word rendered *instruction*, as denoting *castigation*, or *punishment*, and according to that explanation the meaning would be, that he announces to them certain punishment if they continued in sin; he made it as certain to them as if it were ratified by a *seal*. So Rosenmüller and Mercer. Schultens supposes it to be equivalent to *inspires* them, or communicates instruction by inspiration as if it were confirmed and ratified by a seal. He observes that the Arabic word *hhatham* is often used in the Koran, meaning *to inspire*. The LXX. render it, αὐτοὺς ἐξεφόβησεν—"he terrifies them"—where they evidently read יְחִתֵּם instead of יַחְתֹּם. The sense is, that God communicates warnings to men on their beds, in a manner as solemn and impressive as if it were ratified with a seal, and made as secure as possible.

17. *That he may withdraw man* from his *purpose*. Marg. *work*. The sense is plain. God designs to warn him of the consequences of executing a plan of iniquity. He alarms him by showing him that his course will lead to punishment, and by representing to him in the night visions, the dreadful woes of the future world into which he is about to plunge. The *object* is to deter him from committing the deed of guilt which he had contemplated, and to turn him to the paths of righteousness. Is it unreasonable to suppose that the same thing *may* occur now, and that God *may* have a purpose in the dreams

18 He keepeth back his soul from the pit, and his life from [1] perishing by the sword.

[1] *passing by.*

19 He [a] is chastened also with pain upon his bed, and the multitude of his bones with strong *pain,*

[a] Ps.107.17.

which often visit the man who has formed a plan of iniquity, or who is living a life of sin? It cannot be doubted that such men often have alarming dreams; that these dreams are such as are fitted to deter them from the commission of their contemplated wickedness; and that in fact they not unfrequently do it. What shall hinder us from supposing that God *intends* that the workings of the mind when the senses are locked in repose, shall be the means of alarming the guilty, and of leading them to reflection? Why should not *mind* thus be its own admonisher, and be made the instrument of restraining the guilty then, as really as by its sober reasonings and reflections when awake? Many a wicked man has been checked in a career of wickedness by a frightful dream; and not a few have been brought to a degree of reflection which has resulted in sound conversion by the alarm caused on the mind by having the consequences of a career of wickedness traced out in the visions of the night. The case of Colonel Gardiner cannot be forgotten—though in that instance it was rather "a vision of the night" than a dream. He was meditating an act of wickedness, and was alone in his room awaiting the appointed hour. In the silence of the night, and in the solitude of his room, he *seemed* to see the Saviour on the cross. This view, however, it may be accounted for, restrained him from the contemplated act of wickedness, and he became an eminently pious man; see Doddridge's Life of Col. Gardiner. The mind, with all its faculties, is under the control of God, and no one can demonstrate that he does not make its actings, even in the wanderings of a dream, the designed means of checking the sinner, and of saving the soul. ¶ *And hide pride from man.* Probably the particular thing which Elihu here referred to, was pride and arrogance *towards God;* or an insolent bearing towards him, and a reliance on one's own merits. This was the particular thing in Job which Elihu seems to have thought required animadversion, and probably he meant to intimate that all men had such communications from God by dreams as to save them from such arrogance.

18. *He keepeth back his soul from the pit.* The word *soul* in the Hebrew is often equivalent to *self,* and the idea is, that he keeps *the man* from the pit in this manner. The *object* of these warnings is to keep him from rushing on to his own destruction. The word rendered *pit*—שחת, properly means *a pit,* or *pitfall,* in which traps are laid for wild animals; Ps. vii. 15; ix. 15; then a cistern that is miry; Job ix. 31; a prison, Isa. li. 14; then the grave, or sepulchre, as being often a cavern; Job xvii. 13; Ps. xxx. 9; see ver. 28, 30, of this chapter. It evidently means here *the grave,* and the sense is, that God thus warns men against pursuing a course of conduct which would lead them to destruction, or would speedily terminate their lives. ¶ *And his life from perishing by the sword.* Marg. *passing by.* The meaning of the Hebrew may be, "to keep his life from *passing away* by the sword;" as if the sword were the means by which the life or soul *passed* from the body. The word rendered *sword* here—שׁלח is from שׁלח—*to send, cast, hurl,* and the reference is rather to something *sent,* as of an arrow, dart, javelin, than to a sword. The sense is not materially varied, and the idea referred to is that of a violent death. The meaning is, that God by these warnings would keep a man from such a course of life as would lead to a death by violence—either by punishment for his crime, or by being cut off in war.

19. *He is chastened also with pain.* As another means of checking and

20 So that his life abhorreth
bread, and his soul [1] dainty meat.
21 His flesh is consumed away,
that it cannot be seen; and
his bones *that* were not seen, stick
out.
22 Yea, his soul draweth near
unto the grave, and his life to the
destroyers.

[1] *meat of desire.*

restraining him from the commission of sin. When the warnings of the night fail, and when he is bent on a life of sin, then God lays him on a bed of pain, and he is brought to reflection there. There he has an opportunity to think of his life, and of all the consequences which must follow from a career of iniquity. This involves the main inquiry before the disputants. It was, why men were afflicted. The three friends of Job had said that it was a full proof of wickedness, and that when the professedly pious were afflicted it was demonstrative of insincerity and hypocrisy. Job had called this position in question, and proved that it could not be so, but still was at a loss *why* it was. Elihu now says, that affliction is a part of *a disciplinary government;* that it is one of the means which God adopts, when warnings are ineffectual, to restrain men and to bring them to reflection and repentance. This appears to have been a view which was almost entirely new to them. ¶ *And the multitude of his bones with strong* pain. The *bones,* as has before been remarked, it was supposed might be the seat of the acutest pain; see Notes on chap. xxx. 17; comp. chap. xx. 11; vii. 15; xxx. 30. The meaning here is, that the frame was racked with intense suffering in order to admonish men of sin, to save them from plunging into deeper transgression, and to bring them to repentance.

20. *So that his life abhorreth bread.* It is a common effect of sickness to take away the appetite. Elihu here regards it as a part of the wholesome discipline of the sufferer. He has no relish for the comforts of life. ¶ *And his soul dainty meat.* Marg. *meat of desire.* The Hebrew is, "food of desire." The word rendered *meat* (מאכל) does not denote animal food only, but any kind of food. So the old English word *meat* was used. The idea is, that the sick man loathes the most delicate food. It is a part of his discipline that the pleasure which he had in the days of his health is now taken away.

21. *His flesh is consumed away, that it cannot be seen.* He wastes away. His flesh, once vigorous, beautiful, and fair, now disappears. This is not a mere description of the nature of his sickness, but it is a description of the disciplinary arrangements of God. It is an important part of his affliction, as a part of the discipline, that his flesh vanishes, and that his appearance is so changed that he becomes repulsive to the view. ¶ *And his bones* that *were not seen, stick out.* His bones were before invisible. They were carefully concealed by the rounded muscle, and by the fat which filled up the interstices, so that they were not offensive to the view. But now the protuberances of his bones can be seen, for God has reduced him to the condition of a skeleton. This is one of the common effects of disease, and this shows the strength of the discipline which God contemplates. The parts of the human frame which in health are carefully hid from the view, as being unsightly, become now prominent, and can be hidden no longer. *One* design is to humble us; to take away the pride which delighted in the round and polished limb, the rose on the cheek, the ruby lip, and the smooth forehead; and to show us what we shall soon be in the grave.

22. *Yea, his soul draweth near unto the grave.* That is, he himself does, for the word *soul* is often used to denote self. ¶ *And his life to the destroyers*—לַמְמִתִים. Literally, "to those causing death." The interpretation commonly given of this is, "the angels of death" who were supposed to come to close human life; comp. 2 Sam. xxiv. 16, 17. But it

23 If there be a messenger with him, an interpreter, one among a thousand, to show unto man his uprightness;

probably refers to diseases and pangs as having power to terminate life, and being the cause of the close of life. The meaning is, that the afflicted man comes very near to those acute sufferings which terminate life, and which by personification are here represented as the authors of death.

23. *If there be a messenger with him.* This part of the speech of Elihu has given rise to scarcely less diversity of opinion, and to scarcely less discussion, than the celebrated passage in chap. xix. 25—27. Almost every interpreter has had a peculiar view of its meaning, and of course it is very difficult, if not impossible, to determine its true sense. Before the opinions which have been entertained are specified, and an attempt made to determine the true sense of the passage, it may be of interest to see how it is presented in the ancient versions, and what light they throw on it. The Vulgate renders it, "If there is for him an angel speaking, one of thousands, that he may announce the righteousness of the man; he will pity him, and say, Deliver him that he descends not into corruption: I have found him in whom I will be propitious to him"—*inveni in quo ei propitior.* The Septuagint translators render it, "If there be a thousand angels of death (*ἄγγελοι θανατηφόροι*), not one of them can [mortally] wound him (*τρώσῃ αὐτόν*). If he determine in his heart to turn to the Lord, when he shall have shown man his charge against him, and shown his folly, he will support him that he may not fall to death, and renew his body, like plastering on a wall (*ὥσπερ ἀλοιφὴν ἐπὶ τοίχου*), and will fill his bones with marrow, and make his flesh soft like an infant." The Chaldee renders it, "If there is merit (זכותא) in him, an angel is prepared, a comforter (פרקליטא, *Paraclete,*) [Gr. *παράκλητος*], one among a thousand accusers (קטיגורא, [Gr. *κατήγορός*], that he may announce to man his rectitude. And he spares him, and says, Redeem him, that he may not descend to corruption; I have found a ransom." Schultens has divided the opinions which have been entertained of the passage into three classes. They are, I. The opinions of those who suppose that by the messenger, or angel, here, there is reference to a *man.* Of those who hold this opinion, he enumerates no less than *seven* classes. They are such as these: (1) those who hold that the man referred to is some distinguished instructor sent to the sick to teach them the will of God, an opinion held by Munster and Isidorus; (2) those who refer it to a prophet, as Junius et Tremillius; (3) Codurcus supposes that there is reference to the case of Abimelech, who was made sick on account of Sarah, and that the man referred to was a prophet, who announced to him that God was righteous; Gen. xx. The 4th and 5th cases slightly vary from these specified. (6) Those who hold that Elihu referred to himself as being the angel, or messenger, that God had sent to make known to Job the truth in regard to the divine government, and the reason why he afflicts men. Of this opinion was Gusset, and we may add that this is the opinion of Umbreit. (7) Those who suppose that some faithful servant of God is intended, without specifying who, who comes to the sick and afflicted, and announces to them the reason of the divine dispensations. II. The second class of opinions is, that *an angel* is referred to here, and that the meaning is, that God employs angelic beings to communicate his will to men, and especially to the afflicted—to make known to them the reason why they are afflicted, and the assurance that he is willing to show mercy to them if they will repent. Of those who hold this, Schultens mentions (1) the LXX, who render it, "the angels of death;" (2) the Chaldee Paraphrast, who understands it of the "comforting angel"—the Paraclete; (3) the opinion of Mercer, who supposes it to refer to

a good angel, who, though there be a thousand of a contrary description, if he announces the will of God, and shows the true reason why he afflicts men, may be the means of reclaiming them ; (4) the opinion of Clerc, who regards it as a mere *hypothesis* of Elihu, saying that *on the supposition* that an angel would thus visit men, they might be reclaimed ; (5) the opinion of Grotius, who supposes it refers to angels regarded as mediators, who perform their office of mediation in two ways—by admonishing men, and by praying for them. This was also the opinion of Maimonides. (6) The opinion of Jerome, who supposes that it refers to the angel standing in the presence of God, and who is employed by him in admonishing and correcting mankind. III. The third class of opinions consists of those who refer it to the Messiah. Of those who have held this opinion, the following may be mentioned: Cocceius — *of course ;* Calovius, Schmidius, and Augustine. Amidst this diversity of sentiment, it is difficult, if not impossible, to determine the real meaning of the passage. The *general* sentiment is indeed plain. It is, that God visits men with affliction in order to restrain them from sin, and to correct them when they have erred. It is not from hostility to them ; not from mere justice ; not because he delights in their sufferings ; and not because he wishes to cut them off. They may suffer much and long, as Job had done, without knowing the true reason why it was done. They may form erroneous views of the design of the divine administration, and suppose that God is severe and harsh. But *if* there shall come a messenger, in such circumstances, who shall explain the reason of the divine dealings, and show to the sufferer on what principles God inflicts pain ; and if the sufferer shall hear the message, and acquiesce in the divine dealings, *then* God would be willing to be merciful. He would say that he was satisfied ; the object of the affliction was accomplished, and he would restore the afflicted to health, and bestow upon him the most satisfactory evidences of his own favour. An examination of the particular words and phrases occurring in the passage, may elucidate more clearly this general idea, and lead us to its true interpretation. The word translated *messenger* (מַלְאָךְ, *mălâk*), is that which is usually employed to denote an *angel.* It means, properly, *one who is sent,* from לָאַךְ, *to send;* and is applied (1) to one sent, or a messenger, see chap. i. 14 ; comp. 1 Sam. xvi. 19 ; (2) to a *messenger* sent from God, as e. g. *(a)* to *angels,* since angels were employed on messages of mercy or judgment to mankind, Ex. xxiii. 20; 2 Sam. xxiv. 16, *(b)* to *a prophet* as sent from God, Hag. i. 13 ; Mal. iii. 1 ; *(c)* to *a priest ;* Eccl. v. 6 ; Mal. ii. 7. It is rendered here by Jerome, *angel,* and by the LXX. *angels bringing death.* So far as the *word* is concerned, it may apply to *any* messenger sent from God—whether an angel, a prophet, or the Messiah ; any one who should be commissioned to explain to man the reason why afflictions were sent, and to communicate the assurance that God was ready to pardon. ¶ *An interpreter.* That is, *an angel-interpreter,* or a messenger who should be an interpreter. The word מֵלִיץ, *mēlitz,* is from לוּץ, *lutz,* to *stammer ;* to speak in a barbarous tongue ; and then in Hiphil, to cause to understand a foreign language, or to explain ; to interpret. Hence it means one who explains or interprets that which was obscure ; and may mean here one who explains to the sufferer the true principles of the divine administration, or who *interprets* the design of the divine dealings. In 2 Chron. xxxii. 31, it is rendered "ambassadors"—referring to the ambassadors that came from Babylon to Hezekiah—rendered in the margin, *interpreters ;* in Isa. xliii. 27, it is rendered *teachers,* in the margin *interpreters,* referring to the religious *teachers* of the Jews, or those who were appointed to *explain* the law of God. Gesenius supposes that it means here the same as *intercessor,* or *internuncius,* and that the phrase denotes an *interceding angel,* or one interceding with God for men. But there is no instance in which the word מֵלִיץ, *mēlitz*, is so employed, and such an interpretation is not demanded by the connection here. The idea involved in the word here is immediately explained by Elihu himself. The word denotes one who would " show unto man his uprightness ;" that is, who would be able to vindicate the righteousness of God, and explain his dealings. *This* word, also, may therefore be applicable to a prophet, a sage, an angel, or the Messiah — to any one who would be able to explain and interpret the divine dealings. So far as the *language* is concerned, there is no reason why it should not be applied to Elihu himself. ¶ *One among a thousand.* Such an one as you would scarcely hope to find among a thousand ; that is, one who was endowed with a knowledge of the ways of God, and who was qualified for this work in a much more eminent manner than the mass of men. We have now a similar phrase to denote a man eminent for wisdom, learning, skill, or moral worth. This language is such as would most properly be applicable to a *human* messenger. One would hardly think of making such distinctions among angelic beings, or of implying that any one of them might not be qualified to bear a message to man, or that it was necessary to make such a selection as is implied by the phrase here to explain the dealings of God. ¶ *To show unto man his uprightness.* This is the office which the *interpreting-messenger* was to perform. The " uprightness" referred to here, I suppose, is that of God, and means the rectitude of his doings ; or, in a more general sense, *the justness of his character, the equity of his administration.* So explained, it would mean that the messenger would come to show that *God is worthy of confidence ;* that he is not harsh, stern, severe, and cruel. The afflicted person is supposed to have no clear views on this point, but to regard God as severe and unmerciful. Elihu in this undoubtedly had Job in his eye, as entertaining views of God which were far from correct. What was necessary, he said, was, that some one would come who could show to the sufferer that God is worthy of confidence, and that his character is wholly upright. Prof. Lee interprets this as referring wholly to the Messiah, and as denoting the " righteousness which this Mediator is empowered to give or impute to those who duly seek it ; and thus, as a Mediator, between God and man, to make it out as their due, by means of the ransom so found, offered, and accepted." Noyes explains it as meaning "*his duty;*" that is, " what reason and religion require of a man in his situation ; repentance, submission, and prayer to God for pardon." But it seems to me more natural to refer it to the great principles of the divine government, as being worthy of confidence. Those principles it was desirable should be so explained as to inspire such confidence, and particularly this was what Elihu supposed was needed by Job. On the whole, then, it seems probable that Elihu, in this passage, by the *messenger* which he mentions, referred to some one who should perform the office which he himself purposed to perform — some man well acquainted with the principles of the divine administration ; who could explain the reasons why men suffer ; who could present such considerations as should lead the sufferer to true repentance ; and who could assure him of the divine mercy. The *reasons* for this interpretation may be summed up in few words. They are, (1.) That this is all that is fairly and necessarily implied in the language, or such an interpretation meets the obvious import of all the expressions, and leaves nothing unexplained. (2.) It accords with what Elihu supposed to be the views of Job. He regarded him as having improper apprehensions of the government of God, and of the reasons why afflictions were sent upon him. He had patiently listened to all that he had to say ; had heard him give utterance to much that seemed to be in the spirit of complaint and murmuring ;

24 Then he is gracious unto him, and saith, Deliver him from going down to the pit; I have found [1] a ransom.

1 or, *an atonement.*

and it was manifest to Elihu that he had not had right apprehensions of the design of trials, and that they had not produced the proper effect on his mind. He still needed some one—an interpreter sent from God—to *explain* all this, and to present such views as should lead him to put confidence in God as a God of mercy and equity. (3.) It accords with the character which Elihu had assumed, and which he all along maintained. He professed to come from God, chap. xxxii. 8. He was in the place of God, chap. xxxiii. 6. He came to *explain* the whole matter which had excited so long and so warm a debate—a debate to which he had attentively listened, and where neither Job nor his friends had stated the true principles of the divine administration. To represent himself now as having a *clew* to the reason why God afflicts men in this manner, and as being qualified to *explain* the perplexing subject, was in accordance with the character which he maintained. (4.) It accords with the effect which he wished to produce on the mind of Job. He wished to bring him to confide in God; to show *him* that all these mysterious dealings were designed to bring him back to his Creator, and to restore peace and confidence to his agitated and troubled bosom. While Elihu, therefore, advances a general proposition, I doubt not that he meant to represent himself as such a messenger sent from God; and though in the whole of his speech he manifested almost the extreme of modesty, yet he regarded himself as qualified to unravel the mystery. That it refers to the Messiah cannot be demonstrated, and is improbable; for (1.) It is nowhere applied to him in the New Testament—a consideration not indeed decisive, but of some force, since it is not *very safe* to apply passages to him from the Old Testament without such authority. At least, the general rule is to be repudiated and rejected, that every passage is to be supposed to have such a reference which can be possibly made to apply to him, or where the language can be made to describe his person and offices. (2.) The work of the "interpreter," the "angel," or "messenger," referred to here, is not that of the Messiah. The effect which Elihu says would be produced would be, that the life of the sufferer would be spared, his disease removed, and his flesh restored with infantile freshness. But this is not the work which the Redeemer came to perform, and is not that which he actually does. (3) The subject here discussed is not such as is applicable to the work of the Messiah. It is here a question solely *about the design of affliction.* That was the point to be *explained;* and *explanation* was what was needed, and what was proposed to be done. But this is not the peculiar work of the Messiah. His was a much larger, wider office; and even if this had been his whole work, how would the reference to that have met the point under discussion? I am inclined, therefore, to the opinion, that Elihu had himself particularly in his view, and that he meant to represent himself as at that time sustaining the character of a messenger sent from God to explain important principles of his administration.

24. *Then he is gracious unto him.* That is, on the supposition that he hears and regards what the messenger of God communicates. If he rightly understands the reasons of the divine administration, and acquiesces in it, and if he calls upon God in a proper manner (ver. 26), he will show him mercy, and spare him. Or it may mean, that God is in fact gracious to him by sending him a messenger who can come and say to him that it is the divine purpose to spare him; that he is satisfied, and will preserve him from death. If such a messenger should come, and so announce the mercy of God, then he

would return to the vigour of his former days, and be fully restored to his former prosperity. Elihu refers probably to some method of communication, by which the will of God was made known to the sufferer, and by which it was told him that it was God's design not to destroy, but to discipline and save him. ¶ *Deliver him.* Heb. פְּדָעֵהוּ, *redeem him.* The word here used (פָּדָה) properly means to let loose, to cut loose; and then *to buy loose;* that is, to redeem, to ransom for a price. Sometimes it is used in the general sense of freeing or delivering, without reference to a price, comp. Deut. vii. 8; Jer. xv. 21; Ps. xxxiv. 22; Job vi. 23; but usually there is a reference to *a price,* or to some valuable consideration, either expressed or implied; comp. Notes on Isa. xliii. 3. Here the appropriate idea is expressed, for it is said, as a reason for redeeming or rescuing him, "I have found *a ransom.*" That is, the "ransom" is the valuable consideration on account of which he was to be rescued from death. ¶ *From going down to the pit.* The grave; the world of darkness. Notes, ver. 18. That is, he would keep him alive, and restore him again to health. It is possible that by the word *pit* here, there may be a reference to a place of punishment, or to the abodes of the dead as places of gloom and horror, especially in the case of the wicked; but the more probable interpretation is, that it refers to death alone. ¶ *I have found.* That is, there *is* a ransom; or, I have seen a reason why he should not die. The idea is, that God was looking for some reason on account of which it would be proper to release the sufferer, and restore him to the accustomed tokens of his favour, and that such a ransom had now appeared. There was now no necessity why those sufferings should be prolonged, and he could consistently restore him to health. ¶ *A ransom.* Marg. "or, *an atonement.* Heb. כֹּפֶר, *kōphĕr.* On the meaning of this word, see Notes on Isa. xliii. 3. The expression here means that there was something which could be regarded as a valuable consideration, or a reason why the sufferer should not be further afflicted, and why he should be preserved from going down to the grave. What that price, or valuable consideration was, is not specified; and what was the actual idea which Elihu attached to it, it is now impossible with certainty to determine. The connection would rather lead us to suppose that it was something seen *in* the sufferer himself; some change wrought in his mind by his trials; some evidence of acquiescence in the government of God, and some manifestation of true repentance, which was the reason why the stroke of punishment should be removed, and why the sufferer should be saved from death. This might be called by Elihu "a ransom"—using the word in a very large sense. There can be no doubt that such *a fact* often occurs. God lays his hand on his erring and wandering children. He brings upon them afflictions which would consign them to the grave, if they were not checked. Those afflictions are effectual in the case. They are the means of true repentance; they call back the wanderer; they lead him to put his trust in God, and to seek his happiness again in him; and this result of his trials is *a reason* why they should extend no farther. The object of the affliction has been accomplished, and the penitence of the sufferer is a sufficient reason for lightening the hand of affliction, and restoring him again to health and prosperity. This is not properly an *atonement,* or a *ransom,* in the sense in which the word is now technically used, but the Hebrew word here used would not be inappropriately employed to convey such an idea. Thus in Ex. xxxii. 30, the intercession of Moses is said to be that by which an atonement would be made for the sin of the people. "Moses said unto the people, Ye have sinned a great sin; and now I will go up unto the Lord; peradventure I shall make an atonement (אֲכַפְּרָה, *ăkăpp râ,* from כָּפַר, *kâphăr*), for your sin." Here, it is manifest that the act of Moses in making intercession was to be the *public reason,* or the "ransom," why they were not to be punished. So the boldness, zeal, and

25 His flesh shall be fresher than
[1] a child's: he shall return to the
days of his youth:
26 He shall pray unto God, and
he will be favourable unto him;
and he shall see his face with joy:
for he will render unto man his
righteousness.

1 *childhood.*

fidelity of Phinehas in resisting idolatry, and punishing those who had been guilty of it, are spoken of as *the atonement* or *ransom* on account of which the plague was stayed, and the anger of God removed from his people; Num. xxv. 12, 13, "Behold, I give unto him my covenant of peace—because he was zealous for his God, and made an atonement (ויכפר) for the children of Israel." Sept. ἐξιλάσατο. In this large sense, the sick man's repentance might be regarded as the *covering, ransom,* or *public reason* why he should be restored. That word literally means that which *covers,* or *overlays* any thing; and then an atonement or expiation, as being such a covering. See Gen. 20. 16; Ex. xxi. 30. Cocceius, Calovius, and others suppose that the reference here is to the Messiah, and to the atonement made by him. Schultens supposes that it has the same reference by anticipation—that is, that God had *purposed* such a ransom, and that in virtue of the promised and prefigured expiation, he could now show mercy. But it cannot be demonstrated that Elihu had such a reference; and though it was undoubtedly true that God designed to show mercy to men only through that atonement, and that it was, and is, only by this that release is ever given to a sufferer, still, it does not follow that *Elihu* fully understood this. The *general* truth that God was merciful, and that the repentance of the sick man would be followed by a release from suffering, was all that can reasonably be supposed to have been understood at that period of the world. *Now,* we know the reason, the mode, and the extent of the ransom; and taking the words in their broadest sense, we may go to all sufferers, and say, that they may be redeemed from going down to the dark chambers of the eternal pit, for God has found a ransom. *A valuable consideration* has been offered, in the blood of the Redeemer, which is an ample reason why they should not be consigned to hell, if they are truly penitent.

25. *His flesh shall be fresher than a child's.* Marg. *childhood.* The meaning is obvious. He would be restored again to health. The calamity which had been brought upon him for purposes of discipline, would be removed. This was the theory of Elihu in regard to afflictions, and he undoubtedly meant that it should be applied to Job. If he would now, understanding the nature and design of affliction, turn to God, he would be recovered again, and enjoy the health and vigour of his youth. We are not to suppose that this is universally true, though it is undoubtedly often a fact now, that if those who are afflicted become truly penitent, and call upon God, the affliction will be removed. It will have accomplished its object, and may be withdrawn. Hence, they who pray that their afflictions may be withdrawn, should *first* pray that they may accomplish on their own hearts the effect which God designs, producing in them penitence, deadness to the world, and humiliation, and *then* that his hand may be withdrawn. ¶ *He shall return to the days of his youth.* That is, to health and vigour.

26. *He shall pray unto God,* &c. That is, when he fully understands the design of affliction; and when his mind is brought to a proper state of penitence for his past conduct, then he will find God merciful and ready to show him kindness. ¶ *And he shall see his face with joy.* The face of God. That is, he shall be able to look up to him with peace and comfort. This language is similar to that which is so frequently employed in the Scriptures, in which God is said to lift upon us the light of his countenance. The meaning here is, that the afflicted man would be again permitted to look by faith on God, being reconciled to him, and would see in his face no indica-

27 He [1] looketh upon men; and *if any* say, [a] I have sinned, and perverted *that which was* right, and it profited me not;

1 or, *he shall look upon men, and say, I have sinned.* a 1 John 1.9.

tion of displeasure. ¶ *For he will render unto man his righteousness.* He will deal with him in justice and equity. When he sees evidence of penitence, he will treat him accordingly; and if in the afflicted man he discerns true piety, he will regard and treat him as his friend. The meaning is, that if there *is* in the sufferer any sincere love to God, he will not be indifferent to it, but will treat him as possessing it. This is still true, and universally true. If there is in the heart of one who is afflicted any real piety, God will not treat him as an impenitent sinner, but will manifest his mercy to him, and show to him the favours which he confers only on his friends.

27. *He looketh upon men.* Marg. "or, *he shall look upon men, and say, I have sinned.*" Umbreit renders this, Nun singt er jubelnd zu den Menschen—"now he sings joyfully among men." So Noyes, "He shall sing among men, and say." Prof. Lee, "He shall fully consider or pronounce right to men, so that one shall say, I have sinned." Coverdale, "Such a respect hath he unto men. Therefore, let a man confess and say, I have offended." The LXX. render it, Εἶτα τότε ἀπομέμψεται ἄνθρωπος αὐτὸς ἑαυτῷ—"then shall a man blame himself," &c. These various renderings arise from the difference of signification attached to the Hebrew word יָשֹׁר. According to our interpretation, it is derived from שִׁיר—*shir*, to sing, and then the meaning would be, "he sings before men," and thus the reference would be to the sufferer, meaning that he would have occasion to rejoice among men. See Gesenius on the word. According to the other view, the word is derived from שׁוּר—*shūr*, to look round; to care for, or regard; and according to this, the reference is to God, meaning that he carefully and attentively observes men in such circumstances, and, if he sees evidence that there is true penitence, he has compassion and saves. This idea certainly accords better with the scope of the passage than the former, and it seems to me is to be regarded as correct. ¶ *And* if any *say, I have sinned.* Heb. "And says," that is, if the sufferer, under the pressure of his afflictions, is willing to confess his faults, then God is ready to show him mercy. This accords with what Elihu purposed to state of the design of afflictions, that they were intended to bring men to reflection, and to be a means of wholesome discipline. There is no doubt that he meant that all this should be understood by Job as applicable to himself, for he manifestly means to be understood as saying that he had not seen in him the evidence of a penitent mind, such as he supposed afflictions were designed to produce. ¶ *And perverted* that which was *right.* That is, in regard to operations and views of the divine government. He had held error, or had cherished wrong apprehensions of the divine character. Or it may mean, that he had dealt unjustly with men in his intercourse with them. ¶ *And it profited me not.* The word here used (שָׁוָה—*shâvâ*) means properly to be even or level; then to be equal, or of like value; and here may mean, that he now saw that it was no advantage to him to have done wickedly, since it brought upon him such a punishment, or the benefit which he received from his life of wickedness was no equivalent for the pain which he had been called to suffer in consequence of it. This is the common interpretation. Rosenmüller, however, suggests another, which is, that he designs by this language to express his sense of the divine mercy, and that it means "my afflictions are in no sense *equal* to my deserts. I have not been punished as I might justly have been, for God has interposed to spare me." It seems to me, however, that the former interpretation accords best with the meaning of the words and the scope of the passage. It would then be the reflection of a man on the bed of suffering, that

28 He [1] will deliver his soul from
going into the pit, and his life shall
see the light.
29 Lo, all these *things* worketh
[2] God oftentimes with man,
30 To bring back his soul from
the pit, [a] to be enlightened with the
light [b] of the living.
31 Mark well, O Job; hearken
unto me, hold thy peace, and I will
speak.
32 If thou hast any thing to say,

1 or, He *hath delivered my soul, &c. and my life.* 2 *twice* and *thrice.*

a Ps.40.1,2; Is.38.17. *b* Ps.56.13; Acts 26.18.

the course of life which brought him there had been attended with no advantage, but had been the means of plunging him into deserved sorrows from which he could be rescued only by the grace of God.

28. *He will deliver his soul.* Marg. "He *hath delivered my soul.*" There are various readings here in the text, which give rise to this diversity of interpretation. The present reading in the text is נפשי—*my soul;* and according to this, it is to be regarded as the language of the sufferer celebrating the mercy of God, and is language which is connected with the confession in the previous verse, "I have sinned; I found it no advantage; and he hath rescued me from death." Many MSS., however, read נפשו—*his soul;* and according to this, the language would be that of Elihu, saying, that in those circumstances God would deliver him when he made suitable confession of his sin. The sense is essentially the same. The Vulgate has, "He will deliver *his* soul;" the LXX, 'Save *my* soul." ¶ *From going into the pit.* Notes ver. 18. ¶ *And his life shall see the light.* Here there is the same variety of reading which occurs in regard to the word *soul.* The present Hebrew text is (חיתי) "*my* life;" many MSS. read (חיתו) "*his* life." The phrase "to see the light" is equivalent *to live.* Death was represented as going down into regions where there was no ray of light. See chap. iii. 5; x. 21, 22.

29. *Lo, all these* things *worketh God.* That is, he takes all these methods to warn men, and to reclaim them from their evil ways. ¶ *Oftentimes.* Heb. as in the margin, *twice, thrice.* This may be taken either, as it is by our translators, to denote an indefinite number, meaning that God takes *frequent* occasion to warn men, and *repeats* the admonition when they disregard it, or more probably Elihu refers here to the particular methods which he had specified, and which were three in number. First, warnings in the visions of the night, ver 14—17. Second, afflictions, 19—22. Third, the messenger which God sent to make the sufferer acquainted with the design of the affliction, and to assure him that he might return to God, ver. 23—26. So the LXX. understand it, who render it, ὁδοὺς τρεῖς—*three ways,* referring to the three methods which Elihu had specified.

30. *To bring back his soul from the pit.* To keep him from descending to the grave, and to the dark world beneath. He takes these methods of warning men, in order that they may not bring destruction on themselves. See ver. 18 ¶ *To be enlightened with the light of the living.* That he may still enjoy life, and not descend to the world of shades.

31. *Mark well, O Job, hearken unto me,* &c. Elihu designs to intimate that he had much more to say which demanded close attention. He begged, therefore, that Job would hear him patiently through.

32 *If thou hast any thing to say, answer me.* In the previous verse, Elihu had asked that Job would hear all that he had to say. Yet here, in view of what he had said, he asks of him that if there were any thing from which he dissented, he would now express his dissent. We may suppose that he paused at this part of his speech, and as what he had said related particularly to Job, he felt that it was proper that he should have an opportunity to reply ¶ *For I desire to justify thee.* I would do you justice. I would not pervert what you have said, or attribute to you any wrong opinions or any improper motives.

answer me: speak; for I desire to justify thee.

33 If not, hearken unto me: hold thy peace, and I shall teach thee wisdom.

CHAPTER XXXIV.

ANALYSIS OF THE CHAPTER.

ELIHU appears to have paused, to give Job an opportunity to reply to what he had said. When he found that he had nothing to reply, he addresses particularly the friends of Job, designing to vindicate the ways of God, and to examine some of the positions which Job had advanced. He had been grieved and offended that they had not replied to what he considered to be his erroneous sentiments (chap. xxxii. 3), and now he proposes to reply to those sentiments himself, and to show what was the truth in the matter. The chapter contains the following points:

I. The introduction to the speech, in which Elihu addresses himself particularly to the friends of Job, and asks their careful consideration of the whole subject, ver. 1—4.

II. A statement of the sentiments of Job which he considered erroneous, and which he proposed to examine, ver. 5—9. Particularly, Job had said that he was righteous; that God had not dealt with him as he ought to have done; and that there was no advantage in serving God and being pious, since calamities came upon the righteous as well as the wicked, and the wicked under his government fared as well as the righteous.

III. An examination and a refutation of these opinions, ver. 10—30. In doing this, Elihu refers to the following considerations: *(a)* A declaration that God will not do wickedness, and that he cannot pervert judgment. This Elihu seems to consider as indisputable, ver. 10—12. *(b)* God is the absolute and original sovereign of all the earth. No one has *given* him authority to reign, and no one can control him, ver. 13—16. *(c)* There is, therefore, great impropriety in calling in question the dealings of such a sovereign. It would be improper even to arraign an earthly prince, and to accuse him of injustice; and how much more impropriety is there in calling in question the equity of the Great Governor of the universe! ver. 17—19. *(d)* All men are under the notice of God. The wicked cannot escape, and there is no land of darkness where they can be concealed. It cannot be supposed, therefore, that they will escape because God *cannot* ferret them out, and call them to judgment, ver. 20—22. *(e)* God will not lay upon man more than is right, or give him occasion to enter into controversy with him, ver. 23. *(f)* God *in fact* cuts off the wicked. He destroys them in the night; he strikes them suddenly down, and spares the poor and the oppressed who cry unto him. He takes care that the hypocrite shall not reign, and brings upon him deserved punishment, ver. 24—30. By such considerations, Elihu meets the allegations of Job, and endeavours to vindicate the government of God. They are for the most part mere assertions, and in his view the whole subject resolves itself into a matter of sovereignty. The amount of all that he says is, that man should *submit* to God, and that it is *presumption* in him to attempt to call in question the equity of his government.

IV. Elihu now turns again to Job, and appeals to him. He says that the proper course for him, instead of complaining of God, would be to confess that he had done wrong, and to pray that he might be taught to understand that which was now inscrutable to him. He ought not to expect that every thing would be according to his mind. He ought to seek counsel of men of understanding, and listen with deference to their opinions, and not to arrogate all wisdom to himself. Job had erred, in the opinion of Elihu, and had maintained sentiments which tended to vindicate the conduct of wicked men. He had evinced a spirit of rebellion, and multiplied words against God, ver. 31—37. The drift of the whole discourse, therefore, is, to convince Job that he was wrong, and to exhort him to acquiesce in the righteous government of God; to lead him to inquire into the reasons why God had afflicted him, and confess the sins which had been the occasion of his trials.

FURTHERMORE, Elihu answered and said,

Perhaps there may be included also a wish to vindicate him, if he possibly could. He did not desire to dispute for the sake of disputing, or to blame him if he could avoid it, but his aim was the truth; and if he could, he wished to vindicate the character of Job from the aspersions which had been cast upon it.

33. *If not, hearken unto me,* &c. If nothing has been said from which you dissent, then listen to me, and I will explain further the perplexing subject which has excited so much discussion. These remarks of Elihu imply great confidence in the truth of what he had to say, but they are not arrogant and disrespectful. He treats Job with the utmost deference; is willing to hear all that could be said in opposition to his own views, and is desirous of not wounding his feelings, or doing injustice to his cause. It may be supposed that he paused here, to give Job an opportunity to reply, but as he made no remarks, he resumed his discourse in the following chapter. The views which he had expressed were evidently new to Job, and were entirely at variance with those of his three friends, and they appear to have been received by all with profound and respectful silence.

CHAPTER XXXIV.

1. *Furthermore, Elihu answered and said.* That is, evidently, after a pause to see if Job had any thing to reply. The word *answered* in the Scriptures often means "to begin a discourse," though nothing had been said by others; see chap. iii. 2; Isa. xiv. 10; Zech. i. 10; iii. 4; iv. 11, 12. Sometimes it is used with reference to a *subject,* meaning that one replied to what could be suggested on the opposite side. Here it may be understood either in the general sense of beginning a discourse, or more probably as replying to the sentiments which Job

2 Hear my words, O ye wise
men; and give ear unto me, ye that
have knowledge:
3 For the ear trieth words, as the
[1] mouth tasteth meat.
4 Let us chose to us judgment:
let us know among ourselves what
is good.
5 For Job hath said, [a] I am
righteous: and God hath taken
away my judgment.
6 Should I lie against my right?
my wound [2] *is* incurable without
transgression.

1 *pa'ate.* a chap.27.2.
2 *arrow*, chap.6.4.

---

had advanced in the debate with his friends.

2. *Hear my words, O ye wise men.* Addressing particularly the three friends of Job. The previous chapter had been addressed to Job himself. He had stated to him his views of the design of affliction, and he had nothing to reply. He now addresses himself to his friends, with a particular view of examining some of the sentiments which Job had advanced, and of showing where he was in error. He addresses them as "wise men," or *sages*, and as endowed with "knowledge," to conciliate their attention, and because he regarded them as qualified to understand the difficult subject which he proposed to explain.

3. *For the ear trieth words.* Ascertains their meaning, and especially determines what words are worth regarding. The object of this is, to fix the attention on what he was about to say; to get the *ear* so that every word should make its proper impression. The word *ear* in this place, however, seems not to be used to denote the external organ, but the whole faculty of hearing. It is by *hearing* that the meaning of what is said is determined, as it is by the *taste* that the quality of food is discerned. ¶ *As the mouth tasteth meat.* Marg. as in Heb. *palate.* The meaning is, as the organ of taste determines the nature of the various articles of food. The same figure is used by Job in chap. xii. 11.

4. *Let us choose to us judgment.* That is, let us examine and explore what is true and right. Amidst the conflicting opinions, and the sentiments which have been advanced, let us find out what will abide the test of close investigation.

5. *For Job hath said, I am righteous.* see chap. xiii. 18, "I know that I shall be justified;" comp. chap. xxiii. 10, 11, where he says, if he was tried he would come forth as gold. Elihu may have also referred to the general course of remark which he had pursued as vindicating himself. ¶ *And God hath taken away my judgment.* This sentiment is found in chap. xxvii. 2; see Notes on that place.

6. *Should I lie against my right?* These are also quoted as the words of Job, and as a part of the erroneous opinions on which Elihu proposes to comment. These words do not occur, however, as used by Job respecting himself, and Elihu must be understood to refer to what he regarded as the general strain of the argument maintained by him. In regard to the meaning of the words, there have been various opinions. Jerome renders them, "For in judging me there is falsehood — *mendacium est;* my violent arrow [the painful arrow in me] is without any sin." The LXX. "He [the Lord] hath been false in my accusation" — ἐψεύσατο δὲ τῷ κρίματί μου — "my arrow is heavy without transgression." Coverdale, "I must needs be a liar, though my cause be right." Umbreit renders it, "I must lie if I should acknowledge myself to be guilty." Noyes, "Though I am innocent, I am made a liar." Prof. Lee, "Should I lie respecting my case? mine arrow is mortal without transgression." That is, Job said he could not lie about it; he could use no language that would deceive. He felt that a mortal arrow had reached him without transgression, or without any adequate cause. Rosenmüller renders it, "However just may be my cause, I appear to be a liar." That is, he was regarded as guilty, and treated accordingly, however conscious he might be of innocence, and however strenuously he

7 What man *is* like Job, *who*
drinketh up scorning like water;
8 Which goeth in company with
the workers of iniquity, and walketh
with wicked men?
9 For he hath said, It profiteth a
man nothing [a] that he should
delight himself with God.
10 Therefore, hearken unto me,
ye men of [1] understanding: Far
be it from God *that he should do*
wickedness; and *from* the Almighty,
that he should commit iniquity.

a chap.9.22,23. 1 *heart*.

might maintain that he was not guilty. The meaning probably is, "I am held to be a liar. I defend myself; go over my past life; state my course of conduct; meet the accusations of my friends, but in all this I am still held to be a liar. My friends so regard me—for they will not credit my statements, and they go on still to argue as if I was the most guilty of mortals. And God also in this holds me to be a liar, for he treats me constantly as if I were guilty. He hears not my vindication, and he inflicts pain and woe upon me as if all that I had said about my own integrity were false, and I were one of the most abandoned of mortals, so that on all hands I am regarded and treated as if I were basely false." The literal translation of the Hebrew is, "Concerning my judgment [or my cause] I am held to be a liar." ¶ *My wound is incurable.* Marg. as in Heb. *arrow*. The idea is, that a deadly arrow had smitten him, which could not be extracted. So in Virgil.

Hæret lateri letalis arundo. Æn. iv. 73.

The image is taken from an animal that had been pierced with a deadly arrow. ¶ *Without transgression.* Without any sin that deserved such treatment. Job did not claim to be absolutely perfect; he maintained only that the sufferings which he endured were no proper proof of his character; comp. chap. vi. 4.

7. *What man* is *like Job,* who *drinketh up scorning like water?* A similar image occurs in chap. xv. 16. The idea is, that he was full of reproachful speeches respecting God; of the language of irreverence and rebellion. He indulged in it as freely as a man drinks water; gathers up and *imbibes* all the language of reproach that he can find, and indulges in it as if it were perfectly harmless.

8. *Which goeth in company with the workers of iniquity.* That is, in his sentiments. The idea is, that he advocated the same opinions which they did, and entertained the same views of God and of his government. The same charge had been before brought against him by his friends; see Notes on chap. xxi.

9. *For he hath said, It profiteth a man nothing that he should delight himself in God.* That is, there is no advantage in piety, and in endeavouring to serve God. It will make no difference in the divine dealings with him. He will be treated just as well if he lives a life of sin, as if he undertakes to live after the severest rules of piety. Job had not used precisely this language, but in chap. ix. 22, he had expressed nearly the same sentiment. It is probable, however, that Elihu refers to what he regarded as the general scope and tendency of his remarks, as implying that there was no respect paid to character in the divine dealings with mankind. It was easy to pervert the views which Job actually entertained, so as to make him *appear* to maintain this sentiment, and it was probably with a special view to this charge that Job uttered the sentiments recorded in chap. xxi; see Notes on that chapter.

10. *Therefore hearken unto me.* Elihu proceeds now to reply to what he regarded as the erroneous sentiments of Job, and to show the impropriety of language which reflected so much on God and his government. Instead, however, of meeting the *facts* in the case, and showing how the actual course of events could be reconciled with justice, he resolves it all into a matter of sovereignty, and maintains that it is wrong to doubt the rectitude of the dealings of one so

11 For the work [a] of a man shall
he render unto him, and cause
every man to find according to *his*
ways.
12 Yea, surely God will not do
wickedly, neither will the Almighty
pervert judgment.
13 Who hath given him a charge
over the earth? or who hath disposed [1] the whole world?

a Re.22.12.

1 all of it.

mighty as God. In this he pursues the same course substantially which the friends of Job had done, and does little more to solve the real difficulties in the case than they had. The *facts* to which Job had referred are scarcely adverted to; the perplexing questions are still unsolved, and the amount of all that Elihu says is, that God is a sovereign, and that there must be an improper spirit when men presume to pronounce on his dealings. ¶ *Ye men of understanding.* Marg. as in Heb. *men of* "heart." The word *heart* is here used as it was uniformly among the Hebrews; the Jewish view of physiology being that *the heart* was the seat of all the mental operations. They never speak of the head as the seat of the intellect, as we do. The meaning here is, that Elihu regarded them as *sages*, qualified to comprehend and appreciate the truth on the subject under discussion. ¶ *Far be it from God.* Heb. חללה—"profane, unholy." It is an expression of *abhorrence*, as if the thing proposed were profane or unholy: 1 Sam. xx. 2; Gen. xviii. 25; Josh. xxiv. 16. The meaning here is, that the very idea that God would do wrong, or could patronize iniquity, was a profane conception, and was not to be tolerated for a moment. This is true enough, and in this general sentiment, no doubt, Job would himself have concurred.

11. *For the work of a man shall he render unto him.* He shall treat each man as he deserves—and this is the essence of justice. Of the truth of this, also, there could have been no question. Elihu does not, indeed, apply it to the case of Job, but there can be little doubt that he intended that it should have such a reference. He regarded Job as having accused God of injustice, for having inflicted woes on him which he by no means deserved. He takes care, therefore, to state this general principle, that with God there *must* be impartial justice — leaving the application of this principle to the *facts* in the world, to be arranged as well as possible. No one can doubt that Elihu in this took the true ground, and that the great principle is to be held that God *can do no wrong*, and that all the *facts* in the universe MUST be consistent with this great principle, whether we can now see it to be so or not.

12. *Yea, surely God will not do wickedly.* So important does Elihu hold this principle to be, that he repeats it, and dwells upon it. He says, "it *surely* (אמנם) MUST be so." The principle *must* be held at all hazards, and no opinion which contravenes this should be indulged for one moment. His ground of complaint against Job was, that he had not held fast to this principle, but, under the pressure of his sufferings, had indulged in remarks which implied that God *might* do wrong. ¶ *Neither will the Almighty pervert judgment.* As Elihu supposed Job to have maintained; see ver. 5. To "pervert judgment" is to do injustice; to place injustice in the place of right.

13. *Who hath given him a charge over the earth?* That is, he is the great original Proprietor and Ruler of all. He has derived his authority to govern from no one; he is under subjection to no one, and he has, therefore, an absolute right to do his own pleasure. Reigning then with absolute and original authority, no one has a right to call in question the equity of what he does. The argument of Elihu here, that God would do right, is derived solely from his *independence*. If he were a subordinate governor, he would feel less interest in the correct administration of affairs, and might be tempted to commit injuries to gratify the feelings of

14 If he set his heart upon [1] man, *if* he gather unto himself his spirit and his breath;
15 All flesh shall perish together and man shall turn again unto dust.
16 If now *thou hast* understanding, hear this; hearken to the voice of my words:

1 *him.*

his superior. As he is, however, supreme and independent, he cannot be tempted to do wrong by any reference to a superior will; as the universe is that which he has made, and which belongs to him, every consideration would lead him to do right to all. He can have no partiality for one more than another; and there can be no one to whom he would desire to do injustice—for who wishes to injure that which belongs to himself? Prof. Lee, however, renders this, "Who hath set a land in order against him?" He supposes that the remark is designed to show the folly of rebelling against God. But the former interpretation seems better to accord with the scope of the argument. ¶ *Or who hath disposed the whole world?* Who has arranged the affairs of the universe? The word rendered "world," usually means *the habitable earth,* but it is employed here in the sense of the universe, and the idea is, that God has arranged and ordered all things, and that he is the supreme and absolute Sovereign.

14. *If he set his heart upon man.* Marg. as in Heb. "upon *him*"—meaning *man.* That is, if he fixes his attention particularly on him, or should form a purpose in regard to him. The argument seems to be this. "If God wished such a thing, and should set his heart upon it, he could easily cut off the whole race. He has power to do it, and no one can deny him the right. Man has no *claim* to life, but he who gave it has a right to withdraw it, and the race is absolutely dependent on this infinite Sovereign. Being such a Sovereign, therefore, and having such a right, man cannot complain of his Maker as unjust, if he is called to pass through trials." Rosenmüller, however, supposes this is to be taken in the sense of severe scrutiny, and that it means, "If God should examine with strictness the life of man, and mark all his faults, no flesh would be allowed to live. All would be found to be guilty, and would be cut off." Grotius supposes it to mean, "If God should regard only himself; if he wished only to be good to himself—that is, to consult his own welfare, he would take away life from all, and live and reign alone." This is also the interpretation of Umbreit, Schnurrer, and Eichhorn. Noyes regards it as an argument drawn from the benevolence of God, meaning if God were severe, unjust, and revengeful, the earth would be a scene of universal desolation. It seems to me, however, that it is rather an argument from the absolute sovereignty or power of the Almighty, implying that man had no right to complain of the divine dealings in the loss of health, property, or friends; for if he chose he might sweep away the whole race, and leave the earth desolate. ¶ *If he gather unto himself his spirit and his breath.* The spirit of man is represented as having been originally given by God, and as returning to him when man dies; Eccl. xii. 7, "Then shall the dust return to the earth as it was; and the spirit shall return unto God who gave it."

15. *All flesh shall perish together.* If God chose, he would have a right to cut down the whole race. How then shall men complain of the loss of health, comforts, and friends, and presume to arraign God as if he were unjust?

16. *If now* thou hast *understanding hear this.* This appears to be addressed to Job. The discourse before this had been directed to his three friends, but Elihu appears here to have turned to Job, and to have made a solemn appeal to him, whether this were not so. In the subsequent verses he remonstrates with him about his views, and shows him that what he had said implied severe reflections on the character and government of God.

17 Shall [a] even he that hateth
right [1] govern? and wilt thou
condemn him that is most just?
18 *Is it fit* to say to a king,
[b] *Thou art* wicked? *and* to princes,
Ye are ungodly?
19 *How much less to him* that
accepteth [c] not the persons of
princes, nor regardeth the rich more
than the poor? for they all *are* the
work of his hands.
20 In a moment shall they die,
and the people shall be troubled at
midnight, and pass away; and
[2] the mighty shall be taken away
without hand.

a 2 Sa.23 3. 1 *bind.* *b* Ex.22.28. *c* Rom.2.11. 1 Pe.1.17. 2 *they shall take away the mighty.*

17. *Shall even he that hateth right govern?* Marg. as in Heb. *bind.* That is, shall he bind by laws. The *argument* in this verse seems to be an appeal to what *must* be the conviction of mankind, that God, the Great Governor of the universe, could not be unjust. This conviction, Elihu appears to have supposed, was so deep in the human mind, that he might appeal even to Job himself for its truth. The question here asked implies that it would be impossible to believe that one who was unjust could govern the universe. Such a supposition would be at variance with all the convictions of the human soul, and all the indications of the nature of his government to be found in his works. ¶ *And wilt thou condemn him that is most just?* The great and holy Ruler of the universe. The argument here is, that Job had *in fact* placed himself in the attitude of condemning him who, from the fact that he was the Ruler of the universe, must be most just. The impropriety of this he shows in the following verses.

18. Is it fit *to say to a king,* Thou art *wicked?* The argument here is this: "There would be gross impropriety in arraigning the conduct of an earthly monarch, and using language severely condemning what he does. Respect is due to those of elevated rank. Their plans are often concealed. It is difficult to judge of them until they are fully developed. To condemn those plans, and to use the language of complaint, would not be tolerated, and would be grossly improper. How much more so when that language relates to the Great, the Infinite God, and to his eternal plans!" It may be added here, in accordance with the sentiment of Elihu, that men often indulge in thoughts and language about God which they would not tolerate respecting an earthly monarch.

19. How much less to him *that accepteth not the person of princes.* To *accept the person* of any one is to treat him with special favour on account of his rank, his wealth, or from favouritism and partiality. This God often disclaims in respect to himself; (comp. Gal. ii. 6; Acts x. 34; 2 Ch. xix. 7; Rom. ii. 11; Eph. vi. 9; Col. iii. 25), and solemnly forbids it in others; see James ii. 1, 3, 9; Lev. xix. 15; Deut. i. 17; xvi. 19. The meaning here is, that God is entirely impartial in his administration, and treats all as they ought to be treated. He shows favour to no one on account of wealth, rank, talent, office, or gay apparel, and he excludes no one from favour on account of poverty, ignorance, or a humble rank in life. This it seems was an admitted sentiment in the time of Elihu, and on the ground of the fact that it was indisputable, he strongly argues the impropriety of calling in question the equity of his administration in language such as that which Job had used. ¶ *For they all* are *the work of his hands.* He regards them all as his creatures. No one has any special claim on him on account of rank, talent, or wealth. Every creature that he has made, high and low, rich and poor, bond and free, may expect that impartial justice will be done him, and that his external circumstances will not control or modify the divine determinations in regard to him, or the divine dealings towards him.

20. *In a moment shall they die.*

21 For his eyes [a] *are* upon the ways of man, and he seeth [b] all his goings.

22 *There is* no darkness, [c] nor shadow of death, where the workers of iniquity may hide [d] themselves.

23 For he will not lay upon man

a 2 Ch.16 9. b Ps. 139.2,3. c Am 9.2,3; He.4.13. d Re.6.15,16.

That is, the rich and the great. They pass suddenly off the stage of action. They have no power to compel God to favour them, and they have no permanency of existence here which can constitute a claim on his special favour. Soon they will lie undistinguished in the dust. All are in his hand ; and when he wills it, they must lie down in the dust together. He exempts none from death ; spares none on account of beauty, rank, wealth, talent, or learning, but consigns all indiscriminately to the grave—showing that he is disposed to treat them all alike. This is urged by Elihu as a proof that God has no partiality, but treats all men as being on the same level—and there is no more striking illustration of this than is furnished by *death*. All die. None are spared on account of title, wealth, rank, beauty, age, or wisdom. All die in a manner that shows that he has no favouritism. The rich man may die with a malady as painful and protracted as the poor man ; the beautiful and accomplished with a disease as foul and loathsome as the beggar. The sad change that the body undergoes in the tomb is as repulsive in the one case as in the other ; and amidst all the splendour of rank, and the magnificence of dress and equipage, God intends to keep the great truth before the minds of men, that they are really on a level, and that all must share at his hand alike. ¶ *And the people shall be troubled.* They shall be shaken, agitated, alarmed. They dread impending danger, or the prospect of sudden destruction. ¶ *At midnight.* The image here is probably taken from an earthquake, or from a sudden onset made by a band of robbers on a village at night. The essential thought is that of the *suddenness* with which God can take away the mighty and the mean together. Nothing can resist him, and as he has this absolute control over men, and deals with all alike, there is great impropriety in complaining of his government. ¶ *And the mighty.* Marg. *They shall take away the mighty.* The idea is, that the great shall be removed—to wit, by sudden death or by overwhelming calamity. The *argument* of Elihu in this passage (ver. 18–20) is, that it would be esteemed great presumption to arraign the conduct of a prince or king, and it must be much more so to call in question the doings of him who is so superior to princes and kings that he shows *them* no partiality on account of their rank, but sweeps them away by sudden calamity as he does the most humble of mankind. ¶ *Without hand.* That is, without any human instrumentality, or without the use of *any* visible means. It is by a word—by an expression of his will—by power where the agency is not seen. The design is, to show that God can do it with infinite ease.

21. *For his eyes* are *upon the ways of man.* None can escape from his notice ; comp. Ps. cxxxix. 2, 3.

22. There is *no darkness.* No dark cavern which can furnish a place of concealment. The guilty usually take refuge in some obscure place where men cannot detect them. But Elihu says that man has no power of concealing himself thus from God. ¶ *Nor shadow of death.* A phrase here signifying deep darkness ; see it explained in the Notes on chap. iii. 5. ¶ *Where the workers of iniquity may hide themselves.* That is, where they may conceal themselves so as not to be detected by God. They may conceal themselves from the notice of man ; they may escape the most vigilant police ; they may elude all the officers of justice on earth. But they cannot be hid from God. There is an eye that sees their lurking places, and there is a hand that will drag them forth to justice.

23. *For he will not lay upon man*

more *than*[a] *right*, that he should
[1] enter into judgment with God.
24 He shall break in pieces
mighty men without [2] number,
and set others in their stead.
25 Therefore he knoweth their
works, and he overturneth *them*
in the night, so that they are
[3] destroyed.

a Is.42.3; 1 Cor.10.13. 1 *go.* 2 *searching out.* 3 *crushed.*

more than right. Very various translations have been given of this verse. According to our common version, it means that God will not deal with man in such a manner as to give him just reason for calling in question the rectitude of the divine dealings. He shall in no case receive more than his sins deserve, so as to give him cause for complaint. This is undoubtedly a correct sentiment; but it may be doubted whether it is the sense conveyed by the original. Umbreit renders it:

Denn er braucht auf einem Mann nicht lang zu achten
Um ihm vor Gott in das Gericht zu ziehen.

"For he needs not long to regard a man in order to bring him before God in judgment"—meaning that he has all power; that he can at once see all his character; and that he can bring him at once to his bar. This translation undoubtedly accords with the general scope of the argument. Noyes renders it:

He needeth not attend long to a man,
To bring him into judgment before God.

Wemyss renders it in a similar way:

He has no need of laborious inquiry,
In order to convict men at his tribunal.

Rosenmüller gives a similar sense to the passage. According to this, the meaning is, that there is no need that God should give long attention to a man, or go into a protracted investigation, in order that he may bring him to judgment. He knows him at a glance. He can at once convict him, and can decide the case in a moment without danger of error. Human tribunals are under a necessity of long and patient investigation, and then are often deceived; but no such necessity, and no such danger, pertains to God. This interpretation agrees with the scope of the passage (comp. Notes on ver. 24), and seems to me to be correct. The Hebrew literally is, "For not upon man will he place [scil. his mind or attention] long that he should go before God in judgment;" that is, there is no need of long and anxious investigation on his part, in order that he may prove that it is right for him to cut man off. He may do it at once, and no one has a right to complain.

24. *He shall break in pieces.* He crushes or destroys the great. He is not intimidated by their wealth, their rank, or their number. ¶ *Without number.* Marg. more correctly, *searching out.* That is, he does it without the protracted process of a judicial investigation. The Hebrew word here used (חקר) means properly *a searching out, an examination;* and the meaning here is, that there is no need of his going into a protracted investigation into the lives of wicked men before he brings them to punishment. He sees them at once; knows all their conduct, and may proceed against them without delay. Hence it is that he comes often in such a sudden manner, and cuts them off. A human tribunál is under a necessity of examining witnesses and of attending to all the palliating circumstances, before it can pronounce a sentence on an offender. But it is not so with God. He judges at once and directly, and comes forth therefore in a sudden manner to cut down the guilty. ¶ *And set others in their stead.* Place others in the situation which they now occupy. That is, he can with the utmost ease make entire revolutions among men.

25. *Therefore he knoweth their works.* Or, "Because he knoweth their works." The word (לכן) here rendered "therefore" is evidently used as denoting that *since* or *because* he was intimately acquainted with all which they did, he could justly bring vengeance upon them without long investigation. ¶ *And he over-*

26 He striketh them as wicked
men in the open [1] sight [a] of others;
27 Because they turned back
[2] from him, and [b] would not consider
any of his ways:
28 So that they cause the cry of
the poor to come unto him, and he
heareth [c] the cry of the afflicted.
29 When he [d] giveth quietness,
who then can make trouble? and
when he hideth [e] *his* face, who then
can behold him? whether *it be*

1 *place of beholders.* 2 *from after.*
a 1 Ti.5.24. b Pr.1.29,30. c Ex.22.27. d Ro.8.31-34. e Ps.143.7.

turneth them *in the night.* Literally, "he turneth night;" meaning, probably, he turns night upon them; that is, he brings calamity upon them. The word *night* is often used to denote calamity, or ruin. Umbreit understands it in the sense of *turning about the night;* that is, that they had covered up their deeds as in the night, but that God *so turns the night about* as to bring them to the light of day. The Vulgate renders it *et ideireo inducit noctem,* "and therefore he brings night;" that is, he brings adversity and ruin. This is probably the correct interpretation. ¶ *So that they are destroyed.* Marg. *crushed.* The idea is, that when God thus brings adversity upon them, they are prostrated beneath his power.

26. *He striketh them as wicked men.* Literally, "Under the wicked, or on account of the wicked, he smites them." That is, he deals with them *as if* they were wicked; he regards and treats them as such. He deals with them *under* the general character of wicked men, and punishes them accordingly. ¶ *In the open sight of others.* Marg. as in Heb. *in the place of beholders.* The idea is, that it is done openly or publicly. Their sins had been committed in secret, but they are punished openly. The manifestation of the divine displeasure is in the presence of spectators, or is so open and public, that it cannot but be seen. It is very probable that in all this description Elihu had his eye upon the public calamities which had come upon Job, and that he meant to include him among the number of mighty men whom God thus suddenly overturned.

27. *Because they turned back from him.* Marg. *from after him.* That is, they receded, or went away from God. ¶ *And would not consider any of his ways.* They would not regard or attend to any of his commands. The word *way,* in the Scriptures, is often used to denote *religion.* A *way* denotes the course of life which one leads; the path in which he walks. The "ways of God" denote his course or plan, his precepts or laws; and to depart from them, or to disregard them, is only another mode of saying that a man has no religion.

28. *So that they cause the cry of the poor to come unto him.*—Their character is that of oppressors. They take away the rights of the poor; strip away their property without any just claims, and cause them to pour out their lamentations before God. ¶ *And he heareth the cry of the afflicted.* They oppress the poor so that they appeal unto him, but God hears their cry, and brings punishment upon the oppressor. This is *a general remark* thrown in here, meaning that God *always* regards the cry of the oppressed. Its bearing on the case before us is, that God hears the appeal which the oppressed make to him, and as a consequence brings calamity upon those who are guilty of wrong.

29. *When he giveth quietness.* That is, when God designs to give rest, comfort, ease, or prosperity in any way to a man. The Hebrew word here used may refer to any kind of ease, rest, or peace. The idea which Elihu intends to convey is, that God has all things under his control, and that he can bring prosperity or adversity upon an individual or a nation at his own pleasure. ¶ *Who then can make trouble?* Literally, "Who can condemn, or hold guilty" — רשע. The sense is, that no one can overwhelm him with the consciousness of guilt, to whom God intends to give

done against a nation, or against a man only:
30 That the hypocrite reign not, lest the people [a] be ensnared.
31 Surely it is meet to be said unto God, I [b] have borne *chastisement*, I will not offend *any more:*

a 1 Ki.12 28. b Da.9.7—14.

the peace resulting from his favour and friendship. Or, no one can bring calamities upon a man *as if* he were guilty, or so as to *show* that he is guilty, when God intends to treat him as if he were not. This is as true now as it was in the time of Elihu. When *God* designs to give peace to a man's soul, and to impart to him the evidence that his sins are forgiven, there is no one who can excite in his mind the conviction of guilt, or take away the comfort that God gives. When he designs to *treat* a man as if he were his friend, and to impart to him such evidences of his favour as shall convince the world that he is his friend, there is no one who can prevent it. No one can so calumniate him, or so prejudice the world against him, or so arrest the descending tokens of the divine favour, as to turn back the proof of the favour of God; comp. Prov. xvi. 7. ¶ *And when he hideth* his *face.* To *hide the face,* is a common expression in the Scriptures to denote calamity, distress, and the want of spiritual comfort, as the expression "to lift up the light of the countenance" is a common phrase to denote the opposite; comp. chap. xiii. 24. ¶ *Who then can behold him?* An expression denoting that no one can then have cheering and elevating views of God. No one can then have those clear conceptions of his character and government which will give peace to the soul. *This* is also as true now as it was in the time of Elihu. We are dependent on God himself for any just views of his own character, for any elevating and purifying conceptions of his government and plans, and for any consolation flowing in upon our souls from the evidence that he is our friend. ¶ *Whether* it be done *against a nation, or against a man only.* The same truth pertains to nations and to individuals. The same laws respecting the sources of peace and happiness apply to both. Both are alike dependent on God, and neither can secure permanent peace and prosperity without him. Both are alike at his sovereign disposal; and neither can originate permanent sources of prosperity. This, too, is as true now as it was in the time of Elihu. Nations are more prone to forget it than individuals are, but still it is a great truth which should never be forgotten, that neither have power to originate or perpetuate the means of happiness, but that both are alike dependent on God.

30. *That the hypocrite reign not.* All this is done to prevent wicked men from ruling over the people. The remarks of Elihu had had respect much to princes and kings, and he had shown that however great they were, they were in the hands of God, and were wholly at his disposal. He *now* says that the design of his dealings with them was to prevent their oppressing their fellow-men. The general scope of the remarks of Elihu is, that God is the universal Sovereign; that he has all men under his control, and that there are none so powerful as to be able to resist his will. The remark in this verse is thrown in, not as illustrating this general sentiment, but to show what was *in fact* the aim for which he thus interposed—to save men from being oppressed and crushed by those in authority. ¶ *Lest the people be ensnared.* Heb. "From their being snarers of the people." He thrusts down the mighty, in order that they may not be left to take the people as wild beasts are taken in the toils. They were disposed to make use of their power to oppress others, but God interposes, and the people are saved. For a fuller view of this verse, see the remarks of Rosenmüller.

31. *Surely it is meet to be said unto God.* It is evident that this verse commences a new strain of remark, and that it is designed particularly to bring Job to proper reflections in view

32 *That which* I see not, teach
[a] thou me: if I have done iniquity,
I [b] will do no more.

a Ps.32 8. b Ep.4 22.

of what had occurred. There has been, however, much diversity of opinion about the meaning of this and the following verses. Schultens enumerates no less than *fifteen* different interpretations which have been given of this verse. The *general* meaning seems to be, that a man who is afflicted ought to submit to God, and not to murmur or complain. He ought to suppose that there is some good reason for what God does, and to be resigned to his will, even where he cannot *see* the reason of his dispensations. The drift of all the remarks of Elihu is, that God is a great and inscrutable Sovereign; that he has a right to reign, and that man should submit unqualifiedly to him. In this passage he does not reproach Job harshly. He does not say that he had been guilty of great crimes. He does not affirm that the sentiments of the three friends of Job were correct, or maintain that Job was a hypocrite. He states a *general* truth, which he considers applicable to all, and says that it becomes all who are afflicted to submit to God, and to resolve to offend no more; to go to God with the language of humble confession, and when every thing is dark and gloomy in the divine dealings to implore *his* teachings, and to entreat him to shed light on the path. Hence he says, "It is meet or proper to use this language before God. It becomes man. He should presume that God is right, and that he has some good reasons for his dealings, though they are inscrutable. Even when a sufferer is not to be reckoned among the most vile and wicked; when he is conscious that his general aim has been to do right; and when his external character has been fair, it is to be *presumed to be possible* that he may have sinned. He may not have wholly known himself. He may have indulged in things that were wrong without having been scarcely conscious of it. He may have loved the world too much; may have fixed his affections with idolatrous attachment on his property or friends; may have had a temper such as ought not to be indulged; or he may have relied on what he possessed, and thus failed to recognize his dependence on God. In such cases, it becomes man to have so much confidence in God as to go and acknowledge *his right* to inflict chastisement, and to entreat him to teach the sufferer *why* he is thus afflicted." ¶ *I have borne* chastisement. The word *chastisement* is not in the Hebrew. The Hebrew is simply נשאתי—*I have borne*, or *I bear*. Umbreit renders it, "I repent." Some word like *chastisement* or *punishment* must be understood after "I have borne." The idea evidently is, that a man who is afflicted by God, even when he cannot see the reason *why* he is afflicted, and when he is not conscious that he has been guilty of any particular sin that led to it, should be willing to regard it as *a proof* that he is guilty, and should examine and correct his life. But there is a great variety of opinion in regard to the meaning of this passage—no less than fifteen different interpretations being enumerated by Schultens. ¶ *I will not offend* any more. לא אחבל—"I will not act wickedly; I will no more do corruptly." The sense is, that his afflictions should lead him to a resolution to reform his life, and to sin no more. This just and beautiful sentiment is as applicable to us now as it was to the afflicted in the time of Elihu. It is a common thing to be afflicted. Trial often comes upon us when we can see no particular sin which has led to it, and no special reason why *we* should be afflicted rather than others. We should, however, regard it as a proof that there is something in our hearts or lives which may be amended, and should endeavour to ascertain what it is, and resolve to offend no more. Any one, if he will examine himself carefully, can find sufficient reasons why *he* should be visited with the rod of chastisement, and though we may not be able to see why others are preserved from such calamities, yet we can see that there are reasons in abun-

33 *Should it be* [1] according to thy mind? he will recompense it, whether thou refuse, or whether thou choose; and not I: therefore speak what thou knowest.

[1] *from with thee.*

dance why *we* should be recalled from our wanderings.

32. That which *I see not, teach thou me.* That is, in regard to my errors and sins. No prayer could be more appropriate than this. It is language becoming every one who is afflicted, and who does not see clearly the reason why it is done. The sense is, that with a full belief that he is liable to error and sin, that he has a wicked and deceitful heart, and that God never afflicts without reason, he should go to him and ask him to show him *why* he has afflicted him. He should not murmur or repine; he should not accuse God of injustice or partiality; he should not attempt to cloak his offences, but should go and entreat him to make him acquainted with the sins of heart and life which have led to these calamities. Then only will he be in a state of mind in which he will be likely to be profited by trials. ¶ *If I have done iniquity, I will do no more.* Admitting the possibility that he had erred. Who is there that cannot appropriately use this language when he is afflicted?

33. Should it be *according to thy mind?* Marg. as in Heb. "from with thee"—המעמך. There has been much diversity of opinion in regard to the meaning of this verse. It is exceedingly obscure in the original, and has the appearance of being a proverbial expression. The general sense seems to be, that God will not be regulated in his dealings by what may be the views of man, or by what man might be disposed to choose or refuse. He will act according to his own views of what is right and proper to be done. The phrase, "should it be according to thy mind," means that it is not to be expected that God will consult the views and feelings of man rather than his own. ¶ *He will recompense it.* He will visit with good or evil, prosperity or adversity, according as he shall judge to be right. ¶ *Whether thou refuse, or whether thou choose.* Whatever may be your preferences or wishes. He will act according to his own views of right. The idea is, that God is absolute and independent, and does according to his own pleasure. He is a just Sovereign, dispensing his favours and appointing calamity, not according to the will of individual men, but holding the scales impartially, and doing what *he* esteems to be right. ¶ *And not I.* Rosenmüller, Drusius, De Wette, and Noyes, render this, "And not he," supposing that it refers to God, and means that the arrangements which are to affect men should be as *he* pleases, and not such as *man* would prefer. Umbreit explains it as meaning, "It is for you to determine in this matter, not for me. You are the person most interested. I am not particularly concerned. Do you, therefore, speak and determine the matter, if you know what is the truth." The Vulgate renders it, "Will God seek that from thee because it displeases thee? For thou hast begun to speak, not I: for if thou knowest any thing better, speak." So Coverdale, "Wilt thou not give a reasonable answer? Art thou afraid of any thing, seeing thou beganne st first to speak, and not I?" The great difficulty of the whole verse may be seen by consulting Schultens, who gives no less than *seventeen* different interpretations, which have been proposed—his own being different from all others. He renders it, "Lo, he will repay you in your own way; for thou art full of sores—*namque subulceratus es:* which, indeed, thou hast chosen, and not I—and what dost thou know? speak." I confess that I cannot understand the passage, nor do any of the interpretations proposed seem to be free from objections. I would submit the following, however, as a paraphrase made from the Hebrew, and differing somewhat from any interpretation which I have seen, as possibly expressing the true sense of the whole verse. "Shall it be from thee that God will send retribution on it [that is, on human conduct], because thou refusest or art

34 Let men of [1] understanding
tell me, and let a wise man hearken
unto me.
35 Job hath spoken without
[a] knowledge, and his words *were*
without wisdom.

36 My [2] desire *is, that* Job may
be tried unto the end, because of
his answers for wicked men.
37 For he addeth rebellion unto
his sin; he clappeth *his hands*
amongst us, and multiplieth his
words against God.

1 *heart.* a chap.38.2
2 or, *My father, let Job be tried.*

reluctant, or because it is not in accordance with thy views? For thou must choose, and not I. Settle this matter, for it pertains particularly to you, and not to me, and what thou knowest, speak. If thou hast any views in regard to this, let them be expressed, for it is important to know on what principles God deals with men."

34, 35. *Let men of understanding.* Marg. as in Heb. *heart.* The *heart,* as there has been frequent occasions to remark, in the Scriptures is often used to denote the seat of the mind or soul, as the head is with us. Rosenmüller, Umbreit, and Noyes, render this passage as if it were to be taken in connection with the following verse, "Men of understanding will say, and a wise man who hears my views will unite in saying, 'Job has spoken without knowledge, and his words are without wisdom.'" According to this, the two verses express a sentiment in which Elihu supposes every wise man who had attended to him would concur, that what Job had said was not founded in knowledge or on true wisdom.

36. *My desire* is. Marg. "or, *my father, let Job be tried.*" This variation between the text and the margin, arises from the different interpretations affixed to the Hebrew word אבי —*ābi.* The Hebrew word commonly means "father," and some have supposed that that sense is to be retained here, and then it would be a solemn appeal to God as his Father—expressing the earnest prayer of Elihu that Job might be fully tried. But the difficulties in this interpretation are obvious. (1.) Such a mode of appeal to God occurs nowhere else in the book, and it is little in the spirit of the poem. No particular reason can be assigned why that solemn appeal should be made here, rather than in many other places. (2.) The name *Father,* though often given to God in the Scriptures, is not elsewhere given to him in this book. The probability is, therefore, that the word is from אבה—*to breathe after, to desire,* and means that Elihu *desired* that Job should have a fair trial. No other similar form of the word, however, occurs. The Vulgate renders it, *Pater mi, my father;* the LXX., "But learn, Job, no more to make reply like the foolish;" the Chaldee, צבינא—*I desire.* ¶ *May be tried.* That his views may be fully canvassed and examined. He had expressed sentiments which Elihu thought should not be allowed to pass without the most careful examination into their truth and bearing. ¶ *Unto the end.* In the most full and free manner; that the matter should be pursued as far as possible, so that it might be wholly understood. Literally, it means *for ever*—עד־נצח. ¶ *Because of* his *answers for wicked men.* Because of the views which he has expressed, which seem to favour the wicked. Elihu refers to the opinions advanced by Job that God did not punish men in this life, or did not deal with them according to their characters, which *he* interpreted as giving countenance to wickedness, or as affirming that God was not the enemy of impiety. The Vulgate renders this, "My Father, let Job be tried to the end; do not cease from the man of iniquity;" but the true meaning doubtless is, that Job had uttered sentiments which Elihu understood to favour the wicked, and he was desirous that every trial should be applied to him which would tend to correct his erroneous views.

37. *For he addeth rebellion unto his sin.* To the sin which he has formerly committed, and which has brought

CHAPTER XXXV.

ANALYSIS OF THE CHAPTER.

THIS chapter comprises the third speech of Elihu, in which he examines one of the opinions which he understood Job to advance. It consists of two parts—(1.) A statement of the opinion which he understood Job to maintain, ver. 1—3. This was, that his righteousness was more than God's; and that it was no advantage to be pious, for his religion did not save him at all from affliction. This Elihu regarded as a severe reflection on God and his government, and to this (2.) he replies. His reply consists of two parts. *First* (ver. 4—12), that God is supreme. He is so exalted that he cannot be affected by what man does; he reaps no benefit from the service of man, and cannot be injured in any way if he is sinful. He cannot be influenced, therefore, in his dealings by any selfish principles, or any self-interest in the matter. It ought to be *presumed*, therefore, that he is impartial, and there ought to be submission to him. The *second* consideration which Elihu adduces (ver. 13—16) is, that if God does *not* at once interpose and relieve a sufferer; if he does not hear his prayer and take away his calamities, it ought to be supposed that it *may possibly* be because the prayer is not offered in a proper spirit and manner. It ought not at once to be inferred that God is wrong; or that he is indifferent to the character of men, or that it is of no advantage to be pious, but that it may be because there is an improper temper of mind in him who prays. Confidence ought still to be reposed in God, and it *ought* to be supposed that there may be some other reason why he does not interpose and hear the prayer of the sufferer than that he is indifferent to the welfare of his true friends. Elihu concludes, therefore (ver. 16), that Job had spoken without a proper understanding of the subject, and that his argument was rash and vain.

ELIHU spake, moreover, and said,

2 Thinkest thou this to be right, *that* thou saidst, [a] My righteousness *is* more than God's?

a chap. 9.17—34; 16.12—17; 27.2-6.

these trials upon him, he now adds the sin of murmuring and rebellion against God. Of Job, this was certainly not true to the extent which Elihu intended, but it is a very common case in afflictions. A man is visited with calamity as a chastisement for his sins. Instead of searching out the cause why he is afflicted, or bowing with resignation to the superior wisdom of God when he cannot *see* any cause he regards himself as unjustly dealt with; complains of the government of God as severe, and gives *occasion* for a severer calamity in some other form. The result is often that he is visited with severe affliction, and is made to see both his original offence and the accumulated guilt which has made a new form of punishment necessary. ¶ *He clappeth* his hands *amongst us.* To clap the hands is either a signal of applause or triumph, or a mark of indignation, Num. xxiv. 10, or of derision, chap. xxvii. 23. It seems to be used in some such sense here, as expressing contempt or derision for the sentiments of his friends. The meaning is, that instead of treating the subject under discussion with a calm spirit and a disposition to learn the truth and profit by it, he had manifested in relation to the whole matter great disrespect, and had conducted like one who attempts to silence others, or who shows his contempt for them by clapping his hands at them. It is scarcely necessary to say, that, notwithstanding all the professed candour and impartiality of Elihu, this is a most unfair representation of the general spirit of Job. That he had sometimes given vent to improper feelings there can be no doubt, but nothing had occurred to justify this statement. ¶ *And multiplieth his words against God.* That is, his arguments are against the justice of his government and dealings. In the peculiar phrase here used—"he multiplieth *words,*" Elihu means, probably, to say, that there was more of *words* than of argument in what Job had said, and that he was not content even with expressing his improper feelings once, but that he piled words on words, and epithet on epithet, that he might more fully give utterance to his reproachful feelings against his Maker.

CHAPTER XXXV.

1. *Elihu spake.* Heb. ויען—"And he *answered;*" the word *answer* being used, as it is often in the Scriptures, to denote the commencement of a discourse. We may suppose that Elihu had paused at the close of his second discourse, possibly with a view to see whether there was any disposition to reply.

2. *Thinkest thou this to be right?* This is the point which Elihu now proposes to examine. He, therefore, solemnly appeals to Job himself to determine whether he could himself say that he thought such a sentiment correct. ¶ That *thou saidst, My righteousness* is *more than God's.* Job had nowhere said this in so many words,

3 For thou saidst, What [a] advantage will it be unto thee? *and*, What profit shall I have *if* [1] *I be cleansed* from my sin?

4 I will [2] answer thee, and thy companions with thee.

5 Look unto the heavens, and see; and behold the clouds, *which* are higher than thou.

a chap.31.2,&c. 1 or, by it *more than by my sin.* 2 *return to thee words.*

but Elihu regarded it as the substance of what he had said, or thought that what he had said amounted to the same thing. He had dwelt much on his own sincerity and uprightness of life; he had maintained that he had not been guilty of such crimes as to make these calamities deserved, and he had indulged in severe reflections on the dealings of God with him; comp chap ix. 30—35; x. 13—15. All this Elihu interprets as equivalent to saying, that he was more righteous than his Maker. It cannot be denied that Job had given occasion for this interpretation to be put on his sentiments, though it cannot be supposed that he would have affirmed this in so many words.

3. *For thou saidst.* Another sentiment of a similar kind which Elihu proposes to examine. He had already adverted to this sentiment of Job in chap. xxxiv. 9, and examined it at some length, and had shown in reply to it that God could not be unjust, and that there was great impropriety when man presumed to arraign the justice of the Most High. He now adverts to it again in order to show that God could not be benefited or injured by the conduct of man, and that he was, therefore, under no inducement to treat him otherwise than impartially. ¶ *What advantage will it be unto thee?* see Notes on chap. xxxiv. 9. The phrase "unto thee," refers to Job himself. He had said this to himself; or to his own soul. Such a mode of expression is not uncommon in the Scriptures. ¶ And, *What profit shall I have* if I be cleansed *from my sin?* Marg. "or, by it *more than by my sin.*" The Hebrew will admit of either of these interpretations, and the sense is not materially varied. The idea is, that as to good treatment or securing the favour of God under the arrangements of his government, a man might just as well be wicked as righteous. He would be as likely to be prosperous in the world, and to experience the tokens of the divine favour. Job had by no means advanced such a sentiment; but he had maintained that he was treated *as if* he were a sinner; that the dealings of Providence were *not* in this world in accordance with the character of men; and this was interpreted by Elihu as maintaining that there was no advantage in being righteous, or that a man might as well be a sinner. It was for such supposed sentiments as these, that Elihu and the three friends of Job charged him with giving "answers" for wicked men, or maintaining opinions which went to sustain and encourage the wicked; see chap. xxxiv. 36.

4. *I will answer thee.* Marg. *return to thee words.* Elihu meant to explain this more fully than it had been done by the friends of Job, and to show where Job was in error. ¶ *And thy companions with thee.* Eliphaz, in chap. xxii. 2, had taken up the same inquiry, and proposed to discuss the subject, but he had gone at once into severe charges against Job, and been drawn into language of harsh crimination, instead of making the matter clear, and Elihu now proposes to state just how it is, and to remove the objections of Job. It may be doubted, however, whether he was much more successful than Eliphaz had been. The doctrine of the future state, as it is revealed by Christianity, was needful to enable these speakers to comprehend and explain this subject.

5. *Look unto the heavens, and see.* This is the commencement of the reply which Elihu makes to the sentiment which he had understood Job to advance, and which Eliphaz had proposed formerly to examine. The general object of the reply is, to show that God is so great that he cannot be affected with human conduct, and

6 If thou sinnest, what dost thou
against him? [a] or *if* thy transgressions be multiplied, what dost thou
unto him?
7 If [b] thou be righteous, what
givest thou him? or what receiveth
he of thine hand?
8 Thy wickedness *may hurt* a
man as thou *art*, and thy righteousness *may profit* the son of
man.

a Je.7.19. b Ps.16.2; Pr.9.12.

that he has no interest in treating men otherwise than according to character. He is so exalted that their conduct cannot reach and affect his happiness. It ought to be *presumed*, therefore, since there is no motive to the contrary, that the dealings of God with men would be impartial, and that there *would* be an advantage in serving him—not because men could lay him under *obligation*, but because it was right and proper that such advantage should accrue to them. To impress this view on the mind, Elihu directs Job and his friends to look to the heavens—so lofty, grand, and sublime; to reflect how much higher they are than man; and to remember that the great Creator is *above* all those heavens, and *thus* to see that he is so far exalted that he is not dependent on man; that he cannot be affected by the righteousness or wickedness of his creatures; that his happiness is not dependent on them, and consequently that it is to be presumed that he would act impartially, and treat all men as they deserved. There *would* be, therefore, an advantage in serving God. ¶ *And behold the clouds.* Also far above us, and seeming to float in the heavens. The sentiment here is, that one view of the astonishing display of wisdom and power above us must extinguish every feeling that he will be influenced in his dealings as men are in theirs, or that he can gain or suffer any thing by the good or bad behaviour of his creatures.

6. *If thou sinnest, what doest thou against him?* This should not be interpreted as designed to justify sin, or as saying that there is no evil in it, or that God does not regard it. That is not the point or scope of the remark of Elihu. His object is to show that God is not influenced in his treatment of his creatures as men are in their treatment of each other. He has no *interest* in being partial, or in treating them otherwise than they deserve. If they sin against him his happiness is not so marred that he is under any inducement to interpose *by passion*, or in any other way than that which is *right*.

7. *If thou be righteous, what givest thou him?* The same sentiment substantially as in the previous verses. It is, that God is supreme and independent. He does not desire such benefits from the services of his friends and is not so dependent on them, as to be induced to interpose in their favour, in any way beyond what is strictly proper. It is to be presumed, therefore, that he will deal with them according to what is right, and as it is right that they should experience proofs of his favour, it followed that there *would be* advantage in serving him, and in being delivered from sin; that it *would be* better to be holy than to lead a life of transgression. This reasoning seems to be somewhat abstract, but it is correct, and is as sound now as it was in the time of Elihu. There is no reason why God should not treat men according to their character. He is not so under obligations to his friends, and has not such cause to dread his foes; he does not derive so much benefit from the one, or receive such injury from the other, that he is under any inducement to swerve from strict justice; and it follows, therefore, that where there *ought* to be reward there will be, where there *ought* to be punishment there will be, and consequently that there *is* an advantage in being righteous.

8. *Thy wickedness* may hurt *a man as thou* art. That is, it may injure him, but not God. He is too far exalted above man, and too independent of man in his sources of happiness, to be affected by what he can do. The object of the whole

9 By reason of the multitude of oppressions they make *the oppressed* to cry; they cry out by reason of the arm of the mighty:

10 But none saith, Where *is* God my Maker, who giveth songs in the night;

---

passage (ver. 6–8) is, to show that God is independent of men, and is not governed in his dealings with them on the principles which regulate their conduct with each other. One man may be greatly benefited by the conduct of another, and may feel under obligation to reward him for it; or he may be greatly injured in his person, property, or reputation, by another, and will endeavour to avenge himself. But nothing of this kind can happen to God. If he rewards, therefore, it must be of his grace and mercy, not because he is laid under obligation; if he inflicts chastisement, it must be because men deserve it, and not because God has been injured. In this reasoning Elihu undoubtedly refers to Job, whom he regards as having urged a *claim* to a different kind of treatment, because he supposed that he *deserved* it. The general principle of Elihu is clearly correct, that God is entirely independent of men; that neither our good nor evil conduct can effect his happiness, and that consequently his dealings with us are those of impartial justice.

9. *By reason of the multitude of oppressions they make* the oppressed *to cry.* It is not quite easy to see the connection which this verse has with what goes before, or its bearing on the argument of Elihu. It seems, however, to refer to the *oppressed in general*, and to the fact, to which Job had himself adverted (chap. xxiv. 12), that men are borne down by oppression and that God does not interpose to save them. They are suffered to remain in that state of oppression—trodden down by men, crushed by the arm of a despot, and overwhelmed with poverty, sorrow, and want, and God does not interpose to rescue them. He looks on and sees all this evil, and does not come forth to deliver those who thus suffer. This is a common case, according to the view of Job; this was his own case, and he could not explain it, and in view of it he had indulged in language which Elihu regarded as a severe reflection on the government of the Almighty. He undertakes, therefore, to *explain the reason* why men are permitted thus to suffer, and why they are not relieved. In the verse before us, he states *the fact*, that multitudes *do* thus suffer under the arm of oppression—for that fact could not be denied; in the following verses, he states *the reason* why it is so, and that reason is, that they do not apply in any proper manner to God, who could "give songs in the night," or joy in the midst of calamities, and who could make them acquainted with the nature of his government as intelligent beings, so that they would be able to understand it and acquiesce in it. The phrase "the multitude of oppressions" refers to the numerous and repeated calamities which tyrants bring upon the poor, the down-trodden, and the slave. The phrases "to cry" and "they cry out," refer to the lamentations and sighs of those under the arm of the oppressor. Elihu did not dispute the truth of *the fact* as it was alleged by Job. That fact could not then be doubted any more than it can now, that there were many who were bowed down under burdens imposed by hard-hearted masters, and groaning under the government of tyrants, and that all this was seen and permitted by a holy God. This fact troubled Job—for he was one of this general class of sufferers; and this fact Elihu proposes to account for. Whether his solution is satisfactory, however, may still admit of a doubt.

10. *But none saith.* That is, none of the oppressed and down-trodden say. This is the solution which Elihu gives of what appeared so mysterious to Job, and of what Elihu regarded as the source of the bitter complaints of Job. The solution is, that when men are oppressed they do not apply to God with a proper spirit, and look to him that they may find relief. It was

11 Who teacheth us more than the beasts of the earth, and maketh us wiser than the fowls of heaven?

12 There they cry, but none giveth answer, because of the pride of evil men.

a principle with Elihu, that if when a man was afflicted he would apply to God with a humble and penitent heart, he would hear him, and would withdraw his hand; see this principle fully stated in chap. xxxiii. 19—26. This Elihu now says, was not done by the oppressed, and this, according to him, is the reason why the hand of God is still upon them. ¶ *Where is God my Maker.* That is, they do not appeal to God for relief. They do not inquire for him who alone can help them. This is the reason why they are not relieved. ¶ *Who giveth songs in the night.* Night, in the Scriptures, is an emblem of sin, ignorance, and calamity. Here *calamity* is particularly referred to; and the idea is, that God can give joy, or impart consolation, in the darkest season of trial. He can impart such views of himself and his government as to cause the afflicted even to rejoice in his dealings; he can raise the song of praise even when all external things are gloomy and sad; comp. Acts xvi. 25. There is great beauty in this expression. It has been verified in thousands of instances where the afflicted have looked up through tears to God, and their mourning has been turned into joy. Especially is it true under the gospel, that in the day of darkness and calamity, God puts into the mouth the language of praise, and fills the heart with thanksgiving. No one who has sought comfort in affliction with a right spirit has found it withheld, and all the sad and sorrowful may come to God with the assurance that he can put songs of praise into their lips in the night of calamity; comp. Ps. cxxvi. 1, 2.

11. *Who teacheth us more than the beasts of the earth.* Who is able to teach us more than the irrational creation; that is, in regard to the nature and design of affliction. They suffer without knowing why. They are subjected to toil and hardships; endure pain, and die, without any knowledge why all this occurs, and without any rational view of the government and plans of God. It is not, or need not be so, says Elihu, when man suffers. He is intelligent. He can understand why he is afflicted. He has only to make use of his superior endowments, and apply to his Maker, and he will see so much of the reason of his doings that he will acquiesce in the wise arrangement. Perhaps there is an implied reflection here on those who suffered generally, as if they manifested no more intelligence than the brute creation. They make no use of their intellectual endowments. They do not examine the nature of the divine administration, and they do not apply to God for instruction and help. If they should do so, he would teach them so that they would acquiesce and rejoice in his government and dealings. According to this view, the meaning is, that if men suffer without relief and consolation, it is to be attributed to their stupidity and unwillingness to look to God for light and aid, and not at all to his injustice.

12. *There they cry.* They cry out in the language of complaint, but not for mercy. ¶ *Because of the pride of evil men.* That is, of their own pride. The pride of men so rebellious, and so disposed to complain of God, is the reason why they do not appeal to him to sustain them and give them relief. This is still as true as it was in the time of Elihu. The pride of the heart, even in affliction, is the true reason with multitudes why they do not appeal to God, and why they do not pray. They have valued themselves on their independence of spirit. They have been accustomed to rely on their own resources. They have been unwilling to recognize their dependence on any being whatever. Even in their trials, the heart is too wicked to acknowledge God, and they would be ashamed to be known to do what they regard as so weak a thing as *to pray.* Hence they murmur in their afflictions; they

13 Surely God will not [a] hear vanity, neither will the Almighty regard it.

14 Although thou sayest thou shalt not see him; *yet* [b] judgment *is* before him; therefore trust thou in him.

15 But now, because *it is* not

a Is.1.15. b Ps.77.5—10.

---

linger on in their sufferings without consolation, and then die without hope. However inapplicable, therefore, this solution of the difficulty may have been to the case of Job, it is *not* inapplicable to the case of multitudes of sufferers. *Many of the afflicted have no peace or consolation in their trials—no "songs in the night"—* BECAUSE THEY ARE TOO PROUD TO PRAY!

13. *Surely God will not hear vanity.* A vain, hollow, heartless petition. The object of Elihu here is to account for the reason why sufferers are not relieved—having his eye, doubtless, on the case of Job as one of the most remarkable of the kind. The solution which he here gives of the difficulty is, that it is not consistent for God to hear a prayer where there is no sincerity. Of the *truth* of the remark there can be no doubt, but he seems to have taken it for granted that all prayers offered by unrelieved sufferers are thus insincere and hollow. This was needful in his view to account for the fact under consideration, and this he *assumes* as being unquestionable. Yet the very point indispensable to make out his case was, that *in fact* the prayers offered by such persons *were* insincere.

14. *Although thou sayest thou shalt not see him.* This is addressed to Job, and is designed to entreat him to trust in God. Elihu seems to refer to some remark that Job had made, like that in chap. xxiii. 8, seq., where he said that he could not come near him, nor bring his cause before him. If he went to the east, the west, the north, or the south, he could not see him, and could get no opportunity of bringing his cause before him; see Notes on that place. Elihu here says that though it is true in fact that God is invisible, yet this ought not to be regarded as a reason why he should not confide in him. The argument of Elihu here—which is undoubtedly sound—is, that the fact that God is invisible should not be regarded as any evidence that he does not attend to the affairs of men, or that he is not worthy of our love. ¶ *Judgment is before him.* He is a God of justice, and will do that which is right. ¶ *Therefore trust him.* Though he is invisible, and though you cannot bring your cause directly before him. The word which is here used (תְּחוֹלֵל, from חִיל) means to turn around; to twist; to be firm—as a rope is that is twisted; and then to wait or delay—that is, to be firm in patience. Here it may have this meaning, that Job was to be firm and unmoved, patiently waiting for the time when the now invisible God would interpose in his behalf, though he could not now see him. The idea is, that we may trust the *invisible God*, or that we should patiently *wait* for him to manifest himself in our behalf, and may leave all our interests in his hands, with the feeling that they are entirely safe. It must be admitted that Job had not learned this lesson as fully as it might have been learned, and that he had evinced an undue anxiety for some public *manifestation* of the favour and friendship of God, and that he had not shown quite the willingness which he should have done to commit his interests into his hands, though he was unseen.

15. *But now, because* it is *not so.* This verse, as it stands in our authorized translation, conveys no intelligible idea. It is evident that the translators meant to give a literal version of the Hebrew, but without understanding its sense. An examination of the principal words and phrases may enable us to ascertain the idea which was in the mind of Elihu when it was uttered. The phrase in the Hebrew here (ועתה כי־אין) may mean, "but now it is as nothing," and is to be connected with the following clause, denoting, "now it is comparatively nothing that he

so, [1] he hath visited in his anger;
yet he [2] knoweth *it* [a] not in great
extremity:
16 Therefore doth Job open his
mouth in vain: he multiplieth
words without knowledge.

CHAPTER XXXVI.

ANALYSIS OF THE CHAPTER.

This chapter is the commencement of the fourth speech of Elihu, which continues to the close of chap. xxxvii., when the subject is taken up by God himself. The object of this whole speech is to vindicate the justice of God in his dealings; and this is done mainly by showing that he has shown so much wisdom in the creation and government of the world, that men ought to have confidence in him, and to submit to him. This argument is pressed particularly in chap. xxxvi. 26—33, and in the whole of chap. xxxvii., where Elihu goes into an examination of the things in the works of God which show his inscrutable wisdom.

In this chapter, the argument consists of the following parts:

I. The introduction—where Elihu proposes to speak on behalf of God, and says that he will not deal in common place remark, but will bring his illustrations from subjects beyond the ordinary range of thinking. The idea is, that he has some views of the divine government which show that God is great, and just, and wise, and has a claim to confidence, ver. 1—4.

II. He affirms that God is just in his dealings; that he is the watchful guardian over the conduct of men; that whether men be on the throne or bound in fetters and chains, he equally observes them, and deals justly

1 i. e. *God.* 2 i. e. *Job.* *a* Hos. 11. 8, 9.

has visited you in his anger;" that is, the punishment which he has inflicted on you is almost as nothing compared with what it might have been, or what you have deserved. Job had complained much, and Elihu says to him, that so far from having cause of complaint, his sufferings were as nothing — scarcely worth noticing, compared with what they might have been. ¶ *He hath visited in his anger;* Marg. i. e. *God.* The word rendered "hath visited" (פָּקַד) means to visit for any purpose—for mercy or justice; to review, take an account of, or investigate conduct. Here it is used with reference to punishment — meaning that the punishment which he had inflicted was trifling compared with the desert of the offences. ¶ *Yet he knoweth* it *not.* Marg. i. e. *Job.* The marginal reading here is undoubtedly erroneous. The reference is not to Job, but to God, and the idea is, that he did not *know*, that is, did not *take full account* of the sins of Job. He passed them over, and did not bring them all into the account in his dealings with him. Had he done this, and marked every offence with the utmost strictness and severity, his punishment would have been much more severe. ¶ *In great extremity.* The Hebrew here is בַּפַּשׁ מְאֹד. The word פַּשׁ *pash*, occurs nowhere else in the Hebrew. The Septuagint renders it *παράπτωμα*, *offence*, and the Vulgate *scelus*, i. e. *transgression*. The authors of those versions evidently read it as if it were פֶּשַׁע, *iniquity;* and it may be that the final ע has been dropped, like שַׁו for שָׁוְא, in Job xv. 31. *Gesenius.* Theodotion and Symmachus in like manner render it *transgression*. Others have regarded it as if from פוּשׁ *to be proud*, and as meaning *in pride* or *arrogance;* and others, as the Rabbins generally, as if from פּוּשׁ, *to disperse*, meaning *on account* of the *multitude*, scil. of transgressions. So Rosenmüller, Umbreit, Luther, and the Chaldee. It seems probable to me that the interpretation of the Septuagint and the Vulgate is the correct one, and that the sense is, that he "does not take cognizance severely (מְאֹד) of transgressions;" that is, that he had not done it in the case of Job. This interpretation agrees with the scope of the passage, and with the view which Elihu meant to express—that God, so far from having given any just cause of complaint, had not even dealt with him as his sins deserved. Without any impeachment of his wisdom or goodness, his inflictions *might* have been far more severe.

16. *Therefore.* In view of all that Elihu had now said, he came to the conclusion that the views of Job were erroneous, and that he had no just cause of complaint. He had suffered no more than he had deserved; he might have obtained a release or mitigation if he had applied to God; and the government of God was just, and was every way worthy of confidence. The remarks of Job, therefore, complaining of the severity of his sufferings and of the government of God, were not based on knowledge, and had in fact no solid foundation.

with them; and that if they had been guilty of crime he takes measures to reclaim them, and to bring them to forsake their iniquity, ver. 5—14.

III. He affirms that God deals gently with the poor, the humble, and the contrite; and that if Job had manifested that spirit, he would have been merciful to him, and would have brought him out of his calamities. Having stated this general principle, he concludes that the true reason why Job continued thus to be afflicted was, that he was obstinate, and refused to repent of his sins under the chastisement of the divine hand, ver. 15—17. In this the view which Elihu takes of the nature and design of affliction differs from that taken by the friends of Job. *They* held that it was full proof of guilt and hypocrisy, *he* maintained that it was disciplinary in its nature; *they* affirmed that it demonstrated only that the sufferer was a sinner, *he* that if the sufferer was penitent he might again obtain the divine favour; *they* maintained that the true cause of the severe and protracted nature of the sufferings of Job was that he *had been* in his former life a man of eminent guilt, *Elihu* maintained that the reason why he suffered so much and so long was because the discipline had failed of its object, and he did not return with a humble and penitent heart to God.

IV. Elihu, therefore, exhorts Job with great earnestness to beware lest his obstinacy end in his ruin. God would not change, and if he persevered in his unyielding state of mind, the result must be destruction. That destruction was so great, that if it came upon him a great ransom could not rescue him; great riches could not save from it, nor the forces of strength recover him, ver. 18—21.

V. He then reminds Job that God is wise. None could teach like him; none had prescribed his way for him; and it became man to magnify his Maker, and to acknowledge him, ver. 22—25.

VI. The chapter is closed by the commencement of an argument respecting the inscrutable dealings of God, ver. 26—33. This argument is continued through the next chapter, and consists of appeals to his works, as being beyond our comprehension. Elihu refers, in this chapter, to the rain, the dew, the clouds, the light, the thunder, and the vapour, to show that we cannot understand his works. The design of the whole of this argument is to show that God is far above us; and that we should, therefore, bow with submission to his will; see chap. xxxvii. 23, 24.

ELIHU also proceeded and
said,
2 Suffer me a little, and I will
shew thee that [1] *I have* yet to speak
on God's behalf.

1 there are *yet words for God.*

CHAPTER XXXVI.

1. *Elihu also proceeded.* Heb. *added*—ויסף. Vulg. *addens*; LXX. Προσθεὶς—*adding*, or *proceeding*. The Hebrew commentators remark that this word is used because this speech is *added* to the number which it might be supposed he would make. There had been *three* series of speeches, by Job and his friends, and in each one of them Job had spoken three times. Each one of the three friends had also spoken thrice, except Zophar, who failed to reply when it came to his turn. Elihu had also now made three speeches, and here he would naturally have closed, but it is remarked that he *added* this to the usual number.

2. *Suffer me a little.* Even beyond the regular order of speaking; or, allow me to go on though I have fully occupied my place in the *number* of speeches. Jarchi remarks that this verse is *Chaldaic*, and it is worthy of observation that the principal words in it are not those ordinarily used in Hebrew to express the same thought, but are such as occur in the Chaldee. The word rendered *suffer* (כתר) has here a signification which occurs only in Syriac and Chaldee. It properly means in Hebrew, to *surround*, in a hostile sense; Judges xx. 43; Ps. xxii. 12; then in Hiph. to crown one's self. In Syriac and Chaldee, it means *to wait*—perhaps from the idea of going round and round—and this is the meaning here. He wished them not to remit their attention, but to have patience with what he would yet say. ¶ *And I will show thee that.* Marg. "there are *yet words for God.*" The Hebrew is, "And I will show you that there are yet words for God;" that is, that there were yet many considerations which could be urged in vindication of his government. The idea of Elihu is not so much that *he* had much to say, as that in fact there was much that *could be* said for him. He regarded his character and government as having been attacked, and he believed that there were ample considerations which could be urged in its defence. The word which is here rendered "I will show thee" (אחוך), is also Chaldee in its signification. It is from חוה (*Chald.*) not used in Kal, but it occurs in other forms in the Chaldee portion of the Scriptures; see Dan. ii. 11, 16, 24, 27. The use of these Chaldee words is somewhat remarkable, and perhaps may throw some light on the question about the time and place of the composition of the book.

3 I will fetch my knowledge from afar, and will ascribe righteousness to my Maker.

4 For truly my words *shall* not be false; he that is perfect in knowledge *is* with thee.

5 Behold, God *is* mighty, and despiseth not *any; he* [a] *is* mighty in strength *and* [1] wisdom.

a Jer.32.19. 1 heart.

3. *I will fetch my knowledge from afar.* What I say shall not be mere commonplace. It shall be the result of reflection on subjects that lie out of the ordinary range of thought. The idea is, that he did not mean to go over the ground that had been already trodden, or to suggest such reflections as would occur to any one, but that he meant to bring his illustrations from abstruser matters, and from things that had escaped their attention. He in fact appeals to the various operations of nature — the rain, the dew, the light, the instincts of the animal creation, the vicissitudes of the seasons, the laws of heat and cold, and shows that all these prove that God is inscrutably wise and gloriously great. ¶ *And will ascribe righteousness to my Maker.* That is, I will show that these things to which I now appeal, *prove* that he is righteous, and is worthy of universal confidence. Perhaps, also, he means to contrast the result of his reflections with those of Job. He regarded him as having charged his Maker with injustice and wrong. Elihu says that it was a fixed principle with him to ascribe righteousness to God, and that he believed it could be fully sustained by an appeal to his works. Man should *presume* that his Maker is good, and wise, and just; he should be *willing* to find that he is so; he should *expect* that the result of the profoundest investigation of his ways and works will prove that he is so—and in such an investigation he will never be disappointed. A man is in no good frame of mind, and is not likely to be led to any good result in his investigations, when he *begins* his inquiries by believing that his Maker is unjust, and who *prosecutes* them with the hope and expectation that he will find him to be so. Yet do men never do this?

4. *For truly my words* shall *not be false.* This is designed to conciliate attention. It is a professed purpose to state nothing but truth. Even in order to vindicate the ways of God he would state nothing but what would bear the most rigid examination. Job had charged on his friends a purpose "to speak wickedly for God;" to make use of unsound arguments in vindicating his cause, (see Notes on chap. xiii. 7, 8), and Elihu now says that *he* will make use of no such reasoning, but that all that he says shall be founded in strict truth. ¶ *He that is perfect in knowledge* is *with thee.* This refers undoubtedly to Elihu himself, and is a claim to a clear understanding of the subject. He did not doubt that he was right, and that he had some views which were worthy of their attention. The main idea is, that he was of *sound* knowledge; that his views were not sophistical and captious; that they were founded in truth, and were worthy, therefore, of their profound attention.

5. *Behold, God* is *mighty.* This is the first consideration which Elihu urges, and the purpose seems to be to affirm that God is so great that he has no occasion to modify his treatment of any class of men from a reference to himself. He is wholly independent of all, and can therefore be impartial in his dealings. If it were otherwise; if he were dependent on men for any share of his happiness, he might be tempted to show special favour to the great and to the rich; to spare the mighty who are wicked, though he cut off the poor. But he has no such inducement, as he is wholly independent; and it is to be presumed, therefore, that he treats all impartially; see Notes on chap. xxxv. 5—8. ¶ *And despiseth not* any. None who are poor and humble. He does not pass them by with cold neglect because they are poor and powerless, and turn his attention to the great and mighty because he is depen-

6 He preserveth not the life of
the wicked: but giveth right to
the [1] poor.
7 He [a] withdraweth not his eyes
from the righteous: but with kings
are they on the throne; yea, he
doth establish them for ever, and
they are exalted.
8 And if [b] *they be* bound in

1 or, *afflicted*. *a* He.13.5. *b* Ps.107.10.

dent on them. ¶ He is *mighty in wisdom*. Marg. *heart*. The word *heart* in Hebrew is often used to denote the intellectual powers; and the idea here is, that God has perfect wisdom in the management of his affairs. He is acquainted with all the circumstances of his creatures, and passes by none from a defect of knowledge, or from a want of wisdom to know how to adopt his dealings to their condition.

6. *He preserveth not the life of the wicked*. Elihu here maintains substantially the same sentiment which the three friends of Job had done, that the dealings of God in this life are in accordance with character, and that strict justice is thus maintained. ¶ *But giveth right to the poor*. Marg. "or *afflicted*." The Hebrew word often refers to the afflicted, to the humble, or the lowly; and the reference here is to the *lower classes* of society. The idea is, that God deals justly with them, and does not overlook them because they are so poor and feeble that they cannot contribute any thing to him. In this sentiment Elihu was undoubtedly right, though, like the three friends of Job, he seems to have adopted the principle that the dealings of God here are according to the *characters* of men. He had some views in advance of theirs. He saw that affliction is designed for *discipline* (chap. xxxiii.); that God is willing to show mercy to the sufferer on repentance; that he is not dependent on men, and that his dealings *cannot* be graduated by any reference to what he would receive or suffer from men; but still he clung to the idea that the dealings of God here are a proof of the character of the afflicted. What was mysterious about it he resolved into sovereignty, and showed that man *ought* to be submissive to God, and to *believe* that he was qualified to govern. He lacked the views which Christianity has furnished, that the inequalities that appear in the divine dealings here will be made clear in the retributions of another world.

7. *He withdraweth not his eyes from the righteous*. That is, he constantly observes them, whether they are in the more elevated or humble ranks of life. Even though he afflicts them, his eye is upon them, and he does not forsake them. It will be remembered that one of the difficulties to be accounted for was, that they who professed to be righteous are subjected to severe trials. The friends of Job had maintained that such a fact was in itself proof that they who professed to be pious were not so, but were hypocrites. Job had verged to the other extreme, and had said that it looked as if God had forsaken those that loved him, and that there was no advantage in being righteous; Notes, chap. xxxv. 2. Elihu takes a middle ground, and says that neither was the correct opinion. It is true, he says, that the righteous are afflicted, but they are not forsaken. The eye of God is still upon them, and he watches over them, whether on the throne or in dungeons, in order *to bring good results* out of their trials. ¶ *But with kings* are they *on the throne*. That is, if the righteous are in the state of the highest earthly honour and prosperity, God is with them, and is their protector and friend. The same thing Elihu, in the following verses, says is true respecting the righteous, when they are in the most down-trodden and depressed condition. ¶ *Yea, he doth establish them for ever*. The meaning of this is, that they are regarded by God with favour. When righteous kings *are* thus prospered, and have a permanent and peaceful reign, it is God who gives this prosperity to them. They are under his watchful eye, and his protecting hand.

fetters, *and* be holden in cords of affliction :

9 Then he sheweth them their work and their transgressions that they have exceeded.

10 He openeth also their ear to discipline, and commandeth that they return from iniquity.

11 If they obey and serve *him*, they shall spend their days in prosperity, and their years in pleasures :

12 But if they obey not, they shall perish [1] by the sword, and they shall die without knowledge.

1 *pass away.*

---

8. *And if* they be *bound in fetters.* That is, if the righteous are thrown into prison, and are subjected to oppressions and trials, or if they are chained down, as it were, on a bed of pain, or crushed by heavy calamities, the eye of God is still upon them. Their sufferings should not be regarded either as proof that they are hypocrites, or that God is regardless of them, and is indifferent whether men are good or evil. The true solution of the difficulty was, that God was then accomplishing purposes of discipline, and that happy results would follow if they would receive affliction in a proper manner.

9. *Then he showeth them their work.* What their lives have been. This he does either by a messenger sent to them (chap. xxxiii. 23), or by their own reflections (chap. xxxiii. 27), or by the influences of his Spirit leading them to a proper review of their lives. The object of their affliction, Elihu says, is to bring them to see what their conduct has been, and to reform what has been amiss. It should not be interpreted either as proof that the afflicted are eminently wicked, as the friends of Job maintained, or as furnishing an occasion for severe reflections on the divine government, such as Job had indulged in. It is all consistent with an equitable and kind administration ; with the belief that the afflicted have true piety—though they have wandered and erred ; and with the conviction that God is dealing with them in mercy, and not in the severity of wrath. They need only recal the errors of their lives ; humble themselves, and exercise true repentance, and they would find afflictions to be among even their richest blessings. ¶ *Transgressions that they have exceeded.* Or, rather, "he shows them their transgressions that *they have been very great ;*" that they have made themselves great, mighty, strong—יתגברו. The idea is, that their transgressions had been allowed to accumulate, or to become strong, until it was necessary to interpose in this manner, and check them by severe affliction. All this was consistent, however, with the belief that the sufferer was truly pious, and might find favour if he would repent.

10. *He openeth also their ear to discipline.* To teaching ; or he makes them willing to learn the lessons which their afflictions are designed to teach ; comp. Notes on chap. xxxiii. 16.

11. *If they obey and serve* him. That is, if, as the result of their afflictions, they repent of their sins, seek his mercy, and serve him in time to come, they shall be prospered still. The design of affliction, Elihu says, is, not to cut them off, but to bring them to repentance. This sentiment he had advanced and illustrated before at greater length ; see Notes on chap. xxxiii. 23–28. The object of all this is, doubtless, to assure Job that he should not regard his calamities either as proof that he had never understood religion—as his friends maintained ; or that God was severe, and did not regard those that loved and obeyed him—as Job had seemed to suppose ; but that there was something in his life and conduct which made discipline necessary, and that if he would repent of that, he would find returning prosperity, and end his days in happiness and peace.

12. *But if they obey not.* If those who are afflicted do not turn to God, and yield him obedience, they must expect that he will continue their calamities until they are cut off.

13 But the hypocrites in heart heap [a] up wrath; they cry not when he bindeth them:

a Rom.2.5.

14 They [1] die in youth, [b] and their life *is* among the [2] unclean.

1 *their soul dieth.* b Ps 55.23. 2 *Sodomites*, De.23.17.

¶ *They shall perish by the sword.* Marg. as in Heb. *pass away.* The word rendered *sword* (שלח) means properly *any thing sent*—as a spear or an arrow—*a missile*—and then an instrument of war in general. It may be applied to any weapon that is used to produce death. The idea here is, that the man who was afflicted on account of the sins which he had committed, and who did not repent of them and turn to God, would be cut off. God would not withdraw his hand unless he acknowledged his offences. As he had undertaken the work of discipline, he could not consistently do it, for it would be in fact *yielding* the point to him whom he chastised. This *may* be the case now, and the statement here made by Elihu may involve a principle which will explain the cause of the death of many persons, even of the professedly pious. They are devoted to gain or amusement; they seek the honours of the world for their families or themselves, and in fact they make no advances in piety, and are doing nothing for the cause of religion. God lays his hand upon them at first gently. They lose their health, or a part of their property. But the discipline is not effectual. He then lays his hand on them with more severity, and takes from them an endeared child. Still, all is ineffectual. The sorrow of the affliction passes away, and they mingle again in the gay and busy scenes of life as worldly as ever, and exert no influence in favour of religion. Another blow is needful, and blow after blow is struck; but nothing overcomes their worldliness, nothing makes them devotedly and sincerely useful, and it becomes necessary to remove them from the world. ¶ *They shall die without knowledge.* That is, without any true knowledge of the plans and government of God, or of the reasons why he brought these afflictions upon them. In all their sufferings they never *saw* the design. They complained, and murmured, and charged God with severity, but they never understood that the affliction was intended for their own benefit.

13. *But the hypocrites in heart heap up wrath.* By their continued impiety they lay the foundation for increasing and multiplied expressions of the divine displeasure. Instead of confessing their sins when they are afflicted, and seeking for pardon; instead of returning to God and becoming truly his friends, they remain impenitent, unconverted, and are rebellious at heart. They complain of the divine government and plans, and their feelings and conduct make it necessary for God farther to interpose, until they are finally cut off and consigned to ruin. Elihu had stated what was the effect in two classes of persons who were afflicted. There were those who were truly pious, and who would receive affliction as sent from God for purposes of discipline, and who would repent and seek his mercy; ver. 11. There were those, as a second class, who were openly wicked, and who would not be benefited by afflictions, and who would thus be cut off, ver. 12. He says, also, that there was a third class—the class of hypocrites, who also were not profited by afflictions, and who would only by their perverseness and rebellion heap up wrath. It is *possible* that he may have designed to include Job in this number, as his three friends had done, but it seems more probable that he meant merely to suggest to Job that there *was* such a class, and to turn his mind to the *possibility* that he might be of the number. In explaining the design and effect of afflictions, it was at least proper to refer to this class, since it could not be doubted that there *were* men of this description. ¶ *They cry not when he bindeth them.* They do not cry to God with the language of

15 He delivereth the [1] poor in his affliction, and openeth their ears in oppression:

1 or, *afflicted*.

16 Even so would he have removed thee out of the strait *into* a broad [a] place, where *there is* no

a Ps.31.8

penitence when he binds them down by calamities; see ver. 8.

14. *They die in youth*. Marg. *their soul dieth*. The word *soul* or *life* in the Hebrew is used to denote one's self. The meaning is, that they would soon be cut down, and share the lot of the openly wicked. If they amended their lives they might be spared, and continue to live in prosperity and honour; if they did not, whether openly wicked or hypocrites, they would be early cut off. ¶ *And their life is among the unclean*. Marg. *Sodomites*. The idea is, that they would be treated in the same way as the most abandoned and vile of the race. No special favour would be shown to them because they were *professors* of religion, nor would this fact be a shield against the treatment which they deserved. They could not be classed with the righteous, and must, therefore, share the fate of the most worthless and wicked of the race. The word rendered *unclean* (קְדֵשִׁים) is from קָדַשׁ—*kâdhăsh*, to be pure or holy; and in Hiph. to regard as holy, to consecrate, or devote to the service of God, as *e. g.* a priest; Ex. xxviii. 41; xxix. 1. Then it means to consecrate or devote to *any* service or purpose, as to an idol god. Hence it means one consecrated or devoted to the service of Astarte, the goddess of the Sidonians, or Venus, and as this worship was corrupt and licentious, the word means one who is licentious or corrupt; comp. Deut. xxiii. 18; 1 Kings xiv. 24; Gen. xxxviii. 21, 22. Here it means the licentious, the corrupt, the abandoned; and the idea is, that if hypocrites did not repent under the inflictions of divine judgment, they would be dealt with in the same way as the most abandoned and vile. On the evidence that licentiousness constituted a part of the ancient worship of idols, see Spencer *de Legg. ritual. Hebræor.* Lib. ii. cap. iii. pp. 613, 614, Ed. 1732. Jerome renders this, *inter effæminatos*. The LXX. strangely enough, "Let their life be wounded *by angels*."

15. *He delivereth the poor in his affliction*. Marg. " or afflicted." This accords better with the usual meaning of the Hebrew word (עני), and with the connection. The inquiry was not particularly respecting the *poor*, but the *afflicted*, and the sentiment which Elihu is illustrating is, that when the afflicted call upon God he will deliver them. The object is to induce Job to make such an application to God that he might be rescued from his calamities, and be permitted yet to enjoy life and happiness. ¶ *And openeth their ears*. Causes them to understand the nature of his government, and the reasons why he visits them in this manner: comp. chap. xxxiii. 16, 23–27. The sentiment here is a mere repetition of what Elihu had more than once before advanced. It is his leading thought; the *principle* on which he undertakes to explain the reason why God afflicts men, and by which he proposes to remove the difference between Job and his friends. ¶ *In oppression*. This word expresses too much. It refers to God, and implies that there was something oppressive, harsh, or cruel in his dealings. This is not the idea of Elihu in the language which he uses. The word which he uses here (לחץ) means that which crushes; then straits, distress, affliction. Jerome, *in tribulatione*. The word *affliction* would express the thought.

16. *Even so would he have removed thee*. That is, if you had been patient and resigned, and if you had gone to him with a broken heart. Having stated the *principles* in regard to affliction which he held to be indisputable, and having affirmed that God was ever ready to relieve the sufferer if he would apply to him with a proper spirit, it was natural to infer from this that the reason why Job *continued* to suffer was, that he did not manifest a proper spirit in his trials. Had he done this,

straitness; and [1] that which should
be set on thy table [a] *should be* full
of fatness.
17 But thou hast fulfilled the
judgment of the wicked: judgment
and justice [2] take *hold on thee.*
18 Because *there is* wrath, *beware*
lest he take thee away with *his*
stroke: then a great ransom cannot
[3] deliver thee.

1 *the rest of thy table.* *a* Ps.23.5.
2 or, *should uphold* thee. 3 *turn thee aside.*

Elihu says, the hand of God would have been long since withdrawn, and his afflictions would have been removed. ¶ *Out of the strait* into *a broad place.* From the narrow, pent-up way, where it is impossible to move, into a wide and open path. Afflictions are compared with a narrow path, in which it is impossible to get along; prosperity with a broad and open road in which there are no obstructions; comp. Ps. xviii. 19; xxxi. 8. ¶ *And that which should be set on thy table.* Marg. *the rest of thy table.* The Hebrew word (נחת—from נוח, *to rest,* and in Hiph. to set down, to cause to rest) means properly *a letting,* or *setting down;* and then that which is set down—as *e. g.* food on a table. This is the idea here, that the food which would be set on his table would be rich and abundant; that is, he would be restored to prosperity, if he evinced a penitent spirit in his trials, and confessed his sins to God. The same image of piety occurs in Ps. xxiii. 5, "Thou preparest a table before me in the presence of mine enemies."

17. *But thou hast fulfilled the judgment of the wicked.* Rosenmüller explains this as meaning, "If under divine inflictions and chastisements you wish to imitate the obduracy of the wicked, then the cause and the punishment will mutually sustain themselves; that is, the one will be commensurate with the other." But it is not necessary to regard this as a *supposition.* It has rather the aspect of an affirmation, meaning to express the fact that Job *had,* as Elihu feared, evinced the same spirit in his trials which the wicked do. He had not seen in him evidence of penitence and of a desire to return to God, but had heard complaints and murmurings, such as the wicked indulge in. He had "filled up," or "fulfilled," the judgment of the wicked; that is, he had in no way come short of the opinion which *they* expressed of the divine dealings. Still it is possible that the word "if" may be here understood, and that Elihu means merely to state that *if* Job should manifest the same spirit with the wicked, instead of a spirit of penitence, he would have reason to apprehend the same doom which they experience. ¶ *Judgment and justice take* hold on thee. Marg. "or, *should uphold thee.*" The Hebrew word here rendered *take*—יתמכו, is from תמך—to take hold of, to obtain, to hold fast, to support. Rosenmüller and Gesenius suppose that the word here has a *reciprocal* sense, and means they take hold of each other, or sustain each other. Prof. Lee renders it, "Both judgment and justice will uphold this;" that is, the sentiment which he had just advanced, that Job had filled up the judgment of the wicked. Umbreit renders it, "If thou art full of the opinion of the wicked, then the opinion and justice will rapidly follow each other."

Doch wenn du voll bist von des Frevlers Urtheil,
So werden Urtheil und Gericht schnell auf einander folgen.

According to this the meaning is, that if Job held the opinions of wicked men, he must expect that these opinions would be rapidly followed by judgment, or that they would go together, and support each other. This seems to me to be in accordance with the connection, and to express the thought which Elihu meant to convey. It is a sentiment which is undoubtedly true—that if a man holds the sentiments, and manifests the spirit of the wicked, he must expect to be treated as they are.

18. *Because* there is *wrath.* That is, the wrath of God is to be dreaded. The meaning is, that if Job persevered in the spirit which he had manifested, he had every reason to expect

19 Will he esteem thy riches? [a] *no,* not gold, nor all the forces of strength.

20 Desire not the night, when people are cut off in their place.

a Pr.11.4.

that God would suddenly cut him off. He might now repent and find mercy, but he had shown the spirit of those who were rebellious in affliction, and if he persevered in that, he had nothing to expect but the wrath of God. ¶ *With* his *stroke.* With his smiting or chastisement; comp. chap. xxxiv. 26. ¶ *Then a great ransom cannot deliver thee.* Marg. *turn thee aside.* The meaning is, that a great ransom could not prevent him from being cut off. On the meaning of the word *ransom,* see Notes on chap. xxxiii. 24. The idea here is, not that a great ransom could not deliver him *after* he was cut off and consigned to hell—which would be true; but that when he had manifested a spirit of insubmission a little longer, nothing could save him from being cut off from the land of the living. God would not spare him on account of wealth, or rank, or age, or wisdom. None of these things would be a *ransom* in virtue of which his forfeited life would be preserved.

19. *Will he esteem thy riches?* That is, God will not regard thy riches as a reason why he should not cut you off, or as a ransom for your forfeited life. The reference here must be to the fact that Job *had been* a rich man, and the meaning is, either that God would not spare him because he *had been* a rich man, or that if he had now all the wealth which he once possessed, it would not be sufficient to be a ransom for his life. ¶ *Nor all the forces of his strength.* Not all that gives power and influence to a man—wealth, age, wisdom, reputation, authority, and rank. The meaning is, that God would not regard any of these when a man was rebellious in affliction, and refused in a proper manner to acknowledge his Maker. Of the truth of what is here affirmed, there can be no doubt. Riches, rank, and honours cannot redeem the life of a man. They do not save him from the grave, and from all that is gloomy and revolting there. When God comes forth to deal with mankind, he does not regard their gold, their rank, their splendid robes or palaces, but he deals with them as *men*—and the gay, the beautiful, the rich, the noble, moulder back, under his hand, to their native dust, in the same manner as the most humble peasant. How forcibly should this teach us not to set our hearts on wealth, and not to seek the honours and wealth of the world as our portion!

20. *Desire not the night.* That is, evidently, *the night of death.* The darkness of the night is an emblem of death, and it is not uncommon to speak of death in this manner; see John ix. 4, "The night cometh, when no man can work." Elihu seems to have supposed that Job might have looked forward to death as to a time of release; that so far from *dreading* what he had said would come, that God would cut him off at a stroke, it might be the very thing which he desired, and which he anticipated would be an end of his sufferings. Indeed Job had more than once expressed some such sentiment, and Elihu designs to meet that state of mind, and to charge him not to look forward to death as relief. If his present state of mind continued, he says, he would perish under the "wrath" of God; and death in such a manner, great as might be his sufferings here, could not be desirable. ¶ *When people are cut off in their place.* On this passage, Schultens enumerates no less than *fifteen* different interpretations which have been given, and at the end of this enumeration remarks that he "waits for clearer light to overcome the shades of this night." Rosenmüller supposes it means, "Long not for the night, in which nations go under themselves;" that is, in which they go down to the inferior regions, or in which they perish. Noyes renders it, "To which nations are taken away to their place." Umbreit renders it, "Pant not for the night, to go down to the people who dwell under thee;" that is, to the Shades, or to

21 Take heed, regard not iniquity: for this hast thou chosen rather than affliction.

22 Behold, God *a* exalteth by his power: who teacheth *b* like him?

a Da.4.25,32. *b* Ps.94.12.

those that dwell in Sheol. Prof. Lee translates it, "Pant not for the night, for the rising of the populace from their places." Coverdale, "Prolong not thou the time, till there come a night for thee to set other people in thy stead." The LXX. "Do not draw out the night, that the people may come instead of them;" that is, to their assistance. Dr. Good, "Neither long thou for the night, for the vaults of the nations underneath them;" and supposes that the reference is to the *catacombs*, or mummy-pits that were employed for burial-places. These are but specimens of the interpretations which have been proposed for this passage, and it is easy to see that there is little prospect of being able to explain it in a satisfactory manner. The principal difficulty in the passage is in the word rendered *cut off*, (עלות) which means *to go up, to ascend*, and in the incongruity between that and the word rendered *in their place* (תחתם), which literally means *under them*. A literal translation of the passage is, "Do not desire the night to ascend to the people under them;" but I confess I cannot understand the passage, after all the attempts made to explain it. The translation given by Umbreit, seems best to agree with the connection, but I am unable to see that the Hebrew would bear this. See, however, his Note on the passage. The word עלה he understands here in the sense of *going away*, or *bearing away*, and the phrase the "people under them," as denoting the *Shades* in the world beneath us. The whole expression then would be equivalent to a wish *to die*—with the expectation that there would be a change for the better, or a release from present sufferings. Elihu admonishes Job not to indulge such a wish, for it would be no gain for a man to die in the state of mind in which he then was.

21. *Take heed, regard not iniquity.* That is, be cautious that in the view which you take of the divine government, and the sentiments which you express, you do not become the advocate of iniquity. Elihu apprehended this from the remarks in which he had indulged, and regarded him as having become the advocate of the same sentiments which the wicked held, and as in fact manifesting the same spirit. It is well to put a man who is afflicted on his guard against this, when he attempts to reason about the divine administration. ¶ *For this hast thou chosen rather than affliction.* That is, you have chosen rather to give vent to the language of complaint, than to bear your trials with resignation. "You have chosen rather to accuse divine Providence than to submit patiently to his chastisements." *Patrick.* There was too much truth in this remark about Job; and it is still not an uncommon thing in times of trial, and indeed in human life in general. Men often prefer iniquity to affliction. They will commit crime rather than suffer the evils of poverty; they will be guilty of fraud and forgery to avoid apprehended want. They will be dishonest to their creditors rather than submit to the disgrace of bankruptcy. They will take advantage of the widow and the fatherless rather than suffer themselves. *Sin is often preferred to affliction;* and many are the men who, to avoid calamity, would not shrink from the commission of wrong. Especially in times of trial, when the hand of God is laid on men, they *prefer* a spirit of complaining and murmuring to patient and calm resignation to the will of God. They seek relief even in complaining; and think it *some* alleviation of their sufferings that they can *find fault with God.* "They who choose iniquity rather than affliction, make a very foolish choice; they that ease their cares by sinful pleasures, escape their troubles by sinful projects, and evade sufferings for righteousness' sake by sinful compliances against their consciences; these make a choice they will repent of, for there is more

23 Who hath enjoined him his way? or who can say, Thou hast wrought iniquity?

24 Remember that thou magnify [a] his work, which men behold.

[a] Ps.118.2,8.

evil in the least sin than in the greatest affliction." *Henry*.

22. *Behold, God exalteth by his power.* The object of Elihu is now to direct the attention of Job to God, and to show him that he has evinced such power and wisdom in his works, that we ought not to presume to arraign him, but should bow with submission to his will. He remarks, therefore, that God *exalts*, or rather that God *is exalted*, or *exalts himself* (ישׂגיב) by his power. In the exhibition of his power, he thus shows that he is great, and that men ought to be submissive to him. In support of this, he appeals, in the remainder of his discourse, to the *works* of God as furnishing extraordinary proofs of power, and full demonstration that God is exalted far above man. ¶ *Who teacheth like him?* The LXX. render this, δυνάστης—"Who is so powerful as he?" Rosenmüller and Umbreit render it *Lord:* "Who is Lord like him?" But the Hebrew word (מורה) properly means *one who instructs*, and the idea is, that there is no one who is qualified to give so exalted conceptions of the government of God as he is himself. The object is to direct the mind to him as he is revealed in his works, in order to obtain elevated conceptions of his government.

23. *Who hath enjoined him his way?* Who hath prescribed to him what he ought to do? Who is superior to him, and has marked out for him the plan which he ought to pursue? The idea is, that God is supreme and independent; no one has advised him, and no one has a right to counsel him. Perhaps, also, Elihu designs this as a reproof to Job for having complained so much of the government of God, and for being disposed, as he thought, to *prescribe* to God what he should do. ¶ *Who can say, Thou hast wrought iniquity?* Thou hast done wrong. The object of Elihu is here to show that no one has a right to say this; no one could, in fact, say it. It was to be regarded as an indisputable point that God is always right, and that however dark his dealings with men may seem, the *reason* why they are mysterious *never is, that God is wrong*.

24. *Remember that thou magnify his work.* Make this a great and settled principle, to remember that God is *great* in all that he does. He is exalted far above us, and all his works are on a scale of vastness corresponding to his nature, and in all our attempts to judge of him and his doings, we should bear this in remembrance. He is not to be judged by the narrow views which we apply to the doings of men, but by the views which ought to be taken when we remember that he presides over the vast universe, and that as the universal Parent, he will consult the welfare of the whole. In judging of his doings, therefore, we are not to place ourselves in the centre, or to regard ourselves as the *whole* of the creation, but we are to remember that there are other great interests to be regarded, and that his plans will be in accordance with the welfare of the whole. One of the best rules for taking a proper estimate of God is that proposed here by Elihu—to remember that HE IS GREAT. ¶ *Which men behold.* The Vulgate renders this, *de quo cecinerunt viri*—"concerning which men sing." The LXX., ὧν ἦρξαν ἄνδρες—"over which men rule." Schultens accords with the Vulgate. So Coverdale renders it, "Whom all men love and praise." So Herder and Noyes understand it, "Which men celebrate with songs." This difference of interpretation arises from the ambiguity of the Hebrew word (שׁררו) some deriving it from שׁור—*shūr*, to go round about, and then to survey, look upon, examine; and some from שׁיר—*shir, to sing, to celebrate.* The word will admit of either interpretation, and either will suit the connection. The sense of *seeing* those works, however, better

25 Every man may see it; man
may behold *it* afar off.
26 Behold, God *is* great, and we
know *him* not; neither [a] can the
number of his years be searched
out.
27 For he maketh small the
drops of water: they pour down

a Ps.102.24.

agrees with what is said in the following verse, and perhaps better suits the connection. The object of Elihu is not to fix the attention on the fact that men *celebrate* the works of God, but to turn *the eyes to the visible creation,* as a proof of the greatness of the Almighty.

25. *Every man may see it.* That is, every man may look on the visible creation, and see proofs there of the wisdom and greatness of God. All may look on the sun, the moon, the stars; all may behold the tempest and the storm; all may see the lightning and the rain, and may form some conception of the majesty of the Most High. The idea of Elihu here is, that every man might trace the evidences that God is great in his works. ¶ *Man may behold* it *afar off.* His works are so great and glorious that they make an impression even at a vast distance. Though we are separated from them by a space which surpasses the power of computation, yet they are so great that they fill the mind with vast conceptions of the majesty and glory of their Maker. This is true of the heavenly bodies; and the more we learn of their immense distances from us, the more is the mind impressed with the greatness and glory of the visible creation.

26. *Behold, God* is *great, and we know* him *not.* That is, we cannot fully comprehend him; see Notes on chap. xi. 7—9. ¶ *Neither can the number of his years be searched out.* That is, he is eternal. The object of what is said here is to impress the mind with a sense of the greatness of God, and with the folly of attempting fully to comprehend the reason of what he does. Man is of a few days, and it is presumption in him to sit in judgment on the doings of one who is from eternity. We may here remark that the doctrine that there is an Eternal Being presiding over the universe, was a doctrine fully held by the speakers in this book—a doctrine far in advance of all that philosophy ever taught, and which was unknown for ages in the lands on which the light of revelation never shone.

27. *For he maketh small the drops of water.* Elihu now appeals, as he proposed to do, to the works of God, and begins with what appeared so remarkable and inexplicable, the wisdom of God in the rain and the dew, the tempest and the vapour. That which excited his wonder was, the fact in regard to the suspension of water in the clouds, and the distilling of it on the earth in the form of rain and dew. This very illustration had been used by Eliphaz for a similar purpose (Notes, chap. v 9,10), and whether we regard it as it *appears* to men without the light which science has thrown upon it, or look at the manner in which God suspends water in the clouds and sends it down in the form of rain and dew, with all the light which has been furnished by science, the fact is one that evinces in an eminent degree the wisdom of God. The word which is rendered "maketh small" (גרע), means properly *to scrape off, to detract, to diminish, to take away from.* In Piel, the form used here, it means, according to Gesenius, *to take to one's self, to attract;* and the sense here, according to this, is, that God attracts, or draws upwards the drops of water. So it is rendered by Herder, Noyes, Umbreit, and Rosenmüller. The idea is, that he *draws up* the drops of the water to the clouds, and then pours them down in rain. If the meaning in our common version be retained, the idea would be, that it was proof of great wisdom in God that the water descended in *small drops,* instead of coming down in a deluge; comp. Notes on chap. xxvi. 8. ¶ *They pour down rain.* That is, the clouds pour down the rain. ¶ *According to the vapour*

rain [a] according to the vapour
thereof.
28 Which the clouds do drop
and distil upon man abundantly.
29 Also can *any* understand the
spreadings of the clouds, *or* the
noise of his tabernacle?
30 Behold, he spreadeth [b] his
light upon it, and covereth the
[1] bottom of the sea.

a Ps.147.8. *b* Lu.17.24. 1 *roots.*

thereof—לְאֵדוֹ. The idea seems to be, that the water thus drawn up is poured down again in the form of a *vapoury rain*, and which does not descend in torrents. The subject of admiration in the mind of Elihu was, that water should evaporate and ascend to the clouds, and be held there, and then descend again in the form of a gentle rain or fine mist. The reason for admiration is not lessened by becoming more fully acquainted with the laws by which it is done than Elihu can be supposed to have been.

28. *Upon man abundantly.* That is, upon many men. The clouds having received the ascending vapour, retain it, and pour it down copiously for the use of man. The arrangement, to the eye even of one who did not understand the scientific principles by which it is done, is beautiful and wonderful; the beauty and wonder are increased when the laws by which it is accomplished are understood. Elihu does not attempt to explain the *mode* by which this is done. The *fact* was probably all that was then understood, and that was sufficient for his purpose. The LXX. have given a translation of this verse which cannot be well accounted for, and which is certainly very unlike the original. It is, "But when the clouds cast a shade over the dumb creation, he impresseth a care on beasts, and they know the order for retiring to rest—κοίτης τάξιν. At all these things is not their understanding confounded? And is not thy heart starting from thy body?"

29. *Also, can* any *understand the spreadings of the clouds?* The outspreading—the manner in which they expand themselves over us. The idea is, that the manner in which the clouds seem to *spread out*, or unfold themselves on the sky, could not be explained, and was a striking proof of the wisdom and power of God. In the early periods of the world, it could not be expected that the causes of these phenomena would be known. Now that the causes *are* better known, however, they do not less indicate the wisdom and power of God, nor are these facts less fitted to excite our wonder. The simple and beautiful laws by which the clouds are suspended; by which they roll in the sky; by which they spread themselves out—as in a rising tempest, and by which they seem to unfold themselves over the heavens, should increase, rather than diminish, our conceptions of the wisdom and power of the Most High. ¶ Or, *the noise of his tabernacle.* Referring, doubtless, to thunder. The clouds are represented as a tent or pavilion spread out for the dwelling of God (comp. Notes on Isa. xl. 22), and the idea here is, that the noise made in a thunder-storm is in the peculiar dwelling of God. Herder well expresses it, "The fearful thunderings in his tent," comp. Ps. xviii. 11:

He made darkness his secret place,
His pavilion round about him were dark
waters and thick clouds of the skies.

The sense here is, Who can understand and explain the cause of thunder? The object of Elihu in this is, to show how great and incomprehensible is God, and nature furnishes few more impressive illustrations of this than the crash of thunder.

30. *Behold, he spreadeth his light upon it.* That is, upon his tabernacle or dwelling-place—the clouds. The allusion is to lightning, which flashes in a moment over the whole heavens. The image is exceedingly beautiful and graphic. The idea of *spreading out* the light in an instant over the whole of the darkened heavens, is that which Elihu had in his mind, and which impressed him so forcibly. On the difficulty in regard to the translation of the Septuagint here, see Schleusner on the word ἠδῶ. ¶ *And covereth the*

31 For by them [a] judgeth he the people; he [b] giveth meat in abundance.

32 With clouds he covereth the light; and commandeth it *not to shine*, by *the cloud* that cometh betwixt.

a De.8.2,15. *b* Ps.136.25; Acts 14.17.

bottom of the sea. Marg. *roots.* The word *roots* is used to denote the bottom, as being the lowest part of a thing—as the roots of a tree. The meaning is that he covers the lowest part of the sea with floods of waters; and the object of Elihu is to give an exalted conception of the greatness of God, from the fact that his agency is seen in the highest and the lowest objects. He spreads out the clouds, thunders in his tabernacle, diffuses a brilliant light over the heavens, and at the same time is occupied in covering the bottom of the sea with the floods. He is Lord over all, and his agency is seen every where. The highest and the lowest objects are under his control, and his agency is seen above and below. On the one hand, he covers the thick and dense clouds with light; and on the other, he envelopes the depth of the ocean in impenetrable darkness.

31. *For by them judgeth he the people.* By means of the clouds, the rain, the dew, the tempest, and the thunderbolt. The idea seems to be, that he makes use of all these to execute his purposes on mankind. He can either make them the means of imparting blessings, or of inflicting the severest judgments. He can cause the tornado to sweep over the earth; he can arm the forked lightning against the works of art; he can withhold rain and dew, and spread over a land the miseries of famine. ¶ *He giveth meat in abundance.* That is, by the clouds, the dew, the rain. The idea is, that he can send timely showers if he chooses, and the earth will be clothed with plenty. All these things are under his control, and he can, as he pleases, make them the means of comfort to man, or of punishing him for his sins; comp. Ps. lxv. 11—13.

32. *With clouds he covereth the light.* The Hebrew here is, על־כפים —"upon his hands." Jerome, *In manibus abscondit lucem,* "he hideth the light in his hands." Sept., Ἐπὶ χειρῶν ἐκάλυψε φῶς—"he covereth the light in his hands." The allusion is, undoubtedly, to the lightning, and the image is, that God takes the lightning in his hands, and directs it as he pleases. There has been great variety however, in the exposition of this verse and the following. Schultens enumerates no less than *twenty-eight* different interpretations, and almost every commentator has had his own view of the passage. It is quite evident that our translators did not understand it, and were not able to make out of it any tolerable sense. What idea they attached to the two verses (32, 33), it would be very difficult to imagine, for what is the meaning (ver. 33) of the phrase, "the cattle also concerning the vapour?" The general sense of the Hebrew appears to be, that God controls the rapid lightnings which appear so vivid, so quick, and so awful; and that he executes his own purposes with them, and makes them, when he pleases, the instruments of inflicting punishment on his foes. The object of Elihu is to excite admiration of the greatness of God who is *able* thus to control the lightning's flash, and to make it an obedient instrument in his hands. The particular expression before us, "By his hands he covereth the light," seems to mean that he seizes or holds the lightning in his hands *(Herder)*, or that he covers over his hands *with* the lightning *(Umbreit)*, and has it under his control. Prof. Lee supposes that it means, that he holds the lightning in the palms of his hands, or between his two hands, as a man holds a furious wild animal which he is about to let loose for the purpose of destroying. With this he compares the expression of Shakspeare, "Cry havock, and let slip the dogs of war." There can be no doubt, I think, that the phrase means that God has the lightning under his control, that it is in his hands, and that he directs it as

33 The noise *a* thereof sheweth concerning it, the cattle also concerning [1] the vapour.

a 1 Ki.18.41,45. [1] *that which goeth up.*

he pleases. According to Umbreit (Note) the allusion is to the *double use* which God makes of light, in one hand holding the lightning to destroy his foes, and in the other the light of the sun to bless his friends, as he makes use of the rain either for purposes of destruction or mercy. But this idea is not conveyed in the Hebrew. ¶ *And commandeth it* not to shine. The phrase " not to shine" is not in the Hebrew, and destroys the sense. The simple idea in the original is, " he commandeth it ;" that is, he has it under his control, directs it as he pleases, makes use even of the forked lightning as an instrument to execute his pleasure. ¶ *By* the cloud *that cometh betwixt.* The words " the cloud " are also inserted by our translators, and destroy the sense. There is no allusion to a cloud, and the idea that the light is intercepted by any object is not in the original. The Hebrew word (במפגיע) means *in occurring, in meeting,* in striking upon, (from פגע—to strike upon, to impinge to fall upon, to light upon), and the sense here would be well expressed by the phrase "*in striking.*" The idea is exactly that which we have when we apply the word *strike* or *struck* to lightning, and the meaning is, that he gives the lightning commandment *in striking,* or when *it strikes.* Nothing could better answer the purpose of an illustration for Elihu in exciting elevated views of God, for there is no exhibition of his power more wonderful than that by which he controls the lightning.

33. *The noise thereof showeth concerning it.* The word "*noise*" here has been inserted by our translators as a version of the Hebrew word (רעו), and if the translators attached any idea to the language which they have used, it seems to have been that the noise attending the lightning, that is, the thunder, furnished an illustration of the power and majesty of God. But it is not possible to educe this idea from the original, and perhaps it is not possible to determine the sense of the passage. Herder renders it, " He pointeth out to them the wicked." Prof. Lee, " By it he announceth his will." Umbreit, " He makes known to it his friend ;" that is, he points out his friend to the light, so that it may serve for the happiness of that friend. Noyes, " He uttereth to him his voice ; to the herds and the plants." Rosenmüller, " He announces what he has decreed against men, and the flocks which the earth has produced." Many other expositions have been proposed, and there is no reasonable ground of hope that an interpretation will be arrived at which will be free from all difficulty. The principal difficulty in this part of the verse arises from the word רעו, rendered in our version, " The noise thereof." This may be from רוע, and may mean a *noise,* or *outcry,* and so it is rendered here by Gesenius, " He makes known to him his thunder, *i. e.* to man, or to his enemies." Or the word may mean *his friend,* as the word רע is often used ; Job ii. 11 ; xix. 21 ; Prov. xxvii. 17 ; Cant. v. 16 ; Hos. iii. 1. Or it may denote *will, thought, desire;* Ps. cxxxix. 2, 17. A choice must be made between these different meanings according to the view entertained of the scope of the passage. To me it seems that the word "*friend*" will better suit the connection than any one of the other interpretations proposed. According to this, the idea is, that God points out *his friends* to the lightning which he holds in his hand, and bids it spare them. He has entire control of it, and can direct it where he pleases, and instead of sending it forth to work indiscriminate destruction, he carefully designates those on whom he wishes it to strike, but bids it spare his friends. ¶ *The cattle also concerning the vapour.* Marg. *that which goeth up.* What idea the translators attached to this phrase it is impossible now to know, and the probability is, that being conscious of utter inability to give *any* meaning to the passage, they endeavoured to translate the *words* of the original as

CHAPTER XXXVII.

ANALYSIS OF THE CHAPTER.

THIS chapter is a continuation of the argument commenced in the previous chapter to demonstrate the majesty and glory of God. The object is to show that his works are past finding out, and that therefore it becomes man to bow with submission under the dealings of his hand; see the analysis of chap. xxxvi. In the prosecution of this argument, Elihu refers to the following things as illustrating the majesty of God, and as showing how incomprehensibly wise he is. To the tempest, or thunder storm, ver. 1—5; to the snow and rain, ver. 6—8; to the whirlwind, the cold, and the frost, ver. 9—13; to the phenomena of the clouds, ver. 14—16; to his own garments as imparting heat to the body, ver. 17; to the sky, spread out like a molten looking-glass, ver. 18; to the bright light on the clouds and to the fair weather that comes out of the North, ver. 21, 22. In view of all this, he says that he was unable to speak of God in any adequate manner (ver. 19, 20; that we cannot hope to find him out, and that we ought to fear him, and to believe that he is wise and impartial in all his doings.

AT this also my heart trembleth,
a and is moved out of his place.

a Da.10.7,8; Mat.28 2-4; Ac.16.26-29.

literally as possible. Coverdale evidently felt the same perplexity, for he renders it, "The rising up thereof showeth he to his friends and to the cattle." Indeed almost every translator and expositor has had the same difficulty, and each one has proposed a version of his own. An examination of the *words* employed is the only hope of arriving at any satisfactory view of the passage. The word rendered *cattle* (מִקְנֶה), means properly, (1,) expectation, hope, confidence; Ezek. 28. 26; Ezra x. 2; (2,) a gathering together, a collection, as (*a*) of waters, Gen. i. 10; Ex. vii. 19, (*b*) a gathering together, a collection, or company of men, horses, &c.—a caravan. So it may possibly mean in 1 Kings x. 28, where interpreters have greatly differed. The word *cattle*, therefore, by no means expresses its usual signification. That would be better expressed by *gathering, collecting*, or *assembling*. The word rendered *also* (אַף), denotes (1,) also, even, more, besides, &c., and (2,) *the nose*, and then *anger*—from the effect of anger in producing hard breathing, Prov. xxii. 24; Deut. xxxii. 22; xxix. 20. Here it may be rendered, without impropriety, *anger*, and then the phrase will mean, "the collecting, or gathering together of anger." The word rendered *vapour* (עוֹלֶה—if from עלה), means that which *ascends*, and would then mean any thing that ascends—as smoke, vapour; or as Rosenmüller supposes, what *ascends*, or *grows* from the ground—that is, plants and vegetables, And so Umbreit, *das Gewächs*—"plants of any kind." *Note*. But with a slight variation in the pointing עַוְלָה—instead of עוֹלֵה), the word means *evil, wickedness, iniquity*—whence our word *evil*; Job xxiv. 20; vi. 29; xi. 14; xiii. 7; and it may, without impropriety, be regarded as having this signification here, as the points have no authority. The meaning of the whole phrase then will be, "the gathering, or collecting of his wrath is upon evil, *i. e.* upon the wicked;" and the sense is, that while, on the one hand, God, who holds the lightning in his hands, points out to it his friends, so that they are spared; on the other hand the gathering together, or the condensation, of his wrath is upon the evil. That is, the lightnings—so vivid, so mighty, and apparently so wholly beyond law or control, are under his direction, and he makes them the means of executing his pleasure. His friends are spared; and the condensation of his wrath is on his foes. This exposition of the passage accords with the general scope of the remarks of Elihu, and this view of the manner in which God controls even the lightning, was one that was adapted to fill the mind with exalted conceptions of the majesty and power of the Most High.

CHAPTER XXXVII.

1. *At this also*. That is, in view of the thunder-storm, for it is that which Elihu is describing. This description was commenced in chap. xxxvi. 29, and is continued to ver. 5 of this chapter, and should not have been separated by the division into chapters. Elihu sees a tempest rising. The clouds gather, the lightnings flash, the thunder rolls, and he is awed as with the conscious presence of God. There is nowhere to be found a more graphic and impressive description of a thunder-storm than this; comp. Herder on Heb. Poetry, vol. i., 85,

2 Hear [1] attentively the noise of
his voice, and the sound *that* goeth
out of his mouth.
3 He directeth it under the whole
heaven, and his [2] lightning unto
the [3] ends of the earth.
4 After it a voice [a] roareth: he
thundereth [b] with the voice of his
excellency; and he will not stay
them when his voice is heard.

1 *hear in hearing.* 2 *light.* 3 *wings.* a Ps.68.33. b Ps.29.3.

seq., by Marsh, Burlington, 1833. ¶ *My heart trembleth.* With fear. He refers to the palpitation or increased action of the heart produced by alarm. ¶ *And is moved out of his place.* That is, by violent palpitation. The heart seems to leave its calm resting-place, and to burst away by affright. The increased action of the heart under the effects of fear, as described here by Elihu, has been experienced by all. The *cause* of this increased action is supposed to be this. The immediate effect of fear is on the extremities of the nerves of the system, which are diffused over the whole body. The first effect is to prevent the circulation of the blood to the extremities, and to drive it back to the heart, and thus to produce paleness. The blood thus driven back on the heart produces an increased action there to propel it through the lungs and the arteries, thus causing at the same time the increased effort of the heart, and the rapid action of the lungs, and of course the quick breathing and the palpitation observed in fear. See Scheutzer, Physica. Sacra, *in loc.* An expression similar to that which occurs here, is used by Shakspeare, in Macbeth:

"Why do I yield to that suggestion,
Whose horrid image doth unfix my hair,
And make my seated heart knock at my ribs
Against the use of nature."

2. *Hear attentively.* Marg. as in Heb. *hear in hearing;* that is, hear with attention. It has been supposed by many, and not without probability, that the tempest was already seen rising, out of which God was to address Job (chap. xxxviii.), and that Elihu here calls the special attention of his hearers to the gathering storm, and to the low muttering thunder in the distance. ¶ *The noise of his voice.* Thunder is often represented as the voice of God, and this was one of the most natural of all suppositions when its nature was little understood, and is at all times a beautiful poetic conception; see the whole of Ps. xxix. The word rendered "noise" (רֹגֶז), means properly *commotion,* that which is fitted to produce perturbation, or disquiet (see chap. iii. 17, 26; Isa. xiv. 3), and is here used to denote the commotion, or *raging* of thunder. ¶ *And the sound.* The word here used (הֶגֶה) means properly a *muttering growling*—as of thunder. It is often used to denote sighing, moaning, and meditation, in contradistinction from clear enunciation. Here it refers to the thunder which seems to mutter or growl in the sky.

3. *He directeth it under the whole heaven.* It is under the control of God, and he directs it where he pleases. It is not confined to one spot, but seems to be murmuring from every part of the heavens. ¶ *And his lightning.* Marg. as in Heb. *light.* There can be no doubt that the lightning is intended. ¶ *Unto the ends of the earth.* Marg. as in Heb. *wings.* The word *wings* is given to the earth from the idea of its being spread out or expanded like the wings of a bird; comp. chap. xxxviii. 13; Ezek. vii. 2. The earth was spoken of as an expanse or plain that had corners or boundaries (Notes on Isa. xi. 12; xxiv. 16; xlii. 5), and the meaning here is, that God spread the lightning at pleasure over the whole of that vast expanse.

4. *After it a voice roareth.* After the lightning; that is, the flash is seen before the thunder is heard. This is apparent to all, the interval between the lightning and the hearing of the thunder depending on the distance. Lucretius, who has referred to the same fact, compares this with what occurs when a woodman is seen at a distance to wield an axe. The glance of the axe is seen long before the sound of the blow is heard:

5 God thundereth marvellously with his voice; great things doeth he, [a] which we cannot comprehend.

[a] Ec.3.11; Ro.11.33.

Sed tonitrum fit uti post auribus accipiamus,
Fulgere quam cernunt oculi, quia semper ad aures
Tardius adveniunt, quam visum, quam moveant res.
Nunc etiam licet id cognoscere, cædere si quem
Ancipiti videas ferro procul arboris actum,
Ante fit, ut cernas ictum, quam plaga per aures
Det sonitum: Sic fulgorem quoque cernimus ante. Lib. vi.

¶ *He thundereth with the voice of his excellency.* That is, with a voice of majesty and grandeur. ¶ *And he will not stay them.* That is, he will not hold back the rain, hail, and other things which accompany the storm, when he begins to thunder. *Rosenmüller.* Or, according to others, he will not hold back and restrain the lightnings when the thunder commences. But the connection seems rather to demand that we should understand it of the usual accompaniments of a storm—the wind, hail, rain, &c. Herder renders it, "We cannot explore his thunderings." Prof. Lee, "And none can trace them, though their voice be heard." According to him, the meaning is, that "great and terrific as this exhibition of God's power is, still the progress of these, his ministers, cannot be followed by the mortal eye." But the usual interpretation given to the Hebrew word is that of *holding back*, or *retarding*, and this idea accords well with the connection.

5. *God thundereth marvellously.* He thunders in a wonderful manner. The idea is, that the voice of his thunder is an amazing exhibition of his majesty and power. ¶ *Great things doeth he, which we cannot comprehend.* That is, not only in regard to the thunder and the tempest, but in other things. The description of the storm properly ends here, and in the subsequent verses Elihu proceeds to specify various other phenomena, which were wholly incomprehensible by man. The reference here to the storm, and to the other grand and incomprehensible phenomena of nature, is a most appropriate introduction to the manifestation of God himself as described in the next chapter, and could not but have done much to prepare Job and his friends for that sublime close of the controversy.

The passage before us (chap. xxxvi. 29–33; xxxvii. 1—5), is probably the earliest description of a thunder-storm on record. A tempest is a phenomenon which must early have attracted attention, and which we may expect to find described or alluded to in all early poetry. It may be interesting, therefore, to compare this description of a storm, in probably the oldest poem in the world, with what has been furnished by the masters of song in ancient and modern times, and we shall find that in sublimity and beauty the Hebrew poet will suffer nothing in comparison. In one respect, which constitutes the chief sublimity of the description, he surpasses them all; I mean in the recognition of God. In the Hebrew description, God is every where in the storm. He excites it; he holds the lightnings in both hands; he directs it where he pleases; he makes it the instrument of his pleasure and of executing his purposes. Sublime, therefore, as is the description of the storm itself, furious as is the tempest; bright as is the lightning; and heavy and awful as is the roar of the thunder, yet the description derives its chief sublimity from the fact that *God* presides over all, riding on the tempest and directing the storm as he pleases. Other poets have rarely attempted to give this direction to the thoughts in their description of a tempest, if we may except Klopstock, and they fall, therefore, far below the sacred poet. The following is the description of a storm by Elihu, according to the exposition which I have given:

Who can understand the outspreading of the clouds,
And the fearful thunderings in his pavilion?
Behold, he spreadeth his light upon it;
He also covereth the depths of the sea.
By these he executeth judgment upon the people,

By these he giveth food also in abundance.
With his hands he covereth the lightning,
And commandeth it where to strike.
He pointeth out to it his friends—
The collecting of his wrath is upon the wicked.
At this also my heart palpitates,
And is moved out of its place.
Hear, O hear, the thunder of his voice!
The muttering thunder that goes from his mouth!
He directeth it under the whole heaven,
And his lightning to the ends of the earth.
After it, the thunder roareth;
He thundereth with the voice of his majesty,
And he will not restrain the tempest when his voice is heard.
God thundereth marvellously with his voice;
He doeth wonders, which we cannot comprehend.

The following is the description of a tempest by Æschylus, in the Prometh. Desm., beginning,

—Χθὼν σεσάλευται·
Βρυχία δ' ἠχὼ παραμυκᾶται
Βροντῆς, κ.τ.λ.

———"I feel in very deed
The firm earth rock: the thunder's deepening roar
Rolls with redoubled rage; the bickering flames
Flash thick; the eddying sands are whirled on high;
In dreadful opposition, the wild winds
Rend the vex'd air; the boisterous billows rise
Confounding earth and sky: the impetuous storm
Rolls all its terrible fury." *Potter.*

Ovid's description is the following:

Æthera conscendit, vultumque sequentia traxit
Nubila; queis nimbos, immistaque fulgura ventis
Addidit, et tonitrus, et inevitabile fulmen.
Meta. ii.

The description of a storm by Lucretius, is the following:

Præterea persæpe niger quoque per mare nimbus
Ut picis è cœlo demissum flumen, in undas
Sic cadit. et fertur tenebris, procul et trahit atram
Fulminibus gravidam tempestatem, atque procellis,
Ignibus ac ventis cum primus ipse repletus:
In terris quoque ut horrescant ac tecta requirant.
Sic igitur supra nostrum caput esse putandum est
Tempestatem altam. Neque enim caligine tanta
Obruerat terras, nisi inædificata supernè
Multa forent multis exempto nubila sole.
Lib. vi.

The well-known description of the storm by Virgil is as follows:

Nimborum in patriam, loca foeta furentibus austris,
Æoliam venit. Hic vasto Rex Æolus antro
Luctantis ventos tempestatesque sonoras
Imperio premit, ac vinclis et carcere frenat.
Illi indignantes, magno cum murmure, montis
Circum claustra fremunt. Celsa sedet Æolus arce,
Sceptra tenens: mollitque animos, et temperat iras.
———Venti, velut agmine facto,
Qua data porta, ruunt, et terras turbine perflant.
Incubuere mari, totumque à sedibus imis,
Unà Eurusque Notusque ruunt, creberque procellis
Africus, et vastos volvunt ad litora fluctus.
Æn. i. 51—57, 82—86.

One of the most sublime descriptions of a storm to be found any where, is furnished by Klopstock. It contains a beautiful recognition of the presence and majesty of God, and a most tender and affecting description of the protection which his friends experience when the storm rushes by. It is in the Frühlingsfeier—a poem which is regarded by many as his master-piece. A small portion of it I will transcribe:

Wolken strömen herauf!
Sichtbar ist; der kommt, der Ewige!
Nun schweben sie, rauschen sie, wirbeln die Winde!
Wie beugt sich der Wald! Wie hebet sich der Strom!
Sichtbar, wie du es Sterblichen seyn kannst,
Ja, das bist du, sichtbar, Unendlicher!

Zürnest du, Herr,
Weil Nacht dein Gewand ist?
Diese Nacht ist Segen der Erde.
Vater, du Zürnest nicht!

Seht ihr den Zeugen des Nahen, den zücken den Strahl?
Hört ihr Jehovah's Donner?
Hört ihr ihn? hört ihr ihn.
Der erschütternden Donner des Herrn?
Herr! Herr! Gott!
Barmhertzig, und gnädig!
Angebetet, gepriesen,
Sey dein herrlicher Name!

Und die Gewitterwinde! Sie tragen den Donner!
Wie sie rauschen! Wie sie mit lawter Woge den Wald durchströmen!
Und nun schwiegen sie. Langsam wandelt
Die schwartze Wolke.

Seht ihr den neuen Zeugen des Nahen, den fliegenden Strahl!
Höret ihr hoch in Wolke den Donner des Herrn?
Er ruft: Jehova! Jehova!
Und der geschmetterte Wald dampft!

Aber nicht unsre Hütte
Unser Vater gebot
Seinem Verderber,
Vor unsrer Hütte vorüberzugehn!

6 For he saith to the snow, Be thou *on* the earth; [1] likewise to the small rain, and to the great rain of his strength.

1 and to the shower of rain, and to the showers of rain of his strength.

7 He sealeth up the hand of every man, that [a] all men may know his work.

a Ps.109.27.

6. *For he saith to the snow.* That is, the snow is produced by the command of God, and is a proof of his wisdom and greatness. The idea is, that the formation of snow was an illustration of the wisdom of God, and should teach men to regard him with reverence. It is not to be supposed that the laws by which snow is formed in the atmosphere were understood in the time of Elihu. The fact that it seemed to be the effect of the immediate creation of God, was the principal idea in the mind of Elihu in illustrating his wisdom. But it is not less fitted to excite our admiration of his wisdom now that the laws by which it is produced are better understood; and in fact the knowledge of those laws is adapted to elevate our conceptions of the wisdom and majesty of Him who formed them. The investigations and discoveries of science do not *diminish* the proofs of the Creator's wisdom and greatness, but every new discovery tends to change blind admiration to intelligent devotion; to transform wonder to praise. On the formation of snow, see Notes on chap. xxxviii. 22. ¶ *Be thou* on *the earth.* There is a strong resemblance between this passage and the sublime command in Gen. i. 3, "And God said, Let there be light, and there was light." Each of them is expressive of the creative power of God, and of the ease with which he accomplishes his purposes. ¶ *Likewise to the small rain.* Marg. *and to the shower of rain, and to the showers of rain of his strength.* The word which is here used in the Hebrew (גשם), means *rain* in general, and the phrase "small rain" (מטר גשם), seems to be used to denote the *rain* simply, without reference to its violence, or to its being copious. The following phrase, "the great rain of his strength" (מטרות עזו גשם), refers to the rain when it has increased to a copious shower. The idea before the mind of Elihu seems to have been that of a shower, as it commences and increases until it pours down torrents, and the meaning is, that alike in the one case and the other, the rain was under the command of God, and obeyed his will. The whole description here is that which pertains to winter, and Elihu refers doubtless to the copious rains which fell at that season of the year.

7. *He sealeth up the hand of every man.* That is, in the winter, when the snow is on the ground, when the streams are frozen, and when the labours of the husbandman cease. The idea of "sealing up the hand" is derived from the common purpose of a seal, to make fast, to close up, to secure (comp. Notes chap. ix. 7; xxxiii. 16), and the sense is, that the hands can no more be used in ordinary toil. Every man in the snow and rain of winter is prevented from going abroad to his accustomed toil, and is, as it were, *sealed up* in his dwelling. The idea is exquisitely beautiful. God confines men and beasts in their houses or caves, until the winter has passed by. ¶ *That all men may know his work.* The LXX. render this, "That every man may know his own weakness"—ἀσθένειαν. Various interpretations have been given of the passage, but our common version has probably expressed in the main the true sense, that God thus interrupts the labours of man, and confines him in his home, that he may feel his dependence on God, and may recognize the constant agency of his Creator. The Hebrew literally is, "For the knowledge of all the men of his making;" that is, that all the men whom he has created may have knowledge. The changing seasons thus keep before us the constant evidence of the unceasing agency of God in his works, and prevent the feeling which we might have, if every thing was uniform that the universe was under the control of *fate.* As it is, the succession

8 Then the beasts go [a] into dens, and remain in their places.

9 Out of the [1] south cometh the whirlwind; and cold out of the [2] north.

[a] Ps.104.22. 1 *chamber*. 2 *scattering* winds.

of the seasons, the snow, the rain, the dew, and the sunshine, all bear marks of being under the control of an intelligent Being, and are so regulated that we need not forget that his unceasing agency is constantly round about us. It may be added, that when the farmer in the winter is laid aside from his usual toil, and confined to his dwelling, it is a favourable time for him to meditate on the works of God, and to acquaint himself with his Creator. The labours of man are thus interrupted; the busy affairs of life come to a pause, and while nature is silent around us, and the earth wrapped in her fleecy mantle forbids the labour of the husbandman, every thing invites to the contemplation of the Creator, and of the works of his hands. The winter, therefore, might be improved by every farmer to enlarge his knowledge of God, and should be regarded as a season wisely appointed for him to cultivate his understanding and improve his heart.

8. *Then the beasts go into dens.* In the winter. This fact appears to have been early observed, that in the season of cold the wild animals withdrew into caves, and that many of them became torpid. This fact Elihu adverts to as an illustration of the wisdom and greatness of God. The proof of his superintending care was seen in the fact that they withdrew from the cold in which they would perish, and that provision is made for their continuance in life at a time when they cannot obtain the food by which they ordinarily subsist. In that torpid and inactive state, they need little food, and remain often for months with almost no nourishment.

9. *Out of the south.* Marg. *chamber.* Jerome, *ab interioribus—from the interior,* or *inner places.* Sept. Ἐκ ταμιείων—*from their chambers issue sorrows*—ὀδύνας. The Hebrew word here used (חֶדֶר) denotes properly an apartment, or chamber, especially an inner apartment, or a chamber in the interior of a house or tent: Gen. xliii. 30; Judges xvi. 9, 12. Hence it means a bed-chamber, 2 Sam. iv. 7, or a female apartment or harem, Cant. i. 4; iii. 4. In chap. ix. 9, it is connected with the *south*—"the chambers of the south" (see Notes on that place), and means some remote, hidden regions in that quarter. There can be little doubt that the word "*south*" is here also to be understood, as it stands in contrast with a word which properly denotes the north. Still there may have been reference to a supposed opinion that whirlwinds had their origin in deep, hollow caves, and that they were owing to the winds which were supposed to be pent up there, and which raged tumultuously until they broke open the doors of their prison, and then poured forth with violence over the earth; comp. the description of the storm in Virgil, as quoted above in ver. 5. There are frequent allusions in the Scriptures to the fact that whirlwinds come from the South; see Notes on Isa. xxi. 1; comp. Zech. ix. 14. Savary says of the south wind, which blows in Egypt from February to May, that it fills the atmosphere with a fine dust, rendering breathing difficult, and that it is filled with an injurious vapour. Sometimes it appears in the form of a furious whirlwind, which advances with great rapidity, and which is highly dangerous to those who traverse the desert. It drives before it clouds of burning sand; the horizon appears covered with a thick veil, and the sun appears red as blood. Occasionally whole caravans are buried by it in the sand. It is possible that there may be reference to such a whirlwind in the passage before us; comp. Burder, in Rosenmüller's Alte u. neue Morgenland. No. 765. ¶ *The whirlwind;* see Notes on chap. i. 19; xxx. 22. ¶ *And cold out of the north.* Marg. *scattering* winds. The Hebrew word here used (מְזָרִים) means literally, *the scattering,* and is hence used for the north winds, says Gesenius which

10 By the breath of God frost [a] is given; and the breadth of the waters is straitened.

a Ps.147.16, 17.

11 Also by watering he wearieth the thick cloud; he scattereth his [1] bright cloud.

1 *the cloud of his light.*

scatter the clouds, and bring severe cold. Umbreit thinks the word is used to denote the north, because we seem to see the north winds strewed on the clouds. Probably the reference is to the north wind as scattering the snow or hail on the ground. Heated winds come from the south; but those which scatter the snow, and are the source of cold, come from the north. In all places north of the equator it is true that the winds from the northern quarter are the source of cold. The idea of Elihu is, that all these things are under the control of God, and that these various arrangements for heat and cold are striking proofs of his greatness.

10. *By the breath of God frost is given.* Not by the violent north wind, or by the whirlwind of the south, but God seems to *breathe* in a gentle manner, and the earth is covered with hoary frost. It appears in a still night, when there is no storm or tempest, and descends upon the earth as silently as if it were produced by mere breathing. Frost is congealed or frozen *dew.* On the formation and cause of dew, see Notes on chap. xxxviii. 28. The figure is poetical and beautiful. The slight motion of the air, even when the frost appears, seems to be caused by the *breathing* of God. ¶ *And the breadth of the waters is straitened.* That is, is contracted by the cold; or is frozen over. The waters are *compressed* into a solid mass (במוצק), or are in a state of *pressure* or *compression*—for so the word here used means. What were before expanded rivers or arms of the sea, are now compressed into solid masses of ice. This, also, is proof of the greatness and power of God, for though the cause was not understood by Elihu, yet there was no doubt that it was produced by his agency. Though the *laws* by which this occurs are now better understood than they were then, it is no less clearly seen that it is by his agency; and all the light which we obtain in regard to the laws by which these things occur, only serve to exalt our conceptions of the wisdom and greatness of God.

11. *Also by watering.* Very various interpretations have been given of this phrase. Herder renders it, "His brightness rendeth the clouds." Umbreit, Und Heiterkeit vertreibt die Wolke—"and serenity or clearness drives away the clouds." Prof. Lee, "For irrigation is the thick cloud stretched out." Rosenmüller, "Splendour dispels the clouds." Luther, "The thick clouds divide themselves that it may be clear." Coverdale, "The clouds do their labour in giving moistness." The Vulgate, "The grain desires the clouds," and the LXX. "The cloud forms the chosen"—ἐκλεκτον. This variety of interpretation arises from the uncertainty of the meaning of the original word—ברי. According to the Chaldee and the Rabbins, this word means *clearness, serenity* of the heavens, and then the whole clause is to be rendered, "serenity dispelleth the cloud." Or the word may be formed of the preposition ב *Beth,* and רי *Ri,* meaning *watering* or *rain,* the same as רוי *Revi.* The word does not occur elsewhere in Hebrew, and hence it is not easy to determine its meaning. The weight of authority is in favour of *serenity,* or *clearness*—meaning that the thick, dark cloud is driven away by the *serenity or clearness of the atmosphere*—as where the clear sky seems to light up the heavens and to drive away the clouds. This idea seems, also, to be demanded by the parallelism, and is also more poetical than that in the common version. ¶ *Wearieth.* Or removes, or scatters. The *verb* here used (טרח) occurs nowhere else in the Scriptures, though *nouns* derived from the verb are found in Isa. i. 14, rendered *trouble,* and Deut. i. 12, rendered *cumbrance.* In Arabic it means *to cast down, to pro-*

12 And it is turned round about by his counsels; that they may do [a] whatsoever he commandeth them upon the face of the world in the earth.

13 He causeth it to come whether [1] for correction,[b] or for his land, [c] or for mercy.[d]

a Ps.148.8. 1 *a rod.* *b* 1 Sa 12.18; Is.29.6. *c* 1 Ki.18.45. *d* Joel 2.23.

ject, and hence to lay upon as a burden. But the word may mean to impel, drive forward, and hence the idea that the dark thick cloud is propelled or driven forward by the serenity of the sky. This *appears* to be so, and hence the poetic idea as it occurred to Elihu. ¶ *He scattereth his bright cloud.* Marg. *the cloud of his light.* The idea seems to be, that "his light," that is, the light which God causes to shine as the tempest passes off, seems to scatter or disperse the cloud. The image before the mind of Elihu probably was, that of a departing shower, when the light seems to rise behind it, and as it were to expel the cloud or to drive it away. We are not to suppose that this is philosophically correct, but Elihu represents it as it *appeared*, and the image is wholly poetical.

12. *And it is turned round about.* The word here rendered "*it*" (הוּא) may refer either to the *cloud*, and then it will mean that it is driven about at the pleasure of God; or it may refer to God, and then it will mean that *he* drives it about at pleasure. The sense is not materially varied. The use of the Hebrew participle rendered "turned about" (in Hithpael), would rather imply that it refers to the cloud. The sense then is, that it turns *itself* round about—referring to the appearance of a cloud in the sky that rolls itself about from one place to another. ¶ *By his counsels.* By the counsels or purposes of God. It is not by any agency or power of its own, but it is by laws such as he has appointed, and so as to accomplish his will. The object is to keep up the idea that God presides over, and directs all these things. The word which is rendered *counsels* (תחבולות) means properly *a steering, guidance, management*, Prov. xi. 14. It is usually applied to the act of steering, as a vessel, and then to prudent management, wise counsel, skilful measures. It is rendered *wise counsels*, and *counsels*, Prov. i. 5; xi. 14; xii. 5; xxiv. 6, and *good advice*, Prov. xx. 18. It does not elsewhere occur in the Scriptures. The word is derived from חֶבֶל—*hhēbēl*, a rope, or חֹבֵל—*hhōbēl*, *a sailor, pilot*, and hence the idea of *steering*, or *directing*. The meaning is, that the movements of the clouds are entirely under the *direction* of God, as the vessel is of the pilot or helmsman. The LXX. appear not to have understood the meaning of the word, and have not attempted to translate it. They retain it in their version, writing it, ϑεϊβουλαϑὼϑ, showing, among other instances, how the Hebrew was *pronounced* by them. ¶ *That they may do whatsoever he commandeth them;* see Ps. cxlvii. 17, 18. The idea is, that even the *clouds*, which appear so capricious in their movements, are really under the direction of God, and are accomplishing his purposes. They do not move at hap-hazard, but they are under the control of one who intends to accomplish important purposes by them. Elihu had made this observation respecting the lightning (chap. xxxvi. 30—33), and he now says that the same thing was true of the clouds. The investigations of science have only served to confirm this, and to show that even the movements of the clouds are regulated by laws which have been ordained by a Being of infinite intelligence.

13. *He causeth it to come.* That is, the rain, or the storm. It is entirely under the hand of God, like the lightning (chap. xxxvi. 30), and designed to accomplish *his* purposes of mercy and of justice. ¶ *Whether for correction.* Marg. as in Heb. *a rod.* The *rod* is often used as an emblem of punishment. The idea is, that God, when he pleases, can send the rain upon the earth for the purpose of executing punishment. So he did on the old world (Gen. vii. 11, 12), and

14 Hearken unto this, O Job; stand still, and consider the wondrous works of God.
15 Dost thou know when God disposed them, and caused the light of his cloud to shine;
16 Dost thou know the balancings of the clouds, the wondrous

so the overflowing flood is often now sent to sweep away the works of man, to lay waste his fields, and to cut off the wicked. ¶ *Or for his land.* When necessary to render the land productive. He waters it by timely rains. It is called "*his* land," meaning that the earth belongs to the Lord, and that he cultivates it as his own; Ps. xxiv. 1. ¶ *Or for mercy.* In kindness and benignity to the world. But for this, the earth would become baked and parched, and all vegetation would expire. The idea is, that the rains are entirely under the control of God, and that he can make use of them to accomplish his various purposes — to execute his judgments, or to express his benignity and love. These various uses to which the lightning, the storm, and the rain could be made subservient under the divine direction, seem to have been one of the main ideas in the mind of Elihu, showing the supremacy and the majesty of God.

14. *Hearken unto this, O Job.* That is, to the lesson which such events are fitted to convey respecting God. ¶ *Stand still.* In a posture of reverence and attention. The object is to secure a calm contemplation of the works of God, so that the mind might be filled with suitable reverence for him.

15. *Dost thou know when God disposed them?* That is, the winds, the clouds, the cold, the snow, the sky, &c. The question refers to the *manner* in which God arranges and governs them, rather than to the *time* when it was done. So the Hebrew implies, and so the connection demands. The question was not whether Job knew *when* all this was done, but whether he could explain *how* it was that God thus arranged and ordered the things referred to. Elihu asks him whether he could *explain* the manner in which the balancings of the clouds were preserved; in which the lightnings were directed; in which his garments were warm, and in which God had made and sustained the sky? The LXX. render this, "We know that God hath disposed his works—that he hath made light out of darkness." ¶ *And caused the light of his cloud to shine.* That is, Canst thou explain the cause of lightning? Canst thou tell how it is that it seems to break out of a dark cloud? Where has it been concealed? And by what laws is it now brought forth? Elihu assumes that all this was done by the agency of God, and since, as he assumes to be true, it was impossible for men to explain the manner in which it was done, his object is to show that profound veneration should be shown for a God who works in this manner. Somewhat more is known now of the laws by which lightning is produced than there was in the time of Job; but the question may still be asked of man, and is as much fitted to produce awe and veneration as it was then, whether he understands the way in which God produces the bright lightning from the dark bosom of a cloud. Can he tell what is the exact agency of the Most High in it? Can he explain all the laws by which it is done?

16. *Dost thou know the balancings of the clouds?* That is, Dost thou know how the clouds are poised and suspended in the air? The difficulty to be explained was, that the clouds, so full of water, did not fall to the earth, but remained suspended in the atmosphere. They were poised and moved about by some unseen hand. Elihu asks what kept them there; what prevented their falling to the earth; what preserved the equilibrium so that they did not all roll together. The phenomena of the *clouds* would be among the first that would attract the attention of man, and in the early times of Job it is not to be supposed that the subject could be explained. Elihu assumes that they were held in

works of him which is perfect in knowledge?

17 How thy garments *are* warm, when he quieteth the earth by the south *wind?*

18 Hast thou with him spread

the sky by the power of God, but what was the nature of his agency, he says, man could not understand, and hence he infers that God should be regarded with profound veneration. *We* know more of the facts and laws respecting the clouds than was understood then, but our knowledge in this, as in all other things, is fitted only to exalt our conceptions of the Deity, and to change blind wonder into intelligent adoration. The *causes* of the suspension of the clouds are thus stated in the Edinburgh Encyclopedia, Art. Meteorology: "When different portions of the atmosphere are intermixed so as to produce a deposition of moisture;" (comp. Notes on chap. xxxviii. 28), "the consequence will be the formation of a cloud. This cloud, from its increased specific gravity, will have a tendency to sink downwards; and were the lower strata of the air of the same temperature with the cloud, and saturated with moisture, it would continue to descend till it reached the surface of the earth—in the form of rain, or what is commonly called mist. In general, however, the cloud in its descent passes through a warmer region, when the condensed moisture again passes into a vapour, and consequently ascends till it reaches a temperature sufficiently low to recondense it, when it will begin again to sink. This oscillation will continue till the cloud settles at the point where the temperature and humidity are such as that the condensed moisture begins to be dissipated, and which is found on an average to be between two and three miles above the surface of the earth." By such laws the "balancing" of the clouds is secured, and thus is shown the wisdom of Him that is "perfect in knowledge." ¶ *The wondrous works of him that is perfect in knowledge.* Particularly in the matter under consideration. He who can command the lightning, and hold the clouds suspended in the air, Elihu infers must be perfect in knowledge. To a Being who can do this, every thing must be known. The reasoning of Elihu here is well-founded, and is not less forcible now than it was in the time of Job.

17. *How thy garments* are *warm.* What is the reason that the garments which we wear produce warmth? This, it would seem, was one of the philosophical questions which were asked at that time, and which it was difficult to explain. Perhaps it has never occurred to most persons to ask this apparently simple question, and if the inquiry were proposed to them, plain as it seems to be, they would find it as difficult to give an answer as Elihu supposed it would be for Job. Of the *fact* here referred to that the garments became oppressive when a sultry wind came from the south, there could be no dispute. But what was the precise *difficulty* in explaining the fact, is not so clear. Some suppose that Elihu asks this question sarcastically, as meaning that Job could not explain the simplest matters and the plainest facts; but there is every reason to think that the question was proposed with entire seriousness, and that it was supposed to involve real difficulty. It seems probable that the difficulty was not so much to explain why *the garments* should become oppressive in a burning or sultry atmosphere, *as to show how the heated air itself was produced.* It was difficult to explain why cold came out of the north (ver. 9); how the clouds were suspended, and the lightnings caused (ver. 11, 15, 16); and it was not less difficult to show what produced uncomfortable heat when the storms from the north were allayed; when the earth became quiet, and when the breezes blowed from the south. This would be a fair question for investigation, and we may readily suppose that the causes then were not fully known. ¶ *When he quieteth the earth.* When the piercing blast from the north dies away, and the wind comes round to the south, producing a more gentle,

[a] out the sky, *which is* strong, *and* as a molten looking-glass?

a Isa. 40. 22; 44. 24.

19 Teach us what we shall say unto him: *for* we cannot order *our speech* by reason of darkness.

but a sultry air. It was true not only that the whirlwind came from the south (ver. 9), but also that the heated burning air came also from that quarter, Luke xii. 55. *We* know the reason to be that the equatorial regions are warmer than those at the north, and especially that in the regions where Job lived the air becomes heated by passing over extended plains of sand, but there is no reason to suppose that this was fully understood at the time referred to here.

18. *Hast thou with him spread out the sky?* That is, wert thou employed with God in performing that vast work, that thou canst explain how it was done? Elihu here speaks of the sky as it *appears,* and as it is often spoken of, as an *expanse* or solid body spread out over our heads, and as sustained by some cause which is unknown. Sometimes in the Scriptures it is spoken of as a curtain (Notes, Isa. xl. 22); sometimes as a "firmament," or a solid body spread out (Sept. Gen. i. 6, 7); sometimes as a fixture in which the stars are placed (Notes, Isa. xxxiv. 4), and sometimes as a scroll that may be rolled up, or as a garment, Ps. cii 26. There is no reason to suppose that the true cause of the appearance of an expanse was understood at that time, but probably the prevailing impression was that the sky was *solid,* and was a fixture in which the stars were held. Many of the ancients supposed that there were *concentric spheres,* which were transparent but solid, and that these spheres revolved around the earth carrying the heavenly bodies with them. In one of these spheres, they supposed, was the sun; in another the moon; in another the fixed stars; in another the planets; and it was the harmonious movement of these concentric and transparent orbs which it was supposed produced the "music of the spheres." ¶ Which is *strong.* Firm, compact. Elihu evidently supposed that it was *solid.* It was so firm that it was self-sustained. ¶ And *as a molten looking-glass.* As a mirror that is made by being fused or cast. The word "glass" is not in the original, the Hebrew denoting simply *seeing,* or *a mirror* (ראי). Mirrors were commonly made of plates of metal highly polished; see Notes on Isa. iii. 23; comp. Wilkinson's Manners and Customs of the Ancient Egyptians, vol. iii. p. 365. Ancient mirrors were so highly polished that in some which have been discovered at Thebes the lustre has been partially restored, though they have been buried for many centuries. There can be no doubt that the early apprehension in regard to the sky was, that it was a solid expanse, and that it is often so spoken of in the Bible. There is, however, no *direct declaration* that it *is* so, and whenever it is so spoken of, it is to be understood as *popular* language, as we speak still of the *rising* or *setting* of the sun, though we know that the language is not philosophically correct. The design of the Bible is not to teach science, but religion, and the speakers in the Bible were allowed to use the language of common life—just as scientific men in fact do now.

19. *Teach us what we shall say unto him.* This seems to be addressed to Job. It is the language of Elihu, implying that he was overawed with a sense of the majesty and glory of such a God. He knew not in what manner, or with what words to approach such a Being, and he asks Job to inform him, if he knew. ¶ *We cannot order* our speech *by reason of darkness.* Job had repeatedly professed a desire to bring his cause directly before God, and to argue it in his presence. He felt assured that if he could do that, he should be able so to present it as to obtain a decision in his favour; see Notes on chap. xiii. 3, 18—22. Elihu now designs, indirectly, to censure that confidence. He says that he and his friends were so overawed by the majesty of God, and felt themselves so ignorant and so ill qualified to judge of him and his

20 Shall it be told him that I speak? If a man speak, surely he shall be swallowed up.

21 And now *men* see not the bright light which *is* in the clouds; but the wind passeth, and cleanseth them.

works, that they would not know what to say. They were in darkness. They could not understand even the works of his hands which were directly before them, and the most common operations of nature were inscrutable to them. How then could they presume to arraign God? How could they manage a cause before him with any hope of success? It is scarcely necessary to say, that the state of mind referred to here by Elihu is that which should be cultivated, and that the feelings which he expresses are those with which we should approach the Creator. We need some one to teach us. We are surrounded by mysteries which we cannot comprehend, and we should, therefore, approach our Maker with profound reverence and submission.

20. *Shall it be told him that I speak?* Still the language of profound awe and reverence, as if he would not have it even intimated to God that he had presumed to say *any thing* in regard to him, or with a view to explain the reason of his doings. ¶ *If a man speak*. That is, if he attempt to speak with God; to argue a case with him; to contend with him in debate; to oppose him. Elihu had designed to reprove Job for the bold and presumptuous manner in which he had spoken of God, and for his wish to enter into a debate with him in order to vindicate his cause. He now says, that if any one should attempt this, God had power at once to destroy him; and that such an attempt would be perilous to his life. But other interpretations have been proposed, which may be seen in Rosenmüller, Umbreit, and Lee. ¶ *Surely he shall be swallowed up*. Destroyed for his presumption and rashness in thus contending with the Almighty. Elihu says that on this account he would not dare to speak with God. He would fear that he would come forth in his anger, and destroy him. How much man by nature instinctively feels, when he has any just views of the majesty of God, that he needs a Mediator!

21. *And now* men *see not the bright light which* is *in the clouds*. Either the lightning that plays on the clouds in an approaching tempest, or a glorious light spread over the sky on the approach of God. There is reason to believe that as Elihu delivered the sentiments recorded in the close of this chapter, he meant to describe God as if he were seen to be approaching, and that the symbols of his presence were discovered in the gathering tempest and storm. He is introduced in the following chapter with amazing sublimity and grandeur to speak to Job and his friends, and to close the argument. He comes in a whirlwind, and speaks in tones of vast sublimity. The tokens of his coming were now seen, and as Elihu discerned them he was agitated, and his language became abrupt and confused. His language is just such as one would use when the mind was overawed with the approach of God—solemn, and full of reverence, but not connected, and much less calm than in his ordinary discourse. The close of this chapter, it seems to me, therefore, is to be regarded as spoken when the tempest was seen to be gathering, and when in awful majesty God was approaching, the lightnings playing around him, the clouds piled on clouds attending him, the thunder reverberating along the sky, and an unusual brightness evincing his approach; Notes, ver. 22. The idea here is, that men could not steadfastly behold that bright light. It was so dazzling and so overpowering that they could not gaze on it intently. The coming of such a Being arrayed in so much grandeur, and clothed in such a light, was fitted to overcome the human powers. ¶ *But the wind passeth, and cleanseth them.* The wind passes along and makes them clear. The idea seems to be, that the wind appeared to sweep

22 [1] Fair weather cometh out of the north; with God *is* terrible majesty.

[1] *Gold.*

along over the clouds as the tempest was rising, and they seemed to open or disperse in one part of the heavens, and to reveal in the opening a glory so bright and dazzling that the eye could not rest upon it. That light or splendour made in the opening cloud was the symbol of God, approaching to wind up this great controversy, and to address Job and his friends in the sublime language which is found in the closing chapters of the book. The word rendered *cleanseth* (טהר) means properly to shine, to be bright; and then to be pure or clean. Here the notion of shining or brightness is to be retained; and the idea is, that a wind appeared to pass along, removing the cloud which seemed to be a veil on the throne of God, and suffering the visible symbol of his majesty to be seen through the opening; see Notes on chap. xxvi. 9, "He holdeth back the face of his throne, and spreadeth his cloud upon it."

22. *Fair weather.* Marg. *gold*, The Hebrew word (זהב) properly means *gold*, and is so rendered by the Vulgate, the Syriac, and by most versions. The LXX. render it, νέφη χρυσαυγοῦντα, "clouds shining like gold." The Chaldee, אסתנרא, the north wind, Boreas. Many expositors have endeavoured to show that gold was found in the northern regions (see Schultens, *in loc.*); and it is not difficult so to establish that fact as to be a confirmation of what is here said, on the supposition that it refers literally to gold. But it is difficult to see why Elihu should here make a reference to the source where *gold* was found, or how such a reference should be connected with the description of the approaching tempest, and the light which was already seen on the opening clouds. It seems probable to me that the idea is wholly different and that Elihu means to say that a bright, dazzling light was seen in the northern sky *like burnished gold*, which was a fit symbol of the approaching Deity. This idea is hinted at in the Septuagint, but it has not seemed to occur to expositors. The image is that of the heavens darkened with the tempest, the lightnings playing, the thunder rolling, and *then* the wind seeming to brush away the clouds in the north, and disclosing in the opening a bright, dazzling appearance like burnished gold, that bespoke the approach of God. The word is never used in the sense of *fair weather*. An ancient Greek tragedian, mentioned by Grotius, speaks of *golden air*—χρυσωπὸς αἰθήρ. Varro also uses a similar expression—aurescit aër, *the air becomes like gold.* So Thomson, in his Seasons:

> But yonder comes the powerful king of day
> Rejoicing in the east. The lessening cloud,
> The kindling azure, and the mountain's brow,
> *Illumed with fluid gold*, his near approach
> Betoken glad. *Summer.*

¶ *Out of the north.* That is, the symbol of the approaching Deity appears in that quarter, or God was seen to approach from the north. It may serve to explain this, to remark that among the ancients the northern regions were regarded as the residence of the gods, and that on the mountains in the north it was supposed they were accustomed to assemble. In proof of this, and for the reasons of it, see Notes on Isa. xiv. 13. From that region Elihu sees God now approaching, and directs the attention of his companions to the symbols of his advent. It is this which fills his mind with so much consternation, and which renders his discourse so broken and disconnected. Having, in a manner evincing great alarm, directed their attention to these symbols, he concludes what he has to say in a hurried manner, and God appears, to close the controversy. ¶ *With God is terrible majesty.* This is not a declaration asserting this of God in general, but as he then appeared. It is the language of one who was overwhelmed with his awful majesty, as the brightness of his presence was seen on the tempest.

23 *Touching* the Almighty, we
[z] cannot find him out: *he is* excellent in [b] power, and in judgment,
[c] and in plenty of justice: [d] he
will not afflict. [e]

24 Men do therefore [f] fear him;
he respecteth not any *that are*
wise [g] of heart.

a 1 Ti.6.16. *b* Ps. 62.11; 66.3. *c* Ps. 99.4. *d* Isa.45.19. *e* La.3.33. *f* Mat.10.28. *g* Mat.11.25; 1 Co.1.26.

23. Touching *the Almighty, we cannot find him out;* see Notes, chap. xi. 7—9. This sentiment accords with all that Elihu had said, and indeed is what he designed particularly to enforce. But it has a peculiar emphasis here, where God is seen approaching in visible splendour, encompassed with clouds and tempests, and seated on a throne of burnished gold. *Such* a God, Elihu says, it was impossible to comprehend. His majesty was overwhelming. The passage is much more impressive and solemn, and accords much better with the original, by omitting the words which our translators have introduced and printed in italics. It would then be,

The Almighty!—We cannot find him out!
Great in power, and in justice, and in righteousness!

Thus it expresses the overwhelming emotion, the awe, the alarm produced on the mind of one who saw God approaching in the sublimity of the storm. ¶ He is *excellent in power.* He *excels,* or is vast and incomprehensible in power. ¶ *And in judgment.* That is, in justice. ¶ *And in plenty of justice.* Heb., "in multitude of righteousness." The meaning is, that there was an overflowing fulness of righteousness; his character was entirely righteous, or that trait *abounded* in him. ¶ *He will not afflict.* Or, he will not oppress, he will not crush. It was true that he *did afflict* men, but the idea is, that there was not harshness or oppression in it. He would not do it for the mere sake of producing affliction, or when it was not deserved. Some MSS. vary the reading here so as to mean "he will not answer;" that is, he will not give any account of what he does. The change has relation only to the points, but the above is the usual interpretation, and accords well with the connection.

24. *Men do therefore fear him.* There is reason why they should fear him, or why they should treat him with reverence. ¶ *He respecteth not any* that are *wise of heart.* He pursues his own plans, and forms and executes his own counsels. He is not dependent on the suggestions of men, and does not listen to their advice. In his schemes he is original and independent, and men should therefore regard him with profound veneration. This is the sum of all that Elihu had to say—that God was original and independent; that he did not ask counsel of men in his dealings; that he was great, and glorious, and inscrutable in his plans; and that men therefore should bow before him with profound submission and adoration. It was to be *presumed* that he was wise and good in all that he did, and to this independent and almighty Sovereign man ought to submit his understanding and his heart. Having illustrated and enforced this sentiment, Elihu, overwhelmed with the awful symbols of the approaching Deity, is silent, and God is introduced to close the controversy.

CHAPTER XXXVIII.

ANALYSIS OF THE CHAPTER.

In the previous chapter, God is represented as approaching in a tempest. While the lightnings were playing, and the thunders rolling, a bright, golden light is seen in the north, indicating the approach of the Most High. Elihu is overpowered with his majesty, and concludes his speech in a brief, hurried, and agitated manner; see Notes on chap. xxxvii. 21—24. Even while he is thus speaking, God appears, and addresses Job from the midst of the storm, and puts an end to this protracted controversy. He is introduced in circumstances of the highest sublimity, and at a time when all the speakers must have felt that his interposition was

CHAPTER XXXVIII.

1. *Then the* Lord *answered Job.* This speech is addressed particularly to Job, not only because he is the principal personage referred to in the book, but particularly because he had indulged in language of murmuring and complaint. God designed to bring him to a proper state of mind before he appeared openly for his vindication. It is the purpose of God, in his dealings with his people, *to bring them to a proper state of mind*

desirable. The friends of Job had not been able to maintain their position, and had been silenced. Job, though he had silenced them, had not been able to explain the facts which were constantly occurring, and which had constituted the basis of the argument of his friends. Both they and he had evinced, to a considerable extent, an improper spirit in what they had said, and it was appropriate that the divine views should be expressed in regard to their opinions and their temper. Elihu had interposed, and had professed his ability to explain every thing which was dark in the debate. He had, however, advanced but one new thought, that calamity was designed to be disciplinary, and was not to be regarded as certain proof of the character of him who was afflicted. Beyond this he was unable to offer any explanation; and supposing that Job had not submitted as a good man should under afflictions, *he* had concluded also that Job lacked the proper spirit of piety, and joined with the friends of Job in the language of severe reproach. But in the great matters pertaining to the divine administration which had given so much perplexity, Elihu had no explanation to make, and all that he could say was that God was so mighty that man *ought* to submit to him.

At this stage of the argument the Almighty himself appears, and addresses Job from the midst of the tempest. He does not indeed appear, as Job had anticipated he would, to vindicate him at once; see Notes on chap. xix. 25, seq. His first object is to bring Job to a proper state of mind; to reprove the boldness and presumption with which he had spoken of the divine dealings; and to show him how utterly incompetent he was to judge of the ways of God. At the close of the scene, however, he expresses his approbation of the general spirit of Job in preference to that of his friends, and restores him to more than his former prosperity.

It is remarkable that in this discourse even God himself does not *explain* the difficulties which had so much embarrassed Job and his friends. He does not state why the wicked are so much prospered, or why the righteous suffer so much; he does not show how the sufferings of the good are consistent with his approbation of their conduct, nor does he refer to the retributions of the future world. He does not say that the inequalities here will be adjusted there; that the wicked who are prospered here will be punished there; or that the righteous who suffer here will receive an ample compensation there. This, which we might have anticipated, and which would be the way in which *we* would now endeavour to meet the difficulties of the case, would have been far in advance of the state of knowledge then possessed in the world, and would have been anticipating the high and sublime revelations reserved for Christianity. It was not the purpose of God *then* to reveal the doctrine of the future state, and to communicate those sublime truths which now console us in our afflictions, and which, amidst the inequalities of the present state of trial, lead us to look forward to another world. Those truths were appropriately reserved for the brighter period in the history of the world, when the light of Christianity would arise. Truth has been communicated to mankind *gradually*, and however easy it would have been for God to have communicated the truths which we now have in the earliest stages of society, and however much suffering they might have alleviated, yet God chose to leave the subject of revelation as he did science, morality, the arts of life, and civil government, *to gradual and slow development*. Elementary truths were communicated at first, and by degrees those truths were enlarged until the perfect light arose.

In the conceptions of the nature of the divine government, therefore, among the patriarchs, we are not to look for the elevated views which we have under the gospel, and we are not to expect to find the same hopes and promises to cheer them in their afflictions which we enjoy. There was indeed enough of truth revealed to preserve them from utter despondency, and to save the soul; but the system of divine truth was not fully disclosed to them. Accordingly, in this discourse of the Almighty, we do not meet with the same truths which we are permitted to contemplate under the Christian revelation. We are not directed to the same views of the designs of affliction, nor the same topics of consolation. We are not told of the future state, nor of the benefits which flow from trial there, nor of the consolations of the Holy Spirit, nor of the blessings of redemption. One great thought is held up to view, *that there ought to be submission to that God who had shown himself to be so great and wise.* The appeal is made to his works; to the vastness of his wisdom; to the evidences of his power; to the fact that there was so much in his doings that was above the comprehension of man; and hence there is inferred the impropriety of arraigning him in regard to his moral government, or of sitting in judgment on his dealings. Profound submission to such a God is demanded, and men should acquiesce in the belief that he is right, even though *the reasons* of his doings are not disclosed. God is supreme, and should be adored; his wisdom is incomprehensible, and it is presumptuous to arraign it; his power is infinite, and man cannot resist it; and his providential care is universal, and man should trust him. The single lesson, therefore, which seems to be designed to be taught, is, THAT WE ARE TO SUBMIT TO THE WILL OF GOD. We are to do this, not because we see the reasons of his doings, and not because we are to be rewarded for it, and not because there is nothing dark in his dispensations, but because he is God, and has a right to do his pleasure.

In this chapter, the appeal is made to a great variety of subjects to show how great and incomprehensible he is. God does not vindicate his own dealings, but he requires Job, who had spoken so confidently and rashly, to attempt to give an explanation of some of the works of nature which are constantly presented to view. The argument is, that if he was unable to explain those things which are before the eyes, it was presumption of the highest kind to complain of the secret counsels and purposes of the Almighty. If his natural government could not be comprehended or explained in regard to the phenomena which are constantly occurring, how much less could man hope to understand the principles of his moral administration. In illustrating and enforcing this, God appeals to the following things:—To the creation of the earth, ver. 4—7; to the sea, and the wisdom evinced in fixing its bounds, ver. 8—11; to the formation of light, and the manner in which it is distributed over the earth, ver. 12—15; to the supplies of water for the ocean, ver. 16; to the deep caverns of the region of death, ver. 17; to the extent of the earth, ver. 18; to the sources of light and of darkness, ver. 19—21; to the formation of snow and hail, ver. 22, 23; to the lightning, the storm, and the showers of rain, ver. 24—28; to the formation of ice, ver. 29, 30; to the rising and setting of the stars, and their influence over the world, ver 31—35; to the wisdom which he has given to man, ver. 36; to the clouds, ver. 37, 38; to the instincts of animals, and the laws by which they are governed, ver. 39—41.

THEN the LORD answered Job out of the whirlwind, and said,

---

before he appears as their vindicator and friend, and hence their trials are often prolonged, and when he appears, he seems at first to come only to rebuke them. Job had indulged in very improper feelings, and it was needful that those feelings should be subdued before God would manifest

2 Who *is* this that darkeneth counsel by words [a] without knowledge?

a chap. 34.35; 35.16.

3 Gird up now thy loins like a man; for I will demand of thee, and [1] answer thou me.

1 *make me known.*

himself as his friend, and address him in words of consolation. ¶ *Out of the whirlwind.* The tempest; the storm—probably that which Elihu had seen approaching, chap. xxxvii. 21—24. God is often represented as speaking to men in this manner. He spake amidst lightnings and tempests on Mount Sinai (Ex. xix. 16—19), and he is frequently represented as appearing amidst the thunders and lightnings of a tempest, as a symbol of his majesty; comp. Ps. xviii. 9—13; Hab. iii. 3—6. The word here rendered *whirlwind* means rather *a storm, a tempest.* The LXX. render this verse, "After Elihu had ceased speaking, the Lord spake to Job from a tempest and clouds."

2. *Who* is *this.* Referring doubtless to Job, for he is specified in the previous verse. Some have understood it of Elihu (see Schultens), but the connection evidently demands that it should be understood as referring to Job. The object was, to reprove him for the presumptuous manner in which he had spoken of God and of his government. It was important before God manifested his approval of Job, that he should declare his sense of what he had said, and show him how improper it was to indulge in language such as he had used. ¶ *That darkeneth counsel.* That makes the subject darker. Instead of explaining the reason of the divine dealings, and vindicating God from the objections alleged against him and his government, the only tendency of what he had said had been to make his government appear dark, and severe, and unjust in the view of his friends. It might have been expected of Job, being a friend of God, that all that he said would have tended to inspire confidence in him, and to explain and vindicate the divine dealings; but God had seen much that was the very reverse. Even the true friends of God, in the dark times of trial, may say much that will tend to make men doubt the wisdom and goodness of his government, and to prejudice the minds of the wicked against him. ¶ *By words without knowledge.* Words that did not contain a true explanation of the difficulty. They conveyed no light about his dealings; they did not tend to satisfy the mind, or to make the subject more clear than it was before. There is much of this kind of speaking in the world; much that is written, and much that falls from the lips in debate, in preaching, and in conversation, that explains nothing, and that even leaves the subject more perplexed than it was before. We see from this verse that God does not and cannot approve of such "words." If his friends speak, they should vindicate his government; they should at least express their conviction that he is *right;* they should aim to explain his doings, and to show to the world that they are reasonable. If they cannot do this, they should adore in silence. The Saviour never spoke of God in such a way as to leave any doubt that his ways could be vindicated, never so as to leave the impression that he was harsh or severe in his administration, or so as to lend the least countenance to a spirit of murmuring and complaining.

3. *Gird up now thy loins like a man.* To gird up the loins, is a phrase which has allusion to the mode of dress in ancient times. The loose flowing robe which was commonly worn, was fastened with a girdle when men ran, or laboured, or engaged in conflict; see Notes on Matth. v. 38—41. The idea here is, "Make thyself as strong and vigorous as possible; be prepared to put forth the highest effort." God was about to put him to a task which would require all his ability—that of explaining the facts which were constantly occurring in the universe. The whole passage is ironical. Job had undertaken to tell

4 Where [a] wast thou when I laid the foundations of the earth? declare, if thou [1] hast understanding.

5 Who hath laid the measures thereof, if thou knowest? or who hath stretched the line upon it?

6 Whereupon are the [2] foundations thereof [3] fastened? or who laid the corner-stone thereof,

a Pr.8.22,30. 1 *knowest.* 2 *sockets.* 3 *made to sink.*

what he knew of the divine administration, and God now calls upon him to show his claims to the office of such an expositor. So wise a man as he was, who could pronounce on the hidden counsels of the Most High with so much confidence, could assuredly explain those things which pertained to the visible creation. The phrase "like a man" means boldly, courageously; comp. Notes, 1 Cor. xvi. 13. ¶ *I will demand of thee, and answer thou me.* Marg. as in Heb., *make me known.* The meaning is, "I will submit some questions or subjects of inquiry to you for solution. Since you have spoken with so much confidence of my government, I will propose some inquiries as a test of your knowledge."

4. *Where wast thou when I laid the foundations of the earth?* The first appeal is to the creation. The question here, "Where wast thou?" implies that Job was not present. He had not then an existence. He could not, therefore, have aided God, or counselled him, or understood what he was doing. How presumptuous, therefore, it was in one so short-lived to sit in judgment on the doings of him who had formed the world! How little could he expect to be able to know of him! The expression, "laid the foundations of the earth," is taken from building an edifice. The foundations are first laid, and the superstructure is then reared. It is a poetic image, and is not designed to give any intimation about the actual process by which the earth was made, or the manner in which it is sustained. ¶ *If thou hast understanding.* Marg. as in Heb. *if thou knowest.* That is, "Declare how it was done. Explain the manner in which the earth was formed and fixed in its place, and by which the beautiful world grew up under the hand of God." If Job could not do this, what presumption was it to speak as he had done of the divine administration!

5. *Who hath laid the measures thereof.* That is, as an architect applies his measures when he rears a house. ¶ *If thou knowest.* Or rather, "for thou knowest." The expression is wholly ironical, and is designed to rebuke Job's pretensions of being able to explain the divine administration. ¶ *Or who hath stretched the line upon it.* As a carpenter uses a line to mark out his work; see Notes on Isa. xxviii. 17. The earth is represented as a building, the plan of which was laid out beforehand, and which was then made according to the sketch of the architect. It is not, therefore, the work of chance or fate. It is laid out and constructed according to a wise plan, and in a method evincing infinite skill.

6. *Whereupon are the foundations.* Marg. *sockets.* The Hebrew word (אדן) means a basis, as of a column, or a pedestal; and then also the foundation of a building. The language here is evidently figurative, comparing the earth with an edifice. In building a house, the securing of a proper foundation is essential to its stability; and here God represents himself as rearing the earth on the most permanent and solid basis. The word is not used in the sense of *sockets,* as it is in the margin. ¶ *Fastened.* Marg. *made to sink.* The margin rather expresses the sense of the Hebrew word—הטבעו. It is rendered *sink* and *sunk* in Ps. lxix. 2, 14; ix. 15; Lam. ii. 9; Jer. xxxviii. 6, 22; *drowned* in Ex. xv. 4; and *were settled* in Prov. viii. 25. The word does not elsewhere occur in the Scriptures, and the prevailing sense is that of *sinking,* or *settling down,* and hence to *impress*—as a seal *settles down* into wax. The reference

7 When the morning-stars [a] sang together, and all the sons of God shouted for joy?

a Rev.2.28.

here is to a foundation-stone that sinks or settles down into clay or mire until it becomes solid. ¶ *Or who laid the corner stone thereof.* Still an allusion to a building. The corner-stone sustains the principal weight of an edifice, as the weight of two walls is concentrated on it, and hence it is of such importance that it should be solid and firmly fixed. The question proposed for the solution of Job is, On what the earth is founded? On this question a great variety of opinions was entertained by the ancients, and of course no correct solution could be given of the difficulty. It was not known that it was suspended and held in its place by the laws of gravitation. The meaning here is, that if Job could not solve this inquiry, he ought not to presume to sit in judgment on the government of God, and to suppose that he was qualified to judge of his secret counsels.

7. *When the morning-stars.* There can be little doubt that angelic beings are intended here, though some have thought that the *stars* literally are referred to, and that they seemed to unite in a chorus of praise when another world was added to their number. The Vulgate renders it, *astra matutina, morning-stars;* the LXX. Ὅτε ἐγενήθησαν ἄστρα—*when the stars were made;* the Chaldee, "the stars of the zephyr," or morning—כּוֹכְבֵי צַפְרָא. The comparison of a prince, a monarch, or an angel, with a *star*, is not uncommon; comp. Notes on Isa. xiv. 12. The expression "the *morning-stars*" is used on account of the beauty of the principal star which, at certain seasons of the year, leads on the morning. It is applied naturally to those angelic beings that are of distinguished glory and rank in heaven. That it refers to the angels, seems to be evident from the connection; and this interpretation is demanded in order to correspond with the phrase "sons of God" in the other member of the verse. ¶ *Sang together.* United in a grand chorus or concert of praise. It was usual to celebrate the laying of a corner-stone, or the completion of an edifice, by rejoicing; see Zech. iv. 7; Ezra iii. 10. ¶ *And all the sons of God.* Angels—called the sons of God from their resemblance to him, or their being created by him. ¶ *Shouted for joy.* That is, they joined in praise for so glorious a work as the creation of a new world. They saw that it was an event which was fitted to honour God. It was a new manifestation of his goodness and power; it was an enlargement of his empire; it was an exhibition of benevolence that claimed their gratitude. The expression in this verse is one of uncommon, perhaps of unequalled beauty. The time referred to is at the close *of the creation of the earth,* for the whole account relates to the formation of this world, and not of the stars. At that period, it is clear that other worlds had been made, and that there were holy beings then in existence who were of such a rank as appropriately to be called "morning-stars" and "sons of God." It is a fair inference therefore, that the *whole* of the universe was not made at once, and that the earth is one of the last of the worlds which have been called into being. No one can demonstrate that the work of creation may not now be going on in some remote part of the universe, nor that God may not yet form many more worlds to be the monuments of his wisdom and goodness, and to give occasion for augmented praise. Who can tell but that this process may be carried on for ever, and that new worlds and systems may continue to start into being, and there be continually new displays of this inexhaustible goodness and wisdom of the Creator? When this world was made, there was occasion for songs of praise among the angels. It was a beautiful world. All was pure, and lovely, and holy. Man was made like his God, and every thing was full of love. Surveying the beautiful scene, as the world arose under the plastic

8 Or *who* shut up the sea with
doors, when it brake forth, *as if* it
had issued out of the womb?
9 When I made the cloud the
garment thereof, and thick darkness a swaddling-band for it,
10 And brake [1] up for it my

[1] *established my decree upon it.*

hand of the Almighty—its hills, and vales, and trees, and flowers, and animals, there was occasion for songs and rejoicings in heaven. Could the angels have foreseen, as perhaps they did, what was to occur here, there was also occasion for songs of praise such as would exist in the creation of no other world. This was to be the world of redeeming love; this the world where the Son of God was to become incarnate and die for sinners; this the world where an immense host was to be redeemed to praise God in a song unknown to the angels—the song of redemption, in the sweet notes which shall ascend from the lips of those who shall have been ransomed from death by the great work of the atonement.

8. *Or* who *shut up the sea with doors.* This refers also to the act of the creation, and to the fact that God fixed limits to the raging of the ocean. The word "doors" is used here rather to denote *gates,* such as are made to shut up water in a dam. The Hebrew word properly refers, in the dual form which is used here (דלתים), to *double doors,* or to folding doors, and is also applied to the gates of a city; Deut. iii. 5; 1 Sam. xxiii. 7; Isa. xlv. 1. The idea is, that the floods were bursting forth from the abyss or the centre of the earth, and were checked by placing gates or doors which restrained them. Whether this is designed to be a poetic or a real description of what took place at the creation, it is not easy to determine. Nothing forbids the idea that something like this may have occurred when the waters in the earth were pouring forth tumultuously, and when they were restrained by obstructions placed there by the hand of God, as if he had made *gates* through which they could pass only when he should open them. This supposition also would accord well with the account of the flood in Gen. vii. 11, where it is said that "the fountains of the great deep were broken up," as if those flood-gates had been opened, or the obstructions which God had placed there had been suffered to be broken through, and the waters of their own accord flowed over the world. We know as yet too little of the interior of the earth, to ascertain whether this is to be understood as a literal description of what actually occurred. ¶ *When it brake forth,* as if *it had issued out of the womb.* All the images here are taken from child-birth. The ocean is represented as being born, and then as invested with clouds and darkness as its covering and its swaddling-bands. The image is a bold one, and I do not know that it is any where else applied to the formation of the ocean.

9. *When I made the cloud the garment thereof.* Referring to the garment in which the new-born infant is wrapped up. This image is one of great beauty. It is that of the vast ocean just coming into being, with a cloud resting upon it and covering it. Thick darkness envelopes it, and it is swathed in mists; comp. Gen. i. 2, "And darkness was upon the face of the deep." The *time* here referred to is that before the light of the sun arose upon the earth, before the dry land appeared, and before animals and men had been formed. Then the new-born ocean lay carefully enveloped in clouds and darkness under the guardian care of God. The dark night rested upon it, and the mists hovered over it.

10. *And brake up for it my decreed* place. Marg. *established my decree upon it.* So Herder, "I fixed my decrees upon it." Luther renders it, "Da ich ihm den Lauf brach mit meinem Damm"—"then I broke its course with my barrier." Umbreit renders it, "I measured out to it my limits;" that is, the limits or bounds which I judged to be proper. So the

decreed *place*, and set bars and doors.

11 And said, Hitherto shalt thou come, but no further; and here shall [1] thy proud waves be stayed? [a]

12 Hast thou commanded the

[1] *the pride of thy waves.*

[a] Ps.89.9.

Vulgate, *Circumdedi illud terminis meis*—"I surrounded it with my limits," or with such limits as I chose to affix. The LXX. render it, "I placed boundaries to it." Coverdale, "I gave it my commandment." This is undoubtedly the sense which the connection demands; and the idea in the common version, that God had broken up his fixed plans in order to accommodate the new-born ocean, is not in accordance with the parallelism. The Hebrew word (שׁבַר) indeed commonly means to break, to break in pieces. But, according to Gesenius, and as the place here demands, it may have the sense of measuring off, defining, appointing, "from the idea of breaking into portions;" and then the sense will be, "I measured for it [the sea] my appointed bound." This meaning of the word is, however, more probably derived from the Arabic, where the word *shabar*, means *to measure with the span* (*Castell*), and hence the idea here of measuring out the limits of the ocean. The sense is, that God *measured out* or determined the limits of the sea. The idea of *breaking up* a limit or boundary which had been before fixed, it is believed, is not in the text. The word rendered "my decreed place" (חֻקִּי) refers commonly to a law, statute, or ordinance, meaning originally any thing that was *engraved* (חָקַק) and then, because laws were engraved on tablets of brass or stone, any statute or decree. Hence it means any thing prescribed or appointed, and hence a *bound*, or *limit;* see Notes on chap. xxvi. 10; comp. Prov. viii. 29, "When he gave to the sea his decree (חֻקּוֹ) that the waters should not pass his commandment." The idea in the passage before us is, that God fixed the limits of the ocean by his own purpose or pleasure. ¶ *And set bars.* Doors were formerly fastened, as they are often now, by cross-bars; and the idea here is, that God had inclosed the ocean, and so fastened the doors whence it would issue out, that it could not pass.

11. *And said, Hitherto shalt thou come.* This is a most sublime expression, and its full force can be felt only by one who has stood on the shores of the ocean, and seen its mighty waves roll towards the beach as if in their pride they would sweep every thing away, and how they are checked by the barrier which God has made. A voice seems to say to them that they may roll in their pride and grandeur so far, but no farther. No increase of their force or numbers can sweep the barrier away, or make any impression on the limits which God has fixed. ¶ *And here shall thy proud waves be stayed.* Marg. as in Heb., *the pride of thy waves.* A beautiful image. The waves seem to advance in pride and self-confidence, as if nothing could stay them. They come as if exulting in the assurance that they will sweep every thing away. In a moment they are arrested and broken, and they spread out humbly and harmlessly on the beach. God fixes the limit or boundary which they are not to pass, and they lie prostrate at his feet.

12. *Hast thou commanded the morning since thy days.* That is, in thy lifetime hast thou ordered the light of the morning to shine, and directed its beams over the world? God appeals to this as one of the proofs of his majesty and power—and who can look upon the spreading light of the morning and be insensible to the force and beauty of the appeal? The transition from the ocean to the morning may have been partly because the light of the morning is one of the striking exhibitions of the power of God, and partly because in the creation of the world the light of the sun was made to dawn soon after the gathering together of the waters into seas; see Gen. i. 10, 14. The phrase

morning since thy days; *and* caused the day-spring to know his place :
13 That it might take hold of
the [1] ends of the earth, that the wicked might be shaken out of it ?
14 It is turned as clay *to* the seal;
and they stand as a garment.

[1] wings.

"since thy days," implies that the laws determining the rising of the sun were fixed long before the time of Job. It is asked whether this had been done since he had an existence, and whether he had an agency in effecting it—implying that it was an ancient and established ordinance long before he was born. ¶ *Caused the day-spring to know his place.* The "day-spring" (שחר) means the aurora, the dawn, the morning. The mention of its "*place*" here seems to be an allusion to the fact that it does not always occupy the same position. At one season of the year it appears on the equator, at another north, and at another south of it, and is constantly varying its position. Yet it always knows its *place.* It never fails to appear where by the long-observed laws it ought to appear. It is regular in its motions, and is evidently under the control of an intelligent Being, who has fixed the laws of its appearing.

13. *That it might take hold of the ends of the earth.* Marg. as in Heb. *wings.* Wings are in the Scriptures frequently given to the earth, because it seems *to be spread out,* and the expression refers to its *extremities.* The language is derived from the supposition that the earth was a plain, and had limits or bounds. The idea here is, that God causes the light of the morning suddenly to spread to the remotest parts of the world, and to reveal every thing which was there. ¶ *That the wicked might be shaken out of it.* Out of the earth ; that is, by the light which suddenly shines upon them. The sense is, that the wicked perform their deeds in the darkness of the night, and that in the morning light they flee away. The effect of the light coming upon them is to disturb their plans, to fill them with alarm, and to cause them to flee. The idea is highly poetic. The wicked are engaged in various acts of iniquity under cover of the night. Robbers, thieves, and adulterers, go forth to their deeds of darkness as though no one saw them. The light of the morning steals suddenly upon them, and they flee before it under the apprehension of being detected. "The dawn," says Herder, "is represented as a watchman, a messenger of the Prince of heaven, sent to chase away the bands of robbers." It may illustrate this to observe that it is still the custom of the Arabs to go on plundering excursions before the dawn. When on their way this faithful watchman, the aurora, goes out to spread light about them, to intimidate them, and to disperse them ; comp. Notes on chap. xxiv. 13—17.

14. *It is turned as clay* to *the seal.* A great variety of interpretations has been given to this passage. Schultens enumerates no less than *twenty,* and of course it is not easy to determine the meaning. The LXX. render it, "Didst thou take clay of the earth, and form an animal, and place on the earth a creature endowed with speech?" Though this would agree well with the connection, yet it is a wide departure from the Hebrew. The reference is, undoubtedly, to some effect or impression produced upon the earth by the light of the morning, which bears a resemblance, in some respects, to the impression produced on clay by a seal. Probably the idea is, that the spreading light serves to render visible and prominent the forms of things, as the seal when impressed on clay produces certain figures. The following cut, representing ancient seals, may enable us the better to understand the passage :

Babylonian Seals.
a a, Babylonian cylinders; *b*, cylinder with modern handle fitted to it; *c c*, wax impressions.

In this cut it will be seen that one form of the seal (the Babylonian, *a*) was an engraved cylinder, fixed on an axle, with a handle in the manner of a garden roller, which produced the impression *by being rolled on the softened wax*. Mr. Rich (Second Memoir on the Ruins of Babylon, p. 59) remarks, "The Babylonian cylinders are among the most interesting and remarkable of the antiques. They are from one to three inches in length; some are of stone, and others apparently of paste or composition of various kinds. Sculptures from several of these cylinders have been published in different works. Some of them have cuneiform writing," [for the "arrow-headed" character, p. 48], "but it has the remarkable peculiarity that it is reversed, or written from right to left, every other kind of cuneiform writing being incontestably to be read from left to right. This can only be accounted for by supposing that they were intended *to roll off impressions*. The cylinders are said to be chiefly found in the ruins of Jabouiga. The people of America are fond of using them as amulets, and the Persian pilgrims who came to the shrines of Ali and Hossein frequently carry back with them some of these curiosities." The following cut will greatly assist in furnishing an idea of the impression produced by one of the cylinder-seals in the possession of Mr. Rich.

Impression from a Cylinder Seal.

15 And from the wicked their light is withholden, and the high arm [a] shall be broken.

[a] Ps.10.15.

It may be observed, also, in the explanation of the passage, that clay was often used for the purpose of a seal in Oriental countries. The manner in which it was used was to daub a mass of it over the door or lock of a house, a caravansera, a room, or any place where any thing valuable was deposited, and to impress upon it a rude seal. This indeed would not make the goods safe from a robber, but it would be an indication that the place is not to be entered, and show that if it had been entered it was by violence; comp. Matth. xxvii. 66. This impression on clay would be produced by the "revolving" or Babylonian seal, by *turning it about,* or *rolling it* on clay, and thus bringing the figures out prominently, and this will explain the passage here. The passing of the light over the earth in the morning, seems to be like rolling a cylinder-seal on soft clay. It leaves distinct impressions; raises up prominent figures; gives form and beauty to what seemed before a dark undistinguished mass. The word rendered "it is turned" (תתהפך), means properly "it turns itself"—and the idea is that, like the revolving seal, it seems to roll over the face of the earth, and to leave a distinct and beautiful impression. Before, the face of the earth was obscure. Nothing, in the darkness of the night, could be distinguished. Now, when the dawn arises and the light spreads abroad, the figures of hills, and trees, and tents, and cities, rise before it as if a seal had been rolled on yielding clay. The image is one, therefore, of high poetic character, and of great beauty. If this be the correct interpretation, the passage does not refer to the revolution of the earth on its axis, or to any change in appearance or form which it assumes when the wicked are shaken out of it, as Schultens supposes, but to the beautiful change in appearance which the face of the earth seems to undergo when the aurora passes over it. ¶ *And they stand as a garment.* This passage is perhaps even more difficult than the former part of the verse. Prof. Lee renders it, "And that men be set up as if accoutred for battle," and according to him the idea is, that men, when the light shines, set themselves up for the prosecution of their designs. Coverdale renders it, "Their tokens and weapons hast thou turned like clay, and set them up again as the changing of a garment." Grotius supposes it means that things by the aurora change their appearance and colour like a variegated garment. The true idea of the passage is probably that adopted by Schultens, Herder, Umbreit, Rosenmüller, and Noyes, that it refers to the beautiful appearance which the face of nature seems to put on when the morning light shines upon the world. Before, all was dark and undistinguished. Nature seemed to be one vast blank, with no prominent objects, and with no variety of colour. When the light dawns on the earth, the various objects—the hills, trees, houses, fields, flowers, seem to *stand forth,* or *to raise themselves up* (יתיצבו), and to put on the appearance of gorgeous and variegated vestments. It is as if the earth were *clothed* with beauty, and what was before a vast blank were now arrayed in splendid vestments. Thus understood, there is no need of supposing that garments were ever made, as has been sometimes supposed, with so much inwrought silver and gold that they would *stand upright themselves.* It is a beautiful conception of poetry—that the spreading light seems to clothe the dark world with a gorgeous robe, by calling forth the objects of creation from the dull and dark uniformity of night to the distinctness of day.

15. *And from the wicked their light is withholden.* While the light thus spreads over the earth, rendering every object beautiful and blessing the righteous, light and prosperity are withheld from the wicked; see Notes on chap. xxiv. 17. Or, the meaning may be, that when the light shines upon the world, the wicked, accus-

16 Hast thou entered into the springs of the sea? or hast thou walked in the search of the depth?

17 Have the gates [a] of death been opened unto thee? or hast thou seen the doors of the shadow of death?

a Ps.9.13.

tomed to perform their deeds in the night, flee from it, and retreat to their dark hiding-places. ¶ *And the high arm.* Of the wicked. The arm is a symbol of strength. It is that by which we accomplish our purposes, and the idea here is, that the haughty power of the oppressor shall be crushed. The *connection* here seems to be this. In ver. 12—14, there is a beautiful description of the *light,* and of its effects upon the appearance of natural objects. It was such as to clothe the world with beauty, and to fill the heart of the pious with gladness. In order now to show the greatness of the punishment of the wicked, it is added that all this beauty will be hidden from them. They will be driven away by the light into their dark hiding-places, and will be met there with the withdrawal of all the tokens of prosperity, and their power will be crushed.

16. *Hast thou entered into the springs of the sea?* The word here rendered *springs* (נבך), occurs nowhere else in the Scriptures. It is rendered by the Vulgate *profunda, the deep parts;* and by the LXX. πηγὴν—*fountains.* The reference seems to be to the deep fountains at the bottom of the sea, which were supposed to supply it with water. A large portion of the water of the ocean is indeed conveyed to it by rivers and streams that run on the surface of the earth. But it is known, also, that there are fountains at the bottom of the ocean, and in some places the amount of water that flows from them is so great, that its action is perceptible at the surface. One such fountain exists in the Atlantic ocean near the coast of Florida. ¶ *Or hast thou walked in the search of the depth?* Or, rather, in the deep places or caverns of the ocean. The word rendered "*search*" here (חקר), means *searching, investigation,* and then an object that is to be searched out, and hence that which is obscure, remote, hidden. Then it may be applied to the deep caverns of the ocean, or the bottom of the sea. This is to man unsearchable. No line has been found long enough to fathom the ocean, and of course what is there is unknown. It is adduced, therefore, with great propriety as a proof of the wisdom of God, that he could look on the deep caverns of the ocean, and was able to search out all that was there. A sentiment similar to this occurs in Homer, when speaking of Atlas:

> Ὅστε θαλάσσης
> Πάσης βένθεα οἶδεν. Odys. i. 5.
>
> "Who knows the depths of every sea."

17. *Have the gates of death been opened unto thee.* That is, the gates of the world where death reigns; or the gates that lead to the abodes of the dead. The allusion here is to *Sheol,* or *Hades,* the dark abodes of the dead. This was supposed to be beneath the ground, and was entered by the grave, and was inclosed by gates and bars; see Notes on chap. x. 21, 22. The transition from the reference to the bottom of the sea to the regions of the dead was natural, and the mind is carried forward to a subject farther beyond the ken of mortals than even the unfathomable depths of the ocean. The idea is, that God saw all that occurred in that dark world beneath us, where the dead were congregated, and that his vast superiority to man was evinced by his being able thus to penetrate into, and survey those hidden regions. It is common in the classic writers to represent those regions as entered by *gates.* Thus Lucretius, i. 1105,

> ——Haec rebus erit pars janua leti,
> Hae se turba foras dabit omnis materaï.
>
> ——"The doors of death are ope,
> And the vast whole unbounded ruin whelms."
> Good.

So Virgil, Æn. ii. 661,

> ——Patet isti janua leto.
> "The door of death stands open."

¶ *Or hast thou seen the doors of the*

18 Hast thou perceived the
breadth of the earth? declare, if
thou knowest it all.
19 Where *is* the way *where* light
dwelleth? and *as for* darkness,
where *is* the place thereof,
20 That thou shouldest take it [1] to
the bound thereof, and that thou

1 or, *at*.

---

shadow of death? The doors which lead down to the gloomy realms where death spreads its dismal shades. This expression is more emphatic than the former, for the word צַלְמָוֶת—*tzalmaveth,* "shadow of death," is more intensive in its meaning than the word מָוֶת—*maveth,* "death." There is the superadded idea of a deep and dismal shadow; of profound and gloomy darkness; see the word explained in the Notes on chap. iii. 5; comp. chap. x. 21, 22. Man was unable to penetrate those gloomy abodes and to reveal what was there; but God saw all with the clearness of noon-day.

18. *Hast thou perceived the breadth of the earth?* How far the earth extends. To see the force of this, we must remember that the early conception of the earth was that it was a vast plain, and that in the time of Job its limits were unknown. One of the earliest and most obvious inquiries would naturally be, What was the extent of the earth? By what was it bounded? And what was the character of the regions beyond those which were then known? All this was hidden from man at that time, and God, therefore, asks with emphasis whether Job had been able to determine this great inquiry. The knowledge of this is put on the same foundation as that of the depths of the sea, and of the dark regions of the dead, and in the time of Job the one was as much unknown as the other. God, who knew all this, must, therefore, be infinitely exalted above man.

19. *Where* is *the way* where *light dwelleth?* Or, rather, where is the way or path *to* the place where light dwells? Light is conceived of as coming from a great distance, and as having a place which might be regarded as its home. It comes in the morning, and is withdrawn at evening, and it *seems* as if it came from some far distant dwelling-place in the morning to illuminate the world, and then retired to its home in the evening, and thus gave place for darkness to visit the earth. The idea is this, "Dost thou know, when the light withdraws from the world, to what place it betakes itself as its home? Canst thou follow it to its distant abodes, and tell where they are? And when the shadows of night come forth, and take its place, canst thou tell whence *they* come; and when they withdraw again in the morning, canst thou follow them, and tell where they are congregated together to abide?" The thought is highly poetic, and is not to be taken literally. The meaning is, that God only could know what was the great fountain of light, and where that was; and the question substantially may be asked of man with as much force and propriety now as in the time of Job. Who knows what is the great fountain of light to the universe? Who knows what light *is?* Who can explain the causes of its rapid flight from world to world? Who can tell what supplies it, and prevents it from being exhausted? Who but God, after all the discoveries of science, can fully understand this? ¶ *And* as for *darkness, where* is *the place thereof?* Darkness here is personified. It is represented as having a place of abode as coming forth to take the place of light when that is withdrawn, and again as retiring to its dwelling when the light reappears.

20. *That thou shouldest take it to the bounds thereof.* Marg. "or, *at*." The sense seems to be this: God asks Job whether he was so well acquainted with the sources of light, and the place where it dwelt, that he could take it under his guidance and *reconduct* it to its place of abode. ¶ *And that thou shouldest know the paths* to *the house thereof?* The same idea is repeated here. Light has a home; a place of abode. It was far distant—in some region unknown to man. Did

shouldest know the paths *to* the house thereof?

21 Knowest thou *it*, because thou wast then born? or *because* the number of thy days *is* great?

22 Hast thou entered into the treasures of the snow, or hast thou seen the treasures of the hail.

Job know the way in which it came, and the place where it dwelt so well, that he could conduct it back again to its own dwelling? Umbreit, Noyes, and Herder, suppose that this is to be understood ironically.

> "For thou hast reached its boundaries!
> For thou knowest the path to its dwelling!"

But it has been commonly regarded as a question, and thus understood it accords better with the connection.

21. *Knowest thou* it, *because thou wast then born?* This may either be a question, or it may be spoken ironically. According to the former mode of rendering it, it is the same as asking Job whether he had lived long enough to understand where the abode of light was, or whether he had an existence when it was created, and knew where its home was appointed. According to the latter mode, it is keen sarcasm. "Thou must know all this, for thou art so old. Thou hast had an opportunity of observing all this, for thou hast lived through all these changes, and observed all the works of God." This latter method of interpreting it is adopted by Umbreit, Herder, Noyes, Rosenmüller, and Wemyss. The former, however, seems much better to accord with the connection, and with the dignity and character of the speaker. It is not desirable to represent God as speaking in the language of irony and sarcasm unless the rules of interpretation imperatively demand it.

22. *Hast thou entered into the treasures of snow?* Snow is here represented as something which is *laid up* like treasure, and kept in reserve for use when God shall require it. Silver and gold were thus laid up for occasions when they would be wanted, and the figurative sentiment here is, that snow and hail were thus preserved for the use to which the Almighty might devote them, or for those great occasions when it would be proper to bring them forth to execute his purposes. Of course, it was to be expected that God would speak in the language which men commonly used when speaking of his works, and would not go into a philosophical or scientific explanation of the phenomena of nature. His object was not to teach science, but to produce a solemn impression of his greatness, and *that* is secured by such an appeal whether the laws of nature are understood or not. The simple appeal to Job here is, whether he could explain the phenomena of snow and hail? Could he tell how they were formed? Whence they came? Where they were preserved, and how they were sent forth to execute the purposes of God? The idea is, that all that pertained to the snow was distinctly understood by God, and that these were facts which Job did not know of, and which he could not explain. The effect of time and of scientific investigation, in this as in other cases to which reference is made in this book, has been only to increase the force of this question. The effect of the discoveries which are made in the works of God is not to diminish our sense of his wisdom and majesty, but to change mere wonder to praise; to transform blind amazement to intelligent adoration. Every new discovery of a law of nature is fitted more to impress the mind with awe, and at the same time it becomes the basis of a new act of intelligent confidence in God. This is true of *snow* as of other things. In the time and country of Job it came doubtless from the north. Vast quantities seemed to be poured forth from those regions at certain seasons of the year, as if it were reserved there in vast store-houses, or treasuries. Science has however told us that it is congealed vapour formed in the air, by the vapour being frozen there before it is collected into drops large

enough to form hail. In the descent of the vapour to the earth it is frozen and descends in the numerous variety of crystallized forms in which the flakes appear. Perhaps there is nothing more fitted to excite pleasing conceptions of the wisdom of God—not even the variety of beauty in flowers —than the various forms of crystals in which snow appears. Those crystals present an almost endless variety of forms. Descartes and Dr. Hook were among the first whose minds seem to have been drawn to the figures of the crystals in snow, and since their investigations the subject has excited great interest in others. Captain Scoresby, who gave much attention to this subject and to other arctic phenomena, has given a delineation of ninety-six of these crystals, a portion of which will be found in the annexed cut.

He adds, " The extreme beauty and the endless variety of the microsopic objects perceived in the animal and vegetable kingdoms, are perhaps fully equalled, if not surpassed, in both particulars of beauty and variety, by

23 Which *a* I have reserved against the time of trouble, against the day of battle and war?

a Ex.9.18,24; Jos.10.11; Is.30.30; Rev.16.21.

the crystals of snow. The principal configurations are the stelliform and the hexagonal; though almost every variety of shape of which the generating angle of 60° and 120° are susceptible, may, in the course of a few years' observation, be discovered. Some of the general varieties in the figures of the crystals may be referred to the temperature of the air; but the particular and endless modifications of the same classes of crystals can only be referred to the will and pleasure of the First Great Cause, whose works, even the most minute and evanescent, and in regions the most remote from human observation, are altogether admirable." See the *Edinburgh Encyclopedia*, art. *Snow.* ¶ *Or hast thou seen the treasures of the hail.* As if the hail were reserved in storehouses, like the weapons of war, to be called forth when God should please, in order to execute his purposes. Hail—so well known in its nature and form—consists of masses of ice or frozen vapour, falling from the clouds in showers or storms. These masses consist of little spherules united, but not all of the same consistence; some being as hard and solid as perfect ice, others soft like frozen snow. Hail-stones assume various figures; some are round, others angular, others pyramidal, others flat, and sometimes they are stellated, with six radii, like crystals of snow. *Ency. as quoted in Webster's Dic.* Snow and hail are formed in the clouds when they are at an elevation where the temperature is below 32° The particles of moisture become congealed and fall to the earth. When the temperature below the clouds is more than 32°, the flakes of snow often melt, and descend in the form of rain. But hailstones, from their greater solidity and more rapid descent, often reach the earth even when the temperature is much higher; and hence we have storms of hail in the summer. The difference in the formation of snow and hail is, that in the former case the vapour in the clouds is congealed before it is collected into drops; in the case of hail, the vapour is collected into drops or masses, and then frozen. "If we examine," says Mr. Leslie, "the structure of a hailstone, we shall perceive a snowy kernel encased by a harder crust. It has very nearly the appearance of a drop of water suddenly frozen, the particles of air being driven from the surface towards the centre, where they form a spongy texture. This circumstance suggests the probable origin of hail, which is perhaps occasioned by rain falling through a dry and very cold stratum of air." *Edin. Ency., Art. Meteorology.* All the facts about the formation of hail were unknown in the time of Job, and hence God appeals to them as evidence of his superior wisdom and greatness, and in proof of the duty of man to submit to him. These phenomena, which were constantly occurring, man could not explain; and how much less qualified, therefore, was he to sit in judgment on the secret counsels of the Almighty! The same observation may be made now, for though science has done *something* to explain the laws by which snow and hail are formed, yet those discoveries have tended to enlarge our conceptions of the wisdom of God, and have shown us, to an extent which was not then suspected, how much is still unknown. We see a few of the *laws* by which God does these things, but who is prepared to explain *these laws themselves*, or to tell *why* and *how* the particles of vapour arrange themselves into such beautiful crystallized forms?

23. *Which I have reserved.* As if they were carefully treasured up to be brought forth as they shall be needed. The idea is, that they were entirely under the direction of God. ¶ *The time of trouble.* Herder "the time of need." The meaning probably is, that he had kept them in reserve for the time when he wished to bring calamity on his enemies, or that he made use of them to punish his foes; comp. Notes on chap. xxxvi

24 By what way is the light parted, *which* scattereth the east wind upon the earth?

25 [a]Who hath divided a watercourse for the overflowing of waters; or a way for the lightning of thunder;

a ch 28.26.

31—33. ¶ *Against the day of battle and war.* Hailstones were employed by God sometimes to overwhelm his foes, and were sent against them in time of battle; see Josh. x. 11; Ex. ix. 22—26; Ps. xviii. 12, 13; comp. Notes on Isa. xxix. 6.

24. *By what way is the light parted.* The reference here is to the light of the morning, that seems to come from one point, and to spread itself at once over the whole earth. It seems to be collected in the east, or, as it were, *condensed* or *concentrated* there, and then to *divide itself*, and to expand over the face of the world. God here asks Job whether he could explain this, or show in what manner it was done. This was one of the subjects which might be supposed early to excite inquiry, and is one which can be as little explained now as then. The causes of the propagation of light, which seems to proceed from a centre and to spread rapidly in every direction, are perhaps as little known now as they were in the time of Job. Philosophy has done little to explain this, and the *mode* in which light is made to travel in eight minutes from the sun to the earth—a distance of ninety millions of miles—and the manner in which it is "divided" or "parted" from that great centre, and spread over the solar system, is as much of a real mystery as it was in the days of Job, and the question proposed here may be asked now with as much emphasis as it was then. ¶ Which *scattereth the east wind upon the earth.* According to this translation, the idea would be that somehow light is the cause of the east wind. But it may be doubted whether this is the true interpretation, and whether it is meant to be affirmed that light has any agency in causing the wind to blow. Herder renders it,

"When doth the light divide itself,
When the east wind streweth it upon the earth?"

According to this, the idea would be that the light of the morning seemed to be borne along by the wind. Umbreit renders it, "Where is the way upon which the east wind flows forth upon the earth?" That is, the east wind, like the light, comes from a certain point, and seems to spread abroad over the world; and the question is, whether Job could explain this? This interpretation is adopted by Rosenmüller and Noyes, and seems to be demanded by the parallelism, and by the nature of the case. The cause of the rapid spreading of the wind from a certain point of the compass, was involved in as much obscurity as the propagation of the light, nor is that cause much better understood now. There is no reason to suppose that the spread of the light has any particular agency in causing the east wind, as our common version seems to suppose, nor is that idea necessarily in the Hebrew text. The *east* wind is mentioned here either because the *light* comes from the east, and the wind from that quarter was more naturally suggested than any other, or because the east wind was remarkable for its violence. The idea that a strong east wind was somehow connected with the dawn of day or the rising of the sun, was one that prevailed, at least to some extent, among the ancients. Thus Catullus (lxiv. 270, seq.) says:

Hîc qualis flatu placidum mare matutino
Horrificans zephyrus proclivas incitat undas
Aurora exoriente, vagi sub lumina solis

25. *Who hath divided a watercourse for the overflowing of waters.* That is, for the waters that flow down from the clouds. The idea seems to be this, that the waters of heaven, instead of pouring down in floods, or all coming down together, seemed to flow in certain canals formed for them; as if they had been cut out through the clouds for that purpose. The causes of rain, the manner in which water was suspended in the clouds, and the reasons why the rain did not come

26 To cause it to rain [a] on the
earth, *where* no man *is; on* the
wilderness, wherein *there is* no
man.
27 To satisfy [b] the desolate and
waste *ground;* and to cause the
bud of the tender herb to spring
forth?
28 Hath the rain a father? or
who hath begotten the drops of
dew?

a Ps.147.8; Je.14.22. b Ps.107.35.

down altogether in floods, early attracted attention, and gave occasion to investigation. The subject is more than once referred to in this book; see Notes on chap. xxvi. 8. ¶ *Or a way for the lightning of thunder.* For the *thunder-flash.* The idea is this: a path seems to be opened in the dark cloud for the passage of the flash of lightning. How such a path was made, by what agency or by what laws, was the question proposed for inquiry. The lightning seemed at once to burst through the dark cloud where there was no opening and no sign of a path before, and pursue its zig-zag journey as if all obstructions were removed, and it passed over a beaten path. The question is, Who could have traced out this path for the thunder-flash to go in? Who could do it but the Almighty? And still, with all the light that science has cast on the subject, we may repeat the question.

26. *To cause it to rain on the earth,* where *no man is.* This is designed to heighten the conception of the power of God. It could not be pretended that this was done by man, for the rain was caused to fall in the desolate regions where no one dwelt. In the lonely desert, in the wastes remote from the dwellings of men, the rain is sent down, evidently by the providential care of God, and far beyond the reach of the agency of man. There is very great beauty in this whole description of God as superintending the falling rain far away from the abodes of men, and in those lonely wastes pouring down the waters, that the tender herb may spring up, and the flowers bloom under his hand. All this may seem to be *wasted,* but it is not so in the eye of God. Not a drop of rain falls in the sandy desert or on the barren rock, however useless it may seem to be, that is not seen to be of value by God, and that is not designated to accomplish some important purpose there.

27. *To satisfy the desolate and waste* ground. As if it lifted an imploring voice to God, and he sent down the rain to satisfy it. The desert is thus like a thirsty pilgrim. It is parched, and thirsty, and sad, and it appeals to God, and he meets its wants, and satisfies it. ¶ *Or to cause the bud of the tender herb to spring forth.* In the desert. There God works alone. No man is there to cultivate the extended wilds, and yet an unseen agency is going forward. The grass springs up; the bud opens; the leaf expands; the flowers breathe forth their fragrance as if they were under the most careful cultivation. All this must be the work of God, since it cannot even be pretended that *man* is there to produce these effects. Perhaps one would be more deeply impressed with a sense of the presence of God in the pathless desert, or on the boundless prairie, where no man is, than in the most splendid park, or the most tastefully cultivated garden which man could make. In the one case, the hand of God alone is seen; in the other, we are constantly admiring the skill of man.

28. *Hath the rain a father?* That is, it is produced by God and not by man. No one among men can claim that he causes it, or can regard it as his offspring. The idea is, that the production of *rain* is among the proofs of the wisdom and agency of God, and that it is caused in a way that demonstrates his own agency. It is not by any power of man; and it is not in such a way as to constitute a relation like that between a father and a son. The rain is often appealed to in this book as something whose cause man could not explain, and as demonstrating the wisdom and supremacy of God. Among philosophic and contemplative minds

it would early excite inquiry, and give occasion for wonder. What caused it? Whence came the water which fell? How was it suspended? How was it borne from place to place? How was it made to descend in drops, and why was it not poured down at once in floods? Questions like these would early excite inquiry, and we are not to suppose that in the time of Job science was so far advanced that they could be answered; see Notes on chap. xxvi. 8; comp. ver. 37 of this chapter. The laws of the production of rain are now better understood, but like all other laws discovered by science, they are adapted to elevate, not to diminish, our conceptions of the wisdom of God. It may be of interest, and may serve to explain the passages in this book which refer to *rain*, as illustrating the wisdom of God, to state what is now the commonly received theory of its cause. That theory is the one proposed by Dr. James Hutton, and first published in the Philosophical Transactions of Edinburgh, in 1784. In this theory it is supposed that the cause consists in the vapour that is held dissolved in the air, and is based on this principle—*that the capacity of the air for holding water in a state of vapour increases in a greater ratio than its temperature;* that is, that if there are two portions of air which would contain a certain quantity of water in solution if both were heated in an equal degree, the capacity for holding water would be alike; but if one of them be heated more than the other, the amount of water which it would hold in solution is not exactly in proportion to the heat applied, but increases much more rapidly than the heat. It will hold much more water when the temperature is raised than is proportionate to the amount of heat applied. From the experiments which were made by Saussure and others, it was found that while the temperature of the air rises in arithmetical progression, the dissolving power of the air increases nearly in geometrical progression; that is, if the temperature be represented by the figures 2, 4, 6, 8, 10, &c., the capacity for holding moisture will be nearly represented by the figures 2, 8, 16, 32, 64, &c. Rain is caused in the following manner. When two portions of air of different temperature, and each saturated with moisture, are intermixed, the quantity of moisture in the air thus intermixed, in consequence of the decrease of temperature, will be greater than the air will contain in solution, and will be condensed in a cloud or precipitated to the earth. This law of nature was of course unknown to Job, and is an arrangement which could have been formed only by the all-wise Author of nature; see *Edin. Ency., Art. Meteorology*, p. 181. ¶ *Or who hath begotten the drops of the dew?* Who has produced them—implying that they were caused only by the agency of God. No one among mortals could claim that he had caused the dew to fall. God appeals to the *dew* here, the causes of which were then unknown, as an evidence of his wisdom and supremacy. Dew is the moisture condensed from the atmosphere, and that settles on the earth. It usually falls in clear and calm nights, and is caused by a reduction of the temperature of that on which the dew falls. Objects on the surface of the earth become colder than the atmosphere above them, and the consequence is, that the moisture that was suspended in the atmosphere near the surface of the earth is condensed—in the same way as in a hot day moisture will form on the outside of a tumbler or pitcher that is filled with water. The coldness of the vessel containing the water condenses the moisture that was suspended in the surrounding atmosphere. The *cold*, therefore, which accompanies dew, precedes instead of following it. The *reason* why the surface of the earth becomes cooler than the surrounding atmosphere at night, so as to form dew, has been a subject of considerable inquiry. The theory of Dr. Wells, which is now commonly adopted, is, that the earth is continually radiating its heat to the high and colder regions of the atmosphere; that in the day-time the effects of this radiation are not sensible, being more than counterbalanced by the greater influx of heat from the

29 Out of whose womb came the
ice? and the hoary frost [a]of heaven,
who hath gendered it?
30 The waters are hid as *with* a
stone, and the face of the deep is
[1]frozen.
31 Canst thou bind the sweet influences of [2] Pleiades, [b]or loose the
bands of [3]Orion?

a chap. 37.10 1 *taken.*
2 *Cimah,* or *the seven stars.*
b chap. 9.9; Amos 5.8. 3 *Cecil.*

direct influence of the sun; but that during the night, when the counteracting cause is removed, these effects become sensible, and produce the reduction of temperature which causes dew. The surface of the earth becomes cool by the heat which is radiated to the upper regions of the atmosphere, and the moisture in the air adjacent to the surface of the earth is condensed. This occurs only in a clear and calm night. When the sky is cloudy, the clouds operate as a *screen,* and the radiation of the heat to the higher regions of the atmosphere is prevented, and the surface of the earth and the surrounding atmosphere are kept at the same temperature; see the *Edin. Ency., Art. Meteorology,* pp. 185-188. Of course, these laws were unknown to Job, but now that they are known to us, they constitute not less properly a proof of the wisdom of God.

29. *Out of whose womb came the ice?* That is, who has caused or produced it? The idea is, that it was not by any human agency, or in any known way by which living beings were propagated. ¶ *And the hoary frost of heaven.* Which seems to fall from heaven. The sense is, that it is caused wholly by God; see Notes, chap. xxxvii. 10.

30. *The waters are hid as* with *a stone.* The solid ice is laid as a stone upon them, wholly concealing them from view. ¶ *And the face of the deep is frozen.* Marg. *taken.* The idea is, they seem to take hold of one another (יתלכדו); they hold together, or cohere. The formation of *ice* is thus appealed to as a proof of the wisdom of God, and as a thing which Job could not explain. No man could produce this effect: nor could Job explain how it was done.

31. *Canst thou bind the sweet influences of Pleiades?* The seven stars. On the meaning of the word used here (כימה, *kimâh*), see Notes on chap. ix. 9. In regard to the meaning of the word rendered *sweet influences,* there has been considerable variety of interpretation. The LXX. render it, "Dost thou understand the band (δεσμὸν) of Pleiades?" The Hebrew word (מעדנות) is naturally derived from a word signifying *pleasures,* or *delights* (מעדן, from עדן, to be soft, or pliant; to enjoy pleasure or delight; hence the word *Eden*), and then it would mean, as in our translation, the delightful influences of the Pleiades; or the influences supposed to be produced by this constellation in imparting happiness, particularly the pleasures enjoyed in the spring time, when that constellation makes its appearance. But Gesenius supposes that the word is derived from ענד, *ânădh,* to bind, and that it is used by transposition for מענדות, *măănăddoth.* It would then refer to the "bands of Pleiades," and the question would be whether Job had created the *band* which united the stars composing that constellation in so close union; whether he had bound them together in a cluster or bundle. This idea is adopted by Rosenmüller, Umbreit, and Noyes. Herder renders it, "the brilliant Pleiades." The word "bands" applied to the Pleiades is not unfrequently used in Persian poetry. They were spoken of as a band or ornament for the forehead—or compared with a headband made up of diamonds or pearls. Thus Sadi, in his Gulistan, p. 22, (Amsterdam, 1651), speaking of a garden, says, "The earth is strewed, as it were, with emeralds, and the bands of Pleiades appear upon the boughs of the trees." So Hafiz, another Persian poet, says, in one of his odes, "Over thy songs Heaven has strewed the bands of the Pleiades as a seal of immortality." The Greenlanders call the Pleiades killukturset, a name given to them because they appear to be bound together. *Egede's*

32 Canst thou bring forth [1] Mazzaroth in his season? or canst
thou [2] guide Arcturus with his sons?

1 or, *the twelve signs.*

2 guide *them.*

Account of the Greenland Mission, p. 57; see Rosenmüller, *Alte u. neue Morgenland*, No. 768. There seems, however, no good reason for departing from the usual meaning of the word, and then the reference will be to the time when the Pleiades or the seven stars make their appearance — the season of spring. Then the winter disappears; the streams are unlocked; the earth is covered with grass and flowers; the air is sweet and balmy; and a happy influence seems to set in upon the world. There *may* be some allusion here to the influence which the stars were supposed to exert over the seasons and the affairs of this world, but it is not *necessary* to suppose this. All that is required in the interpretation of the passage is, that the appearance of certain constellations was *connected with* certain changes in the seasons; as with spring, summer, or winter. It was not unnatural to infer from that fact, that the constellations exerted an influence in causing those changes, and hence arose the pretended science of astrology. But there is no necessary connection between the two. The Pleiades appear in the spring, and seem to lead on that joyous season. These stars, so closely set together, seem to be *bound to one another* in a sisterly union (*Herder*), and thus joyously usher in the spring. God asks Job whether *he* were the author of that band, and had thus united them for the purpose of ushering in happy influences on the world. ¶ *Or loose the bands of Orion.* In regard to this constellation, see Notes on chap. ix. 9. The word *bands* here has been supposed to refer to the *girdle* with which it is usually represented. Orion is here described as a man girded for action, and is the pioneer of winter. It made its appearance early in the winter, and was regarded as the precursor of storms and tempests; see the quotations in the Notes on chap. ix. 9. Thus appearing in the autumn, this constellation seems to lead on the winter. It comes with strength. It spreads its influence over the air, the earth, the waters, and binds every thing at its pleasure. God here asks Job whether *he* had power to disarm this giant; to unloose his girdle; to divest him of strength; to control the seasons? Had *he* power over summer and winter, so as to cause them to go or come at his bidding, and to control all those laws which produced them?

32. *Canst thou bring forth Mazzaroth in his season?* Marg. "*the twelve signs;*" that is, the twelve signs of the zodiac. There has been much diversity of opinion about the meaning of this word. It occurs nowhere else in the Scriptures, and of course it is not easy to determine its signification. The LXX. retain the word μαζουρὼθ, without attempting to translate it. Jerome renders it, *Luciferum* —*Lucifer*, the morning-star. The Chaldee, שטרי מזליא—*the constellations of the planets.* Coverdale, "the morning-star;" and so Luther renders it. Rosenmüller, *signa celestia* —*the celestial signs*, and so Herder, Umbreit, Gesenius, and Noyes, "*the zodiac.*" Gesenius regards the word מזרות—*mazzaroth*, as the same as מזלות *mazzaloth*, properly *lodgings, inns;* and hence the *lodgings* of the sun, or the places or *houses* in which he appears in the heavens, and thus as meaning the signs in the zodiac. Most of the Hebrew interpreters adopt this view, but it rests on no certain foundation, and as we are not certain as to the meaning of the word, the only safe way is to retain the original, as is done in our common version. I do not see how it is possible to determine its meaning with certainty, and probably it is to be regarded as a name given to some constellation or cluster of stars supposed to exert an influence over the seasons, or connected with some change in the seasons, which we cannot now accurately understand. ¶ *Or canst thou guide Arcturus?* On the constellation "Arcturus" (עיש)—*aish*), see Notes on chap. ix. 9. The word ren-

33 Knowest thou the ordinances [a] of heaven? canst thou set the dominion thereof in the earth?

a Je.31.35,36.

34 Canst thou lift up thy voice to the clouds, that abundance of waters may cover thee?

dered "guide" in the text, is in the margin "guide them." The Hebrew is, "and *ăish* upon [or near—עַל] her sons, canst thou lead them?" Herder and Umbreit render it, "And lead forth the Bear with her young," or her children. The reference is to the constellation Arcturus, or Ursa Major, in the northern sky. The 'sons" referred to are the stars that accompany it, probably the stars that are now called the "tail of the bear." *Umbreit.* Another interpretation is suggested by Herder, which is that this constellation is represented as a nightly wanderer—a mother, who is seeking her lost children, the stars that are no longer visible, and that thus revolves around the heavens. But the probable reference is to the constellation conducted round and round the pole as by some unseen hand, like a mother with her children, and the question is, whether Job had skill and power to do this? God appeals to it as a manifestation of his majesty and power, and as far above the skill of man. Who ever looked upon that beautiful constellation and marked its regular revolutions, without feeling that its position and movements were such as God only could produce?

33. *Knowest thou the ordinances of heaven?* The laws or statutes by which the motions of the heavenly bodies are governed. These were wholly unknown in the time of Job, and the discovery of some of those laws—for only a few of them are yet known—was reserved to be the glory of the modern system of astronomy. The suggestion of the great principles of the system gave immortality to the name Copernicus; and the discovery of those laws in modern times has conferred immortality on the names of Brahè, Kepler, and Newton. The laws which control the heavenly bodies are the most sublime that are known to man, and have done more to impress the human mind with a sense of the majesty of God than any other discoveries made in the material universe. Of course, all those laws were known to God himself, and he appeals to them in proof of his greatness and majesty. The grand and beautiful movements of the heavenly bodies in the time of Job were fitted to produce admiration; and one of the chief delights of those that dwelt under the splendour of an Oriental sky was to contemplate those movements, and to give names to those moving lights. The discoveries of science have enlarged the conceptions of man in regard to the starry heavens far towards immensity; have shown that these twinkling lights are vast worlds and systems, and at the same time have so disclosed the laws by which they are governed as to promote, where the heart is right, intelligent piety, and elevate the mind to more glorious views of the Creator. ¶ *Canst thou set the dominion thereof in the earth?* That is, "dost thou assign the dominion of the heavens over the earth?" The reference is, undoubtedly, to the influence of the heavenly bodies upon sublunary objects. The exact extent of that cannot be supposed to have been known in the days of Job, and it is probable that much more was ascribed to the influence of the stars on human affairs than the truth would justify. Nor is its extent now known. It *is* known that the moon has an influence over the tides of the ocean; it may be that it has to some extent over the weather; and it is not impossible that the other heavenly bodies may have some effect on the changes observed in the earth which is not understood. Whatever it is, it was and is all known to God, and the idea here is, that it was a proof of his immense superiority over man.

34. *Canst thou lift up thy voice to the clouds, that abundance of waters may cover thee?* That is, canst thou command the clouds so that they shall send down abundant rain?

35 Canst thou send lightnings, that they may go, and say unto thee, [1] Here we *are?*

1 *Behold us.*

36 Who hath put wisdom in the inward [a] parts? or who hath given understanding to the heart?

a Ps.51.6.

Bouillier supposes that there is an allusion here to the incantations which were pretended to be practised by the Magi, by which they claimed the power of producing rain at pleasure; comp. Jer. xiv. 22, "Are there any among the vanities of the Gentiles [the idols that they worship] that can cause rain? Art not thou he, O Lord our God?" The idea is, that it is God only who can cause rain, and that the control of the clouds from which rain descends is wholly beyond the reach of man.

35. *Canst thou send lightnings?* That is, lightning is wholly under the control of God. So it is now; for after all that man has done to discover its laws, and to guard against it, yet still man has made no advances towards a power to wield it, nor is it possible that he ever should. It is *one* of the agencies in the universe that is always to be under the divine direction, and however much man may subsidize to his purposes wind, and water, and steam, and air, yet there can be no prospect that the forked lightning can be seized by human hands and directed by human skill to purposes of utility or destruction among men; comp. Notes on chap. xxxvi. 31—33. ¶ *And say unto thee, Here we* are. Marg. *Behold us.* That is, we are at your disposal. This language is derived from the condition of servants presenting themselves at the call of their masters, and saying that they stood ready to obey their commands; comp. 1 Sam. iii. 4, 6, 9; Isa. vi. 8.

36. *Who hath put wisdom in the inward parts?* There is great variety in the interpretation of this passage. Jerome renders it, Quis posuit in visceribus hominis sapientiam? Vel quis dedit gallo intelligentiam? "Who hath put wisdom in the inner parts of man? Or who has given to the cock intelligence?" The LXX. as strangely, "Who hath given to women skill in weaving, and a knowledge of the art of embroidering?" One of the Targums renders it, "Who has given to the woodcock intelligence that he should praise his Master?" Herder renders it,

"Who gave understanding to the flying clouds,
Or intelligence to the meteors of the air?"

Umbreit,

"Who placed wisdom in the dark clouds?
Who gave understanding to the forms of the air?"

Schultens and Rosenmüller explain it of the various phenomena that appear in the sky—as lightning, thunder, meteoric lights, &c. So Prof. Lee explains the words as referring to the "tempest" and the "thunder-storm." According to that interpretation, the idea is, that these phenomena appear to be endowed with intelligence, There is proof of plan and wisdom in their arrangement and connection, and they show that it is not by chance that they are directed. One reason assigned for this interpretation is, that it accords with the connection. The course of the argument, it is remarked, relates to the various phenomena that appear in the sky—to the lightnings, tempests, and clouds. It is unnatural to suppose that a remark would be interposed here respecting the intellectual endowments of man, when the appeal to the clouds is again (ver. 37) immediately resumed. There can be no doubt that there is much weight in this observation, and that the connection demands this interpretation, and that it should be adopted if the words which are used will admit of it. The only difficulty relates to the words rendered "inward parts," and "heart." The former of these (טחות) according to the Hebrew interpreters, is derived from טוח—*tuahh*, to cover over, to spread, to besmear: and is hence given to the veins, because covered with fat. It occurs only in this place, and in Ps. li. 6, "Behold thou desirest truth in the *inward parts,*" where it undoubtedly refers to the seat of the affections

37 Who can number the clouds in wisdom? or who can [1] stay the bottles of heaven,

38 When the dust [2] groweth into hardness, and the clods cleave fast together?

1 *cause to lie down.*

2 *is poured,* or, *is turned into mire.*

or thoughts in man. The *verb* is often used as meaning to daub, overlay, or plaster, as in Lev. xiv. 42; Ezek. xxii. 28; xiii. 12, 14. Schultens, Lee, Umbreit, and others, have recourse in the explanation to the use of the Arabic word of the same letters with the Hebrew, meaning *to wander, to make a random shot,* &c., and thence apply it to lightning, and to meteors. Umbreit supposes that there is allusion to the prevalent opinion in the East that the clouds and the phenomena of the air could be regarded as furnishing prophetic indications of what was to occur; or to the custom of predicting future events by the aspects of the sky. It is a sufficient objection to this, however, that it cannot be supposed that the Almighty would lend his sanction to this opinion by appealing to it as if it were so. After all that has been written on the passage, and all the force of the difficulty which is urged, I do not see evidence that we are to depart from the common interpretation, to wit, that God means to appeal to the fact that he has endowed man with intelligence as a proof of his greatness and supremacy. The connection is, indeed, not very apparent. It may be, however, as Noyes suggests, that the reference is to the mind of Job in particular, and to the intelligence with which he was able to perceive, and in some measure to comprehend, these various phenomena. The connection may be something like this: "Look to the heavens, and contemplate these wonders. Explain them, if possible; and then ask who it is that has so endowed the mind of man that it *can* trace in them such proofs of the wisdom and power of the Almighty. The phenomena themselves, and the capacity to contemplate them, and to be instructed by them, are alike demonstrations of the supremacy of the Most High." ¶ *Understanding to the heart.* To the mind. The common word to denote *heart*—לֵב is not used here, but a word (שֶׂכְוִי from שׂכה) meaning to look at, to view; and hence denoting the mind; the intelligent soul. *Gesenius.*

37. *Who can number the clouds?* The word here rendered *clouds* (שְׁחָקִים) is applied to the clouds as made up of *small particles*—as if they were composed of fine dust, and hence the word *number* is applied to them, not as meaning that the clouds themselves were innumerable, but that no one could estimate the number of particles which enter into their formation. ¶ *In wisdom.* By his wisdom. Who has sufficient intelligence to do it? ¶ *Or who can stay the bottles of heaven?* Marg. as in Heb. *cause to lie down.* The clouds are here compared with bottles, as if they held the water in the same manner; comp. Notes on chap. xxvi. 8. The word rendered "stay" in the text, and in the margin "cause to lie down," is rendered by Umbreit, "pour out," from an Arabic signification of the word. Gesenius supposes that the meaning to "pour out" is derived from the idea of "causing to lie down," from the fact that a bottle or vessel was made to lie down or was inclined to one side when its contents were poured out. This explanation seems probable, though there is no other place in the Hebrew where the word is used in this signification. The sense of pouring out agrees well with the connection.

38. *When the dust groweth into hardness.* Marg. "*is poured,* or, *is turned into mire.*" The words here used relate often to metals, and to the act of pouring them out when fused, for the purpose of casting. The proper idea here is, "when the dust flows into a molten mass;" that is, when wet with rain it flows together and becomes hard. The sense is, that the rain operates on the clay as heat does on metals, and that when it is dissolved it flows together and thus becomes a solid mass. The object is to compare the effect of rain with the

39 Wilt thou hunt the prey for
the [a] lion? or fill the [1] appetite of
the young lions,
40 When they couch in *their* dens
and abide in the covert to lie in wait?
41 Who provideth for the raven
[b] his food? when his young ones
cry unto God, they wander for lack
of meat.

a Ps.104.21. 1 *life*. *b* Ps.147.9; Lu.12.24

usual effect in casting metals. ¶ *And the clods cleave fast together.* That is, they are run together by the rain. They form one mass of the same consistency, and then are baked hard by the sun.

39. *Wilt thou hunt the prey for the lion?* The appeal here is to the *instincts* with which God has endowed animals, and to the fact that he had so made them that they would secure their own food. He asks Job whether he would undertake to do what the lion did by instinct in finding his food, and by his power and skill in seizing his prey. There was a wise adaptation of the lion for this purpose which man could neither originate nor explain. ¶ *Or fill the appetite of the young lions.* Marg. as in Heb. *life*. The word *life* is here used for hunger, as the appetite is necessarily connected with the preservation of life. The meaning here is, "Wouldst thou undertake to supply his wants? It is done by laws, and in a manner which thou canst not explain. There are in the arrangement by which it is accomplished marks of wisdom which far surpass the skill of man to originate, and the instinct and power by which it is done are proof of the supremacy of the Most High." No one can study the subject of the instincts of animals, or become in the least acquainted with Natural History, without finding every where traces of the wisdom and goodness of God.

40. *When they couch in* their *dens.* For the purpose of springing upon their prey. ¶ And *abide in the covert to lie in wait?* The usual posture of the lion when he seeks his prey. He places himself in some unobserved position in a dense thicket, or crouches upon the ground so as not to be seen, and then springs suddenly upon his victim. The common method of the lion in taking his prey is to spring or throw himself upon it from the place of his ambush, with one vast bound, and to inflict the mortal blow with one stroke of his paw. If he misses his aim, however, he seldom attempts another spring at the same object, but deliberately returns to the thicket in which he lay in concealment. See the habits of the lion illustrated in the Edin. Ency., Art. *Mazology*.

41. *Who provideth for the raven his food?* The same thought is expressed in Ps. cxlvii. 9,

> He giveth to the beast his food,
> And to the young ravens which cry.

Comp. Matth. vi. 26. Scheutzer (*in loc.*) suggests that the reason why the *raven* is specified here rather than other fowls is, that it is an offensive bird, and that God means to state that no object, however regarded by man, is beneath *his* notice. He carefully provides for the wants of all his creatures. ¶ *When his young ones cry unto God, they wander for lack of meat.* Bochart observes that the raven expels the young from the nest as soon as they are able to fly. In this condition, being unable to obtain food by their own exertions, they make a croaking noise, and God is said to hear it, and to supply their wants. *Noyes.* There are various opinions expressed in regard to this subject by the Rabbinical writers, and by the ancients generally. Rabbi Eliezer (cap. 21) says that, "When the old ravens see the young coming into the world which are not black, they regard them as the offspring of serpents, and flee away from them, and God takes care of them." Rabbi Solomon says that in this condition they are nourished by the flies and worms that are generated in their nests, and the same opinion was held by the Arabian writers, Haritius, Alkuazin, and Damir. Among the fathers of the church, Chrysostom, Olympiodorus, Gregory, and Isidorus, supposed that they were nurtured by dew descending from heaven. Pliny

CHAPTER XXXIX.

ANALYSIS OF THE CHAPTER.

THE argument in proof of the divine wisdom and greatness, which was commenced at ver. 39 of the previous chapter, is continued in this. The argument is drawn from the instincts, habits, and power of the animal creation. It is, in substance, that the arrangements for the preservation of the brutes, their instincts and the power which they exhibit, far surpass all the wisdom and skill of man to have imparted them. He could not even *explain* those things which God had made. In the prosecution of this argument, God appeals (1.) To the wild goats of the rocks, and the hinds, and to the paternal care and tenderness with which he regards them, ver. 1—4. (2.) To the wild ass exulting in his freedom, scorning restraint, and roaming at large in the wilderness and in the extended plains, ver. 5—8. (3.) To the unicorn, and to his great strength, far surpassing that of man, and to the fact that he could not be subjugated as other animals are, and made subservient to the purposes of agriculture, ver. 9—12. (4.) To the wings and feathers of the ostrich. Especially, God asks of Job whether *he* had ordained the remarkable laws by which she was governed in reference to her young, and which were so unlike the usual habits of the animal creation, ver. 13—18. (5.) To the horse—his strength, his majesty, his courage, his impatience for battle, ver. 19—25. (6.) To the hawk, evincing consummate wisdom in its instincts, ver. 26. (7.) To the eagle—the king of birds, and to the laws by which it secures its food. By an appeal to the habits and instincts of these animals, God designs to impress the mind with the conviction of his wisdom and greatness, and to show to man how incompetent he is to pronounce on his doings.

KNOWEST thou the time when the wild goats of the rock bring forth? *or* canst thou mark when the hinds [a] do calve?

a Ps.29.9.

(Lib. x. c. 12) says, that the old ravens expel the strongest of their young from the nest, and compel them to fly. This is the time, according to many of the older commentators, when the young ravens are represented as calling upon God for food. See Scheutzer, Physica Sacra, *in loc.* and Bochart, Hieroz. P. ii. L. ii. c. ii. I do not know that there is now supposed to be sufficient evidence to substantiate this fact in regard to the manner in which the ravens treat their young, and all the circumstances of the place before us will be met by the supposition that young birds seem to call upon God, and that he supplies their wants. The last three verses in this chapter should not have been separated from the following. The appeal in this is to the animal creation, and this is continued through the whole of the next chapter. The proper place for the division would have been at the close of verse 38, where the argument from the great laws of the material universe was ended. Then commences an appeal to his works of a higher order—the region of instinct and appetites, where creatures are governed by other than mere physical laws.

CHAPTER XXXIX.

1. *Knowest thou the time when the wild goats of the rock bring forth?* That is, the particular season when the mountain goats bring forth their young. Of domestic animals—the sheep, the tame goat, &c., the habits would be fully understood. But the question here relates to the animals that roamed at large on inaccessible cliffs; that were buried in deep forests; that were far from the dwellings and observation of men; and the meaning is, that there were many facts in regard to such points of Natural History which Job could not explain. God knew all their instincts and habits, and on the inaccessible cliffs, in the deep dell, in the dark forest, he was with them, and they were the objects of his care. He not only regarded the condition of the domestic animals that had been brought into the service of man, and where man perhaps *might* be disposed to claim that they owed much of their comfort to *his* care, but he regarded also the wild, wandering beast of the mountain, where no such pretence could be advanced. The providence of God is over them; and in the periods of their lives when they seem most to need attention, when every shepherd and herdsmen is most solicitous about his flocks and herds, then God is present, and his care is seen in their preservation. The particular point in the inquiry here is, not in regard to the *time* when these animals produced their young or the period of their gestation, which might probably be known, but in regard to the attention and care which was needful for them when they were so far removed from the observance of man, and had no human aid. The "wild goat of the rock" here referred to, is, doubtless, the Ibex, or mountain goat, that has its dwellings among

2 Canst thou number the months *that* they fulfil? or knowest thou the time when they bring forth?

3 They bow themselves, they bring forth their young ones, they cast out their sorrows.

---

the rocks, or in stony places. The Hebrew term is יעל — *yâēl*, or *yaal*, from יעל—*yáăl, to ascend, to go up.* They had their residence in the lofty rocks of mountains; Ps. civ. 18. "The high hills are a refuge for the wild goats." Heb. "For the goats of the rocks"—יעלים סלעים. So in 1 Sam. xxiv. 2. [3.] "Saul went to seek David and his men *upon the rocks of the wild goats;*" that is, where were the wild goats—היעלים. For a description of the *wild goat,* see Bochart, Hieroz. P. i. Lib. iii. c. xxiii. The animal here referred to is, doubtless, the same which Burckhardt saw on the summit of Mount St. Catharine, adjacent to Mount Sinai, and which he thus describes in his Travels in Syria, p. 571: "As we approached the summit of the mountain (St. Catharine, adjacent to Mount Sinai), we saw at a distance a small flock of mountain goats feeding among the rocks. One of our Arabs left us, and by a widely circuitous route endeavoured to get to the leeward of them, and near enough to fire at them. He enjoined us to remain in sight of them, and to sit down in order not to alarm them. He had nearly reached a favourable spot behind a rock, when the goats suddenly took to flight. They could not have seen the Arab, but the wind changed, and thus they smelt him. The chase of the beden, as the wild goat is called, resembles that of the chamois of the Alps, and requires as much enterprise and patience. The Arabs make long circuits to surprise them, and endeavour to come upon them early in the morning, when they feed. The goats have a leader who keeps watch, and on any suspicious smell, sound, or object, makes a noise, which is a signal to the flock to make their escape. They have much decreased of late, if we may believe the Arabs; who say that fifty years ago, if a stranger came to a tent, and the owner of it had no sheep to kill, he took his gun and went in search of a beden. They are, however, even now more common here than in the Alps, or in the mountains to the east of the Red Sea. I had three or four of them brought to me at the convent, which I bought at three-fourths of a dollar each. The flesh is excellent, and has nearly the same flavour as that of the deer. The Bedouins make water bags of their skins, and rings of their horns, which they wear on their thumbs. When the beden is met with in the plains, the dogs of the hunters easily catch him; but they cannot come up with him among the rocks, where he can make leaps of twenty feet." ¶ Or *canst thou mark when the hinds do calve?* The reference here is to the special care and protection of God manifested for them. The meaning is, that this animal seems to be always timid and apprehensive of danger, and that there is special care bestowed upon an animal so defenceless in enabling it to rear its young. The word *hinds* denotes the deer, the fawn, the most timid and defenceless, perhaps, of all animals.

2. *Canst thou number the months,* &c. That is, as they wander in the wilderness, as they live in inaccessible crags and cliffs of the rocks, it is impossible for man to be acquainted with their habits as he can with those of the domestic animals.

3. *They bow themselves.* Literally they *curve* or bend themselves; that is, they draw their limbs together. ¶ *They cast out their sorrows.* That is, they cast forth the *offspring* of their pains, or the young which cause their pains. The idea seems to be, that they do this without any of the care and attention which shepherds are obliged to show to their flocks at such seasons. They do it when God only guards them; when they are in the wilderness or on the rocks far away from the abodes of man. The leading thought in all this seems to be, that the tender care of God was over his creatures, in the most peril-

4 Their young ones are in good liking, they grow up with corn; they go forth, and return not unto them.

5 Who hath sent out the wild ass [a] free? or who hath loosed the bands of the wild ass?

a Je. 2 24; Ho. 8.9.

ous and delicate state, and that all this was exercised where man could have no access to them, and could not even observe them.

4. *Their young ones are in good liking.* Heb. "they are fat;" and hence it means that they are strong and robust. ¶ *They grow up with corn.* Herder, Gesenius, Noyes, Umbreit, and Rosenm ller render this, "in the wilderness," or "field." The proper and usual meaning of the word here used (בַּר) is corn, or grain; but in Chaldee it has the sense of *open fields*, or *country*. The same idea is found in the Arabic, and this sense seems to be required by the connection. The idea is not that they are nurtured with *grain*, which would require the care of man, but that they are nurtured under the direct eye of God far away from human dwellings, and even when they go away from their dam and return no more to the place of their birth. This is one of the instances, therefore, in which the connection seems to require us to adopt a signification that does not elsewhere occur in the Hebrew, but which is found in the cognate languages. ¶ *They go forth, and return not unto them.* God guards and preserves them, even when they wander away from their dam, and are left helpless. Many of the young of animals require long attention from man, many are kept for a considerable period by the side of the mother, but the idea here seems to be, that the young of the wild goat and of the fawn are thrown early on the providence of God, and are protected by him alone. The particular care of Providence over these animals seems to be specified because there are no others that are exposed to so many dangers in their early life. "Every creature then is a formidable enemy. The eagle, the falcon, the osprey, the wolf, the dog, and all the rapacious animals of the cat kind, are in continual employment to find out their retreat. But what is more unnatural still, the stag himself is a professed enemy, and she [the hind] is obliged to use all her arts to conceal her young from him, as from the most dangerous of her pursuers." *Goldsmith's Nat. His.*

5. *Who hath sent out the wild ass free?* For a description of the wild ass, see Notes on chap. xi. 12. On the meaning of the word rendered *free* (חָפְשִׁי), see Notes on Isa. lviii. 6. These animals commonly "inhabit the dry and mountainous parts of the deserts of Great Tartary, but not higher than about lat. 48°. They are migratory, and arrive in vast troops to feed, during the summer, on the tracts to the north and east of the sea of Aral. About autumn they collect in herds of hundreds, and even thousands, and direct their course southward towards India to enjoy a warm retreat during winter. But they more usually retire to Persia, where they are found in the mountains of Casbin; and where part of them remain during the whole year. They are also said to penetrate to the southern parts of India, to the mountains of Malabar and Golconda. These animals were anciently found in Palestine, Syria, Arabia Deserta, Mesopotamia, Phrygia, and Lycaonia, but they rarely occur in those regions at the present time, and seem to be almost entirely confined to Tartary, some parts of Persia and India, and Africa. Their manners resemble those of the wild horse. They assemble in troops under the conduct of a leader or sentinel; and are extremely shy and vigilant. They will, however, stop in the midst of their course, and even suffer the approach of man for an instant, and then dart off with the utmost rapidity. They have been at all times celebrated for their swiftness. Their voice resembles that of the common ass, but is shriller." *Rob. Calmet.* The Onager or wild ass is doubtless "the parent stock from which we have derived the useful domestic ani-

6 Whose [a]house I have made the
wilderness, and the [1]barren land his
dwellings.
7 He scorneth the multitude of
the city, neither regardeth he the
crying of the [2]driver.
8 The range of the mountains *is*
his pasture, and he searcheth after
every green thing.

a chap.24.5. 1 *salt places.* 2 *exactor,* chap.3.18.

---

mal, which seems to have degenerated the farther it has been removed from its parent seat in Central Asia. It is greatly distinguished in spirit and grace of form from the domestic ass. It is taller and more dignified; it holds the head higher, and the legs are more elegantly shaped. Even the head, though large in proportion to the body, has a finer appearance, from the forehead being more arched; the neck by which it is sustained is much longer, and has a more graceful bend. It has a short mane of dark and woolly hair; and a stripe of dark bushy hair also runs along the ridge of the back from the mane to the tail. The hair of the body is of a silver gray, inclining to flaxen colour in some parts, and white under the belly. The hair is soft and silken, similar in texture to that of the camel."—*Pict. Bible.* It is of this animal, so different in spirit, energy, agility, and appearance, from the domestic animal of that name, that we must think in order to understand this passage. We must think of them fleet as the wind, untamed and unbroken, wandering over vast plains in groups and herds, assembled by thousands under a leader or guide, and bounding off with uncontrollable rapidity on the approach of man, if we would feel the force of the appeal which is here made. God asks of Job whether *he*—who could not even subdue and tame this wild creature—had ordained the laws of its freedom; had held it as a captive, and then set it at liberty to exult over boundless plains in its conscious independence. The idea is, that it was one of the creatures of God, under *no* laws but such as *he* had been pleased to impose upon it, and wholly beyond the government of man. ¶ *Or who hath loosed the bands of the wild ass?* As if he had been once a captive, and then set free. The illustration is derived from the feeling which attends a restoration to liberty. The freedom of this animal *seems* to be as productive of exhilaration as if it had been a prisoner or slave, and had been suddenly emancipated.

6. *Whose house I have made.* God had appointed its home in the desert. ¶ *And the barren land his dwellings.* Marg. as in Heb. *salt places.* Such places were usually barren. Ps. cvii. 34, "He turneth a fruitful land into *barrenness.*" Heb. *saltness.* Thus Virgil, Geor. ii. 238-240,

> Salsa autem tellus, et quæ perhibetur amara,
> Frugibus infelix: ea nec mansuescit arando;
> Nec Baccho genus, aut pomis sua nomina servat.

Comp. Pliny, Nat. His. 31, 7, Deut. xxix. 23.

7. *He scorneth the multitude of the city.* That is, he sets all this at defiance; he is not intimidated by it. He finds his home far away from the city in the wild freedom of the wilderness. ¶ *Neither regardeth he the crying of the driver.* Marg. *exactor.* The Hebrew word properly means a collector of taxes or revenue, and hence an oppressor, and a driver of cattle. The allusion here is to a driver, and the meaning is, that he is not subject to restraint, but enjoys the most unlimited freedom.

8. *The range of the mountains* is *his pasture.* The word rendered *range* (יְתוּר), means properly a *searching out,* and then that which is obtained by search. The word *range* expresses the idea with sufficient exactness. The usual range of the wild ass is the mountains. Pallas, who has given a full description of the habits of the Onager, or wild ass, states, that it especially loves desolate hills as its abode. *Acts of the Society of Sciences of St. Petersburg, for the year* 1777.

9 Will the unicorn [a] be willing to serve thee, or abide by thy crib?

a De.33.17; Ps.92.10.

9. *Will the unicorn be willing to serve thee?* In the previous part of the argument, God had appealed to the lion, the raven, the goats of the rock, the hind, and the wild ass; and the idea was, that in the instincts of each of these classes of animals, there was some special proof of wisdom. He now turns to another class of the animal creation in proof of his own supremacy and power, and lays the argument in the great strength and in the independence of the animal, and in the fact that man had not been able to subject his great strength to the purposes of husbandry. In regard to the animal here referred to, there has been great diversity of opinion among interpreters, nor is there as yet any one prevailing sentiment. Jerome renders it *rhinoceros*; the LXX., μονόκερως, *the unicorn*; the Chaldee and the Syraic retain the Hebrew word; Gesenius, Herder, Umbreit, and Noyes, render it *the buffalo*; Schultens, *alticornem*; Luther and Coverdale, *the unicorn*; Rosenmüller, *the onyx*, a large and fierce species of the antelope; Calmet supposes that the rhinoceros is intended; and Prof. Robinson, in an extended appendage to the article of Calmet (art. Unicorn), has endeavoured to show that the wild buffalo is intended. Bochart, also, in a long and learned argument, has endeavoured to show that the rhinoceros cannot be meant. Hieroz. P. i. Lib. iii. chap. xxvi. He maintains that a species of antelope is referred to, the *rim* of the Arabs. De Wette (Com. on Ps. xxii. 21) accords with the opinion of Gesenius, Robinson, and others, that the animal referred to is the buffalo of the Eastern continent, the *bos bubalus* of Linnæus, an animal which differs from the American buffalo only in the shape of the horns and the absence of the dewlap. The word which occurs here, and which is rendered *unicorn* (רים *rēm*, or ראם *rěēm*), is used in the Scriptures only in the following places, where in the singular or plural it is uniformly rendered *unicorn*, or *unicorns*—Num. xxiii. 22; Deut. xxxiii. 17; Job xxxix. 9, 10; Ps. xxii. 21; xxix. 6; xcii. 10; and Isa. xxxiv. 7. By a reference to these passages, it will be found that the animal had the following characteristics. (1.) It was distinguished for its *strength*; see ver. 11 of this chapter. Num. xxiii. 22, "He [that is, Israel, or the Israelites] hath as it were the strength of an unicorn—ראם, *rěēm*. In Num. xxiv. 8, the same declaration is repeated. It is true that the Hebrew word in both these places (תּוֹעֲפֹת) may denote *rapidity of motion, speed;* but in this place the notion of *strength* must be principally intended, for it was of the *power* of the people, and their ability manifested in the number of their hosts, that Balaam is speaking. Bochart, however (Hieroz. P. i. Lib. iii. c. xxvii.), supposes that the word means, not strength, or agility, but *height*, and that the idea is, that the people referred to by Balaam was a lofty or elevated people. If the word means *strength*, it was most appropriate to compare a vast host of people with the vigour and force of an untamable wild animal. The idea of *speed* or of *loftiness* does not so well suit the connection. (2.) It was an animal that was not subjected to the service of tilling the soil, and that was supposed to be incapable of being so trained. Thus in the place before us it is said, that he could not be so domesticated that he would remain like the ox at the crib; that he could not be yoked to the plough; that he could not be employed and safely left to pursue the work of the field; and that he could not be so subdued that it would be safe to attempt to bring home the harvest by his aid. From all these declarations, it is plain that he was regarded as a wild and untamed animal; an animal that was not then domesticated, and that could not be employed in husbandry. This characteristic would agree with either the antelope, the onyx, the buffalo, the rhinoceros, or the supposed unicorn. With which of them it will *best* accord,

we may be able to determine when all his characteristics are examined. (3.) The strength of the animal was in his horns. This was one of his peculiar characteristics, and it is evidently by this that he is designed to be distinguished. Deut. xxxiii. 17, "His glory is like the firstling of a bullock, and his horns like the horns of unicorns." Ps. xcii. 10, "My horn shalt thou exalt like the horn of an unicorn." Ps. xxii. 21, "Thou hast heard me [saved me] from the horns of the unicorns." It is true, indeed, as Prof. Robinson has remarked (Calmet, art. *Unicorn*), the word *reem* has in itself no reference to *horns*, nor is there in the Hebrew an illusion any where to the supposition that the animal here referred to has only *one* horn. Wherever, in the Scriptures, the animal is spoken of with any allusion to this member, the expression is in the plural, *horns*. The only variation from this, even in the common version, is in Ps. xcii. 10, where the Hebrew is simply, "My horn shalt thou exalt like an unicorn," where the word *horn*, as it stands in the English version, is not expressed. There is, indeed, in this passage, some obvious allusion to the *horns* of this animal, but all the force of the comparison will be retained if the word inserted in the ellipsis is in the plural number. The horn or horns of the *reem* were, however, beyond question, the principal seat of strength, and the instruments of assault and defence. See the passage in Deut. xxxiii. 17, "With them he shall push the people together to the ends of the earth." (4.) There was some peculiar majesty or dignity in the horns of this animal that attracted attention, and that made them the proper symbol of dominion and of royal authority. Thus in Ps. xcii. 10, "My horn shalt thou exalt like the horn of an unicorn," where the reference seems to be to a kingly authority or dominion, of which the horn was an appropriate symbol. These are all the characteristics of the animal referred to in the Scriptures, and the question is, With what known animal do they best correspond? The principal animals referred to by those who have examined the subject at length are, the onyx or antelope; the buffalo; the animal commonly referred to as the unicorn, and the rhinoceros. The principal characteristic of the *unicorn* was supposed to be, that it had a long, slender horn projecting from the *forehead;* the horn of the rhinoceros is on the *snout*, or the nose. I. In regard to the antelope, or the *rim* of the modern Arabs, supposed by Bochart to be the animal here referred to, it seems clear that there are few characteristics in common between the two animals. The onyx or antelope is not distinguished as this animal is for strength, nor for the fact that it is peculiarly untamable, nor that its strength is in its horns, nor that it is of such size and proportions that a comparison would naturally be suggested between it and the ox. In all that is said of the animal, we think of one greater in bulk, in strength, in untamableness, than the onyx; an animal more distinguished for conquest and subduing other animals before him. Bochart has collected much that is fabulous respecting this animal, from the Rabbins and the Arabic writers, which it is not needful here to repeat; see the Hieroz. P. i. Lib. iii. c. xxvii.; or Scheutzer, Physi. Sac. on Num. xxiii. 22. II. The claims of the *buffalo* to be regarded as the animal here referred to, are much higher than those of the onyx, and the opinion that this is the animal intended is entertained by such names as those of Gesenius, De Wette, Robinson, Umbreit, and Herder. But the objections to this seem to me to be insuperable, and the arguments are not such as to carry conviction. The principal objections to the opinion are (1.) that the account in regard to the horns of the *reem* by no means agrees with the fact in regard to the bison, or buffalo. The buffalo is an animal of the cow kind (Goldsmith), and the horns are short and crooked, and by no means distinguished for strength. They do not in fact surpass in this respect the horns of many other animals, and are not such as would occur ordinarily as the prominent characteristic in their description. It is true that there are instances where the horns of the wild buffalo are large, but this does not appear to be the case ordinarily. Mr. Pennant mentions a pair of horns in the British Museum, which are six feet and a half long, and the hollow of which will hold five quarts. Father Lobo affirms that some of the horns of the buffaloes in Abyssinia will hold ten quarts; and Dillon saw some in India that were ten feet long. But these were manifestly extraordinary cases. (2.) The animal here referred to was evidently a stronger and a larger animal than the wild ox or the buffalo. "The Oriental buffalo appears to be so closely allied to our common ox, that without an attentive examination it might be easily mistaken for a variety of that animal. In point of size, it is rather superior to the ox; and upon an accurate inspection, it is observed to differ in the shape and magnitude of the head, the latter being larger than in the ox." *Robinson, in Calmet.* The animal here referred to was such as to make the contrast particularly striking between him and the ox. The latter could be employed for labour; the former, though greatly superior in strength, could not. (3.) The reem, it was supposed, could not be tamed and made to subserve domestic purposes. The buffalo, however, can be made as serviceable as the ox, and is actually domesticated and employed in agricultural purposes. Niebuhr remarks that he saw buffaloes not only in Egypt, but also at Bombay, Surat, on the Euphrates, Tigris, Orontes, and indeed in all marshy regions and near large rivers. Sonnini remarks that in Egypt the buffalo, though but recently domesticated, is more numerous than the common ox, and is there equally domestic, and in Italy they are known to be commonly employed in the Pontine marshes, where the fatal nature of the climate acts on common cattle, but affects buffaloes less. It is true that the animal has been comparatively recently domesticated, and that it was doubtless known in the time of Job only as a wild, savage, ferocious animal; but still the description here is that of an animal not only that *was not* then tamed, but obviously of one that could not well be employed in domestic purposes. We are to remember that the language here is that of God himself, and that therefore it may be regarded as descriptive of what the essential nature of the animal was, rather than what it was supposed to be by the persons to whom the language was addressed. One of the principal arguments alleged for supposing that the animal here referred to by the *reem* was the buffalo, is, that the rhinoceros was probably unknown in the land where Job resided, and that the unicorn was altogether a fabulous animal. This difficulty will be considered in the remarks to be made on the claims of each of those animals. III. It was an early opinion, and the opinion was probably entertained by the authors of the Septuagint translation, and by the English translators as well as by others, that the animal here referred to was the *unicorn*. This animal was long supposed to be a fabulous animal, and it has not been until recently that the evidences of its existence have been confirmed. These evidences are adduced by Rosenmüller, *Morgenland*, ii. p. 269, *seq.*, and by Prof. Robinson, *Calmet*, pp. 908, 909. They are, summarily, the following: (1.) Pliny mentions such an animal, and gives a description of it, though from his time for centuries it seems to have been unknown. *His. Nat.* 8, 21. His language is, Asperrimam autem feram monocerotem reliquo corpore equo similem, capite cervo, pedibus elephanti, cauda apro, mugitu gravi, uno cornu nigro media fronte cubitorum duum eminente. Hanc feram vivam negant capi. "The unicorn is an exceeding fierce animal, resembling a horse as to the rest of his body, but having the head like a stag, the feet like an elephant, and the tail like a wild boar; its roaring is loud; and it has a black horn of about two cubits projecting from the middle of the forehead." (2.) The figure of the unicorn, in various attitudes, according to Niebuhr, is depicted on almost all the staircases in the ruins of Persepolis. *Reisebeschreib.* ii. S. 127. (3.) In 1530, Ludovico de Bartema, a Roman patrician, visited Mecca under the assumed character of a Mussulman, and among other curiosities that he mentions, he says, " On the other side of the caaba is a walled court, in which we saw two unicorns that were pointed out to us as a rarity; and they are indeed truly remarkable. The larger of the two is built like a three-year-old colt, and has a horn upon the forehead about three ells long. This animal has the colour of a yellowish-brown horse, a head like a stag, a neck not very long, with a thin mane; the legs are small and slender like those of a hind or roe; the hoofs of the fore feet are divided, and resemble the hoofs of a goat. Rosenmüller, *Alte u. neue Morgenland,* No. 377. Th. ii. S. 271, 272. (4.) Don Juan Gabriel, a Portuguese colonel, who lived several years in Abyssinia, assures us that in the region of Agamos, in the Abyssinian province of Damota, he had seen an animal of the form and size of a middle-sized horse, of a dark, chestnut-brown colour, and with a whitish horn about five spans long upon its forehead; the mane and tail were black, and the legs long and slender. Several other Portuguese, who were placed in confinement upon a high mountain in the district Namna, by the Abyssinian king Saghedo, related that they had seen at the mountain several unicorns feeding. These accounts are confirmed by Father Lobo, who lived for a long time as a missionary in Abyssinia. (5.) Dr. Sparrman, the Swedish naturalist, who visited the Cape of Good Hope and the adjacent regions in 1772-1776, gives, in his Travels, the following account:—Jacob Kock, an observing peasant on Hippopotamus river, who had travelled over a considerable part of Southern Africa, found on the face of a perpendicular rock, a drawing made by the Hottentots of an animal with a single horn. The Hottentots told him that the animal there represented was very like the horse on which he rode, but had a straight horn upon the forehead. They added, that these one-horned animals were rare; that they ran with great rapidity, and that they were very fierce. (6.) A similar animal is described as having been killed by a party of Hottentots in pursuit of the savage Bushmen in 1791. The animal resembled a horse, was of a light grey colour, and with white stripes under the jaw. It had a single horn directly in front, as long as one's arm, and at the base about as thick. Towards the middle the horn was somewhat flattened, but had a sharp point; it was not attached to the bone of the forehead, but was fixed only in the skin. The head was like that of the horse, and the size about the same. These authorities are collected by Rosenmüller, *Alte u. neue Morgenland,* vol. ii. p. 269, *seq.*, ed. Leipz. 1818. (7.) To these proofs one other is added by Prof. Robinson. It is copied from the Quarterly Review for Oct. 1820 (vol. xxiv. p. 120), in a notice of Frazer's Tour through the Himalaya mountains. The information is contained in a letter from Maj. Latter, commanding in the rajah of Sikkim's territories, in the hilly country east of Nepaul. This letter states that the unicorn, so long considered as a fabulous animal, actually exists in the interior of Thibet, where it is well known to the inhabitants. " In a Thibetian manuscript," says Maj. Latter, " containing the names of different animals, which I procured the other day from the hills, the unicorn is classed under the head of those whose hoofs are divided: it is called the one-horned *tso'po.* Upon inquiring what kind of an animal it was, to our astonishment, the person who brought the manuscript described exactly the unicorn of the ancients; saying that it was a native of the interior of Thibet, about the size of a *tattoo* (a horse from twelve to thirteen hands high,) fierce and extremely wild; seldom if ever caught alive, but frequently shot; and that the flesh was used for food. They go together in herds, like wild buffaloes, and are frequently to be met with on the borders of the great desert, in that part of the country inhabited by wandering Tartars." (8.) To these proofs I add another, taken from the Narrative of the Rev. John Campbell, who thus speaks of it, in his "Travels in South Africa," vol. ii. p. 294. "While in the Mashow territory, the Hottentots brought in a head different from any rhinoceros that had been previously killed. The common African rhinoceros has a crooked horn resembling a cock's spur, which rises about nine or ten inches above the nose, and inclines backward; immediately behind this is a short thick horn. But the head they brought us had a straight horn projecting three feet from the forehead, about ten inches above the tip of the nose. The projection of this great horn very much resembles that of the fanciful unicorn in the British arms. It has a small, thick, horny substance, eight inches long, immediately behind it, and which can hardly be observed on the animal at the distance of one hundred yards, and seems to be designed for keeping fast that which is penetrated by the long horn; so that this species must look like the unicorn (in the sense 'one-horned') when running in the field. The head resembled in size a nine-gallon cask, and measured three feet from the mouth to the ear; and being much larger than that of the one with the crooked horn, and which measured eleven feet in length, the animal itself must have been still larger and more formidable. From its weight, and the position of the horn, it appears capable of overcoming any creature hitherto known." A fragment of the skull, with the horn, is deposited in the Museum of the London Missionary Society. These testimonies from so many witnesses from different parts of the world, who write without concert, and yet who concur so almost entirely in the account of the size and figure of the animal, leave little room to doubt its real existence. That it is not better known, and that its existence has been doubted, is not wonderful. It is to be remembered that all accounts agree in the representation that it is an animal whose residence is in deserts or mountains, and that large parts of Africa and Asia are still unexplored. We are to remember, also, that the *giraffe* has been discovered only within a few years, and that the same is true of the *gnu*, which till recently was held to be a fable of the ancients. At the same time, however, that the existence of such an animal as that of the unicorn is in the highest degree probable, it is clear that it is *not* the animal referred to in the passage before us; for (1.) It is in the highest degree improbable that it was so well known as is supposed in the description here; and (2.) the characteristics do not at all agree with the account of the *reem* of the Scriptures. Neither in regard to the size of the animal, its strength, or the strength of its horns, does it coincide with the account of that animal in the Bible. IV. If neither of the opinions above referred to be correct, then the only remaining opinion that has weight is, that it refers to the rhinoceros. Besides the considerations above suggested, it may be added that the characteristics of the animal given in the Scriptures all agree with the rhinoceros. In size, strength, wildness, untamableness, and in the power and use of the horn, those characteristics agree accurately with the rhinoceros. The only argument of much weight against this opinion is presented by Prof. Robinson in the following language: "The *reem* was obviously an animal well known to the Hebrews, being every where mentioned with other animals common to the country, while the rhinoceros was never an inhabitant of the country, is nowhere else spoken of by the sacred writers, nor, according to Bochart, either by Aristotle in his treatise of animals, nor by Arabian writers." In reply to this we may observe, (1.) that the *reem* is mentioned in the Scriptures only in seven places (see above), showing at least that it was probably an animal not *very well known* in that country, or it would have been oftener alluded to; (2.) it is not clear that in those places it is "every where mentioned with other animals common to that country," as in the passage before us there is no allusion to any domestic animal; nor is there in Num. xxiii. 22; xxiv. 8; Ps. xcii. 10. In

Ps. xxii. 21, they are mentioned in the same verse with "lions;" in Ps. xxix. 6, in connection with "calves;" and in Isa. xxxiv. 7, with bullocks and bulls —wild animals inhabiting Idumea. But the entire account is that of an animal that was untamed and that was evidently a foreign animal. (3.) What evidence is there that the Hebrews were well acquainted, as Prof. Robinson supposes, with *the wild buffalo?* Is this animal an inhabitant of Palestine? Is it "elsewhere" mentioned in the Scriptures? Is there any more evidence from the Bible that they were acquainted with it than with the rhinoceros? (4.) It cannot be reasonably supposed that the Hebrews were so unacquainted with the rhinoceros that there could be no allusion to it in their writings. This animal was found in Egypt and in the adjacent countries, and whoever was the writer of the book of Job, there are frequent references in the book to what was well known in Egypt; and at all events, the Hebrews had lived too long in Egypt, and had had too much intercourse with the Egyptians, to be wholly ignorant of the existence and general character of an animal well known there, and we *in fact* find just about as frequent mention of it as we should on this supposition. It does not seem, therefore, to admit of reasonable doubt that the rhinoceros is referred to in the passage before us. This animal, next to the elephant, is the most powerful of animals. It is usually about twelve feet long; from six to seven feet high; and the circumference of its body is nearly equal to its length. Its bulk of body, therefore, is about that of the elephant. Its head is furnished with a horn, growing from the snout, sometimes three and a half feet long. This horn is erect, and perpendicular to the bone on which it stands, and it has thus a greater purchase or power than it could have in any other position. *Bruce.* Occasionally it is found with a double horn, one above the other, though this is not common. The horn is entirely solid, formed of the hardest bony substance, and so firmly growing on the upper maxillary bone as seemingly to make but a part of it, and so powerful as to justify all the allusions in the Scriptures to the horn of the *reem.* The skin of this animal is naked, rough, and knotty, lying upon the body in folds, and so thick as to turn the edge of a scimetar, or to resist a musket-ball. The legs are short, strong, and thick, and the hoofs divided into three parts, each pointing forward. It is a native of the deserts of Asia and Africa, and is usually found in the extensive forests which are frequented by the elephant and the lion. It has never been domesticated; never employed in agricultural purposes; and thus, as well as in size and strength, accords with the account which is given of the animal in the passage before us. The following cut will furnish a good illustration of this animal:

¶ *Be willing to serve thee.* In ploughing and harrowing thy land, and conveying home the harvest, ver. 12. ¶ *Or abide by thy crib.* As the ox will. The word here used (יָלִין) means properly to pass the night; and then to abide, remain, dwell. There is propriety in retaining here the original

10 Canst thou bind the unicorn with his band in the furrow? or will he harrow the valleys after thee?

11 Wilt thou trust him, because his strength *is* great? or wilt thou leave thy labour to him?

12 Wilt thou believe him, that he will bring home thy seed, and gather *it into* thy barn?

13 *Gavest thou* the goodly wings unto the peacocks? or [1] wings and feathers unto the ostrich?

1 or, *the feathers of the stork and ostrich.*

---

meaning of the word, and the sense is, Can he be domesticated or tamed? The rhinoceros never has been.

10. *Canst thou bind the unicorn with his band in the furrow?* That is, with the common traces or cords which are employed in binding oxen to the plough, ¶ *Or will he harrow the valleys after thee?* The word "valleys" here is used to denote such ground as was capable of being ploughed or harrowed. Hills and mountains could not thus be cultivated, though the spade was in common use in planting the vine there, and even in preparing them for seed, Isa. vii. 25. The phrase "after thee" indicates that the custom of driving cattle in harrowing then was the same as that practised now with oxen, when the person who employs them goes in advance of them. It shows that they were entirely under subjection, and it is here implied that the *reem* could not be thus tamed.

11. *Wilt thou trust him?* As thou dost the ox. In the domestic animals great confidence is of necessity placed, and the reliance on the fidelity of the ox and the horse is not usually misplaced. The idea here is, that the unicorn could not be so tamed that important interests could be safely intrusted to him. ¶ *Because his strength is great?* Wilt thou consider his strength as a reason why important interests might be intrusted to him? The strength of the ox, the camel, the horse, and the elephant was a reason why their aid was sought by man to do what he could not himself do. The idea is, that man could not make use of the same reason for employing the rhinoceros. ¶ *Wilt thou leave thy labour to him?* Or, rather, the *avails* of thy labour—the harvest.

12. *Wilt thou believe him?* That is, wilt thou *trust* him with the productions of the field? The idea is, that he was an untamed and unsubdued animal. He could not be governed, like the camel or the ox. If the sheaves of the harvest were laid on him, there would be no certainty that he would convey them where the farmer wished them. ¶ *And gather* it into *thy barn?* Or, rather, "to thy threshing-floor," for so the word here used (גרן) means. It was not common to gather a harvest into a *barn*, but it was usually collected on a hard-trod place and there threshed and winnowed. For the use of the word, see Ruth iii. 2; Judges vi. 37; Num. xviii. 30; Isa. xxi. 10.

13. Gavest thou *the goodly wings unto the peacocks?* In the previous verses the appeal had been to the wild and untamable animals of the desert. In the prosecution of the argument, it was natural to allude to the feathered tribes which resided there also, and which were distinguished for their strength or fleetness of wing, as proof of the wisdom and the superintending providence of God. The idea is, that these animals, far away from the abodes of man, where it could not be pretended that man had any thing to do with their training, had habits and instincts peculiar to themselves, which showed great variety in the divine plans, and at the same time consummate wisdom. The appeal in the following verses (13—18) is to the remarkable habits of the *ostrich*, as illustrating the wisdom and the superintending providence of God. There has been very great variety in the translation of this verse, and it is important to ascertain its real meaning, in order to know whether there is any allusion here to the *peacock*, or whether it refers wholly to the *ostrich*. The LXX. did not understand the passage, and a *part* of the words they endeavoured to translate, but the others are retained without any at-

tempt to explain them. Their version is, Πτέρυξ τερπομένων νεέλασσα, ἐὰν συλλάβῃ ἀσίδα καὶ νέσσα—"the wing of the exulting Neelassa if she conceives [or comprehends] the Asis and Nessa." Jerome renders it, "The wing of the ostrich is like the wings of the falcon and the hawk." Schultens renders it, "The wing of the ostrich is exulting; but is it the wing and the plumage of the stork?" He enumerates no less than *twenty* different interpretations of the passage. Herder renders it,

> "A wing with joyous cry is uplifted yonder;
> Is it the wing and feather of the ostrich?"

Umbreit renders it,

> "The wing of the ostrich, which lifts itself joyfully,
> Does it not resemble the tail and feather of the stork?"

Rosenmüller renders it,

> "The wing of the ostrich exults!
> Truly its wing and plumage is like that of the stork!"

Prof. Lee renders it, "Wilt thou confide in the exulting of the wings of the ostrich? Or in her choice feathers and head-plumage, when she leaveth her eggs to the earth," &c. So Coverdale renders it, "The ostrich (whose feathers are fairer than the wings of the sparrow-hawk), when he hath laid his eggs upon the ground, he breedeth them in the dust, and forgetteth them." In none of these versions, and in none that I have examined except that of Luther and the common English version, is there any allusion to the *peacock;* and amidst all the variety of the rendering, and all the difficulty of the passage, there is a common sentiment that the *ostrich* alone is referred to as the particular subject of the description. It is certain that the description proceeds with reference only to the habits of the ostrich, and it is very evident to my mind that in the whole passage there is no allusion whatever to the *peacock*. Neither the scope of the passage, nor the words employed, it is believed, will admit of such a reference. There is great difficulty in the Hebrew text, which no one has been able fully to explain, but it is sufficiently clear to make it manifest that the ostrich, and not the peacock, is the subject of the appeal. The word which is rendered *peacock*, רננים—*rĕnânim*, is derived from רנן—*rânăn*, *to give forth a tremulous and stridulous sound;* and then to give forth the voice in vibrations; to shake or trill the voice; and then, as in lamentation or joy the voice is often given forth in that manner, the word comes to mean to utter cries of joy; Isa. xii. 6; xxxv. 6; and also cries of lamentation or mourning, Lam. ii. 19. The prevailing sense of the word in the Scriptures is to rejoice; to shout for joy; to exult. The name is here given to the bird referred to, evidently from the *sound* which it made, and probably from its exulting or joyful cry. The word does not elsewhere occur in the Scriptures as applicable to a bird, and there is no reason whatever, either from its etymology, or from the connection in which it is found here, to suppose that it refers to the peacock. Another reason is suggested by Scheutzer (Phys. Sac. *n loc.*), why the peacock cannot be intended here. It is, that the peacock is originally an East Indian fowl, and that it was imported at comparatively a late period in the Jewish history, and was doubtless unknown in the time of Job. In 1 Kings x. 22, and 2 Chron. ix. 21, it appears that *peacocks* were among the remarkable productions of distant countries that were imported for use or luxury by Solomon, a fact which would not have occurred had they been common in the patriarchal times. To these reasons to show that the peacock is not referred to here, Bochart, whose chapters on the subject deserve a careful attention (Hieroz. P. ii. L. ii. c. xvi. xvii.), has added the following: (1.) That if the peacock had been intended here, the allusion would not have been so brief. Of so remarkable a bird there would have been an extended description as there is of the ostrich, and of the unicorn and the horse. If the allusion is to the peacock, it is by a bare mention of the name, and by no argument, as in other cases, from the habits and instincts of the fowl. (2.) The word which is here used as a description of the bird referred to, רננים—*rĕnânim*, derived from the musical properties of the bird, is by no means applicable to the peacock. It is of all fowls, perhaps, least distinguished for beauty of voice. (3.) The property ascribed to the fowl here of "exulting in the *wing*," by no means agrees with the peacock. The glory and beauty of that bird is in the *tail*, and not in the *wing*. Yet the *wing* is here, from some cause, particularly specified. Bochart has demonstrated at great length, and with entire clearness, that the peacock was a foreign fowl, and that it must have been unknown in Judea and Arabia, as it was in Greece and Rome, at a period long after the time in which the book of Job is commonly supposed to have been written. The proper translation of the Hebrew here then would be, "The wing of the exulting fowls *moves joyfully*"—נעלסה. The attention seems to be directed to the *wing*, as being lifted up, or as vibrating with rapidity, or as being *triumphant* in its movement in eluding the pursuer. It is not its *beauty* particularly that attracts the attention, but its exulting, joyful, triumphant, appearance. ¶ *Or wings and feathers unto the ostrich?* Marg. "or, *the feathers of the stork and ostrich*." Most commentators have despaired of making any sense out of the Hebrew in this place, and there have been almost as many conjectures as there have been expositors. The Hebrew is, אם־אברה חסידה ונצה. A literal translation of it would be, "Is it the wing of the stork, and the plumage," or feathers? The object seems to be to institute a comparison of some kind between the ostrich and the stork. This comparison, it would seem, relates partly to the wings and plumage of the two birds, and partly to their habits and instincts; though the latter point of comparison appears to be couched in the mere *name*. So far as I can understand the passage, the comparison relates *first* to the wings and plumage. The point of vision is that of the *sudden appearance* of the ostrich with exulting wing, and the attention is directed to it as in the bounding speed of its movements when in rapid flight. In this view the usual *name* is not given to the bird—יענה בנות, Isa. xiii. 21; xxxiv. 13; xliii. 20; Jer. l. 39, but merely the name of fowls making a stridulous or whizzing sound—רננים. The question is then asked whether *it has the wing and plumage of the stork*—evidently implying that the wing of the stork might be supposed to be adapted to such a flight, but that it was remarkable that *without* such wings the ostrich was able to outstrip even the fleetest animal. The question is designed to turn the attention to the fact that the ostrich accomplishes its flight in this remarkable manner *without* being endowed with wings like the stork, which is capable of sustaining by its wings a long and rapid flight. The *other* point of the comparison seems couched in the *name* given to the stork, and the design is to contrast the habits of the ostrich with those of this bird—particularly in reference to their care for their young. The name given to the stork is חסידה—*hhasida*, meaning literally *the pious*, a name usually given to it—*avis pia*, from its tenderness toward its young—a virtue for which it was celebrated by the ancients, Pliny *Hist. Nat.* x; Aelian *Hist. An.* 3, 23. On the contrary, the Arabs call the ostrich the *impious* or *ungodly* bird, on account of its neglect and cruelty towards its young. The *fact* that the ostrich thus neglects its young, is dwelt upon in the passage before us (ver. 14—17), and in this respect she is placed in strong contrast with the stork. The verse then, I suppose, may be rendered thus:

> "A wing of exulting fowls moves joyfully!
> Is it the wing and the plumage of the pious bird?"

meaning that both in regard to the wing and the habits of the two there was a strong contrast, and yet designing to show that what seems to be a defect in the size and vigour of the wing, and what seems to be stupid forgetfulness of the bird in regard to its young, is proof of the wisdom of the Creator, who has so made it as to be able to outstrip the fleetest horse, and to be adapted to its shy and timid mode of life in the desert. The ostrich, whose principal characteristics are beautifully and strikingly detailed in this passage in Job, is a native of the torrid regions of Arabia and Africa. It is the largest of the feathered tribes and is the connecting link between quadrupeds and fowls. It has the general properties and outlines of a bird, and yet retains many of the marks of the quadruped. In appearance, the ostrich resembles the camel, and is almost as tall; and in the East is called "the camel-bird." (*Calmet.*) It is covered with a plumage that resembles hair more nearly than feathers; and its internal parts bear as near a resemblance to those of the quadruped as of the bird creation. *Goldsmith.* See also Poiret's *Travels in the Barbary States,* as quoted by Rosenmüller, *Alte u. neue Morgenland,* No. 770. A full description is there given of the appearance and habits of the ostrich. Its head and bill resemble those of a duck; the neck may be compared with that of the swan, though it is much longer; the legs and thighs resemble those of a hen, but are fleshy and large. The end of the foot is cloven, and has two very large toes, which like the leg are covered with scales. The height of the ostrich is usually seven feet from the head to the ground; but from the back it is only four, so that the head and the neck are about three feet long. From the head to the end of the tail, when the neck is stretched in a right line, the length is seven feet. One of the wings with the feathers spread out is three feet in length. At the end of the wing there is a species of spur almost like the quill of a porcupine. It is an inch long, and is hollow, and of a bony substance. The plumage is generally white and black, though some of them are said to be gray. There are no feathers on the sides of the thighs, nor under the wings. It has not, like most birds, feathers of various kinds, but they are all bearded with detached hairs or filaments, without consistence and reciprocal adherence. The feathers of the ostrich are almost as soft as down, and are therefore wholly unfit for flying, or to defend the body from external injury. The feathers of other birds have the webs broader on one side than the other, but those of the ostrich have the shaft exactly in the middle. In other birds, the filaments that compose the feathers of the wings are firmly attached to each other, or are *hooked together,* so that they are adapted to catch and resist the air; on those of the ostrich no such attachments are found. The consequence is, that they cannot oppose to the air a suitable resistance, as is the case with other birds, and are therefore incapable of flying, and in fact never mount on the wing. The wing is used (see Notes on ver. 18) only to *balance* the bird, and to aid it in *running.* The great size of the bird—weighing seventy-five or eighty pounds—would require an immense power of wing to elevate it in the air, and it has, therefore, been furnished with the means of surpassing all other animals in the rapidity with which it runs, so that it may escape its pursuers. The ostrich is made to live in the wilderness, and it was called by the ancients "a lover of the deserts." It is shy and timorous in no common degree, and avoids the cultivated fields and the abodes of man, and retreats into the utmost recesses of the desert. In those dreary wastes its subsistence is the few tufts of coarse grass which are scattered here and there, but it will eat almost any thing that comes in its way. It is the most voracious of animals, and will devour leather, glass, hair, iron, stones, or any thing that is given. Valisnieri found the first stomach filled with a quantity of incongruous substances; grass, nuts, cords, stones, glass, brass, copper, iron, tin, lead, and wood, and among the rest, a piece of stone that weighed more than a pound. It would seem that the ostrich is obliged to fill up the great capacity of its stomach in order to be at ease; but that, nutritious substances not occurring, it pours in whatever is at hand to supply the void. The flesh of the ostrich was forbidden by the laws of Moses to be eaten (Lev. xi. 13), but it is eaten by some of the savage nations of Africa, who hunt them for their flesh, which they regard as a dainty. The principal value of the ostrich, how-

14 Which leaveth her eggs in the earth, and warmeth them in dust.

ever, and the principal reason why it is hunted. is in the long feathers that compose the wing and the tail, and which are used so extensively for ornaments. The anci nts used these plumes in their helmets ; the ladies, in the East, as well as in the West, use them to decorate their persons, and they have been extensively employed also as badges of mourning on hearses. The Arabians assert that the ostrich never drinks, and the chosen place of its habitation—the waste, sandy desert – seems to confirm

Ostrich.

the assertion. As the ostrich, in the passage before us, is contrasted with

White Stork.

the stork, the accompanying illustrations will serve to explain the passage.

14. *Which leaveth her eggs in the earth.* That is, she does not build a nest, as most birds do, but deposits her eggs in the sand. The ostrich, Dr. Shaw remarks, lays usually from thirty to fifty eggs. The eggs are very large, some of them being above five inches in diameter, and weighing fifteen pounds.—*Goldsmith.* "We are not to consider," says Dr. Shaw, "this large collection of eggs as if they were all intended for a brood. They are the greatest part of them reserved for food, which the dam breaks, and disposeth of according to the number and cravings of her young ones." The idea which seems to be conveyed in our common version is, that the ostrich deposits her eggs in the sand, and then leaves them, without further care, to be hatched by the heat of the sun. This idea is not, however, necessarily implied in the original, and is contrary to fact. The truth is, that the eggs are deposited with great care, and with so much attention to the manner in which they are placed, that a line drawn from those in the extremities would just touch the tops of the intermediate ones (see Damir, as quoted by Bochart, *Hieroz.* P. ii. Lib. ii. c. xvii. p. 253), and that they are hatched, as the eggs of other birds are, in a great measure by the heat imparted by the incubation of the parent bird. It is true that in the hot climates where these birds live, there is less necessity for constant incubation than in colder latitudes, and that the parent bird is more frequently absent ; but she is accustomed regularly to return at night, and carefully broods over her eggs. See Le Valliant, *Travels in the Interior of Africa,* ii. 209, 305. It is true also that the parent bird wanders sometimes far from the place where the eggs are deposited, and forgets the place, and in this case if another nest of eggs is seen, she is not concerned whether they are her own or not, for she is not endowed with the power of distinguishing between her own eggs and those of

15 And forgetteth that the foot may crush them, or that the wild beast may break them.
16 She is hardened [a] against her young ones, as though *they were* not hers; her labour is in vain without fear;

a La.4.3.

another. This fact seems to have given rise to all the fables stated by the Arabic writers about the stupidity of the ostrich; about her leaving her eggs; and about her disposition to sit on the eggs of others. Bochart has collected many of these opinions from the Arabic writers, among which are the following: Alkazuinius says, "They say that no bird is more foolish than the ostrich, for while it forsakes its own eggs, it sits on the eggs of others; whence the proverb, "Every animal loves its own young except the ostrich." Ottomanus says, "Every animal loves its own progeny except the ostrich. But that pertains only to the male. For although the common proverb imputes folly to the female, yet with her folly she loves her young, and feeds them, and teaches them to fly, the same as other animals." Damir, an Arabic writer, says, "When the ostrich goes forth from her nest, that she may seek food, if she finds the egg of another ostrich, she sits on that, and forgets her own. And when driven away by hunters, she never returns; whence it is that she is described as foolish, and that the proverb in regard to her has originated." ¶ *And warmeth them in dust.* The idea which was evidently in the mind of the translators in this passage was, that the ostrich left her eggs in the dust to be hatched by the heat of the sun. This is not correct, and is not necessarily implied in the Hebrew, though undoubtedly the heat of the sand is made to contribute to the process of hatching the egg, and allows the parent bird to be absent longer from her nest than birds in colder climates. This seems to be all that is implied in the passage.

15. *And forgetteth that the foot may crush them.* She lays her eggs in the sand, and not, as most birds do, in nests made on branches of trees, or on the crags of rocks, where they would be inaccessible, *as if* she was forgetful of the fact that the wild beast might pass along and crush them. She often wanders away from them, also, and does not stay near them to guard them, as most parent birds do, *as if* she were unmindful of the danger to which they might be exposed when she was absent. The *object* of all this seems to be, to call the attention to the *peculiarity* in the natural history of this bird, and to observe that there were laws and arrangements in regard to it which seemed to show that she was deprived of wisdom, and yet that every thing was so ordered as to prove that she was under the care of the Almighty. The *great variety* in the laws pertaining to the animal kingdom, and especially their want of resemblance to what would have occurred to man, seems to give the peculiar force and point to the argument here used.

16. *She is hardened against her young ones.* The obvious meaning of this passage, which is a fair translation of the Hebrew, is, that the ostrich is destitute of natural affection for her young; or that she treats them as if she had not the usual natural affection manifested in the animal creation. This sentiment also occurs in Lam. iv. 3, "The daughter of my people is become cruel, like the ostriches in the wilderness." This opinion is controverted by Buffon, but seems fully sustained by those who have most attentively observed the habits of the ostrich. Dr. Shaw, as quoted by Paxton, and in Robinson's Calmet, says, "On the least noise or trivial occasion she forsakes her eggs or her young ones, to which perhaps she never returns; or if she does, it may be too late either to restore life to the one, or to preserve the lives of the others." "Agreeable to this account," says Paxton, "the Arabs meet sometimes with whole nests of these eggs undisturbed, some of which are sweet and good, and others addle and corrupted; others again have their young ones of different growths, according to the

17 Because God hath deprived her of wisdom, neither [a] hath he imparted to her understanding.

[a] chap.35.11.

18 What time she lifteth up herself on high, she scorneth the horse and his rider.

time it may be presumed they have been forsaken by the dam. They oftener meet a few of the little ones, not bigger than well-grown pullets, half-starved, straggling and moaning about like so many distressed orphans for their mothers." ¶ *Her labour is in vain without fear.* Herder renders this, "In vain is her travail, but she regards it not." The idea in the passage seems to be this; that the ostrich has not that *apprehension* or *provident care* for her young which others birds have. It does not mean that she is an animal remarkably bold and courageous, for the contrary is the fact, and she is, according to the Arabian writers, timid to a proverb; but that she has none of the anxious solicitude for her young which others seem to have,—the dread that they may be in want, or in danger, which leads them, often at the peril of their own lives, to provide for and defend them.

17. *Because God hath deprived her of wisdom,* &c. That is, he has not imparted to her the wisdom which has been conferred on other animals. The meaning is, that all this remarkable arrangement, which distinguished the ostrich so much from other animals, was to be traced to God. It was not the result of chance; it could not be pretended that it was by a human arrangement, but it was the result of divine appointment. Even in this apparent destitution of wisdom, there were reasons which had led to this appointment, and the care and good providence of God could be seen in the preservation of the animal. Particularly, though apparently so weak, and timid, and unwise, the ostrich had a noble bearing (ver. 18), and when aroused, would scorn the fleetest horse in the pursuit, and show that she was distinguished for properties that were expressive of the goodness of God towards her, and of his care over her.

18. *What time she lifteth up herself on high.* In the previous verses reference had been made to the fact that in some important respects the ostrich was inferior to other animals, or had peculiar laws in regard to its habits and preservation. Here the attention is called to the fact that, notwithstanding its inferiority in some respects, it had properties such as to command the highest admiration. Its lofty carriage, the rapidity of its flight, and the proud scorn with which it would elude the pursuit of the fleetest coursers, were all things that showed that God had so endowed it as to furnish proof of his wisdom. The phrase "what time she lifteth up herself," refers to the fact that she raises herself for her rapid flight. It does not mean that she would mount on her wings, for this the ostrich cannot do; but to the fact that this timid and cowardly bird would, when danger was near, rouse herself, and assume a lofty courage and bearing. The word here translated "lifteth up" (תַּמְרִיא) means properly *to lash, to whip,* as a horse, to increase its speed, and is here supposed by Gesenius to be used as denoting that the ostrich by flapping her wings lashes herself up as it were to her course. All the ancient interpretations, however, as well as the common English version, render it as if it were but another form of the word רוּם, *rūm, to raise one's self up,* or *to rise up,* as if the ostrich aroused herself up for her flight. Herder renders it, "At once she is up, and urges herself forward." Taylor (in Calmet) renders it,

> "Yet at the time she haughtily assumes courage;
> She scorneth the horse and his rider."

The leading idea is, that she rouses herself to escape her pursuer; she lifts up her head and body, and spreads her wings, and then bids defiance to any thing to overtake her. ¶ *She scorneth the horse and his rider.* In the pursuit. That is, she runs faster than the fleetest horse, and easily escapes. The extraordinary rapidity of

19 Hast thou given the horse strength? hast thou clothed his neck with thunder?

the ostrich has always been celebrated, and it is well known that she can easily outstrip the fleetest horse. Its swiftness is mentioned by Xenophon, in his Anabasis; for, speaking of the desert of Arabia, he says, that ostriches are frequently seen there; that none could overtake them; and that horsemen who pursued them were obliged soon to give over, "for they escaped far away, making use both of their feet to run, and of their wings, when expanded, as a sail, to waft them along." Marmelius, as quoted by Bochart (see above), speaking of a remarkable kind of *horses*, says, "that in Africa, Egypt, and Arabia, there is but one species of that kind which they call the Arabian, and that those are produced only in the deserts of Arabia. Their velocity is wonderful, nor is there any better evidence of their remarkable swiftness, than is furnished when they pursue the camel-bird." It is a common sentiment of the Arabs, Bochart remarks, that there is no animal which can overcome the ostrich in its course. Dr. Shaw says, "Notwithstanding the stupidity of this animal, its Creator hath amply provided for its safety by endowing it with extraordinary swiftness, and a surprising apparatus for escaping from its enemy. 'They, when they raise themselves up for flight, laugh at the horse and his rider.' They afford him an opportunity only of admiring at a distance the extraordinary agility, and the stateliness likewise of their motions, the richness of their plumage, and the great propriety there was in ascribing to them *an expanded, quivering wing*. Nothing, certainly, can be more entertaining than such a sight; the wings, by their rapid but unwearied vibrations, equally serving them for sails and for oars; while their feet, no less assisting in conveying them out of sight, are no less insensible of fatigue." *Travels*, 8vo., vol. ii. p. 343, as quoted by Noyes. The same representation is confirmed by the writer of a voyage to Senegal, who says, "She sets off at a hand gallop; but after being excited a little, she expands her wings, as if to catch the wind, and abandons herself to a speed so great, that she seems not to touch the ground. I am persuaded she would leave far behind the swiftest English courser." *Rob. Calmet*. Buffon also admits that the ostrich runs faster than the horse. These unexceptionable testimonies completely vindicate the assertion of the inspired writer. The proofs and illustrations here furnished at considerable length are designed to show that the statements here made in the book of Job are such as are confirmed by all the investigations in Natural History since the time the book was written. If the statements are to be regarded as an indication of the progress made in the science of Natural History at the time when Job lived, they prove that the observations in regard to this animal had been extensive and were surprisingly accurate. They show that the minds of sages at that time had been turned with much interest to this branch of science, and that they were able to describe the habits of animals with an accuracy which would do the highest credit to Pliny or to Buffon. If, however, the account here is to be regarded as the mere result of inspiration, or as the language of God speaking and describing what *he* had done, then the account furnishes us with an interesting proof of the inspiration of the book. Its minute accuracy is confirmed by all the subsequent inquiries into the habits of the animal referred to, and shows that the statement is based on simple truth. The general remark may here be made, that all the notices in the Bible of the subjects of science —which are indeed mostly casual and incidental—are such as are confirmed by the investigations which science in the various departments makes. Of what other ancient book but *the Bible* can this remark be made?

19. *Hast thou given the horse strength?* The incidental allusion to the horse in comparison with the ostrich in

the previous verse, seems to have suggested this magnificent description of this noble animal—a description which has never been surpassed or equalled. The *horse* is an animal so well known, that a particular description of it is here unnecessary. The *only* thing which is required is an explanation of the phrases here used, and a confirmation of the particular qualities here attributed to the war-horse, for the description here is evidently that of the horse as he appears in war, or as about to plunge into the midst of a battle. The description which comes the nearest to this before us, is that furnished in the well known and exquisite passage of Virgil, *Georg.* iii. 84, seq.:

—tum, si qua sonum procul arma dedêre,
Stare loco nescit, micat auribus, et tremit artus,
Collectumq; premens volvit sub naribus ignem.
Densa juba, et dextro jactata recumbat in armo.
At duplex agitur, per lumbos spina; cavatque
Tellurem, et solido graviter sonat ungula cornu.

"But at the clash of arms, his ear afar
Drinks the deep sound, and vibrates to the war;
Flames from each nostril roll in gathered stream,
His quivering limbs with restless motion gleam;
O'er his right shoulder, floating full and fair,
Sweeps his thick mane, and spreads his pomp of hair;
Swift works his double spine; and earth around
Rings to his solid hoof that wears the ground."
Sotheby.

Many of the circumstances here enumerated have a remarkable resemblance to the description in Job. Other descriptions and correspondences between this passage and the classic writers may be seen at length in Bochart, *Hieroz.* P. i. L. i. c. viii.; in Scheutzer, *Physica Sacra, in loc.;* and in the *Scriptorum variorum Sylloge* (*Vermischte Schriften,* Goetting. 1782), of Godofr. Less. A full account of the habits of the horse is also furnished by Michaelis in his "Dissertation on the most ancient history of horses and horse-breeding," &c. Appendix to Art. clxvi. of the Commentary of the Laws of Moses, vol. ii. According to the results of the investigations of Michaelis, Arabia was not, as is commonly supposed, the native country of the horse, but its origin is rather to be sought in Egypt; and in the account which is given of the riches of Job, chap. i. 3; xlii. 12, it is remarkable that the *horse* is not mentioned. It is, therefore, in a high degree probable that the horse was not known in his time as a domestic animal, and that, in his country at least, it was employed chiefly in war. ¶ *Hast thou clothed his neck with thunder?* There seems to be something incongruous in the idea of making *thunder* the *clothing* of the neck of a horse, and there as been considerable diversity in the exposition of the passage. There is evidently some allusion to the *mane,* but exactly in what respect is not agreed. The LXX. render it, "Hast thou clothed his neck with terror"—φόβον? Jerome refers it to the *neighing* of the horse—*aut circumdabis collo ejus hinnitum* Prof. Lee renders it, "Clothest thou his neck with scorn?" Herder, "And clothed its neck with its flowing mane." Umbreit, "Hast thou clothed his neck with loftiness?" Noyes, "Hast thou clothed his neck with its quivering mane?" Schultens, *convestis cervicem ejus tremore alacri*—"with rapid quivering;" and Dr. Good, "with the thunder-flash." In this variety of interpretation, it is easy to perceive that the common impression has been that the *mane* is in some way referred to, and that the allusion is not so much to *a sound* as of thunder, as to some *motion* of the mane that attracted attention. The mane adds much to the majesty and beauty of the horse, and perhaps it was in some way decorated by the ancients so as to set it off with increased beauty. The word which is here used, and which is rendered *thunder* (רעמה), is from the verb רעם, *râ'm,* meaning to rage, to roar, as applied to the sea, Ps. xcvi. 11; xcviii. 7, and then to thunder. It has also the idea of *trembling* or *quaking,* Ezek. xxvii. 35, and also of provoking to anger, 1 Sam. i. 6. The verb and the noun are more commonly referred to *thunder* than any thing else, Job xxxvii. 4, 5; xl. 9; 2 Sam. xxii. 14; 1 Sam. ii. 10; vii. 10; Ps. xviii. 13; xxix. 3; lxxvii. 18; civ. 7; Isa. xxix. 6. A full investigation of the meaning of the passage may be seen

20 Canst thou make him afraid as a grasshopper? the glory of his nostrils [1] is terrible.

1 *terrors.*

in Bochart, *Hieroz.* P. i. Lib. ii. c. viii. It seems to me to be very difficult to determine its meaning, and none of the explanations given are quite satisfactory. The *word used* requires us to understand the appearance of the neck of the horse as having some resemblance to *thunder*, but in what respect is not quite so apparent. It may be this; the description of the war-horse is that of an animal fitted to inspire terror. He is caparisoned for battle; impatient of restraint; rushing forward into the thickest of the fight; tearing up the earth; breathing fire from his nostrils; and it was not unnatural, therefore, to compare him with the tempest. The majestic neck, with the erect and shaking mane, is likened to the thunder of the tempest that shakes every thing, and that gives so much majesty and fearfulness to the gathering storm, and the description seems to be this —that his very neck is fitted to produce awe and alarm, like the thunder of the tempest. We are required, therefore, it seems to me, to adhere to the proper meaning of the word; and though in the coolness of criticism there may *appear* to be something incongruous in the application of *thunder* to the neck of the horse, yet it might not appear to be so if we saw such a war-horse—and if the thought, not an unnatural one, should strike us, that in majesty and fury he bore a strong resemblance to an approaching tempest.

20. *Canst thou make him afraid as a grasshopper?* Or, rather, *as a locust*—כארבה. This is the word which is commonly applied to the locust considered as *gregarious*, or as appearing in great numbers (from רבה, *to be multiplied*). On the variety of the species of locusts, see Bochart, *Hieroz.* P. ii. Lib. iv. c. 1, seq. The Hebrew word here rendered "make afraid" (רעש) means properly *to be moved, to be shaken*, and hence to tremble, to be afraid. In Hiphil, the form used here, it means to cause to tremble, to shake; and then *to cause to leap*, as a horse; and the idea here is, Canst thou cause the horse, an animal so large and powerful, to leap with the agility of a locust? See Gesenius, *Lex.* The allusion here is to the leaping or moving of the locusts as they advance in the appearance of squadrons or troops; but the comparison is not so much that of a *single* horse to a single *locust*, as of *cavalry* or a company of war-horses to an army of locusts; and the point of comparison turns on the elasticity or agility of the motion of cavalry advancing to the field of battle. The sense is, that *God* could cause that rapid and beautiful movement in animals so large and powerful as the horse, but that it was wholly beyond the power of man to effect it. It is quite common in the East to compare a horse with a locust, and travellers have spoken of the remarkable resemblance between the *heads* of the two. This comparison occurs also in the Bible; see Joel ii. 4, "The appearance of them is as the appearance of horses; and as horsemen so shall they run;" Rev. ix. 7. The Italians, from this resemblance, call the locust *cavaletta*, or little horse. Sir W. Ouseley says, "Zakaria Cavini divides the locusts into two classes, like horsemen and footmen, 'mounted and pedestrian.'" Niebuhr says that he heard from a Bedouin near Bassorah, a particular comparison of the locust with other animals; but he thought it a mere fancy of the Arabs, till he heard it repeated at Bagdad. He compared the head of a locust to that of a horse, the breast to that of a lion, the feet to those of a camel, the belly with that of a serpent, the tail with that of a scorpion, and the feelers with the hair of a virgin; see *Pict. Bib.* on Joel ii. 4. ¶ *The glory of his nostrils is terrible.* Marg. as in Heb., *terrors.* That is, it is fitted to inspire terror or awe. The reference is to the wide-extended and fiery looking nostrils of the horse when animated, and impatient for action. So Lucretius, L. v.:

21 He[1] paweth in the valley, and
rejoiceth in *his* strength; he goeth
[a] on to meet the [2] armed men.
22 He mocketh at fear, and is
not affrighted; neither turneth he
back from the sword.
23 The quiver rattleth against him,
the glittering spear and the shield.
24 He swalloweth the ground
with fierceness and rage; neither
believeth he that *it is* the sound of
the trumpet.

1 or, His feet *dig*. a Je.8.6. 2 *armour*.

Et fremitum patulis sub naribus edit ad arma.

So Virgil, *Georg.* iii. 87:

Collectumque premens voluit sub naribus ignem.

Claudian, in iv. *Consulatu Honorii*:

Ignescunt patulæ nares.

21. *He paweth in the valley.* Marg. "or, His feet *dig*." The marginal reading is more in accordance with the Hebrew. The reference is to the well known fact of the *pawing* of the horse with his feet, as if he would dig up the ground. The same idea occurs in Virgil, as quoted above:

cavatque
Tellurem, et solido graviter solat ungula cornu.

Also in Apollonius, L. iii. *Argonauticon*:

Ὡς δ' ἀρήϊος ἵππος, ἐελδόμενος πολεμοῖο,
Σκαρθμῷ ἐπιχρεμέθων κρούει πέδον.

"As a war-horse, impatient for the battle,
Neighing beats the ground with his hoofs"

¶ *He goeth on to meet the armed men.* Marg. *armour*. The margin is in accordance with the Hebrew, but still the idea is substantially the same. The horse rushes on furiously against the weapons of war.

22. *He mocketh at fear.* He laughs at that which is fitted to intimidate; that is, he is not afraid. ¶ *Neither turneth he back from the sword.* He rushes on it without fear. Of the fact here stated, and the accuracy of the description, there can be no doubt.

23. *The quiver rattleth against him.* The quiver was a case made for containing arrows. It was usually slung over the shoulder, so that it could be easily reached to draw out an arrow. Warriors on horseback, as well as on foot, fought with bows and arrows, as well as with swords and spears; and the idea here is, that the war-horse bore upon himself these instruments of war. The rattling of the quiver was caused by the fact that the arrows were thrown somewhat loosely into the case or the quiver, and that in the rapid motion of the warrior they were shaken against each other. Thus Virgil, *Æn.* ix. 660:

—pharetramque fugâ sensere sonantem.

Silius, L. 12:

Plena tenet et resonante pharetra.

And again:

Turba ruunt stridentque sagittiferi coryti.

So Homer (*Iliad, a.*), when speaking of Apollo:

Τόξ' ὤμοισιν ἔχων, ἀμφηρεφέα τε φαρέτρην·
Ἔκλαγξαν δ' ἄρ' ὀϊστοὶ ἐπ' ὤμων χωομένοιο.

See Scheutzer's *Phys. Sac.*, *in loc.*

24. *He swalloweth the ground.* He seems as if he would absorb the earth. That is, he strikes his feet into it with such fierceness, and raises up the dust in his prancing, as if he would devour it. This figure is unusual with us, but it is common in the Arabic. See Schultens, *in loc.*, and Bochart, *Hieroz*, P. i. L. ii. c. viii. pp. 143—145. So Statius:

Stare loco nescit, pereunt vestigia mille
Ante fugam, absentemque ferit gravis ungula campum.

Th' impatient courser pants in every vein,
And pawing seems to beat the distant plain;
Hills, vales, and floods, appear already cross'd,
And ere he starts a thousand steps are lost.
POPE.

¶ *Neither believeth he that* it is *the sound of the trumpet.* This translation by no means conveys the meaning of the original. The true sense is probably expressed by Umbreit. "He standeth not still when the trumpet soundeth;" that is, he becomes impatient; he no longer *confides* in the voice of the rider and remains submissive, but he becomes excited by the martial clangour, and rushes into the midst of the battle. The Hebrew word which is employed (יאמין) means properly to prop, stay,

25 He saith among the trumpets,
Ha, ha; and he smelleth the battle
afar off, the thunder of the captains
and the shouting.

26 Doth the hawk fly by thy
wisdom, *and* stretch her wings toward the south?

---

support; then to believe, to be firm, stable; and is that which is commonly used to denote an act of *faith*, or as meaning *believing*. But the original sense of the word is here to be retained, and then it refers to the fact that the impatient horse no longer stands still when the trumpet begins to sound for battle.

25. *He saith among the trumpets, Ha, ha.* That is, "When the trumpet sounds, his voice is heard *as if* he said, Aha—or said that he heard the sound calling him to the battle." The reference is to the impatient neighing of the war horse about to rush into the conflict. ¶ *And he smelleth the battle afar off.* That is, he snuffs, as it were, for the slaughter. The reference is to the effect of an approaching army upon a spirited war-horse, as if he perceived the approach by the sense of smelling, and longed to be in the midst of the battle. ¶ *The thunder of the captains.* Literally "the war-cry of the princes." The reference is to the loud voices of the leaders of the army commanding the hosts under them. In regard to the whole of this magnificent description of the war-horse, the reader may consult Bochart, *Hieroz.* P. i. L. ii. c. viii., where the phrases used are considered and illustrated at length. The leading idea here is, that the war-horse evinced the wisdom and the power of God. His majesty, energy, strength, impatience for the battle, and spirit, were proofs of the greatness of Him who had made him, and might be appealed to as illustrating His perfections. Much as men admire the noble horse, and much as they take pains to train him for the turf or for battle, yet how seldom do they refer to it as illustrating the power and greatness of the Creator; and, it may be added, how seldom do they use the horse as if he were one of the grand and noble works of God!

26. *Doth the hawk fly by thy wisdom.* The appeal here is to the hawk, because it is among the most rapid of the birds in its flight. The particular thing specified is its *flying*, and it is supposed that there was something peculiar in that which distinguished it from other birds. Whether it was in regard to its speed, to its manner of flying, or to its habits of flying at periodical seasons, may indeed be made a matter of inquiry, but it is clear that the particular thing in this bird which was adapted to draw the attention, and which evinced peculiarly the wisdom of God, was connected with its flight. The word here rendered *hawk*, (נֵץ, *nētz*) is probably *generic*, and includes the various species of the falcon or hawk tribe, as the jer-falcon, the goshawk, the sparrow-hawk, the lanner, the saker, the hobby, the kestril, and the merlin. Not less than one hundred and fifty species of the hawk, it is said, have been described, but of these many are little known, and many of them differ from others only by very slight distinctions. They are birds of prey, and, as many of them are endowed with remarkable docility, they are trained for the diversions of *falconry*—which has been quite a science among sportsmen. The falcon, or hawk, is often distinguished for fleetness. One, belonging to a Duke of Cleves, flew out of Westphalia into Prussia in one day; and in the county of Norfolk (England) one was known to make a flight of nearly thirty miles in an hour. A falcon which belonged to Henry IV. of France, having escaped from Fontainebleau, was found twenty-four hours after in Malta, the space traversed being not less than one thousand three hundred and fifty miles; being a velocity of about fifty-seven miles an hour, on the supposition that the bird was on the wing the whole time. It is this remarkable velocity which is here appealed to as a proof of the divine wisdom. God asks Job whether *he* could have formed these birds for their rapid flight. The wisdom and

27 Doth the eagle mount up [1] at thy command, and make her nest on [a] high?
28 She dwelleth and abideth on the rock, upon the crag of the rock, and the strong place.
29 From thence she seeketh the prey, *and* her eyes behold afar off.

1 *by thy mouth.* a Je.49.16; Ob.4.

skill which has done this is evidently far above any that is possessed by man. ¶ *And stretch her wings toward the south.* Referring to the fact that the bird is migratory at certain seasons of the year. It is not here merely the *rapidity* of its flight which is referred to, but that remarkable instinct which leads the feathered tribes to seek more congenial climates at the approach of winter. In no way is this to be accounted for, except by the fact that God has so appointed it. This great law of the winged tribes is one of the clearest proofs of divine wisdom and agency.

27. *Doth the eagle mount up at thy command?* Marg. as in Heb., *by thy mouth.* The meaning is, that Job had not power to direct or order the eagle in his lofty flight. The eagle has always been celebrated for the height to which it ascends. When Ramond had reached the summit of Mount Perdu, the highest of the Pyrenees, he perceived no living creature but an eagle which passed above him, flying with inconceivable rapidity in direct opposition to a furious wind. *Edin. Ency.* "Of all animals, the eagle flies highest; and from thence the ancients have given him the epithet of *the bird of heaven.*" *Goldsmith.* What is particularly worth remarking here is, the accuracy with which the descriptions in Job are made. If these are any indications of the progress of the knowledge of Natural History, that science could not have been then in its infancy. Just the things are adverted to here which all the investigations of subsequent ages have shown to characterize the classes of the feathered creation referred to. ¶ *And make her nest on high.* "The nest of the eagle is usually built in the most inaccessible cliff of the rock, and often shielded from the weather by some jutting crag that hangs over it." *Goldsmith.* "It is usually placed horizontally, in the hollow or fissure, of some high and abrupt rock, and is constructed of sticks of five or six feet in length, interlaced with pliant twigs, and covered with layers of rushes, heath, or moss. Unless destroyed by some accident, it is supposed to suffice, with occasional repairs, for the same couple during their lives." *Edin. Ency.*

28. *She dwelleth and abideth on the rock.* "He rarely quits the mountains to descend into the plains. Each pair live in an insulated state, establishing their quarters on some high and precipitous cliff, at a respectful distance from others of the same species." *Edin. Ency.* They seem to occupy the same cliff, or place of abode, during their lives; and hence it is that they are represented as having a permanent abode on the lofty rock. In Damir it is said that the blind poet Besar, son of Jazidi, being asked, if God would give him the choice to be an animal, what he would be, said that he would wish to be nothing else than an *alokab,* a species of the eagle, for they dwelt in places to which no wild animal could have access. Scheutzer, *Phys. Sac. in loc.* The word rendered "*abideth*" means commonly *to pass the night,* and here refers to the fact that the high rock was its constant abode or dwelling. By night as well as by day, the eagle had his home there. ¶ *Upon the crag of the rock.* Heb., "Upon the *tooth* of the rock"—from the resemblance of the crag of a rock to a tooth.

29. *From thence she seeketh the prey,* and *her eyes behold afar off.* "When far aloft, and no longer discernible by the human eye, such is the wonderful acuteness of its sight, that from the same elevation it will mark a hare, or even a smaller animal, and dart down on it with unerring aim." *Edin. Ency.* "Of all animals, the eagle has the quickest eye; but his sense of smelling is far

30 Her young ones also suck up blood: and where *a* the slain *are*, there *is* she.

a Mat.24.28; Lu.17.37.

inferior to that of the vulture. He never pursues, therefore, but in sight." *Goldsmith.* This power of sight was early known, and is celebrated by the ancients. Thus Homer, *Il.* ῤ'. ver. 674.

> —ὥστ' αἰετός ὅν ῥά τε φασὶν
> Ὀξύτατον δέρκεσθαι ὑπουρανίων πετεηνῶν.

" As the eagle of whom it is said that it enjoys the keenest vision of all the fowls under heaven."

So Aelian, H. L. i. 32. Also Horace *Serm.* L. i. Sat. 3:

> —tam cernit acutùm
> Quam aut aquila, aut serpens Epidaurus.

The Arabic writers say that the eagle can see "four hundred parasangs." *Damir*, as quoted by Scheutzer. It is now ascertained that birds of prey search out or discern their food rather by the sight than the smell. No sooner does a camel fall and die on the plains of Arabia, than there may be seen in the far-distant sky apparently a black speck, which is soon discovered to be a vulture hastening to its prey. From that vast distance the bird, invisible to human eye, has seen the prey stretched upon the sand and immediately commences toward it its rapid flight.

30. *Her young ones also suck up blood.* The word here used (יְעַלְעוּ) occurs nowhere else in the Scriptures. It is supposed to mean, to sup up greedily; referring to the fact that the young ones of the eagle devour blood voraciously. They are too feeble to devour the flesh, and hence they are fed on the blood of the victim. The strength of the eagle consists in the beak, talons, and wings; and such is their power, that they are able to convey animals of considerable size, alive, to their places of abode. They often bear away in this manner, lambs, kids, and the young of the gazelle. Three instances, at least, are known, where they have carried off children. In the year 1737, in Norway, a boy upwards of two years of age was carried off by an eagle in the sight of his parents. Anderson, in his history of Iceland, asserts that in that island children of four and five years of age have experienced the same fate; and Ray mentions that in one of the Orkneys an infant of a year old was seized in the talons of an eagle, and conveyed about four miles to its eyry. *Edin. Ency.* The principal food of the *young* eagle is blood. The *proof* of this fact may be seen in Scheutzer's *Phys. Sac., in loc.* ¶ *And where the slain* are, *there* is *she.* Heb., *the slain*; referring perhaps primarily to a field of battle—where horses, camels, and men, lie in confusion. It is not improbable that the Saviour had this passage in view when he said, speaking of the approaching destruction of Jerusalem, "For wheresoever the carcase is, there will the eagles be gathered together;" Matth. xxiv. 28. Of the *fact* that they thus assemble, there can be no doubt. The *argument* in proof of the wisdom and majesty of the Almighty in these references to the animal creation, is derived from their strength, their instincts, and their peculiar habits. We may make two remarks, in view of the argument as here stated. (1.) One relates to the remarkable *accuracy* with which they are referred to. The statements are not vague and general, but are minute and characteristic, about the habits and the instincts of the animals referred to. The very things are selected which are now known to distinguish those animals, and which are not found to exist in the same degree, if at all, in others. Subsequent investigations have served to confirm the accuracy of these descriptions, and they may be taken now as a correct account *even to the letter* of the natural history of the different animals referred to. If, therefore, as has already been stated, this is to be regarded as an indication of the state of natural science in the time of Job, it shows quite an advanced state; if it is *not* an indication of the existing state of knowledge in his time, if there was no such acquaintance with the animal creation as the result of observation, then it shows that these

CHAPTER XL.

ANALYSIS OF CHAPTERS XL. AND XLI.

These chapters consist of the following parts:

I. God rebukes Job for the spirit which he had manifested, and especially for his presumption in contending with him, and for the impropriety of the language in which he had indulged, and which was the same as "reproving" God, ver. 1, 2.

II. Job confesses his guilt. He had on a former occasion expressed his desire to carry his cause immediately before God (chap. xiii. 3, 21, 22.), and to argue it there. He was sure that he could be able to vindicate himself, and show that he did not deserve the peculiar calamities which had come upon him, and which were appealed to by his friends as full proof that he was a wicked man. Now, however, overpowered by the majesty of God, and by the argument which he had used, he is silent. He does not adventure to go into the argument. He confesses that he is vile, and says that he would lay his hand upon his mouth. He *had* spoken repeatedly, but he could proceed no farther, ver. 3—5.

III. God then pursues and completes the argument which he had commenced, in proof of his own majesty and glory. The argument is continued through this and the following chapter, and comprises the following subjects, viz.:

(1.) An appeal to the power and majesty of God, ver. 7—14. That power was displayed in his arm in executing judgments; in his thunder; in casting down the proud; and in trampling the wicked in the dust. God says that if Job could put forth power like this then he would confess that his own hand could save him.

(2.) He appeals to the *behemoth*, and this chapter concludes with a detailed description of this animal of immense strength, which might be regarded as in some sort an illustration of the mighty power of the Most High, ver. 15—24.

(3.) The whole argument is closed (chap. xli.) by an appeal to the *leviathan*, as the chief among the works of God, and as showing his dominion over the sea. This immense sea-monster is described at length, and in the most sublime manner; and the *argument* is, that a Being who could form such an animal, and control him, must be a Being of infinite majesty and glory, before whom man should bow down with profound reverence and silence. This sublime argument is not so conducted as to remove or explain the difficulties which pressed upon the minds of Job and his friends. No statements are made respecting the reason of afflictions; the question whether trials are evidence of the moral character of the sufferer is not decided, and no reference is made to the future state, and to the fact that all these inequalities would be adjusted there. The object of the whole argument is to produce an overwhelming sense of the majesty and glory of God; to show the impropriety of complaining and murmuring against the government of one so exalted and so powerful; and to inculcate the duty of calm acquiescence in the expressions of his will. The object was not to disclose all the light in regard to the difficult questions about the government of God which *could be* communicated, nor to anticipate the glorious truths which were reserved for the Christian revelation, but to produce a state of submission *to the will of God*. It was to make men feel that God had a right to reign, and that they were to be submissive, not because they saw the *reasons* of his doings, but because *such was* HIS WILL. This is still a proper ground of argument with the afflicted, and is often in fact about all that can be referred to

MOREOVER, the LORD answered Job and said,
2 Shall he that contendeth [a] with the Almighty instruct *him?* he that reproveth God, let him answer it.

a chap. 33.13; Is. 45.9.

were truly the words of God, and are to be regarded as direct inspiration. At all events, the statement was evidently made under the influence of inspiration, and is worthy of the origin which it claims. (2.) The second remark is, that the progress of discovery in the science of natural history has only served to confirm and expand the argument here adverted to. Every new fact in regard to the habits and instincts of animals is a new proof of the wisdom and greatness of God; and we may appeal now, with all the knowledge which we have on these subjects, with unanswerable force to the habits and instincts of the wild goats of the rock, the wild ass, the rhinoceros, the ostrich, the horse, the hawk, and the eagle, as each one furnishing some striking and peculiar proof of the wisdom, goodness, superintending providence and power of the great Creator.

CHAPTER XL.

1. *Moreover, the* LORD *answered Job.* The word *answered* is used here as it is often in the Scriptures, not to denote a reply to what had been immediately said, but to take up or continue an argument. What God said here was designed as a reply to the spirit which Job had so frequently manifested.

2. *Shall he that contendeth with the Almighty instruct* him? Gesenius renders this, "Contending shall the reprover of God contend with the Almighty?" Prof. Lee, "Shall one by contending with the Almighty correct this?" On the grammatical construction, see Gesenius on the word יסור, and Rosenmüller and Lee, *in loc.* The meaning seems to be this: "Will he who would enter into a controversy with the Almighty now presume to instruct him? He that was so desirous of arguing his cause with God, will he now answer?" All the language here used is taken from courts, and is such as I have had frequent occasion to explain in these Notes. The reference is to the fact that Job had so often expressed a wish to carry his

3 Then Job answered the LORD,
and said,
4 Behold, I am vile : [a] what shall
I answer thee? I will lay [b] mine
hand upon my mouth.
5 Once have I spoken ; but I will
not answer : yea, twice ; but I will
proceed no further.

[a] Ezr.9 6 ; chap. 42.6 ; Ps. 51.4 ; Is. 6.5 ; 64.6 ; Da. 9 5,7 ; Lu. 18.13. [b] chap. 29.9 ; Mi. 7.16 ; Zech. 2.13 ; Ro. 3.19

---

cause, as before a judicial tribunal, directly up to God. He had felt that *if* he could get it there, he could so argue it as to secure a verdict in his favour ; that he could set arguments before the Almighty which would secure a reversal of the fearful sentence which had gone out against him, and which had caused him to be held as a guilty man. God now asks whether he who had been so anxious to have a legal argument, and to carry his cause himself before God—a man disposed to litigation before God (רב)—was still of the same mind, and felt himself qualified to take upon himself the office of *an instructor, a corrector, an admonisher* (יסור) of God? He had the opportunity now, and God here paused, after the sublime exhibition of his majesty and power in the previous chapters, to give him an opportunity, as he wished, to carry his cause directly before him. The result is stated in ver. 3, 4. Job had now nothing to say. ¶ *He that reproveth God.* Or rather, "He that is disposed to carry his cause before God," as Job had often expressed a wish to do. The word here used (יכח) is often employed, especially in Hiphil, in a *forensic sense,* and means *to argue, to show, to prove* any thing ; then *to argue down, to confute, to convict;* see Job vi. 25 ; xiii. 15 ; xix. 5 ; xxxii. 12 ; Prov. ix. 7, 8 ; xv. 12 ; xix. 25. It is evidently used in that sense here—a Hiphil participle (מוכיח)—and refers, not to any man in general who reproves God, but to Job in particular, as having expressed a wish to carry his cause before him, and to argue it there. ¶ *Let him answer it.* Or rather, "Let him answer *him.*" That is, "Is he now ready to answer? There is now an opportunity for him to carry his cause, as he wished, directly before God. Is he ready to embrace the opportunity, and to answer now what the Almighty has said? This does not mean, then, as the common version would seem to imply, that the man who reproves God must be held responsible for it, but that Job, who had expressed the wish to carry his cause before God, had now an opportunity to do so. That this is the meaning, is apparent from the next verses, where Job says that he was confounded, and had nothing to say.

4. *Behold, I am vile : what shall I answer thee?* "Instead of being able to argue my cause, and to vindicate myself as I had expected, I now see that I am guilty, and I have nothing to say." He had argued boldly with his friends. He had, before them, maintained his innocence of the charges which they brought against him, and had supposed that he would be able to maintain the same argument before God. But when the opportunity was given, he felt that he was a poor, weak man ; a guilty and miserable offender. It is a very different thing to maintain our cause before God, from what it is to maintain it before men ; and though we may attempt to vindicate our own righteousness when we argue with our fellow-creatures, yet when we come to maintain it before God we shall be dumb. On earth, men vindicate themselves ; what will they do when they come to stand before God in the judgment? ¶ *I will lay mine hand upon my mouth.* An expression of silence. Catlin, in his account of the Mandan Indians, says that this is a common custom with them when any thing wonderful occurs. Some of them laid their hands on their mouths and remained in this posture by the hour, as an expression of astonishment at the wonders produced by the brush in the art of painting ; comp. Notes on chap. xxi. 5 ; xxix. 9.

5. *Once have I spoken.* That is, in vindicating myself. He had once spoken of God in an irreverent and improper manner, and he now saw it. ¶ *But I will not answer.* I will not

6 Then [a] answered the LORD unto Job out of the whirlwind, and said,

a chap. 38.1, &c.

now answer, as I had expressed the wish to do. Job now saw that he had spoken in an improper manner, and he says that he would not repeat what he had said. ¶ *Yea, twice.* He had not only offended once, as if in a thoughtless and hasty manner, but he had repeated it, showing deliberation, and thus aggravating his guilt. When a man is brought to a willingness to confess that he has done wrong *once*, he will be very likely to see that he has been guilty of more than one offence. One sin will draw on the remembrance of another; and the gate once open, a flood of sins will rush to the recollection. It is not common that a man can so *isolate* a sin as to repent of that alone, or so look at one offence against God as not to feel that he has been often guilty of the same crimes. ¶ *But I will proceed no further.* Job felt doubtless that if he should allow himself to speak again, or to attempt now to vindicate himself, he would be in danger of committing the same error again. He now saw that God was right; that he had himself repeatedly indulged in an improper spirit, and that all that became him was a penitent confession in the fewest words possible. We may learn here, (1.) That a view of God is fitted to produce in us a deep sense of our own sins. No one can feel himself to be in the presence of God, or regard the Almighty as speaking to him, without saying, "Lo I am vile!" There is nothing so much fitted to produce a sense of sinfulness and nothingness as a view of God. (2.) The world will be dumb at the day of judgment. They who have been most loud and bold in vindicating themselves will then be silent, and will confess that they are vile, and the whole world "will become guilty before God." If the presence and the voice of God produced such an effect on so good a man as Job, what will it not do on a wicked world? (3.) A true penitent is disposed to use but few words; "God be merciful to me a sinner," or, "lo, I am vile," is about all the language which the penitent employs. He does not go into long arguments, into metaphysical distinctions, into apologies and vindications, but uses the simplest language of confession, and then leaves the soul, and the cause, in the hands of God. (4.) Repentance consists in stopping where we are, and in resolving to add no more sin. "I have erred," is its language. "I will not add to it, I will do so no more," is the immediate response of the soul. A readiness to go into a vindication, or to expose one's self to the danger of sinning again in the same way, is an evidence that there is no true repentance. Job, a true penitent, would not allow himself even to *speak again* on the subject, lest he should be guilty of the sin which he had already committed. (5.) In repentance we must be willing to retract our errors, and confess that we were wrong—no matter what favourite opinions we have had, or how tenaciously and zealously we have defended and held them. Job had constructed many beautiful and eloquent arguments in defence of his opinions; he had brought to bear on the subject all the results of his observation, all his attainments in science, all the adages and maxims that he had derived from the ancients, and from a long intercourse with mankind, but he was now brought to a willingness to confess that his arguments were not solid, and that the opinions which he had cherished were erroneous. It is often more difficult to abandon *opinions* than *vices*; and the proud philosopher when he exercises repentance has a more difficult task than the victim of low and debasing sensuality. His opinions are his idols. They embody the results of his reading, his reflections, his conversation, his observation, and they become a part of himself. Hence it is, that so many abandoned sinners are converted, and so few philosophers; that religion spreads often with so much success among the obscure and the openly wicked, while so few of the "wise men of the world" are called and saved.

6. *Then answered the Lord unto*

7 Gird up thy loins now like a
man: I will demand of thee, and
declare thou unto me.
8 Wilt thou also disannul my
judgment? wilt thou condemn me,
that thou mayest be righteous?
9 Hast thou an arm like God?
or canst thou thunder with a
voice [a] like him?
10 Deck thyself now *with* majesty [b] and excellency; and array
thyself with glory and beauty.

a Ps.29.3,4.

b Ps. 93.1; 104.1.

Job out of the whirlwind; see Notes on chap. xxxviii. 1. God here resumes the argument which had been interrupted in order to give Job an opportunity to speak and to carry his cause before the Almighty, as he had desired, see ver. 2. Since Job had nothing to say, the argument, which had been suspended, is resumed and completed.

7. *Gird up thy loins now like a man.* An expression taken from the ancient mode of dress. That was a loose, flowing robe, which was secured by a girdle when travelling, or when one entered upon any thing requiring energy; see Notes on Matth. v. 38—41. The meaning here is, "Prepare thyself for the highest effort that can be made. Put forth all your strength, and explain to me what will now be said;" comp. Notes on Isa. xli. 21. ¶ *I will demand of thee.* Heb. "I will ask of thee." That is, I will submit some questions to you to be answered. ¶ *And declare thou unto me.* Heb. "Cause me to know." That is, furnish a satisfactory answer to these inquiries, so as to show that you understand the subject. The object is to appeal to the proofs of divine wisdom, and to show that the whole subject was far above human comprehension.

8. *Wilt thou disannul my judgment?* Wilt thou *reverse* the judgment which I have formed, and show that it should have been different from what it is? This was implied in what Job had undertaken. He had complained of the dealings of God, and this was the same as saying that he could show that those dealings should have been different from what they were. When a man murmurs against God, it is always implied that he supposes he could show why his dealings should be different from what they are, and that they should be reversed. ¶ *Wilt thou condemn me, that thou mayest be righteous?* Or, rather, probably, "Wilt thou show that I am wrong because thou art superior in justice?" Job had allowed himself to use language which strongly implied that God was improperly severe. He had regarded himself as punished far beyond what he deserved, and as suffering in a manner which justice did not demand. All this implied that *he* was more righteous in the case than God, for when a man allows himself to vent such complaints, it indicates that he esteems himself to be more just than his Maker. God now calls upon Job to maintain this proposition, since he had advanced it, and to urge the arguments which would prove that *he* was more righteous in the case than God. It was proper to demand this. It was a charge of such a nature that it could not be passed over in silence, and God asks, therefore, with emphasis, whether Job now supposed that he could institute such an argument as to show that he was right and his Maker wrong.

9. *Hast thou an arm like God?* The arm is the symbol of strength. The question here is, whether Job would venture to compare his strength with the omnipotence of God? ¶ *Or canst thou thunder with a voice like him?* Thunder is a symbol of the majesty of the Most High, and is often spoken of as the voice of God; see Ps. xxix. The question here is, whether Job could presume to compare himself with the Almighty, whose voice was the thunder?

10. *Deck thyself now* with *majesty and excellency.* That is, such as God has. Put on every thing which you can, which would indicate rank, wealth, power, and see whether it could all be compared with the majesty of God; comp. Ps. civ. 1, "O Lord my God, thou art very great; thou art clothed with honour and majesty."

11 Cast abroad the rage of thy wrath: and behold every one *that is* proud, and abase him.
12 Look on every one *that is* [a] proud, *and* bring him low; and tread down the wicked in their place.
13 Hide them in the dust together; *and* bind their faces in secret.
14 Then will I also confess unto thee that thine own right hand can save thee.
15 Behold now [1] behemoth, which I made with thee; he eateth grass as an ox.

a Ex.18.11.
1 or, *the elephant*, as some think.

---

11. *Cast abroad the rage of thy wrath.* That is, as God does. Show that the same effects can be produced by *your* indignation which there is in his. God appeals here to the effect of his displeasure in prostrating his foes as one of the evidences of his majesty and glory, and asks Job, if he would compare himself with him, to imitate him in this, and produce similar effects. ¶ *And behold every one* that is *proud, and abase him.* That is, *look* upon such an one and bring him low, or humble him by a look. It is implied here that God could do this, and he appeals to it as a proof of his power.

12. *And tread down the wicked in their place.* Even in the very place where they are, crush them to the dust, as God can. It is implied that God was able to do this, and he appeals to it as a proof of his power.

13. *Hide them in the dust together*; comp. Isa. ii. 10. The meaning seems to be, that God had power to prostrate the wicked in the dust of the earth, and he calls upon Job to show *his* power by doing the same thing. ¶ And *bind their faces in secret.* The word *faces* here is probably used (like the Greek πρόσωπα) to denote *persons.* The phrase "to bind them," is expressive of having them under control or subjection; and the phrase "in secret" may refer to some secret or safe place—as a dungeon or prison. The meaning of the whole is, that God had power to restrain and control the haughty and the wicked, and he appeals to Job to do the same.

14. *Then will I also confess unto thee,* &c. If you can do all this, it will be full proof that you can save yourself, and that you do not need the divine interposition. If he could do all this, then it might be admitted that he was qualified to pronounce a judgment on the divine counsels and dealings. He would then show that he had qualifications for conducting the affairs of the universe.

15. *Behold now behemoth.* Marg. "or, *the elephant*, as some think." In the close of the argument, God appeals to *two* animals as among the chief of his works, and as illustrating more than any others his power and majesty—the behemoth and the leviathan. A great variety of opinions has been entertained in regard to the animal referred to here, though the *main* inquiry has related to the question whether the *elephant* or the *hippopotamus* is denoted. Since the time of Bochart, who has gone into an extended examination of the subject (*Hieroz.* P. ii. L. ii. c. xv.), the common opinion has been that the latter is here referred to. As a *specimen* of the method of interpreting the Bible which has prevailed, and as a proof of the slow progress which has been made towards settling the meaning of a difficult passage, we may refer to some of the opinions which have been entertained in regard to this animal. They are chiefly taken from the collection of opinions made by Schultens, *in loc.* Among them are the following: (1.) That wild animals in general are denoted. This appears to have been the opinion of the translators of the Septuagint. (2.) Some of the Rabbins supposed that a huge monster was referred to, that ate every day "the grass of a thousand mountains." (3.) It has been held by some that the wild bull was referred to. This was the opinion particularly of Sanctius. (4.) The common opinion, until the time of Bochart, has been that the elephant was meant. See the particular authors who have

held this opinion enumerated in Schultens. (5.) Bochart maintained, and since his time the opinion has been generally acquiesced in, that the *river-horse* of the Nile, or the hippopotamus, was referred to. This opinion he has defended at length in the *Hieroz.* P. ii. L. v. c. xv. (6.) Others have held that some "hieroglyphic monster" was referred to, or that the whole description was an emblematic representation, though without any living original. Among those who have held this sentiment, some have supposed that it is designed to be emblematic of the old Serpent; others, of the corrupt and fallen nature of man; others, that the proud, the cruel, and the bloody are denoted; most of the "Fathers" supposed that the devil was here emblematically represented by the behemoth and the leviathan; and one writer has maintained that Christ was referred to! To these opinions may be added the supposition of Dr. Good, that the behemoth here described is at present a genus altogether extinct, like the mammoth, and other animals that have been discovered in fossil remains. This opinion is also entertained by the author of the article on *Mazology*, in the Edinburgh Encyclopædia, chiefly for the reason that the description of the *tail* of the behemoth (ver. 17) does not well accord with the hippopotamus. There must be admitted to be some plausibility in this conjecture of Dr. Good, though perhaps I shall be able to show that there is no necessity for resorting to this supposition. The word *behemoth* (בהמות), used here in the plural number, occurs often in the singular number, to denote a dumb beast, usually applied to the larger kind of quadrupeds. It occurs very often in the Scriptures, and is usually translated *beast,* or collectively *cattle.* It usually denotes land animals, in opposition to birds or reptiles. See the Lexicons, and Taylor's *Hebrew Concordance*. It is rendered by Dr. Nordheimer (*Heb. Con.*) in this place, *hippopotamus*. The plural form is often used (comp. Deut. xxxii. 24; Job xii. 7; Jer. xii. 4; Hab. ii. 17; Ps. l. 10), but in no other instance is it employed as a proper name. Gesenius supposes that under the form of the word here used, there lies concealed some Egyptian name for the hippopotamus, "so modified as to put on the appearance of a Semitic word. Thus the Ethiopian *pehemout* denotes *water-ox,* by which epithet (*bomarino*) the Italians also designate the hippopotamus." The translations do not afford much aid in determining the meaning of the word. The LXX. render it, θηρία, *wild beasts;* Jerome retains the word, *Behemoth;* the Chaldee, בעירא, *beast;* the Syriac retains the Hebrew word; Coverdale renders it, "cruel beast;" Prof. Lee, "the beasts;" Umbreit, *Nilpferd,* "Nile-horse;" and Noyes, "river-horse." The only method of ascertaining, therefore, what animal is here intended, is to compare carefully the characteristics here referred to with the animals now known, and to find in what one these characteristics exist. We may here safely *presume* on the entire accuracy of the description, since we have found the previous descriptions of animals to accord entirely with the habits of those existing at the present day. The illustration drawn from the passage before us, in regard to the nature of the animal, consists of two parts. (1.) The *place* which the description occupies in the argument. That it is an *aquatic* animal, seems to follow from the plan and structure of the argument. In the two discourses of JEHOVAH (chap. xxxviii.—xli.), the appeal is made, first, to the phenomena of nature (chap. xxxviii.); then to the beasts of the earth, among whom the *ostrich* is reckoned (chap. xxxix. 1—25); then to the fowls of the air (chap. xxxix. 26–30); and then follows the description of the behemoth and the leviathan. It would seem that an argument of this kind would not be constructed without some allusion to the principal wonders of the deep; and the fair presumption, therefore, is, that the reference here is to the principal animals of the aquatic race. The argument in regard to the nature of the animal from the *place* which the description occupies, seems to be confirmed by the fact that the account of the behemoth is immediately followed by that of the leviathan — beyond all question an aquatic monster. As they are here grouped together in the argument, it is probable that they belong to the same class; and if by the leviathan is meant the *crocodile,* then the presumption is that the river-horse, or the hippopotamus, is here intended. These two animals, as being Egyptian wonders, are everywhere mentioned together by ancient writers; see Herodotus, ii. 69—71; Diod. Sic. i. 35; and Pliny, *Hist. Nat.* xxviii. 8. (2.) The character of the animal may be determined from the *particular things* specified. Those are the following: (*a*) It is an amphibious animal, or an animal whose usual resort is the river, though he is occasionally on land. This is evident, because he is mentioned as lying under the covert of the reed and the fens; as abiding in marshy places, or among the willows of the brook, (ver. 21, 22), while at other times he is on the mountains, or among other animals, and feeds on grass like the ox, ver. 15, 20. This account would not agree well with the elephant, whose residence is not among marshes and fens, but on solid ground. (*b*) He is not a carnivorous animal. This is apparent, for it is expressly mentioned that he feeds on grass, and no allusion is made to his at any time eating flesh, ver. 15, 20. This part of the description would agree with the elephant as well as with the hippopotamus. (*c*) His strength is in his loins, and in the navel of his belly, ver. 16. This would agree with the hippopotamus, whose belly is equally guarded by his thick skin with the rest of his body, but is not true of the elephant. The strength of the elephant is in his head and neck, and his weakest part, the part where he can be most successfully attacked, is his belly. There the skin is thin and tender, and it is there that the rhinoceros attacks him, and that he is even annoyed by insects. Pliny, Lib. viii. c. 20; Ælian, Lib. xvii. c. 44; comp. Notes on ver. 16. (*d*) He is distinguished for some peculiar movement of his tail—some slow and stately motion, or a certain *inflexibility* of the tail, like a cedar. This will agree with the account of the hippopotamus; see Notes on ver. 17. (*e*) He is remarkable for the strength of his bones, ver. 18. (*f*) He is remarkable for the quantity of water which he drinks at a time, ver. 23; and (*g*) he has the power of forcing his way, chiefly by the strength of his nose, through snares by which it is attempted to take him, ver. 24. These characteristics agree better with the hippopotamus than with any other known animal; and at present critics, with few exceptions, agree in the opinion that this is the animal which is referred to. As additional reasons for supposing that the *elephant* is not referred to, we may add, (1.) that there is no allusion to the proboscis of the elephant, a part of the animal that could not have failed to be alluded to if the description had pertained to him; and (2.) that the elephant was wholly unknown in Arabia and Egypt. The hippopotamus (Ἱπποπόταμος) or *river horse* belongs to the mammalia, and is of the order of the *pachydermata,* or thick-skinned animals. To this order belong also the elephant, the tapirus, the rhinoceros, and the swine. *Edin. Ency.,* art. *Mazology.* The hippopotamus is found principally on the banks of the Nile, though it is found also in the other large rivers of Africa, as the Niger, and the rivers which lie between that and the Cape of Good Hope. It is not found in any of the rivers which run north into the Mediterranean except the Nile, and there only at present in that portion which traverses Upper Egypt; and it is found also in the lakes and fens of Ethiopia. It is distinguished by a broad head; its lips are very thick, and the muzzle much inflated; it has four very large projecting curved teeth in the under jaw, and four also in the upper; the skin is very thick, the legs short, four toes on each foot inverted with small hoofs, and the tail is very short. The appearance of the animal, when on land, is represented as very uncouth, the body being very large, flat, and round, the head enormously large in proportion, the feet as disproportionably short, and the armament of teeth in its mouth truly formidable. The length of a male has been known to be seventeen feet, the height seven, and the circumference fifteen; the head three feet and a half, and the mouth about two feet in width. Mr. Bruce mentions some in the lake Tzana that were twenty feet in length. The whole animal is covered with short hair, which is more thickly set on the under than the upper parts. The general colour of the animal is brownish. The skin is exceedingly tough and strong, and was used by the ancient Egyptians for the manufacture of shields. They are timid and sluggish on land, and when pursued they betake themselves to the water, plunge in, and walk on the bottom, though often compelled to rise to the surface to take in fresh air. In the day-time they are so much afraid of being discovered, that when they rise for the purpose of breathing, they only put their noses out of the water; but in rivers that are unfrequented by mankind they put out the whole head. In shallow rivers they make deep holes in the bottom to conceal their bulk. They are eaten with avidity by the inhabitants of Africa. The following account of the capture of a hippopotamus serves greatly to elucidate the description in the book of Job, and to show its correctness, even in those points which have formerly been regarded as poetical exaggerations. It is translated from the travels of M. Küppell, the German naturalist, who visited Upper Egypt, and the countries still farther up the Nile, and is the latest traveller in those regions. (*Reisen in Nubia, Kordofan, &c.*, Frankf. 1829, p. 52, *seq.*) "In the province of Dongola, the fishermen and hippopotamus hunters form a distinct class or caste; and are called in the Berber language *Hauauit* (pronounced *Howowit.*) They make use of a small canoe, formed from a single tree, about ten feet long, and capable of carrying two, and at most three men. The harpoon which they use in hunting the hippopotamus has a strong barb just back of the blade or sharp edge; above this a long and strong cord is fastened to the iron, and to the other end of this cord a block of light wood, to serve as a buoy, and aid in tracing out and following the animal when struck. The iron is then slightly fastened upon a wooden handle, or lance, about eight feet long. The hunters of the hippopotamus harpoon their prey either by day or by night; but they prefer the former, because they can then better parry the ferocious assaults of the enraged animal. The hunter takes in his right hand the handle of the harpoon, with a part of the cord; in his left the remainder of the cord, with the buoy. In this manner he cautiously approaches the creature as it sleeps by day upon a small island, or he watches at night for those parts of the shore where he hopes the animal will come up out of the water, in order to feed in the fields of grain. When he has gained the desired distance (about seven paces), he throws the lance with his full strength; and the harpoon, in order to hold, must penetrate the thick hide and into the flesh. The wounded beast commonly makes for the water, and plunges beneath it in order to conceal himself; the handle of the harpoon falls off, but the buoy swims, and indicates the direction which the animal takes. The harpooning of the hippopotamus is attended with great danger, when the hunter is perceived by the animal before he has thrown the harpoon. In such cases the beast sometimes rushes, enraged, upon his assailant, and crushes him at once between his wide and formidable jaws—an occurrence that once took place during our residence near Shendi. Sometimes the most harmless objects excite the rage of this animal; thus, in the region of Amera, a hippopotamus once craunched, in the same way, several cattle that were fastened to a water-wheel. So soon as the animal has been successfully struck, the hunters hasten in their canoe cautiously to approach the buoy, to which they fasten a long rope; with the other end of this they proceed to a large boat or bark, on board of which are their companions. The rope is now drawn in; the pain thus occasioned by the barb of the harpoon excites the rage of the animal, and he no sooner perceives the bark, than he rushes upon it ; seizes it, if possible, with his teeth ; and sometimes succeeds in shattering it, or oversetting it. The hunters, in the meantime, are not idle ; they fasten five or six other harpoons in his flesh, and exert all their strength, by means of the cords of these, to keep him close alongside of the bark, in order thus to diminish, in some measure, the effects of his violence. They endeavour, with a long sharp iron, to divide the *ligamentum lugi*, or to beat in the skull—the usual modes in which the natives kill this animal. Since the carcase of a full-grown hippopotamus is too large to be drawn out of the water without quite a number of men, they commonly cut up the animal, when killed, in the water, and draw the pieces ashore. In the whole Turkish province of Dongola, there are only one or two hippopotami killed annually. In the years 1821—23, inclusive, there were nine killed four of which were killed by us. The flesh of the young animal is very good eating ; when full grown, they are usually very fat, and their carcase is commonly estimated as equal to four or five oxen. The hide is used only for making whips, which are excellent ; and one hide furnishes from three hundred and fifty to five hundred of them. The teeth are not used. One of the hippopotami which we killed was a very old male, and seemed to have reached his utmost growth. He measured, from the snout to the end of the tail, about fifteen feet, and his tusks, from the root to the point, along the external curve, twenty-eight inches. In order to kill him, we had a battle with him of four hours long, and that too in the night. Indeed, he came very near destroying our large bark, and with it, perhaps, all our lives. The moment he saw the hunters in the small canoe, as they were about to fasten the long rope to the buoy, in order to draw him in, he threw himself with one rush upon it, dragged it with him under water, and shattered it to pieces. The two hunters escaped the extreme danger with great difficulty. Out of twenty-five musket-balls which were fired into the monster's head, at the distance of five feet, only one penetrated the hide and the bones near the nose ; so that every time he breathed he snorted streams of blood upon the bark. All the other balls remained sticking in the thickness of his hide. We had at last to employ a small cannon, the use of which at so short a distance had not before entered our minds ; but it was only after five of its balls, fired at the distance of a few feet, had mangled, most shockingly, the head and body of the monster, that he gave up the ghost. The darkness of the night augmented the horrors and dangers of the contest. This gigantic hippopotamus dragged our large bark at will in every direction of the stream ; and it was in a fortunate moment for us that he yielded, just as he had drawn the bark among a labyrinth of rocks, which might have been so much the more dangerous, because, from the great confusion on board, no one had observed them. Hippopotami of the size of the one above described cannot be killed by the natives, for want of a cannon. These animals are a real plague to the land, in consequence of their voraciousness. The inhabitants have no permanent means of keeping them away from their fields and plantations ; all that they do is to make a noise during the night with a drum, and to keep up fires in different places. In some parts the hippopotami are so bold that they will yield up their pastures, or places of feeding, only when a large number of persons come rushing upon them with sticks and loud cries." The method of taking the hippopotamus by the Egyptians was the following : "It was entangled by a running noose, at the extremity of a long line wound upon a reel, at the same time that it was struck by the spear of the chasseur. This weapon consisted of a broad, flat blade, furnished with a deep tooth or barb at the side, having a strong rope of considerable length attached to its upper end, and running over the notched summit of a wooden shaft, which was inserted into the head or blade, like a common javelin. It was thrown in the same manner, but on striking, the shaft fell and the iron head alone remained in the body of the animal, which, on receiving the wound, plunged into deep water, the rope having been immediately let out. When fatigued by exertion, the hippopotamus was dragged to the boat, from which it again plunged, and the same was repeated until it became perfectly exhausted: frequently receiving additional wounds, and being entangled by other nooses, which the attendants held in readiness, as it was brought within their reach." Wilkinson's *Manners and Customs of the Ancient Egyptians*, vol. iii. pp. 70, 71. The following sketch of the taking of a hippopotamus, from a drawing at Thebes, will illustrate this interesting subject:

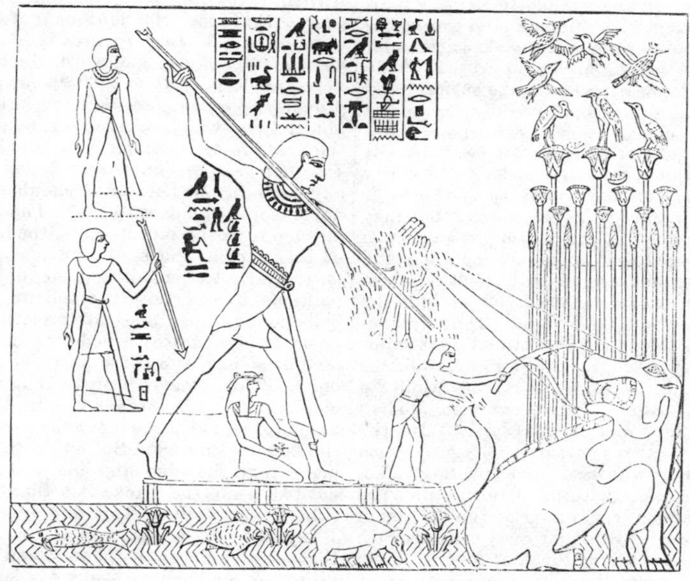

EGYPTIAN SPEARING HIPPOPOTAMUS.

"The chasseur is here in the act of throwing the spear at the hippopotamus, which he has already wounded with three other blades indicated by the ropes he holds in his left hand, and an attendant endeavours to throw a noose over its head as he strikes it for the fourth time."—Wilkinson's *Manners and Customs of the Ancient Egyptians*, vol. iii.

¶ *Which I made with thee.* That is, either "I have made him as well as you, have formed him to be a fellow-creature with thee," or, "I have made him *near* thee"—to wit, in Egypt. The latter Bochart supposes to be the true interpretation, though the former is the more natural. According to that, the meaning is, that God was the Creator of both; and he calls on Job to contemplate the power and greatness of a fellow-creature, though a brute, as illustrating his own power and majesty. The annexed engraving—the figures drawn from the living animal—shows the general appearance of the massive and unwieldy hippopotamus. The huge head of

16 Lo now, his strength *is* in his loins, and his force *is* in the navel of his belly.

17 He [1] moveth his tail like a cedar: the sinews of his stones are wrapped together.

1 or, *setteth up*.

the animal, from the prominency of its eyes, the great breadth of its muzzle, and the singular way in which the jaw is placed in the head, is almost grotesque in its ugliness. When it opens its jaws its enormously large mouth and tongue, pinkish and fleshy, and armed with tusks of most formidable character, is particularly striking. In the engraving hippopotami are represented as on a river bank asleep, and in the water, only the upper part of the head appearing above the surface, and an old animal is conveying her young one on her back down the stream. ¶ *He eateth grass as an ox.* This is mentioned as a remarkable property of this animal. The *reasons* why it was regarded as so remarkable may have been, (1) that it might have been supposed that an animal so huge and fierce, and armed with such a set of teeth, would be carnivorous, like the lion or the tiger; and (2) it was remarkable that an animal that commonly lived in the water should be graminivorous, as if it were wholly a land animal. The common food of the hippopotamus is *fish*. In the water they pursue their prey with great swiftness and perseverance. They swim with much force, and are capable of remaining at the bottom of a river for thirty or forty minutes. On some occasions three or four of them are seen at the bottom of a river, near some cataract, forming a kind of line, and seizing upon such fish as are forced down by the violence of the stream. *Goldsmith.*—But it often happens that this kind of food is not found in sufficient abundance, and the animal is then forced on land, where it commits great depredations among plantations of sugar-cane and grain. The fact here adverted to, that the food of the hippopotamus is grass or herbs, is also mentioned by Diodorus—Κατανέμεται τόν τε σῖτον καὶ τόν χόρτον. The same thing is mentioned also by Sparrmann, *Travels through South Africa*, p. 563, Germ. Trans.

16. *Lo now, his strength* is *in his loins.* The inspection of the figure of the hippopotamus will show the accuracy of this. The strength of the elephant is in the neck; of the lion in the paw; of the horse and ox in the shoulders; but the principal power of the river-horse is in the loins; comp. Na. ii. 1. This passage is one that proves that the elephant cannot be referred to. ¶ *And his force* is *in the navel of his belly.* The word which is here rendered *navel* (שְׁרִיר) means properly *firm, hard, tough,* and in the plural form, which occurs here, means the *firm,* or *tough* parts of the belly. It is not used to denote the *navel* in any place in the Bible, and should not have been so rendered here. The reference is to the muscles and tendons of this part of the body, and perhaps particularly to the fact that the hippopotamus, by crawling so much on his belly among the stones of the stream or on land, acquires a peculiar hardness or strength in those parts of the body. This clearly proves that the elephant is not intended. In that animal, this is the most tender part of the body. Pliny and Solinus both remark that the elephant has a thick, hard skin on the back, but that the skin of the belly is soft and tender. Pliny says (*Hist. Nat.* Lib. viii. c. 20), that the rhinoceros, when about to attack an elephant, "seeks his belly, as if he knew that that was the most tender part." So Ælian, *Hist.* Lib. xvii. c. 44; see Bochart, as above.

17. *He moveth his tail like a cedar.* Marg. "*setteth up*." The Hebrew word (חָפֵץ) means *to bend, to curve;* and hence it commonly denotes *to be inclined, favourably disposed, to desire or please.* The obvious meaning here is, that this animal had some remarkable power of *bending* or *curving* its tail, and that there was some resemblance in this to the motion of the cedar-tree when moved by the wind. In *what* this resemblance consisted, or *how* this was a proof of its power, it is

18 His bones *are as* strong pieces of brass: his bones *are* like bars of iron.

---

not quite easy to determine. Rosenmüller says that the meaning is, that the tail of the hippopotamus was "smooth, round, thick, and firm," and in this respect resembled the cedar. The tail is short—being, according to Abdollatiph (see Ros.), about half a cubit in length. In the lower part, says he, it is thick, "equalling the extremities of the fingers;" and the idea here, according to this, is, that this short, thick, and apparently firm tail, was bent over by the will of the animal as the wind bends the branches of the cedar. The point of comparison is not the *length*, but the fact of its being easily bent over or curved at the pleasure of the animal. Why this, however, should have been mentioned as remarkable, or how the power of the animal in this respect differs from others, is not very apparent. Some, who have supposed the elephant to be here referred to, have understood this of the proboscis. But though *this would be* a remarkable proof of the power of the animal, the language of the original will not admit of it. The Hebrew word (זנב) is used only to denote the tail. It is *possible* that there may be here an allusion to the unwieldy nature of every part of the animal, and especially to the thickness and inflexibility of the skin; and what was remarkable was, that notwithstanding this, this member was entirely at its command. Still, the reason of the comparison is not very clear. The description of the movement of the *tail* here given, would agree much better with some of the extinct orders of animals whose remains have been recently discovered and arranged by Cuvier, than with that of the hippopotamus. Particularly, it would agree with the account of the ichthyosaurus (see Buckland's *Geology*, *Bridgewater Treatise*, vol. i. 133, *seq.*), though the other parts of the animal here described would not accord well with this. ¶ *The sinews of his stones are wrapped together.* Good renders this, *haunches;* Noyes, Prof. Lee, Rosenmüller, and Schultens, *thighs;* and the LXX. simply, "his sinews." The Hebrew word here used (פחד) means properly *fear, terror,* Ex. xv. 16; Job xiii. 11; and, according to Gesenius, it then means, since *fear* is transferred to cowardice and shame, any thing which *causes* shame, and hence the secret parts. So it is understood here by our translators; but there does not seem to be any good reason for this translation, but there is every reason why it should *not* be thus rendered. The *object* of the description is to inspire a sense of the *power* of the animal, or of his capacity to inspire terror or dread; and hence the allusion here is to those parts which were fitted to convey this dread, or this sense of his power—to wit, his strength. The usual meaning of the word, therefore, should be retained, and the sense then would be, "the sinews of his terror," that is, of his parts fitted to inspire terror, "are wrapped together;" are firm, compact, solid. The allusion then is to his thighs or haunches, as being formidable in their aspect, and the seat of strength. The sinews or muscles of these parts seemed to be like a hard-twisted rope; compact, firm, solid, and such as to defy all attempts to overcome them.

18. *His bones* are as *strong pieces of brass.* The circumstance here adverted to was remarkable, because the common residence of the animal was the water, and the bones of aquatic animals are generally hollow, and much less firm than those of land animals. It should be observed here, that the word rendered *brass* in the Scriptures most probably denotes *copper.* Brass is a compound metal, composed of copper and zinc; and there is no reason to suppose that the art of compounding it was known at as early a period of the world as the time of Job. The word here translated "strong pieces" (אפיק) is rendered by Schultens *alvei*—*channels*, or *beds,* as of a rivulet or stream; and by Rosenmüller, Gesenius, Noyes, and Umbreit, *tubes*—supposed to allude to the fact

19 He *is* the chief of the ways of
God: he that made him can make
his sword to approach *unto him.*
20 Surely the mountains bring
him forth food, [a] where all the
beasts of the field play.
21 He lieth under the shady trees,
in the covert of the reed, and fens.

a Ps.104.14.

---

that they seemed to be hollow tubes of brass. But the more common meaning of the word is *strong, mighty,* and there is no impropriety in retaining that sense here; and then the meaning would be, that his bones were so firm that they seemed to be made of solid metal.

19. *He* is *the chief of the ways of God.* In size and strength. The word rendered "chief" is used in a similar sense in Num. xxiv. 20, "Amalek was the *first* of the nations;" that is, one of the most powerful and mighty of the nations. ¶ *He that made him can make his sword approach* unto him. According to this translation, the sense is, that God had power over him, notwithstanding his great strength and size, and could take his life when he pleased. Yet this, though it would be a correct sentiment, does not seem to be that which the connection demands. That would seem to require some allusion to the strength of the animal; and accordingly, the translation suggested by Bochart, and adopted substantially by Rosenmüller, Umbreit, Noyes, Schultens, Prof. Lee, and others, is to be preferred—"He that made him furnished him with a sword." The allusion then would be to his strong, sharp teeth, bearing a resemblance to a sword, and designed either for defence or for the purpose of cutting the long grass on which it fed when on the land. The propriety of this interpretation may be seen vindicated at length in Bochart, *Hieroz.* P. ii. Lib. v. c. xv. pp. 766, 762. The ἅρπη—the *harpe, i. e.* the sickle or scythe, was ascribed to the hippopotamus by some of the Greek writers. Thus Nicander, *Theriacŏn,* ver. 566:

"Ἢ ἵππου, τὸν Νεῖλος ὑπὲρ Σάϊν αἰθαλόεσσαν
Βόσκει, ἀρούρησιν δὲ κακὴν ἐπιβάλλεται
ἍΡΠΗΝ.

On this passage the Scholiast remarks, "The ἅρπη, *harpe,* means a sickle, and the teeth of the hippopotamus are so called—teaching that this animal consumes (τρώγει) the harvest." See Bochart also for other examples. A slight inspection of the *cut* will show with what propriety it is said of the Creator of the hippopotamus, that he had armed him with a sickle, or sword.

20. *Surely the mountains bring him forth food.* That is, though he lies commonly among the reeds and fens, and is in the water a considerable portion of his time, yet he also wanders to the mountains, and finds his food there. But the point of the remark here does not seem to be, that the mountains brought forth food for him, but that he gathered it *while all the wild beasts played around him, or sported in his very presence.* It was remarkable that an animal so large and mighty, and armed with such a set of teeth, should not be carnivorous, and that the wild beasts on the mountains should continue their sports without danger or alarm in his very presence. This fact could be accounted for partly because the *motions* of the hippopotamus were so very slow and clumsy that the wild beasts had nothing to fear from him, and could easily escape from him if he were disposed to attack them, and partly from the fact that he seems to have *preferred* vegetable food. The hippopotamus is seldom carnivorous, except when driven by extreme hunger, and in no respect is he formed to be a beast of prey. In regard to *the fact* that the hippopotamus is sometimes found in mountainous or elevated places, see Bochart.

21. *He lieth under the shady trees.* Referring to his usually inactive and lazy life. He is disposed to lie down in the shade, and especially in the vegetable growth in marshy places on the banks of lakes and rivers, rather than to dwell in the open field or in the upland forest. This account agrees well with the habits of the hippopotamus. The word here and in ver.

22 The shady trees cover him
with their shadow ; the willows of
the brook compass him about.
23 Behold, he [1] drinketh up a
river, *and* hasteth not : he trusteth
that he can draw up Jordan into
his mouth.

[1] *oppresseth.*

22 rendered *shady trees* (צאלים), is by Gesenius, Noyes, Prof. Lee, and Schultens, translated *lotus*, and *wild lotus*. The Vulgate, Syriac, Rosenmüller, Aben-Ezra, and others, render it *shady trees*. It occurs nowhere else in the Scriptures, and it is difficult, therefore, to determine its meaning. According to Schultens and Gesenius, it is derived from the obsolete word צאל, *tzâăl, to be thin, slender ;* and hence in Arabic it is applied to the *wild lotus* – a plant that grows abundantly on the banks of the Nile, and that often serves the wild beasts of the desert for a place of retreat. It is not very important whether it be rendered the *lotus*, or *shades*, though the probable derivation of the word seems to favour the former. ¶ *In the covert of the reed.* It is well known that *reeds* abounded on the banks of the Nile. These would furnish a convenient and a natural retreat for the hippopotamus. ¶ *And fens*, בצה—*marsh, marshy places.* This passage *proves* that the elephant is not here referred to. He is never found in such places.

22. *The shady trees.* Probably the *lote-trees ;* see on ver. 21. The same word is here used. ¶ *The willow-trees of the brook.* Of the *stream*, or *rivulet.* The Hebrew word (נחל) means rather *a wady ;* a gorge or gulley, which is swollen with torrents in the winter, but which is frequently dry in summer ; see Notes on chap. vi. 15. Willows grew commonly on the banks of rivers. They could not be cultivated in the desert ; Isa. xv. 7.

23. *Behold he drinketh up a river.* Marg. *oppresseth.* The margin expresses the proper meaning of the Hebrew word, עשק. It usually means to oppress, to treat with violence and injustice ; and to defraud, or extort. But a very different sense is given to this verse by Bochart, Gesenius, Noyes, Schultens, Umbreit, Prof. Lee, and Rosenmüller. According to the interpretation given by them the meaning is, " The stream overfloweth, and he feareth not ; he is secure, even though Jordan rush forth even to his mouth." The reference then would be, not to the fact that he was greedy in his mode of drinking, but to the fact that this huge and fierce animal, that found its food often on the land, and that reposed under the shade of the lotus and the papyrus, could live in the water as well as on the land, and was unmoved even though the impetuous torrent of a swollen river should overwhelm him. The *names* by which this translation is recommended are a sufficient guarantee that it is not a departure from the proper meaning of the original. It is also the most natural and obvious interpretation. It is impossible to make good sense of the phrase " he *oppresseth* a river ;" nor does the word used properly admit of the translation " he drinketh up." The word *river* in this place, therefore (נהר), is to be regarded as in the nominative case to יעשק, and the meaning is, that when a swollen and impetuous river rushes along and bears all before it, and, as it were, *oppresses* every thing in its course, he is not alarmed ; he makes no effort to flee ; he lies perfectly calm and secure. What was *remarkable* in this appears to have been, that an animal that was so much on land, and that was not properly a fish, should be thus calm and composed when an impetuous torrent rolled over him. The LXX. appear to have been aware that this was the true interpretation, for they render this part of the verse, Ἐὰν γένηται πλημμύρα, κ. τ. λ.—" Should there come a flood, he would not regard it." Our common translation seems to have been adopted from the Vulgate—*Ecce absorbebit fluvium.* ¶ *He trusteth that he can draw up Jordan into his mouth.* Or, rather, " He is confident [*i. e.* unmoved] though Jordan should rush forth to his mouth." The idea is, that though the whole river Jordan should seem to pour down upon him *as if* it were

24 He [1] taketh it with his eyes: *his* nose pierceth through snares.

CHAPTER XLI.

ANALYSIS OF THE CHAPTER.

For a general view of the design of this chapter, see the Analysis of chap. xl. The argument in this chapter is derived wholly from the leviathan, and relates to the following points.—He cannot be taken with a hook or with a cord, ver. 1, 2; he will not be tamed, or come and submit himself to man, ver. 3—5, he cannot be served up at a banquet, ver. 6; his head cannot be pierced with barbed irons, ver. 7; and the sight of him was enough to deter one from an attempt to take him, ver. 8—10. God then appeals to the particular parts of the animal, and goes into a minute description of him. He says he will not conceal his parts that are so fitted to excite terror and admiration, ver. 11, 12. He refers particularly to his mouth and teeth, ver. 13, 14; to his scales, ver. 15—17; to his eyes like the eyelids of the morning, ver. 18; to the smoke and fire that seemed to go out of his mouth and nostrils, ver. 19—21; to the strength of his neck and the compactness of his flesh, ver. 22—24; to his irresistible power, and to the fact that he disregarded all the usual weapons for taking wild beasts, ver. 25—30; and to his appearance when he moves through the deep, ver. 31, 32. It is then added (ver. 33, 34), that there is nothing on earth like him, and that among the most proud works of God he is a king.

1, or *Will* any *take him in his sight*, or *bore* his *nose with a gin?* chap. 41.1,2.

about to rush into his mouth, it would not disturb him. Even such an impetuous torrent would not alarm him. Being amphibious, he would not dread what would fill a land animal with alarm. There is no evidence that the hippopotamus was ever found in the river Jordan, nor is it necessary to suppose this in order to understand this passage. The mention of the Jordan shows indeed that this river was known to the writer of this book, and that it was probably written by some one who resided in the vicinity. In speaking of this huge foreign animal, it was not unnatural to mention a river that was familiarly known, and to say that he would not be alarmed should such a river rush suddenly and impetuously upon him. Even though the hippopotamus is an inhabitant of the Nile, and was never seen in the Jordan, it was much more natural to mention this river in this connection than the Nile. It was better known, and the illustration would be better understood, and to an inhabitant of that country would be much more striking. I see no reason, therefore, for the supposition of Bochart and Rosenmüller, that the Jordan here is put for any large river. The illustration is just such as one would have used who was well acquainted with the Jordan—that the river horse would not be alarmed even though such a river should pour impetuously upon him.

24. *He taketh it with his eyes.* Marg. "Or, *will* any *take him in his sight*, or, *bore* his *nose with a gin!*" From this marginal reading it is evident that our translators were much perplexed with this passage. Expositors have been also much embarrassed in regard to its meaning, and have differed much in their exposition. Rosenmüller supposes that this is to be regarded as a question, and is to be rendered, "Will the hunter take him while he sees him?"—meaning that he could not be taken without some snare or guile. The same view also is adopted by Bochart, who says that the hippopotamus could be taken only by some secret snare or pitfall. The common mode of taking him, he says, was to excavate a place near where the river horse usually lay, and to cover it over with reeds and canes, so that he would fall into it unawares. The meaning then is, that the hunter could not approach him openly and secure him while he saw him, but that some secret plan must be adopted to take him. The meaning then is, "Can he be taken when he sees the hunter?" ¶ His *nose pierceth through snares.* Or rather, "When taken in snares, can any one pierce his nose?" That is, Can the hunter even then pierce his nose so as to put in a ring or cord, and lead him wherever he pleases? This was the common method by which a wild animal was secured when taken (see Notes on Isa. xxxvii. 29), but it is here said that this could not be done to this huge animal. He could not be subdued in this manner. He was a wild, untamed and fierce animal, that defied all the usual methods by which wild beasts were made captive. In regard to the difficulty of taking this animal, see the account of the method by which it is now done, in the Notes on ver. 15. That account shows that there is a striking accuracy in the description

CANST thou draw out [1] leviathan [a] with an hook? or his tongue with a cord *which* thou [2] lettest down?

1 i. e. *a whale*, or, *a whirlpool*. *a* Ps.104 26; Isa.27.1. 2 *drownest*.

CHAPTER XLI.

1. *Canst thou draw out.* As a fish is drawn out of the water. The usual method by which fish were taken was with a hook; and the meaning here is, that it was not possible to take the leviathan in this manner. The whole description here is of an animal that lived in the water. ¶ *Leviathan.* Much has been written respecting this animal, and the opinions which have been entertained have been very various. Schultens enumerates the following classes of opinions in regard to the animal intended here. 1. The opinion that the word leviathan is to be retained, without attempting to explain it—implying that there was uncertainty as to the meaning. Under this head he refers to the Chaldee and the Vulgate, to Aquila and Symmachus, where the word is retained, and to the Septuagint, where the word Δράκοντα, *dragon*, is used, and also the Syriac and Arabic, where the same word is used. 2. The fable of the Jews, who mention a serpent so large that it encompassed the whole earth. A belief of the existence of such a marine serpent or monster still prevails among the Nestorians. 3. The opinion that the whale is intended. 4. The opinion that a large fish called *Mular*, or *Musar*, which is found in the Mediterranean, is denoted. This is the opinion of Grotius. 5. The opinion that the crocodile of the Nile is denoted. 6. The opinion of Hasaeus, that not the whale is intended, but the *Orca*, a sea-monster armed with teeth, and the enemy of the whale. 7. Others have understood the whole description as allegorical, as representing monsters of iniquity; and among these, some have regarded it as descriptive of the devil! See Schultens. To these may be added the description of Milton:

> ——that sea-beast
> Leviathan, which God of all his works
> Created hug'st that swim the ocean-stream,
> Him, haply, slumb'ring on the Norway foam,
> The pilot of some small night-foundered skiff
> Deeming some island, oft, as seamen tell,
> With fixed anchor in his scaly rind
> Moors by his side under the lee, while night
> Invests the sea, and wished morn delays.
> *Par. Lost*, B. i.

For a full investigation of the subject, Bochart may be consulted, *Hieroz.* P. ii. Lib. v. c. xvi—xviii. The conclusion to which he comes is, that the crocodile of the Nile is denoted; and in this opinion critics have generally, since his time, acquiesced. The opinions which are entitled to most attention are those which regard the animal here described as either the whale or the crocodile. The objections to the supposition that the whale is intended are such as the following: (1.) That the whale tribes do not inhabit the Mediterranean, much less the rivers which empty into it—with which alone it is supposed Job could have been acquainted. (2.) That the animal here described differs from the whale in many essential particulars. "This family of marine monsters have neither proper snout nor nostrils, nor proper teeth. Instead of a snout, they have a mere spiracle, or blowing-hole, with a double opening on the top of the head; and for teeth, a hard expanse of horny laminæ, which we call whalebone, in the upper jaw. The eyes of the common whale, moreover, instead of answering the description here given, are most disproportionately small, and do not exceed in size those of the ox. Nor can this monster be regarded as of fierce habits or unconquerable courage; for instead of attacking the larger sea-animals for plunder, it feeds chiefly on crabs and medusas, and is often itself attacked by the ork or grampus, though less than half its size." *Dr. Good.* These considerations seem to be decisive in regard to the supposition that the animal here referred to is the whale. In fact, there is almost nothing in the description that corresponds with the whale, except the size. The whole account, on the contrary, agrees well with the crocodile; and there are several considerations which may be suggested, before we proceed with the exposition, which correspond with the supposition that this is the animal intended. They are such as these : (1.) The crocodile is a natural inhabitant of the Nile and of other Asiatic and African rivers, and it is reasonable to suppose that an animal is referred to that was well known to one who lived in the country of Job. Though the Almighty is the speaker, and could describe an animal wholly unknown to Job, yet it is not reasonable to suppose that such an unknown animal would be selected. The appeal was to what he knew of the works of God. (2.) The general description agrees with this animal. The leviathan is represented as wild, fierce, and ungovernable ; as of vast extent, and as terrible in his aspect ; as having a mouth of vast size, and armed with a formidable array of teeth ; as covered with scales set near together like a coat of mail, as distinguished by the fierceness of his eyes, and by the frightful aspect of his mouth ; as endowed with great strength, and incapable of being taken in any of the ordinary methods of securing wild beasts. This general description agrees well with the crocodile. These animals are found in the rivers of Africa, and also in the southern rivers of America, and are usually called the alligator. In the Amazon, the Niger, and the Nile, they occur in great numbers, and are usually from eighteen to twenty-seven feet long ; and sometimes lying as close to each other as a raft of timber. *Goldsmith.* The crocodile grows to a great length, being sometimes found thirty feet long from the tip of the snout to the end of the tail ; though its most usual length is about eighteen or twenty feet. " The armour, with which the upper part of the body is covered, may be numbered among the most elaborate pieces of Nature's mechanism. In the full-grown animal it is so strong and thick as easily to repel a musket-ball. The whole animal appears as if covered with the most regular and curious carved work. The mouth is of vast width, the gape having a somewhat flexuous outline, and both jaws being furnished with very numerous, sharp-pointed teeth. The number of teeth in each jaw is thirty or more, and they are so disposed as to alternate with each other when the mouth is closed. The legs are short, but strong and muscular. In the glowing regions of Africa, where it arrives at its full strength and power, it is justly regarded as the most formidable inhabitant of the rivers." Shaw's *Zoology,* vol. iii. p. 184. The crocodile seldom, except pressed with hunger, or for the purpose of depositing its eggs, leaves the water. Its usual method is to float along the surface, and seize whatever animals come within its reach ; but when this method fails, it then goes nearer the bank. There it waits, among the sedges, for any animal that may come down to drink, and seizes upon it, and drags it into the water. The tiger is thus often seized by the crocodile, and dragged into the river and drowned. (3.) A third reason for supposing that the crocodile is here intended, arises from the former conclusion concerning the *behemoth,* chap. xl. 15, *seq.* The description of the leviathan immediately follows that, and the presumption is that they were animals that were usually found inhabiting the same district of country. If, therefore, the behemoth be the hippopotamus, there is a presumption that the leviathan is the crocodile—an inhabitant of the same river, equally amphibious, and even more terrible. " And this consideration," says the Editor of the Pictorial Bible, " is strengthened, when we consider that the two animals were so associated by the ancients. Some of the paintings at Herculaneum represent Egyptian landscapes, in which we see the crocodile lying among the reeds, and the hippopotamus browsing upon the plants on an island. So also in the famous Mosaic pavement at Præneste, representing the plants and animals of Egypt and Ethiopia, the river-horse and the crocodile are associated in the same group, in the river Nile." The crocodile was formerly found in abundance in Lower Egypt and the Delta, but it now limits the extent of its visits northward to the districts about Manfaloot, and the hippopotamus is no longer seen in Lower Ethiopia. Neither the hippopotamus nor the crocodile appear to have been eaten by the ancient Egyptians. Pliny mentions the medicinal properties of both of them (xxviii. 8), and Plutarch affirms that the people of Apollinopolis used to eat the crocodile (*de Isid.* s. 50); but this does not appear to have been a usual custom. Herodotus says that "some of the Egyptians consider the crocodile sacred, while others make war upon it; and those who live about Thebes and the lake Moeris (in the Arsinoïte *nome*), hold it in great veneration," ii. 69. In some cases the crocodile was treated with the greatest respect, and kept up at considerable expense; it was fed and attended with the most scrupulous care; geese, fish, and various meats were dressed purposely for it; they ornamented its head with ear-rings and its feet with bracelets and necklaces of gold and artificial stones; it was rendered tame by kind treatment, and after death the body was embalmed in a sumptuous manner. This was particularly the case in the Theban, Ombite, and Arsinoïte nomes, and at a place now called Maabdeh, opposite the modern town of Manfaloot, are extensive grottoes cut far into the limestone mountain, where numerous crocodile mummies have been found, perfectly preserved and evidently embalmed with great care. In other parts of Egypt, however, the animal was held in the greatest abhorrence, and so they lost no opportunity of destroying it. See Wilkinson's *Manners and Customs of the Ancient Egyptians*, vol. iii. p. 75, *seq.* The engraving opposite represents Egyptian crocodiles (*Crocodilus vulgaris*) disporting themselves on the banks of the Nile, or basking in the sun—one of their favourite practices. The figures were drawn from living animals. —The word here rendered *leviathan* (לויתן) occurs only in this place and in chap. iii. 8; Ps. lxxiv. 14; civ. 26; Isa. xxvii. 1. In all these places it is rendered leviathan, except in Job iii. 8, where it is rendered in the text, "their mourning," in the margin, *leviathan;* see Notes on that verse, and comp. Notes on Isa. xxvii. 1. The connection of the word with the root is not certainly known. Gesenius regards it as derived from לוה, to join one's self to any one, and then to wreathe, to fold, to curve; and in Arabic *to weave, to twist,* as a wreath or garland; and that the word is applied to an animal that is *wreathed,* or that gathers itself *in folds*—a *twisted animal.* In chap. iii. 8, the word is used to denote some huge, untamable, and fierce monster, and will agree there with the supposition that the crocodile is intended; see Notes on that place. In Ps. lxxiv. 14. the allusion is to Pharaoh, compared with the leviathan, and the passage would agree best with the supposition that the allusion was to the crocodile. The crocodile was an inhabitant of the Nile, and it was natural to allude to that in describing a fierce tyrant of Egypt. In Ps. civ. 26, the allusion is to some huge animal of the deep, particularly of the Mediterranean, and the language would apply to any sea-monster. In Isa. xxvii. 1. the allusion is to the king and tyrant that ruled in Babylon, as compared with a dragon or fierce animal; comp. Notes on that passage, and Rev. xii. Any of these passages will accord well with the supposition that the crocodile is denoted by the word, or that some fierce, strong, and violent animal that could involve itself, or that had the appearance of an extended serpent, is referred to. The resemblance between the animal here described and the crocodile, will be farther indicated by the Notes on the particular descriptions in the chapter. ¶ *With an hook.* Implying that the animal here referred to was aquatic, and that it could not be taken in the way in which fish were usually caught. It is known now that the crocodile is occasionally taken with a hook, but this is not the usual method, and there is no evidence that it was practised in the time of Job. Herodotus says that it was one of the methods which were used in his time. "Among the various methods," says he, "that are used to take the crocodile, I shall relate only

2 Canst thou put an hook [a] into his nose? or bore his jaw through with a thorn?

a Isa.37.29.

3 Will he make many supplications unto thee? will he speak soft *words* unto thee?

one which deserves most attention; they fix a hook (ἄγκιστρον) on a piece of swine's flesh, and suffer it to float into the middle of the stream. On the banks they have a live hog, which they beat till it cries out. The crocodile, hearing the noise, makes towards it, and in the way encounters and devours the bait. They thus draw it on shore, and the first thing they do is to fill its eyes with clay; it is thus easily manageable, which it otherwise would not be." B. ii. 70. "The manner of taking it in Siam is by throwing three or four strong nets across a river at proper distances from each other, so that if the animal breaks through the first, it may be caught by one of the rest. When it is first taken it employs the tail, which is the grand instrument of its strength, with great force; but after many unsuccessful struggles, the animal's strength is at length exhausted. Then the natives approach their prisoner in boats, and pierce him with their weapons in the most tender parts, till he is weakened with the loss of blood." *Goldsmith.* From ancient sculptures in Egypt, it appears that the common method of attacking the crocodile was with a spear, transfixing it as it passed beneath the boat in shallow water, See Wilkinson's *Manners and Customs of the Ancient Egyptians*, vol. iii. p. 75, *seq.* The most common method of taking the crocodile now is by shooting it. *Pococke.* It is quite clear, therefore, that, agreeably to what is said in the passage before us, the common method of taking it was not by a hook, and it is probable that in the time of Job this method was not practised. ¶ *Or his tongue with a cord* which *thou lettest down.* Or rather, "Canst thou sink his tongue with a cord?"—that is, Canst thou tame him by a thong or bit thrust into his mouth? *Gesenius.* The idea is that of *pressing down* the tongue with a cord, so that he would be tractable.

2. *Canst thou put a hook into his nose.* Or rather, a *rope*, or *cord.* The word here used (אגמון) means a caldron, or kettle (Job xli. 20), also a reed, or bulrush, growing in marshy places, and thus a rope made of reeds, a rush-cord. The idea is, that he could not be led about by a cord, as tame animals may be. Mr. Vansittart, however, supposes that the words here are expressive of ornaments, and that the allusion is to the fact mentioned by Herodotus, that the crocodile was led about by the Egyptians as a divinity, and that in this state it was adorned with rings and various stately trappings. There can be no doubt that such a fact existed, but this does not accord well with the scope of the passage here. The object is to impress the mind of Job with a sense of the strength and untamableness of the animal, not to describe the honours which were paid to it. ¶ *Or bore his jaw through with a thorn.* Or with a *ring.* The word here properly means a thorn, or thorn-bush, Job xxxi. 40; Prov. xxvi. 9; and then also a ring that was put through the nose of an animal, in order to secure it. The instrument was probably made sharp like a thorn or spike, and then bent so as to become a ring; comp. Isa. xxxvii. 29. Mr. Bruce, speaking of the manner of fishing in the Nile, says that when a fisherman has caught a fish, he draws it to the shore, and puts a strong iron ring into its jaw. To this ring is fastened a rope by which the fish is attached to the shore, which he then throws again into the water. *Rosenmüller.*

3. *Will he make many supplications unto thee?* In the manner of a captive begging for his life. That is, Will he quietly submit to you? Prof. Lee supposes that there is an allusion here to the well-known cries of the dolphin when taken; but it is not necessary to suppose such an allusion. The idea is, that the animal here referred to would not tamely submit to his captor. ¶ *Will he speak soft*

4 Will he make a covenant with thee? wilt thou take him for a servant for ever?
5 Wilt thou play with him as *with* a bird? or wilt thou bind him for thy maidens?

6 Shall thy companions make a banquet of him? shall they part him among the merchants?
7 Canst thou fill his skin with barbed irons? or his head with fish-spears?

---

words *unto thee?* Pleading for his life in tones of tender and plaintive supplication.

4. *Will he make a covenant with thee?* That is, Will he submit himself to thee, and enter into a compact to serve thee? Such a compact was made by those who agreed to serve another; and the idea here is, that the animal here referred to could not be reduced to such service—that is, could not be tamed. ¶ *Wilt thou take him for a servant for ever?* Canst thou so subdue him that he will be a perpetual slave? The meaning of all this is, that he was an untamable animal, and could not be reduced, as many others could, to domestic use.

5. *Wilt thou play with him as* with *a bird?* A bird that is tamed. The art of taming birds was doubtless early practised, and they were kept for amusement. But the leviathan could not thus be tamed. ¶ *Or wilt thou bind him for thy maidens?* For their amusement. For such purposes doubtless, birds were caught and caged. There is great force in this question, on the supposition that the crocodile is intended. Nothing could be more incongruous than the idea of securing so rough and unsightly a monster for the amusement of tender and delicate females.

6. *Shall thy companions make a banquet of him?* This is one of the "vexed passages" about which there has been much difference of opinion. Gesenius renders it, "Do the companions (*i. e.* the fishermen in company) lay snares for him?" So Noyes renders it. Dr. Harris translates it, "Shall thy partners spread a banquet for him?" The LXX. render it, "Do the nations feed upon him?" The Vulgate, "Will friends cut him up?" that is, for a banquet. Rosenmüller renders it, "Will friends feast upon him?" The word rendered "thy companions" (חברים) means properly those joined or associated together for any purpose, whether for friendship or for business. It may refer here either to those associated for the purpose of fishing or feasting. The word "thy" is improperly introduced by our translators, and there is no evidence that the reference is to the companions or friends of Job, as that would seem to suppose. The word rendered "make a banquet" (יכרו) is from כרה, *kârâ, to dig*, and then to make a plot or device against one—derived from the fact that a *pitfall* was dug to take animals (Ps. vii. 15; lvii. 6; comp. Job vi. 27); and according to this it means, "Do the companions, *i. e.* the fishermen in company, lay snares for him?" The word, however, has another signification, meaning to buy, to purchase, and also to give a feast, to make a banquet, perhaps from the idea of *purchasing* the provisions necessary for a banquet. According to this, the meaning is, "Do the companions, *i. e.* those associated for the purpose of feasting, make a banquet of him?" Which is the true sense here it is not easy to determine. The majority of versions incline to the idea that it refers to a feast, and means that those associated for eating do not make a part of their entertainment of him. This interpretation is the most simple and obvious. ¶ *Shall they part him among the merchants?* That is, Shall they cut him up and expose him for sale? The word rendered "merchants" (כנענים) means properly *Canaanites*. It is used in the sense of *merchants*, or *traffickers*, because the Canaanites were commonly engaged in this employment; see Notes on Isa. xxiii. 8. The crocodile is never made a part of a banquet, or an article of traffic.

7. *Canst thou fill his skin with barbed irons?* Referring to its thickness and impenetrability. A common

8 Lay thine hand upon him, remember the battle, do no more.
9 Behold, the hope of him is in
vain: shall not *one* be cast down
even at the sight of him?
10 None *is so* fierce that dare stir
him up: who then is able to stand
before me?
11 Who [a] hath prevented me,
that I should repay *him? whatsoever is* under the whole heaven is
mine.[b]

a Ro.11.35. *b* Ex.19.5; De.10.14; Ps. 50.12; 1 Cor.10.26,28.

method of taking fish is by the spear; but it is here said that the leviathan could not be caught in this manner. The common method of taking the crocodile now is by shooting him; see Notes on ver. 1. Nothing is more remarkable in the crocodile than the thick and impenetrable skin with which it is covered; and the description here will agree better with this animal than with any other. ¶ *Or his head with fish spears.* The word here rendered "fish-spears" (צלצל) means properly a *tinkling*, *clanging*, as of metal or arms, and then any tinkling instrument. Here it evidently refers to some metal spear, or harpoon, and the name was given to the instrument on account of its clanging noise. The LXX. render this strangely, referring it to the "Phenicians," or merchants mentioned in the previous verse—"With their whole fleet they could not carry the first skin of his tail, nor his head in their fishing-barks."

8. *Lay thine hand upon him.* Prof. Lee renders this, very improperly, as it seems to me, "Lay thine hand on thy mouth respecting him," supposing it means that he should be awed into silence by dread of the animal referred to. But the meaning of the passage evidently is, "Endeavour to seize him by laying the hand on him, and you will soon desist from the fearful conflict, and will not renew it." ¶ *Remember the battle.* Remember what a fearful conflict will ensue. Perhaps there is an allusion to some fact fresh in the mind of Job, where such an attempt had been made to secure the leviathan, attended with fearful disaster to those who had made the attempt. ¶ *Do no more.* Or, rather, "Thou wilt not do it again." That is, he would be deterred from ever renewing the attempt, or the conflict would be fatal to him.

9. *Behold, the hope of him is in vain.* That is, the hope of taking him is vain. ¶ *Shall not* one *be cast down even at the sight of him?* So formidable is his appearance, that the courage of him who would attack him is daunted, and his resolution fails. This agrees well also with the crocodile. There is perhaps scarcely any animal whose appearance would be more likely to deter one from attacking him.

10. *None* is so *fierce that dare stir him up.* No one has courage to rouse and provoke him. ¶ *Who then is able to stand before me?* The meaning of this is plain. It is, "If one of my creatures is so formidable that man dare not attack it, how can he contend with the great Creator? This may perhaps be designed as a reproof of Job. He had expressed a desire to carry his cause before God, and to urge argument before him in vindication of himself. God here shows him how hopeless must be a contest with the Almighty. Man trembles and is disarmed of his courage by even the sight of one of the creatures of God. Overpowered with fear, he retires from the contemplated contest, and flees away. How then could he presume to contend with God? What hope could he have in a contest with him?

11. *Who hath prevented me?* As this verse is here rendered, its meaning, and the reason why it is introduced, are not very apparent. It almost looks, indeed, as if it were an interpolation, or had been introduced from some other place, and torn from its proper connection. Dr. Harris proposes to remove the principal difficulty by translating it,

"Who will stand before me, yea, presumptuously?
Whatsoever is beneath the whole heaven is mine.

12 I will not conceal his parts, nor his power, nor his comely proportion.

I cannot be confounded at his limbs and violence,
Nor at his power, or the strength of his frame."

It may be doubted, however, whether the original will admit of this translation. Rosenmüller, Umbreit, and Noyes, unite in supposing the meaning to be, "Who has done me a favour, that I must repay him?" But perhaps the true idea of the passage may be arrived at by adverting to the meaning of the word rendered "prevented"—קדם. It properly means in Piel, to go before; to precede; to anticipate, Ps. xvii. 13; cxix. 148. Then it means to rush upon suddenly; to seize; to go to meet any one either for succour, Ps. lix. 11, or for a different purpose. Isa. xxxvii. 33, "No shield shall come up against her." יקדמנה *i. e.* against the city. So Job xxx. 27, "The days of affliction *prevented* me." A similar meaning occurs in the Hiphil form in Amos ix. 10, "The evil shall not overtake us nor *prevent* us;" that is, shall not rush upon us as if by anticipation, or when we are off our guard. If some idea of this kind be supposed to be conveyed by the word here, it will probably express the true sense. "Who is able to seize upon me suddenly, or when I am off my guard; to anticipate my watchfulness and my power of resistance so as to *compel* me to recompense him, or so to overmaster me as to lay me under obligation to confer on him the favours which he demands?" There may be an allusion to the manner in which wild beasts are taken, when the hunter springs his gin suddenly, anticipates the power of the animal, rushes unexpectedly upon him, and compels him to yield. God says that no one could thus surprise and overpower him. Thus explained, the sentiment agrees with the argument which the Almighty is presenting. He is showing his right to reign and do all his pleasure. He appeals, in proof of this, to his great and mighty works, and especially to those specimens of the animal creation which *man* could not tame or overcome. The argument is this: "If man cannot surprise and subdue these creatures of the Almighty, and compel *them* to render him service, how can he expect to constrain the Creator himself to be tributary to him, or to grant him the favours which he demands?" ¶ Whatsoever is *under the whole heaven is mine.* That is, "All belong to me; all are subject to me; all are mine, to be conferred on whom I please. No one can claim them as his own; no one can wrest them from me." This claim to the proprietorship of all created things, is designed *here* to show to Job that over a Being thus supreme man could exert no control. It is his duty, therefore, to submit to him without a murmur, and to receive with gratitude what he chooses to confer.

12. *I will not conceal his parts.* This is the commencement of a more particular description of the animal than had been before given. In the previous part of the chapter, the remarks are general, speaking of it merely as one of great power, and not to be taken by any of the ordinary methods. A description follows of the various parts of the animal, all tending to confirm this general impression, and to fill the hearer with a deep conviction of his formidable character. The words rendered, "I will not conceal," mean, "I will not be silent;" that is, he would speak of them. The description which follows of the "parts" of the animal refers particularly to his mouth, his teeth, his scales, his eyelids, his nostrils, his neck, and his heart. ¶ *Nor his comely proportion.* The crocodile is not an object of beauty, and the animal described here is not spoken of as one of beauty, but as one of great power and fierceness. The phrase here used (חִין עֶרְכּוֹ) means properly "the grace of his armature," or the beauty of his armour. It does not refer to the beauty of the animal as such, but to the armour or defence which it had. Though there might be no

13 Who can discover the face of
his garment? or who can come *to*
him [1] with his double bridle?
14 Who can open the doors of
his face? his teeth *are* terrible
round about.
15 *His* scales [2] *are his* pride,
shut up together *as with* a close
seal.

1 or, *within*.
2 *strong pieces of shields*.

beauty in an animal like the one here described, yet there might be a "grace" or fitness in its means of defence which could not fail to attract admiration. This is the idea in the passage. So Gesenius, Umbreit, and Noyes render it.

13. *Who can discern the face of his garment?* Literally, "Who can reveal the face, *i. e.* the appearance, of his garment?" This "garment" is undoubtedly his skin. The meaning seems to be, "His hard and rough skin is his defence, and no one can so strip off that as to have access to him." The word rendered "discover" (גלה) means to make naked; then to reveal; and the idea is, that he cannot be made naked of that covering, or deprived of it so that one could attack him. ¶ *Or who can come* to him *with his double bridle?* Marg. *within.* Gesenius renders this, "The doubling of his jaws;" that is, his double row of teeth. Umbreit, "His double bit." Noyes, "Who will approach his jaws?" So Rosenmüller. Schultens and Prof. Lee, however, suppose it means that no one can come near to him and *double the bit* upon him, *i. e.* cast the bit or noose over his nose, so as to secure him by doubling it, or passing it around him. The former seems to me to be the true meaning. "Into the doubling of his jaws, who can enter?" That is, Who will dare approach a double row of teeth so formidable? The word rendered "bridle" (רסן) means properly a curb or halter, which goes over a horse's nose, and hence a bit or bridle. But it may be used to denote the interior of the mouth, the jaws, where the bit is placed, and then the phrase denotes the double row of teeth of the animal. Thus the description of the "parts of defence" of the animal is kept up.

14. *Who can open the doors of his face?* His mouth. The same term is still used to denote the mouth—from its resemblance to a door. The idea is, that no one would dare to force open his mouth. This agrees better with the crocodile than almost any other animal. It would not apply to the whale. The crocodile is armed with a more formidable set of teeth than almost any other animal; see the description in the Notes on ver. 1. Bochart says that it has sixty teeth, and those much larger than in proportion to the size of the body. Some of them, he says, stand out; some of them are serrated, or like a saw, fitting into each other when the mouth is closed; and some come together in the manner of a comb, so that the grasp of the animal is very tenacious and fearful; see a full description in Bochart.

15. His *scales* are his *pride.* Marg. *strong pieces of shields.* The literal translation of this would be, "Pride, the strong of shields;" that is, the strong shields. There can be no doubt that there is reference to the scales of the animal, as having a resemblance to strong shields laid close to each other. But there is considerable variety of opinion as to its meaning. Umbreit and Prof. Lee take the word here rendered "pride" (גאוה) to be the same as (גוה), *back*, and then the meaning would be that his back was armed as with a shield—referring, as Prof. Lee supposes, to the dorsal fin of the whale. But there is no necessity for this supposition, and it cannot be denied that it is somewhat forced. The *connection* requires that we should understand it, not of the dorsal fin, but of the scales; for a description immediately follows in continuation of this, which will by no means apply to the fin. The obvious and proper meaning is, that the pride or glory of the animal—that on which his safety depended, and which was the most remarkable thing about him—was his *scales,* which were laid together like

16 One is so near to another, that no air can come between them.

17 They are joined one to another, they stick together that they cannot be sundered.

18 By his neesings a light doth shine, and his eyes *are* like the eyelids of the morning.

19 Out of his mouth go burning lamps, *and* sparks of fire leap out.

---

firm and compact shields, so that nothing could penetrate them. This description accords better with the crocodile than with any other animal. It is covered with scales, "which are so hard as to resist a musket-ball." *Ed. Ency.* The description cannot be applied to a whale, which has no scales; and accordingly Prof. Lee supposes that the reference in this verse and the two following is not to the *scales*, but to the *teeth*, and to "the setting in of the dorsal fin!" ¶ *Shut up together.* Made close or compact. ¶ As with *a close seal.* As if they had been sealed with wax, so that no air could come between them.

17. *They are joined one to another.* Literally, "A man with his brother;" that is, each one is connected with another. There is no natural fastening of one scale with another, but they lie so close and compact that they seem thus to be fastened down on one another; see Bochart on this verse. It is this which makes the crocodile so difficult to be killed. A musket-ball will penetrate the skin under the belly, which is there less firmly protected; and accordingly the efforts of those who attempt to secure them are directed to that part of the body. A ball in the eye or throat will also destroy it, but the body is impervious to a spear or a bullet.

18. *By his neesings a light doth shine.* The word rendered "neesings" means properly *sneezing*, and the literal sense here would be, "His sneezings, light shines." Coverdale renders it, "His nesinge is like a glisteringe fyre." Bochart says that the meaning is, "that when the crocodile sneezes, the breath is driven through the nostrils with such force that it seems to scintillate, or emit fire." Probably the meaning is, that when the animal emits a sudden sound, like sneezing, the fire seems to flash from the eye. There is some quick and rapid motion of the eyes, which in the rays of the sun seem to flash fire. The sneezing of the crocodile is mentioned by Aristotle. *Prof. Lee.* Amphibious animals, the longer they hold their breath under water, respire so much the more violently when they emerge, and the breath is expelled suddenly and with violence. *Schultens.* This is the action here referred to—the strong effort of the animal to recover breath when he rises to the surface, and when in the effort the eyes seem to scintillate, or emit light. ¶ *And his eyes* are *like the eyelids of the morning.* The "eyelids of the morning" is a beautiful poetic phrase quite common in Hebrew poetry. The eyes of the crocodile are small, but they are remarkable. When he lifts his head above water, his staring eyes are the first things that strike the beholder, and may then with great beauty be compared with the morning light. There is a remarkable coincidence here, in the fact that when the Egyptians would represent the morning by a hieroglyphic, they painted a crocodile's eye. The reason assigned for this was, that before the whole body of the animal appeared, the eyes seemed to rise from the deep; see Bochart on the passage, *Hieroz.*, and also Horapollo, *Hieroglyph.* i. c. 65.

19. *Out of his mouth go burning lamps.* The word "lamps" here is probably used to denote *torches*, or *fire-brands.* The animal is here described as in pursuit of his prey on land; and the description is exceedingly graphic and powerful. His mouth is then open; his jaws are distended; his breath is thrown out with great violence; his blood is inflamed, and the animal seems to vomit forth flames. The description is of course to be regarded as figurative. It is such as one would be likely to give

20 Out of his nostrils goeth smoke, as *out* of a seething-pot or caldron.
21 His breath kindleth coals, and a flame goeth out of his mouth.
22 In his neck remaineth strength, and sorrow [1] is turned into joy before him.

1 *rejoiceth.*

---

who should see a fierce animal pressing on in pursuit of its prey. ¶ And *sparks of fire leap out.* There is an appearance like sparks of fire. The animal, with an open throat highly inflamed, seems to breathe forth flames. The figure is a common one applied to a war-horse. Thus Ovid:

> "From their full racks the generous steeds retire,
> Dropping ambrosial foam and *snorting fire.*'
> Dr. Good.

The same thing is remarked by Achilles Tatius, of the hippopotamus, "With open nostrils, and breathing smoke like fire (πυρώδη καπνόν) as from a fountain of fire." And in Eustathius it is said, "They have an open nostril, breathing forth smoke like fire from a furnace"—πυρώδη καπνόν, ὡς ἐκ καμίνου πνέοντα. See Bochart.

20. *Out of his nostrils goeth smoke;* see the quotations on ver. 19. This appearance of the crocodile, or alligator, has been often noticed. Bertram, in his *Travels in North and South Carolina,* p. 116, says, "While I was seeking a place of rest, I encountered an alligator that in the neighbouring lake rushed through the canes that grew on its banks. He inflated his enormous body, and swung his tail high in the air. A thick smoke streamed from his wide-open nostrils, with a sound that made the earth tremble." Rosenmüller, *Alte u. neue Morgenland,* No. 778. ¶ *As out of a seething-pot.* A pot that is boiling. Literally, "a blown pot;" that is, a pot under which the fire is *blown,* or kindled. ¶ *Or caldron.* Any kettle. The same word is used to denote a reed or bulrush, or a rope made of reeds, Isa. ix. 14; Job xli. 1.

21. *His breath kindleth coals.* It seems to be a flame, and to set on fire all around it. So Hesiod, *Theog.* i. 319, describing the creation of the Chimera, speaks of it as

> πνέουσαν ἀμαιμάκετον πῦρ.

"breathing unquenchable fire." So Virgil, *Georg.* ii. 140:

> Hæc loca non tauri spirantes naribus ignem
> Invertêre.
>
> "Bulls breathing fire these furrows ne'er have known." Warton.

A similar phrase is found in a sublime description of the anger of the Almighty, in Ps. xviii. 8:

> There went up a smoke out of his nostrils,
> And fire out of his mouth devoured:
> Coals were kindled by it.

22. *In his neck remaineth strength.* That is, strength is *permanently residing* there. It is not assumed for the moment, but his neck is so constructed as to be the abode of strength. The word here rendered "remaineth" (ילין), means properly to pass the night; then to abide or dwell; and there is a designed contrast here with what is said of "sorrow" in this verse. This description of strength residing in the neck, agrees well with the crocodile; see the figure of the animal on p. 255. It is not easy, however, to see how this is applicable to the whale, as Prof. Lee supposes. The whale is endowed, indeed, with great strength, as Prof. Lee has shown, but that strength is manifested mainly by the stroke of the tail. ¶ *And sorrow is turned into joy before him.* Marg. *rejoiceth.* The proper meaning of the word here used (תדוץ) is *to dance, to leap, to skip;* and the sense is, that "terror dances before him." It does not refer to the motion of the animal, as if he were brisk and rapid, but it is a poetic expression, as if terror played or pranced along wherever he came. Strength *resided* in his neck, but his approach made terror and alarm play before him wherever he went; that is, produced terror and dread. In his neck is permanent, calm strength; before him, every thing trembles and is agitated. The beauty of the passage lies in this contrast between the strength and firmness which

23 The [1] flakes of his flesh are joined together: they are firm in themselves; they cannot be moved.
24 His heart is as firm as a stone; yea, as heard as a piece of the nether *millstone.*
25 When he raiseth up himself, the mighty are afraid; by reason of breakings they purify themselves.

[1] *fallings.*

---

repose calmly in the neck of the animal, and the consternation which he everywhere produces, causing all to tremble as he approaches. Bochart has well illustrated this from the classic writers.

23. *The flakes of his flesh are joined together.* Marg. *fallings.* The Hebrew word here used means any thing *falling,* or *pendulous,* and the reference here is, probably, to the pendulous parts of the flesh of the animal; the flabby parts; the dew-laps. In animals commonly these parts about the neck and belly are soft, pendulous, and contribute little to their strength. The meaning here is, that in the leviathan, instead of being thus flabby and pendulous, they were compact and firm. This is strikingly true of the crocodile. The belly is, indeed, more soft and penetrable than the other parts of the body, but there is nothing like the soft and pendulous dew-laps of most animals.

24. *His heart is as firm as a stone.* As hard; as solid. Bochart remarks that the word *heart* here is not to be regarded as denoting the *courage* of the animal, as it sometimes does, but the heart literally. The statement occurs in the description of the various parts of the animal, and the object is to show that there was peculiar firmness or solidity in every one of his members. There is peculiar firmness or strength needed in the *hearts* of all animals, to enable them to propel the blood through the arteries of the body; and in an animal of the size of the crocodile, it is easy to see that the heart must be made capable of exerting vast force. But there is no reason to suppose that the affirmation here is made on the supposition that there is need of extraordinary strength in the heart to propel the blood. The doctrine of the circulation of the blood was not then known to mankind, and it is to be presumed that the argument here would be based on what *was* known, or what might be easily observed. The presumption therefore is, that the statement here is based on what had been *seen* of the remarkable compactness and firmness of the heart of the animal here referred to. Probably there was nothing *so* peculiar in the heart of the crocodile that this description would be applicable to that animal alone, but it is such doubtless as would apply to the heart of any animal of extraordinary size and strength. ¶ *Yea, as hard as a piece of the nether* millstone. The mills commonly used in ancient times were hand-mills; see a description of them in the Notes on Matth. xxiv. 41. *Why* the lower stone was the hardest, is not quite apparent. Perhaps a more solid stone might have been chosen for this, because it was supposed that there was more wear on the lower than the upper stone, or because its weight would make the machine more solid and steady.

25. *When he raiseth up himself.* When he rouses himself for an attack or in self-defence. ¶ *The mighty are afraid.* The Vulgate renders this "*angels.*" The meaning is, that he produces alarm on those who are unaccustomed to fear. ¶ *By reason of breakings they purify themselves.* This, though a literal translation, conveys no very clear idea, and this rendering is not necessary. The word rendered "breakings" (שֶׁבֶר) means properly a breaking, breach, puncture; a breaking down, destruction; and then it may mean *a breaking down of the mind, i. e. terror.* This is evidently the meaning here. "By reason of the prostration of their courage, or the crushing of the mind by alarm." The word rendered "purify themselves" (חטא) means in Kal *to miss,* as a mark; to sin; to err. In the form of Hithpael, which occurs here, it means to miss one's way; *to lose*

26 The sword of him that layeth
at him cannot hold; the spear, the
dart, nor the [1] habergeon.
27 He esteemeth iron as straw,
and brass as rotten wood.
28 The arrow cannot make him
flee: sling-stones are turned with
him into stubble.
29 Darts are counted as stubble;
he laugheth at the shaking of a
spear.
30 Sharp [2] stones are under him;
he spreadeth sharp pointed things
upon the mire.

1 or, *breastplate.*
2 *pieces of potsherd.*

---

one's self; and it may refer to the astonishment and terror by which one is led to miss his way in precipitate flight. *Gesenius.* The meaning then is, "They lose themselves from terror." They know not where to turn themselves; they flee away with alarm; see Rosenmüller *in loc.*

26. *The sword of him that layeth at him.* The word "sword" here (חרב) means undoubtedly *harpoon,* or a sharp instrument by which an attempt is made to pierce the skin of the monster. ¶ *Cannot hold.* That is, in the hard skin. It does not penetrate it. ¶ *The spear, the dart.* These were doubtless often used in the attempt to take the animal. The meaning is, that *they* would not hold or stick to the animal. They flew off when hurled at him. ¶ *Nor the habergeon.* Marg. *breastplate.* Noyes, *javelin.* Prof. Lee, *lance.* Vul., *thorax, breastplate.* So the LXX., θώρακα. The word here used (שריה), the same as שריון (1 Sam. xvii. 5, 38; Neh. iv. 16; 2 Chron. xxvi. 14), means properly a *coat of mail,* and is so called from its shining—from שרה, *to shine.* It is not used in the sense of spear or javelin elsewhere, though perhaps it may have that meaning here—denoting a *bright* or *shining* weapon. This agrees best with the connection.

27. *He esteemeth iron as straw.* He regards instruments made of iron and brass as if they were straw or rotten wood. That is, they make no impression on him. This will agree better with the crocodile than any other animal. So hard is his skin, that a musket-ball will not penetrate it; see numerous quotations proving the hardness of the skin of the crocodile, in Bochart.

28. *The arrow.* Heb. "the son of the bow." So Lam. iii. 13, *margin.* This use of the word *son* is common in the Scriptures and in all Oriental poetry. ¶ *Sling-stones.* The sling was early used in war and in hunting, and by skill and practice it could be so employed as to be a formidable weapon; see Judg. xx. 16; 1 Sam. xvii. 40, 49. As one of the weapons of attack on a foe it is mentioned here, though there is no evidence that the sling was ever actually used in endeavouring to destroy the crocodile. The meaning is, that all the common weapons used by men in attacking an enemy had no effect on him. ¶ *Are turned with him into stubble.* Produce no more effect on him than it would to throw stubble at him.

29. *Darts are counted as stubble.* The word rendered "darts" (תותח) occurs nowhere else in the Scriptures. It is from יתח, obs. root, to beat with a club. The word here probably means clubs. Darts and spears are mentioned before, and the object seems to be to enumerate all the usual instruments of attack. The singular is used here with a plural verb in a collective sense.

30. *Sharp stones are under him.* Marg. as in Heb., "*pieces of potsherd.*" The Hebrew word (חדוד, *khăddûdh*), means sharp, pointed; and the phrase here used means *the sharp points of a potsherd,* or broken pieces of earthenware. The reference is, undoubtedly, to the scales of the animal, which were rough and pointed, like the broken pieces of earthenware. This description would not agree with the whale, and indeed will accord with no other animal so well as with the crocodile. The meaning is, that the under parts of his body, with which he rests upon the mire, are made up of sharp, pointed things, like broken

31 He maketh the deep to boil
like a pot: he maketh the sea like
a pot of ointment.
32 He maketh a path to shine
after him; *one* would think the
deep *to be* hoary.
33 Upon earth there is not his
like, who [1] is made without fear.

1 or, *behave themselves with fear.*

---

pottery. ¶ *He spreadeth sharp pointed things upon the mire.* That is, when he rests or stretches himself on the mud or slime of the bank of the river. The word here used and rendered "sharp pointed things" (חָרוּץ) means properly something *cut in;* then something sharpened or pointed; and is used to denote *a threshing sledge;* see this instrument described in Notes on Isa. xxviii. 27, 28; xli. 15. It is not certain, however, that there is any allusion here to that instrument. It is rather to any thing that is rough or pointed, and refers to the lower part of the animal as having this character. The Vulgate renders this, "Beneath him are the rays of the sun, and he reposeth on gold as on clay." Dr. Harris, Dr. Good, and Prof. Lee, suppose it refers to what the animal lies on, meaning that he lies on splinters of rock and broken stone with as much readiness and ease as if it were clay. But the above seems to me to be the true interpretation. It is that of Gesenius, Rosenmüller, and Umbreit. Grotius understands it as meaning that the weapons thrown at him lie around him like broken pieces of pottery.

31. *He maketh the deep to boil like a pot.* In his rapid motion through it. The word "deep" (מְצוּלָה) may refer to any deep place—either of the sea, of a river, or of mire, Ps. lxix. 2. It is applied to the depths of the sea, Jonah ii. 3; Micah vii. 19; but there is nothing in the word that will prevent its application to a large river like the Nile—the usual abode of the crocodile. ¶ *He maketh the sea.* The word "sea" (יָם) is often applied to a large river, like the Nile or the Euphrates; see Notes, Isa. xix. 5. ¶ *Like a pot of ointment.* When it is mixed, or stirred together. Bochart supposes that there is an allusion here to the smell of musk, which it is said the crocodile has, and by which the waters through which he passes seem to be perfumed. But the allusion seems rather to be merely to the fact that the deep is agitated by him when he passes through it, as if it were stirred from the bottom like a pot of ointment.

32. *He maketh a path to shine after him.* This refers doubtless to the white foam of the waters through which he passes. If this were spoken of some monster that commonly resides in the ocean, it would not be unnatural to suppose that it refers to the phosphoric light such as is observed when the waters are agitated, or when a vessel passes rapidly through them. If it refers, however, to the crocodile, the allusion must be understood of the hoary appearance of the Nile or the lake where he is found. ¶ One *would think the deep* to be *hoary.* Homer often speaks of the sea as πολιὴν θάλασσαν—"the hoary sea." So Apollonius, speaking of the Argonauts, Lib. i. 545:

—μακραὶ δ' αἰὲν ἐλευκαίνοντο κέλευθοι—
"the long paths were always white"

So Catullus, in *Epith. Pelei:*

Totaque remigio spumis incanuit unda.

And Ovid, *Epis. Œno:*

—remis eruta canet aqua.

The rapid motion of an aquatic animal through the water will produce the effect here referred to.

33. *Upon earth there is not his like.* Heb., "Upon the dust." The meaning is, that no other animal can be compared with him; or the land does not produce such a monster as this. For size, strength, ferocity, courage, and formidableness, no animal will bear a comparison with him. This can be true only of some such fierce creature as the crocodile. ¶ *Who is made without fear.* Marg. "Or, *behave themselves with fear.*" The meaning is, that he is created not to be afraid; he has no dread of others In this respect he is unlike other ani-

34 He beholdeth all high *things:* he *is* a king over all the children of pride.

---

mals. The LXX. render this, "He is made to be sported with by my angels."

34. *He beholdeth all high* things. That is, he looks down on every thing as inferior to him. ¶ *He* is *a king over all the children of pride.* Referring, by "the children of pride," to the animals that are bold, proud, courageous—as the lion, the panther, &c. The lion is often spoken of as "the king of the forest," or "the king of beasts," and in a similar sense the leviathan is here spoken of as at the head of the animal creation. He is afraid of none of them; he is subdued by none of them; he is the prey of none of them. The whole argument, therefore, closes with this statement, that he is at the head of the animal creation; and it was by this magnificent description of the power of the creatures which God had made, that it was intended to impress the mind of Job with a sense of the majesty and power of the Creator. It had the effect. He was overawed with a conviction of the greatness of God, and he saw how wrong it had been for him to presume to call in question the justice, or sit in judgment on the doings, of such a Being. God did not, indeed, go into an examination of the various points which had been the subject of controversy; he did not explain the nature of his moral administration so as to relieve the mind from perplexity; but he evidently meant to leave the impression that he was vast and incomprehensible in his government, infinite in power, and had a right to dispose of his creation as he pleased. No one can doubt that God *could* with infinite ease have so explained the nature of his administration as to free the mind from perplexity, and so as to have resolved the difficulties which hung over the various subjects which had come into debate between Job and his friends. *Why* he did not do this, is nowhere stated, and can only be the subject of conjecture. It is possible, however, that the following suggestions may do something to show the reasons why this was not done. (1.) We are to remember the early period of the world when these transactions occurred, and when this book was composed. It was in the infancy of society, and when little light had gleamed on the human mind in regard to questions of morals and religion. (2.) In that state of things, it is not probable that either Job or his friends would have been able to comprehend the principles in accordance with which the wicked are permitted to flourish and the righteous are so much afflicted, if they had been stated. Much higher knowledge than they then possessed about the future world was necessary to understand the subject which then agitated their minds. It could not have been done without a very decided reference to the future state, where all these inequalities are to be removed. (3.) It has been the general plan of God to communicate knowledge by degrees; to impart it when men have had full demonstration of their own imbecility, and when they feel their need of divine teaching; and to reserve the great truths of religion for an advanced period of the world. In accordance with this arrangement, God has been pleased to keep in reserve, from age to age, certain great and momentous truths, and such as were particularly adapted to throw light on the subjects of discussion between Job and his friends. They are the truths pertaining to the resurrection of the body; the retributions of the day of judgment; the glories of heaven and the woes of hell, where all the inequalities of the present state may receive their final and equal adjustment. These great truths were reserved for the triumph and glory of Christianity; and to have stated them in the time of Job, would have been to have anticipated the most important revelations of that system. The truths of which *we* are now in possession would have relieved much of the perplexity then felt, and solved most of those questions; but the world was not then in the proper state for their revelation. (4.) It was a very important lesson to be taught

CHAPTER XLII.

ANALYSIS OF THE CHAPTER.

This closing chapter of the book is composed partly of poetry and partly of prose. The first part comprises the first six verses, and consists of the confession of Job that he had erred. He is convinced by the reasoning of the Almighty that all things are under his control, and that none of his purposes can be hindered (ver. 2, *margin*); he acknowledges that he himself had uttered things which he did not understand, and had undertaken the discussion of things which were too high for him, and deserved the reproof of having "darkened counsel by words without knowledge," ver. 3; he confesses his error in having with so bold and irreverent a spirit called on God to enter on a trial, and having wished to argue his case himself before God (see Notes on ver. 4); he says that he now has new views of the Almighty—as different from those which he formerly had, as was that between a thing of which a man had only a distant rumour and what he saw, ver. 5; and now having "seen" God, he saw himself to be vile, and repented in dust and ashes. Thus the effect which it was desired to produce on Job was accomplished. The improprieties in which he had indulged were rebuked; he was brought to true repentance, and showed that he was truly a good man, and that, notwithstanding all that he had said under excited feeling, and in the bitterness of his anguish, he had at heart a profound reverence for God, and supreme submission to his will.

The second part of the chapter (ver. 7—16) is in prose, and contains the statement of the result of the whole trial. The Almighty pronounces the friends of Job to be in error in the opinions which they had maintained respecting his dispensations, and decides in favour of Job in the controversy, ver. 7. This decision involves the conclusion that trials in this life are *not* certain indications of character; that the fact that a man suffers much is no evidence that he is eminently wicked; and that prosperity is no clear proof that a man is the object of the divine favour. As the friends of Job had defended many sentiments which were erroneous, and manifested a spirit eminently wrong, it was adjudged that it was proper that a sacrifice should be made in acknowledgment of their error; and as they had done much to pain and grieve the heart of Job; and as some act of deference and respect was due to him from them, they are commanded to take a sacrifice of seven bullocks and seven rams, and to go to Job, that he might offer the sacrifice, and intercede for them, ver. 8, 9. The account of the returning prosperity of Job completes the book, ver. 10—16. He is restored to double his former possessions; is honoured with the returning affection of all his kindred; is consoled by their sympathy and enriched with their offerings; is blessed with a second family as numerous as the former; lives till he sees a numerous and happy posterity; and dies at last honoured and full of days.

THEN Job answered the LORD and said,

men, to bow with submission to a sovereign God, without knowing the reason of his doings. No lesson, perhaps, could be learned of higher value than this. To a proud, self-confident, philosophic mind, a mind prone to rely on its own resources, and trust to its own deductions, it was of the highest importance to inculcate the duty of submission to *will* and to *sovereignty*. This is a lesson which we often have to learn in life, and which almost all the trying dispensations of Providence are fitted to teach us. It is not because God *has* no reason for what he does; it is not because he intends we shall never *know* the reason; but it is because it is our *duty* to bow with submission to his will, and to acquiesce in his right to reign, even when we cannot see the reason of his doings. Could we *reason it out*, and then submit *because* we saw the reason, our submission would not be to our Maker's pleasure, but to the deductions of our own minds. Hence, all along, he so deals with man, by concealing the reason of his doings, as to bring him to submission to his authority, and to humble all human pride. To this termination all the reasonings of the Almighty in this book are conducted; and after the exhibition of his power in the tempest, after his sublime description of his own works, after his appeal to the numerous things which are in fact incomprehensible by man, we feel that God IS GREAT—that it is presumptuous in man to sit in judgment on his works—and that the mind, no matter what he does, should bow before him with profound veneration and silence. These are the great lessons which we are every day called to learn in the actual dispensations of his providence; and the *arguments* for these lessons were never elsewhere stated with so much power and sublimity as in the closing chapters of the book of Job. *We* have the light of the Christian religion; we can look into eternity, and see how the inequalities of the present order of things can be adjusted there; and we have sources of consolation which neither Job nor his friends enjoyed; but still, with all this light, there are numerous cases where we are required to bow, not because we see the *reason* of the divine dealings, but because such is the *will* of God. To us, in such circumstances, this argument of the Almighty is adapted to teach the most salutary lessons.

CHAPTER XLII.

2. *I know that thou canst do every*

2 I know that thou [a] canst do
every *thing*, and *that* no thought, [1]
can be withholden from thee.
3 Who [b] *is* he that hideth counsel
without knowledge? therefore
have I uttered that I understood
not; things too wonderful [c] for me,
which I knew not.
4 Hear, I beseech thee, and I
will speak: I [d] will demand of
thee, and declare thou unto me.

a Ge.18.14; Is.43.13; Mat.19.26.
1 or, *of thine can be hindered.* b chap.38.2,3.
c Ps.131.1; 139.6. d chap.40.7.

---

thing. This is said by Job in view of what had been declared by the Almighty in the previous chapters. It is an acknowledgment that God was omnipotent, and that man ought to be submissive, under the putting forth of his infinite power. One great object of the address of the Almighty was to convince Job of his majesty, and that object was fully accomplished. ¶ *And that no thought.* No purpose or plan of thine. God was able to execute all his designs. ¶ *Can be withholden from thee.* Marg. "or, *of thine can be hindered.*" Literally, *cut off*—בצר. The word, however, means also *to cut off access to*, and then to prevent, hinder, restrain. This is its meaning here; so Gen. xi. 6, "Nothing will be restrained (יבצר) from them, which they have imagined to do."

3. *Who is he that hideth counsel without knowledge?* This is repeated from chap. xxxviii. 2. As used there these are the words of the Almighty, uttered as a reproof of Job for the manner in which he had undertaken to explain the dealings of God; see Notes on that verse. As repeated here by Job, they are an acknowledgment of the truth of what is there implied, that *he* had been guilty of hiding counsel in this manner, and the repetition here is a part of his confession. He acknowledges that he *had* entertained and expressed such views of God as were in fact clothing the whole subject in darkness instead of explaining it. The meaning is, "Who indeed is it, as thou saidst, that undertakes to judge of great and profound purposes without knowledge? *I am that presumptuous man?*" *Ilgen.* ¶ *Therefore have I uttered that I understood not.* I have pronounced an opinion on subjects altogether too profound for my comprehension. This is the language of true humility and penitence, and shows that Job had at heart a profound veneration for God, however much he had been led away by the severity of his sufferings to give vent to improper expressions. It is no uncommon thing for even good men to be brought to see that they have spoken presumptuously of God, and have engaged, in discussions and ventured to pronounce opinions on matters pertaining to the divine administration, that were wholly beyond their comprehension.

4. *Hear, I beseech thee, and I will speak.* This is the language of humble, docile submission. On former occasions he had spoken confidently and boldly of God; he had called in question the equity of his dealings with him; he had demanded that he might be permitted to carry his cause before him, and argue it there himself; Notes, chap. xiii. 3, 20—22. Now he is wholly changed. His is the submissive language of a docile child, and he begs to be permitted to sit down before God, and humbly to inquire of *him* what was truth. *This is true religion.* ¶ *I will demand of thee.* Or rather, "I will *ask* of thee." The word "demand" implies more than there is of necessity in the original word (שאל). That means simply to *ask*, and it may be done with the deepest humility and desire of instruction. That was now the temper of Job. ¶ *And declare thou unto me.* Job was not now disposed to debate the matter, or to enter into a controversy with God. He was willing to sit down and receive instruction from God, and earnestly desired that he would *teach* him of his ways. It should be added, that very respectable critics suppose that in this verse Job designs to make confession of the impropriety of his language on former occasions, in the presumptuous and irreverent manner in which he had demanded a trial of argument with God. It would

5 I have heard of thee by the hearing of the ear: but now mine eye seeth thee.

6 Wherefore [a] I abhor *myself*, and repent in dust and ashes.[b]

a Ez.9.4; chap.40.4; Ps.51 17; Je.31.19; Ja.4.10. b Da.9.3; Mat.11.21.

then require to be rendered as a quotation from his own words formerly.

> "I have indeed uttered what I understood not,
> Things too wonderful for me, which I know not,
> (When I said) Hear now, I will speak,
> I will demand of thee, and do thou teach me."

This is adopted by Umbreit, and has much in its favour that is plausible; but on the whole the usual interpretation seems to be most simple and proper.

5. *I have heard of thee by the hearing of the ear.* Referring to the indistinct views which we have of any thing by merely hearing of it, compared with the clear apprehension which is furnished by sight. Job had had such views of God as one may obtain by being told of him; he now had such views as are furnished by the sight. The meaning is, that his views of God before were dark and obscure. ¶ *But now mine eye seeth thee.* We are not to suppose that Job means to say that he actually *saw* God, but that his apprehensions of him were clear and bright *as if* he did. There is no evidence that God appeared to Job in any visible form. He is said, indeed, to have spoken from the whirlwind, but no visible manifestation of JEHOVAH is mentioned.

6. *Wherefore I abhor* myself. I see that I am a sinner to be loathed and abhorred. Job, though he did not claim to be perfect, had yet unquestionably been unduly exalted with the conception of his own righteousness, and in the zeal of his argument, and under the excitement of his feelings when reproached by his friends, had indulged in indefensible language respecting his own integrity. He now saw the error and folly of this, and desired to take the lowest place of humiliation. Compared with a pure and holy God, he saw that he was utterly vile and loathsome, and was not unwilling now to confess it. ¶ *And repent.* Of the spirit which I have evinced; of the language used in self-vindication; of the manner in which I have spoken of God. Of the general sentiments which he had maintained in regard to the divine administration as contrasted with those of his friends he had no occasion to repent, for they were correct (ver. 8), nor had he occasion to repent *as if* he had never been a true penitent or a pious man. But he now saw that in the spirit which he had evinced under his afflictions, and in his argument, there was much to regret; and he doubtless saw that there had been much in his former life which had furnished occasion for bringing these trials upon him, over which he ought now to mourn. ¶ *In dust and ashes.* In the most lowly manner, and with the most expressive symbols of humiliation. It was customary in times of grief, whether in view of sin or from calamity, to sit down in ashes (see Notes, chap. ii. 8; comp. Dan. ix. 3; Jonah iii. 6; Matth. xi. 21); or on such an occasion the sufferer and the penitent would strew ashes over himself; comp. Isa. lviii. 5. The philosophy of this was—like the custom of wearing *black* for mourning apparel—that the external appearance ought to correspond with the internal emotions, and that deep sorrow would be appropriately expressed by disfiguring the outward aspect as much as possible. The sense here is, that Job meant to give expression to the profoundest and sincerest feelings of penitence for his sins. From this effect produced on his mind by the address of the Almighty, we may learn the following lessons: (1.) That a correct view of the character and presence of God is adapted to produce humility and penitence; comp. chap. xl. 4, 5 This effect was produced on the mind of Peter when, astonished by a miracle wrought by the Saviour which none but a divine being could have wrought, he said, "Depart from me, for I am a sinful man, O Lord;" Luke v. 8. The same effect was produced on the mind of

7 And it was *so*, that after the LORD had spoken these words unto Job, the LORD said to Eliphaz the Temanite, My wrath is kindled against thee and against thy two friends: for ye have not spoken of me [a] *the thing that* is right, as my servant Job *hath*.

a Ps.51.4.

Isaiah after he had seen Jehovah of Hosts in the temple: "Then said I, Wo is me, for I am undone; because I am a man of unclean lips, and I dwell in the midst of a people of unclean lips; for mine eyes have seen the king, the Lord of Hosts;" Isa. vi. 5. No man can have any elevated views of his own importance or purity, who has right apprehensions of the holiness of his Creator. (2.) Such a view of the presence of God will produce what no *argument* can in causing penitence and humility. The friends of Job had reasoned with him in vain to secure just this state of mind; they had endeavoured to convince him that he was a great sinner, and *ought* to exercise repentance. But he met argument with argument; and all their arguments, denunciations, and appeals, made no impression on his mind. When, however, God manifested himself to him, he was melted into contrition, and was ready to make the most penitent and humble confession. So it is now. The arguments of a preacher or a friend often make no impression on the mind of a sinner. He can guard himself against them. He can meet argument with argument, or can coolly turn the ear away. But he has no such power to resist God, and when *he* manifests himself to the soul, the heart is subdued, and the proud and self-confident unbeliever becomes humbled, and sues for mercy. (3.) A good man will be willing to confess that he is vile, when he has any clear views of God. He will be so affected with a sense of the majesty and holiness of his Maker, that he will be overwhelmed with a sense of his own unworthiness. (4.) The most holy men may have occasion to repent of their presumptuous manner of speaking of God. We all err in the same way in which Job did. We reason about God with irreverence; we speak of his government as if we could comprehend it; we discourse of him as if he were an equal; and when we come to have any just views of him, we see that there has been much improper boldness, much self-confidence, much irreverence of thought and manner, in our estimation of the divine wisdom and plans. The bitter experience of Job should lead us to the utmost carefulness in the manner in which we speak of our Maker.

7. *And it was* so, *that after the* LORD *had spoken these words unto Job.* Had the matter been left according to the record in ver. 6, a wholly erroneous impression would have been made. Job was overwhelmed with the conviction of his guilt, and had nothing been said to his friends, the impression would have been that he was wholly in the wrong. It was important, therefore, and was indeed essential to the plan of the book, that the divine judgment should be pronounced on the conduct of his three friends. ¶ *The* LORD *said to Eliphaz the Temanite.* Eliphaz had been uniformly first in the argument with Job, and hence he is particularly addressed here. He seems to have been the most aged and respectable of the three friends, and in fact the speeches of the others are often a mere echo of his. ¶ *My wrath is kindled.* Wrath, or anger, is often represented as enkindled, or burning. ¶ *For ye have not spoken of me* the thing that is *right, as my servant Job* hath. This must be understood *comparatively*. God did not approve of *all* that Job had said, but the meaning is, that his general views of his government were just. The main position which he had defended in contradistinction from his friends was correct, for his arguments tended to vindicate the divine character, and to uphold the divine government. It is to be remembered, also, as Bouiller has remarked, that there was a great difference in the circumstances of Job and the three friends—circumstances

8 Therefore take unto you now [a] seven bullocks and seven rams, and go to my servant Job, and offer up for yourselves a burnt offering; and my servant Job shall pray [b] for you; for [1] him will I accept: lest I deal with you *after your* folly, in that ye have not spoken of me *the thing which is* right, like my servant Job.

a Nu.23.1. *b* Ja.5.16; 1 John 5.16.

1 *his face,* or, *person,* 1 Sa.25.35; Mal.1.8.

modifying the degrees of blameworthiness chargeable to each. Job uttered indeed, some improper sentiments about God and his government; he expressed himself with irreverence and impatience; he used a language of boldness and complaint wholly improper, but this was done in the agony of mental and bodily suffering, and when provoked by the severe and improper charges of hypocrisy brought by his friends. What *they* said, on the contrary, was unprovoked. It was when they were free from suffering, and when they were urged to it by no severity of trial. It was, moreover, when every consideration required them to express the language of condolence, and to comfort a suffering friend.

8. *Therefore take unto you.* Or, *for* yourselves. ¶ *Seven bullocks and seven rams.* The number *seven* was a common number in offering animals for sacrifice; see Lev. xxiii. 18; Num. xxix. 32. It was not a number, however, confined at all to Jewish sacrifices, for we find that Balaam gave the direction to Balak, king of Moab, to prepare just this number for sacrifice. "And Balaam said unto Balak, Build me here seven altars, and prepare me here seven oxen and seven rams;" Num. xxiii. 1, 29. The number *seven* was early regarded as a perfect number, and it was probably with reference to this that that number of victims was selected, with an intention of offering a sacrifice that would be complete or perfect. ¶ *And go to my servant Job.* An acknowledgment of his superiority. It is probably to be understood, also, that Job would act as the officiating priest in offering up the sacrifice. It is observable that no allusion is made in this book to the priestly office, and the conclusion is obvious that the scene is laid before the institution of that office among the Jews; comp. Notes on chap. i. 5. ¶ *And offer up for yourselves.* That is, by the aid of Job. They were to make the offering, though Job was evidently to be the officiating priest. ¶ *A burnt-offering;* Notes, chap. i. 5. ¶ *And my servant Job shall pray for you.* In connection with the offering, or as the officiating priest. This is a beautiful instance of the nature and propriety of intercession for others. Job was a holy man; his prayers would be acceptable to God, and his friends were permitted to avail themselves of his powerful intercession in their behalf. It is also an instance showing the nature of the patriarchal worship. It did not consist merely in offering sacrifices. Prayer was to be connected *with* sacrifices, nor is there any evidence that bloody offerings were regarded as available in securing acceptance with God, except in connection with fervent prayer. It is also an instance showing the nature of the patriarchal *piety.* It was *presumed* that Job would be ready to do this, and would not hesitate thus to pray for his "friends." Yet it could not be forgotten how much they had wounded his feelings; how severe had been their reproaches; nor how confidently they had maintained that he was an eminently bad man. But it was presumed now that Job would be ready to forgive all this; to welcome his friends to a participation in the same act of worship with him, and to pray for them that their sins might be forgiven. Such is religion, alike in the patriarchal age and under the gospel, prompting us to be ready to forgive those who have pained or injured us, and making us ready to pray that God would pardon and bless them. ¶ *For him will I accept.* Marg. *his face,* or *person.* So the Hebrew. So in Gen. xix. 21 (*marg.*) comp. Deut. xxviii. 50. The word *face* is thus used to denote the *person,* or man. The meaning is, that Job

9 So Eliphaz the Temanite, and
Bildad the Shuhite, and Zophar the
Naamathite, went and did according as the LORD commanded them: the LORD [a] also accepted [1] Job.
10 And the LORD turned [b] the
captivity of Job, when he prayed for his friends: also the LORD [2] gave Job twice as much as he had before.
11 Then came there unto him
all [c] his brethren, and all his sisters, and all they that had been of his acquaintance before, and did eat bread with him in his house; and they bemoaned him, and comforted him over all the evil that the LORD had brought upon him: every man also gave him a piece of money, and every one an ear-ring of gold.

a Pr.3.11, 12. 1 *the face of Job.* b Ge.20.17; Ps.14.7,126.1. 2 *addeth all that* had been to *Job unto the double.* c chap.19.13.

was so holy and upright that God would regard his prayers. ¶ *Lest I deal with you* after your *folly.* As their folly had deserved. There is particular reference here to the sentiments which they had advanced respecting the divine character and government.

9. *The* LORD *also accepted Job.* Marg. as in ver. 8, *the face of.* The meaning is, that he accepted his prayers and offerings in behalf of his friends.

10. *And the* LORD *turned the captivity of Job.* Restored him to his former prosperity. The language is taken from restoration to country and home after having been a captive in a foreign land. This language is often applied in the Scriptures to the return of the Jews from their captivity in Babylon, and some writers have made use of it as an argument to show that Job lived *after* that event. But this conclusion is unwarranted. The language is so general that it might be taken from the return from *any* captivity, and is such as would naturally be employed in the early periods of the world to denote restoration from calamity. It was common in the earliest ages to convey captives in war to the land of the conqueror, and thus make a land desolate by the removal of its inhabitants; and it would be natural to use the language expressive of their return to denote a restoration from *any* great calamity to former privileges and comforts. Such is undoubtedly its meaning as applied to the case of Job. He was restored from his series of protracted trials to a state of prosperity. ¶ *When he prayed for his friends.* Or after he had prayed for his friends. It is not implied of necessity that his praying for them had any particular effect in restoring his prosperity. ¶ *Also the* LORD *gave Job twice as much as he had before.* Marg. *added all that* had been to *Job unto the double.* The margin is a literal translation, but the meaning is the same. It is not to be understood that this occurred at once—for many of these blessings were bestowed gradually. Nor are we to understand it in every respect literally—for he had the same number of sons and daughters as before; but it is a general declaration, and was true in all essential respects.

11. *Then came there unto him all his brethren,* &c. It seems remarkable that none of these friends came near to him during his afflictions, and especially that his *sisters* should not have been with him to sympathize with him. But it was one of the bitter sources of his affliction, and one of the grounds of his complaint, that in his trials his kindred stood aloof from him; so in chap. xix. 13, 14, he says, "He hath put my brethren far from me, and mine acquaintance are verily estranged from me. My kinsfolk have failed, and my familiar friends have forgotten me." It is not easy to account for this. It may have been, however, that a part were kept from showing any sympathy, in accordance with the general fact that there are always professed friends, and sometimes kindred, who forsake a man in affliction; and that a part regarded him as abandoned by God, and forsook him on that account—

from a mistaken view of what they regarded as duty, that they ought to forsake one whom God had forsaken. When his calamities had passed by, however, and he again enjoyed the tokens of the divine favour, all returned to him full of condolence and kindness; part, probably, because friends always cluster around one who comes out of calamity and rises again to honour, and the other portion because they supposed that as *God* regarded him now with approbation, it was proper for *them* to do it also. A man who has been unfortunate, and who is visited with returning prosperity, never lacks friends. The rising sun reveals many friends that darkness had driven away, or brings to light many—real or professed—who were concealed at midnight. ¶ *And did eat bread with him in his house.* An ancient token of friendship and affection; comp. Ps. xli. 9; Prov. ix. 5; xxiii. 6; Jer. xli. 1. ¶ *And every man also gave him a piece of money.* This is probably one of the earliest instances in which *money* is mentioned in history. It is, of course, impossible now to determine the form or value of the "piece of money" here referred to. The Hebrew word (קְשִׂיטָה, *kesitah*), occurs only in this place and in Gen. xxxiii. 19, where it is rendered "pieces of money," and in Josh. xxiv. 32, where it is rendered "pieces of silver." It is evident, therefore, that it was one of the earliest names given to coin, and its use here is an argument that the book of Job is of very early origin. Had it been composed at a later age, the word *shekel*, or some word in common use to denote money, would have been used. The Vulgate here renders the word *ovem*, a sheep; the LXX. in like manner, *ἀμνάδα, a lamb;* and so also the Chaldee. In the margin, in both the other places where the word occurs (Gen. xxxiii. 19; Josh. xxiv. 32), it is also rendered *lambs*. The reason why it is so rendered is unknown. It may have been supposed that in early times a sheep or lamb having something like a fixed value, might have been the standard by which to estimate the value of other things; but there is nothing in the etymology of the word to support this interpretation. The word in Arabic (*kasat*) means to divide out equally, to measure; and the Hebrew word probably had some such signification, denoting that which was measured or weighed out, and hence became the name of a certain *weight* or *amount* of money. It is altogether probable that the first money consisted of a certain amount of the precious metals *weighed out*, without being *coined* in any way. It is not an improbable supposition, however, that the figure of a sheep or lamb was the first figure stamped on coins, and this may be the reason why the word here used was rendered in this manner in the ancient versions. On the meaning of the word, Bochart may be consulted, *Hieroz.* P. i. Lib. c. xliii. pp. 433—437; Rosenmüller on Gen. xxxiii. 19; Schultens *in loco;* and the following work in Ugolin's *Thes. Antiq. Sacr.* Tom. xxviii., *Otthonis Sperlingii Diss. de nummis non cusis*, pp. 251—253, 298—306. The arguments of Bochart to prove that this word denotes a piece of money, and not a lamb, as it is rendered by the Vulgate, the LXX. the Syriac, the Arabic, and by Onkelos, are briefly, (1.) That in more than an hundred places where reference is made in the Scriptures to a lamb or a sheep, this word is not used. Other words are constantly employed. (2.) The testimony of the Rabbins is uniform that it denotes a piece of money. Rabbi Akiba says that when he travelled into Africa he found there a coin which they called *kesita*. So R. Solomon, and Levi Ben Gerson, in their commentaries, and Kimchi, Pomarius, and Aquinas, in their Lexicons. (3.) The authority of the Masorites in relation to the Hebrew word is the same. According to Bochart the word is the same as קְשָׁט, *kashat* or קֹשֶׁט, *koshet*, changing שׂ for שׁ. The word means true, sincere, Ps. lx. 6; Prov. xxii. 21. According to this, the name was given to the coin because it was made of pure metal—unadulterated silver or gold. See this argument at length in Bochart.

12 So [a] the LORD blessed the latter end of Job more than his beginning: for he had [b] fourteen thousand sheep, and six thousand camels, and a thousand yoke of oxen, and a thousand she-asses.

13 He had also seven sons and three daughters.

a De.8.16; chap. 8.7; Ja.5.11.

b chap.1.3.

(4.) The feminine form of the noun used here shows that it does not mean a lamb—it being wholly improbable that the friends of Job would send him ewe lambs only. (5.) In the early times of the patriarchs—as early as the time of Jacob—money was in common use, and the affairs of merchandise were conducted by that as a medium; Gen. xvii. 12, 13; xlvii. 16. (6.) The statement in Acts vii. 16, leads to the supposition that *money* is referred to by the word as used in Gen. xxxiii 19. If, as is there supposed, the purchase of the same field is referred to in Gen. xxiii. 16, and xxiii. 19, then it is clear that money is referred to by the word. In Gen. xxiii. 16 it is said that Abraham paid for the field of Ephron in Macpelah "four hundred shekels of silver, current money with the merchant." And if the same purchase is referred to in both these places, then by a comparison of the two, it appears that the *kesita* was heavier than the shekel, and contained about four shekels. It is not easy, however, to determine its value. ¶ *And every one an ear-ring of gold.* The word rendered "ear-ring" (נזם) may mean a ring for the nose (Gen. xxiv. 47; Isa. iii. 21; Prov. xi. 22; Hos. ii. 13), as well as for the ear, Gen. xxxv. 4. The word *ring* would better express the sense here without specifying its particular use; comp. Judg. viii. 24, 25; Prov. xxv. 12. Ornaments of this kind were much worn by the ancients (comp. Isa. iii; Gen. xxiv. 22), and a contribution of these from each one of the friends of Job would constitute a valuable property; comp. Ex. xxxii. 2, 3. It was not uncommon for friends thus to bring presents to one who was restored from great calamity. See the case of Hezekiah, 2 Chron. xxxii. 23.

12. *So the* LORD *blessed the latter end of Job.* To wit, by giving him double what he had possessed before his calamities came upon him; see ver. 10. ¶ *For he had fourteen thousand sheep,* &c. The possessions which are here enumerated are in each instance just twice as much as he possessed in the early part of his life. In regard to their value, and the rank in society which they indicated, see Notes on chap. i. 3. The only thing which is omitted here, and which it is not said was doubled, was his "household," or "husbandry" (chap. i. 3, *margin*), but it is evident that this must have been increased in a corresponding manner to have enabled him to keep and maintain such flocks and herds. We are not to suppose that these were granted to him at once, but as he lived an hundred and forty years after his afflictions, he had ample time to accumulate this property.

13. *He had also seven sons and three daughters.* The same number which he had before his trials. Nothing is said of his wife, or whether these children were, or were not, by a second marriage. The last mention that is made of his wife is in chap. xix. 17, where he says that "his breath was strange to his wife, though he entreated her for the children's sake of his own body." The character of this woman does not appear to have been such as to have deserved farther notice than the fact, that she contributed greatly to increase the calamities of her husband. It falls in with the design of the book to notice her only in this respect, and having done this, the sacred writer makes no farther reference to her. The strong presumption is, that the second family of children was by a second marriage. See Prof. Lee on Job, p. 26. It would not, however, have fallen in with the usual manner in which *a wife* is mentioned in the Scriptures, to represent her removal as *in any circumstances* a felicitous event, and, as it could have been represented in no other light, if it had

14 And he called the name of the first Jemima; and the name of the second, Kezia; and the name of the third, Keren-happuch.

---

actually occurred, it is delicately passed over in silence. Even under all these circumstances—with a former wife who was impious and unfeeling; who served only to aggravate the woes of her holy and much afflicted husband; who saw him pass through his trials without sympathy and compassion—a second marriage is not mentioned as a desirable event, nor is it referred to as one of the grounds on which Job could felicitate himself on his return to prosperity. The children are mentioned; the whole reference to the second marriage relation, if it occurred, is delicately passed over. Under no circumstances would the sacred penman mention it as an event laying the ground for felicitation.

14. *And he called the name of the first, Jemima.* It is remarkable that in the former account of the family of Job, the names of none of his children are mentioned, and in this account the names of the daughters only are designated. *Why* the names of the daughters are here specified, is not intimated. They are significant, and they are *so* mentioned as to show that they contributed greatly to the happiness of Job on the return of his prosperity, and were among the chief blessings which gladdened his old age. The name *Jemima* (ימימה) is rendered by the Vulgate *Diem,* and by the LXX. Ἡμέραν, *Day.* The Chaldee adds this remark: "He gave her the name Jemima, because her beauty was like the day." The Vulgate, Septuagint, and Chaldee, evidently regarded the name as derived from יום, *yom,* day, and this is the most natural and obvious derivation. The name thus conferred would indicate that Job had now emerged from the *night* of affliction, and that returning light shone again on his tabernacle. It was usual in the earliest periods to bestow names because they were significant of returning prosperity (see Gen. iv. 25), or because they indicated hope of what would be in their time (Gen. v. 29), or because they were a pledge of some permanent tokens of the divine favour; see Notes on Isa. viii. 18. Thomas Roe remarks (*Travels,* 425), that among the Persians it is common to give names to their daughters derived from spices, unguents, pearls, and precious stones, or any thing which is regarded as beautiful or valuable. See Rosenmüller, *Alte u. neue Morgenland,* No. 779. ¶ *And the name of the second Kezia.* The name *Kezia* (קציעה) means *cassia,* a bark resembling cinnamon, but less aromatic. *Gesenius.* It grew in Arabia, and was used as a perfume. The Chaldee Paraphrast explains this as meaning that he gave her this name because "she was as precious as cassia." Cassia is mentioned in Ps. xlv. 8. as among the precious perfumes. "All thy garments smell of myrrh, and aloes, and cassia." The agreeableness or pleasantness of the perfume was the reason why the name was chosen to be given to a daughter. ¶ *And the name of the third, Keren-happuch.* Properly, "*horn of stibium.*" The *stibium* (פוך, *puch*), was a paint or dye made originally, it is supposed, from sea-weed, and afterwards from antimony, with which females tinged their eye-lashes; see Notes on Isa. liv. 11. It was esteemed as an ornament of great beauty, chiefly because it served to make the eye appear larger. Large eyes are considered in the East as a mark of beauty, and the painting of black borders around them gives them an enlarged appearance. It is remarkable that this species of ornament was known so early as the time of Job, and this is one of the cases, constantly occurring in the East, showing that fashions there do not change. It is also remarkable that the fact of painting in this manner should have been considered so respectable as to be incorporated into the name of a daughter; and this shows that there was no attempt at *concealing* the habit. This also accords with the customs which prevail still in the East. With us, the materials

15 And in all the land were no women found *so* fair as the daughters of Job; and their father gave them inheritance among their brethren.

16 After this lived Job an hun-

and instruments of personal adorning are kept in the back-ground, but the Orientals obtrude them constantly on the attention, as objects adapted to suggest agreeable ideas. The *process* of painting the eye is described by a recent traveller to be this: "The eye is closed, and a small ebony rod

Painted Face.

smeared with the composition is squeezed between the lids so as to tinge the edges with the colour. This is considered to add greatly to the brilliancy and power of the eye, and to deepen the effect of the long black eye-lashes of which the Orientals are proud. The same drug is employed on their eye-brows; used thus, it is

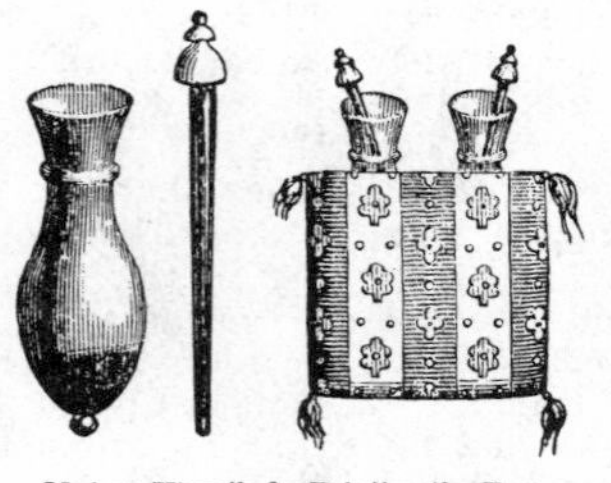

Modern Utensils for Painting the Eyes.

intended to elongate, not to elevate the arc, so that the inner extremities are usually represented as meeting between the eyes. To Europeans the effect is at first seldom pleasing; but it soon becomes so." The foregoing cuts give a representation of the vessels of stibium now in use.

15. *And their father gave them inheritance among their brethren.* This is mentioned as a proof of his special regard, and is also recorded because it was not common. Among the Hebrews the daughter inherited only in the case where there was no son, Num. xxvii. 8. The property was divided equally among the sons, with the exception that the eldest received a double portion; see Jahn's *Bib. Arch.* § 168. This custom, prevailing still extensively in the East, it seems existed in the time of Job, and it is mentioned as a remarkable circumstance that he made his daughters heirs to his property with their brothers. It would also be rather implied in the passage before us that they were equal heirs.

16. *After this Job lived an hundred and forty years.* As his age at the time his calamities commenced is not mentioned, it is of course impossible to determine how old he was when he died. The LXX., however, have undertaken to determine this, but on what authority is unknown. They render this verse, "And Job lived after this affliction an hundred and seventy years: so that all the years that he lived were two hundred and forty." According to this, his age would have been seventy when his afflictions came upon him; but this is a mere conjecture. Why the authors of that version have added thirty years to the time which he lived after his calamities, making it an hundred and seventy instead of an hundred and forty as it is in the Hebrew text, is unknown. The supposition that he was about seventy years of age when his calamities came upon him, is not an unreasonable one. He had a family of ten children, and his sons were

dred and forty years, and saw his sons, and his sons' sons, *even* four generations.

17 So Job died, [a] *being* old and full of days.

a chap. 5.26.

grown so as to have families of their own, chap. i. 4. It should be remembered, also, that in the patriarchal times, when men lived to a great age, marriages did not occur at so early a period of life as they do now. In this book, also, though the age of Job is not mentioned, yet the uniform representation of him is that of a man of mature years; of large experience and extended observation; of one who had enjoyed high honour and a wide reputation as a sage and a magistrate; and when these circumstances are taken into the account, the supposition of the translators of the Septuagint, that he was seventy years old when his afflictions commenced, is not improbable. If so, his age at his death was two hundred and ten years. The age to which he lived is mentioned as remarkable, and was evidently somewhat extraordinary. It is not proper, therefore, to assume that this was the ordinary length of human life at that time, though it would be equally improper to suppose that there was any thing like miracle in the case. The fair interpretation is, that he reached the period of old age which was then deemed most honourable; that he was permitted to arrive at what was then regarded as the outer limit of human life; and if this be so, it is not difficult to determine *about* the time when he lived. The length of human life, after the flood, suffered a somewhat regular decline, until, in the time of Moses, it was fixed at about threescore years and ten, Ps. xc. 10. The following instances will show the regularity of the decline, and enable us, with some degree of probability, to determine the period of the world in which Job lived. Noah lived 950 years; Shem, his son, 600; Arphaxad, his son, 438 years; Salah, 433 years; Eber, 464; Peleg, 239; Reu, 239; Serug, 230; Nahor, 248; Terah, 205; Abraham, 175; Isaac, 180; Jacob, 147; Joseph, 110; Moses, 120; Joshua, 110. Supposing, then, the age of Job to have been somewhat unusual and extraordinary, it would fall in with the period somewhere in the time between Terah and Jacob; and if so, he was probably contemporary with the most distinguished of the patriarchs. ¶ *And saw his sons*, &c. To see one's posterity advancing in years and honour, and extending themselves in the earth, was regarded as a signal honour and a proof of the divine favour in the early ages. Gen. xlviii. 11, "And Israel said unto Joseph, I had not thought to see thy face; and lo, God hath also showed me thy seed." Prov. xvii. 6, "Children's children are the crown of old men." Ps. cxxviii. 6, "Yea, thou shalt see thy children's children;" comp. Ps. cxxvii. 5; Gen. xii. 2; xvii. 5, 6; Job v. 25; and Notes on Isa. liii. 10.

17. *So Job died*, being *old and full of days*. Having filled up the ordinary term of human life at that period of the world. He reached an honoured old age, and when he died was not prematurely cut down. He was *regarded* as an old man. The translators of the Septuagint, at the close of their version, make the following addition: "And it is written that he will rise again with those whom the Lord will raise up." This is translated out of a Syrian book. "He dwelt indeed in the land of Ausitis, on the confines of Idumea and Arabia. His first name was Jobab; and having married an Arabian woman, he had by her a son whose name was Ennon. He was himself a son of Zare, one of the sons of Esau; and his mother's name was Bosorra; so that he was the fifth in descent from Abraham. And these were the kings who reigned in Edom, over which country he also bore rule. The first was Balak, the son of Beor, and the name of his city was Dannaba. And after Balak, Jobab, who is called Job; and after him, Asom, who was governor (ἡγεμών) from the region of Thaimanitis; and

after him, Adad, son of Barad, who smote Madian in the plain of Moab; and the name of his city was Getham. And the friends who came to him were Eliphaz of the sons of Esau, the king of the Thaimanites; Bildad, the sovereign (τύραννος) of the Saucheans; and Sopher, the king of the Manaians." What is the authority for this statement is now entirely unknown, nor is it known whence it was derived. The remark with which it is introduced, that it is written that he would be raised up again in the resurrection, looks as if it were a forgery made after the coming of the Saviour, and has much the appearance of being an attempt to support the doctrine of the resurrection by the authority of this ancient book. It is, at all events, an unauthorized addition to the book, as nothing like it occurs in the Hebrew.

CONCLUDING REMARKS.

We have now gone through with an exposition of the most ancient book in the world, and the most difficult one in the sacred volume. We have seen how sagacious men reason on the mysterious events of Divine Providence, and how little light can be thrown on the ways of God by the profoundest thinking, or the acutest observation. We have seen a good man subjected to severe trials by the loss of all his property and children, by a painful and loathsome disease, by acute mental sorrows, by the reproaches of his wife, by the estrangement of his surviving kindred, and then by the laboured efforts of his friends to prove that he was a hypocrite, and that all his calamities had come upon him as a demonstration that he was at heart a bad man. We have seen that man struggling with those arguments; embarrassed and perplexed by their ingenuity; tortured by the keenness of the reproaches of his friends; and under the excitement of his feelings, and the pressure of his woes, giving vent to expressions of impatience and irreverent reflection on the government of God, which he afterwards had occasion abundantly to regret. We have seen that man brought safely through all his trials; showing that, after all that *they* had said and that *he* had said and suffered, he was a good man. We have seen the divine interposition in his favour at the close of the controversy; the divine approbation of his general character and spirit; and the divine goodness shown him in the removal of his calamities, in his restoration to health, in the bestowment on him of double his former possessions; and in the lengthening out his days to an honoured old age. In his latter days we have seen his friends coming around him again with returning affection and confidence; and a happy family growing up to cheer him in his declining years, and to make him honoured in the earth. In view of all these things, and especially of the statements in the chapter which closes the book, we may make the following remarks:

(1.) The upright will be ultimately honoured by God and man. God may bring afflictions upon them, and they may *seem* to be objects of his displeasure; but the period will arrive when he will show them marks of his favour. This may not *always*, indeed, be in the present life, but there will be a period when all these clouds will be dissipated, and when the good, the pious, the sincere friends of God, shall enjoy the returning tokens of his friendship. If his approbation of them is declared in no intelligible way in this life, it will be at the day of judgment in a more sublime manner even than it was announced to Job; if the whole of this life should be dark with storms, yet there is a heaven where, through eternity, there will be pure and unclouded day. In like manner, honour will be ultimately shown to the good and just by the world. At present friends may withdraw; enemies may be multiplied; suspicions may attach to a man's name; calumny and slander may come over his reputation like a mist from the ocean. But things will ultimately work themselves right. A man in the end will have all the reputation which he ought to have. He who has a character that *ought* to be loved, honoured, and remembered, will be loved, honoured, and remembered; and he who has such a character that he ought to be hated or forgotten, will be. It may not *always*, indeed, be in the present life; but there is a current of public favour and esteem setting towards a good man while living, which always comes up to him when he is dead. The world will do justice to his character; and a holy man, if calumniated while he lives, may safely commit his character to God and to the "charitable speeches" (*Bacon,*) of men, and to distant times, when he dies. But in most instances, as in the case of Job, if life is lengthened out, the calumniated, the reproached, and the injured, will find justice done them before they die. Reproaches in early or middle life will be succeeded by a fair and wide reputation in old age; the returning confidence of friends will be all the compensation which this world can furnish for the injury which was done, and the evening of life spent in the enjoyment of friendship and affection, will but precede the entrance on a better life, to be spent in the eternal friendship of God and of all holy beings.

(2.) We should adhere to our integrity when passing through trials. They may be long and severe. The storm that rolls over us may be very dark, and the lightning's flash may be vivid, and the thunder deep and long. Our friends may withdraw and reproach us; those who should console us may entreat us to curse God and die; one woe may succeed another in rapid succession, and each successive stroke be heavier than the last; years may roll on in which we may find no comfort or peace; but we should not despair. We should not let go our integrity. We should not blame our Maker. We should not allow the language of complaint or murmuring to pass our lips, nor ever doubt that God is good and true. There is a good reason for all that he does; and in due time we shall meet the recompense of our trials and our fidelity. No pious and submissive sufferer ever yet failed of ultimately receiving the tokens of the divine favour and love.

(3.) The expressions of divine favour and love are not to be expected in the midst of angry controversy and heated debate. Neither Job nor his friends appear to have enjoyed communion with God, or to have tasted much of the happiness of religion, while the controversy was going on. They were excited by the discussion; the argument was the main thing; and on both sides they gave vent to emotions that were little consistent with the reigning love of God in the heart, and with the enjoyment of religion. There were high words; mutual criminations and recriminations; strong doubts expressed about the sincerity and purity of each other's character; and many things were said on both sides, as there usually is in such cases, derogatory to the character and government of God. It was only after the argument was closed, and the disputants were silenced, that God appeared in mercy to them, and imparted to them the tokens of his favour. Theological combatants usually enjoy little religion. In stormy debate and heated discussion there is usually little communion with God and little enjoyment of true piety. It is rare that such discussions are carried on without engendering feelings wholly hostile to religion; and it is rare that such a controversy is continued long, in which much is not said on both sides injurious to God—in which there are not severe reflections on his government, and in which opinions are not advanced which give abundant occasion for bitter regret. In a heated argument a man becomes insensibly more concerned for the success of his cause than for the honour of God, and will often advance sentiments even severely reflecting on the divine government, rather than confess the weakness of his own cause, and yield the point in debate. In such times it is not an inconceivable thing that even good men should be more anxious to maintain their own opinions than to vindicate the cause of God, and would be more willing to express hard sentiments about their Maker than to acknowledge their own defeat.

(4.) From the chapter before us (xlii. 11), we are presented with an interesting fact, such as often occurs. It is this: friends return to us, and become exceedingly kind *after* calamity has passed by. The kindred and acquaintances of Job withdrew when his afflictions were heavy upon him; they returned only with returning prosperity. When afflicted, they lost their interest in him. Many of them, perhaps, had been dependent on him, and when his property was gone, and he could no longer aid them, they disappeared of course. Many of them, perhaps, professed friendship for him *because* he was a man of rank, and property, and honour; and when he was reduced to poverty and wretchedness, they also disappeared of course. Many of them, perhaps, had regarded him as a man of piety; but when these calamities came upon him, in accordance with the common sentiments of the age, they regarded him as a bad man, and they also withdrew from him of course. When there were evidences of returning prosperity, and of the renewed favour of God, these friends and acquaintances again returned. Some of them doubtless came back *because* he was thus restored. "Swallow-friends, that are gone in the winter, will return in the spring, though their friendship is of little value." *Henry*. That portion of them who had been sincerely attached to him as a good man, though their confidence in his piety had been shaken by his calamities, now returned, doubtless with sincere hearts, and disposed to do him good. They contributed to his wants; they helped him to begin the world again; they were the means of laying the foundation of his future prosperity; and in a time of real need their aid was valuable, and they did all that they could to minister consolation to the man who had been so sorely afflicted. In adversity, it is said, a man will know who are his real friends. If this is true, then this distinguished and holy patriarch had few friends who were truly attached to him, and who were not bound to him by some consideration of selfishness. Probably this is always the case with those who occupy prominent and elevated situations in life. True friendship is oftenest found in humble walks and in lowly vales.

(5.) We should overcome the unkindness of our friends by praying for them; see Notes on chap. xlii. 8, 10. This is the true way of meeting harsh reproaches and unkind reflections on our character. Whatever may be the severity with which we are treated by others; whatever charges they may bring against us of hypocrisy or wickedness; however ingenious may be their arguments to prove this, or however cutting their sarcasm and retorts, we should never refuse to pray for them. We should always be willing to seek the blessing of God upon them, and be ready to bear them on our hearts before the throne of mercy. It is one of the privileges of good men thus to pray for their calumniators and slanderers; and one of our highest honours, and it may be the source of our highest joys, is that of being made the instruments of calling down the divine blessing on those who have injured us. It is not that we delight to triumph over them; it is not that we are now proud that *we* have the evidence of divine favour; it is not that we exult that they are humbled, and that we now are exalted; it is that we may be the means of permanent happiness to those who have greatly injured us.

(6.) The last days of a good man are not unfrequently his best and happiest days. The early part of his life may be harassed with cares; the middle may be filled up with trials; but returning prosperity may smile upon his old age, and his sun go down without a cloud. His heart may be weaned from the world by his trials; his true friends may have been ascertained by their adhering to him in reverses of fortune, and the favour of God may so crown the evening of his life, that to him, and to all, it shall be evident that he is ripening for glory. God is often pleased also to impart unexpected comforts to his friends in their old age; and though they have suffered much and lost much, and thought that they should never "again see good," yet he often disappoints the expectations of his people, and the most prosperous times come when they thought all their comforts were dead. In the trials through which we pass in life, it is not improper to look forward to brighter and better days, as to be yet possibly our portion in this world; at all events, if we are the friends of God, we may look forward to certain and enduring happiness in the world that is to come.

(7.) The book, through whose exposition we have now passed, is a most beautiful and invaluable argument. It relates to the most important subject that can come before our minds—the government of God, and the principles on which his administration is conducted. It shows how this appeared to the reflecting men of the earliest times. It shows how their minds were perplexed with it, and what difficulties attended the subject after the most careful observation. It shows how little can be accomplished in removing those difficulties by human reasoning, and how little light the most careful observation, and the most sagacious reflections, can throw on this perplexing subject. Arguments more beautiful, illustrations more happy, sentiments more terse and profound, and views of God more large and comprehensive, than those which occur in this book, can be found in no works of philosophy; nor has the human mind in its own efforts ever gone beyond the reasonings of these sages in casting light on the mysterious ways of God. They brought to the investigation the wisdom collected by their fathers and preserved in proverbs; they brought the results of the long reflection and observation of their own minds; and yet they threw scarce a ray of light on the mysterious subject before them, and at the close of their discussions we feel that the whole question is just as much involved in mystery as ever. So we feel at the end of all the arguments of man without the aid of revelation, on the great subjects pertaining to the divine government over this world. The reasonings of philosophy now are no more satisfactory than were those of Eliphaz, Zophar, and Bildad, and it may be doubted whether, since this book was written, the slightest advance has been made in removing the perplexities on the subject of the divine administration, so beautifully stated in the book of Job.

(8.) The reasonings in this book show the desirableness and the value of revelation. It is to be remembered that the place which the reasonings in this book should be regarded as occupying, is properly *before* any revelation had been given to men, or before any was recorded. If it is the most ancient book in the world, this is clear; and in the volume of revealed truth it should be regarded as occupying the first place in the order in which the books of revelation were given to man. As introductory to the whole volume of revelation—for so it should be considered—the book of Job is of inestimable worth and importance. It shows how *little* advance the human mind can make in questions of the deepest importance, and what painful perplexity is left after all the investigations that man can make. It shows what clouds of obscurity rest on the mind, whenever man by himself undertakes to explain and unfold the purposes of Deity. It shows how little philosophy and careful observation can accomplish to explain the mysteries of the divine dealings, and to give the mind solid peace in the contemplation of the various subjects that so much perplex man. There was no better way of showing this than that adopted here. A great and good man falls. His comforts all depart. He sinks to the lowest degree of wretchedness. To explain this, and all kindred subjects, his own mind is taxed to the utmost, and four men of distinguished sagacity and extent of observation are introduced—the representatives of the wisdom of the world—to explain the fact. They adduce all that they had learned by tradition, and all that their own observation had suggested, and all the considerations which reason would suggest to them; but all in vain. They make no advances in the explanation, and the subject at the close is left as dark as when they began. Such an effect, and such a train of discussion, is admirably fitted to prepare the mind to welcome the teachings of revelation, and to be grateful for that volume of revealed truth which casts such abundant light on the questions that so perplexed these ancient sages. Before the book of revelation was given, it was well to have on record the result of the best efforts which man could make to explain the mysteries of the divine administration.

As a specimen of early poetry, and an illustration of the early views of science and the state of the arts, of incomparable beauty and sublimity, also, this book is invaluable. Almost four thousand years have passed away since this patriarch lived, and since the arguments recorded in the book were made and recorded. Men have made great advances since in science and the arts. The highest efforts, probably, of which the human mind is capable, have since been made in the department of poetry, and works have been produced destined certainly to live on to the consummation of all things. But the sublimity and beauty of the poetry in this book stand still unsurpassed, unrivalled. As a mere specimen of composition, apart from all the questions of its theological bearing; as the oldest book in the world; as reflecting the manners, habits, and opinions of an ancient generation; as illustrating more than any other book extant the state of the sciences, the ancient views of astronomy, geology, geography, natural history, and the advances made in the arts, this book has a higher value than can be attached to any other record of the past, and demands the profound attention of those who would make themselves familiar with the history of the race. The theologian should study it as an invaluable introduction to the volume of inspired truth; the humble Christian, to obtain elevated views of God; the philosopher, to see how little the human mind can accomplish on the most important of all subjects without the aid of revelation; the child of sorrow, to learn the lessons of patient submission; the man of science, to know what was understood in the far distant periods of the past; the man of taste, as an incomparable specimen of poetic beauty and sublimity. It will teach invaluable lessons to each advancing generation; and to the end of time true piety and taste will find consolation and pleasure in the study of the BOOK OF JOB. God grant that this effort to explain it may contribute to this result. To that God who inclined my heart to engage in the attempt to explain this ancient book, and who has given me health, and strength, and the means to prosecute the study with advantage, I now devote this exposition. I trust it may do good to others; it has been profitable and pleasant to my own soul.

THE END OF THE NOTES.

NEW TRANSLATION OF THE BOOK OF JOB.

PART I.

CHAP. I.

1 There was a man in the land of Uz whose name was Job.
2 And that man was sincere and upright; and one that feared God and
3 avoided evil. And there were born unto him seven sons and three
daughters. His possessions were seven thousand sheep, and three thousand camels, and five hundred yoke of cattle, and five hundred she-asses, and a very numerous household; so that this man was the greatest of all the sons of the East.
4 And his sons went and made a feast in their houses, each in his day, and they sent and invited their three sisters to eat and drink with them.
5 And when the days of feasting had gone round, Job sent for them and sanctified them, and he rose up early in the morning, and offered burnt-offerings according to the number of them all; for Job said, It may be that my sons have sinned, and have cursed God in their hearts. Thus did Job constantly.
6 And there was a day when the sons of God came to present themselves before JEHOVAH, and Satan came also among them.
7 And JEHOVAH said to Satan, From whence dost thou come? And Satan answered JEHOVAH and said, From rapidly going to and fro in the earth, and walking up and down in it.
8 And JEHOVAH said to Satan, Hast thou attentively observed my servant
Job? For there is none like him upon the earth, a man sincere and
9 upright, fearing God, and avoiding evil. And Satan answered JEHOVAH
10 and said, Is it for nothing that Job fears God? Hast thou not made a
hedge around him, and around his house, and around all his possessions?
The work of his hands thou hast blessed, and his possessions spread over
11 the land. But now only put forth thine hand and smite all that he
12 possesses, and he will curse thee to thy face. And JEHOVAH said to
Satan, Lo, all which he has is in thy power; but upon himself lay not thy
hand. So Satan went forth from the presence of JEHOVAH.
13 And the day came when his sons and his daughters were eating and
14 drinking wine in the house of their elder brother; and a messenger
came to Job, and said, The cattle were ploughing, and the she-asses,
15 feeding beside them, and the Sabeans rushed upon them, and took them
away, and slew the young men with the edge of the sword; and I only
16 am escaped by myself to tell thee. While he was yet speaking, there
came also another, and said, The fire of God hath fallen from heaven,

and burned up the sheep, and the servants, and consumed them; and I
17 only have escaped by myself to tell thee. While he was yet speaking,
there came also another, and said, The Chaldeans made out three bands,
and rushed upon the camels, and took them, and slew the young men
with the edge of the sword; and I only am escaped by myself to tell
18 thee. And while he was yet speaking, there came also another and said,
Thy sons and thy daughters were eating, and drinking wine in the house
19 of their elder brother, and lo! there came a great wind from across the
desert, and smote upon the four corners of the house, and it fell upon
the young men, and they are dead; and I only am escaped by myself to
20 tell thee. Then Job arose, and rent his mantle, and shaved his head,
21 and fell upon the ground, and worshipped, and said, Naked came I forth
from the womb of my mother, and naked I shall return there! Jehovah
gave, and Jehovah hath taken away; blessed be the name of Jehovah.
22 In all this Job did not sin, and he attributed no wrong to God.

Chap. II.

1 And there was a day when the sons of God came to present themselves
before Jehovah, and Satan came also among them, to present himself
2 also before Jehovah. And Jehovah said to Satan, Whence dost thou
come? And Satan answered Jehovah and said, From rapidly going to
3 and fro in the earth, and walking up and down in it. And Jehovah
said to Satan, Hast thou attentively observed my servant Job, that
there is none like him upon the earth, a man sincere and upright, fearing God and avoiding evil? And still he holdeth fast his integrity,
although thou didst excite me against him to destroy him without cause.
4 And Satan answered Jehovah and said, Skin for skin; and all which
5 pertains to a man will he give for his life. But put forth now thine
hand, and smite his bone and his flesh, and he will curse thee to thy
6 face. And Jehovah said unto Satan, Behold he is in thy hand. Only
7 spare his life. And Satan went out from the presence of Jehovah, and
smote Job with a painful ulcer from the sole of his foot unto his crown.
8 And he took a piece of broken earthen ware to scrape himself with, and
he sat down among the ashes.
9 Then said his wife unto him, Dost thou still retain thine integrity;
10 Curse God, and die. But he said unto her, Thou talkest as one of the
foolish women talk. Shall we then receive good from God, and shall
we not receive evil? In all this, Job sinned not with his lips.
11 And the three friends of Job heard of all the evil which had befallen
him, and they came every man from his home: Eliphaz the Temanite,
and Bildad the Shuhite, and Zophar the Naamathite, for they had
agreed to come together to condole with him, and to comfort him.
12 And they lifted up their eyes afar off, and they did not know him. Then
they lifted up their voices and wept, and they rent each one his mantle,

13 and they threw dust upon their heads towards heaven. And they sat
down with him upon the ground seven days and seven nights, and no
one spake a word to him, for they saw that his grief was very great.

PART II.

THE ARGUMENT OR CONTROVERSY IN VERSE. Chap. iii—xlii. 6

The first series in the controversy. Chap. iii.—xiv.

THE COMPLAINT OF JOB. Chap. iii.

1 At length Job opened his mouth, and cursed his day.
2 And Job exclaimed and said,
3 O that the day might have perished in which I was born;
And the night which said, "A male child is conceived!"
4 That day—let it be darkness!
Let not God inquire after it from on high!
Yea, let not the light shine upon it!
5 Let darkness and the shadow of death stain it;
Let a cloud dwell upon it;
Let whatever darkens the day terrify it.
6 That night—let darkness seize upon it!
Let it not rejoice among the days of the year!
Let it not come into the number of the months!
7 O that night! let it be desolate!
Let there come in it no sound of joy!
8 Let them who curse the day curse it;
They who are skilful to rouse up Leviathan!
9 Let the stars of its twilight be darkened;
Let it long for the light, and there be none;
Neither let it see the eye-lids of the morning!
10 Because it closed not the doors of the womb to me
And caused not trouble to be hid from mine eyes!
11 Why did I not expire from my birth?
When I came from the womb why did I not die?
12 Why did the knees anticipate me?
And why the breasts that I should suck?
13 For now should I lie down and be quiet;
I should sleep; then should I be at rest.
14 With kings and counsellors of the earth,
Who build lonely places for themselves;
15 Or with princes that had gold,

And who filled their houses with silver;
16 Or as a hidden abortion I had not been,
As infants which never saw the light.
17 There the wicked cease from troubling:
And there the weary are at rest.
18 There the prisoners rest together;
They hear not the voice of the oppressor.
19 The small and the great are there;
And the servant is free from his master.
20 Why doth He give light to him that is in misery,
And life to the bitter in spirit;
21 Who long for death, and it is not;
And dig for it more than for hid treasures;
22 Who rejoice exceedingly—
Yea, they exult when they can find a grave?
23 Why to the man whose path is hid,
And whom God hath hedged up?
24 For my sighing comes before I eat,
And my groans are poured forth as the billows.
25 For I had a great dread, and it came upon me;
And what I shuddered at overtook me.
26 I have no peace, and I have no quiet, and I have no respite,
And such misery as makes me tremble comes.

CHAPTER IV. V.

The first series in the controversy continued.

THE FIRST SPEECH OF ELIPHAZ IN REPLY TO JOB.

1 Then answered Eliphaz the Temanite and said:
2 If one attempt a word with thee, wilt thou take it ill?
Yet who can refrain from speaking?
3 Lo, thou hast admonished many,
And the feeble hands thou hast strengthened;
4 The stumbling thy words have upheld,
And to the feeble knees thou hast given strength.
5 But now [affliction] has come upon thee, and thou faintest,
It toucheth thee, and thou art troubled.
6 Is not thy confidence and thy expectation [founded on] thy fear of God,
And on the integrity of thy ways?
7 Remember, I pray thee, who ever perished being innocent?
Or where were the righteous cut off?

8 According to what I have seen, they who plough iniquity,
And sow mischief, reap the same.
9 By the blast of God they perish,
And by the breath of his nostrils are they consumed.
10 The roaring of the lion and the voice of the fierce lion [are silenced],
And the teeth of the young lions are broken out.
11 The old lion perishes for want of prey,
And the whelps of the lioness are scattered abroad.
12 Unto me an oracle was secretly imparted,
And mine ear caught a gentle whisper of it.
13 In distracted thoughts among the visions of the night,
When profound sleep falleth upon men,
14 Fear came upon me, and trembling,
Which made all my bones to quake.
15 Then a spirit glided along before my face,
The hair of my flesh stood on end :
16 It stood—but its form I could not discern ;
A spectre was before mine eyes ;
There was silence, and I heard a voice—
17 Shall feeble man be more just than God ?
Shall man be more pure than his Maker ?
18 Behold, in his servants he putteth no confidence,
And his angels he chargeth with frailty ;
19 How much more true is this of those who dwell in houses of clay
Whose foundation is in the dust !
They are crushed before the moth-worm !
20 Between morning and evening they are destroyed ;
Without any one regarding it they perish for ever.
21 Is not the excellency that is in them torn away ?
They die before they have become wise.

CHAP. V.

1 Call now ! Is there any one who will respond to thee ?
And to which of the holy ones wilt thou look ?
2 Truly wrath destroyeth the fool ;
And indignation kills the man easily seduced [to sin].
3 I have seen the fool taking root ;
But soon I pronounced his habitation accursed.
4 His children are far from safety ;
They are crushed in the gate, and there is no deliverer.
5 His harvest the hungry man devours,
And even to the thorns he seizes it,
And the thirsty swallow up their wealth.
6 For though affliction cometh not from the dust,

And trouble does not sprout up from the ground;
7 For though man is born unto trouble
As the sparks elevate their flight;
8 Nevertheless I would seek unto God,
And to God would I commit my cause,
9 Who doeth great things and unsearchable,
Marvellous things without number;
10 Who giveth rain upon the face of the [cultivated] earth,
And sendeth waters upon the out-places;
11 Who advances the lowly to high places,
And the dejected are elevated to prosperity;
12 Who disappointeth the purposes of the crafty,
And their hands cannot accomplish their design;
13 Who taketh the wise in their own craftiness,
And precipitateth the counsels of intriguers.
14 They meet with darkness in the day-time,
And grope at noon as if it were night.
15 And he saveth from the sword, from their mouth,
And from the hand of the mighty, the poor.
16 So the poor hath hope,
And iniquity stoppeth her mouth.
17 Behold, happy is the man whom God correcteth,
And the chastening of the Almighty do not despise.
18 For he bruiseth, and he bindeth up;
He woundeth, and his hands heal.
19 In six troubles he will deliver thee,
Yea, in seven evil shall not touch thee.
20 In famine he will redeem thee from death,
And in war from the power of the sword.
21 From the scourge of the tongue shalt thou be hid,
Nor be afraid of devastation when it cometh.
22 At devastation, and at famine thou shalt laugh,
Nor shalt thou dread the wild beasts of the land.
23 For thou shalt form an alliance with the stones of the field,
And the beasts of the field shall be at peace with thee.
24 Thou shalt know that thy tent is secure,
And thou shalt return to thy dwelling, and not miss it.
25 And thou shalt know that thy posterity shall be numerous,
And thine offspring like plants upon the earth.
26 Thou shalt come in full age to the grave,
As a shook of grain that is gathered in its season.
27 Lo! This we have searched out. So it is;
Hear! and know thou it for thyself.

CHAPTER VI. VII.

The first series in the controversy continued.

THE REPLY OF JOB TO ELIPHAZ.

1 And Job answered, and said:
2 O that my grief were weighed thoroughly!
That they would put my calamities in the balance together!
3 For now would they be heavier than the sands of the sea;
Therefore are my words swallowed up.
4 For the arrows of the Almighty are within me,
Their poison drinketh up my spirit:
The terrors of God set themselves in array against me.
5 Doth the wild ass bray in the midst of grass?
Or loweth the ox over his fodder?
6 Can that which is insipid be eaten without salt?
Is there any taste in the white of an egg?
7 The things which my soul abhors to touch
Are become my sorrowful food.
8 O that I might have my request,
And that God would grant my desire,
9 That it would please God to crush me,
That he would let loose his hand and cut me off!
10 Then there would be yet comfort to me;
Yea, I would exult in my anguish—
Let him spare not—
For I have not concealed the words of the Holy One.
11 What is my strength, that I should hope?
And what is my end, that I should be patient?
12 Is my strength the strength of stones?
Is my flesh brass?
13 Alas, my help is not in myself!
Deliverance has fled from me.
14 To the afflicted kindness should be shown by his friend;
But he has forsaken the fear of the Almighty.
15 My brethren are faithless as a brook,
Like the streams of the valley that pass away;
16 Which are turbid by means of the [melted] ice,
In which the snow is hid [by being dissolved].
17 In the time when they become warm, they evaporate;
When the heat cometh they are dried up from their place.

18 The channels of their way wind round about;
They go into nothing—and are lost.
19 The caravans of Tema look;
The travelling companies of Sheba expect to see them.
20 They are ashamed that they have relied on them;
They come even to the place, and are confounded.
21 For now ye also are nothing:
Ye see my calamity, and shrink back.
22 Have I said, Bring me a gift?
Or, from your property make me a present?
23 Or, deliver me from the hand of an enemy?
Or, from the hand of the violent rescue me?
24 Teach me, and I will be silent;
And wherein I have erred cause me to understand.
25 How powerful are words of truth!
But what doth your reproaching demonstrate?
26 Do you think to reprove mere words?
The words of a man in despair [should be regarded] as the wind.
27 Truly against the fatherless ye would spring [a net],
And ye dig a pitfal for your neighbour.
28 Now, therefore, if you please, look closely upon me,
For if I speak falsehood it will be manifest to you.
29 Return now, let it not be assumed to be evil;
Return again, for my vindication is in it [in my argument].
30 Is there iniquity in my tongue?
Cannot my taste discern that which is simple?

CHAP. VII.

1 Is there not an appointed service to man upon earth?
Are not his days as the days of an hireling?
2 As the servant pants for the evening shadow,
And as the hireling anxiously expects his wages,
3 Thus am I made to inherit comfortless months,
And nights of anguish are appointed to me.
4 If I lie down, then I say,
When shall I arise, and the night flee away?
And I am full of restlessness until the dawn.
5 My flesh is clothed with worms, and clods of dust;
My skin becomes rigid, and is loathsome.
6 My days are swifter than a weaver's shuttle;
They are consumed without hope.
7 O remember that my life is wind;
Mine eye shall not return to see good!
8 The eye of him that hath seen me shall see me no more;

Thine eyes are upon me—and I am not!
9 A cloud wasteth and vanisheth away—
So he that goes down to the grave cometh up again no more.
10 He shall not return again to his house,
And his dwelling-place shall know him no more.
11 Therefore I will not refrain my mouth;
I will speak in the anguish of my spirit,
I will cry out in the bitterness of my soul.
12 Am I a sea, or a sea monster,
That thou settest a watch over me?
13 When I say my couch shall console me,
My bed shall lighten my complaint,
14 Then dost thou scare me with dreams,
And with visions dost thou terrify me;
15 So that my soul chooseth strangling—
Death—rather than these bones.
16 I loathe [life]; I would not live always
Let me alone, for my days are vanity.
17 What is man that thou shouldst make him of so great importance,
And that thou shouldst set thy heart towards him?
18 That thou shouldst visit him every morning,
And prove him every moment?
19 How long ere thou wilt look away from me,
And let me alone that I may swallow down my spittle?
20 Have I sinned; what have I done to thee?
O thou Watcher of man!
Why dost thou set me up before thyself for a mark,
So that I am a burden to myself?
21 And why dost thou not pardon my transgression,
And suffer my guilt to pass away?
For soon shall I sleep in the dust:
In the morning thou shalt seek me, and I shall not be.

CHAPTER VIII.

The first series in the controversy continued.

THE FIRST SPEECH OF BILDAD THE SHUHITE.

1 Then answered Bildad the Shuhite, and said:
2 How long wilt thou speak these things?
And the words of thy mouth be a mighty wind?
3 Doth God pervert judgment?

Or will the Almighty pervert justice?
4 Since thy children have sinned against him,
And he hath cast them away on account of their transgression,
5 Yet if thou wouldst seek early unto God,
And make thy supplication to the Almighty,
6 If thou wert pure and upright,
Even now would he arouse himself for thee,
And would make prosperous thy righteous habitation.
7 Although thy beginning should be small,
Yet thy latter end would greatly increase.
8 For inquire, I pray thee, of the former age,
Yea, apply thyself to the examination of their forefathers;
9 (For we are but of yesterday, and we know nothing,
For our days upon earth are a shadow;)
10 Shall they not teach thee, and tell thee,
And utter words from their hearts?
11 "Can the paper reed grow up without mire?
"Can the bulrush grow up without water?
12 "Even yet in its greenness, and uncut,
"It withereth before any other herb.
13 "Such are the ways of all who forget God;
"So perishes the hope of the hypocrite.
14 "His hope shall rot,
"And his trust shall be the building of the spider.
15 "He shall lean upon his building and it shall not stand;
"He shall grasp it, but it shall not endure.
16 "He is green before the sun rises,
"And his branches go forth over his garden.
17 "Over the heap [of stones] his roots are entwined,
"They look to the pile of stones [for a support].
18 "Yet the sun shall absorb it from its place,
"And shall refuse to own it, saying, 'I never saw thee!'
19 "Lo! such is the joy of his course!
"Yet from the dust others shall spring up."
20 Behold, God will not cast away a perfect man;
Nor will he lend his aid to the wicked.
21 While he filleth thy mouth with laughter,
And thy lips with triumph.
22 They that hate thee shall be clothed with shame,
And the tent of the wicked shall not be!

CHAPTER IX.

The first series in the controversy continued.

THE REPLY OF JOB TO BILDAD. Chap. ix. x.

1 Then Job answered, and said:
2 Truly I know that it is so;
And how can man be just before God?
3 If he chooses to enter into a litigation with him,
He cannot answer him to one [charge] of a thousand.
4 Wise in heart! and mighty in strength!
Who hath hardened himself in opposition to him and been successful?
5 He removeth the mountains, and they know it not;
He overturneth them in his wrath.
6 He shaketh the earth out of her place;
And the pillars thereof tremble.
7 He commandeth the sun, and it riseth not;
And he sealeth up the stars.
8 He alone stretches out the heavens;
And walketh upon the high waves of the sea.
9 He maketh Arcturus, Orion,
The Pleiades, and the secret chambers of the South.
10 He doeth great things which there is no searching out;
Yea, marvellous things beyond number.
11 Lo! He passeth by me—and I see him not;
He goeth on—but I do not perceive him.
12 Lo! He taketh away, and who can compel him to restore?
Who can say to him, What doest thou?
13 God will not turn away his anger;
The supporters of pride bow before him.
14 Truly if I should answer him,
I would carefully select my words before him;
15 Whom, though I were innocent I would not answer;
I would cast myself on the mercy of my Judge.
16 Should I call, and he should respond,
I would not believe that he could hear my voice—
17 He who is overwhelming me with a tempest,
And who multiplies my wounds without cause—
18 He that will not suffer me to take my breath,
But who fills me with bitterness.
19 If the contest had respect to strength, lo! how strong is He!

If it relates to justice, who would summon for me the witnesses for trial?
20 Should I justify myself, my own mouth would condemn me.
I perfect! It would prove me perverse.
21 I perfect! I should not know my own soul ;
I should disown my very being!
22 There is but one result ; therefore I maintained it—
The perfect and the wicked he destroyeth alike.
23 If the scourge slayeth suddenly
He laugheth at the sufferings of the innocent.
24 The earth is given into the hands of the wicked ;
The face of its judges he covereth ;
If this be not so, where—who is he?
25 And my days are swifter than a runner ;
They flee away, and they see no good.
26 They pass on like the reed-skiffs ;
As the eagle darting upon his prey.
27 If I say I will forget my complaining,
I will change my sad countenance and brighten up,
28 Still I am in dread of all my sorrows,
I know that thou wilt not hold me innocent.
29 I am held to be guilty ;
Why then should I labour in vain?
30 Should I wash myself in snow-water,
And cleanse my hands in soap,
31 Still thou wilt plunge me into the mire,
So that my own clothes will abhor me.
32 For he is not a man as I am that I should contend with him,
And that we should come together to trial.
33 Neither is there between us any umpire
Who may lay his hand upon both.
34 Let him remove from me his rod,
And let not his terror dismay me,
35 And I will speak and not be afraid of him—
But not thus can I as I am now.

CHAP. X.

1 My soul is weary of my life,
I will give myself up to complaint,
I will speak in the bitterness of my soul.
2 I will say unto God,
Do not merely hold me to be wicked,
Show me the reason why thou dost contend with me.
3 Is it a pleasure for thee to oppress?
To despise the work of thy hands,

And to shine upon the counsel of the wicked?
4 Are thine eyes of flesh?
Dost thou see as man seeth?
5 Are thy days as the days of man?
And thy years as the years of man?
6 That thou seekest after my iniquity,
And searchest after my sin,
7 With thy knowledge that I am not a wicked man,
And that none can deliver out of thy hand?
8 Thy hands have laboriously formed me,
And have made me compact on every part,
And wilt thou destroy me?
9 Remember, I beseech thee, that thou hast made me as clay;
And wilt thou bring me again to dust?
10 Thou didst pour me out as milk,
And curdle me as cheese.
11 With skin and flesh hast thou clothed me,
With bones and sinews hast thou strengthened me.
12 Life and favour thou hast granted me,
And thy care hath preserved my spirit.
13 And these things thou didst hide in thine heart;
I know that this was thy purpose.
14 If I sin, thou dost carefully observe me;
And from my iniquity thou wilt not quit me.
15 If I am wicked, wo is unto me;
And if I am righteous, I cannot lift up my head.
I am full of confusion :—
And see my affliction,
16 For it magnifies itself.
Like a lion thou dost hunt me,
And thou returnest, and thy dealings towards me are marvellous!
17 Thou makest new thy proofs against me,
And increasest thine anger against me :—
The whole army of afflictions is upon me.
18 And why didst thou bring me forth from the womb?
O that I had expired, and that no eye had seen me!
19 I should have been as though I had not been;
I should have been borne from the womb to the grave.
20 Are not my days few?
O spare me, and let me alone, that I may take a little ease,
21 Before I go whence I shall not return,
To the land of darkness and the shadow of death—
22 The land of darkness like the blackness of the shadow of death;
Where there is no order, and where its shining is like blackness.

CHAPTER XI.

The first series in the controversy continued.

THE FIRST SPEECH OF ZOPHAR. Chap. xi.

1 And Zophar the Naamathite answered and said :
2 Shall not the multitude of words be answered ?
Shall the man of mere talk be justified ?
3 Shall thy trifles make men be silent ?
Shalt thou mock and no one put thee to shame ?
4 For thou hast said, My doctrine is pure,
And I am clean in thine eyes.
5 But O that God would speak,
And open his lips with thee ;
6 And would declare to thee the secrets of wisdom,
For they are double what we can understand !
Then shouldst thou know that God had left unnoticed a part of thine iniquities.
7 Canst thou by searching find out God ?
Canst thou find out the Almighty to perfection ?
8 The heights of heaven ! What canst thou do ?
The depths below Sheol ! What canst thou know ?
9 Longer than the earth is its measure ;
And broader than the ocean.
10 If he arrest, and imprison, and bring to trial,
Who then can prevent him ?
11 For he knoweth men of falsehood,
And he seeth iniquity, though he does not seem to notice it.
12 For deceitful man would seem to have a heart,
Though man be born like the colt of a wild ass.
13 If thou prepare thine heart,
And stretch out thine hands towards him ;
14 If the iniquity which is in thine hands thou wilt put far away
And wilt not suffer evil to dwell in thy habitation ;
15 Then shalt thou lift up thy countenance without spot,
And thou shalt be firm, and shalt not fear.
16 For thou shalt forget thy misery ;
Like waters that pass away shalt thou remember it.
17 And thy life shall be bright above the noon-day :
Now thou art now in darkness—but thou shalt be as the morning.
18 And thou shalt be confident, for there will be hope :

Now thou art suffused with shame—but then shalt lie down in safety.
19 Yea, thou shalt lie down, and none shall make thee afraid;
And many shall make suit unto thee.
20 But the eyes of the wicked shall be wearied out;
And they shall find no refuge;
And their hope shall expire.

CHAP. XII. XIII. XIV.

The first series in the controversy continued.

THE ANSWER OF JOB TO ZOPHAR.

CHAP. XII.

1 And Job answered and said:
2 No doubt ye are the people!
And wisdom will die with you!
3 Yet I have understanding as well as you;
I am not inferior to you;
And with whom are there not sayings like these?
4 A mockery to his neighbour am I—
The man calling upon God, and whom he answers—
Derided is the just, the perfect man.
5 He that is ready to slip with his feet,
In the eyes of him that is at ease,
Is as a cast-away torch.
6 The tents of robbers are secure,
They are secure to those who provoke God,
To whose hand God brings in abundance.
7 But now ask the beasts, and they shall teach thee;
And the fowls of heaven, and they shall tell thee.
8 Or speak to the earth, and it shall teach thee.
And the fishes of the sea will declare to thee.
9 Who among all these doth not know.
That the hand of JEHOVAH doeth this?
10 In whose hand is the life of every thing that liveth,
And the breath of all human flesh.
11 Doth not the ear prove words?
And the palate taste its food?
12 With the aged is wisdom,
And in length of days is understanding.
13 With Him are wisdom and strength;
To him pertains counsel and understanding.

14 Lo! he pulleth down, and it cannot be rebuilt;
He shutteth up a man, and there is no opening [for escape].
15 Lo! he restraineth the waters, and they are dried up;
He sendeth them forth, and they desolate the earth.
16 With him are strength and sufficiency;
The deceived and the deceiver are his.
17 He leadeth counsellors away captive,
And judges he maketh fools.
18 The authority of kings he loosens,
And with a cord he bindeth their loins.
19 He leadeth priests away captive,
And the mighty he prostrates.
20 He removeth eloquence from the trusty,
And taketh away discernment from the aged.
21 He poureth contempt upon princes;
And looseth the girdle of the mighty.
22 He revealeth deep things from the midst of darkness;
And bringeth the shadow of death to light.
23 He increaseth nations, and destroyeth them;
He enlargeth nations, and leadeth them back.
24 He taketh away understanding from the chiefs of the people of the earth,
And causeth them to wander in a solitude where there is no path.
25 They grope in darkness, and there is no light;
He maketh them to reel like a drunken man.

Chap. XIII.

1 Lo! all this hath mine eye seen;
Mine ear hath heard and understood it.
2 What ye know, I know also;
I do not fall below you.
3 But O that I might speak to the Almighty;
And I would have pleasure in urging my cause before God.
4 For truly ye are forgers of sophisms,
Physicians of no value all of you!
5 O that ye would be entirely silent,
And it would be your wisdom!
6 Hear, I pray you, my reasoning;
And attend to the arguments of my lips.
7 Will ye speak falsely for God?
For him will ye utter fallacy?
8 Will ye be partial to his person?
Will ye contend for God?
9 Would it be well for you if he should thoroughly search you?
Can you deceive him as man may be deceived?

10 Surely he will rebuke you
If you secretly have respect to persons.
11 Shall not his majesty fill you with reverence?
And his dread fall upon you?
12 Your maxims are parables of ashes;
Your ramparts are ramparts of clay.
13 Hold your peace, and let me speak—
And then let any thing come upon me.
14 In regard to this, I will take my flesh in my teeth,
And my life in my hand.
15 Lo! let him slay me; I will trust in him;
I will vindicate my ways before him.
16 He also shall be to me for salvation;
For an hypocrite shall not come before him.
17 Attentively hear my words,
And my declaration with your ears.
18 Lo! now I have set in order my cause;
I know that I shall be declared just.
19 Who is there that will contend with me?
For then would I be silent—and die.
20 Only do not two things unto me—
Then will I not hide myself from thy presence.
21 Remove thy hand far from me,
And let not thy dread make me afraid!
22 Then call, and I will answer;
Or I will speak, and answer thou me.
23 How many are my iniquities and my sins?
Make me to know my transgression and my sins.
24 Why dost thou hide thy face,
And regard me as thine enemy?
25 Wilt thou break the driven leaf?
Wilt thou pursue the dry stubble?
26 For thou writest bitter things against me,
And makest me to inherit the sins of my youth.
27 Thou placest my feet in the stocks,
And thou watchest all my paths.
Upon the soles of my feet thou dost set a print.
28 Thus man like rottenness decays,
Like a garment that the moth consumes.

CHAP. XIV.

1 Man, the offspring of woman,
Is of few days, and is full of trouble.
2 He cometh forth as a flower, and is cut down;

And he fleeth as a shadow, and doth not stay.
3 And dost thou indeed open thine eyes upon such an one,
And bring me to trial with thee?
4 Who can produce a clean thing from an unclean?
Not one.
5 Since his days are fixed,
The number of his months is with thee,
Thou hast affixed his limits which he cannot pass,
6 O turn from him, and leave him,
That he may enjoy his day, as [that of] a hireling.
7 For there is hope of a tree,
If it be cut down that it will flourish again,
And that its tender branch will not fail.
8 Though its root grow old in the earth,
And its trunk die on the ground,
9 From the vapour of water it will spring up again,
And put forth boughs as a young plant.
10 But man dieth, and he is gone—
Yea, man expires—and where is he?
11 The waters from the lake fail,
And the river is exhausted and dried up,
12 So man lieth down, and riseth not;
Till the heavens be no more they shall not be aroused,
And they shall not be awaked out of their sleep.
13 O that thou wouldst hide me in Sheol!
That thou wouldst conceal me till thine anger be past!
That thou wouldst appoint for me a set time and then remember me!
14 If a man die, shall he live again?
All the days of my hard service will I wait
Till my change come.
15 Do thou call, and I will answer thee;
Show thou compassion to the work of thine hands.
16 For now thou dost number my steps;
Dost thou not watch over my sins?
17 My transgression is sealed up in a bag,
And thou sewest up mine iniquity.
18 And surely the mountain falling comes to nought,
And the rock is removed from its place;
19 The waters wear away the stones,
The floods wash away the dust of the earth,
And the hope of man thou dost destroy.
20 Thou dost overpower him for ever, and he passes off;
Thou dost change his countenance, and sendest him away.
21 His sons are honoured, but he knoweth it not;

Or they are brought low, but he perceiveth it not.
22 But his flesh shall have pain upon him;
And his soul within him shall mourn.

CHAPTER XV.

The second series in the controversy. Chap. xv.—xxi.

THE SECOND SPEECH OF ELIPHAZ. Chap. xv.

1 And Eliphaz the Temanite answered and said:
2 Should a wise man answer with arguments of wind,
And fill himself with the east wind?
3 Should he reason with words which do not profit,
And in discourses in which there is no benefit?
4 Truly thou dost make religion void;
And dost make prayer useless before God.
5 Yea, thine own mouth proclaimeth thine iniquity,
And thou hast chosen the tongue of the crafty.
6 Thine own mouth condemneth thee, and not I,
And thy lips testify against thee.
7 Art thou the first man that was born?
And wast thou brought forth before the hills?
8 In the council of God hast thou listened?
And hast thou reserved all wisdom to thyself?
9 What dost thou know that we know not also?
What dost thou understand that is not with us?
10 For the old and the hoary-headed are with us—
More venerable in age than thy father.
11 Wilt thou disregard the consolations which God furnishes,
And the words which have been so very gently addressed to thee?
12 Why does thy heart bear thee away?
And why do thine eyes evince so much pride?
13 For against God hath thy spirit replied,
And thou hast brought forth [hard] speeches from thy mouth.
14 What is man that he should be pure?
And he that is born of a woman that he should be just?
15 Behold he does not confide in his Holy Ones,
And the heavens are not pure in his eyes.
16 How much more abominable and polluted is man,
Who drinketh iniquity as water!
17 I will show thee; hear me;
That which I have seen I will declare,

18 Which wise men have related,
And which [having received it] of their ancestors they have not concealed,
19 When the land was entirely in their possession,
And a foreigner had not passed among them :
20 "All his days the wicked man is tormented with pain ;
"And the number of his years is unknown to the oppressor.
21 "A fearful sound is in his ears—
"And in his security the destroyer cometh upon him.
22 "He has not confidence that he shall return from darkness :
"And his expectation is the sword.
23 "He wandereth abroad for bread—where is it?
"He knows that a day of darkness is at hand.
24 "Trouble and anguish fill him with dread,
"They prevail against him—as a king prepared for the battle.
25 "For he stretches out his hand against God ;
"And against the Almighty he fortifies himself.
26 "He runneth upon him with outstretched neck,
"With the thick bosses of his shields,
27 "Because he covered his face with fatness,
"And gathered flesh upon his loins ;
28 "Therefore shall he dwell in desolate cities,
"In houses which are not inhabited,
"Which are ready to become a pile of ruins.
29 "He shall not be rich;
"His property shall not remain ;
"His possessions shall not be spread abroad upon the earth.
30 "He shall not escape out of darkness ;
"His branches shall the flame dry up ;
"By the breath of his mouth shall he be taken away.
31 "Let him not trust in vanity. He is deceived.
"Vanity shall be his recompense.
32 "He shall not complete his time ;
"And his branches shall not be green.
33 "He shall cast his unripe fruit as the vine,
"And shed his blossoms like the olive.
34 "For the community of hypocrites shall be desolate ;
"And fire shall consume the tents of bribery.
35 "They conceive mischief ;
"They bring forth vanity ;
"And their breast deviseth deceit."

CHAPTERS XVI. XVII.

THE ANSWER OF JOB.

1 But Job answered, and said:
2 Many such things as these have I heard
Miserable comforters are ye all!
3 Will there be an end to words of wind?
Or what has provoked thee to answer thus?
4 I also could speak as ye do;
If ye were now in my place
I could string together words against you,
And could shake my head at you.
5 But I would strengthen you with my mouth,
And the moving of my lips should sustain you.
6 If I speak, my grief is not staid;
If I forbear, how does it depart from me?
7 For now He hath quite exhausted me;
Thou hast made desolate all my house.
8 For thou hast compressed me, and this is a witness against me;
And my leanness rises up against me, and accuses me to my face
9 In his anger he teareth me, and is become my adversary;
He gnashes upon me with his teeth;
Mine enemy sharpeneth his eyes upon me.
10 They gape upon me with their mouth;
In scorn they smite my cheek;
They have conspired together against me.
11 God hath made me a captive to the unrighteous;
And into the hands of the wicked hath he delivered me.
12 Happy was I—but he crushed me;
He seized me by the neck, and shook me;
He set me up for a mark.
13 His archers came around me;
He transfixed my reins, and did not spare;
My gall hath he poured out upon the ground.
14 He breaketh me with breach upon breach;
He rusheth upon me like a mighty man,
15 I have sewed sackcloth upon my skin;
And degraded my horn in the dust.
16 My face is swollen with grief;
And on my eyelids is the shadow of death.
17 Not because there has been injustice in my hands;

And my prayer hath been pure.
18 O earth, cover not my blood,
Let there be no hiding-place for my cry.
19 Also now behold my evidence is in heaven ;
My witness is on high.
20 My friends are but mockers ;
Mine eye looketh with tears unto God.
21 O that a man might be permitted to contend with God
As the offspring of man does with his neighbour.
22 For the numbered years pass away,
And I am going the way whence I shall not return.

CHAP. XVII.

1 My spirit is exhausted ;
My days are at an end ;
The grave waits for me.
2 Are there not mockers with me ?
And doth not mine eye rest upon their provocations ?
3 Lay down now [O God, a pledge],
Give security for me [in the controversy] with thee ;
Who is he that will strike hands with me ?
4 Behold, thou hast hid their heart from understanding ;
Therefore thou shalt not exalt them.
5 He who discloses his friends to the prey,
The eyes of his children shall fail.
6 Me he has placed for a by-word among the people ;
I am an object of scorn before their face.
7 Mine eye is dim with sorrow,
And all my limbs are like a shadow.
8 The upright shall be amazed at this ;
And the innocent will rouse himself against the wicked.
9 The righteous will hold on his way,
And he that hath clean hands will become stronger and stronger.
10 As for you all, return, and come, I pray,
And I shall not find among you one wise man.
11 My days are passed ;
My plans are at an end—
The cherished purposes of my heart.
12 Night has become day to me
The light bordereth on darkness.
13 Truly I look to Sheol as my home ;
My bed I spread in the place of darkness.
14 To corruption I say, " Thou art my father ;"
To the worm, " My mother, and my sister."

15 And where now is my hope?
And who will see my hope fulfilled?
16 To the bars of Sheol they must descend,
Yea, we shall descend together to the dust.

CHAPTER XVIII.

The second series of the controversy continued.

THE REPLY OF BILDAD TO JOB.

1 Then Bildad the Shuhite answered and said:
2 How long will it be ere you make an end of words?
Use sound arguments, and then we will speak.
3 Why are we regarded as brutes,
And reputed vile in your sight?
4 O Thou that tearest thyself in thine anger!
Must the earth be deserted for thee,
And the rock removed from its place?
5 Behold, the light of the wicked shall be put out;
The flame of his fire shall not shine.
6 Light shall turn to darkness in his tent,
And his lamp over him shall be extinguished.
7 His strong steps shall be straitened,
And his own plans shall cast him down.
8 For he is brought into the net by his own feet,
And into the pitfall he walks.
9 The snare takes him by the heel,
And the gin takes fast hold of him.
10 A net is secretly laid for him in the ground,
And a trap for him in the pathway.
11 Terrors alarm him on every side,
And harass him at his heels.
12 His strength shall be exhausted by hunger,
And destruction shall seize upon his side.
13 It shall devour the vigour of his frame,
The first-born of death shall devour his limbs.
14 His hope shall be rooted out of his tent,
And he shall be brought to the King of Terrors.
15 [Terror] shall dwell in his tent—for it is no longer his;
Sulphur shall be scattered upon his habitation.
16 His roots below, are dried up;
Above, his branches are withered.

17 His memory shall perish from the earth,
And no name shall he have in public places.
18 He shall be driven from light into darkness,
And they shall drive him out of the world.
19 He shall have no son or kinsman among the people,
And there shall be no survivor in his dwelling-place.
20 The dwellers in the East shall be astonished at his day;
They in the West shall be struck with horror.
21 Such are the dwellings of the impious man,
And this the place of him that knows not God.

CHAPTER XIX.

The second series in the controversy continued.

THE REPLY OF JOB TO BILDAD.

1 Then Job answered, and said:
2 How long will ye vex my soul,
And crush me with words?
3 These ten times have ye reviled me,
You are not ashamed to stun me [with reproaches].
4 And be it, indeed, that I have erred;
My error remaineth with myself.
5 Since ye do indeed magnify yourselves against me,
And urge vehemently against me this which is [the ground of] my reproach,
6 Know now that it is God who has overthrown me;
He hath encircled me with his net.
7 Lo, I complain of violence, but I receive no answer;
I cry aloud, but there is no justice.
8 My way he hath hedged up so that I cannot pass,
And in my paths he hath placed darkness.
9 He hath stripped me of my glory,
And taken the crown from my head.
10 He destroys me on every side—and I am gone;
He uprooteth my hope as a tree.
11 His anger burneth against me,
And he regardeth me as an enemy.
12 His troops advance together against me,
They throw up their way against me,
And they encamp round about my dwelling.
13 My brethren he hath put far from me,

And my acquaintances are wholly estranged from me.
14 My neighbours have failed,
And my intimate friends have forgotten me.
15 The foreigners in my house,
Yea, my own maid-servants regard me as a stranger—
I am an alien in their view.
16 I call my servant—and he gives me no answer ;
With my own mouth do I entreat him.
17 My breath is offensive to my wife—
Though I entreated her by [our love for] my own children.
18 Yea, young children despised me ;
I arose, and they spake against me.
19 All my intimate friends abhorred me,
And they whom I loved turned against me.
20 My bone cleaves to my skin and my flesh,
And I have scarcely escaped with the skin of my teeth.
21 Have pity upon me, have pity upon me, O my friends,
For the hand of God hath smitten me !
22 Why do ye persecute me as God does,
And are not satisfied with my flesh ?
23 O that my words were now written !
O that they were engraved on a tablet !
24 That with an iron graver, and with lead,
They were engraven upon a rock for ever !
25 For I know that my Avenger liveth,
And that hereafter he shall stand up upon the earth ;
26 And though after my skin this [flesh] be destroyed,
Yet even without my flesh shall I see God ;
27 Whom I shall see for myself,
And mine eyes shall behold, and not another—
Though my vitals are wasting away within me.
28 Therefore you should say, " Why do we persecute him ?
" Yea, the substance of piety is found in him."
29 Be ye afraid of the sword ;
For malice is a crime for the sword—
That ye may know that there is justice.

CHAPTER XX.

The second series in the controversy continued.

THE REPLY OF ZOPHAR TO JOB.

1 Then Zophar the Naamathite answered and said:
2 My distracted thoughts urge me to reply;
[I reply] from the impetuosity of my feelings.
3 I have heard thy injurious rebuke,
And the emotions of my mind cause me to answer.
4 Knowest thou not that from the most ancient times,
From the time when man was placed upon the earth,
5 That the triumphing of the wicked is short,
And the joy of the hypocrite is but for a moment?
6 Though his greatness mount up to the heavens,
And his excellency unto the clouds,
7 Yet he shall perish forever as the vilest substance:
They who have seen him shall say, Where is he?
8 He shall flee away as a dream, and not be found;
Yea, he shall vanish as a vision of the night.
9 The eye also which saw him shall see him no more,
And his place shall never more behold him.
10 His sons shall seek the aid of the poor,
And their hands shall give back his wealth.
11 His bones are full of his secret sins,
And they shall lie down with him in the dust.
12 Though wickedness be sweet in his mouth,
Though he hide it under his tongue,
13 Though he retain it, and will not part with it,
And keep it long in his mouth,
14 His food shall be changed within him;
It shall become the poison of asps within him.
15 He hath glutted himself with riches,
And he shall vomit them up again:
God shall expel them from him.
16 He shall suck the poison of asps;
The viper's tongue shall destroy him.
17 He shall never look upon the rivulets—
The streams of the valleys—of honey and butter.
18 The fruits of his labour shall he give back, and shall not enjoy them.
As property to be restored shall it be, and he shall not rejoice in it.

19 Because he hath oppressed, and then abandoned the poor,
And seized upon the house which he did not build,
20 Surely he shall not know internal peace,
He shall not save that in which he delights.
21 Nothing of his food shall remain;
Wherefore, his posterity shall not endure.
22 In the fulness of his abundance he shall be in want;
The whole power of wretchedness shall come upon him.
23 Enough indeed shall there be to fill himself—
God shall send upon him the fury of his anger,
And rain it down upon him while he is eating.
24 He shall flee from the iron weapon,
But the bow of brass shall pierce him through.
25 One draws out [the arrow], and it cometh through his body,
The glittering steel cometh out of his gall—
Terrors are upon him!
26 Every kind of calamity is treasured up for him;
A fire not kindled shall consume him;
That shall fare ill which is left in his tent.
27 The heavens shall reveal his iniquity;
And the earth shall rise up against him.
28 The property of his house shall disappear—
Flowing away in the day of the wrath of God.
29 This is the portion of the wicked man from God;
And the inheritance appointed for him by the Almighty.

CHAPTER XXI.

The second series in the controversy concluded.

THE ANSWER OF JOB.

1 But Job answered and said:
2 Hear attentively my speech;
And let this be your consolation.
3 Bear with me, and I will speak;
And after I have spoken, mock on!
4 As for me, is my argument before man?
And if this be so, why should not my spirit be in anguish?
5 Look on me, and be astonished!
And lay your hand on your mouth!
6 When I think on it, I am confounded;
And trembling seizes on my flesh.

7 Why is it that the wicked live,
Grow old, yea, are mighty in wealth?
8 Their children are established before them, and with them,
And their posterity before their eyes.
9 Their houses are safe from alarms,
And the rod of God is not upon them.
10 Their cattle conceive and fail not;
Their heifer calveth, and casteth not her young.
11 They send forth their little ones like a flock,
And their children sportively play.
12 They exhilarate themselves with the tabor and harp,
And rejoice at the sound of the pipe.
13 They spend their days in [the enjoyment of] good,
And in an instant they go down to the grave.
14 And they say to God, "Depart from us;
"We desire not the knowledge of thy ways.
15 "Who is the Almighty that we should serve him,
"And what will it profit us if we pray unto him?"
16 "Lo, their good" [you say] "is not in their own hand"—
(Far from me be the defence of the wicked;)
17 [But] how often does it occur that the light of the wicked is put out,
And that destruction cometh upon them,
And that God distributeth to them sorrows in his wrath?
18 How often are they as stubble before the wind,
And as chaff that the storm carrieth away
19 [You say] "God layeth up his iniquity for his children;
"He rewardeth him, and he shall know it.
20 "His eyes shall see his destruction,
"And he shall drink of the wrath of the Almighty.
21 "For what is his happiness in his family after him,
"When the number of his own months are cut off in the midst?"
22 [But I reply] Who shall impart knowledge to God,
To him who judgeth the highest!
23 One dieth in the fulness of his prosperity,
Being wholly at ease and quiet—
24 His watering-places for flocks abound with milk,
And his bones are moist with marrow;
25 And another dieth in the bitterness of his soul,
And never tasteth pleasure.
26 Alike they lie down in the dust,
And the worm covereth them.
27 Lo! I know your thoughts,
And the devices by which you wrong me.
28 For ye say, "Where is the house of the prince?

"And where the dwelling-place of the wicked?"
29 Have ye not inquired of the travellers,
And will you not admit their testimony,
30 That the wicked man is kept for the day of destruction,
And that he shall be brought forth in the day of fierce wrath?
31 Who charges him with his way to his face?
And who recompenses to him that which he has done?
32 And he shall be borne [with honour] to the grave;
And [friends] shall watch tenderly over his tomb.
33 Sweet to him shall be the clods of the valley;
Every man shall go out to honour him,
And of those before him there shall be no number.
34 And why then do you offer me vain consolations—
Since in your responses there is error?

CHAPTER XXII.

The third series in the controversy. Chap. xxii—xxxi.

THE THIRD SPEECH OF ELIPHAZ.

1 Then Eliphaz the Temanite answered and said:
2 Can a man then be profitable to God,
As a wise man may be profitable to himself?
3 Is it a pleasure to the Almighty if thou be just,
Or gain to him shouldst thou make thy ways perfect?
4 Will he contend with thee because he feareth thee—
With THEE will he enter into judgment?
5 Is not thy wickedness great?
Is there any end to thy sins?
6 For thou hast taken a pledge of thy brother unjustly,
And stripped off the clothing of the destitute.
7 Thou hast not given water to the weary to drink,
And from the hungry thou hast withholden bread.
8 But the man of power had the land;
The man of rank dwelt in it.
9 Thou hast sent widows away empty,
And the arms of the fatherless thou hast broken.
10 Therefore snares are round about thee,
And sudden fear troubleth thee.
11 Or darkness, so that thou canst not see,
And floods of waters cover thee.
12 Is not God in the height of heaven?

And behold the stars, how high they are!
13 And [hence] thou sayest, "How doth God know?
"And can he judge behind the thick darkness?
14 "Thick clouds are a covering to him, that he cannot see;
"And he walketh upon the arch of heaven."
15 But hast thou marked the ancient way
Which wicked men have trodden?
16 Who were huddled together [by the waters] in a moment,
And whose foundations the flood swept away?
17 Who said unto God, "Depart from us;"
And [who asked] what the Almighty could do for them?
18 And yet he filled their houses with good things!
Far from me be the counsel of the wicked!
19 The righteous see it, and rejoice;
And the innocent hold them in derision [saying:]
20 "Truly our adversary is destroyed!
"The fire hath consumed their abundance!"
21 Acquaint now thyself with him, and thou shalt have peace;
And thus shall good come unto thee.
22 Receive, I pray thee, the law from his mouth,
And lay up his words in thine heart.
23 If thou return to the Almighty thou shalt be built up:
If thou put away iniquity from thy tabernacle,
24 And cast to the dust thy precious treasure,
And to the stones of the brooks [again] the gold of Ophir,
25 Then shall the Almighty be thy precious treasure,
And shall be to thee piles of silver.
26 For then shalt thou have delight in the Almighty,
And shalt lift up thy face unto God.
27 Thou shalt pray unto him, and he shall hear thee,
And thou shalt perfect [the object of] thy vows.
28 Thou shalt form a purpose and it shall be accomplished,
And upon thy ways shall the light shine.
29 When [other men] are cast down,
Thou shalt say, "Cheer up!"
And the dejected thou shalt save.
30 Thou shalt deliver even the guilty man—
He shall be saved by the purity of thy hands.

CHAP. XXIII.

The third series of the controversy continued.

THE ANSWER OF JOB. Chap. xxiii. xxiv.

1 Then Job answered and said :
2 Even to-day is my complaint bitter ;
The hand that is upon me is heavier than my groaning.
3 O that I knew where I might find him
That I might come even to his seat !
4 I would order my cause before him,
And fill my mouth with arguments ;
5 I would know the words which he would answer me,
And understand what he would say unto me.
6 Would he contend with me with his mighty power ?
No : he would give me strength.
7 There the righteous man might argue the case before him ;
And I should be delivered for ever from him who would judge me.
8 But, behold, I go to the East, and he is not there,
And to the West, but I cannot perceive him ;
9 To the North, where he doth work, but I cannot behold him,
He hideth himself in the South, but I cannot see him.
10 But he knoweth my way ;
When he has tried me, I shall come forth as gold.
11 On his steps my foot hath seized ;
His way I have kept, and have not turned from it.
12 The commandment of his lips I have not neglected ;
More than every purpose of my own have I regarded the words of his mouth,
13 But he is of one [purpose], and who can turn him ?
And what he desireth, that he doeth.
14 He performeth the thing that is appointed for me ;
And there are many such purposes in his mind.
15 Therefore I am troubled before him ;
When I consider, I am afraid of him.
16 For God maketh my heart faint,
And the Almighty troubleth me ;
17 Because I was not taken away before darkness came,
And he hath not hidden the cloud from mine eyes.

CHAP. XXIV.

1 Why, since no events are hidden from the Almighty,
Do not his friends see his judgments?
2 They [the wicked] remove the landmarks;
They drive off the flock and pasture it.
3 They drive away the ass of the fatherless;
They take the widow's ox for a pledge.
4 They push the needy from the way;
The poor of the earth hide themselves together.
5 Behold, like wild asses of the desert, they go forth to their employment,
Rising early in the morning to plunder;
The desert furnishes food to them and their children.
6 They reap their grain in the field [of others],
And they gather the vintage of the oppressor.
7 They cause the naked to lodge without clothing,
And without covering in the cold.
8 They are wet with the showers of the mountains,
And embrace the rock for want of a shelter.
9 They tear away the fatherless from the breast,
And of the poor they exact a pledge.
10 They cause him to go naked without clothing;
And they are made to carry the sheaf hungry.
11 They cause them to express oil within their walls;
They tread their wine-presses, and yet suffer thirst.
12 From the city mortals groan,
And the soul of the wounded crieth out;
But God does not lay this guilt to heart.
13 Others hate the light;
They know not its ways;
They abide not in its paths.
14 At early dawn rises the murderer;
He kills the poor and the needy;
In the night he is as a thief.
15 The eye of the adulterer waits for the twilight,
Saying, "No eye will see me,"
And he puts a mask upon his face.
16 In the dark they dig through houses;
In the day-time they shut themselves up;
They are strangers to the light.
17 For the morning is to them the very shadow of death;
For they are familiar with the terrors of the shadow of death.
18 They are like a light boat on the face of the waters;
Accursed is their lot in the earth;
On the way of vineyards they look not.

19 Drought and heat steal away the snow waters ;
The grave, in like manner, those who have sinned.
20 The mother soon forgets him ;
The worm feeds sweetly on him ;
He is no more remembered—
Like a decayed tree the wicked man [gently] falls.
21 He oppresseth the barren, that hath not borne,
And doeth not good to the widow.
22 He destroys also the mighty by his power ;
He rises up, and no one is secure of life ;
23 God gives to him security, and he is sustained ;
Yea, his eyes are upon his ways.
24 They are exalted for a little time—and then are not—
They are brought low, and are gathered [to their fathers] like others ;
And like the ripe ears of grain they are cut off.
25 If it be not so, who will confute me,
And show my speech to be worthless ?

CHAPTER XXV.

The third series in the controversy continued.

THE REPLY OF BILDAD TO JOB.

1 Then answered Bildad the Shuhite, and said :
2 Dominion and fear are with Him ;
He maintaineth peace in his high places.
3 Is there any numbering of his armies ?
And upon whom doth not his light arise ?
4 And how then can man be righteous before God ?
And how can he be pure that is born of a woman ?
5 Behold, even the moon is not bright ;
And the stars are not pure in his sight.
6 How much less man that is a worm !
And the son of man that is a reptile !

CHAPTER XXVI.

The third series in the controversy concluded.

ANSWER OF JOB. Chap. xxvi.—xxxi.

1 Then Job answered and said :
2 How hast thou helped the weak,

And strengthened the feeble arm?
3 How hast thou counselled the ignorant,
And declared wisdom in abundance?
4 To whom hast thou uttered these words,
And whose spirit went from thee?
5 The Shades tremble from beneath,
The waters, and their inhabitants.
6 Sheol is naked before him,
And destruction hath no covering.
7 He stretcheth out the North over empty space,
And hangeth the earth upon nothing.
8 He bindeth up the waters in his thick clouds,
And the cloud is not rent under them.
9 He withdraweth the face of his throne,
And spreadeth his cloud upon it.
10 He hath drawn a circular bound upon the waters,
To the confines of the light and darkness.
11 The pillars of heaven tremble,
And are astonished at his rebuke,
12 By his power he stilleth the sea,
And by his wisdom he scourgeth its pride.
13 By his spirit he hath garnished the heavens;
His hand hath formed the fleeing serpent.
14 Lo, these are but the outlines of his ways;
And how faint the whisper which we hear of him!
[Should he speak with] the thunder of his power, who could understand him?

CHAP. XXVII.

1 Moreover, Job continued his discourse, and said:
2 As God liveth, who has rejected my cause,
And the Almighty, who has embittered my spirit,
3 As long as I have life in me,
And the breath imparted by God is in my nostrils,
4 My lips shall not speak wickedness,
Nor my tongue utter deceit.
5 Far be it from me that I should acknowledge you to be correct;
Till I die I will assert my integrity.
6 My righteousness I hold fast, and will not loose my grasp;
My heart shall not reproach me for any part of my life.
7 Let mine enemy be as the wicked,
And he that riseth up against me as the unrighteous.
8 For what is the hope of the hypocrite when [God] cuts him off,

When he taketh away his life?
9 Will God listen to his cry
When trouble cometh upon him?
10 Will he delight himself in the Almighty?
Will he call at all times upon God?
11 I will teach you by the operations of God;
That which is with the Almighty I will not conceal.
12 Behold, ye yourselves have all seen it;
And why do you cherish such vain opinions [saying]:
13 "This is the portion of a wicked man from God;
"And the inheritance which oppressors receive from the Almighty—
14 "If his children are multiplied, it is for the sword;
"And his offspring shall not be satisfied with bread.
15 "His survivors shall be buried by Death,
"And his widows shall not weep.
16 "Though he heap up silver as the dust,
"And prepare raiment as the mire,
17 "He may prepare it, but the just shall wear it,
"And the innocent shall share the silver.
18 "He buildeth his house like the moth,
"Or like a shed which a watchman maketh.
19 "The rich man lieth down, and is not buried
"In the twinkling of an eye he is no more.
20 "Terrors come upon him like waters;
"In the night a tempest stealeth him away.
21 "The East wind carrieth him away, and he departeth;
" And it sweeps him away from his place.
22 "For God shooteth at him, and does not spare;
"He would gladly escape out of his hand.
23 "Men clap their hands at him;
"They hiss him away from his place."

CHAPTER XXVIII.

1 Truly there is a vein for silver,
And a place for gold where they refine it.
2 Iron is obtained from the earth,
And ore is fused into copper.
3 Man putteth an end to darkness,
And completely searches every thing—
The rocks—the thick darkness—and the shadow of death.
4 He sinks a shaft far from a human dwelling;
They, unsupported by the feet, hang suspended;

Far from men they swing to and fro.
5 The earth—out of it cometh bread;
And when turned up beneath, it resembles fire.
6 Its stones are the place of sapphires,
And gold dust pertains to it.
7 The path thereto no bird knoweth,
And the vulture's eye hath not seen it.
8 The fierce wild beasts have not trodden it;
And the lion hath not walked over it.
9 Man layeth his hand upon the flinty rock;
He upturneth mountains from their foundations.
10 He cutteth out canals among the rocks,
And his eye seeth every precious thing.
11 He restraineth the streams from trickling down,
And bringeth hidden things to light.
12 But where shall wisdom be found?
And where is the place of understanding?
13 Man knoweth not the price thereof;
Nor can it be found in the land of the living.
14 The deep saith, It is not in me;
And the sea saith, It is not with me.
15 The pure gold cannot purchase it;
And silver cannot be weighed out as its price.
16 It cannot be estimated by the gold of Ophir;
By the precious onyx, or the sapphire.
17 Gold and the crystal are not to be compared with it;
And jewels of fine gold cannot buy it.
18 No mention shall be made of coral or of crystal,
For the price of wisdom is above rubies.
19 The topaz of Cush cannot equal it;
Nor can it be purchased with pure gold.
20 Whence, then, cometh wisdom?
And where is the place of understanding?
21 Since it is concealed from the eyes of all the living,
And hidden from the fowls of the air.
22 Destruction and Death say,
"We have heard [only] a rumour of it with our ears."
23 God causes its way to be understood,
And he knows its place.
24 For he looketh to the ends of the earth;
[All] that is under the whole heavens he seeth.
25 When to the winds he gave weight,
And when he measured out the waters
26 When he prescribed laws for the rain,

And a path for the thunder-flash ;
27 Then he saw it, and he made it known ;
He prepared it, and he also searched it out.
28 And he said to man—
"Lo ! the fear of the Lord—that is wisdom ;
"And departure from evil is understanding."

CHAP. XXIX.

1 Moreover, Job continued his discourse, and said .
2 O that I were as in months past,
As in the days when God was my protector !
3 When his lamp shone over my head,
And when by his light I walked through darkness !
4 As I was in the days of my strength,
When God abode in my tent as a friend !
5 When the Almighty was yet with me,
And my children were round about me !
6 When I washed my steps in cream,
And the rock poured me out rivers of oil !
7 When I went forth to the gate through the city,
And prepared my seat in the public place,
8 The young men saw me, and respectfully retired before me,
And the aged arose, and stood;
9 The princes refrained from speaking,
And laid their hand upon their mouth.
10 The voice of counsellors was silent,
And their tongue cleaved to the roof of their mouth.
11 For the ear heard, and it blessed me ;
And the eye saw, and it bore witness to me.
12 For I rescued the poor when they cried,
And the fatherless, when there was none to help him.
13 The blessing of him that was ready to perish came upon me,
And I caused the heart of the widow to sing with joy.
14 I put on righteousness, and it clothed me ;
And justice was my robe and diadem.
15 I was eyes to the blind,
And feet was I to the lame ;
16 I was a father to the poor,
And the cause of the unknown I searched out.
17 And I broke the teeth of the wicked,
And from their teeth I plucked away the spoil.
18 Then said I, "I shall die in my nest ;
"I shall multiply my days as the sand."
19 My root was exposed to the waters,

The dew lay all night on my branches.
20 My glory was fresh in me,
And my bow gathered strength in my hand.
21 To me men gave ear and waited,
And were silent at my counsel
22 After my words they made no reply,
And my speech dropped upon them.
23 And they waited for me as for the rain;
And they opened their mouths wide as for the latter rain.
24 Did I smile upon them, they confided not [in their plans],
And the light of my countenance they could not cast down.
25 I chose out their way, and sat as a chief;
I dwelt as a king in the midst of an army,
And as a comforter among mourners.

CHAP. XXX.

1 But now they who are younger than I have me in derision,
Whose fathers I would have disdained to set with the dogs of my flock
2 Yet the strength of their hands, what is it to me,
In whom vigour is perished?
3 On account of hunger and famine they are wholly emaciated;
Gnawing in the wilderness—
In the shades of desolation and waste.
4 Who pluck up the salt-wort among the bushes,
And the root of the Retem is their food.
5 They were driven from among men;
They shouted after them as after a thief.
6 They dwell in horrid valleys,
In the holes of the earth, and in the rocks.
7 Among the bushes they brayed;
Under the thorns they were huddled together.
8 Children of the fool; yea, children of those without a name,
They were driven out of the land.
9 And now I am become their song;
Yea, I am their by-word.
10 They abominate me, they stand aloof from me,
They forbear not to spit before my face!
11 For they let loose all restraint, and afflict me;
They also cast off the bridle before me.
12 On my right hand rises up the low brood;
They trip up my feet;
They cast up against me ways for my destruction.
13 They break up my path;
They help forward my ruin—

Men who have no helper!
14 As through a wide breach they came upon me,
They rolled themselves tumultuously along with the ruins!
15 Terrors are turned upon me,
They pursue my generous nature as the wind;
And my welfare has passed away as a cloud.
16 And now my soul is poured out upon me;
The days of affliction have taken hold upon me.
17 At night my bones are pierced through;
And my jaws take no rest.
18 By its great power [disease] has become my garment;
It girds me about like the mouth of my tunic.
19 He hath cast me into the mire,
And I am become like dust and ashes.
20 I cry unto thee, but thou dost not hear me;
I stand up, but thou dost not regard me.
21 Thou art become cruel unto me;
With thy strong hand thou dost persecute me.
22 Thou liftest me up to the wind; thou causest me to ride upon it;
Thou causest me to melt away; thou terrifiest me.
23 For I know that thou wilt bring me to death;
And to the house appointed for all living.
24 Nevertheless over the ruins he will not stretch out his hand,
If when he destroys there is prayer among them.
25 Did not I weep for him that was in trouble?
Was not my soul grieved for the poor?
26 When I looked for good, then evil came;
When I looked for light, then came darkness.
27 My bowels boil, and rest not;
The days of anguish have come upon me.
28 I am become black, but not by the sun;
I stand up and weep in the congregation.
29 I am become a brother to the jackal,
And a companion to the ostrich.
30 My skin is black upon me:
And my bones burn with heat.
31 My harp also is turned to mourning,
And my pipe to notes of grief.

Chap. XXXI.

1 I made a covenant with mine eyes;
How then could I think upon a virgin?
2 For what portion should I have from God above,
And what would be my inheritance from the Almighty on high?

3 Is not destruction for the wicked,
And strange punishment for the workers of iniquity?
4 Does he not see my ways,
And number all my steps?
5 If I have walked with falsehood,
And if my foot hath hasted after deception,
6 Let Him weigh me in an even balance,
And let God know my integrity.
7 If my steps have turned aside from the way,
And my heart have followed my eyes,
And any stain have cleaved to my hand,
8 Then may I sow, and another reap,
And then may my harvests be rooted up!
9 If my heart have been enticed by a woman;
Or if I have laid wait at my neighbour's door,
10 Then let my wife be a mill-wench to another,
And let others bow down upon her.
11 For this is a heinous crime;
Yea, this would be iniquity to be punished by the judges.
12 For it is a fire that would burn to destruction.
And root out all my increase.
13 If I have refused justice to my man-servant or maid-servant
When they had a cause with me,
14 What shall I do when God riseth up?
And when he visiteth, what shall I answer him?
15 Did not He that made me in the womb make him?
Did not the same One fashion us in the womb?
16 If I have withheld the poor from their desire,
Or caused the eyes of the widow to fail;
17 If I have eaten my morsel alone,
And the fatherless hath not eaten of it;
18 (For from my youth he [the orphan] grew up with me, as with a father,
And I was her guide [of the widow] from my earliest days);—
19 If I have seen any one perishing for want of clothing,
Or any poor man without covering;
20 If his loins have not blessed me,
And if he has not been warmed with the fleece of my sheep,
21 If I have lifted up my hand against the fatherless,
Because I saw that I had help in the gate;
22 Then may my shoulder fall from the blade,
And mine arm be broken from the upper-bone!
23 For destruction from God was a terror to me;
And before his majesty I could not do it.
24 If I have made gold my trust,

Or said to the fine gold, Thou art my confidence;
25 If I rejoiced because my wealth was great,
And because mine hand had found much;
26 If I beheld the sun when it shined,
And the moon advancing in its brightness,
27 And my heart has been secretly enticed,
And my mouth has kissed my hand—
28 This also would have been a crime to be punished by the judge,
For I should have denied the God who is above.
29 If I have rejoiced at the destruction of him that hated me,
And exulted when evil came upon him—
30 But no! I have not suffered my mouth to sin
By imprecating a curse on his soul;—
31 If my domestics could not at all times say,
"Who will show an instance when we have not been satisfied from his hospitable table?"*
32 The stranger did not lodge in the street,
My doors I opened to the traveller;
33 If I have covered my transgressions as Adam,
By concealing my iniquity in my bosom,
34 Then let me be confounded before a great multitude!
Let the contempt of families crush me!
Yea, let me keep silence, and never go out of my door!
35 O that He would hear me!
Behold my defence! May the Almighty answer me!
Would that He who contends with me would write down his charge;
36 Truly upon my shoulder would I bear it;
I would bind it upon me as a diadem!
37 I would tell the number of my steps to him;
Like a prince would I approach him!
38 If my land cry out against me,
And the furrows likewise complain;
39 If I have eaten its fruits without payment,
And extorted the living of its owners;
40 Let thistles grow up instead of wheat,
And noxious weeds instead of barley.

* This translation is more paraphrastic than I have made in any other instance, but it was not easy to express the sense by a literal rendering

CHAPTER XXXII.

SPEECH OF ELIHU.

1 So these three men ceased to answer Job, because he was righteous in
2 his own eyes. Then was kindled the anger of Elihu, the son of Barachel the Buzite, of the family of Ram; against Job was his anger
3 kindled, because he vindicated himself more than God. Also against
his three friends was his anger kindled, because they had not found an
4 answer, and yet had condemned Job. Now Elihu had waited till Job
5 had spoken, because they were older than himself. When Elihu saw
that there was no answer in the mouth of these three men, then his
6 anger was kindled. Then Elihu, the son of Barachel the Buzite,
answered and said:

I am young, and ye are very old;
Therefore I was afraid,
And durst not make known to you my opinion.
7 I said, "Days should speak,
"And multitude of years should teach wisdom."
8 But there is a spirit in man;
And the Inspiration of the Almighty giveth him understanding.
9 Great men are not always wise;
Neither do the aged always understand what is right.
10 Therefore I said, "Hearken unto me;
"I also will declare mine opinion."
11 Behold, I waited for your words;
I listened for your arguments,
While ye searched out what to say.
12 Yea, I have attended to you;
And behold there is no one that hath refuted Job,
Or answered his words:—
13 Lest ye should say, "We have found out wisdom;"—
God only can subdue him; not man.
14 Now, he did not direct his discourse against me;
And I will not answer him with speeches like yours.
15 They were confounded; they answered no more;
They put words far from them.
16 And I waited, although they did not speak;
Although they stood still, and answered no more.
17 Even I will answer now on my part;
Even I will show mine opinion.

18 For I am full of words ;
The spirit within me doth constrain me.
19 Behold I am as wine which has no vent ;
I am ready to burst like new bottles.
20 I will speak that I may breathe more freely,
I will open my lips and reply.
21 May I not be partial to any man's person !
And let me not flatter any one !
22 For I cannot flatter—
In a little time my Maker will bear me away !

Chap. XXXIII.

1 Hear, therefore, O Job, I beseech thee, my discourse,
And to all my words give ear.
2 Behold now I open my mouth,
My tongue now speaks in my mouth.
3 My words shall be in the uprightness of my heart,
And my lips shall speak knowledge in its purity.
4 The Spirit of God hath made me,
And the breath of the Almighty hath given me life.
5 If thou art able, answer me ;
Set [thy words] in array before me ; stand firm !
6 Lo ! I, according to thy request, am in the place of God ;—
Yet from clay am I also formed.
7 Lo ! my terror shall not make thee afraid ;
And my hand shall not be heavy upon thee.
8 Surely thou hast said in my hearing,
And I have heard the voice of thy words,
9 "I am pure, and without transgression ;
"I am innocent, and there is no iniquity in me.
10 "Behold, He seeketh causes of enmity against me,
"He regardeth me as his enemy,
11 "He putteth my feet in the stocks ;
"He watcheth all my paths."
12 Behold, in this thou art not right—I will answer thee—
For God is greater than man.
13 Why dost thou strive against him ?
For he doth not give account of any of his doings.
14 For God speaketh once,
Yea twice, when man regardeth it not.
15 In a dream, in a vision of the night,
When deep sleep falleth upon men,
In slumberings upon the bed,
16 Then he openeth the ears of men,

And sealeth instruction unto them ;
17 That He may turn man from his purpose,
And hide pride from man.
18 He keepeth him back from the pit,
And his life from perishing by a violent death.
19 He is also chastened with pain upon his bed,
And the multitude of his bones with violent suffering,
20 So that his life abhorreth bread,
And his soul the choicest food.
21 His flesh is consumed so that it cannot be seen,
And his bones that were invisible are naked.
22 And his soul draweth near to the pit,
And his life to the destroyers.
23 If there be with him a messenger [of God],
An interpreter—one among a thousand—
To announce to man his uprightness,
24 Then will he be gracious unto him, and say,
"Deliver him from going down to the pit ;
"I have found a ransom."
25 His flesh shall become fresher than a child's ;
He shall return to the days of his youth.
26 He shall pray unto God and he will be merciful to him
And he shall see his face with joy,
For he deals with men in equity.
27 He looketh attentively on man,
And when he says,
"I have sinned, and acted perversely,
"And it has been no advantage to me,"
28 Then he delivers his soul from going down to the pit,
And his life beholds the light.
29 Lo, all these things doeth God,
Twice, yea thrice, with man,
30 That he may bring him back from the pit,
To enjoy the light of life.
31 Mark well, O Job, hearken unto me !
Keep silence, and I will speak.
32 If thou hast any thing to say, answer me:
Speak, for I desire to do thee justice.
33 But if not, do thou listen to me ;
Attend, and I will teach thee wisdom.

Chap. XXXIV.

1 And Elihu proceeded, and said :
2 Hear my words, ye wise men ;

And ye that have knowledge, give ear to me.
3 For the ear trieth words,
As the mouth tasteth meat.
4 Let us choose to ourselves what is right;
Let us know among ourselves what is good.
5 For Job hath said, "I am righteous;
"And God hath taken away my right."
6 In respect to my cause I am regarded as a liar,
"The arrow in me is fatal—though I am free from transgression."
7 What man is like Job,
Who drinketh up scorning like water;
8 Who keepeth company with the workers of iniquity,
And walketh with wicked men?
9 For he hath said, "It is no advantage to a man
"When he is in friendship with God."
10 Wherefore hearken unto me, ye men of understanding.
Far be iniquity from God!
And injustice far from the Almighty!
11 For he will render to man his work,
And requite every man according to his way.
12 Surely God will not do wickedly,
Nor will the Almighty pervert justice.
13 Who hath committed to him the charge of the earth?
Or who hath arranged the whole world?
14 If he form such a purpose in regard to man,
The spirit and the breath he will gather to himself;
15 All flesh will expire together,
And man will return to the dust.
16 If thou hast understanding, hear this;
Hearken to the voice of my words!
17 Shall he that hateth justice govern?
Wilt thou condemn him that is supremely just?
18 Is it proper to say to a king, "Thou art wicked?"
Or to princes, "Ye are unrighteous?"
19 How much more to him that shows no partiality to princes,
Nor regards the rich more than the poor?
For they are all the work of his hands.
20 In a moment they die,
And at midnight are the people shaken and pass away;—
Yea, the mighty are destroyed without hand.
21 For his eyes are upon the ways of men,
He seeth all their steps.
22 There is no darkness nor shadow of death
Where the workers of iniquity may hide themselves.

23 For he needeth not long to regard man
To bring him before God in judgment.
24 He dasheth in pieces the mighty without inquiry,
And setteth others in their stead.
25 For he knoweth their works,
And he bringeth night upon them, and they are crushed.
26 On account of their being wicked he smiteth them
In the presence of beholders,
27 Because they turned away from him,
And had no regard to his ways,
28 And caused the cry of the poor to come before him ;—
For the cry of the oppressed he heareth.
29 When he giveth rest, who then can make trouble ?
And when he hideth his face, who then can behold him ?
And this in respect to a nation and an individual alike,
30 That the wicked should no more reign,
Nor be snares to the people.
31 Surely it is proper to say to God,
"I have received chastisement ; I will no more offend.
32 "What I see not, teach thou me ;
"If I have done iniquity, I will do so no more."
33 Shall it be from thee that God recompenses it [human conduct] because thou dost refuse ?
For thou must choose, and not I,
And what thou knowest, speak.
34 Men of understanding will say to me,
And the man of wisdom who has heard me,
35 "Job hath spoken without knowledge,
And his words are without wisdom."
36 My desire is that Job may be fully tried
On account of his answers for wicked men.
37 For he hath added rebellion to his sin ;
He clappeth his hands among us,
And multiplieth his words against God.

CHAP. XXXV.

1 And Elihu proceeded and said :
2 Thinkest thou this to be right
When thou saidst, "I am more righteous than God ?"
3 For thou hast said [to thyself] "What advantage will it be to thee ?
"What profit shall I have more than if I had not sinned ?"
4 I will answer thee,
And thy companions with thee.
5 Look up to the heavens, and see !

And behold the clouds, which are high above thee !
6 If thou sinnest, what doest thou against Him ?
And if thy transgressions be multiplied, what dost thou do to Him ?
7 If thou art righteous, what dost thou give Him ?
Or what does He receive at thy hand ?
8 Thy wickedness can injure only a man like thyself.
And thy righteousness profit only a son of man.
9 Men are made to cry out [indeed] on account of the multitude of their wrongs ;
They cry out on account of the arm of the mighty.
10 But none saith, " Where is God my maker,
" Who in the night of calamity giveth songs ?
11 " Who would teach us more than the beasts of the earth,
" And make us wiser than the fowls of heaven."
12 Then they cry aloud, but he giveth no answer,
On account of the pride of [such] wicked men.
13 For God will not hear vain supplication,
Nor will the Almighty regard it.
14 Although thou sayest that thou canst not see him,
Yet justice is with him ; only wait thou for him.
15 But now the visitations of his anger are almost as nothing ;
And he has not taken cognizance with strictness of transgression.
16 Job hath opened his mouth without understanding ;
He hath multiplied words without knowledge.

CHAP. XXXVI.

1 Elihu also proceeded and said :
2 Bear with me a little farther, and I will show you,
For there is much yet to be said for God.
3 I will bring my knowledge from afar,
And will ascribe righteousness to my Maker.
4 For truly my words shall not be false ;
One perfect in knowledge is with thee.
5 Behold, God is great, and despiseth not any
Great is he in strength of understanding.
6 He preserveth not the life of the wicked ;
He doeth justice to the oppressed.
7 He withdraweth not his eyes from the righteous ;
But with kings are they upon the throne,
And he establisheth them for ever, and they are exalted.
8 And if [the righteous] are bound in fetters,
And holden in the cords of affliction,
9 Then he showeth them their deeds,
And their transgressions that they have been great.

10 He openeth also their ear to instruction,
And commandeth them to turn from iniquity.
11 If they obey and serve him they spend their days in prosperity
And their years in pleasure.
12 But if they will not obey they perish with the sword,
And they die without knowledge.
13 But the hypocrites in heart treasure up wrath ;
They cry not [to God] when he bindeth them.
14 They die in their youth ;
And their life [is closed] with the grossly impure,
15 He delivereth the afflicted in their distress,
And openeth their ears in their trials.
16 In like manner he would have removed thee from a pent-up way
To a broad place where there is not straitness,
And the provision of thy table would have been full of fatness.
17 But if thou dost fully hold the sentiments of the wicked,
Such sentiments and justice will be close together.*
18 For there is wrath ; beware lest he take thee away with his stroke
Then a great ransom cannot save thee.
19 Will he esteem thy riches ?
No ! not gold, nor all the abundance of wealth.
20 Long not for the night,
To go to the people beneath them.
21 Take heed ! regard not iniquity,
For this hast thou preferred to affliction.
22 Behold, God is exalted in his power ;
Who is a teacher like him ?
23 Who hath appointed him his way ?
And who can say, " Thou hast done iniquity ?"
24 Forget not thou to magnify his work,
On which men look †
25 All men see it ;
Mortals behold it from afar.
26 Lo, God is great, and we know him not ;
The number of his years is unsearchable.
27 For he draweth up the drops of water,
They distil rain in its vapour,
28 Which the clouds pour down ;
They pour it upon man in abundance.
29 Who also can understand the outspreading of the clouds,
And the fearful thunderings in his pavilion ?

* Or, will sustain each other

† That is, the works of the visible creation.

30 Behold, he spreadeth his light upon it ;
He also covereth the depths of the sea.
31 By these he executeth judgment upon the people ;
By these also he giveth food in abundance.
32 With his hands he covereth the lightning,
And commandeth it where to strike.
33 He pointeth out to it his friends—
The collecting of his wrath is upon the wicked.

Chap. XXXVII.

1 At this also my heart palpitates,
And is moved out of its place.
2 Hear, O hear the thunder of his voice !
The muttering thunder that goes from his mouth !
3 He directeth it under the whole heaven,
And his lightning to the ends of the earth.
4 After it, the thunder roareth ;
He thundereth with the voice of his majesty,
And he will not restrain the tempest when his voice is heard.
5 God thundereth marvellously with his voice
He doeth wonders which we cannot comprehend.
6 For he saith to the snow, " Be thou on the earth,"
To the pouring forth of the rain, also ; even the pouring forth of his mighty rains.
7 He sealeth up the hand of every man,
That all the men whom he has made may have knowledge.
8 Then the beasts go into their dens,
And abide in their caverns.
9 Out of the South cometh the whirlwind,
And cold out of the North.
10 By the breath of God the frost is produced,
And the broad waters become compressed.
11 Serenity also expels the thick cloud ;
His light scatters the cloud,
12 And it is turned about by his direction,
To execute all that he has commanded upon the face of the habitable world.
13 Whether for correction, or for his land, or for mercy,
He causeth it to come.
14 Give ear, O Job, to this ;
Stand and consider the wonderful works of God.
15 Dost thou know how God arranges these things,
And how he causes the lightning to flash from the dark cloud ?
16 Dost thou understand how the clouds are suspended,

The wondrous works of Him that is perfect in wisdom?
17 How thy garments become warm,
When he maketh the earth sultry by the South wind?
18 Hast thou aided him in spreading out the firmament,
That stands strong, like a molten mirror?
19 Teach us what we shall say unto him;
We cannot address him by reason of darkness.
20 Shall it be told him that I have presumed to speak?
Surely if a man should speak to him, he would be destroyed.
21 And now—men cannot look upon the bright splendour that is on the clouds,
For the wind passeth along, and maketh an opening!
22 Golden splendour approaches from the North:—
How fearful is the majesty of God!
23 The Almighty!—we cannot find him out!
Great in power, and in justice, and vast in righteousness!
He does not oppress!
24 Wherefore men should be filled with awe;
The wise in heart he does not regard.

CHAPTER XXXVIII.

JEHOVAH'S FIRST ADDRESS TO JOB. Chap. xxxviii., xxxix.

1 Then Jehovah answered Job out of the storm, and said:
2 Who is this that darkeneth counsel by words without knowledge?
3 Gird up now thy loins like a man;
I will put questions to thee, and do thou inform me
4 Where wast thou when I founded the earth?
Declare, if thou hast knowledge!
5 Who then fixed the measure of it? For thou knowest!
Who stretched the line upon it?
6 Upon what are its foundations settled?
Or who laid its corner-stone?
7 When the morning stars sang together,
And all the sons of God shouted for joy?
8 Who shut up the sea with doors
In its bursting forth as from the womb?
9 When I made the cloud its garment,
And swathed it in thick darkness:
10 I measured out for it my limits,
And fixed its bars and doors;
11 And said, Thus far shalt thou come, but no further,

And here shall thy proud waves be stayed!
12 Hast thou, in thy life, given commandment to the morning,
Or caused the dawn to know its place,
13 That it may seize on the far corners of the earth,
And scatter the robbers before it?
14 It turns itself along like clay under a seal,
And all things stand forth as if in gorgeous apparel.
15 But from the wicked their light is withheld,
And the high arm is broken.
16 Hast thou penetrated to the springs of the sea,
And hast thou walked about in the recesses of the deep?
17 Have the gates of death been opened to thee,
Or hast thou seen the gates of the shadow of death?
18 Hast thou observed the breadths of the earth?
Declare, if thou knowest it all.
19 Where is the way to the dwelling-place of light?
And the darkness—where is its place—
20 That thou couldst conduct it to its limits,
And that thou shouldst know the path to its dwelling?
21 Didst thou know this because thou wast then born,
Or because the number of thy days is great?
22 Hast thou been into the store-houses of snow,
Or seen the store-houses of hail,
23 Which I have reserved until the time of trouble,
To the day of battle and war?
24 By what way is the light distributed,
And how is the East wind spread abroad upon the earth?
25 Who hath divided for the shower a channel,
And who hath made a path for the thunder flash,
26 To give rain to a land where there is no man,
Upon the desert where no one dwells;
27 To saturate the desert and the barren place,
And to cause the bud of the tender herb to germinate?
28 Hath the rain a father?
And who hath begotten the drops of the dew?
29 From whose womb came the ice?
The hoar frost of heaven—who gave it birth?
30 The waters are hid as under a stone;
And the surface of the deep becomes a solid mass.
31 Canst thou bind the sweet influences of Pleiades,
Or loose the bands of Orion?
32 Canst thou bring forth Mazzaroth in his season,
Or lead forth the Bear with her young?
33 Knowest thou the laws of the heavens,

Or hast thou appointed their dominion over the earth?
34 Canst thou lift up thy voice to the clouds,
So that the overflowings of the waters shall cover thee?
35 Canst thou send forth the lightnings, so that they shall go,
And shall say to thee, "Here we are?"
36 Who hath imparted understanding to thy inward parts?
Or given intelligence to thy mind?
37 Who can number the clouds by wisdom?
And who can empty the bottles of heaven,
38 When the dust flows into a molten mass,
And the clods cleave fast together?
39 Canst thou hunt for the lion his prey?
And the hunger of the young lions canst thou satisfy,
40 When they crouch in their dens,
And lie in wait in the thicket?
41 Who provideth for the raven his food,
When his young cry unto God,
And wander for lack of food?

CHAP. XXXIX.

1 Knowest thou the time when the wild goats of the rock bring forth?
Or canst thou observe the birth-throes of the hind?
2 Canst thou number the months that they fulfil;
Knowest thou the season when they bring forth?
3 They bow themselves; they give birth to their young;
They cast forth their sorrows.
4 Their young ones increase in strength;
They grow up in the wilderness;
They go from them and return no more.
5 Who hath sent forth the wild ass free?
Or who hath loosed the bands of the wild ass?
6 Whose home I have made the wilderness,
And his dwellings the barren land.
7 He scorneth the uproar of the city;
The cry of the driver he heedeth not.
8 The range of the mountains is his pasture;
He searcheth after every green thing.
9 Will the unicorn be willing to serve thee?
Will he abide through the night at thy crib?
10 Wilt thou bind him with his band in the furrow
And will he harrow the valleys after thee?
11 Wilt thou trust him because his strength is great
Or wilt thou commit thy labour to him?
12 Wilt thou have confidence in him to bring in thy grain,

And to gather it to thy threshing-floor?
13 A wing of exulting fowls moves joyfully!
Is it the wing and the plumage of the stork?
14 She leaveth her eggs upon the ground,
And upon the dust she warmeth them,
15 And forgetteth that the foot may crush them,
And that the wild beast may break them.
16 She is hardened towards her young, as if they were not hers;
In vain is her travail, and without solicitude;
17 Because God hath withheld wisdom from her,
And hath not imparted to her understanding.
18 In the time when she raiseth herself up on high,
She laugheth at the horse and his rider.
19 Hast thou given the horse his strength?
Hast thou clothed his neck with thunder?
20 Dost thou make him leap as the locust?
How terrible is the glory of his nostrils!
21 He paweth in the valley; he exulteth in his strength;
He goeth forth into the midst of arms,
22 He laugheth at fear, and is nothing daunted;
And he turneth not back from the sword.
23 Upon him rattleth the quiver,
The glittering spear and the lance.
24 In his fierceness and rage he devoureth the ground,
And will no longer stand still when the trumpet sounds.
25 When the trumpet sounds he saith, "Aha!"
And from afar he snuffeth the battle—
The war-cry of the princes, and the battle-shout.
26 Is it by thy understanding that the hawk flieth,
And spreadeth his wings toward the South?
27 Is it at thy command that the eagle mounteth up,
And that he buildeth his nest on high?
28 He inhabiteth the rock, and abideth there—
Upon the crag of the rock, and the high fortress.
29 From thence he spieth out his prey;
His eyes discern it from afar.
30 His young ones greedily gulp down blood;
And where the slain are, there is he.

CHAPTER XL.

JEHOVAH'S SECOND ADDRESS TO JOB. Chap. xl., xli.

1 Moreover JEHOVAH answered Job, and said:
2 Will he that would enter into an argument with the Almighty now instruct him?
Will he that wished to carry his cause before God now reply?
3 Then Job answered JEHOVAH and said:
4 Behold, I am vile! What can I answer thee?
I will lay my hand upon my mouth.
5 Once did I speak; but I will not answer again:
Yea, twice; but I will add no more.
6 Then JEHOVAH answered Job out of the whirlwind and said:
7 Gird up now thy loins like a man!
I will ask of thee, and do thou instruct me!
8 Wilt thou reverse my judgment?
Wilt thou show that I am wrong because thou art righteous?
9 Hast thou an arm like God?
Or canst thou thunder with a voice like him?
10 Adorn thyself now with grandeur and majesty,
And array thyself with splendour and glory.
11 Let loose the fury of thy wrath!
Look upon every one that is proud and abase him!
12 Look upon every one that is proud and bring him low!
Yea, tread down the wicked in their place!
13 Hide them in the dust together!
Bind them in the dungeon!
14 Then will I also give thee praise,
For thine own right hand can save thee.
15 Behold now Behemoth which I have made, as well as thyself;
He feedeth on grass like the ox.
16 Behold now his strength is in his loins;
And his vigour in the muscles of his belly.
17 He bendeth his tail like the cedar;
The sinews of his haunches are twisted together.
18 His bones are like strong pieces of brass:
His bones are like bars of iron.
19 He is chief among the works of God;
He that made him has furnished him [as] with a sword.
20 For the mountains bring him forth food,
Where all the beasts of the field play.

21 He lieth under the lotus-trees,
In the covert of the roots and fens.
22 The lotus-trees cover him with their shade;
The willows of the brook compass him about.
23 Lo! should a river rush upon him, he is not alarmed;
He is unmoved should the Jordan rush upon his mouth.
24 Who can take him when he is on his guard?
Or when taken in snares, who can pierce his nose?

CHAP. XLI.

1 Canst thou draw forth Leviathan with an hook,
Or press down his tongue with a cord?
2 Canst thou put a rope into his nose?
Or pierce his jaw with a ring?
3 Will he make many supplications unto thee?
Will he speak soft words unto thee?
4 Will he make a covenant with thee?
Canst thou take him for a servant forever?
5 Canst thou play with him as with a bird?
Or canst thou bind him for thy maidens?
6 Do men in company make a banquet of him?
Do they divide him among the merchants?
7 Canst thou fill his skin with barbed irons?
Or his head with fish spears?
8 Lay thine hand upon him; remember the fierce conflict:—
Thou wilt not do it again.
9 Behold the hope of [taking] him is vain;
Is it not dissipated at his very appearance?
10 None is so courageous that he dare arouse him;—
And who then is he that can stand before me?
11 Who can come upon me by surprise that I should recompense him?
All under the whole heavens is mine.
12 I will not be silent concerning his parts,
And his power, and the fitness of his armature.
13 Who can strip off the surface of his garment?
Who can come near to the doubling of his jaws?
14 Who can open the doors of his face?
The rows of his teeth are terrible
15 His strong shields are his pride—
Shut up together as with a close seal.
16 They are joined one to another,
So that no air can come between them.
17 They cleave fast to each other;
They take hold on one another, so that they cannot be separated.

18 In his sneezing light is caused to shine,
And his eyes are like the eyelids of the morning.
19 Out of his mouth go forth torches;
Sparks of fire leap forth.
20 Out of his nostrils goeth smoke,
As from a boiling pot or caldron.
21 His breath kindleth coals,
And a flame issueth out of his mouth.
22 In his neck dwelleth strength;
Before him danceth Terror.
23 The dewlaps of his flesh cleave fast together;
They are firm upon them; they cannot be moved.
24 His heart is solid like a stone;
Yea, solid like the nether millstone.
25 When he riseth up the mighty are afraid;
Yea, they lose themselves from terror,
26 The sword of him that attacks him will not adhere;
Nor will the spear, the dart, or the javelin.
27 He regardeth iron as straw,
And brass as rotten wood.
28 The arrow will not put him to flight;
Sling-stones turn themselves into stubble in respect to him:
29 Clubs are regarded by him as stubble;
He laugheth at the shaking of a spear.
30 Under him are sharp potsherds;
He spreadeth out his rough parts upon the mire.
31 He maketh the deep to boil like a pot;
He maketh the sea like a pot of ointment.
32 After him he leaves a shining path—
So that one would think the deep to be hoary.
33 Upon the earth there is not his like;
He is made to be destitute of fear.
34 On every high thing he looketh down;
King over all the sons of pride.

CHAPTER XLII.

THE RESPONSE AND PENITENT CONFESSION OF JOB. Ver. 1—6.

1 Then Job answered JEHOVAH, and said:
2 I know that thou canst do every thing,
And that no purpose of thine can be prevented.
3 "Who is he [indeed] that darkeneth counsel by words without knowledge?"

I have indeed uttered what I understood not ;
Things too wonderful for me, which I knew not.
4 Hear then, I beseech thee, and I will speak ;
I will ask thee, and do thou instruct me ;
5 I have heard of thee by the hearing of the ear
But now mine eye seeth thee ;
6 Wherefore I abhor myself,
And repent in dust and ashes.

PART III.

THE CONCLUSION IN PROSE. Ver. 7—16.

7 And it came to pass after JEHOVAH had spoken these words to Job, that
JEHOVAH said to Eliphaz the Temanite. "My wrath is kindled against
thee and thy two friends, for ye have not spoken concerning me that
8 which is right, as my servant Job hath. Therefore take for yourselves
seven bullocks and seven rams, and go to my servant Job and offer for
yourselves a burnt-offering ; and Job my servant shall pray for you –
for to him will I have regard—lest I should recompense to you your
folly. For ye have not spoken concerning me that which is right, as
9 my servant Job hath." So Eliphaz the Temanite, and Bildad the
Shuhite, and Zophar the Naamathite, went and did as JEHOVAH com-
10 manded them ; and JEHOVAH had respect to Job. And JEHOVAH turned
the captivity of Job when he prayed for his friends, and JEHOVAH gave
11 him double of what he had before. Then came to him all his brethren,
and all his sisters, and all his former acquaintances, and ate bread with
him in his house ; and they condoled with him and comforted him over
all the evil that JEHOVAH had brought upon him ; and every one gave
12 him a piece of money, and every one a ring of gold. So JEHOVAH
blessed the latter days of Job more than his beginning ; for he had
fourteen thousand sheep, six thousand camels, a thousand yoke of oxen,
13 and a thousand she-asses. He had also seven sons and three daughters.
14 And he called the name of the first Jemima, of the second Kezia, and
15 of the third Keren-happuch. And in all the land were no women found
so beautiful as the daughters of Job ; and their father gave them an
16 inheritance among their brethren. And Job lived after this an hundred
and forty years, and saw his sons, and his sons' sons, even four genera-
17 tions. And Job died, being old and full of days.

W9-ATE-640

Angry Adolescents

Angry Adolescents

Ronald Goldman

Professor of Education at La Trobe University, Australia

Beverley Hills

Sage Publications, Inc.

For information address:

SAGE PUBLICATIONS, INC.
275 South Beverley Drive
Beverley Hills, California 90212

Printed in Great Britain

International Standard Book Number 0-8039 0026-0

Library of Congress Catalog Card No. 71-82897

Second Printing

To Jean, Tony and Becca,
Michael and Kathleen

Contents

Introduction

The boys were either openly hostile or unco-operative and sullen; the girls egging the boys to violent behaviour. I first saw twenty of these angry adolescents outside the village hall, throwing stones at the windows, breaking each pane of glass with evident enjoyment. The local residents did not interfere but stayed quietly behind their curtains, looking out nervously at the damage these angry adolescents were causing. As a new resident I was disturbed by this incident, not only by the young people's destructive behaviour but also by the apparent helplessness of the adult community.

This book is the story of these adolescents and of how a Youth Club began with such an unpromising membership and developed in a village in the Home Counties, some forty miles from London, just outside normal commuter territory. I have called the village by the fictitious name of Berrocfield, but all the facts and events really happened and only the names of places and people are invented. This account is of possible interest for various reasons. Firstly, as one who has helped in the training of voluntary and professional youth leaders for some years I have been aware that the literature on adolescents generally and youth work in particular tends to become outdated quickly. The best books on the subject seem to have been written from the late 1940s up to the middle 1950s. The speed of social change has quickened in the last ten years, so that the society in which adolescents grow up today is very different from that of a decade ago. Adolescents are very sensitive reflectors of the society to which they belong and it is evident that as society changes, some changes in adolescent behaviour are to be expected. There is a dearth of literature to help leaders of young people reared in an affluent society. Many of the difficulties experienced with modern adolescents in groups are comparatively recent, and some guidance is needed for those who try to help young people today. Much has been written here and in America about the psychology of adolescence, but very little has been documented by readable descriptions of individual adolescents, particularly how they behave in their leisure time and in small membership groups. This book is written with the intention of helping to repair this gap by a detailed account of a group of adolescents and how they behaved in a certain situation in the years of the mid-sixties.

This account may also be relevant because the club activities at Berrocfield were of an experimental nature. Beginning in a fairly primitive old army hut the club now occupies modern premises with a cycle speedway track at the rear and a multi-purpose sports area, floodlit by a shilling-in-the-slot meter arrangement, so that a wide range of sports from tennis and netball to five-a-side football can be played throughout the year. Experimental activities are not confined to club nights, but go on at other times during the week and weekends, and it will be an encouragement to leaders of various types of clubs to know the wide variety of ventures possible in a quite ordinary youth club with a limited membership.

Another reason for this book is that it provides a number of case studies of individual adolescents, many of whom had varying problems to handle, as well as general descriptions of group behaviour. Difficult home backgrounds, low intellectual ability, poor motivation to school-work, the leaving of school at the first opportunity, the taking of unskilled and often well-paid jobs, made dealing with these young people very perplexing and unpredictable. Many of them were problems to leaders in the club, because the young people were problems to themselves. At times, worn out and disillusioned, we were tempted to respond to their violence, their disregard for elementary values and their difficult behaviour, by permanently closing the club. We did, in fact, close the club temporarily on several occasions. That we persisted was due to no particular merit on our part, but because we realized that the youth club was the one association available in the community in which some social education was possible, informal and transitory though it was.

It is difficult to know how typical these adolescents are, whose group and individual behaviour is described in this book. Certainly many of them reveal the classical dilemmas of adolescence outlined in many academic books on the subject. But of greater importance they also disclosed the problems of growing up in the 1960s which the newer problems of affluence, easy ownership of vehicles and earlier maturing appear to create.

Some criticism might be expressed that Berrocfield is very untypical since not many adolescents are reared in country villages with a total population of about two thousand. Country people, it may be argued, are also very different in the ways in which they behave, the values they hold and in their rhythm of life. In certain remote country areas in Dorset, Wales or the Yorkshire moors this argument may still have some point, but in country areas within easy access of large towns and particularly near London it is doubtful if 'country people' really exist, in the way they existed up to a few years ago. The greater availability of motor-cars, motor cycles and scooters, the advent of mass media, especially television, and the availability of jobs in nearby towns, mean that the vast majority of those who live in the countryside are town-orientated in their thinking and their behaviour. The majority of members of the Berrocfield Club have always lived in moderately sized council housing estates, more resembling suburbia than country dwellings. Currently only two out of some fifty or sixty regular members work in countryside occupations, such as farming or forestry. The rest work in factories, offices, garages, shops, laundries and other occupations in nearby towns. It seems to me that a clear distinction between town and country no longer exists. In Berrocfield I could discern much the same social patterns as I saw in Birmingham and between adolescents in these two places there appeared to be no startling or significant differences other than the obvious regional ones.

I have tried to make this book readable to the general reader who is interested in young people, not only to those engaged in youth work. It is therefore written in non-technical language, although my professional concerns as an educational psychologist are very evident. In the first chapter I have described the area in which the young people of Berrocfield live, work and spend their leisure, with some general sociological assessment of the district. There then follows the narrative of how the youth club began and developed into what it is today. The home and educational influences at work on the members are explained and some description of varying behaviour patterns in relation to money, sex, employment and other aspects occupy most of the remaining pages.

Experimental centres for the unattached adolescent, book-bars for students, special interest clubs and many other flexible forms of catering for young people are needed and will be tried in the future. Yet most of the work with adolescents after they leave school will continue to be done in comparatively small youth groups, in town and country. Within the conventional structure of the Youth Service we need to sharpen our objectives, to know the differing needs of each new generation of adolescents and to provide programmes and activities which will help them, in terms of the Albemarle Report,[1] to associate together, train to some purpose and be challenged to grow into mature men and women. I hope that this book will help, in some small way, all who deal with young people to realize these aims.

Didsbury College of Education
Manchester

RONALD GOLDMAN

[1] *The Youth Service in England and Wales*, London, H.M.S.O., 1958. Cmnd. 929.

1 Berrocfield in its Social Setting

In a report on a new town, an adolescent described it as 'a graveyard with lights'. In less succinct and less polite language the adolescents living in Berrocfield regarded it, until very recently, as a graveyard *without* lights.

Berrocfield is not so much a village as a series of villages surrounding a common. The old centre of the village was at one time the parish church with a post office and general grocery store, a blacksmiths, now a small foundry, and a cluster of houses round the church. The real and effective centre of the village today is Upper Berrocfield, with a public house, two shops, including a post office–general store, a police house, three garages and the village hall and youth centre. The housing here is predominantly a council estate and of the two thousand population in the Berrocfield parish, some fourteen hundred are concentrated in Upper Berrocfield. The majority of the people concentrated there are working class, mainly unskilled and semi-skilled workers and their families. The men travel some distance to their work in nearby towns, the nearest industries being a paper mill, a cable manufacturing plant, floor tile producers and government equipment plants. Work on the roads or in agriculture are the occupations of very few.

More recently a new estate has been built at Upper Berrocfield, of privately-owned bungalows and small detached houses, so that about sixty middle-class families have been added to the population in the last two years. The men are mainly office workers, executives or salesmen connected with local industries and most of them have still to plant roots in village life. As we shall see later, the social life of the village is fairly tightly structured and activities tend to be in homogeneous social groups. The significance of this does not escape the adolescents.

The rest of the population not living at Old Berrocfield and Upper Berrocfield, are situated in small cottages or clusters of council houses at Berrocfield Green, Berrocfield Moss and the Dell. Of these the most coherently organized concentration of houses is to be found at the Dell, which despite its quaint and rural name is largely composed of a group of cheap and unattractive council houses. The majority of members of the youth club come from the two council estates at the Dell and Upper Berrocfield. In between these main centres of population detached houses of varying size, occupied by upper and middle-class families, surround the common. These range from managing director's mansions and the lord of the manor's 'hall' to small houses and bungalows, many of which are occupied by ex-naval, air force and army officers and their wives, or retired gentlefolk. I am not sure whether the term 'retired' gentlefolk is an appropriate one, since many of them do not appear to have had an occupation from which to retire, but the term 'gentlefolk' is still in use as a description of nice, well-bred people 'from the right stock'.

Out of a population of two thousand one would expect to find an adolescent age group numbering about two hundred or about ten per cent of the total. An informal census revealed this to be the approximate number of young people in the community, but many of these were not potential members of a youth group for one of two reasons. Many lived in remote corners of the parish and had no transport to get up to Upper Berrocfield. Moreover those from upper and middle-class families, were away at school for most of the year and during the holidays created their own socially distinct groups, meeting in each other's houses, organizing tennis parties on private courts, and other activities. The church, which might have provided a common meeting ground, had no plan or clear intention to achieve the mixing of young people from each side of the social fence. Among young people on the council estates there was a strongly expressed hostility to 'them' who 'spoke posh'. I well remember organizing a cycle-cross on the common—a cross-country cycle run on a time trial basis through a series of 'slalom' gates—for the youth club, when by accident a small group of teenage pony riders cut across the course. They received loud curses and verbal abuse from the club members, and for a long time afterwards they mimicked the accents and mimed the genteel gestures of the intruders. But these meetings were rare and accidental simply because social events were organized in such a way as to contain the groups distinctly from each other.

This was noticeable in relation to the schools. Prior to our arrival in Berrocfield the village school, a voluntary aided Church of England primary school at Old Berrocfield, took in the children of the lower social groups from the surrounding area. There was a complete lack of upper class and an almost complete absence of children from middle-class homes in the school, since the tradition was to send such children to local kindergarten or play groups, largely run by untrained, inefficient but well-meaning teachers. One of these private schools was moderately well run, the headmistress was a qualified trained teacher, and there was a happy spirit between children and their teachers. The remaining two, however, were not only grossly inefficient, but rather unhappy travesties of education, the children at a very young age being taught prematurely their alphabets (modern reading methods seemed to be unknown) and their arithmetic tables. This never ceases to amaze me—the foolishness of parents prepared to pay for such bad schools, simply because their children associated with their kind of people. It was a source of amazement to them, in return, that we should send our children to the village school. When, in fact, after buying my house I enquired where the nearest schools were, one gentleman told me of the private schools available. 'But what about the local village school?' I asked. A look of extreme puzzlement appeared on his face and slowly comprehension dawned. 'Oh, the local school,' he said, then speaking in early-nineteenth-century terms, added, 'Yes, there is a local Dame School down in the old part of the village. That's not the sort of place for our kind of people.'

Apart from the children of a librarian and one or two others, all the children in the village school had fathers who were unskilled or semi-skilled labourers working in factories in nearby towns. This absence of high-social groups affected the school considerably, since the stimulus of very bright pupils was lacking and the physical amenities were fairly primitive. There was a mixture of trained and untrained 'supply' teachers, considerable over-crowding and, until recently, primitive earth closets. The social cleavage, seen in the primary school, was naturally extended into the secondary age levels. The lower-social groups at first went at eleven years of age to an all-age school in a nearby town and when a new secondary modern school opened nearby they transferred there. Only one or two ever went to take grammar school places at Oldington, some seven miles away. The children from the higher-social groups went to preparatory, day or boarding, schools from about the age of nine and thence to boarding schools at thirteen. The two groups of children rarely met, either socially or educationally, except by accident in a local shop or on the common.

Much has been written about the social and educational

disadvantages of the working-class urban child[1] but little about similar disadvantages of the rural child. The same ghetto-like situation existed in Berrocfield as in Crown Street, Liverpool, even though green fields were close and there appeared, superficially it transpired, to be a greater physical freedom. The children and adolescents are reared in a one-class society, a powerful system of taboos and segregation operates socially and this segregation does appear to have a psychological effect upon the adolescents particularly. Many of them expressed the view that they were second-class citizens, educationally and socially inferior, and this attitude was markedly noticeable towards their schooling. Achievements were very poor, school was left at the earliest opportunity and there was a high incidence of violent behaviour on the part of the boys and of precocious sexual activity on the part of the girls.

When we arrived in the village more than half the boys who initially belonged to the youth club were delinquent, some officially under the probation service and others marginally, indulging in behaviour which was a nuisance to a large number of people, such as creating noise late at night, knocking on doors and running away, and putting fireworks through letterboxes. This aggressive behaviour will be illustrated in detail later but the causes seemed to me to be due partly to the lack of leisure facilities in the village, partly due to the home background of some of the young people but also partly due to the incoherent hostility many of them experienced about their poor social status. Aggressiveness was most marked in the presence of strangers or with those they regarded as belonging to the other side of the social fence. It was persistently expressed towards my wife and myself in the initial eighteen months of the club's history.

[1] Mays, J. B., *Education and the Urban Child*, Liverpool University Press, 1962. Douglas, J. W. B., *The Home and the School*, MacGibbon & Kee, 1964.

One social factor is probably significant in the situation as we first found it. Some of the council houses were occupied by local people, indigenous to the area, whose families had been farm workers for generations. Many of the families did not originate in the area, but came as migrant workers moving to the South during the war or settling in the parish immediately after the war. Coming from Ireland and Wales originally many of them were homeless and occupied, as squatters, an old army camp on Berrocfield Common vacated by the army as soon as the invasion of Normandy began. Conditions were very primitive and somewhat squalid. Some of the older adolescents in the club had actually been born in this camp in 1945 or 1946, before the families were moved to the new council estate in Upper Berrocfield. These formed a hard core of families with fairly low standards of living, some drunkenness and violent behaviour, which tended to set the tone of the estate. This behaviour was inevitably reflected in their children—who were very wild, needing strong discipline in school—and generated an anti-social temper in their adolescents.

On the estate were many with good standards who were concerned to help their children, but as often happens in communities of this kind, there was little effective leadership and the turbulent elements tended to dominate the scene. This was very noticeable among the young people, where the leadership, such as it was, was mostly exercised by strong, aggressive delinquents or near-delinquents.

This was particularly important in a community where there were few leisure facilities. The nearest towns, little more than overgrown villages, were five miles away. The most attractive, from the adolescents' viewpoint—because it had two cafes and one of them had a jukebox—could be reached by private vehicle easily, but public transport only ran every two hours. Even so, the nearest place possessing a cinema, dance hall or swimming bath was more than seven miles away, and the better of two centres was a large town of about 100,000 population, which entailed a very difficult journey involving two bus rides. These two centres were the places to visit on Saturdays and Sundays but were rarely visited at other times, due often to inertia and lack of enterprise. Few of the young people had visited London, although this was only an hour away on cheap excursion fares.

In Berrocfield itself the leisure facilities in the old part of the village consisted of a football field adjacent to the church hall, which acted as a changing room when matches were played, and a rapidly deteriorating playground for children. This playground was practically unused since the bulk of the children lived more than two miles away in Upper Berrocfield. The result was that the equipment of swings, see-saw and slide were in poor shape, the use of the slide tending, for example, to produce a multiple splintered bottom. There was a thriving football club, the team being mainly young adult men, although two of the older adolescents played for the team when there were vacancies. The Berrocfield team had a local reputation for nastiness, bad temper and fighting, which was reproduced in the youth club team in its initial stages. A cricket pitch of sorts existed at Berrocfield Moss, and a team composed of adult men of varying ages had a desultory existence. Both cricket and football teams were solidly working class and were based upon a local public house.

There was a village hall in Upper Berrocfield for general use by the village, as opposed to the church hall in Old Berrocfield used mainly for church purposes. This village hall was essentially an old army prefabricated hut, set on brick pillars, in a small field on land adjacent to the common.

By the time we came to the village it was in a state of advanced decay. It smelled of damp and it was drab and dismal inside. The accommodation was a long, narrow room, with a kitchen at one end having a primitive serving hatch, and a small committee room at the other end. The heating and lighting were very poor, and insulation non-existent so that it was very cold in winter and very warm on hot days in summer. Mercifully, this building came to a timely end, for it was a most inadequate place for a general village social hall and a youth centre.

Organizations which used the village hall were the Women's Institute, a dramatic society and a horticultural society, consisting mainly of middle-class members. The working-class groups used the hall for regular weekly whist drives, bingo evenings, sporadic Saturday dances and occasional wedding receptions. Apart from these events the hall was little used. This situation was to change with the building of a new village hall and youth centre on the same site.

The only regular organization for adolescents was a cycle speedway club, the members of which with some real initiative had built themselves a cinder track on land marginal to the common. It was waste land rather remote and inaccessible to the village, with no shelter or toilet facilities, but here the club entertained visiting league teams from May until October each year on alternate Sundays. This group was formed initially by the parents of two adolescent boys 'to give them something to do' and the composition of the group was largely late adolescents or young adult men, a few of them married. There was some overlap between this group and the football team. As a self-help club it had had a chequered career for finance was not easy, and since few younger members were encouraged it tended to become a closed in-group, ageing from an adolescent to a young adult club. As with the football team, they were in constant trouble about discipline, since disagreements with visiting teams were frequent, and riders were suspended from time to time because of fights or bad language breaking out. Nevertheless, the club continues to this day and provides a stimulating focus of activity for the pedal-cycle enthusiasts of the village.

It is difficult to evaluate the impact of the churches upon the village. The Church of England had its main centre in the old village, with both services moderately attended, interestingly with the same social division evident: morning service was mainly attended by gentry, and the evening by 'the others'—simply because a bus was available and picked people up at various points in the village. In the last two years a new church has been built in Upper Berrocfield, which holds monthly services and has a church room attached. This is the centre for morning Sunday School. Children attend, but fall off by the age of ten with the occasional young adolescent girl remaining as a helper. There was at one time a monthly 'Youth Service' at which the lessons and the collection were done by the young people. This had little attraction for the adolescents, and the 'youth' represented were rarely older than thirteen years.

Once we got to know and understand our members it soon became clear that many were hostile to the established church, some of them because 'it's all out of date' or 'it's so bloody dull' but many of them recognized quite perceptively that the church was basically not on their side of the social fence. It did not escape their notice that St. Jason's, the new church at Upper Berrocfield, was often referred to by church people as 'the mission church', much as a West End London congregation might have paternal responsibility for a mission in the East End. What was interpreted as a patronizing attitude was resented by some of the more vocal adolescents. 'What do they want to call it a bloody mission for?' said one of them. 'Do they think we're savages or something?' This was, indeed, exactly how many of the higher-social groups regarded the council estate tenants. There was a Congregational Chapel in Berrocfield Green and a small Baptist Chapel in a rather remote hamlet, maintained by small groups of devout families, but having no programmes for young people.

In brief then we see the picture of a geographically scattered community, with a few leisure facilities for young adults and the elderly, but virtually none for the fourteen to twenty year age group. These lived in a community socially divided, not only geographically, conscious of their inferior position in relation to schooling and housing, and resentful of this. A great deal of anti-social behaviour was evident and how this affected the activity of the young people once a youth club was formed can be seen in the following chapter.

2 How the Youth Club Began

In the 1950s three youth clubs had been run in Berrocfield with varied results. The first, run for a short time by a teacher, closed when she left the area. The numbers were small and little is known of this club other than that it experienced severe problems of rowdy and uncontrolled behaviour from the members. The second club was much more successful, and was run by a man with considerable youth club experience, who despite many behaviour problems on the part of members, succeeded in carrying out a varied programme with a large number of outdoor activities. Records show that there were camping and canal trips, visits to London and other activities available. Again, the club was short-lived because the leader, who did this work entirely voluntarily in his spare time, moved from the area to take another job.

The immediately preceding attempt to restart the club was a brave effort by a retired civil servant, often in poor health, whose life was made into a weekly hell by violent and uncontrolled behaviour on the part of the boys. There are varied stories related, how accurate it is hard to determine, about the wild events on Tuesday evenings at the village hall. These stories ranged from those about speakers of some eminence who came to address 'the children' on varied topics and who were never able to speak for more than five minutes above the din, to a final catastrophic evening when a member drove his motor-bike and side-car clean through the flimsy partitions of the hall, leaving it in an extremely precarious condition, likely to collapse at any time. It was about this time that the committee decided to build a new village hall, and perhaps the motor-cyclist contributed more creatively to the future centre than he realized. The club closed abruptly since no-one could control the members.

My wife and I had lived in the village for almost a year when the local area youth officer called, since he had heard I was interested in setting up a club. This was largely due to it being known that I had run clubs before and both of us had helped train professional youth leaders at Westhill College of Education in Birmingham. Before the area youth officer's visit we had become aware that the village had a 'youth problem'. For long periods of time two local telephone boxes were out of order due to all the glass in them being broken or the coin boxes forced open. Seats on the common had on several occasions been deliberately sawn in half. Private telephone services had been interrupted since several hundred feet of wire had been cut in various places for re-sale purposes. The common, which in places grew highly inflammable brushwood, had on two occasions in the autumn been set alight by youths exploding fireworks. Dustbins turned over and emptied, anonymous knocks on doors of isolated houses, breaking and entering into houses temporarily unoccupied, were frequent events. The local policeman did his best to cope with all this but boys were adept at dodging him.

Several times I had observed the policeman talking with small groups of boys, who were unco-operative, insolent and openly hostile to him. The police house at that time was on the Upper Berrocfield council estate and he and his family led a most uncomfortable existence. He eventually transferred to another village, and a younger man came, but he in turn became rapidly disillusioned by the blatant disregard for order in the village and he too transferred. The latest incumbent of the post happily arrived as a police house was made available off the estate so that his domestic life was not subject to undue strain. By this time the new club was well under way and behaviour problems among the young people, for various reasons, were not quite so intense.

My wife and I were therefore aware of the difficulties of many adolescents in the community and the bitterness of many adults towards them. Although involved in a very demanding professional life ourselves, we felt something constructive would have to be done. It was plain that, although some of the young people came from problem families, many of them were from settled and satisfactory backgrounds. The real problem was lack of leisure facilities and the aimlessness which followed from this was easily exploited by the proportion of disturbed and difficult adolescents in the village. The young people needed somewhere to associate, where they could be adolescents together and naturally participate in activities which would involve, challenge and educate them. Although I am a professional educator myself I did not think of the word 'educate' in a formal learning sense. Education conjures up teaching formal subjects or depressing raffia work of a type pointless with modern adolescents. Informal education, in which learning is social rather than academic, is the aim of the youth service, and this was plainly our intention when we looked at the possibility of setting up a club in the village.

I have, further, always regarded club work as an educational activity, rather than a welfare or rescue service. Our motives in Berrocfield were not to cure delinquents, nor to provide 'a street with a roof'. We felt that in any community its adolescents have a right to a place where they could associate and enjoy each other's company. A club's function, as the Albemarle Report observes, is to provide the equivalent services a good student union provides in a university or college. Because these wider social and educational aims were central to our thinking we rejected the idea of a boys' club, which many well-meaning people advised us to begin with 'because it's the boys who are the problem' and planned for a mixed club. We have never seen the logic of single-sex clubs, an historical hangover from the public school approach to settlement work and a general fear of sexual misdemeanours. If we were to educate socially young people towards maturity, it seemed a contradiction to do this in anything other than a mixed club. And it soon became evident that the girls in the village were as much in need of this kind of education as were the boys.

Our first step in agreeing to start a club was to consult with the previous management committee. This was an over-large body elected from various village groups, including some of the parents of the adolescents, and we had been warned that some of them were very awkward people. This proved to be quite untrue. We found them to be sincere, helpful and concerned people, but genuinely puzzled to know what to do. It was accepted that a new committee was needed, an 'advisory' rather than a 'management' body, and we were left a free hand to form this new advisory committee. We made the point that until a new village hall and youth centre were provided, we could expect continued disorders, since the old village hall invited destructive activities, and we were shortly to be proved right. We inherited a certain amount of battered equipment, an old dart board without darts, table tennis nets but no bats or table, some tatty cricket pads and several pairs of boxing gloves. The only useful item was an old electric record player, and this had a limited life of less than three months due both to inherent defects and the boisterous behaviour of some members.

We prepared to begin some kind of group activities in the autumn of 1960. It seemed sensible at the time, in the light of experience of previous clubs, to allow a few months for my wife and me, as the initiators of a new club, to get to know the young people and to try to win their confidence, without starting an official youth club. We looked for some device which would commit neither us, as leaders, nor they as members, to a continuing association. If the first experiment failed then we were free to try some other approach. The approach decided upon, was a dancing class 'for young people aged 14 to 20' which was to go on for an hour and a half, once a week, for twelve weeks. To some this may seem a curious choice, but it was done deliberately to attract a proportion of girls, as well as boys, and provide a period of getting to know the young people not so long in duration to be a strain but long enough for us to get acquainted. Moreover, through the Further Education Service of the county and funds left over from the old club we were able to pay for the services of a most able instructress, a young woman of considerable attraction and charm, who had just left the Physical Education Corps of the army. She was therefore capable of looking after herself and running the session, leaving us to organize, collect the weekly charge of two shillings each person, and establish what contacts we could with the young people.

In the two post offices at Upper Berrocfield and the Dell we displayed prominent notices and sent a printed letter to every known member of the previous clubs, from a list of about forty names. Despite all the careful thought and planning which had gone into preparing these exploratory meetings, we began with what we thought at the time was a complete débâcle. Only ten young people turned up on what proved to be the coldest and wettest evening of the autumn. The hall was at its bleakest and most depressing. As they came in I asked each one to fill in a form, but for five out of the ten I had to fill the forms in for them myself. Some of this was due to obstinacy on their part but for some it was to avoid embarrassment. At thirteen and fourteen years of age a few of them could not read the form or could only sign their names. Neither the small numbers, nor the hall itself were insurmountable problems, but the absence of the instructress was. We waited for her with growing dismay and by eight fifteen—we had begun at seven thirty—it was obvious she wasn't going to come.

The customers, all aged around early adolescence, did not appear worried by this and were content to sit listening to some records. The one real communication of the evening was by a boy of fifteen who told me, 'We're used to the buggers not turning up *for us*.' It so happened that the instructress had genuinely mixed up the dates and mercifully arrived on time the following week, but it was hardly a promising start. It has been my golden rule in youth work to always be there at times stated and never to break a promise with young people, however inconvenient it is to keep one's word. They are so prone to this themselves that they need a constant visible reminder that there are adults in the world who can be relied upon and only reliable people, in my view, prepared to keep their word, should be involved in youth work. Because of the bad start, we had to convince these adolescents over the next two years that we really meant what we said. Once they knew this and trusted us we had the beginnings of a good youth community.

The ten who arrived the first evening were four girls and six boys. Two of the girls were grammar school pupils and after seeing the rest of the company never came near us again, not even when we had established a flourishing youth club. The other two apparently sophisticated girls were Kay and Karen, two friends from the Upper Berrocfield council estate, aged thirteen but declaring themselves to be fourteen years old. The six boys were known to be 'trouble-makers' and it was with these that the real struggle was to develop after a watchful interval of three weeks. Even so, on the first evening we were not without incident, for as it was going dark, all the lights went out. Fortunately as basic equipment I had a torch in my pocket and was able to provide some light. I quickly learned that this was no accident, but that a master switch was a tempting lever beside the fuseboxes at the far end of the building in the committee rooms. By the following week I had it all boxed in and fastened with a padlock, but this still did not prevent the boys from clicking the lights off by the front door whenever they thought they were unobserved.

Three of the boys who came that first night had a continuous attendance for the twelve weeks, never missing a meeting but never dancing or taking part in the official proceedings. They were much given to marginal larking about, showing off to but not mixing with the girls, interfering with lights, windows, doors, heating and refreshments. When reinforced by further disturbing elements they made a quite formidable group to deal with. Jim, Dave and Steve were from the 'E' stream in secondary modern school and felt incompetent in almost everything they did except creating difficulties for others, for which they had a remarkable aptitude. Since they were very good at this one talent they exercised it to the full. The other three boys, Tom, Joe and Bill, were in a slightly older age group—sixteen to seventeen—and had obviously more contact with the girls. As older boys too, they were much taken with the attractive instructress, and danced with her at every opportunity. Joe, an ex-Grammar school boy, was weak and easily led by the other two, who were not as intelligent but possessed of very quick physical reflexes. These two were to be the major problem in the next few weeks since they were anxious to provoke a fight with me, to try me out and flex their hardening muscles at me. Yet these two were eventually to become the backbone of the youth club and our close personal friends.

The second October evening saw the arrival on time, much to our relief, of the dancing instructress. Word had got round that it might be 'good for a bit of a giggle' and seventeen customers arrived. There were nine new members, the two grammar school girls having left us. The small group of noisy, active, non-participant boys was joined by three friends, two of whom were brothers on probation, notorious in the neighbourhood for rough and unpredictable behaviour. Both these brothers were to have a constant record of delinquency and crime over the next few years, and I was to visit them on several occasions in borstals and prisons all over the country. Ricky and Tim were alike in colouring, of dark and swarthy countenance, rather like gypsy boys, but dissimilar in build and features. It is probable they had different fathers. They appeared at the dancing sessions and paid their money after several attempts at evasion, playing no part in the official proceedings. They had long, curly hair, with sideburns, fashionable at that time, leather jackets, jeans and studded buckle belts round the waist. I was disconcerted to notice each of them had a knife slung from the belt, and in any argument it was obvious that the other boys were afraid of the two brothers, with good reason.

Another newcomer was Alf—the oldest boy of the group at the age of eighteen—an amiable simple gangling lad, regarded as a good-natured clown by the rest. He was totally illiterate (school records confirm this and an I.Q. of 87), but smartly dressed and very popular since he was the owner of three second-hand cars. Within a month he tried to sell one of them to me, a not unattractive Morris Saloon. His explanations of how he came to own it were transparently untrue and I expressed no interest. He took this refusal as amiably as he took everything. I only once saw him put out and that was when he was thrown over by a girl. He had a new one the following week, his love life consisting in a continuous string of new girls, the turnover being at a similar rate to his ownership of cars. In fact, the two types of relationship seemed to correspond closely.

Among the new girls who arrived on the second occasion were four from the Dell, and we had to provide transport to get them home. Since we did this initially in our own car we soon got to know them. They all came from the council estate, were still at school, for which they always expressed nothing but negative feelings, and were aged thirteen to fourteen. Dressed for their dancing evening they could have been mistaken for eighteen-year-olds. The morning after club I would sometimes see them catching the bus for the secondary school, dressed in gym slips and blazers, and the contrast was most marked. Girls at school and young women at leisure, a superficial sophistication being adopted for evening activities, the behaviour put on and discarded with their clothes. Mary and Celeste were two friends of well below average intelligence; Mary was to marry at seventeen, in a state of advanced pregnancy and Celeste at eighteen in a similar condition. They went steady with the boys who were to marry them and there was never any question of casual sex. Pamela, on the other hand, was at thirteen known as the local tart, who was an easy target for any interested boy. She was living with grandparents, but the exact relationship was difficult to determine; an emotionally insecure girl, given to overweight, she was more interested in older men outside the club than in adolescent boys. By contrast Jane had a settled home, was a thoroughly wholesome girl, dark and attractive, extroverted and interested in boys, but keeping them at a respectable distance. At the time of writing she is aged twenty and engaged to be married to a boy she has been going out with for several years.

It was with this kind of clientele we began and were to continue until Christmas, the numbers rising gradually to a nightly attendance of about twenty-five. The first three weeks were of watchful mistrust on both sides, the official dancing taking place with a short break for refreshments, and about half the group, mainly girls, participating in the activity. The boys for the most part spent most of their time talking and laughing somewhat self-consciously in a corner, with the occasional forage inside and outside the building, to see what diversions could be engaged upon.

Their attitudes to us as leaders were disconcertingly and openly hostile, and they were anxious to try us out to see how much divergent behaviour we were prepared to take. We began with no rules, other than the basic requirement that everyone should pay their weekly two shillings, rather letting the situation and their behaviour determine further rules if they were necessary. About payment most of them paid up quite cheerfully, but a few argued about it each time and one or two were hostile and suspicious that we were in it for the profit. Bill told me at the third session, with an angry sneer, that he came because there was nothing else to do in the village but he knew we weren't interested in young people but only 'to pay for that bloody car of yours out there'. As a sign of hostility we found in the first weeks chewing gum smeared over the windscreen and whenever the car wasn't clean, several messages of a sexual nature were written on the dust. Curiously, no one ever deflated the tyres, possibly because we took some members home in it and this would have obviously been an action contrary to their own interests.

In the fourth week, the inevitable trial of strength occurred, with the ringleader and his two satellites, Tom and Joe, in support. Ricky, the younger of the two delinquent brothers, was larking about at the top end of the hall. Thinking he was unobserved, he threw his knife at the ceiling and smashed an electric light bulb. Immediately, I walked over and said, 'That bulb will cost two and sixpence to replace. You must pay me now or we will have to close down for the evening.' The dancing stopped and the whole group of twenty gathered round, enjoying the scene and speculating about what was going to happen. Ricky refused to pay, saying no one could prove he had done the damage. I told him I had seen it happen, he was directly responsible and should pay. Ricky jeered, 'You've no witnesses 'ave yer? Anyway, yer can't make me pay.' 'All right,' I said, 'if you won't pay we'll stop activities for tonight and close down until somebody pays.' At this, Bill, who had been getting angrier with every remark, pushed right up against me, thrust his face close to mine and seized the lapels of my jacket. 'Oo do yer think you are, givin' orders and bloody well squeezing money out of us? 'E's always being picked on. Why can't you leave 'im alone?' The crowd, now a mob, knowing Bill to be the local tough boy given to frequent punch-ups, sensed blood and did what they could to foment the trouble. My wife was about to go for the police, but the police house was a quarter of a mile away, and it was a dark night pouring with rain.

There is no doubt I was afraid, but I was determined not to show it and to both calm down the atmosphere and still firmly enforce the payment for damage or close the session. 'If you'll kindly put me down we can talk about it.' Everybody laughed and it relieved the tension a little. Bill let go of my lapels but still wanted to be aggressive. 'I'll punch your bloody face in if you try and be superior with me,' he said. 'Look, Bill, if you punch me, I'll not fight you because I think you'd win, especially if your mates join in. But we'll have to close up here for as long as it takes me to recover, and you won't be here when we open again because I'd prefer charges of assault against you.' 'There's no witnesses, your wife can't testify,' he said triumphantly, 'and no one here will split. They'll say you attacked me first.' I looked round and knew there wasn't a member in the room who would help me. But he had forgotten the dancing instructress, whom he liked dancing with, who spoke up and said she would be a witness in my favour.

Tactically, that decided the matter. Ricky still refused to pay. I immediately closed the session half way through though it was, and said we would remain closed until payment was made. Bill and his friends stalked off muttering they'd get me outside and the mob melted away. My wife and I and Miss H. were all trembling and it seemed the whole venture was at an end. We took the records and record player out to the car, expecting some violence in the dark, but mercifully they had all gone home.

Two evenings later three members from the Dell came to see us. They badly wanted the activity to continue and a 'real youth club' after Christmas if we would consider it; they were willing to pay for the half-crown's worth of damage. For them to pay the money when we knew who the culprit was, seemed all wrong, we explained. If Ricky himself were to come, acknowledge that he had done the damage and pay for it, then we would consider not only opening the Friday dancing sessions but starting a youth club after Christmas. They went away and we sat waiting for a week. Meanwhile, Friday came and went and several members turned up, expected the session to begin and were furious to find the hall closed. Their anger began to turn not so much against us but against the one who had done the damage. What pressures were brought to bear upon Ricky I do not know; undoubtedly he was made to feel responsible and he didn't like feeling unpopular, after the initial incident which made him feel important.

Three days later he came to our home very cheerfully accepting the blame and paid over the money. He listened while I quietly explained why we could not allow damage in the hall, and in the best Western saloons the sheriff made them leave their guns at the door. He promised no knife-throwing in the future. Before he left I asked him was he free for an hour to help me get a letter out so we could tell people there would be a session on the coming Friday? He said he was and watched me type out a letter on a stencil and put it on the duplicating machine. He turned the handle and fed in the paper while I addressed the envelopes. This may have been the first time an adult had asked him for help and he seemed to enjoy the occasion. He had a cup of coffee before he left and I felt some useful contact had been made. The letter we ran off stated:

Dear Member,

The dancing sessions will begin again this Friday. We are very sorry not to have opened last Friday but glad that the damage has been paid for by the member responsible. Two basic rules must be kept.

1. If damage to the hall occurs it must be repaired or paid for, or the hall committee will refuse us the right to use it.
2. Our car should not be interfered with otherwise we cannot help members to get to and from the hall in it.

If you have any ideas for other activities, other than dancing, we will try to arrange them.

Your friends,

Ronald and Jean Goldman

Next Friday represented a new beginning and we felt round one had been won. The idea of a youth club after Christmas was being talked about and most of them were very anxious to found a regular club. So we began the dancing again and the atmosphere by contrast was calmer, more relaxed, as though tension had been catalysed by the violence and threat of violence. Club work is such, however, that events are unpredictable and even when things appear to go well the possibilities two jumps ahead must be prepared for.

Tom, one of the tough, older boys, took me up on making suggestions for more activities than dancing. 'What have you to suggest?' 'Well, what about table tennis and darts then?' 'If you can see the darts are kept under control I'll see to it,' I said. By the following week we had secured a new table-tennis table, with full equipment, and the old dart board was supplemented by two sets of darts. These activities did not run at all smoothly, for the unintelligent group did throw the darts around at random when in a wild mood and were only checked by a thump from Tom who didn't want to lose the use of this additional equipment. Squabbles over table tennis were frequent, no one wanting a rota system or a time limit, but everyone complaining that the older boys monopolized the table for too long. I did nothing about this, suggesting that if they wanted fair shares of time they ought to agree to a system of some kind. 'You tell us what system to have,' they asked. 'No, I'm sorry, that's your job, not mine,' and they spent a frustrating six weeks before they tried to control the situation. Once they decided to organize some system there was only occasional trouble.

As the village hall where we met was no more than an enlarged wooden hut, and Guy Fawkes night fell on the night after our Friday session, we were naturally somewhat concerned about fireworks being let off in the hall or car park, near the petrol tanks of cars. By this time, in the middle of each evening, we established a tradition of announcements which were listened to with good humour provided they did not exceed about ninety seconds. We were later to develop notice boards and other more effective means of communication. So on the week prior to November 4th I said tersely 'No fireworks in the hall or car park please. There's a dangerous risk of fire. Thank you.'

The following week lots of bangs and explosions occurred on the road outside and in the adjacent field, none fortunately in the restricted areas I had named, until a quarter of an hour before the end of our session. There was a loud report from the car park and a fleeing group of boys, giggling and catcalling, rapidly disappeared into the dark. It was almost certainly Dave, Jim and Steve. At once I stopped the record player and said, 'Someone has let off a banger in the car park. That's the end for tonight. Good night everyone.' A rather sullen group went out, Bill, vociferous and angry again, had a go at me, a string of abusive statements having nothing to do with the firework episode. It was interesting and informative because he vocalized a great deal of class-hostility, which I am sure most of the others felt but could not express. It is worth summarizing:

> 'Who do you think you are, ordering us about? Yer only in it for the money, all these two bobs, where do they go to I'd like to know? It's orlright with yer posh voice and yer big house (4 bedrooms) and car (a Ford Anglia).

You're just a bloody Conservative and don't know what it is to work hard for yer living. . . .'

My wife quietly stopped the flow of abuse, censored here to be printable, by saying her husband left school at fourteen, didn't go to a grammar school and worked as an errand boy. 'In fact,' she said, 'some of you have better paid jobs than he had when he left school.' The wind was taken out of his sails. From that week on I also put up a sheet titled, 'Where Your Money Goes', showing all payments and receipts. Despite the two shilling charge it soon became obvious that we were not paying our way but the costs were being subsidized by what was left from the funds of the previous youth club.

However, closing down the club for that last quarter of an hour had a salutary effect. We reopened normally the next week, about ten members arriving half an hour late to express their annoyance. It was at the end of that evening we invited them to our home for an extra session next Tuesday if they'd like to bring their favourite records. We could have a record evening and drink coffee. My wife and I felt this might break down the barriers a little to make them feel we trusted them in our home, rather than an impersonal place like the village hall.

We had a thatched house, Tudor construction, with a huge open fire place and, with the early December cold outside, we had a large log burning in the grate. The whole group turned up and we had a hectic two hours, the girls coping well in the kitchen and everyone wandering round anywhere they pleased so long as they didn't go upstairs and disturb the children. We learned afterwards that this, for most of them, was the first non-council house they had ever been in and certainly the first time someone from a professional occupation had invited them home. They were insatiably curious about the furniture, our books and records, the wine cupboard—on which we kept a careful eye—the bathroom and the crockery we used. As usual they were boisterously cheerful, smoking and eating greedily, but we felt round two had been won successfully. We had been warned that we were foolish and were inviting disaster. The one mishap of the evening was that Ricky and Tim, the two brothers, arrived in their working clothes—straight off a coal lorry—and leaned against the virgin white walls of the lounge. This black mark was more easily rectified than other behaviour they later exhibited.

Gradually their picture of us was developed, as we wished it to develop, of friendly, disinterested but firm adults, who kept their word, keeping some kind of order and wanting to provide a meeting place for young people. This was not accomplished overnight, nor achieved in the first three months, but it was beginning by the time the dancing class ended. Without anyone having noticed we had begun a club with dancing receding into a marginal activity, table tennis, darts and card-playing now regular events, and talking, drinking orange squash or coffee, and just meeting with friends became the central occupations.

We still endured the occasional outbreak of anti-social amusements. Damage was done to the hall, for example when a boy burst the lock on the ladies' lavatories and, with unexpected velocity, rocketed through the glass window opposite. I had tabulated the cost of every breakable item in the hall and kept a list of prices in my pocket, making people pay up on the spot. The lock cost 2s. 9d. and the window 12s. 6d. This instantaneous quick justice was accepted and if the culprit could not always be named, the group paid a penny or so as a kind of corporate responsibility fund. This was needed after a most spectacular event occurred when several of them got up on the roof and one boy, running perilously on an asbestos section, fell bodily through it into the kitchen. The group paid the two pounds for the material and the following Saturday morning formed a work party to make good the damage.

The Youth Club really began before the initial experiment of the dancing class had ended. The first real event as a club was a Christmas party, suggested by the members themselves, particularly thought of as a suitable time to make a presentation to Miss H. Joe made himself responsible for the decorations. He charged us £2 2s. 8d. for them, showing me appropriate receipts, but I was convinced at the time able to make a sizeable profit for himself by 'fiddling' the receipts. Some years later in a moment of candour he told me this was so. The girls bought Miss H. a box of chocolates and provided refreshments in abundance. It was an interesting party, lots of horse-play, throwing sticky buns about, intense and continuous activity under the mistletoe and most organized party games ending in a shambles because everyone would try to cheat. Behaviour was not improved by visits during the evening to the Queen's Head, the nearest public house, just down the road from the village hall. Two boys came back drunk to the point of insensibility, fortunately too far gone to be violent, one of them being sick all over the kitchen floor.

At the party we announced our intention to open a club if they were interested, and in the token ninety seconds for announcements said we would be opening on the first Thursday in February. The month would give us time to plan, form a members' committee and an advisory committee. A gesture which encouraged us at the end of the party was that a group of members went carol singing, raised fourteen shillings and next evening proudly and triumphantly gave us the money, asking it to be donated to the new village hall fund. So we closed the first few months' sessions feeling we had established contact, formed some kind of relationships which were beginning to bear fruit and we were on the way to beginning a new type of stable organization for the young people of the village. The worst was over, we thought, without serious mishap. But we were wrong. We discovered that the first full year of the officially formed club was to be the worst.

3 The First Year is always the Worst

Having kept a diary of the club work in Berrocfield it is not hard to recapture our feelings as we began the first official club year. We had formed an advisory committee, small in number, but composed of those we knew to be sympathetic to young people and influential in village life. These were the village school headmaster and his wife, the local doctor, the vicar, the local policeman, two members from the previous committee, a local rural district councillor and a representative of the Women's Institute. We also appointed a members' committee. This was not because we had any tendencies towards autocratic rule, but simply because a democratic election was not feasible. The group would not listen long enough to have procedures explained and any election, to be fair to differing ages, sexes and areas of the village would have to be done by a complex arrangement.

So we appointed those whom we felt had emerged as the natural leaders in the time we had known them, particularly some of the difficult ones among the boys such as Bill, Tom and Joe. From the girls Kay and Karen were obvious choices. To represent the extreme east of the village we asked Jack, a big eighteen year old apprentice engineer, who lived in the Dell. This group we called together at our home early in the New Year. It was a nightmarish kind of meeting, the boys showing off before the two girls, with little sensible discussion possible, because like small children they would not listen to each other. Our carefully prepared agenda was soon abandoned and any idea of electing a chairman was left until the end of the meeting. These young people appeared to have no real concern to get down to the hard work of preparing for a new club and no experience of how to run or participate in a meeting of this kind. To get them to discuss and arrive at some concrete suggestions, was like swimming upstream against a fast-running turbulent current. Everything seemed to be treated as a great joke and a good time was had by all, except by my wife and myself, and at the end of the meeting we were little further forward. Two matters at least were settled. The first was that I asked Bill to be Chairman which, in view of his hostility, seemed a wise thing to do, and also asked if they would wish me to be secretary? Both these ideas were agreed to after much fruitless discussion mixed with horse-play. The second matter settled was that we agreed to open a club on February 2nd, provided they would meet again as a committee and decide on some basic matters.

The behaviour at this committee, although personally exasperating, was most interesting. They were plainly trying to test us out, to see how far they could go and to discover what sort of people we really were. As in the previous three months in the hall meetings we had to make it clear we were friendly but firm in our relationships with them. All of them found this difficult, and when we later got to know their homes and families, we could see why this was so. As children and later as adolescents their parents appeared alternately to indulge them to the point of silliness and quite abruptly change from this, if something angered the parents, to the other extreme of punishing them, usually physically with a clip on the side of the head or a beating with a belt. The middle course of adults dealing with them rationally, not indulgently, and using rational sanctions to show our disapproval, seemed to be an experience unknown to them outside school. Even within school we had evidence that some teachers behaved as inconsistently to them as their parents did.

At that first meeting, for example, we patiently prevented them rooting around in our cupboards, whipping out a bottle of wine, and indulging in horse-play which could mark the furniture. We were as good-natured as we could be and simply said if this went on we would have to close the meeting and abandon the idea of a club. We would not allow our personal possessions to be handled in this way. This statement was greeted with hoots of laughter, and no embarrassment; the limits were cheerfully accepted. Their noisy uninhibited chatter seemed to us to be a defence against speaking individually in turn, since they were painfully aware, as Karen put it later, that 'We can't talk proper.' To have spoken individually would have made them self-conscious and inarticulate, and it was only after a long period of building up their confidence that any really rational discussion became possible.

From this meeting I also realized that I had imposed my own assumptions, and the structure for the meeting upon them, when they were quite unready for this. My typed agenda and the rational flow of my own talk merely reinforced their lack of confidence rather than built up a useful experience for them to share. Further, since there was no real club in existence there were no concrete situations to discuss, only abstract and hypothetical ones, so that while they genuinely wanted a youth club, these young people, among the brightest of the group, could not readily see the point of what I wanted them to discuss.

The next members' committee meeting was called for the following week. Half of them, including the new chairman, failed to arrive, so that the meeting as such was abandoned. However, with the four who came we exchanged views at an informal level on concrete subjects, such as the times and hours of opening the new club, subscriptions, arrangements for refreshments, equipment and other matters. Because it was informal and the subjects were concrete, this was a much more fruitful meeting; we learned from this and it was to form the pattern for the next few meetings. They accepted the view that the club should pay its way, including the rent of the hall, and an entrance fee was agreed upon at five shillings, payments in two six-monthly instalments of half-a-crown, plus a weekly subscription of one and sixpence for those at work, or a shilling a week for those still at school. There was some feeling that this was very expensive for, in contrast, in the next village they only paid sixpence a week for their club. We quite deliberately set this as the highest subscription in the County Youth Service, because in our view what is gained too cheaply is not valued highly. Our financial aim was to pay our way and with whatever was left over we would buy equipment, and subsidize interesting activities such as weekend or holiday trips.

We opened on the first Thursday evening in February as we had promised and twenty-five of those who had come to the Christmas party attended. By this time the construction of our new village hall had begun—we always referred to this as 'our new village hall and youth centre'—and drainage trenches and scaffolding constituted a serious hazard in the dark, since the new building came very close to the old one. Several of the boys approached me and asked if we couldn't keep the old hall for the exclusive use of the young people. But the building was in a dreadful state and I felt it important for these young people to learn to share facilities with the rest of the community. It was also important for the community itself, which displayed varied attitudes ranging from indifference to outright hostility to its own adolescents. The opening of the new premises was to be in May so we had only a period of four to five months to endure in the rapidly disintegrating old hall.

Perhaps it would have been wise to have waited since the old hall did invite destructive activities, but we felt it vital to gain some control of the group and some rudiments of self-discipline on the part of members, before we had the confidence to move into premises costing £8,000. This proved to be a useful expenditure of time, and anyway there were no alternatives in a village where nothing at all existed for the young people.

After the organized activity of a dancing class we left each evening's arrangements deliberately formless for the first three weeks. We put up several notices on the entrance door, inside the porch, so that members could not avoid seeing them as they came in. One notice dealt with the times of opening—8 to 10 p.m.—since two hours was a slight extension of the previous sessions and quite long enough as a beginning. Another dealt with the matter of subscriptions, and a further notice announcing,

> 'This club can continue as long as
> (i) the fabric of the hall and
> (ii) the fabric of the youth leaders
> are respected.'

All these notices were noted by members—some who couldn't read, would ask me, 'What's all that, then?' and I would explain—but they were regularly defaced or torn down. We always kept replacements available. A brief announcement was made verbally to say we expected members to get out and put away equipment and, at the end of each evening, sweep up and leave the hall tidy. This last expectation they found very hard to fulfil, because they were very concerned not to do more than their fair share of work, nor to appear too co-operative, since hostility and resistance to authority was the normal group attitude.

At five minutes to ten there would be a sudden move to the door and a group would huddle around the entrance, if the weather was bad outside, or just outside the porch if the weather was pleasant. At first no one would lift a finger to put away table tennis or other equipment, nor sweep the floor littered with a great amount of papers and cigarette ends. We would pack up our small equipment case and the portable material stored at home and stand and wait. Just after ten we would say, 'We'd like some help carrying things out to the car, and the hall needs tidying up.' Usually nothing happened, other than rude or snide remarks. So in the same friendly tones we would say, 'Fine then, if we have to do it all ourselves, then we'll close the club next week to give us time to recover.' On the first week, very reluctantly, two boys and a girl helped. The next week no one responded but just stood around and watched my wife and me do it all. We did it and then announced without any rancour there would be no club the following week. We were, in fact, very annoyed but tried not to show it. Most of the members accepted this news in sullen silence, but a small hostile group followed us out to the car arguing. Bill again threatened a punch up and it was touch and go whether there would be some violence. I said, 'Look, we aren't paid to run this club. We do it so you can have a place to meet every week. It seems only reasonable you help tidy up. You didn't help. That's all right by us if you want it that way, but we feel we need a rest next week, as we warned you.' If there had been the slightest edge to my voice, sarcasm or rancour I am sure they would have assaulted us. But I spoke in a matter of fact voice, got into the car and drove off.

It is interesting to record, some years later, that although we appeared outwardly calm we were very frightened. When we were not afraid, we found much of their behaviour and attitudes really distasteful. They were not only noisy and rude, but untidy and dirty. We would come home, after only two hours, in a state of exhaustion and sometimes even physically sick from the smoky atmosphere, chewing gum and cigarette ends all over the floors and the plain hostility threatening to erupt at any time. We found these young people very hard to like. It was difficult to find positive elements in such a situation; we persevered because occasionally glimpses of likeable traits could be seen.

For one thing there was a tremendous vigour about many of these adolescents which could be observed in the way they danced or played at sport. This was also seen in a whole-hearted love of life, often expressed in anti-social ways, but they were repressed for only limited periods. In other ways they were intensely loyal to their own groups, and while this meant hostility to those outside their groups, there was a fierce allegiance to their mates, which never seemed to waver. These are the working-class qualities which writers like Richard Hoggart[1] and Arnold Wesker[2] want to see retained. The secret of a good youth club in this type of social setting seems to be the harnessing of this exuberance and loyalty to the total youth group rather than allowing it to be squandered on small closed groups, and expressed negatively.

For this first period there was little organized activity and the evenings were spent in sporadic dancing, just listening to pop records, talking round the canteen hatch, playing cards, table tennis and darts, while a few boys discovered the boxing gloves in a cupboard and had a hard work-out in the committee room. So fragile was the wall separating this room from the rest of the hall that on one occasion a boy was knocked right through it. Since many of them sat

[1] *The Uses of Literacy.* [2] *Roots* and *Chips with Everything.*

around and did nothing, coming regularly for this purpose, we let them, but began to invest quite an amount of our funds in good quality magazines for both sexes, such as *Honey* or *Motor-cycle*. Those for girls mainly dealt with clothes and fashion while those for boys were mainly to do with hobbies and sport. We made racks so that these could be attractively displayed, and added a series of paper-back novels and short stories, which we felt would help young people, such as Salinger's *Catcher in the Rye* and *Diary of Ann Frank*.

The reaction to this literature was mixed. Some books were ripped up or despoiled by crude sexual drawings and remarks. Some were just taken and never returned. Gradually the custom grew of reading them on the spot or borrowing them for a week or two. We discovered that for most of them this was the *only* reading material they read, apart from papers like the *Daily Mirror* and the *News of the World*. Only one or two belonged to the public library, which appeared in mobile form on a Tuesday afternoon when they were all at work or school. Just the odd one or two appeared to read books required by further education or day release courses. The destructive reaction remained, gradually becoming less, and we were convinced that we could have done a lot more of this kind of literary activity if we could have spent much more money on paper-back books. Some attractively designed books on Health, Personal Relationships and *How Your Body Works* were in constant demand and needed frequent replacement. When they disappeared we were less concerned with the moral aspect, than that they were being used.

It was slowly established that we meant what we said, and what we did was done with no malice but was always preceded by warnings. It took several closures of the club, as with the issue of clearing away, for this principle of corporate help to dawn on most of them. Some stayed away for the week we reopened by way of a reprisal, but they would drift in again the following week having apparently got their annoyance out of their system. The payment of their subscriptions was made a weekly issue by many of them, the futile argumentative ritual having to be gone through regularly before they would pay up. The vast majority were not short of funds, but withheld payment as long as possible to assert themselves. Again, we were good-natured about it, firmly allowing no credit, not even for the members who slipped in at nine-thirty hoping to be unnoticed or at least argue for a half price reduction. I always kept change for a five pound note readily available, since it was a regular stunt to produce one in payment in the hope that change was not forthcoming. Alf one evening sat in his car in the car park the whole time, with a girl friend, of course, only coming into the hall to use the lavatory or to speak to a friend. After a good-natured argument he would pay up. Some were downright mean and nasty about it, sometimes throwing the money on the floor to make me pick it up. I never picked up the money, treating it as non-payment unless they put it in my hand. Later we handed over the collection of subs to various senior members in turn, but for more than a year we had to keep a visual check on who was present, because the collector would frequently let his personal friends in free, which would have meant a loss of nine or ten shillings to the club each week. It was difficult to persuade them that this was cheating and basically foolish, because they were only cheating themselves.

By the end of February some members of the committee, the girls particularly, wanted some activity of a more feminine kind and after discussions with my wife they thought a few sessions on 'How to Run a Party' would be interesting. The County Youth Service put us in touch with a domestic science teacher, who was married with several children, and she agreed to come out for six weeks to run something for the girls for no longer than an hour each time. She was a bright, gay woman of about forty and the girls took to her at once. Despite the draughty committee room, made draughtier by the boy-shaped hole in the wall, they met and worked out a programme involving 'How to dress and look attractive for a party', 'What to eat and how to make it', 'Whom to invite and how to behave' and 'Planning a party programme'. These sessions then involved a little talk, but mostly activity of a practical nature, such as the skill of make-up, dress-making, wearing jewellery, making attractive lanterns, designing a menu. The idea was to work up to a party on the sixth week given by the girls for the rest of the club.

About eight girls began on this project, four of them attending every session, but the others seemed to lack the concentration required, and were too easily distracted by boys forcing their way in or inviting the girls outside. By further education standards of attendance it was not too successful, but as a first club venture, and knowing the girls and their difficulties, it was highly successful and worthwhile. Youth clubs tend to be led by men, and geared more to boys' than girls' interests, so that something put on especially for the girls—and by the girls, with their final session party—was to be encouraged. More of this kind of informal education on being feminine, in the right sense, and how to fulfil the role of a woman, should not only be part of all club programmes but also form a great deal of the curriculum for most of the girls' last year at school. By conventional and external standards of behaviour the party was rather messy, but for the girls it was a splendid achievement. With gay lanterns and other decorations they made the battered, drab hall attractive and lively. Tastefully decorated tables were loaded with delicacies and a short programme was observed and the girls played their parts very well.

It was marred by a great deal of silly behaviour by some of the less intelligent boys, who seized the sausages on sticks and threw them wildly about the hall. This kind of incident happened frequently as they were egged on by others, and these poor lads were too inarticulate to express themselves socially in any other way. But even they became tired of this pointless horse-play, especially when the girls showed their disapproval. 'Really', said one of the girls, Pamela, who hadn't very high standards herself, 'The kind of people who come here give you a pain up the arse!'

At the beginning of the club's life we had affiliated to the National Association of Youth Clubs. This was little more than a nominal affiliation at first but it meant that our individual members had tangible symbols, such as membership cards and badges, to carry about. Those that had these were very proud of them, especially the badge, purchased at a shilling each. Unfortunately, the entire stock of twenty badges was stolen from my case one evening and we never recovered them. This kind of petty pilfering went on continuously and was a great nuisance. In the canteen, bottles of Pepsi-Cola, cakes, biscuits and crisps incessantly disappeared, mainly through the hands of the adolescents running the canteen for the evening, through the hatch to their personal friends, who would try to reciprocate when it was their turn.

Most items were checkable and where this was so we made people in charge make good their losses, which at least caused them to do some personal costing. It was fatal to let one person get away with anything, simply because it became known to all the members that it was possible. There developed, at one time, a racket on returned Pepsi bottles on which we had had to ask for a threepenny deposit, otherwise members threw them away or smashed them senselessly in the road outside. Someone crawled under the hall and sawed his way into the kitchen, stealing some full but more than a score of empty bottles. The empties were then sold back to us by members at threepence each until we realized more were being returned than we were selling full. If a culprit could not be caught then it was essential that the club corporately should pay for the stolen goods. This happened in the case of the missing badges by increasing everyone's subscription by threepence the following week. Some members refused to do this but came into line when the majority saw the fairness of it. It also meant that whoever had stolen the badges could not successfully sell them to members at reduced rates, because the members had paid for them in part already. We never did know what happened to the badges. I wouldn't be surprised if they were simply thrown out of the window into the long grass outside, as a pointless gesture of aggression.

Up to Easter, after three months, there were individual expressions of friendliness and trust towards us, but as yet there was no corporate loyalty to the club, and we were frequently faced with bad group conduct. We were still personally identified with the other side of the social fence and it was evident that they were hostile to the fact that we lived in an attractive private house and had educated voices. The boys mimicked our speech, although we puzzled them a little on this score since my wife often lapsed into her Scots dialect and I into my native Lancashire. What helped us to handle their continual resentment and the frequent regressive behaviour was to realize that there was nothing personal in all this. We were the nearest available targets for their resentments against authority—parents, teachers, policemen and other figures—and 'the posh toffee-nosed' people who continually made them feel inferior. I suppose we were playing a useful social therapeutic role, the outcome of which was uncertain for some time.

When we reopened after Easter we had only a few weeks to go before the new hall and youth centre was ready. The girls, remembering their happy sessions on 'How to Run a Party', wanted some more sessions specifically on the use of cosmetics. One evening, by arrangement, a very attractive blonde lady arrived amid catcalls and 'How are y' darlin' ' cries from the boys. She organized five evenings for the girls very well and there were no absentees this time, simply because all the girls wanted to know how to look their best. The boys for long periods would hang round the open door of the committee room or peer through the hole in the wall, to watch this mysterious feminine process. The girls about this time decided to take over the canteen arrangements and for the first time offered hot drinks, tea and coffee, which were much more popular than soft drinks.

Membership began to drop slightly as the summer evenings extended in length, so we sought round for a tennis court to organize an activity on another evening. There was then no public tennis court within a five mile radius but plenty of the larger houses had their own private courts. About two fields away was such a house owned by Mr. Sinclair, a London business man, who was chairman of the hall committee and very sympathetic to the young people of the village. He agreed to let his hard tennis court be used by club members every Tuesday evening, provided they did not become a nuisance or cause any damage. We purchased four racquets and a set of tennis balls and announced that we would meet next Tuesday on Mr. Sinclair's court. Specific instructions were given that only those who behaved well and, most importantly, those who wore rubber-soled tennis shoes would be allowed to play.

While one of us was present the Tuesday evening tennis went fairly well, although Mr. Sinclair did complain about cigarette ends and litter and an unused contraceptive found in the summer house overlooking the court. Some Tuesdays neither of us could be there and we asked senior members, principally Bill, Tom and Joe, to be in charge. Physically they could overawe and deal with any recalcitrant members if they wished, but unfortunately they did not wish to incur the unpopularity of keeping the others in order. The result was noise, fighting, dubious activities of a sexual nature in the summer house and many people being allowed to play in shoes and even boots. Because of damage to the court surface Mr. Sinclair finally decided to withdraw the privilege. His action was taken in the usually hostile manner, an attack upon his motives, his class and his wealth, the members betraying not the slightest sense of responsibility for what had happened. I wrote a letter of apology on behalf of the club, and read it aloud to them next club night. I said I would not again ask for such favours. It was the first time I was really angry and I showed it. Whether this did any good or not I do not know but I made it clear that if they were not ashamed of their behaviour I was. It was on this happy note that we took over the new hall and youth centre.

The official opening of the centre was arranged to coincide with a Whit-Monday fête, which was really a dog show and several side shows to raise money, with the ceremonial opening as the climax. The club members were asked to run some of the side shows but it was impossible to persuade them to do this. All when asked said they wouldn't be there on Saturday, but, of course, they all *were* there much to the annoyance of the hall committee. They were unco-operative for various reasons. They could not see any reason for helping an adult group to raise money for the new building, although the ways in which they would benefit were told them several times. There was hostility to the adult leaders of village affairs, because of their differing social class and educated accents. They were also undoubtedly very self-conscious about doing something in public. Even later when members did help at the next annual fête it was noticeable how embarrassed they were, especially when their own age group appeared. They would stand, jeer and guffaw in close proximity for most of the afternoon. It was difficult to explain their natural reticence and the other reasons to the hall committee but I tried nevertheless. The fact that a youth group still existed after several months impressed them, but I was still regarded as something of a theoretical intellectual.

We assumed that our first evening in the new centre was going to be so much easier, but this assumption soon proved a false one. The young people were intensely curious about the new premises which were fairly simple, but luxurious by comparison with the old village hall. A hall, large enough for a badminton court, with a stage at one end and a serving hatch from the kitchen, was the main structure provided. There was a vestibule or entrance hall, off which a narrow passage led to the rear of the stage, two dressing rooms which could be opened out into a committee room, and lavatories across the corridor.

We soon discovered that this spacious lay-out with its unlocked doors provided many opportunities for mischievous behaviour, mainly rushing about the building with fast exits and entrances reminiscent of not so well-timed French bedroom farces. On the first night this resulted in a mounting excitement, bordering on hysteria, which made life exceedingly difficult for those in charge. Damage to the brand new hall was considerable. Two doors were broken off their hinges, one of them splintered up the centre, a medicine ball, of fair size and weight, was thrown through a window, and a boy pitched across the stage by a horse-playing friend plunged his head through the thin plasterboard wall. Everyone denied responsibility for these incidents. To cap it all, the tidying up and putting away arrangements which we thought had been solved permanently again broke down, and we were left at ten o'clock sadly surveying the damage and the mess.

The club closed for two weeks, as we wrote in a letter to members, 'or longer until we have repaired all the damage, and paid for the materials'. We knew that the doors had been damaged by the two delinquent brothers, Ricky and Tim, who with delightful lack of guilt admitted it, but said the doors were too flimsy for a public hall. They were undoubtedly right but we had to win this battle or the club would have been impossible to run. During the two weeks nothing happened and it began to look as though the wild elements had won and the club had ceased its existence after the normal, short, turbulent history. We were surprised on the last day to be visited at home by about twelve members, half the membership, who said they wanted the club to begin again. They had raised about four pounds to pay for damage and would get a small group actually to do the repairs. In a matter of fact tone, careful not to show too much enthusiasm we said, 'All right. In future the fabric of the hall must be respected, or we shall close for a very long time.'

There were difficulties, naturally, in persuading the hall committee to let us continue, in view of the damage done. 'These *children* (sic) don't deserve the use of the hall.' 'They are just a bunch of hooligans not worth helping.' 'No respect for property: wait until they can handle themselves responsibly.' It took a great deal of patient discussion to elicit permission and to recognize that damage, if repaired, was a necessary hazard, important for the young people to handle as part of their social education. There was a real insight achieved at this committee meeting, composed of largely middle-class people, in which most of them saw the point and the cost of what we were trying to do. It was part of *their* social education to understand a different constructive approach to these problems.

When we began again in late May we designed a short course in Judo for the boys, at their own request. An insert in the parish magazine realized scores of mattresses, and with a good instructor available, we were promised some lively evenings. This was almost wrecked at the beginning by the unbending mechanisms of officialdom. When we had run courses for girls we had paid for the instructor, and her travelling expenses, from our own funds. For Judo, using an official instructor, we applied for his fees to be covered. Consequently the night we were to begin the Judo activity, the local further education officer arrived to get the participants to enrol and to fill in the appropriate forms. This could have been better done informally through the club leaders, especially as the officer concerned was a teacher at the local secondary modern school, rather a bully and very unpopular with the pupils. It was not surprising to see the reactions of our members, in the informal atmosphere of the club, when confronted by a teacher associated with the formal educational system, and not the most acceptable one either. They were noisy, obviously ill-at-ease and cheeking back as far as they dared. Some of them immediately left the hall, refusing to return for several weeks. Instead of having the sensitivity to see what was happening, for he should have left and handed over any formal requirements to us, he began to shout and bluster, presumably reproducing his normal inadequate school behaviour where he had some nominal authority. Within five minutes he had no customers left in the hall and he, the Judo instructor and the two leaders were the only people left. I told him in no uncertain terms what had happened, requesting him to clear off and in future transact any formalities by post, or dispense with payment for instruction. He went reluctantly, blaming the members, and myself in particular, apparently quite oblivious to the chaos he had caused.

It took until the end of the evening for several members to return, a small number not returning for several sessions either from fear of meeting him again or out of sheer annoyance. The few members who were very vocal revealed their hostility not only to the teacher concerned but also to school and authority generally. The intensity of their anger was almost unbelievable, but it was plain to me that their self-image as inadequate educational rejects was very evident in this situation. It took a long time for us to live down this episode, and we had to give many assurances that this man would not return. 'We come here to get away from school,' they said. 'We don't want any bloody teachers 'ere!'

Judo continued with moderate success after the initial set-back. During the summer we also began a cricket evening, after the tennis activities collapsed due to damage to the court. The girls would come to watch and giggle, while the boys disported themselves on the green. We had a moderately good cricket square available and some fifteen boys, many of them not club members, came to play but the attendance was increasingly erratic. This undependability was a marked feature of these adolescents for a long period. Frequent promises could never be relied upon, and no one was willing to commit himself more than a few days ahead. This was not due to a full diary of engagements, for their leisure time was spent rather aimlessly. It was rather a fear of being tied down, of missing something new and exciting which might turn up on the spur of the moment—it never did—and a direct unwillingness to be organized.

They were very keen, for example, to hire a bus to go to a Southern seaside resort for a Sunday outing, but five attempts failed simply because those who had signed their names would not pay the fare in advance, the only way of avoiding a substantial financial loss to the club. Again, it required time to educate them to this basic requirement, and even after two years, during which we ran several successful trips, it was still a battle to get money in advance from them. They were not lacking in funds, only in the desire to commit themselves ahead of time.

Our summer programme ended with two interesting events. One was a sausage barbecue, planned to be held in our garden at home. A small number of the girls prepared refreshments, ordered the sausages, and a few of the boys helped me prepare a site for the fire, order charcoal and rig up some primitive equipment. Unfortunately, it rained on the evening of the event, but during the intermittent spells of good weather I was pleased to see Bill organize the cooking, although it was true that he himself appeared to consume an abnormal proportion of the sausages. We had organized bowls on the lawn. We should have realized the hazards involved in this because our less bright, more spirited boys used the woods not for rolling sedately across the grass but rather as cannonballs, hurling them through the air at one another. In an atmosphere rather reminiscent of the battle of Trafalgar, with projectiles whizzing across the garden, it was almost impossible to assert any control. Eventually, we stopped this activity but not before a window and two flower beds had been damaged and a precious wood, one of a set of eight borrowed for the occasion, had been lost. Again, we insisted that damage be paid for and that the wood be found. It took six boys with torches until midnight to find it, lodged in a branch six feet high in a thick briar hedge. We never played bowls again.

The final event at the end of July, as our last evening of the summer, was a resounding success. A club some twenty miles away had a reputation for producing revues, pantomimes and plays up to professional standards. So we invited them to pay us a visit, and to put on a revue, for which we paid the expenses of the bus. The club adult advisory committee and all who had helped begin the club were invited, including all the baby-sitters from the village who had volunteered to help in this way, to release my wife and me on club evenings. Although our own members were embarrassed in the presence of so many adults they thoroughly enjoyed the revue, especially the funny sketches and the attractive long-legged chorus girls. Some of them even asked if they couldn't put on a show like this, which is what we had in mind when we planned the event. So we completed the summer, leaving August and early September in which to recuperate.

When we asked members where they were going for their summer holidays we were appalled by their answers. Only one was thinking of going abroad, and this was left to such haphazard planning that he never got there in the end. A few were going to seaside resorts with parents, who would pay for the holiday but the young people themselves would have to provide about £30 pocket money. When I pointed out they could have a complete holiday in Switzerland for that amount of pocket money they were most disbelieving. There were planted the seeds of an idea for a club skiing holiday the following Easter. The remainder stayed at home for holidays, going out on a few days' trip, mainly involving somewhat aimless visits to the nearby towns. At this point we did not feel strong-minded enough to take them away anywhere, and long-term planning was necessary for this in any case. In the following autumn we began to plan further ahead with holidays in mind.

The new autumn programmes began with a dance, at the members' committee's suggestion. A group called 'The Yogs' of no musical distinction, other than the capacity to produce the required pitch at a suitable volume, were engaged. For us the evening was uneventful and rather dull, but the members thought it a smashing evening. By now over thirty attenders from the village were coming, many of them as rough and tough as our earlier group. Since we could not count on the loyalty of our own group as yet, the coming of new members created problems since these had to go through the process of trying us out, by bad behaviour and activities of a high nuisance value, all very exhausting and difficult. We still had little co-operation in tidying up the hall, the payment of subs, and the running of the canteen. Expressions of hostility, rather than friendliness, were fairly frequent. The uncertainty of what was going to happen each evening and the group's volatile condition did not make club night a welcome prospect. Many times we went out, forcing ourselves from a sense of duty, to open the club.

Because the boys were very anxious to play soccer I arranged a few games with other local clubs and I agreed to referee the matches. The bad spirit among members and in relation to visiting teams, illustrates the uncertainty and immaturity of our group at this time. First, they would squabble among themselves about choosing a team, a great deal of bad feeling being aroused among boys not chosen. Choice was mainly on skill as a footballer, but many times was based upon friendships and often, in marginal cases, boys were chosen for quite wrong reasons. The major figure in this was Bill, a good but selfish player, who constantly chose his cronies. Then on the football field they would play with a mixture of fouling and blatant disregard of the rules, with outbursts of bad temper and fighting with opponents, when they were rightly penalized for infringing the rules. In the first match I refereed I was almost mobbed for sending off one of my own team who was playing dirty football, and only my threat to stop the game completely prevented an outbreak of further violence. Playing to them was important but individual achievement and winning were by far more important. After one match, when I sent off three Berrocfield players, I cancelled the next two matches. And although they would promise to be better sportsmen next time, they were rarely able to keep the promise. The bad spirit was only to cease when some of the older players left the team to play elsewhere and when we substituted seven-a-side football for the normal game.

That autumn was as difficult as the spring but we felt, if respect was growing slowly, we were getting the measure of them. A short but successful series of fencing lessons was given, another dance was arranged by a really good jazz group this time, and we had visited a few well-organized youth clubs in the surrounding area, one of them the revue group who had visited us during the summer. On these visits, despite outbreaks of silly self-conscious behaviour by some of our members, they were learning how other young people conducted themselves. This was why we had arranged these exchange visits with care. Evening activities were still fairly conventional but we were content to provide a social meeting. Most members resisted programmes of any kind and seemed to enjoy chatting, listening to recorded music and drinking coffee or soft drinks. No one seemed to trust us, nor did we feel we could trust more than two or three of them, but we planned after the following Christmas to widen the club programme to weekend and out-of-club visits to plays and films, which were to prove an immediate success.

The one event which changed the club climate to one of corporate loyalty to the club and to us as leaders, was a mass invasion of an aggressive motor-cycle group the week before Christmas. Some forty of these leather-jacketed boys roared up about eight-thirty and began to troop into the hall. In ability and behaviour I assessed them as similar to our own boys, and later evidence proved me correct. I met them in the vestibule and said the club was a private club and I was sorry we couldn't admit them as a group. Forty members were in the hall and our policy about visitors was that they were welcome if invited in twos or threes by individual club members. I was courteous and friendly but firm and, to my relief, the crowd began to move back into the car park. But a persistent group of three began to push against me, using some obscene words to try to provoke me to anger. When they saw this to be useless and I remained firm but reasonable, they too began to leave. It was then I made the foolish mistake of following them beyond the porch into the car park. Sensing with some relief that the episode was over I must have had a slightly triumphant edge to my voice when I said something to them. Immediately, one and then a second turned on me and hit me in the face, then ran off into the night. I staggered back into the hall with blood streaming from my face, and a whole group of members led by Bill rushed out to pursue the attackers.

Before this I had had a hostile group behind me as well as resisting groups in front of me. Now they were outraged that the violence they had promised me themselves had been done by visitors. They never caught the offenders otherwise there would have been a full scale battle in the middle of the village, with possibly serious injury. We learned later that this motor-bike gang were armed with bicycle chains and knives. But our own members were angry at the attack on 'our leader' and the fact that they were forcing their way into 'our club'. This created the spirit so lacking in the first period of our association, so that almost twelve months to the day, the external menace created a unity we had never known before. Despite the physical discomfort of four stitches in my face, it seemed a small price to pay for a youth group loyalty which we had never experienced previously. Individual instances of bad behaviour still continued, because of the personal difficulties of individual members, but from this time the group was behind us helping to order and sustain a youth community. We had arrived at the real beginning.

4 The Second Year – Widening Horizons

We opened in the New Year with some optimism. Despite a Christmas party of a noisy, boisterous and disorganized nature there was an encouraging new attitude to us as the leaders. For the first time most of the young people called us by our first names, something we had encouraged for a few months with little result. The social distance between the adults and Club members previously sensed was now diminished, and it was noticeable how much more relaxed the atmosphere was.

As part of the Christmas celebrations, since 'games' were not too acceptable, and few of the boys danced, the members' committee suggested hiring a film. The one selected, a slapstick comedy called '*Pardners*', featuring Jerry Lewis, produced an interesting reaction. For fifteen minutes the members sat and watched fairly quietly, for the next fifteen they gradually got noisier with catcalls, boos, ribald laughter and comic remarks. By the end of the first reel the dialogue on the film was inaudible and while the reel was being changed there was a general exodus to lavatories, the snack bar and to outside activities. Mercifully, early in the second reel the film snapped and to everyone's relief the showing was abandoned. This restlessness, incidentally, could be observed at any local cinema in the nearby towns during weekend evening performances. Many middle-class adults ceased going to cinemas because they became places too noisy for serious concentration.

For our own members it soon became evident at other film showings, apart from courting couples, or the opportunity the darkness provided for quiet, furtive sexual explorations, that the young people used the film as a visual social background against which they talked, ate sweets and popcorn, had a bit of a giggle, strolled around in the semi-darkness and generally relaxed unself-consciously. For this reason we sometimes put on a film show, but for no longer than one reel, as part of an evening's activities.

This particular Christmas party provided two indications of changed attitudes. The first was the reaction to two boys who returned from the Queen's Head rather drunk, one of them in a very excitable, aggressive mood. Instead of having to deal with them myself (the members' normal reaction was to see if I could handle this on my own) two of our biggest members hustled them outside, jollying them home with firm good humour. We also had a visit, half way through the evening, from a tough-looking group of some ten boys, inhabitants of the nearby village of Chiltham. These were taken in hand by some of our members, instead of being allowed to create awkward situations. It was at once obvious that our own members were concerned to see that no outsiders spoiled the party, for the first time showing some solidarity as a community.

It was with this experience behind us that we began the second year and with some confidence began to plan to use the club as a base for other activities. If we had had a slogan, it would have been 'Widening Horizons'. Our first effort was a trip to the club which had put on the Revue at our club the previous summer, who were presenting a pantomime. We were able, with only a week's notice, to hire a forty-seater bus, and dispose of forty tickets, all paid for in advance, to arrive on time and in good order for the performance. It was an eye-opener to our own group to see a really professional presentation of *Ali-Baba* by young people of their own age group to a packed hall of adults

An interest was voiced once again in drama, dancing and light revue. This was an activity we were to develop later in the club's programme. It was refreshing to see our group behave so well on this occasion, especially after our turbulent history of unpredictable nastiness.

This did not mean, of course, that all was sweetness and light during our normal club evenings. Outbreaks of high spirits inevitably resulted in occasional damage, such as the evening when two fire extinguishers were released and the entrance hall was knee-deep in foam. These kinds of incidents still continued but they were sporadic rather than the regular outbreaks we had known in the first year. Much of it was positive good humour, not negatively destructive, as when we had a visiting cleric. We were discussing the club together when Chris, an amiable but very limited youth of seventeen, fell between us from the stage about three feet above us. He lay on the floor as rigid as a post, moaning, frothing at the mouth and showing only the whites of his eyes. Two of his mates came forward and said to the clergyman, 'Its all right Rev. He often has fits like this.' They picked him up and carried him outside. One minute later Chris was back in the hall, grinning like a Cheshire cat and being slapped on the back in congratulation for a splendid performance.

Before widening horizons too far we began to explore how we could do this locally. On our doorstep was the Common, almost exclusively the reserve for nature lovers and courting couples. Local legend has it that half the population of the county is spawned on Berrocfield Common. However, other activities took place there, one of them being a motor-cycle rally, which made full use of the twists and turns, the ups and downs of a series of old quarries long since overgrown. After the annual event that year I suggested the idea of a cycle-cross, a kind of motor-cycle rally without engines, which could be on a time-trial basis. Members were immediately enthusiastic and said 'What about next Sunday?' We said that it could be organized for the Sunday afternoon if a few volunteers would turn up on Sunday morning to plan the cycle-cross course and mark it out. We would need sixty marked flags for the thirty gates, sticks to which the flags would be attached, some white paint and naturally, a fair selection of bicycles stripped of all accessories, including brakes.

A group of girls set to work at once to cut out and stitch the white flags, from old sheets, and without any prompting, Rob, one of the least intelligent and most difficult boys arrived on the Sunday with sixty flagposts in a huge bundle. He had cut sturdy reeds, about six feet high, from a nearby marsh all on his own. It was the first positive thing I had seen him do and it was the first of many he was to do for the club. At school he was known as 'sullen, unco-operative and irresponsible'. I would have agreed with that description if it had not been for his work for the cycle-cross.

An excited group of twenty boys and girls met me at the Common cross-roads next Sunday morning. They arrived an hour late admittedly, but by their remarks I knew that many had had great difficulty getting up and out on time. Most of their families just lay abed the whole of Sunday morning, after a week of very early rising and hard physical work. Even to get out for eleven o'clock many had to go without breakfast. A twisting, up and down, arduous course was plotted out with the flags of over a mile ending in a track uphill to the finishing line, which for the last hundred yards was ankle deep in mud.

The afternoon event had some thirty contestants, some of whom were not our members but regular riders for the Berrocfield Cycle Speedway team. Our own members took the first two places with the record times of 6 minutes, 15 seconds and 6 minutes, 27 seconds. The course was pedalled at fantastic speeds downhill, without brakes, weaving in and out of trees, over a gravel pit 'lip' into shallow water and uphill; in some places, in order to make good time, the riders had to run carrying their cycles. The only way to complete the course was to run like this through the final sea of mud. It was a very popular event, to be repeated many times during the next two years, without a single injury apart from one sprained ankle; an example of spirited adventure activities of a homespun variety which, after the first event, the young people took over and organized for themselves.

Further afield the boys were invited to play football and the girls had a few netball matches arranged. The girls' sports never really caught on until they got a little older, since they associated these activities with school. Their greatest pleasure was to dress up as glamorously as possible, in attractive clothes and hair styles. The girls rarely went out the night before club, so busy were they washing and setting their hair. It was not surprising that they did not wish to chase about a netball court, nor even the less strenuous sport of table tennis—we were never able to get a girls' table-tennis team—simply because they wanted at all times to seem well-dressed and sophisticated. The stereotype of the mature feminine image often had a limiting effect on their interests, even although the majority were little more than fourteen years of age.

The boys, by contrast, had no such inhibitions about sport, since such activities were consistent with an image of masculinity. Their only problems were turning up punctually for fixtures and behaving in a sportsmanlike manner on the field. Our initial experience of bad temper, fouling and rule breaking at football by our club team was never really overcome. We were suspended from one knock-out contest and debarred from a Sunday league, such was our reputation and behaviour. No appeals to pride, shame or club honour had any effect, so powerful was the Berrocfield tradition of 'playing hard to win'.

After an event the bad feeling sometimes persisted, as when Bill, then the football team captain, set upon a player from an opposing team who had made a remark about 'poor sportsmanship'. It took four adults to prise the two contestants apart. Some after-match events were pleasurable. Once when we played a local brewery on their own ground and after a cold wintry afternoon, covered in mud, we had a beautifully warm communal bath, the size of a small swimming pool six foot deep. Curiously, we had several boys who were very self-conscious when naked. On this and on other occasions they would rather go home cold, muddy and bruised than reveal their physique. The very thin and the overweight particularly avoided this, since they were well aware that their peers would make rude remarks and invent cruel nicknames for any physical differences they could observe.

Slowly we introduced innovations into the club evenings. One was a wall newspaper, which had a chequered career. It was a large plywood notice-board about six feet wide and three feet high. We began by pasting up news clippings and pictures of teenagers, mainly cut-outs from magazines; fashion girls, well-known sportsmen, holiday scenes, all covered the board. Just occasionally a couple of girls would spend an evening covering it with their own clippings and cut-outs. They would suddenly take scissors and paste, together with an armful of newspapers and magazines and spend a frenzied hour of intense activity. *The Berrocfield Wall Newspaper* was always a colourful centre of interest around which members would gather and sometimes discuss items, especially the saucier ones. We never had any pornographic pictures or obscene comments scrawled on the newspaper, although we knew that many of the boys brought a number of salacious pictures to the club. The Wall Newspaper was intended to help those who were not good at writing, even barely literate, to express what they wanted to in a pictorial manner. The occasional adolescent poem or cartoon pasted up anonymously would appear but we felt that the opportunity, even when used sporadically, was worth the effort.

The club clientele had clearly settled down to include the average to backward school pupil, the Newsom child, so aptly referred to in the Report as 'Half our Future'. We had noticed their difficulties in expressing themselves, a self-conscious inarticulateness, which pop music and physical movement helped to release. One evening having watched part of the film *We are the Lambeth Boys* they asked 'Why can't we have a "Natter Time"?' as the Lambeth Club, depicted in the film, had shown. Next club evening some twenty of the members crammed into the committee room for the advertised 'Natter time—8.30 to 9.0—Committee Room—Any topic discussed'. Any attempt at controlled discussion was useless on this first and at many subsequent occasions. As chairman all I tried to do was to drop in the odd but relevant question. At first they were doubtful that I really meant any topic could be discussed and ribald shouts of 'Sex', 'Should we or shouldn't we?', 'Nudist camps' and 'Bird watching' opened the proceedings. Most of these were calculated to be funny but even in our later discussion, eventually after many sessions more orderly in character, the obsessive topic was always sex and personal relationships. Sometimes the girls would get very impatient with the boys whom they accused of 'Making it all a great joke'. Yet I firmly believed it had a most beneficial effect and made articulate what would never have been voiced in a formal discussion. The few occasions when set subjects were announced fell rather flat, even those fairly topical and based upon sensational headlines such as 'The Great Train Robbery', 'How Many Divorces Should Film Stars Have?' and 'Is Religion a Load of Rubbish?'. By contrast the sessions where the participants discussed what they wanted to discuss were far more lively and provocative.

One evening they raised the question of drink and alcoholism, and asked if someone would come and talk to them about it. Remembering how visiting speakers to the club were shouted down after ten minutes or so, I said I had a better idea. I knew the local Temperance Society ran a non-alcoholic drinks bar for local clubs, and suggested we invite them to run such a bar and a demonstration for us. A fortnight later the bar was set up. It proved a great attraction. With some skill the barman poured drinks from what resembled champagne, whisky and wine bottles, all the time commenting on the deliciousness of the apple and fruit juices he was dispensing. In this way the members were drawn in to ask questions and explore the subject they had asked about. Although I am far from being an abstainer, as members well knew, I felt this was a most valuable part of their education. The members, by popular consent, asked the society to put on its 'Soft Drinks Bar' when we held our next dance.

The Natter Time session led to one or two interesting developments. A small group of girls approached me one evening and said they would like to know 'How to speak proper'. I arranged on the following week for a local teacher of English, whom I knew to be very good at informal methods of English Usage, to bring a tape recorder. It was a highly successful session, which led to other similar sessions with the recording machine. The girls' request was based not upon a demand 'to learn English' but basically to give them social confidence. They were very conscious that speech inadequacies betrayed their poor status and were very ambitious to improve themselves. One of these girls' school report noted 'Poor social background, slovenly speech; written English nil.' Yet when well motivated this girl improved so much that she became a leading light in a drama group formed later.

Shortly after this the County annual drama contest for youth clubs was presented. We appeared not to have much talent and our previous announcement about a possible entry evoked no response. But we did get a minibus full of interested members to come with us to watch the county finals in a school a few miles away. Most of those who came were girls, the nucleus being the 'talk proper' group. The finals of the county contest contained a wide variety of items from the formal one act play, to lengthy sketches and pop music ballet and mime. It made a great impression upon our youngsters and for a long period they worked on club-nights and at other times under a county drama instructor. The following year they put on an excellent drama mime and got as far as the finals.

We soon discovered that another insatiable interest of the boys, in addition to sex, was car driving. A few were just of the age to gain a provisional licence, and they were very eager to learn to drive. Some were already having driving lessons at driving schools—the cost appeared to be no problem for those out at work—but belonging to carless families, had no facilities for practising between lessons. I was able to give a few practice sessions to boys, and the occasional girl, who asked. The Common, with long stretches of concrete roads, built during the war for army vehicles, was an ideal practice area. I was most insistent that there were four conditions to this help. One was that

I personally saw their provisional driving licence before every session; two, was that they provide their own 'L' plates; three, that they signed a promise to pay what I might lose on my insurance No Claim Bonus should they damage the car, and finally, pay for a gallon of petrol. When I explained why I had to insist on these conditions they saw the point, but it did not prevent one or two trying to get into the scheme by forged licences or 'I left my licence at home' ploys. Eventually the numbers became too large and a few villagers, who had cars, responded well and took the scheme over from the club.

We were very conscious that doing things for the young people should be linked with some demands for service from them. The tradition of community service on the part of the adolescents was very far off. They would do things to help us, when it was plainly in their self interest. When car driving lessons were being given we never seemed to be short of volunteers to tidy the hall at the end of club night. Curiously, all the helpers seemed to be embryonic car drivers. But when we were asked to creosote part of the village hall roof, which badly needed doing, we got one volunteer for a Saturday afternoon. The job could have been done by four people in about two hours, but it took us very much longer. We tried to be philosophical about this and realized that the success of social education had to be measured in years rather than in months. It does take some maturity for young people to undertake social obligations, something not clearly demonstrated by adults in the community, especially their own parents.

Sometimes a little blackmail in reverse was, we felt, desirable. A boy named Pete, who was a particularly good driver, taking lessons with me, was also a good football player and had signed up for a Saturday match. With the minibus waiting to take the team to this away fixture Pete failed to arrive, and so we drove the minibus to his home to pick him up. He was just coming out of the front door, clad in his best suit, a girl friend on his arm. When reminded of the game, much to the fury of the other ten he calmly said he'd changed his mind and was going to the pictures instead. His mates gave him a verbal lashing which only seemed to increase his determination to go to the pictures. As Pete and his girl walked away I said, 'Oh Pete, I'm afraid I can't be bothered to take you out driving on Sunday. I think I'll go to the pictures.' We drove off without him to the club four miles away. Half an hour later when we were ready to begin the game with ten players, Pete turned up in a taxi, grinning from ear to ear, saying nonchalantly, 'I couldn't let my mates down.'

As the year progressed we widened a few of their horizons by sending two girls on a 'Charm' course, two girls to a Spring School, held in the next County and two boys to a drama course held at Oxford. We had tried to rouse interest in this kind of 'going away' but it proved impossible to fill individual vacancies. For some this meant the first time away from home, out of their own beds, in a strange place, and their reluctance was quite natural. We knew many of them were really frightened at such a prospect and we felt there was some way to overcome their lack of confidence. The solution was so simple we wondered why we had not thought of it before. We simply booked two places, even if it meant paying for them in full, and offered them to two friends, in such a way that they regarded the offer as something of a privilege. It was still a problem getting them to commit themselves a week or two in advance. To ask for them to attend a series, involving a continued commitment over a month or more, seemed to be asking for the impossible.

Two events were interesting, not exactly successful, but

useful experiences. First was a visit from a town club, about nine miles away, on the suggestion of a member whose cousin belonged to the club. The other was to take small select groups, especially our own members' committee, to visit neighbouring clubs. Both involved no special programmes, but it meant two groups of young people mainly strangers to each other, mixing during a normal evening programme. The town club arrived an hour and a half late, the coach having visited at least two public houses on the way. Many of their members were under age for licensed drinks but had nevertheless imbibed. The leader, a man unknown to me, was very apologetic but obviously had little influence or control over his members. Our own members had made special catering arrangements, put on their best clothes and behaviour, and were plainly appalled by the noisy, destructive and thoughtless behaviour of the visitors. It was amusing to us to note their reactions, since the visitors behaved in exactly the same way as our members had behaved less than six months ago in their own club.

We had been visitors on previous occasions at other clubs, but learned that a full bus load was too much for other small clubs to absorb for evening activities. In place of this we visited several clubs, by visits spaced over several months, with only small numbers, no more than could be seated in a minibus. It was never difficult getting enough to go on these occasions, since they were intensely interested in how other young people spent their time. The possibility of meeting new and eligible members of the opposite sex was a strong motivation. Because of its popularity we arranged selective invitations, making sure our members' committee went as often as possible. This paid off well because we usually got them talking with their opposite numbers in the clubs visited, which gave them new ideas and helped them understand the Berrocfield Club more realistically. On one occasion we got talking with a very experienced leader of a club noted for a tough clientele. Bill, our newly-appointed club chairman, listened very carefully to the club's difficulties and how the leader had tried to deal with disorderly and violent members. On the way back to our village Bill sat next to me in the minibus as I drove. He was very thoughtful and broke the silence with 'I suppose I was a bastard like some of his members.' I said, yes I supposed he was and then Bill dropped the subject. It was the nearest to an apology he ever came, but from that time on his behaviour changed in relation to the club. I could now count on his support, although temperamentally he was still unpredictable, and a positive leadership began to emerge.

Perhaps the widest horizon opened to members that second year was the beginning of outdoor pursuits, mainly weekend activities, sailing and mountaineering. Before Easter we displayed a great deal of pictorial material supplied by the Ocean Youth Clubs and various mountain associations. The Ocean Youth Club base at Gosport was not too far distant and a brief film was shown, one routine club night, on sailing. It was possible, for only two or three pounds, to spend a full weekend as part of a mixed crew of twelve, under a professional captain and mate, sailing round the Isle of Wight, receiving instruction and participating in, to them, an adventurous schooner voyage. So it was arranged one Friday in late April for seven members to go, and I would accompany them for their first trip. Five of the toughest boys were to come and I was curious to know how things would work out.

Just before we were due to go I received an urgent telephone call from Chris' sister, saying he had to cancel the trip. I asked if he were ill and the answer was that Chris was fine, but his mother was upset at his going away. I hurried over to the house to find his mother, his sister, his grandma and Chris himself all sitting in tears. At seventeen, a big strong lad, Chris had never been away from home overnight and this was obviously a highly emotional moment for them all. Chris pleaded with me to go without him, rather than 'upset me mam' and the sister pleaded with me to take him because 'he's got to grow up sometime'. It took me forty minutes to persuade the mother to let the boy go, that he wasn't going to drown at sea nor be led into what she thought was a sailor's life of lust and depravity. Yet this was a boy who had been at work for nearly three years, drove a car and generally knew how to look after himself. I finally got his mother to agree and Chris was somewhat ashamed of the emotional scene he had just gone through but relieved to get away. We had difficulties of a similar kind from time to time, and it seemed to be an intense problem, to some working-class mothers particularly, to let their sons and daughters go away. It was a revelation to me simply because the feelings aroused were very intense and revealed how these mothers still regarded them as children, not as young people, as a resistance to their growing up. Curiously, this intensity was to be seen more in relation to boys than girls, an interesting point upon which the Freudian analyst would have something to say.

The journey to Gosport by car and motor bike was uneventful, apart from a supper of fish and chips en route. It was evident that despite their high spirits the party was rather nervous. As we awaited the dinghy at the harbour steps their rather tense verbal banter sounded rather hollow. Heavily laden, the small boats were rowed over to the schooner and soon the charm and cheerfulness of the skipper put them at their ease.

It was a splendid weekend for us all. Both boys and girls enjoyed it to the full; fair weather, blue skies and white cloud, bracing winds and the stinging spray as we cut through the waters. Within hours these intellectually limited youngsters had mastered the nautical language, the mechanical skill of working together and faced cheerfully the chores demanded of them. Mixing with members of other clubs, in the main middle-class in outlook, and with professional sailors, was a real eye-opener to them all.

The only incident to cause concern was in the port on the far side of the Isle of Wight into which we sailed on the Saturday night. The crew put on their best nautical style and left for shore leave at 8 p.m. By 10.30 we found four of the Berrocfield boys in a state of stupor outside the main hotel. We later discovered they had been drinking 'chasers', a whisky followed by a beer. One of them was alleged to have drunk eight of these in the space of an hour. It was a contortionist problem of the first order to carry them down the slippery quayside steps into a tiny rowing boat, row across the harbour and finally haul them up the side of the schooner, by a rope ladder, all in the pitch darkness from a boat bobbing up and down on a heavy swell. Since it proved to be stormy that night, our over-full friends were violently sick and suffered from splitting headaches most of Sunday. It was the best lesson they could have had because not only were they very unpopular with their mates, but they had to clean the smelling mess up in the morning and barely endured the sail back into Gosport.

This was only the first of several parties from the club to go sailing. We never had difficulty in filling our bookings for this event, months ahead, as we had to collect deposits. It illustrated the fact that they were willing to commit themselves well ahead if only they wanted something badly enough. The effect of this activity upon the girls was interesting. Many of them did not wish to go simply because they feared they might not look glamorous after a wave had washed over them. But the two who went on the first trip enthused a number of others. Just about that time a large number of advertisements began to appear in magazines and newspapers showing nautical girls, impeccably dressed, a peaked cap perched at a rakish angle on beautifully coiffeured heads, holding nonchalantly to the rigging of an immaculate white yacht. A few of these on the notice board had a very positive effect, not only on the girls, but also on the boys! The May and July bookings were over-subscribed.

We made two attempts to organize other weekend trips that summer, both of which failed. One was a simple day trip to the seaside, handled competently by a small committee until the venue had to be decided. Then, when the choice was narrowed down to Brighton or Bognor, all hell was let loose. The club was almost equally split between the contenders, neither side able to provide the minimum number to fill a bus—thirty—and neither side willing to concede victory to the other. At first the subject of good-natured banter, each side came out with lapel buttons 'Vote for Brighton' and 'Buy Bognor', but it soon degenerated into a bitter feud in which the labels changed their tone to such epithets as 'Bugger Brighton!' It is not surprising that worn out by the fierce contest, the members were the losers, and no seaside trip took place, not only on that occasion, but never in the ensuing years of the club. In all this it is odd that no third party arose with a compromise candidate.

Another attempt to visit Wales fell through because by the time we were able to secure overnight hostel accommodation, enthusiasm had evaporated. We were caught in the inevitable dilemma of having to book this kind of trip months ahead and the reluctance of the young people to pay a deposit and so firmly commit themselves to going. To overcome this problem we bought a small amount of camping equipment, arranging for this to be supplemented from the County Youth Service in an emergency. With the offer of a club minibus we could then plan a trip on a club night, get our equipment organized and go the following weekend with the minimum of delay and frustration.

Our first essay in mountaineering was a visit to North Wales in the early autumn, when with twelve male members and a packed minibus we drove up on the Friday night. It was to prove the worst weather for months. We pitched in darkness in Snowdonia in the pouring rain with a rising wind, which reached gale force in the early morning. All this with a group quite unskilled in pitching tents in even the fairest conditions. After an hour and a half's tussle with the elements and with some very tired, disgruntled adolescents, we had sufficient coverage to sink into an exhausted sleep, only to be roused again three hours later by the increasing gale. Soaked to the skin, with tents badly mauled, we withdrew in disorder into the nearest barn.

Mercifully, the morning dawned bright and clear and while most of us set about drying out tents, clothing and equipment, a few cooked a tasty breakfast. Despite their countryside experience, these youngsters found this kind of primitive living very difficult and the mountains of Snowdonia rather frightening. The weather being settled at that moment we decided to climb Snowdon, taking the minibus up to the top of the Nant Peris pass. Despite a previous briefing on the need for heavy shoes or boots, a few came in tennis shoes or other unsuitable footgear. Their clothing too was fairly thin but fortunately a few of us had extra pullovers, which came in useful. Rather than take the long, monotonous Pyg Track to the summit, I led them up the Crib Goch ridge, a pleasant scramble on firm rock and, if one chose, on certain portions the track along some parts of the ridge was exposed and exhilarating. Long before we got to the ridge two boys, both of them heavy smokers, were very sick and enquired at what height altitude sickness happened? They were so unaccustomed to exercise of this kind and so physically unfit that I could not disillusion them but assured them that altitude affected different people differently. Along the exposed parts of the ridge, where we met a fierce wind most of them clung feverishly to the rock, but after a while, confidence grew and they began to enjoy the new experience.

Very tired, with blistered feet, they stood on the summit four hours later in rare good humour. A photograph of the party taken on the summit cairn shows their pride in achievement. Unfortunately, the picture could not be sent in to be published in the local weekly paper because Tom and Bill had taken the weekend off and had arranged with their mates at work to sign in for them. They unconvincingly tried to explain to me that unless they got double pay —for work they didn't do—they couldn't possibly have afforded to come to Wales.

The cost of these outside trips, in fact, was very reasonable because to encourage varied and especially new activities the club met half the costs from its funds. We felt this was a rightful priority, an investment in people rather than equipment which was of first importance. The effect upon our relationships with members who went with us on week-end or special trips of various kinds and the relationships between members themselves was most encouraging. On club nights following such a trip the feeling of community was very noticeable and the association of members with each other was at a much more personal level.

During the summer and autumn we experimented with two new activities on club nights. One was outdoor archery in a neighbouring field and a county instructor came for six weeks, during the first hour of the club evening. After a twenty minute curiosity period on the first evening, about ten boys—no girls—stayed the full hour to practise the new sport. Half of these led the instructor quite a dance by mischievous and often dangerous behaviour with the arrows, firing them wildly in several directions including straight up in the air. I was at last called out of the club to deal with the delinquents. With no ill feeling at all they went back into the youth centre leaving five very determined and serious archers. It was successful in so far as the five persisted for the whole course. If the criterion of success was whether or not the course resulted in a permanent recruitment to archery then it was a failure. In all our varied activities of sailing, judo, drama, ballet, mountaineering, swimming, roller and ice skating, archery and fencing we were content if a few members tried them out and found an expression in them, however limited and temporary the interest was. For dull, backward, incoherent and angry adolescents we particularly felt this physical expressiveness of first importance.

Fencing was a case in point. In the autumn a series of sessions was arranged with a working man who had formed a fencing club at a large local factory. This was an important feature of the club fencing—one of the longest lasting activities we had known. It went on for fourteen weeks, and even the girls took an interest. The fact that the instructor was a man who spoke their own local accent, worked with his hands and at a factory in which some of them were employed, was somehow attractive to them. Of course, most of the boys imagined themselves to be real Errol Flynns but this sense of social solidarity was a factor in the activity's popularity. Some months previously we had had the offer of fencing instruction from a retired colonel living in the village. Because he was one of those who complained most frequently and vigorously at hall committees about the youth club, and often expressed the view that what modern youth needed was discipline, I feel we were wise not to accept his offer and to wait until someone more suitable could take it for us. As it was, throughout most of that winter the committee rooms rang to the sound of rapier on rapier and a queue of members waited their turn for half an hour of strenuous activity.

Numbers had now doubled from twenty-four regulars when we first opened to nearly fifty on a good night. Sometimes with visitors, our attendance was as high as sixty, which in our premises was about the maximum we could handle. Occasional atavistic outbursts occurred but they were quickly dealt with. They were not, as before, expressions of destructive or hostile behaviour but sudden uncontrollable outbursts of energy. What was important to us adults was that now club night had no terrors for us. We felt we were among friends who liked and trusted us, and we in our turn enjoyed being with them. It was the kind of youth community we had not thought possible at the outset. A good association of adolescents together was now growing, some sense of self-imposed discipline was evident in their behaviour, and here and there we were beginning to challenge the members to better standards and more adventurous choices.

5 The Third Year – The Crest of the Wave

It would be very pleasant to suggest that our angry adolescents were becoming so responsive to the plans of the Club, largely at this point imposed by the leaders, that all from this time ran smoothly. Although this chapter records a greater participation and a growing sense of communal responsibility, our setbacks were still frequent and sometimes difficult to forecast. At the beginning of our third year it was easy to predict that certain activities were almost doomed to failure. For example, we were approached by the local vicar to give some publicity to the fact that at the local new chapel, just opened, every month a Youth Service would be held and that members of the club might care to participate. It was very evident to me that their hostility to the church was very pronounced, not necessarily because the issue was that of religion but because the church seemed to represent to them a privileged and socially superior group. To this could be added the fact that it had failed to communicate to young people of this age and this ability range.

For the first month or so I went to the service myself. Apart from the few members who were communicants of the church, our members were conspicuous by their absence. The most interesting adaptation of a Youth Service to the needs of modern young people the organizers of this service could think of could be seen in the arrangement for replacing the sermon by a series of slides on such issues as The Church Overseas, or The Leper Colonies in Africa. The quality of the slides was poor, the content extremely dull, and the appeal not calculated to excite modern young people who were used to polished television presentations of a different character. Occasionally one of the girls from the club would persuade a boy to go along to the service. After observing their attempts to find their way through the Book of Common Prayer, sweating with embarrassment, it is not surprising that they rarely came a second time. The notice proclaiming the Monthly Youth Service on our notice board gradually became more and more subject to graffiti interference. Terms such as 'balls to you' and 'rubbish' were fairly frequent. After some three months I withdrew the notice and no contact seemed to be made with the local church at all.

On the other hand the idea of going out of the club to other, more interesting, events was catching on. The most exciting event to lure them to the theatre was a trip to the West End in a minibus to see Arnold Wesker's play *Chips with Everything*. This was the first of a number of visits to the West End, not only to musicals, jazz concerts in the Albert Hall, and other youth events, but visits to the serious theatre. To them the attraction was going up west, having a meal in a posh cafe, and being together as a group. It was very difficult to restrain the boys once we got into the West End from leaving the party to have a good booze-up, and especially the older ones just seeing what 'birds' they could meet in various bars and cafes. But they were restrained by being alone in a big city for the first time and the fear that they might miss the bus home. So on this initial trip to the West End we prepared the programme carefully so that the meal was enjoyed and we all went together to the theatre.

The excitement of the evening was heightened by the fact that the minibus we took on this first occasion belonged to the County Youth Service and was driven by a man extremely nervous and unused to driving in heavy traffic, after the quiet by-roads of one of the Home Counties. He narrowly missed an accident on the way into the city and several times made bad errors of judgment, which I was able to evaluate sitting as I was in the front seat. In fact he did on the way home have an accident, colliding with a large bus, and we had to hire a fresh minibus from a nearby garage to get the party home. The members were somewhat shaken by this event but no one was injured and we never after that used the County minibus.

The visit to the theatre was an enormous success. They were completely ignorant of the kind of person Arnold Wesker was and as far as we knew could not name a single contemporary playwright. But crammed into the gallery as we were, it was fascinating to watch their reactions to a play with very earthy language which focused for them a tremendous amount of their own social hostility. On the language side it was most amusing to see their shock at the corporal in charge of the new recruits to the R.A.F. in this play shouting at them, 'I can see what you do when my back is turned because I have eyeballs in the back of my arse'. This is the kind of language they normally spoke themselves. It was an education to them to see this on the apparently refined West End stage. In the play there is a folk song which is highly emotive in terms of class anger and their response to this kind of situation was very marked. In the bus home before the accident occurred, the conversational topic was most useful since they were talking quite freely about what the play had to say about class divisions and their own personal experiences. It was the first time some of them had begun consciously to recognize their feelings

Our next trip to London was to see Tommy Steele in the musical *Half a Sixpence*, which they all found enjoyable. Again their sense of excitement was heightened because we had written previously to the management stating our party was coming and asking would it be possible for the star of the show to meet them in his dressing-room afterwards? This was arranged and on the night after the performance we had a fascinating twenty minutes talking with this young man, who spoke in their own language and talked about himself and the show and his life as an adolescent in London. He autographed their programmes and they left with the intoxication of having spoken to a real live 'star of stage, screen and television'. Once this series of visits had become established the members began to organize some for themselves and several trips were made to the West End to see Vista-Vision films, pop stars in the Albert Hall on a Sunday afternoon, and other events.

We also began about this time a series of group parties to the local cinema, whenever films were showing which we felt appropriate that they should see. Our first in one of the nearby towns was at a small cinema which catered for re-issues of classical films. The film version of Alan Sillitoe's story *The Loneliness of the Long Distance Runner* was showing and we arranged for a party to go. It was a little different when we went to this local cinema from the conventional and restrained atmosphere of a theatre, for there their normal rowdy and difficult behaviour tended to be reproduced. It was interesting to note that some of the delinquent behaviour of the people in this particular film was equalled by the kind of behaviour in the cinema itself by my particular group. A third of the way through the film some of them were so much of a nuisance that the management called in the police and some of the members of our party were threatened with eviction if they did not quieten down. Mercifully they did so after various crude comments about the police.

I have always felt it is important not to spoil a pleasant and provocative evening by holding an artificial and analytical discussion of a film or play immediately afterwards, unless it naturally arises from the members themselves. It was interesting to note that after the *Loneliness of the Long Distance Runner* was seen nobody wanted to talk about it until some five weeks later. One club night over a cup of coffee the subject arose naturally and became the topic of a very interesting and lively conversation. It was very clear that they identified themselves much more with the Borstal boys in the film as delinquents and sympathized very much with the gesture of defiance of the runner, Tom Courtney, in refusing to complete the course. The views of the Governor and the administrative staff they brushed aside as irrelevant. Perhaps we should quite deliberately provide films and plays by people like Sillitoe and Wesker to help young people to work through their attitudes to authority.

Just about this period when more of the members were meeting for Natter Time and becoming slightly more disciplined verbally, the County arranged a series of discussion group contests, one panel produced by each club, to debate Current Affairs. While all realized that compared with other clubs with a large grammar-school intake our performance was not likely to take us to the finals, we mentioned the possibility of entering the contest. To our surprise a group was formed which met for a series of evenings of intensive preparation. When it came to the first round, what had been previously an inarticulate and a fairly silly, undisciplined group, had welded itself with its own chairman into a group which, while not terribly perceptive in its observations of Current Affairs, were discussing much more freely and with some coherence. Their lack of smooth delivery was often made up by a natural wit and knock-about-humour which frequently came through. On this first occasion they got to the semi-finals and were very pleased with their progress to have got so far. When Christmas came around in this third year it was interesting that they no longer wanted things laid on for them but they themselves wanted some say in the kind of occasion it was to be. They chose a dance, hired a reasonably good pop-group locally, issued tickets, the girls providing refreshments, and apart from one or two outbursts of drunkenness, largely created by outside visitors, this was the most orderly and satisfying occasion that had been organized within the Centre. Certain difficulties arose due to inexperience, such as ordering too much of certain things and not enough of other things, but these were quite easily absorbed in our normal budget.

Another occasion which came near to complete success was the participation in the Drama Festival run by the local county. After seeing the fairly professional group who had visited us and whose pantomime we had witnessed last year, some of our members were extremely keen to produce a formal play. With some help from a local producer, it was decided that a formal play was unsuitable as they would have great difficulties both in selecting an appropriate drama and in memorizing long and complicated dialogue. They finally decided that they should do some movement in mime to music. The whole venture almost collapsed after three sessions of practice in which there were temperamental difficulties by the leading young lady and the jealousy of several of her friends. But due to the inspiration of the local producer, who persisted in calming down the differences that began to arise, the group produced an interesting and most attractively presented 'Jungle Dance' based upon a current pop record. When I saw this mounted in the semi-finals I was most impressed by the artistic choice of costume and the presentation, most of it due to the youngsters themselves. Only half-a-dozen of them were involved directly in the cast but an equal number were responsible for costumes, lighting and technical production. We got to the finals of this contest and were awarded third place, a result which could not possibly have been predicted even twelve months before.

As the summer came round further activities were supplied, two of which were a great success. It is significant that these were suggested by the members themselves and to a large extent organized by them. The first was a barbecue in the ground of the new Village Hall and Youth Centre, during which we invited a university jazz group of really top quality. They were interested in helping young people and came for a nominal fee of 'beer money'. A barbecue pit was dug and well-prepared and there were sausages and other delectables cooked by the boys and tastefully served by the girls. The Committee had also asked, since they had several of them seen this kind of event at seaside holidays, that we should arrange a 'Mystery Tour' on a summer evening if the weather were good. We were able to have a local bus company enter into a flexible arrangement, depending on the weather, to provide a forty-seater bus, which in the event turned out to be crammed with our members. They decided unanimously that we should plot the tour and they should be taken somewhere, if possible, where they had not previously visited. We racked our brains and decided to go by various ways to a small chapel in which there were mural paintings by a leading artist which had taken many years to produce. We could quite easily have gone to a bowling alley in the nearby town or other places obviously attractive to young people, but since we had been given a free choice, we decided this could be an interesting experiment. The coach tour itself was a great success but when we got to the chapel there was some protest at just looking at a crummy church.

On arrival all we said at the outset was that they should go into the chapel, look at it and perhaps then discuss why we had chosen this particular place. Their reactions were very mixed. Some took one look into the chapel without really bothering to examine in detail the beautiful murals, turned about and headed for the nearest public house just across the road. Others wandered round looking at the panels, making rude comments, sometimes of a fairly obscene nature. A small group, however, did sit quietly in the pews and looked at the building and were quite visibly impressed by what they saw. As we journeyed back to the club to spend the last half-an-hour of the evening after the tour, they were somewhat outspoken about our choice and most of them expressed the view that it was a complete waste of time. However, they were not violent and extreme in their views and it was very obvious that they were not universally shared.

Other trips outside the club, not on club evenings, very quickly became popular. Swimming parties on Sunday mornings to the local baths some nine miles away were arranged and eventually these were to develop into quite long journeys into London to swim at the National Recreational Centre at Crystal Palace. These swimming parties were very successful and showed how with even a little organization one could get the best facilities within a reasonable distance. London also provided skating rinks and other towns nearby provided bowling alleys. The bowling movement was just beginning about this time and we were regular visitors at one of these centres. Because the bowling alley movement at that time was associated with America and the drinking of Coca Cola, even if youngsters never participated, they came to watch, to drink light refreshments and to be with their friends.

During that autumn we began gradually to introduce the idea that the club should have a holiday, not necessarily in the summer but perhaps at Easter time. We began this propaganda process by showing a number of short films on ski-ing and on the beauties of Switzerland. At first we had no takers for this idea until we actually produced plans which showed the kind of holidays they could get at a reasonable price. We eventually produced the plan of a visit to the Italian Tyrol in hotel accommodation for a ten days' trip, including eight days at an attractive centre 10,000 ft. high, for a total cost of just under £30. We did not succeed in getting a total party for this trip entirely from our own club, but joined eventually with another club so that we were able to take a party of twenty-five young people to the Italian Tyrol. The ten days were difficult for many people to get away from work, but as we had rather skilfully arranged the time to include the Easter week-end, it meant that only one week's holiday need to be taken off work, leaving another week's holiday free for them to use in the summer. The ski-ing holiday was a perfect combination of fresh air, exercise and activity, and social life, which appealed to these young people. One of the objections which we had to overcome was that ski-ing was only for rich people or those high-up in the social scale. Yet it was most salutary to discover when this trip took place how well they mixed with people of varying social strata. The ski-ing instructors, for example, were young men from the villages with a peasant background and, despite language barriers, it was plain that the boys and girls of the party got on famously with them. It was difficult to break the tradition of only going on a real holiday in the summer-time and it represented something of a sacrifice before they could be persuaded that it was worth taking a holiday at this time of the year, in place of a much longer holiday in the summer. But in view of the fact that they were largely unimaginative and disorganized in planning their own holidays, they took to this extremely well. We had to do quite a lot of spade work with the parents of those interested, who curiously enough, felt that just under £30 was a lot of money to pay for a holiday abroad. This reluctance was not because they were short of money but simply because their traditions still kept them within fairly constricted horizons as far as holidays were concerned.

It was surprising to find that once the decision had been made it was not difficult to get the necessary deposit paid on time, although inevitably there were one or two difficult people who delayed until the very last moment. One of the first payments was made when I was passing through the council estate at Upper Berrocfield. I was called in by Kay's father, a labourer in a local factory in the next village, who asked how much the deposit was for the holiday. Having been told that the sum was £10 down and the remainder to be paid over the next six months, he reached into an old vase on the mantelpiece of this very minute council house, and produced a roll of five-pound notes. I calculated he had at least £300 rolled up there. Without batting an eyelid, he handed the whole amount of £30 to me saying that was the payment, 'Now it's done with!' When I asked him why he left so much money around the house in a place where it was easy to steal, he replied, 'I don't trust them bloody banks. I know where the money is every week.' We contemplated the effect of this upon the young people and what a constant temptation to them it was to have so much in cash standing around.

When it came to the holiday itself and the equipment necessary for the holiday and we assembled on Waterloo Station, we could not tell that our members came from a lower social background at all by the kind of clothes they wore. They were immaculately turned out in ski trousers and anoraks of the latest design and altogether looked like any other ski-ing party crossing over the channel that day.

When it came to actual ski-ing performance on the slopes they were just as good and bad as a normal party. They were prepared to work hard during the day and to relax during the evenings. Tom, who was one of our local athletes, took to ski-ing extremely well. More than half the party gained a bronze medallion as a result of their eight days hard work on skis. In the hotel we were provided with a Social Room, which contained a bar and pleasant seating and lighting, and a juke box. Here most evenings the party assembled with friends acquired during the day. I had previously talked to the youngsters about behaviour and the need to remember most of them were unused to drinking. We had only one serious outburst of bad behaviour and drunkenness on the final night when some of the older boys drank far too heavily and were in a very sorry state the next day. As with the Ocean Youth Club episode, the hangovers they experienced were perhaps the best and most effective lesson they could have learnt. But these social difficulties were only slight compared with the exhilaration which both they and we experienced as we watched them careering down the snow-slopes shouting in regional accents and thoroughly enjoying the challenge and the experience that they were having.

We had one accident when a boy of fairly heavy dimensions fell badly on his leg and broke it. Again it was most touching that most of the party took a day off ski-ing in turn to visit him in the local hospital and then helped him on a very difficult journey by train and boat and train again on the way home. It was not astonishing that we had very few accidents or incidents of this kind simply because for several Saturdays before the holiday the county had provided, in a large school hall some distance away, a serious course in dry ski-ing. This meant rushing about the hall with skis on, gaining enormously in fitness and doing all kinds of preliminary exercises. When the party returned home with bronzed and happy faces they were the object of envy by the rest of the club. The photographs and trophies of the trip were mounted on a display for all the club and the rest of the village community to share. The Italian Tyrol furnished many topics for the following year.

Perhaps one of the most provocative visits to the London theatre was to see the Joan Littlewood production *Oh, What a Lovely War*. This was a most moving experience to those of us who had lived through war, but to these young people what began as an entertainment turned into a disturbing social challenge. This play produced more discussion and excited comment from these young people than anything else they saw. They were very conscious of the possibilities of enormous violence in the world today. Their comments revealed that this kind of social documentary really released in them previously unexpressed fears and feelings. We felt this an important stimulant to supplement the pop shows which they now began to attend regularly from month to month.

Although we were on the crest of a wave both in the internal running of the club and the exciting developments outside, there were some personal tragedies to recall. After a chequered career of violent conflict with the law, the two brothers, Ricky and Tim, were finally apprehended for stealing money out of the poor boxes of churches in the surrounding villages. They had, of course, committed several crimes of this kind and a more serious kind many times before, but this was the first occasion the police had been able to apprehend them with witnesses to support their case. These two boys aged fifteen and seventeen respectively were sent to court and despite all that we could do, after visiting them in temporary detention centres, they were assigned to a Borstal course. I went, taking the President and Secretary of the Club with me, to a detention centre in London from which they were going to be sent out to their permanent Borstal. I managed to ensure that we were received, although we were not relatives. Incidentally, no relatives ever visited them since they came from a disorganized, difficult family. The mother, a dependent and helpless creature, really couldn't be bothered to make the effort for these boys. I was greatly incensed by the attitude of the warden of the detention centre who, when hearing that I was the leader of the youth club and the others were visitors representing the club membership, could only say, 'Well, you seem to have done a hell of a good job on these boys. I don't know why you bother to run a club if this is the result.' I was able to make a suitable reply but observed also the effects of this remark upon those club members who came with me. They immediately became very angry and wanted to have a punch-up with the warden, a response not exactly calculated to win friends and influence people. However, when the two brothers were assigned to their Borstal, which was not too far away, we went once a month with a small group of club members and took chocolates, cigarettes and other articles which the boys enjoyed. The cost of these was entirely raised by the club and it was an important education that some of these boys who were difficult in their behaviour themselves, many of them on probation, should see the functioning of the Law.

This period in which the ideals and experiences of the members were being expanded, took a step further when during that summer we became aware of two things. First, some seven miles away, a school for seriously crippled boys needed some help, and they were designing an outdoors sports area with a dirt-track on which go-kart racing was to be a feature. A fairly large contingent of our members went to visit this school and were determined to help in preparing the outdoor sports area for the crippled boys. The second discovery, which was linked with this, was the fact that a local blacksmith, as a side-line, was himself a manufacturer of go-karts. Some of our members went down and talked to him and he agreed to sell a go-kart to us at cost price so that we could present it to the school. Numbers of meetings were held and arguments were fast and furious as to how they would raise the necessary amount of money, the sum of £25. Eventually they decided not to raise the money by asking other people but by simply organizing a collection among themselves each week until they had collected sufficient funds. The club committee was prepared to make a donation of £5 towards the cost from club funds. This demonstrated to us a responsible attitude to social service and money which was beginning to evolve through our corporate activities. The day was very memorable when we had delivery of the go-kart to our Youth Centre. The total membership of the club on that evening wanted to try it out. Unfortunately the noise was so tremendous and took up the whole evening, the rumour went round the village that we had started a Go-kart Club and were liable to produce this noise every time we met. It took six weeks to persuade the village that the go-kart was only there for that evening and had been presented to a village safely out of earshot.

About this time I was able to invite two people, who were to become the future leaders of the club, during my absence later that year in the United States. When I returned I discovered that they were doing a very good job indeed. One of them was a young local builder whose vehicle, a works minibus, we had been using for some time, and the other was a student from a near-by university who volunteered to do this kind of work as part of his educational course. This additional help was a tremendous move forward for it meant increased activities of an interesting kind, such as the building of our first canoe, a rearrangement of the hall and a different bias to our activities which only fresh minds could bring to an established programme. After three years, two of them of intense strain, we were feeling the need to bring in fresh leadership. We discovered that working with this group was far more demanding than school teaching, which provided a framework of routine. In the club routine was minimal and the unexpected was the norm.

Due to the new leadership we extended activities outside the club as well as inside, including more weekend and more evening activities than the normal programme allowed. It soon became evident that the enthusiasms of the young people were being channelled into a variety of ways which previously had been unthinkable. At the climax of this third year we began to see now the whole attitude of the adolescent group changing, both within the group to each other and towards the community. This outward-looking began to be characteristic of them although they would still lapse into very foolish and childish attitudes. But they could now see the possibilities of new suggestions where before they did not wish to. They made their own suggestions. One of these was that the cycle track speedway which had begun to founder due to its remote position on the common, could be brought on to the land adjacent to the Village Hall and Youth Centre. They even suggested that we might consider floodlighting this area for use in the winter months, and in addition provide a sports area of a hard surface also floodlit, on which seven-a-side football could be played in the winter and basketball and netball for the girls, tennis during the summer months, and many other activities could be held. We devised a scheme designed at a cost of £1900, which also included a playground for pre-school children of a fairly elementary Swedish-type pattern.

Although many of the adults connected with the club and with the community were responsible for raising a lot of the money, the enthusiasm generated by the young people was heartening to see. They took part in much of the planning, the ground-clearing exercises and some of the back-breaking work needed to bring the scheme to fruition. There was also devised an ingenious method of payment for floodlighting by having a shilling-in-the-slot meter available. This meant that outside club hours people could come along and pay in this particular way. In an area very restricted for physical activities it meant that there were now things to do in the village when people could not spare the time to organize activities. We were very pleased to note that this centre became quite well-known in the county and large numbers of leaders and youth organizers came to see this, a monument of what could be done by a few people by their own efforts. Grants were raised through the regular processes of applications to the county under the normal recreational provisions and grants from central government. A large number of local firms were tapped for sums of about £100 and a number of generous donations were made. The youngsters themselves contributed as far as they could, not only to the work of the venture but to its financial support.

So we came to the end of our third year and I was due to leave on a research visit to the United States. The final farewell Christmas party at which I handed over the leadership of the club to my successors was marked by a very good spirit, farewells and presentations were made. We felt here we were leaving a group of friends instead of the enemies who seemed to face us some time before. That evening, lest this be seen complacently, sounded a last reminding note that underneath the surface of friendliness an angry outburst of violence was always possible. A fight broke out in the boys' lavatory, when one of our most violent members assaulted another and broke his nose. The boy was found with blood all over his face and a large mess on the floor where he had vomited. Later we discovered it was one of our Borstal inmates who had come out for a temporary visit, although the boy assaulted would not reveal who it was for fear of reprisals later. I was able by devious ways to get the boy who had done the assault to confess. What had provoked this incident I was never to know but it illustrated that even in this kind of community where one had gone so far, there was still much social education to achieve.

6 'How Unlike the Home Life of Our Dear Queen'

Despite a fairly positive culmination of three years' work it was never easy to understand the young people whom we were trying to serve, and in the long run, to educate. Sociologically they were mainly from a lower social-status group but they were not all from a low-earning group, for many of them and their families enjoyed very high wages. Yet most of them came from home backgrounds and such limited experiences that they could only be described as deprived. The anger which was expressed in much of their behaviour, especially in the early period we had to deal with them, stemmed from their awareness of these deprivations. Often they were imitative patterns of hostility shown by their parents to the rest of society. Some brief description of their home backgrounds may give us some insight into the problems they faced. It is interesting that when one comes into a social situation of this kind, one tends to think only of the problems to be faced in handling them. But it soon became evident to us that our problems were only their problems looked at externally. Some way of understanding them in depth was required if we were to lead them forward into a more responsible and more enjoyable participation in life.

The most violent of the boys were the two brothers, Ricky and Tim, who lived on a council estate with their mother and a series of 'uncles' whose stay tended to be no more than one year at a time. Both boys were illegitimate and there was a third brother of very dark and swarthy countenance, with whom we had little close contact. All three boys looked very different and were thought to be from three totally different fathers. The home was not a home in any sense of the word due to the transient nature of the mother's affections. It was a marvel that she managed to attract any man and such a companion tended to be of very poor calibre, both intellectually and economically. The mother and her three sons were living originally in an old nissen hut on the common and came from a group of fairly militant squatters who had moved in towards the end of the war. It is reported that the Attendance Officer of the area called one day and found them all in bed together, the only way in which they could keep warm, the single room which they inhabited being in an indescribable state of untidiness and filth. There was no income of a regular kind in the family apart from National Assistance and even here the mother, being a pitiful creature who whined and complained her way through life, was not always able to cope with the simple task of collecting what was rightly hers. It was noticeable when they came to the club they always ate a great deal, usually at their friends' expense, and in moments of candour they frequently informed me that they would leave home in the mornings without any breakfast at all and come home to a simple meal of bread, margarine and tea. Whilst they were at school a good meal could be given to them and the Welfare Officers made sure that when they did attend school they got some nutrition of this kind. However, they were frequently truants from school and once they both left school and entered into a shiftless process of moving from one job to another with long periods of unemployment, they were extremely deprived, both in a nutritional and psychological sense.

It was evident in the club and in the school which they had previously attended that they had a following of boys and girls who admired their anti-social ways and their very persuasive talk. With their dark colouring and wide brown eyes, they were most physically attractive and one could see that young people who were perhaps anti-authority themselves were easily attracted to them. Their behaviour in the context of the youth club indicated they resented any kind of authority and were a law unto themselves. No tests run by the Education Authority were available but it was very evident that in a cunning and calculating way both Ricky and Tim were very perceptive boys, but by the very nature of their background were unwilling to work hard and apply themselves to steady employment.

The eldest boy, soon after we came to the village, came to me and wanted to borrow some money for the process of paying off a certain number of debts that he had. I well remember talking with him for something like two hours in my study in which he tried to trick me into loaning him a sum of £5. At one time it became known in the village that I would like to buy a second-hand bicycle and within a few hours of this being known he brought a bicycle round to me for sale. I was extremely dubious as to where he had got it. However, it seemed to me quite respectable and I agreed to pay him a down-payment, but in all one's dealings with Ricky one felt there was a trick hand being played and this created an unfortunate air of distrust. Their violence took many forms so that when they did not get their own way they resorted to threats; their reputation was such that they had been known to have no hesitation in carrying out their threats. On one occasion when I was again being asked to lend him money, I was informed that I had a thatched roof and that it perhaps wouldn't be a traceable action if, 'by accident', my thatched roof was set on fire by a spark from the chimney. Ricky said this with a knowing look in his eye, 'if it happened to be round bonfire night.'

On these occasions the only way I could deal with him was to be equally threatening and show that I meant what I said. Immediately he made this remark to me sitting in the study, I dialled the police station and told the policeman that I had a young man who had made this sort of threat to me and he was sitting right here in the study, but please to register this fact and I would inform him of the name of the young man when next I saw him. This had a visible effect upon Ricky who recognized the ploy I had entered into and immediately respected me for it. Unfortunately most of his peers and many of those at school and on the job who had authority over him tended not to counter his threats in such an immediate or effective manner.

Because of their attractiveness the boys were frequently involved with girls, so that the oldest brother was known to have at least three illegitimate children by girls in a nearby village. Ricky himself became linked with a young lady in service in a local doctor's house and we had a considerable series of discussions with the employers about his regular appearance here and the fact that the girl, quite a pretty girl, wanted to marry him and was quite sure that she could reform him. This particular girl did not succeed any more than anyone else before her had succeeded. During our stay in the village Ricky was in Borstal three times and his brother Tim twice. From my contacts over the last year or so since I left both have begun fairly long sustained periods of imprisonment. Many of us were quite sure that of the two delinquent brothers Ricky was the more good-natured and often carried the can for what people regarded as his obnoxious younger brother. When involved in small group delinquencies and crimes he was easily persuaded to be the 'fall guy', and it is probable that his most recent span in H.M. prisons is due to this good-natured, but foolish acquiescence in guilt. The mother was occasionally violent, and once blacked the schoolmaster's eye because she received no help from him and smashed the furniture in the headmaster's room.

In personal terms while Ricky was reasonably well dressed, Tim was always smelly and dirty and many teachers reported the obnoxious nature of the smell that came from him during school hours. Very few people who dealt with him could dissent from the judgment that he was sly, vicious, and totally unreliable. His school teachers evinced a great sense of relief when he became an almost continuous truant from school.

On the same estate, almost neighbours, lived an overweight dumpy girl, Pam, who came from a similar background. Here she stayed within the care of her grandparents, or alleged grandparents, for people were never quite sure whether she was related to this family or not. The two old people were extremely limited intellectually. It is probable that she was an illegitimate child of her mother, who apparently went to Canada at one stage, the father never being mentioned and never being visible. She was alternately spoiled and beaten by her grandparents and while at times she could be pleasant and co-operative, wishing to gain something by this method, she was usually very noisy, very unco-operative and inclined to incite boys to do things for her she could not achieve for herself. By her activities on the common it was evident that she was very promiscuous and used the club as a means of contact with boys for a long period of time. Pam did not remain a member for more than about eighteen months when she developed contacts with much older men and we could only anticipate that in later years she would mature, as was the case, into a professional prostitute. With this family we could make little impression due to the fact that the grandparents were totally incapable of grasping the nature of the problem.

Pam was firmly planted in the bottom stream of school and she had a great talent for upsetting the rest of the class and expressing her views both verbally and physically. She would threaten both her friends and teachers with all kinds of dire results. She had even been known to threaten the life of teachers anonymously over the telephone or, when she thought she was unobserved in the dark, shouting across the fences of teachers where they lived. It was plainly evident to all of us that here was a classical example of someone starved of affection and seeking by physical and other means to make good her deprivation. Her effect upon the other boys and girls was very disturbing, both as an immoral example to them and as someone who was capable of real leadership in a negative sense. Pamela, indeed, was one of those who almost totally wrecked our plans for running a canteen service for the youngsters because when she helped to run the canteen she would steal, lie and cheat her way to securing things for herself and her friends. It was plainly evident that there was little we could do for this girl within the normal run of youth work, and it was nothing short of a miracle that we were able to minimize her influence upon those who were able to profit from the social experience of the club.

The Jackson family, who supplied two boys to the club, the elder brother Bill, and the younger brother Rob, were quite different in that they experienced a settled home life with regular meals and the boys were always turned out cleanly and smartly. But they were nevertheless troublemakers in the beginning simply because while the mother seemed to provide a stable base, the father was a very bad example. He was a very egotistical man who had social aspirations which were disappointed and he was sour and generally negative in his approach to life. He was a frequent complainer to us as youth leaders that his boys were not getting what they really wanted and it was sometimes evident in the way they came to the club that they had previously been beaten rather viciously by their father. It is not surprising therefore that Bill, the older, stronger brother, found the solution to many of his problems by violent behaviour. He was handsome, well-built, well-co-ordinated, and a natural leader for his group but he had been known to have beaten many boys almost senseless at school, at work and within previous youth clubs, while in the grip of a vicious temper. It was this uncontrollable temper which was the greatest problem we had to face. Although we had long discussions with the parents, it was obvious to us that the ill-temper was part of a family tradition which would take a long time to break, if ever, in the behaviour of the children. I cannot recall, except in the last year, Bill being under any self-control whatever when his will was frustrated, particularly in sport. As a football player he was the dirtiest and most bad-tempered player I had ever seen. This was probably the reason why, although a brilliant player, he had never been signed on by any of the professional clubs to which he applied.

Bill Jackson was unpredictably and incredibly selfish in the way in which he could manipulate a situation to his own benefit, yet when he wished to be charming and co-operative, he was a delightful boy to know. When climbing with us he would sit around and wait for others to make the meals, rarely took his turn at doing the daily chores, and generally showed signs of a conceited and self-centred person. In the latter years of our acquaintanceship he became a very firm friend and even then, when events meant that I had to criticize his actions, as frequently I did, he would sulk for a considerable period before he came back to his normal friendly manner.

His young brother, Rob, suffered from various difficulties,

mainly because of comparison with his brother. Rob was under-sized, not physically well-developed or strong, and compared with Bill, who was extremely intelligent, was by contrast rather dull. His older brother dominated him, not only when he was there but when he was absent, and this boy was so lacking in confidence he found it very difficult to try anything at all. The one thing he was good at was destruction. He managed during the period just before we arrived to set the common on fire, imperilling several houses. When we first formed the club, with a group of similarly limited boys, he created noise, nuisance and distraction continually on club nights. Even so, after a period of time he came to see that this negative behaviour profited little, especially as he became very unpopular with his peers when we had to close the club for short periods due to certain delinquencies and damage perpetrated by him. It was he who volunteered to provide markers at the cycle-cross on the common.

It was our constant practice to reward and praise youngsters of this kind who were probably in need of support and encouragement. After our first eighteen months there we searched the records to discover any way in which honorable mention could be made of Rob's activities in the club. We despaired of finding anything of a positive nature until looking at the subscription records we discovered he was the only member who had put in a one-hundred per cent attendance since the club began. So the following Thursday evening when we held the club we displayed prominently a notice congratulating Rob on his one-hundred per cent achievement, something which no other club member had equalled. One could see his self-confidence boosted considerably by this kind of publicity which on various occasions we were able to produce. Praise seemed to beget better or more positive behaviour and he became one of our most trusted and reliable members in the latter part of our time there.

On the other side of the common in the other housing estate we had a number of problem families. One of these was the Drummond family, who produced a series of illegitimate children. One of these was a very tall good-looking girl of sixteen years. Here again was a disorganized, thriftless and low-intelligence family who acted as a focus of discontent on the estate, the mother being a very aggressive woman who was always demanding her rights. She once came to the club and created a scene for some very trivial reason and it was plain that the girl Joyce was merely reflecting in her difficult behaviour in the club the patterns she had seen in her mother. The Jones, too, who lived next door to them, interacted with themselves and their neighbours in a similar fashion. Two of their adolescent children, a boy and a girl, came to the club. Steve was a particularly detestable and unco-operative boy, who threatened me with a punch-up more than once. On one occasion he pulled a knife out during an argument and I was able to persuade him to give it to me for the rest of that evening. We had a long discussion after that with members who carried knives and came to the amicable solution that in the best Western Saloons, holsters were always left at the door. Even when the initial period of distrust disappeared he was never pleasant to know, he was very moody, sulking for weeks on end. He was not unintelligent for he was quick to assess a situation and to profit from it for his own benefit. But at school he was totally illiterate and even by the time he left had not succeeded in the bare skills of literacy.

It was Steve who always asked me to read notices for him, even though they were presented in the most elementary spelling forms. His mother and father, whenever I visited them, were always telling me what a grave problem he was but that they regarded school as a complete waste of time, so Steve had no incentive and no motivation regarding education to help him develop. His sister Grace, a year younger, had similar attitudes to school and to authority in general. She was very much quieter than Steve but equally difficult to communicate with. She too tended to reproduce the sulky pattern of her family life and bear grudges against large numbers of people, including us. Among the girls, we found Grace the most difficult to contact in any way at all and she would try, even when her friends wanted to go on visits to the theatre or trips elsewhere with the club, to undermine their desire and create negative attitudes in them. Fortunately many of her peers resisted her negative influence and when she found she could not get her own way in discouraging the activities of her friends she left the club and only came very occasionally.

It would appear from the homes described so far that very little positive influence could be exerted by the club. We found, however, that there were some members with very peculiar homes, and with strongly negative influences, who did respond to the new atmosphere we had created. For example, Hermy came from some slum-like cottages within the village and he rarely appeared to have a good meal provided for him. He was a member of a family of eight children, he being the eldest, but despite the fact that none of his family appeared in public well-dressed, he himself was always turned out immaculately. How he was able to do this was a miracle to us, but no one had a shine on his shoes, a crease in his trousers and hair brushed so neatly as Hermy on club nights. It was true of course that if one visited the home on any other night when he was there, he would come to the door as scruffy and slovenly as his brothers and sisters, but outside the home on special occasions he was really outstanding for his sartorial appearance.

There was also a family on the estate which had quite high social aspirations and from this home, clean, tidy, ordered and fairly affluent, Joe appeared. He was later to become a quite astute and able salesman, but because he was a weak character using as a front the violent support of Bill, Ricky and Tim, became one of the greatest nuisances in the first six months of our time with the club. He would quite actively incite other people, older and stronger boys, to create trouble for us, and he did this with great subtlety and in such a way that other people did not always realize that they were being used. He was the one boy who had been to grammar school, although he did not emerge from it with any high achievement. One would naturally have thought there was some leadership of a positive kind possible from so perceptive a boy but he was an exploiter of situations, a weak and unreliable boy, prepared to use his well-meaning but less able companions. There was an element of sadism about his nature and it was quite evident to us that his character deficiencies would persist for a long time. Towards the end of the period when we became more settled as a youth community, he in fact became the secretary of the table-tennis team, arranging fixtures both at home and away. He developed a most responsible and reliable attitude to this particular activity but it was typical of the boy that this was the only area in which he could be reliable simply because it coincided with his own interests and concerns. On visiting the family it was very evident that the lad was the apple of his mother's eye and there was nothing she would not do for him. It came as something of a shock to her to discover from me that her darling boy was among the most difficult of our members and I believe she never forgave me for discussing his problems, which to her appeared to be entirely mythical.

Among the girls we had a surprising number who were

adopted or fostered. Many had been deserted by one or both parents and were living with adoptive grandmothers or aunts. One such girl was Jenny, who was bright, attractive and terribly insecure. Her adoptive grandmother—and we were never sure what was the precise relationship—was continually whining and complaining about the girl's behaviour and the constant complaints from her only seemed to aggravate Jenny's attitudes towards her home. She objected once when the boys were talking about certain people as bastards—a term not used in the context of discussion in any real biological sense but merely as an offensive descriptive term. She was for ever talking about her real mother and father coming to take her away and give her a real home. She was subject to frequent breakdowns in tears and yet she was one who found in many activities of the club a creative kind of real fulfilment. When the first party for the club was planned she was among the leading supporters of the venture, she was the first to go away on a Charm School Course run by the county authorities and she was a leading actress on our first venture on the Youth Entertainments Contest run by the local youth club association. Here we felt, although perhaps it was only a very brief period of her life, was an influence which went beyond the home and provided some positive satisfactions and achievements.

Down in one of the smaller areas of the village, Berrocfield Moss, one of the girls, an only daughter, lived in a small private modern bungalow and was the apple of her mother's and father's eye. She was always thought to be very fond of the boys and it was plain in the club that she was very attractive to the opposite sex. Her parents were very indulgent and invited her to bring her boy friends home and would frequently leave her alone in the house from a very tender age with the current boy friend. It was therefore not surprising that she became pregnant before she reached her seventeenth birthday. This was the subject of great concern and condemnation by the family, who finally accepted the boy and arranged a convenient shot-gun marriage. This boy was one of our own club members, very active and lively, but lacking in any extended intelligence. By the time the girl was nineteen, three children had been born and we hear that currently the boy is out of work and a fourth child is on the way. It was evident that the parents had no clear insight about how to handle the situation and plainly the girl needed some contraceptive advice. Their lack of foresight and intelligence, unfortunately, seemed to render this impossible. Such was the situation in this family that by the age of nineteen Mary, the daughter, looked like a woman of thirty to thirty-five years' old.

A nearby village had a large number of boys for whom that village could not provide a club. As the boys were almost regarded as members of the same parish embracing our own community, which was only a mile away, they were accepted into the Youth Centre. The half-dozen boys came from very similar homes on a council estate, consisting of two bedrooms, which were always over-crowded and spilling over with young children. If the adolescents of our own village had a bad reputation, the adolescents of this particular village had an even worse one. Drunkenness in the village pubs was quite a frequent occurrence, and violence resulting in at least one death had occurred there. This aura of violence and disorder found its way inevitably into the club. Yet this group was to provide the most lively, involved, participation in the physical activities we arranged, particularly mountaineering, ski-ing, visits to the Ocean Youth Clubs and similar activities. They provided a more positive influence, which was perhaps decisive, when I was attacked by our outside visitors of the motor-cycle brigade. And yet, although their behaviour with us began to improve with every night they attended, their behaviour in their own village still remained fairly negative and those in the village reported no change.

The backgrounds which I have outlined here seem to be more negative than positive. 'How unlike the home life of our dear queen,' we might remark, as the Victorian theatre-goer said to her neighbour while watching a melodrama of deceit and violence. The wonder of it is that the outcome of the club was of a positive kind when there were so many negative influences from the home at work.

Many positive and personal results could be enumerated from some of these problem families with the most unpromising background. There was Jane who developed a keen interest in designing clothes, and Jenny developing a real talent for drama and dramatic dance. Ben and Peter and many others gained their driving certificates during their time with us due to our tuition. Jim and Dave began as great nuisances because they had little talent for anything else, yet turned into solid committee members and in the latter years supported positively all activities of the club. Al, who began by merely coming and sitting for twenty evenings in the club without speaking to anyone, gradually became a most enthusiastic camper and mountaineer through the influence of our various trips to North Wales and the Lake District. Jack, beginning as a cheerful do-nothing, grew in confidence and positive attitude, acting as an assistant to the leaders when he reached the age of twenty-one. Jerry, who started as a great mischief maker and breaker of windows, became captain of our seven-a-side football team. These are but few of the achievements which are not measurable but were easily perceived and accounted for the later period of keen co-operative and enthusiastic participation in activities. It took us a long time to appreciate ourselves these positive contributions and visible signs of growing up or maturing. For many in the village, however, these young people remained the symbol of disorder and violence and the attitudes of many in the adult community took a long time to change.

Looking at the family data we accumulated over a long period, it struck us forcibly that the skills of leadership with this group involved informal educational techniques, social work facility and counselling insights. The limited time and skills we were able to bring to bear upon the situation was something, but not really adequate for achieving solid aims in youth work with a group of fifty angry adolescents. For the task required not only direct personal work with the young people themselves, but also a more systematic educational programme for their parents and for the largely unsympathetic and hostile community in which they lived.

7 The Litmus Paper of Society

'Adolescents are the Litmus Paper of Society' has been used to indicate that young people by their behaviour and by their attitudes reveal the nature of the society to which they belong. This point is made very strongly in the Albemarle Report (*The Youth Service in England and Wales*, 1958). Although this was published some ten years ago, it is interesting to look at the assertions of that Report and to compare the adolescents we encountered in Berrocfield. The Report was in fact not only reviewing life in the late 1950s but looking at future trends which they seemed to discern among young people of that time. And certainly many of these trends did appear among the young people who composed the membership of the Berrocfield Club.

This assertion, that adolescents produce in their behaviour a revelation about the society to which they belong and reflect the values and attitudes of the adult population, must be viewed with some caution. For if adolescents reflect adult society, it may be that they only reflect certain portions of adult society with which they are in closest contact and have the closest identification. It was very evident from the Berrocfield young people that their social experience was very limited. If they are to be regarded as the litmus paper of society, it was a very limited, lower working-class stratum of society, its attitudes and values which they reflected.

The first feature which was noticeable about the members of the club was their comparative affluence. I use the word 'comparative' in terms of adolescents ten years previously and my own—and my generation's—relative poverty in my youth. Few of them appeared to be short of money although where payment of club subscriptions was concerned, they were very reluctant to part with it. When it came to expenditure of large sums of money, sometimes of over £10, they appeared to have no difficulty in paying instantly or raising the money very quickly over a short period of time. It was very difficult in any systematic way to assess the amount of money which they had to spend weekly. For the small number who were still at school, the average pocket money they enjoyed from their parents was approximately £1 a week.

The girls at work earned between £4 and £8 a week; a few of them were on shift work and most of them working in shops and factories and laundries in the nearby towns. The boys, who tended to be clustered round the older group, 17 to 21 years, had a much wider range of earnings and the *minimum* wage we discovered of those who were in regular employment was £6 to £7. Some of them who were doing piece work and weekend work were able to earn up to £25 and sometimes a little beyond. It was quite common on club nights to be faced with a £5 or a £10 note when a member had to pay his subscription. This was largely offered in the spirit of bravado in the hope that no change would be available, but we always made sure that it was. Once it had been tried and change was forthcoming promptly this ploy was immediately dropped, to our mutual amusement. We verified the earnings of young people, not merely by asking them, for sometimes members would reveal the full contents of the packet which they had only just opened a few hours before, since club coincided with pay night.

The majority of members kept their entire earnings for themselves, and it was not surprising that they had little real concern for saving or any awareness of the coming limitations of expenditure they would have once they settled down and were married, with the increased financial responsibilities that this involved. Just occasionally we were able to ask parents why they did not subtract from their children's wages a certain amount for housekeeping and even if they were not in need of it themselves for running the house, why they did not bank it for the young people against such times as emergency or holidays when they would be short of money? The reply we almost always received was the superficial one, 'Well, they've earned the money and they should do what they like with it.' Although we pointed out that this was bad for the character of young people from 15 and 16 upwards, the parents seemed to have no insight into the need for financially educating their children in this way.

It is not surprising that these young people could afford various items which were fairly expensive. New clothes, which revealed the latest trends in fashions, were very noticeable, many of the boys appearing to spend more on their appearance than the girls. The leather jackets studded with steel buttons, the drainpipe trousers and the hair fashions were scrupulously regarded and kept very up-to-date by the boys. Record players, records, transistor radios, tape recorders, and various other electronic devices were frequently paraded at the club. The most revealing item of expenditure was the purchase by the boys, as soon as they were able to secure a licence, of a vehicle. Beginning with light mopeds, graduating then to more powerful motorbikes, and then to second-hand cars, the car park outside the village hall and youth centre showed a vast variety of vehicles when the young people assembled. On club nights it was noticeable that our own car was sometimes the smallest of the vehicles parked outside.

In the three years in which we ran the club, and during

which time the adolescent population aged from young adolescents to older adolescents, the vehicles became more in number and more opulent and larger in appearance. It was plain that they were able to afford very expensive holidays but their inability to save and their unwillingness to plan ahead militated against any real provision for the future. A little time later when some of them were married and came to talk with us, they did confide that they had found the adjustment to married life and its financial involvement a great shock. They discovered that on precisely the same wages they were having to provide for a wife, and some of them for small children. Apart from one or two apprentices, most of them were in jobs which would not lead to a future career with any stability. Most of the boys were packers in factories, labourers, odd-job boys and, without their being aware of it, they were enjoying the most affluent period of their lives, when they had the least responsibility and the greatest spending power they would ever have.

The availability of transport in this group in the mid-nineteen sixties gave them a freedom and a mobility young people had not enjoyed previously. Just as motor-bike gangs and large numbers of young people crammed into cars, came and visited our club and created disturbances, we were well aware that some of our own groups were involved in the same activity in nearby villages and towns a little distance away. Frequently, since it was the boys who owned the vehicles, they were used as means of picking up girls and the increased freedom of mobility led, of course, to greater sexual freedom. We were fully aware that frequently boys and girls disappeared from the club, went into a car and drove on to the nearby common and indulged in various sexual activities there, behaviour which on cold winter nights would have been quite unthinkable, if not impossible, without the cover of a vehicle. Although there appeared to be a few members who were promiscuous in their relationship with the other sex, there were quite a number of stable relationships developing during our time there. Frequently a couple would confide in us that they had had sex relations together, but would have been most indignant if they had been accused of promiscuity or even of immorality. Their attitude was simply 'We are going to get married anyway, so why wait?' Reports from various sources would indicate that this has become a widely accepted viewpoint in society at large and the young people appeared to be no better and no worse than their elders in this respect.

Because they were more mobile one would have thought that the greater freedom they enjoyed would have led to a wider variety of social life and social experiment. This was not so because they were in a rather narrow restricted world of going to the pictures, sometimes to the dance hall, and very little else. It took a long patient development of many programmes to open their eyes to the variety of opportunities available to them. Even though the journey into London was only just over an hour-and-a-quarter's drive, not one of them had ever been known to go there except in club groups and parties. Greater freedom therefore did not necessarily mean greater vision or a richer life. It took several years of building up their ideas, exciting their interest, opening new possibilities to them, before they built up the desire and the confidence to do something different.

Perhaps the most obvious reflection of society which emerged from their behaviour was their views about society itself, very strongly flavoured by their sense of being discriminated against and their awareness that they were low in the social scale. It was evident from remarks in the initial two years in which we knew these adolescents that their sense of being rejected or regarded as failures by society caused them deep and continual anger. This anger was seen in their first reactions to us as interested adults. It was also directed towards the rest of the community, particularly the middle class and wealthier portions of the population living outside the village in their detached houses. Our members' attitudes to the police, the symbols of authority, were an expression of this sense of anger which released itself in delinquent and criminal actions over a period of time. The policeman, when we first came to the village, lived on the council estate, and his life was made very difficult by the adults around him because they resented being under continual observation. Since large numbers of the adults were 'in trouble' of some kind, this resentment was natural. P.C. Brown was in fact a very friendly and urbane kind of man, taking much of the abuse and rejection of his own family in his stride; nevertheless, it was a strain upon him and after some three or four years of this he applied for a transfer. The new policeman, a young man with a growing family, lasted only nine months. After this, before another resident policeman could be installed in the village, the police house on the estate was given up and a new police house away from the estate in another part of the village had to be built.

The anger of these young people again erupted in relation to almost any adult whom they thought challenged their self-respect. It certainly spread to school teachers and for most of them their attitudes to school were very poor indeed. Negative remarks about school were frequent. Most of the school rules and the discipline of school were regarded as completely oppressive and for them the rejection of education went with their rejection of discipline. Reports from teachers invariably showed that the hard core of our difficult members from Berrocfield were always a nuisance at the school and teachers expressed a great deal of relief when they left school or were frequent absentees. We were aware that in one case a boy was such a nuisance at school that even the School Attendance Officer turned a blind eye to his non-attendance for a period of more than a year.

In listing the aggressiveness and the anger of these adolescents we do not mean to imply that their anger was in all cases justified. It was plain that many were frustrated by the limitations of ability, imagination and poor home environments. They were merely reflecting something of the frustrations, the unhappiness and the tensions that were evident in their family life. But because they were inarticulate, they released their emotions more freely than if they had possessed a degree of controlled expression. It was through negative behaviour and anti-social actions that they seemed to achieve some kind of relief. Anger and aggression stem from frustration and we can only remark that these youngsters as well as facing the normal frustrations of the young, had further difficult frustrations of a social kind imposed upon them. It is true that they were frequently paranoid at finding slights and persecutions where they did not exist, but this somewhat paranoid condition in itself seemed to have substance. It was very evident that they were talked about by the authorities and by middle-class adults in the community in somewhat contemptuous and negative terms. Their only means of combating this and retaining their self-respect was to be contemptuous and angry in return.

In conversation with many of them it was very clear to us that their self image was a curious mixture. While they tried to retain their ego by tangible achievements, when they could not they found a substitute in the possession of cars, the latest clothes in fashion, and material things.

They were, incidentally, fantastic liars and boasters with each other, claiming to have done the most extraordinary deeds which they had not in fact had the courage to do. They would nevertheless recognize that they were inferior and in many ways their own attitudes to each other showed remarkable insights. Remarks were frequent that they could not 'talk proper', they were nervous when sitting down in a restaurant whenever we went on trips to London or other places, their self-conscious laughter in public places and their unruly behaviour only highlighted their unease. Yet beneath all this there was, in moments of complete enjoyment and unself-consciousness, a refreshing vigour and an honesty which is rare to find. Their moods were like that of any other groups of adolescents, alternately happy and sad, gregarious and lonely, unhelpful and co-operative.

Despite their normality in one respect, they showed alarming symptoms of negative and destructive attitudes which were costly in social adjustment and human happiness. Some of them proved costly to society more directly and it is a sad reflection that if adequate welfare services had been applied to say two or three families in this community, boarding fees at Borstals and prisons for a considerable number might have been avoided. Certainly if a full-time youth leader had been available in the village, possessing proper skills of social work and of counselling, able to devote a good deal of his time not only to the young people but to their families, much of this human waste could have been avoided.

I calculate that good personnel and programme facilities would have cost far less than the £4,750 spent on average each year in prosecuting, remanding, borstalizing and imprisoning our worst members. Our annual grant for the club from the county education funds rarely came to more than £35! As it was we were simply a one-night-a-week community, meeting at weekends for special purposes, when these young people really required a centre to which they could go almost every evening. There was the population to sustain it and the need was there, but the financial resources and the agencies were almost totally absent.

The Albemarle Report highlighted various characteristics of the new generation of adolescents which was beginning to emerge at the end of the 1950s. Certainly our own adolescents at Berrocfield reflected these trends. Despite the fact that many of them came from homes where feeding and nutrition were poor, they were larger, heavier and healthier than previous generations of adolescents. It was also evident that they achieved puberty very early, some of the girls of 13 passing for 16 and 17, and although officially they were not allowed to become members until they were 14, it was evident that pressures to admit them had to be yielded to. Indeed, our girl population in the club only lasted two or three years and it was very rare indeed for a girl to be a club member much after the age of 16. The older boys went out with these girls and gradually paired off as they became regular partners. Once this relationship was established we tended not to see them at the club except occasionally for special events.

The boys were remarkable for their physical agility and despite a few who suffered from obesity and the many who were heavy smokers, kept in very good training by strenuous activities such as football and cycling, and once the club was established, an increasing variety of physical pursuits. The Albemarle Report described a trend which was very evident to us at Berrocfield, that more young people were becoming delinquent and anti-social. One of the first lessons the most aggressive boys taught me when we had established some friendly relationships, was how to get into my car when I had left the key locked inside. A boy with an alleged I.Q. of 82 got into my car in a few seconds, and then demonstrated seven other methods of how it could be done. Included in this was a short course on how to start the car without a key. Neither of these skills were known to me, although I had been a car owner for many years.

Looking at previous national reports on crime and the way in which crime was linked with poverty, it was interesting to notice that delinquency here was obviously not linked with poverty, since very few of these families were really poor. Indeed there were some instances of their criminal and delinquent actions being taken by the most affluent members of the club simply because of the need for excitement and their desire to strike gestures of defiance against what they interpreted to be a hostile world. The national statistics which reveal the school-leaving year as the peak age for boy delinquency, tended to be borne out by the behaviour of our own members. Those in the last year at school and those who had just left school were among the most turbulent and less controllable of the group. The only way in which they could be disciplined and controlled was not by vain verbal appeals but by immediate action which followed any delinquency. Within the club we had to be very rigorous at first and incur a great deal of unpopularity by showing them that if they did not behave well other members would suffer. Consequently instead of showing off and achieving status in the eyes of their peers, they deprived their peers of privileges by closure of the club and thus were rejected or became extremely unpopular until they had put right the damage and apologized for the behaviour which had caused the closure.

The surveys done by Mark Abrams, quoted in the Albemarle Report and elsewhere, seemed to be borne out by the facts we knew about the earnings of young people. Although we had a number of programmes on 'Don't be Exploited. Get Value for what you Buy', we made very little impression in helping these young people to spend responsibly and wisely. They were indeed interested to listen and discuss, when they could control themselves long enough to discuss rationally the implications of higher spending power, but they found it very difficult to discriminate between poor, shoddy goods, the pitfalls of hire purchase and the need to budget carefully while they were young so that they would become wise spenders in the future. Realistic budgeting as part of the curriculum for school-leavers is still surprisingly rare, many secondary schools still continuing the old academic, and to these young people, irrelevant subjects such as history, geography and scripture.

When, indeed, such ideas were put to them their remarks were revealing. 'What the hell's the use of saving when it can all be blown up by a bloody bomb?' and 'Let's enjoy life while we can; you're old at 22.' This sense of the fragility of modern life and the idea that a cosmic disaster might overtake them was very present and comments of this kind came out frequently. It is perhaps important to reflect, before we condemn the transitory and apparently irresponsible attitudes of many young people today, to realize that we ourselves, most adults, were not reared in our most formative years with the possibilities of cosmic disaster before us. Even now most of us tend to reject all thinking about the precarious nature of life and to be unaware that this is an important dimension in young people's thinking. Our members' money was spent frequently on goods which Mark Abrams labels as emotionally weighted or status goods. Because of this they were extremely susceptible to commercial exploitation. Many of them confessed to me that having spent twenty-five guineas on a tape recorder of a rather poor quality, they really did not know how to use it and to get value for their money from it. The most they could hope to use it for was taping pop records but they soon became aware that reproduction was very poor and the results were hardly worth recording.

These young people in Berrocfield could be characterized as having economic power without responsibility. The age when they achieved majority seemed to them to be centuries away. Although they were given some kind of graded recognition at certain ages, being able to obtain a licence for a motor-bike and then a motor-car, the fact that they had no political rights, very few social rights, and many of them no family responsibilities, tended to increase their sense of unreality and their irresponsible behaviour. It was on the club committees and on the club council that many of them for the first time were challenged to be part of a controlled and mutually inter-dependent community. This was why it became extraordinarily difficult to gain a consensus of opinion and ask these young people to stand by it. The indecision and the differences, sometimes about trivial things, were marked, as for example the complete deadlock we ran into whilst arranging a trip to the sea-side because the two factions could not compromise on a third place acceptable to them. Perhaps if the findings of the Latey Committee became law (to allow the age of majority to be 18 years), this may help many young people such as these to understand the nature of their social responsibilities earlier than they do now.

We ourselves were caught in the dilemma of running no club at all if we were to depend upon their complete co-operation, their own suggestions and their own initiative, or taking the reins and guiding them, and pouring in suggestions for a considerable period. Only then were they able to begin to make decisions themselves, to generate ideas on their own and this after a period of three years' strenuous process of informal education, by which time many of the original membership had begun to leave.

Because they felt they had no real stake in society, one of the results of having no real responsibilities, when they were not angry they were sceptical. Their scathing and negative remarks about religion, about the behaviour of adults, and about the hypocrisy of certain respected people in the community, about politics, even about young people themselves, whilst lurid, were usually very close to the bone. It is difficult to see how they could generate any more positive attitudes to life when their total reading seemed to be the *News of the World*, the *Sunday Pictorial* and *Reveille* and other fairly low-grade publications. These emphasize sexual and criminal sensationalism but produce very little real news about normal people. The least we could do in the club work at Berrocfield was to produce a genuine teen-age society rather than the commercially imposed pop-culture which they tended uncritically to accept.

Part of the problem we faced in Berrocfield was not merely the young people and their families, but the attitudes of the more respectable middle class, and we tried quite deliberately to keep this section of the community very well-informed about the activities of the club and from time to time invited influential members from our advisory committee and elsewhere to come to the normal club evenings. With this in mind also we had large notice boards in the village hall and youth centre, which could be read during the rest of the week by the Women's Institute, the Old People's Club, the people who ran the Whist Drive, the Young Farmers' Society and other groups who were continually using the hall. The hall committee itself was basically very sympathetic to the club, but again had to be educated into the fact that if a youth club had to run successfully in the centre there would inevitably be occa-